AMERICA AND ITS DISCONTENTS

DATE DUE

DEMCO 38-297

Xerox College Publishing
Waltham, Massachusetts / Toronto

AMERICA

ROBIE MACAULEY
Playboy Magazine
University of Illinois

AND ITS

LARZER ZIFF
University of California
Berkeley

DISCONTENTS

Foreword

In his brilliant 1929 book titled *Civilization and is Discontents*, Sigmund Freud expressed his dark view of American society, saying, "The present cultural state of America would give us a good opportunity for studying the damage to civilization which is to be feared." Not wishing to "employ American methods," Freud declined to pursue his critique further.

America and its Discontents, published forty-two years later, accepts the challenge of the subject that Freud refused to elaborate on. With perhaps poetic injustice the book appears under a variant of Freud's title. It is designed to explore his broad theme through selected articles, essays, fiction, and verse that demonstrate the multiplicity of America's current discontents.

Not merely an anthology of social criticism, *America and its Discontents* is, more importantly, an examination of cultural phenomena in America in the second half of the twentieth century. These phenomena are analyzed through an objective balance of critical commentary and optimistic outlook toward change. Freud said that the critic — even the most unsparing critic — is no enemy of civilization as long as he demands some plan that would make life on earth happier. Accordingly the critic's aim should be to promote social change by examining problems that can be solved. Once the origins and characteristics of social ills are exposed, Freud adds, "We may expect gradually to carry through such alterations in our civilization as will better satisfy our needs. . . ." He cautions, however, that certain faults are inherent in any civilization; they cannot be eradicated without substituting some entirely different order of life.

The studies in *America and its Discontents* discuss not only such inherent flaws, but also those social ills which could be cured in the foreseeable future. As a rational expression of what we Americans observe most critically in ourselves and our society, this anthology is a mirror of our conscience, a conscience responsive to hope rather than despair.

Table of Contents

1 PERSONAL REVOLUTION

ALDOUS HUXLEY	from *The Doors of Perception* 6
TIMOTHY LEARY	*How to Change Behavior* 22
TOM WOLFE	*What do You Think of My Buddha?* 34
FRANK ZAPPA	*The New Rock* 48
TOM NOLAN	*Groupies: A Story of Our Times* 57
	A Short Anthology of Rock Poetry 70
PETER TOWNSHEND	My Generation 70
TULI KUPFERBERG	Morning Morning 70
BRIAN WILSON	Wonderful 71
BOB DYLAN	Sad-Eyed Lady of the Lowlands 72
LEONARD COHEN	Suzanne 73
SKIP SPENCE	Motorcycle Irene 75
JOE TEX	The Love You Save (May Be Your Own) 76
GRACE SLICK	White Rabbit 77
JOHN LENNON AND PAUL MCCARTNEY	A Day in the Life 78

2 THE ESTABLISHMENT

GERALD GREEN	*The Dispatcher* 86
STEWART ALSOP	*The Sinking Hill* 102
FERDINAND LUNDBERG	*The Cream of the Quest* 116
RICHARD J. BARNET	*The Military-Industrial Complex* 130
RALPH SALERNO AND JOHN S. TOMPKINS	*Crime as a Business* 150

3 SOCIAL AND BIOLOGICAL IDENTITY

D. H. LAWRENCE	*Benjamin Franklin* 166
ERIK H. ERIKSON	*Mom* 174
STUDS TERKEL	*Madison Avenue, Chicago* 181
KENNETH KENNISTON	*Moral Exhaustion and Student Revolution* 189
JULIET MITCHELL	from *Women: The Longest Revolution* 197
LYNN WHITE, JR.	*The Historic Roots of Our Ecologic Crisis* 218
ALDO LEOPOLD	*The Land Ethic* 228

4   **BLACK IDENTITY**

MALCOLM X   *Saved*   247
ELDRIDGE CLEAVER   *The White Race and Its Heroes*   256
STOKELEY CARMICHAEL   *Toward Black Liberation*   267
BLACK PANTHER PARTY   Rules of the Black Panther Party   276
                       What We Want, What We Believe   278
RONALD STEEL   *Letter from Oakland: The Panthers*   280
JAMES BROWN   *Say it Loud — I'm Black and I'm Proud*   287

5   **WAR**

KONRAD LORENZ   *Ecce Homo!*   294
HENRY SLESAR   *The Prisoner*   318
JOSEPH HELLER   Two Selections from *Catch-22*   323
ROBERT ARDREY   *Cain's Children*   330
DAVID INGLIS   *The Outlook for Nuclear Explosives*   339
CARL-GÖRAN HEDÉN   *The Infectious Dust Cloud*   347
                       A Short Anthology of Poems About War   354
RANDALL JARRELL   The Death of the Ball Turret Gunner   354
A. E. HOUSMAN   XXXVI   354
W. B. YEATS   An Irish Airman Foresees his Death   355
SIEGFRIED SASSOON   The General   355

6   **MEDIA**

JAMES RESTON   *The News: What Can Be Done?*   362
STUART B. GLAUBERMAN   *The News from Underground*   375
GILLIAN FREEMAN   *Pornography as a Necessity*   391
PAULINE KAEL   from *I Lost it at the Movies*   398
MARSHALL MCLUHAN   *The TV Mosaic*   407

7   **THE FUTURE**

ARTHUR C. CLARKE   *Hazards of Prophecy:*   425
                           The Failure of Nerve   425
                           The Failure of Imagination   432
HERMAN KAHN AND   from *The Year 2000*   439
ANTHONY J. WEINER
GORDON RATTRAY TAYLOR *New Minds for Old*   452
WILLY LEY   *Atlantropa — the Changed Mediterranean*   479
J. G. BALLARD   *Billenium*   488
ALVIN TOFFLER   from *Future Shock*   500

AMERICA AND ITS DISCONTENTS

PERSONAL REVOLUTION

■ In a passage echoed repeatedly in contemporary writings, Aldous Huxley tells us to take seriously a theory put forth by Henri Bergson. He quotes D. C. Broad:

> The suggestion is that the function of the brain and nervous system and sense organs is in the main *eliminative* and not productive. Each person is at each moment capable of remembering all that has ever happened to him and of perceiving everything that is happening everywhere in the universe. The function of the brain and nervous system is to protect us from being overwhelmed and confused by the mass of largely useless and irrelevant knowledge, by shutting out most of what we should otherwise perceive or remember at any moment, and leaving only that very small and special selection which is likely to be practically useful.

And then he goes on to supply the memorable phrase:

> According to such a theory each one of us is potentially Mind at Large. But in so far as we are animals, our business is at all costs to survive. To make biological survival possible, Mind at Large has to be funnelled through the reducing valve of the brain and nervous system.

"The reducing valve of the brain." Hardly the proper phrase for a faculty that has released man from his primitive fears, generated educational systems that transform infants into civilized adults, and reduced the anarchy of nature to an ordered series of controllable phenomena.

And yet just the right phrase if in the names of civilization, education, and science we have shut down our access to other reservoirs of well-being, other and perhaps better sources of nourishment for our frail existence. What would happen if the function of the reducing valve were reversed? What flows in to compensate for our loss of immediate and practical dominance of our environment?

The answer has long been available from such diverse sources as the great works of Oriental philosophy and the ritualistic practices of American Indian tribes, both long misunderstood by Western man. The answer was ignored for two reasons. First, so deeply immersed did Western man become in his rational systems that he saw them as a "natural" stage of human development and believed practices and attitudes outside the rationalist tradition represented not cultural differences but an inferior level of human development. He was, therefore, incapable of even questioning the superiority of his rational outlook, let alone recognizing an alternative. Second, Western man's understanding of the largest human values was limited ultimately by his medium of intellectual articulation, language; hence, a form of perception accessible chiefly if not solely through nonverbal experience was unintelligible to him.

Four-tenths of a gram of mescalin dissolved in a half-glass of water, says Aldous Huxley, transported him to a new world of golden light and appreciation of what the Zen master said about Buddha. His will was severely impaired as the reducing valve reversed itself, but when the flow was reversed his consciousness, he avers, expanded. Huxley heard being and becoming, the pillars of the temple of Western philosophy, fall, not with a crash but a crumble, as for the first time he saw the flowers in the vase in his study as nothing less and nothing more than what they were, shining with their own inner light in a perpetual perishing that was at the same time pure, a transience that was eternal.

"Feed your head," "Turn on," "Blow your mind," are the racier phrases of the personal revolution against behavior in favor of consciousness, against Mind in Control in favor of Mind at Large. The most obvious instrument of the revolution is a drug that expands consciousness, but as the concept of expanded consciousness takes hold, alternate or supplementary means come into play. Once the concern for behavior, for effective action in the immediate environment, is seen as but one mode of thought rather than the only mode, a number of paths to expansion seem open to the adventurous. In varying degrees and combinations, amplified electric music, the operations of the stroboscopic light, and self-hypnosis may lead to the reversal of the reducing valve.

Involved closely in this reversal is social conduct that is termed misbehavior if not downright illegal action. The unfamiliar (and therefore frightening) methods of mental expansion are more evident to society than their results, and it is against the methods that society reacts. Newspapers are quick to publicize the man who takes a drug and leaps from a window under its influence; they are indifferent to, even incapable of reporting, the experience of such as Aldous Huxley when he swallowed his mescalin.

Moreover, although the revolution in favor of Mind at Large may have been started by genuine seekers, its ranks are swelled by children of affluence who simply feel that their society has paid too high a price for its comforts and gadgets — the price of sexual repression, racial distrust, and technological devastation. While they may not clearly understand expanded consciousness, they think they know all they need to know about the Western World's alternatives. Their endorsement of drug use is really a rejection of conventional life styles. There is in the personal revolution a strong antisocial current, if by social we refer to society as it is now constituted. There is in this attitude a strong flavor of "revolution for the hell of it."

Few of the many observers of the revolution who are disturbed by it can resist believing that what they see and dislike is passing fashion rather than lasting change. The oldest of the games for the middle-class young, they reason, is "*Epater le bourgeois.*" But yesterday's Bohemian is today's banker; they'll come around. The man who observed the turmoil of the twenties and commented, "Many of the people who think they are emancipated are merely unbuttoned," may now again be quoted. Let youth have its fling before it settles, as surely it will, into the tasks of its elders. So goes the pep talk.

And indeed who in the midst of the contemporary ferment can confidently say it is revolution rather than fashion? The usual tests appear to favor the latter conclusion. If it is a genuine change, what is its program? What are the consequences for society at large of this alleged expansion of the individual consciousness?

The answers may seem unsatisfactory, even contradictory. Aldous Huxley might reply that he can only be grateful for having had the experience himself although he hopes that eventually beneficial channels will be opened between society and the country of the higher mind. Timothy Leary reports an experiment — though the results are not yet in — in which "expanded consciousness" may be the key to helping prisoners "play the social game" after their release. But Ken Kesey, in Tom Wolfe's rendering, seems to sum up the main drift of rank-and-file thinking: "He . . . was trying to get them to move off their own snug-harbor dead center, out of the plump little game of being *ersatz* daring and *ersatz* alive, the middle-class intellectual game, and move out to Edge City . . . where it was scary but people were whole people." One way of life is played out; on to another which, indeed, has terrors, but only terror can remind you that you are alive.

The very lack of program in the migration to Edge City, however, is more likely a sign of strength than a result of weakness. Although cultural revolutions are frequently accompanied by political revolutions, they tend to precede them. The new consciousness that evolves from a cultural revolution eventually manifests itself in a changed social order, but the lack of a formula for that new order when the cultural revolution is in progress is not necessarily a sign that profound cultural change is missing.

Here is a Puritan from the American past arguing that consciousness is more important than thought:

There is a twofold understanding or knowledge of good . . . The first, that which is merely speculative and notional; as when a person only speculatively judges that any thing is, which, by the agreement of mankind is called good or excellent, viz., that which is most to general advantage, and between which and a reward there is a suitableness, and the like. And the other is, that which consists in the sense of the heart: as when there is a sense of the beauty, amiableness, or sweetness of a thing; so that the heart is sensible of pleasure and delight in the presence of the idea of it.

Such a belief profoundly modified American social patterns, and although the Puritans may appear to be at the farthest remove from today's expanders of consciousness, the cultural revolution of which they were part brought with it the early Quakers whose women, stripped to the waist, interrupted church services; the Familists who advocated community of love; and the Diggers who practiced community of goods.

This is not to say that the present emphasis on expanded consciousness repeats the pattern of the Puritan insistence on a sense of grace above a sense of social tradition. It is merely to assert that major cultural shifts can take place without the initial accompaniment of clear social or political programs. The lack of such programs and the widespread practice of a number of antisocial activities ranging from the malicious through the naughty to the satiric and the joyful, history reveals, is more indicative of significant change than it is of passing fashion.

For self-aggrandizement as well as self-perpetuation (if, indeed, the two are not the same) society fights back not only by repression, such as undiscriminating drug legislation, and school, club, or hotel rules about hair length, but also by absorption. To assure that the new outlook is merely a fad, the economy makes it fashionable. Expensive boutiques thrive by imitating the second-hand dress shop that brought grandmother's gowns back; beauty parlors make as great a profit artificially providing natural hair styles as they used to earn providing permanent waves; and interior decorators supply psychedelic decors. Hardly an antisocial or self-expressive gesture can be made without its being copied and mass produced.

Increasingly, the young who design the gestures of rebellion are employed to mass-reproduce them. Some refuse but most don't. To an extent, they can argue that taking a lot of money to produce an insulting poster or an outrageous record is a continuation of the "put-on" of society. But if that poster and that record bring in the profits, who is putting on whom? The puppy chases his own tail with increasing frenzy as one girl removes her bathing suit top and goes swimming, whereupon thousands of topless bathing suits are designed, manufactured, advertised, and sold; as one or another group engages in a protest march, whereupon an advertising agency confects a television commercial in which hired models happily seize their banners and in mock-protest proclaim the virtues of the product.

It is in this area rather than that of repression that the principal struggle between the new consciousness and society is taking place. A consumer's economy feeds on changes of fashion and is marvelously adroit at adapting its organism to the surface signs of change. New lifestyles suggest new packages, new products, new services; and the acceptance of the styles for commercial purposes not only compromises the styles but enervates the profounder change they signal. Frank Zappa's records and Ken Kesey's writings sell well.

Finally, then, it is not social rigidity but economic compromise that threatens the personal revolution. Not so much, "Don't behave that way or I'll punish you," as "If you behave that way I'll sell you something to help you do it or hire you to persuade others to do it." The threat is surmountable when one remembers the potential of expanded consciousness. But if history says revolution, modern capitalism says fashion.

Aldous Huxley | from The Doors of Perception

It was in 1886 that the German pharmacologist, Ludwig Lewin, published the first systematic study of the cactus, to which his own name was subsequently given. *Anhalonium Lewinii* was new to science. To primitive religion and the Indians of Mexico and the American Southwest it was a friend of immemorially long standing. Indeed, it was much more than a friend. In the words of one of the early Spanish visitors to the New World, 'they eat a root which they call Peyotl, and which they venerate as though it were a deity.'

Why they should have venerated it as a deity became apparent when such eminent psychologists an Jaensch, Havelock Ellis, and Weir Mitchell began their experiments with mescalin, the active principle of peyotl. True, they stopped short at a point well this side of idolatry; but all concurred in assigning to mescalin a position among drugs of unique distinction. Administered in suitable doses, it changes the quality of consciousness more profoundly and yet is less toxic than any other substance in the pharmacologist's repertory.

Mescalin research has been going on sporadically ever since the days of Lewin and Havelock Ellis. Chemists have not merely isolated the alkaloid; they have learned how to synthesize it, so that the supply no longer depends on the sparse and intermittent crop of a desert cactus. Alienists have dosed themselves with mescalin in the hope thereby of coming to a better, a first-hand understanding of their patients' mental processes. Working unfortunately upon too few subjects within too narrow a range of circumstances, psychologists have observed and catalogued some of the drug's more striking effects. Neurologists and physiologists have found out something about the mechanism of its action upon the central nervous system. And at least one professional philosopher has taken mescalin for the light it may throw on such ancient, unsolved riddles as the place of mind in nature and the relationship between brain and consciousness.

There matters rested until, two or three years ago, a new and perhaps highly significant fact was observed.[1] Actually the fact had been staring

SOURCE: Pp. 11–37 in *The Doors of Perception* by Aldous Huxley. Copyright © 1954 by Aldous Huxley. Reprinted by permission of Mrs. Laura Huxley, Chatto and Windus, Ltd., and Harper and Row, Publishers, Inc.

[1] See the following papers:

Humphrey Osmond and John Smythies, "Schizophrenia: A New Approach," *The Journal of Mental Science*, XCVIII (April, 1952).

everyone in the face for several decades; but nobody, as it happened, had noticed it until a young English psychiatrist, at present working in Canada, was struck by the close similarity, in chemical composition, between mescalin and adrenalin. Further research revealed that lysergic acid, an extremely potent hallucinogen derived from ergot, has a structural biochemical relationship to the others. Then came the discovery that adrenochrome, which is a product of the decomposition of adrenalin, can produce many of the symptoms observed in mescalin intoxication. But adrenochrome probably occurs spontaneously in the human body. In other words, each one of us may be capable of manufacturing a chemical, minute doses of which are known to cause profound changes in consciousness. Certain of these changes are similar to those which occur in that most characteristic plague of the twentieth century, schizophrenia. Is the mental disorder due to a chemical disorder? And is the chemical disorder due, in its turn, to psychological distresses affecting the adrenals? It would be rash and premature to affirm it. The most we can say is that some kind of a *prima facie* case has been made out. Meanwhile the clue is being systematically followed, the sleuths — biochemists, psychiatrists, psychologists — are on the trail.

By a series of, for me, extremely fortunate circumstances I found myself, in the spring of 1953, squarely athwart that trail. One of the sleuths had come on business to California. In spite of seventy years of mescalin research, the psychological material at his disposal was still absurdly inadequate, and he was anxious to add to it. I was on the spot and willing, indeed eager, to be a guinea-pig. Thus it came about that, one bright May morning, I swallowed four-tenths of a gramme of mescalin dissolved in half a glass of water and sat down to wait for the results.

We live together, we act on, and react to, one another; but always and in all circumstances we are by ourselves. The martyrs go hand in hand into the arena; they are crucified alone. Embraced, the lovers desperately try to fuse their insulated ecstasies into a single self-transcendence; in vain. By its very nature every embodied spirit is doomed to suffer and enjoy in solitude. Sensations, feelings, insights, fancies — all these are private and, except through symbols and at second hand, incommunicable. We can pool information about experiences, but never the experiences themselves. From family to nation, every human group is a society of island universes.

Humphrey Osmond, "On Being Mad," *Saskatchewan Psychiatric Services Journal*, Vol. I, No. 2 (September, 1952).

John Smythies, "The Mescalin Phenomena," *The British Journal for the Philosophy of Science*, Vol. III (February, 1953).

Abram Hoffer, Humphrey Osmond, and John Smythies, "Schizophrenia: A New Approach," *The Journal of Mental Science*, Vol. C, No. 418 (January, 1954).

Numerous other papers on the biochemistry, pharmacology, psychology, and neurophysiology of schizophrenia and the mescalin phenomena are in preparation.

Most island universes are sufficiently like one another to permit of inferential understanding or even of mutual empathy or 'feeling into'. Thus, remembering our own bereavements and humiliations, we can condole with others in analogous circumstances, can put ourselves (always, of course, in a slightly Picwickian sense) in their places. But in certain cases communication between universes is incomplete or even non-existent. The mind is its own place, and the places inhabited by the insane and the exceptionally gifted are so different from the places where ordinary men and women live, that there is little or no common ground of memory to serve as a basis for understanding or fellow feeling. Words are uttered, but fail to enlighten. The things and events to which symbols refer belong to mutually exclusive realms of experience.

To see ourselves as others see us is a most salutary gift. Hardly less important is the capacity to see others as they see themselves. But what if these others belong to a different species and inhabit a radically alien universe? For example, how can the sane get to know what it actually feels like to be mad? Or, short of being born again as a visionary, a medium, or a musical genius, how can we ever visit the worlds which, to Blake, to Swedenborg, to Johann Sebastian Bach, were home? And how can a man at the extreme limits of ectomorphy and cerebrotonia ever put himself in the place of one at the limits of endomorphy and viscerotonia or, except within certain circumscribed areas, share the feelings of one who stands at the limits of mesomorphy and somatotonia? To the unmitigated behaviourist such questions, I suppose, are meaningless. But for those who theoretically believe what in practice they know to be true — namely, that there is an inside to experience as well as an outside — the problems posed are real problems, all the more grave for being, some completely insoluble, some soluble only in exceptional circumstances and by methods not available to everyone. Thus, it seems virtually certain that I shall never know what it feels like to be Sir John Falstaff or Joe Louis. On the other hand, it had always seemed to me possible that, through hypnosis, or example, or autohypnosis, by means of systematic meditation, or else by taking the appropriate drug, I might so change my ordinary mode of consciousness as to be able to know, from the inside, what the visionary, the medium, even the mystic were talking about.

From what I had read of the mescalin experience I was convinced in advance that the drug would admit me, at least for a few hours, into the kind of inner world described by Blake and A. E. But what I had expected did not happen. I had expected to lie with my eyes shut, looking at visions of many-coloured geometries, of animated architectures, rich with gems and fabulously lovely, of landscapes with heroic figures, of symbolic dramas trembling perpetually on the verge of the ultimate revelation. But I had not reckoned, it was evident, with the idiosyncrasies of my mental make-up, the facts of my temperament, training, and habits.

I am and, for as long as I can remember, I have always been a poor visualizer. Words, even the pregnant words of poets, do not evoke pictures in my mind. No hypnagogic visions greet me on the verge of sleep. When I recall something, the memory does not present itself to me as a vividly seen event or object. By an effort of the will, I can evoke a not very vivid image of what happened yesterday afternoon, of how the Lungarno used to look before the bridges were destroyed, of the Bayswater Road when the only buses were green and tiny and drawn by aged horses at three and a half miles an hour. But such images have little substance and absolutely no autonomous life of their own. They stand to real, perceived objects in the same relation as Homer's ghosts stood to the men of flesh and blood, who came to visit them in the shades. Only when I have a high temperature do my mental images come to independent life. To those in whom the faculty of visualization is strong my inner world must seem curiously drab, limited, and uninteresting. This was the world — a poor thing but my own — which I expected to see transformed into something completely unlike itself.

The change which actually took place in that world was in no sense revolutionary. Half an hour after swallowing the drug I became aware of a slow dance of golden lights. A little later there were sumptuous red surfaces swelling and expanding from bright nodes of energy that vibrated with a continuously changing, patterned life. At another time the closing of my eyes revealed a complex of grey structures, within which pale blueish spheres kept emerging into intense solidity and, having emerged, would slide noiselessly upwards, out of sight. But at no time were there faces or forms of men or animals. I saw no landscapes, no enormous spaces, no magical growth and metamorphosis of buildings, nothing remotely like a drama or a parable. The other world to which mescalin admitted me was not the world of visions; it existed out there, in what I could see with my eyes open. The great change was in the realm of objective fact. What had happened to my subjective universe was relatively unimportant.

I took my pill at eleven. An hour and half later I was sitting in my study, looking intently at a small glass vase. The vase contained only three flowers — a full-blown Belle of Portugal rose, shell pink with a hint at every petal's base of a hotter, flamier hue; a large magenta and cream-colored carnation; and, pale purple at the end of its broken stalk, the bold heraldic blossom of an iris. Fortuitous and provisional, the little nosegay broke all the rules of traditional good taste. At breakfast that morning I had been struck by the lively dissonance of its colours. But that was no longer the point. I was not looking now at an unusual flower arrangement. I was seeing what Adam had seen on the morning of his creation — the miracle, moment by moment, of naked existence.

'Is it agreeable?' somebody asked. (During this part of the experiment, all conversations were recorded on a dictating machine, and it has been possible for me to refresh my memory of what was said.)

'Neither agreeable nor disagreeable,' I answered. 'It just *is*.'

Istigkeit — wasn't that the word Meister Eckhart liked to use? 'Is-ness.' The Being of Platonic philosophy — except that Plato seems to have made the enormous, the grotesque mistake of separating Being from becoming, and identifying it with the mathematical abstraction of the Idea. He could never, poor fellow, have seen a bunch of flowers shining with their own inner light and all but quivering under the pressure of the significance with which they were charged; could never have perceived that what rose and iris and carnation so intensely signified was nothing more, and nothing less, than what they were — a transience that was yet eternal life, a perpetual perishing that was at the same time pure Being, a bundle of minute, unique particulars in which, by some unspeakable and yet self-evident paradox, was to be seen the divine source of all existence.

I continued to look at the flowers, and in their living light I seemed to detect the qualitative equivalent of breathing — but of a breathing without returns to a starting-point, with no recurrent ebbs but only a repeated flow from beauty to heightened beauty, from deeper to ever deeper meaning. Words like Grace and Transfiguration came to my mind, and this of course was what, among other things, they stood for. My eyes travelled from the rose to the carnation, and from that feathery incandescence to the smooth scrolls of sentient amethyst which were the iris. The Beatific Vision, *Sat Chit Ananda*, Being-Awareness-Bliss — for the first time I understood, not on the verbal level, not by inchoate hints or at a distance, but precisely and completely what those prodigious syllables referred to. And then I remembered a passage I had read in one of Suzuki's essays. 'What is the Dharma-Body of the Buddha?' (The Dharma-Body of the Buddha is another way of saying Mind, Suchness, the Void, the Godhead.) The question is asked in a Zen monastery by an earnest and bewildered novice. And with the prompt irrelevance of one of the Marx Brothers, the Master answers, 'The hedge at the bottom of the garden.' 'And the man who realizes this truth,' the novice dubiously enquires, 'what, may I ask, is he?' Groucho gives him a whack over the shoulders with his staff and answers, 'A golden-haired lion.'

It had been, when I read it, only a vaguely pregnant piece of nonsense. Now it was all clear as day, as evident as Euclid. Of course the Dharma-Body of the Buddha was the hedge at the bottom of the garden. At the same time, and no less obviously, it was these flowers, it was anything that I — or rather the blessed Not-I released for a moment from my throttling embrace — cared to look at. The books, for example, with which my study walls were lined. Like the flowers, they glowed, when I looked at them, with brighter colors, a profounder significance. Red books, like rubies; emerald books; books bound in white jade; books of agate, of aquamarine, of yellow topaz; lapis lazuli books whose color was so intense, so intrinsically meaningful, that they seemed to be on the point of leaving the shelves to thrust themselves more insistently on my attention.

'What about spatial relationships?' the investigator inquired, as I was looking at the books.

It was difficult to answer. True, the perspective looked rather odd, and the walls of the room no longer seemed to meet in right angles. But these were not the really important facts. The really important facts were that spatial relationships had ceased to matter very much and that my mind was perceiving the world in terms of other than spatial categories. At ordinary times the eye concerns itself with such problems as *Where? — How far? — How situated in relation to what?* In the mescalin experience the implied questions to which the eye responds are of another order. Place and distance cease to be of much interest. The mind does its perceiving in terms of intensity of existence, profundity of significance, relationships within a pattern. I saw the books, but was not at all concerned with their positions in space. What I noticed, what impressed itself upon my mind was the fact that all of them glowed with living light and that in some the glory was more manifest than in others. In this context, position and the three dimensions were beside the point. Not, of course, that the category of space had been abolished. When I got up and walked about, I could do so quite normally, without misjudging the whereabouts of objects. Space was still there; but it had lost its predominance. The mind was primarily concerned, not with measures and locations, but with being and meaning.

And along with indifference to space there went an even completer indifference to time.

'There seems to be plenty of it,' was all I would answer when the investigator asked me to say what I felt about time.

Plenty of it, but exactly how much was entirely irrelevant. I could, of course, have looked at my watch; but my watch, I knew, was in another universe. My actual experience had been, was still, of an indefinite duration or alternatively of a perpetual present made up of one continually changing apocalypse.

From the books the investigator directed my attention to the furniture. A small typing-table stood in the centre of the room; beyond it, from my point of view, was a wicker chair and beyond that a desk. The three pieces formed an intricate pattern of horizontals, uprights, and diagonals — a pattern all the more interesting for not being interpreted in terms of spatial relationships. Table, chair, and desk came together in a composition that was like something by Braque or Juan Gris, a still life recognizably related to the objective world, but rendered without depth, without any attempt at photographic realism. I was looking at my furniture, not as the utilitarian who has to sit on chairs, to write at desks and tables, and not as the camera-man or scientific recorder, but as the pure aesthete whose concern is only with forms and their relationships within the field of vision or the picture space. But as I looked, this purely aesthetic Cubist's-eye view gave place to what I can only describe as the sacramental vision of reality. I was back where I had been when I was looking at the flowers — back in a world where everything shone with the Inner Light, and was infinite in its significance. The legs, for example, of that chair — how miraculous their tubularity, how supernatural their polished smoothness! I spent several minutes — or was it several centuries? — not merely gazing at those bamboo legs, but actually *being* them — or rather being myself in them; or, to be still more accurate (for 'I' was not involved in the case, nor in a certain sense were 'they') being my Not-self in the Not-self which was the chair.

Reflecting on my experience, I find myself agreeing with the eminent Cambridge philosopher, Dr. C. D. Broad,

> that we should do well to consider much more seriously than we have hitherto been inclined to do the type of theory which Bergson put forward in connexion with memory and sense perception. The suggestion is that the function of the brain and nervous system and sense organs is in the main *eliminative* and not productive. Each person is at each moment capable of remembering all that has ever happened to him and of perceiving everything that is happening everywhere in the universe. The function of the brain and nervous system is to protect us from being overwhelmed and confused by this mass of largely useless and irrelevant knowledge, by shutting out most of what we should otherwise perceive or remember at any moment, and leaving only that very small and special selection which is likely to be practically useful.

According to such a theory, each one of us is potentially Mind at Large. But in so far as we are animals, our business is at all costs to survive. To make biological survival possible, Mind at Large has to be funnelled through the reducing valve of the brain and nervous system. What comes out at the other end is a measly trickle of the kind of consciousness which will help us to stay alive on the surface of this particular planet. To formulate and express the contents of this reduced awareness, man has invented and endlessly elaborated those symbol-systems and implicit philosophies which we call languages. Every individual is at once the beneficiary and the victim of the linguistic tradition into which he or she has been born — the beneficiary inasmuch as language gives access to the accumulated records of other people's experience, the victim in so far as it confirms him in the belief that reduced awareness is the only awareness and as it bedevils his sense of reality, so that he is all too apt to take his concepts for data, his words for actual things. That which, in the language of religion, is called 'this world' is the universe of reduced awareness, expressed and, as it were, petrified by language. The various 'other worlds', with which human beings erratically make contact are so many elements in the totality of the awareness belonging to Mind at Large. Most people, most of the time, know only what comes through the reducing valve and is consecrated as genuinely real by the local language. Certain persons, however, seem to be born with a kind of by-pass that circumvents the reducing valve. In others temporary by-passes may be acquired either spontaneously, or as the result of deliberate 'spiritual exercises', or through hypnosis, or by means of drugs. Through these permanent or temporary by-passes there flows, not indeed the perception 'of everything that is happening everywhere in the universe' (for the by-pass does not abolish the reducing valve, which still excludes the total content of Mind at Large), but something more than, and above all something different from, the carefully selected utilitarian material which our narrowed, individual minds regard as a complete, or at least sufficient, picture of reality.

The brain is provided with a number of enzyme systems which serve to coordinate its workings. Some of these enzymes regulate the supply of glucose to the brain cells. Mescalin inhibits the production of these enzymes and thus lowers the amount of glucose available to an organ that is in constant need of sugar. When mescalin reduces the brain's normal ration of sugar, what happens? Too few cases have been observed, and therefore a comprehensive answer cannot yet be given. But what happens to the majority of the few who have taken mescalin under supervision can be summarized as follows.

1. The ability to remember and to 'think straight' is little if at all reduced. (Listening to the recordings of my conversation under the influence of the drug, I cannot discover that I was then any stupider than I am at ordinary times.)

2. Visual impressions are greatly intensified and the eye recovers some of the perceptual innocence of childhood, when the sensum was not immediately and automatically subordinated to the concept. Interest in space is diminished and interest in time falls almost to zero.

3. Though the intellect remains unimpaired and though perception is enormously improved, the will suffers a profound change for the worse. The mescalin taker sees no reason for doing anything in particular and finds most of the causes for which, at ordinary times, he was prepared to act and suffer, profoundly uninteresting. He can't be bothered with them, for the good reason that he has better things to think about.

4. These better things may be experienced (as I experienced them) 'out there', or 'in here', or in both worlds, the inner and the outer, simultaneously or successively. That they *are* better seems to be self-evident to all mescalin takers who come to the drug with a sound liver and an untroubled mind.

These effects of mescalin are the sort of effects you could expect to follow the administration of a drug having the power to impair the efficiency of the cerebral reducing valve. When the brain runs out of sugar, the undernourished ego grows weak, can't be bothered to undertake the necessary chores, and loses all interest in those spatial and temporal relationships which mean so much to an organism bent on getting on in the world. As Mind at Large seeps past the no longer watertight valve, all kinds of biologically useless things start to happen. In some cases there may be extra-sensory perceptions. Other persons discover a world of visionary beauty. To others again is revealed the glory, the infinite value and meaningfulness of naked existence, of the given, unconceptualized event. In the final stage of ego-lessness there is an 'obscure knowledge' that All is in all — that All is actually each. This is as near, I take it, as a finite mind can ever come to 'perceiving everything that is happening everywhere in the universe'.

In this context, how significant is the enormous heightening, under mescalin, of the perception of colour! For certain animals it is biologically very important to be able to distinguish certain hues. But beyond the limits of their utilitarian spectrum, most creatures are completely colour blind. Bees, for example, spend most of their time 'deflowering the fresh virgins of the spring'; but, as von Frisch has shown, they can recognize only a very few colours. Man's highly developed colour sense is a biological luxury — inestimably precious to him as an intellectual and spiritual being, but unnecessary to his survival as an animal. To judge by the adjectives which Homer puts into their mouths, the heroes of the Trojan War hardly excelled the bees in their capacity to distinguish colours. In this respect, at least, mankind's advance has been prodigious.

Mescalin raises all colours to a higher power and makes the percipient aware of innumerable fine shades of difference, to which, at ordinary times, he is completely blind. It would seem that, for Mind at Large, the so-called secondary characters of things are primary. Unlike Locke, it evidently feels that colours are more important, better worth attending to than masses, positions, and dimensions. Like mescalin takers, many mystics perceive supernaturally brilliant colours, not only with the inward eye, but even in the objective world around them. Similar reports are made by psychics and sensitives. There are certain mediums to whom the mescalin taker's brief revelation is a matter, during long periods, of daily and hourly experience.

From this long but indispensable excursion into the realm of theory we may now return to the miraculous facts — four bamboo chair legs in the middle of a room. Like Wordsworth's daffodils, they brought all manner of wealth — the gift, beyond price, of a new direct insight into the very Nature of Things, together with a more modest treasure of understanding in the field, especially, of the arts.

A rose is a rose is a rose. But these chair legs were chair legs were St Michael and all angels. Four or five hours after the event, when the effects of a cerebral sugar shortage were wearing off, I was taken for a little tour of the city, which included a visit, towards sundown, to what is modestly claimed to be The World's Biggest Drug Store. At the Back of the W.B.D.S., among the toys, the greeting cards, and the comics stood a row, surprisingly enough, of art books. I picked up the first volume that came to hand. It was on Van Gogh, and the picture at which the book opened was *The Chair* — that astounding portrait of a *Ding an Sich*, which the mad painter saw, with a kind of adoring terror, and tried to render on his canvas. But it was a task to which the power even of genius proved wholly inadequate. The chair Van Gogh had seen was obviously the same in essence as the chair I had seen. But, though incomparably more real than the chair of ordinary perception, the chair in his picture remained no more than an unusually expressive symbol of the fact. The fact had been manifested Suchness; this was only an emblem. Such emblems are sources of true knowledge about the Nature of Things, and this true knowledge may serve to prepare the mind which accepts it for immediate insights on its own account. But that is all. However expressive, symbols can never be the things they stand for.

It would be interesting, in this context, to make a study of the works of art available to the great knowers of Suchness. What sort of pictures did Eckhart look at? What sculptures and paintings played a part in the religious experience of St John of the Cross, of Hakuin, of Hui-neng, of William Law? The questions are beyond my power to answer; but I strongly suspect that most of the great knowers of Suchness paid very little attention to art — some refusing to have anything to do with it at all, others being content with what a critical eye would regard as second-rate, or even tenth-rate, works. (To a person whose transfigured and transfiguring mind can see the All in every *this*, the first-rateness or tenth-rateness of even a religious painting will be a matter of the most sovereign indifference.) Art, I suppose, is only for beginners, or else for those resolute dead-enders, who have made up their minds to be content with the *ersatz* of Suchness, with symbols rather than with what they signify, with the elegantly composed recipe in lieu of actual dinner.

I returned the Van Gogh to its rack and picked up the volume standing next to it. It was a book on Botticelli. I turned the pages. *The Birth of Venus* — never one of my favourites. *Venus and Mars*, that loveliness so passionately denounced by poor Ruskin at the height of his long-drawn sexual tragedy. The marvellously rich and intricate *Calumny of Apelles*. And then a somewhat less familiar and not very good picture, *Judith*. My attention was arrested and I gazed in fascination, not at the pale neurotic heroine or her attendant, not at the victim's hairy head or the vernal landscape in the background, but at the purplish silk of Judith's pleated bodice and long wind-blown skirts.

This was something I had seen before — seen that very morning, between the flowers and the furniture, when I looked down by chance, and went on passionately staring by choice, at my own crossed legs. Those folds in the trousers — what a labyrinth of endlessly significant complexity! And the texture of the grey flannel — how rich, how deeply, mysteriously sumptuous! And here they were again, in Botticelli's picture.

Civilized human beings wear clothes, therefore there can be no portraiture, no mythological or historical story telling without representations of folded textiles. But though it may account for the origins, mere tailoring can never explain the luxuriant development of drapery as a major theme of all the plastic arts. Artists, it is obvious, have always loved drapery for its own sake — or, rather, for their own. When you paint or carve drapery, you are painting or carving forms which, for all practical purposes, are nonrepresentational — the kind of unconditioned forms on which artists even in the most naturalistic tradition like to let themselves go. In the average Madonna or Apostle the strictly human, fully representational element accounts for about ten per cent of the whole. All the rest consists of many coloured variations on the inexhaustible theme of crumpled wool or linen. And these non-representational nine-tenths of a Madonna or an Apostle may be just as important qualitatively as they are in quantity. Very often they set the tone of the whole work of art, they state the key in which the theme is being rendered, they express the mood, the temperament, the attitude to life of the artist. Stoical serenity reveals itself in the smooth surfaces, the broad untortured folds of Piero's draperies. Torn between fact and wish, between cynicism and idealism, Bernini tempers the all but caricatural verisimilitude of his faces with enormous sartorial abstractions, which are the embodiment, in stone or bronze, of the everlasting commonplaces of rhetoric — the heroism, the holiness, the sublimity to which mankind perpetually aspires, for the most part in vain. And here are El Greco's disquietingly visceral skirts and mantles; here are the sharp, twisting, flame-like folds in which Cosimo Tura clothes his figures: in the first, traditional spirituality breaks down into a nameless physiological yearning; in the second, there writhes an agonized sense of the world's essential strangeness and hostility. Or consider Watteau; his men and women play lutes, get ready for balls and harlequinades, embark, on velvet lawns and under noble trees, for the Cythera of every lover's dream; their enormous melancholy and the flayed, excruciating sensibility of their creator find expression, not in the actions recorded, not in the gestures and the faces portrayed, but in the relief and texture of their taffeta skirts, their satin capes and doublets. Not an inch of smooth surface here, not a moment of peace or confidence, only a silken wilderness of countless tiny pleats and wrinkles, with an incessant modulation — inner uncertainty rendered with the perfect assurance of a master hand — of tone into tone, of one indeterminate colour into another. In life, man proposes, God disposes. In the plastic arts the proposing is done by the subject matter; that which disposes is ultimately the artist's temperament, proximately (at least in portraiture, history, and genre) the carved or painted drapery. Between them these two may decree that a *fête galante* shall move to tears, that a crucifixion shall be serene to the point of cheerfulness, that a stigmatization shall be almost intolerably sexy, that the likeness of a prodigy of female brainlessness (I am thinking now of Ingres' incomparable Mme Moitessier) shall express the austerest, the most uncompromising intellectuality.

But this is not the whole story. Draperies, as I had now discovered, are much more than devices for the introduction of non-representational forms into naturalistic paintings and sculptures. What the rest of us see only under the influence of mescalin, the artist is congenitally equipped to see all the time. His perception is not limited to what is biologically or socially useful. A little of the knowledge belonging to Mind at Large oozes past the reducing valve of brain and ego into his consciousness. It is a knowledge of the intrinsic significance of every existent. For the artist as for the mescalin taker, draperies are living hieroglyphs that stand in some peculiarly expressive way for the unfathomable mystery of pure being. More even than the chair, though less perhaps than those wholly supernatural flowers, the folds of my grey flannel trousers were charged with 'isness'. To what they owed this privileged status, I cannot say. Is it, perhaps, because the forms of folded drapery are so strange and dramatic that they catch the eye and in this way force the miraculous fact of sheer existence upon the attention? Who knows? What is important is less the reason for the experience than the experience itself. Poring over Judith's skirts, there in the World's Biggest Drug Store, I knew that Botticelli — and not Botticelli alone, but many others too — had looked at draperies with the same transfigured and transfiguring eyes as had been mine that morning. They had seen the *Istigkeit*, the Allness and Infinity of folded cloth, and had done their best to render it in paint or stone. Necessarily, of course, without success. For the glory and the wonder of pure existence belong to another order, beyond the power of even the highest art to express. But in Judith's skirt I could clearly see what, if I had been a painter of genius, I might have made of my old grey flannels. Not much, heaven knows, in comparison with the reality; but enough to delight generation after generation of beholders, enough to make them understand at least a little of the true significance of what, in our pathetic imbecility, we call 'mere things' and disregard in favour of television.

'This is how one ought to see,' I kept saying as I looked down at my trousers, or glanced at the jewelled books in the shelves, at the legs of my infinitely more than Van-Goghian chair. 'This is how one ought to see, how things really are.' And yet there were reservations. For if one always saw like this, one would never want to do anything else. Just looking, just being the divine Not-self of flower, of book, of chair, of flannel. That would be enough. But in that case what about other people? What about human relations? In the recording of that morning's conversations I find the question constantly repeated, 'What about human relations?' How could one reconcile this timeless bliss of seeing as one ought to see with the temporal duties of doing what one ought to do and feeling as one ought to feel? 'One ought to be able,' I said, 'to see these trousers as infinitely important and human beings as still more infinitely important.' One ought — but in practice it seemed to be impossible. This participation in the manifest glory of things left no room, so to speak, for the ordinary, the necessary concerns of human existence, above all for concerns involving persons. For persons are selves and, in one respect at least, I was not a Not-self, simultaneously perceiving and being the Not-self of the things around me. To this new-born Not-self, the behaviour, the appearance, the very thought of the self it had momentarily ceased to be, and of other selves, its one-time fellows, seemed not indeed distasteful (for distastefulness was not one of the categories in terms of which I was thinking), but enormously irrelevant. Compelled by the investigator to analyse and report on what I was doing (and how I longed to be left alone with Eternity in a flower, Infinity in four chair legs, and the Absolute in the folds of a pair of flannel trousers!) I realized that I was deliberately avoiding the eyes of those who were with me in the room, deliberately refraining from being too much aware of them. One was my wife, the other a man I respected and greatly liked; but both belonged to the world from which, for the moment, mescalin had delivered me — the world of selves, of time, of moral judgements and utilitarian considerations, the world (and it was this aspect of human life which I wished, above all else, to forget) of self-assertion, of cocksureness, of over-valued words, and idolatrously worshipped notions.

At this stage of the proceedings I was handed a large coloured reproduction of the well-known self-portrait by Cézanne — the head and shoulders of a man in a large straw hat, red-cheeked, red-lipped, with rich black whiskers and a dark unfriendly eye. It is a magnificent painting; but it was not as a painting that I now saw it. For the head promptly took on a third dimension and came to life as a small goblin-like man looking out through a window in the page before me. I started to laugh. And when they asked me why, 'What pretensions!' I kept repeating. 'Who on earth does he think he is?' The question was not addressed to Cézanne in particular, but to the human species at large. Who did they all think they were?

'It's like Arnold Bennett in the Dolomites,' I said, suddenly remembering a scene, happily immortalized in a snapshot of A. B. some four or five years before his death toddling along a wintry road at Cortina d'Ampezzo. Around him lay the virgin snow; in the background was a more than gothic aspiration of red crags. And there was dear, kind, unhappy A. B. consciously overacting the role of his favourite character in fiction, himself, the Card in person. There he went, toddling slowly in the bright Alpine sunshine, his thumbs in the arm-holes of a yellow waistcoat which bulged, a little lower down, with the graceful curve of a Regency bow window at Brighton — his head thrown back as though to aim some stammered utterance, howitzerlike, at the blue dome of heaven. What he actually said, I have forgotten; but what his whole manner, air, and posture fairly shouted was, 'I'm as good as those damned mountains'. And in some ways, of course, he was infinitely better; but not, as he knew very well, in the way his favourite character in fiction liked to imagine.

Successfully (whatever that may mean) or unsuccessfully, we all over-act the part of our favourite character in fiction. And in fact, the almost infinitely unlikely fact, of actually being Cézanne makes no difference. For the consummate painter, with his little pipe-line to Mind at Large by-passing the brain-valve and ego-filter, was also and just as genuinely this whiskered goblin with the unfriendly eye.

For relief I turned back to the folds in my trousers. 'This is how one ought to see,' I repeated yet again. And I might have added, 'These are the sort of things one ought to look at.' Things without pretensions, satisfied to be merely themselves, sufficient in their suchness, not acting a part, not trying, insanely, to go it alone, in isolation from the Dharma-Body, in Luciferian defiance of the grace of God.

'The nearest approach to this,' I said, 'would be a Vermeer.'

Yes, a Vermeer. For that mysterious artist was trebly gifted — with the vision that perceives the Dharma-Body as the hedge at the bottom of the garden, with the talent to render as much of that vision as the limitations of human capacity permit, and with the prudence to confine himself in his paintings to the more manageable aspects of reality; for though Vermeer represented human beings, he was always a painter of still life. Cézanne, who told his female sitters to do their best to look like apples, tried to paint portraits in the same spirit. But his pippin-like women are more nearly related to Plato's Ideas than to the Dharma-Body in the hedge. They are Eternity and Infinity seen, not in sand or flower, but in the abstractions of some very superior brand of geometry. Vermeer never asked his girls to look like apples. On the contrary, he insisted on their being girls to the very limit — but always with the proviso that they refrain from behaving girlishly. They might sit or quietly stand but never giggle, never display self-consciousness, never say their prayers or pine for absent sweethearts, never gossip, never gaze enviously at other women's babies, never flirt, never love nor hate nor work. In the act of doing any of these things they would doubtless become more intensely themselves, but would cease, for that very reason, to manifest their divine essential Not-self. In Blake's phrase, the doors of Vermeer's perception were only partially cleansed. A single panel had become almost perfectly transparent; the rest of the door was still muddy. The essential Not-self could be perceived very clearly in things and in living creatures on the hither side of good and evil. In human beings it was visible only when they were in repose, their minds untroubled, their bodies motionless. In these circumstances Vermeer could see Suchness in all its heavenly beauty — could see and, in some small measure, render it in a subtle and sumptuous still life. Vermeer is undoubtedly the greatest painter of human still lives. But there have been others, for example, Vermeer's French contemporaries, the Le Nain brothers. They set out, I suppose, to be genre painters; but what they actually produced was a series of human still lives, in which their cleansed perception of the infinite significance of all things is rendered not, as with Vermeer, by a subtle enrichment of colour, and texture, but by a heightened clarity, and obsessive distinctness of form, within an austere, almost monochromatic tonality. In our own day we have had Vuillard, the painter, at his best, of unforgettably splendid pictures of the Dharma-Body manifested in a bourgeois bedroom, of the Absolute blazing away in the midst of some stockbroker's family in a suburban garden, taking tea.

Ce qui fait que l'ancien bandagiste renie
Le comptoir dont le faste alléchait les passants,
C'est son jardin d'Auteuil, où, veufs de tout encens,
Les Zinnias ont l'air d'être en tôle vernie.

For Laurent Taillade the spectacle was merely obscene. But if the retired rubber goods merchant had sat still enough, Vuillard would have seen in him only the Dharma-Body, would have painted, in the zinnias, the goldfish pool, the villa's Moorish tower and Chinese lanterns, a corner of Eden before the Fall.

But meanwhile my questions remained unanswered. How was this cleansed perception to be reconciled with a proper concern with human relations, with the necessary chores and duties, to say nothing of charity and practical compassion? The age-old debate between the actives and the contemplatives was being renewed — renewed, so far as I was concerned, with an unprecedented poignancy. For until this morning I had known contemplation only in its humbler, its more ordinary forms — as discursive thinking; as a rapt absorption in poetry or painting or music, as a patient waiting upon those inspirations, without which even the prosiest writer cannot hope to accomplish anything; as occasional glimpses, in nature, of Wordsworth's 'something far more deeply interfused'; as systematic silence leading, sometimes, to hints of an 'obscure knowledge'. But now I knew contemplation at its height. At its height, but not yet in its fullness. For in its fullness the way of Mary includes the way of Martha and raises it, so to speak, to its own higher power. Mescalin opens up the way of Mary, but shuts the door on that of Martha. It gives access to contemplation — but to a contemplation that is incompatible with action and even with the will to action, the very thought of action. In the intervals between his revelations the mescalin taker is apt to feel that, though in one way everything is supremely as it should be, in another there is something wrong. His problem is essentially the same as that which confronts the quietist, the *arhat* and, on another level, the landscape painter and the painter of human still lives. Mescalin can never solve that problem: it can only pose it, apocalyptically, for those to whom it had never before presented itself. The full and final solution can be found only by those who are prepared to implement the right kind of *Weltanschauung* by means of the right kind of behaviour and the right kind of constant and unstrained alertness. Over against the quietist stands the active-contemplative, the saint, the man who, in Eckhart's phrase, is ready to come down from the seventh heaven in order to bring a cup of water to his sick brother. Over against the *arhat*, retreating from appearances into an entirely transcendental Nirvana, stands the Bodhisattva, for whom Suchness and the world of contingencies are one, and for whose boundless compassion every one of those contingencies is an occasion not only for transfiguring insight, but also for the most practical charity. And in the universe of art, over against Vermeer and the other painters of human still lives, over against the masters of Chinese and Japanese painting, over against Constable and Turner, against Sisley and Seurat and Cézanne stands the all-inclusive art of Rembrandt. These are enormous names, inaccessible eminences. For myself, on this memorable May morning, I could only be grateful for an experience which had shown me, more clearly than I have ever seen it before, the true nature of the challenge and the completely liberating response.

Let me add, before we leave this subject, that there is no form of contemplation, even the most quietistic, which is without its ethical values. Half at least of all morality is negative and consists in keeping out of mischief. The Lord's prayer is less than fifty words long, and six of those words are devoted to asking God not to lead us into temptation. The one-sided contemplative leaves undone many things that he ought to do; but to make up for it he refrains from doing a host of things he ought not to do. The sum of evil, Pascal remarked, would be much diminished if men could only learn to sit quietly in their rooms. The contemplative whose perception has been cleansed does not have to stay in his room. He can go about his business, so completely satisfied to see and be a part of the divine Order of Things that he will never even be tempted to indulge in what Traherne called 'the dirty Devices of the world'. When we feel ourselves to be sole heirs of the universe, when 'the sea flows in our veins . . . and the stars are our jewels', when all things are perceived as infinite and holy, what motive can we have for covetousness or self-assertion, for the pursuit of power or the drearier forms of pleasure? Contemplatives are not likely to become gamblers, or procurers, or drunkards; they do not as a rule preach intolerance, or make war; do not find it necessary to rob, swindle, or grind the faces of the poor. And to these enormous negative virtues we may add another which, though hard to define, is both positive and important. The *arhat* and the quietist may not practise contemplation in its fullness; but if they practise it at all, they may bring back enlightening reports of another, a transcendent country of the mind;

and if they practise it in the height, they will become conduits through which some beneficent influence can flow out of that other country into a world of darkened selves, chronically dying for lack of it.

Timothy Leary | # How To Change Behavior

It is my plan to talk to you tonight about methods of effecting change — change in man's behavior and change in man's consciousness.

Behavior and consciousness. Please note the paired distinction. Behavior and consciousness. Up until recently I considered myself a behavioral scientist and limited the scope of my work to overt and measurable behavior. In so doing I was quite in the *Zeitgeist* of modern psychology, studying the subject matter which our American predecessors defined some fifty years ago, behavior, routinely following the ground rules they laid down, scrupulously avoiding that which is most important to the subject — his consciousness, concentrating instead, on what is most important to we who seek to observe, measure, manipulate, control and predict — the subject's overt behavior.

This decision to turn our backs on consciousness is, of course, typically western and very much in tune with the experimental, objective bent of Western science. Professor Huston Smith of the Massachusetts Institute of Technology has pointed out some basic differences between Western approach and the philosophies of China and India. Differences which have some importance for the applied psychologist concerned with behavior change. Professor Smith reminds us that our Western culture has stressed measurement and control of objects; whereas China has historically emphasized the rules of the social encounter; and Indian philosophy the development and expansion of human consciousness. Tonight I speak to you from a point midway between the Western and Eastern hemispheres of the cortex presenting a theory and method which is Chinese in that behavior is seen as an intricate social game; Indian in its recognition of consciousness and the need to develop a more cosmic awareness, and finally Western in its concern to do good measurably well.

I plan to present, first, some thoughts on behavior change, then some new conceptions of consciousness and its alteration, and finally some data from recent research in these areas.

SOURCE: *L.S.D.: The Consciousness-Expanding Drug*, edited by David Solomon, 1968.

Behavior and Its Change

Except for reflexes and instinctual reactions and random muscular movements (which fall into the province of physiology) all behavior is learned.

Behavior is therefore artifactual and culturally determined. Behavior sequences might usefully be considered as game sequences.

The use of the word "game" in this sweeping context is likely to be misunderstood. The listener may think I refer to "play" as opposed to the stern, real-life, serious activities of man. But as you shall see I consider the latter as "game."

At this point you are asking for and you deserve a definition. What do I mean by game? A game is a learned cultural sequence characterized by six factors:

1. *Roles:* The game assigns roles to the human beings involved.
2. *Rules:* A game sets up a set of rules which hold only during the game sequence.
3. *Goals:* Every game has its goals or purpose. The goals of baseball are to score more runs than the opponents. The goals of the game of psychology are more complex and less explicit but they exist.
4. *Rituals:* Each game has its conventional behavior pattern not related to the goals or rules but yet quite necessary to comfort and continuance.
5. *Language:* Each game has its jargon. Unrelated to the rules and goals and yet necessary to learn and use.
6. *Values:* Each game has its standards of excellence or goodness.

Baseball and basketball have clearly definable roles, rules, rituals, goals, languages and values. Psychology, religion, politics are games, too, learned, cultural sequences with clearly definable roles, rules, rituals, goals, jargons, values. They are less explicitly formulated than the so-called sports and therein, dear friends, lies the pity. For this simple reason millions have died and we may die tomorrow.

The behavior which psychiatrists label as disease entities can be considered as games, too. Dr. Thomas Szasz, the distinguished psychoanalyst-philosopher, in his book, *The Myth of Mental Illness,* suggests that "hysteria" is the name we give to a certain doctor-patient game involving deceitful helplessness. The "bluff" in poker is a similar deceitful but perfectly legitimate game device. Psychiatry according to this model is behavior-change game.

Far from being frivolous, many so-called "play games" are superior in their behavioral science and in their behavior-change techniques to the "not-called games," such as psychiatry and psychology.

In terms of epistomology and scientific method employed, the "game" of American baseball is superior to any of the so-called behavioral sciences. Baseball officials have classified and they reliably record molecular behavior sequences (the strike, the hit, the double play, etc.). Their compiled records are converted into indices most relevant for summarizing and predicting behavior (RBI, runs batted in; ERA, earned run average, etc.). Baseball employs well-trained raters to judge those rare events which are not obviously and easily coded. Their raters are called umpires.

When we move from behavior science to behavior-change we see that baseball experts have devised another remarkable set of techniques for bringing about the results which they and their subjects look for. Coaching. Baseball men understand the necessity for sharing time and space with their learners, for setting up role models, for feedback of relevant information to the learner, for endless practice of the desired behavior. And most important of all, baseball scientists understand the basic, cosmic lesson of percentage: that the greatest player gets on the average one hit in three tries, the winning team loses at least one game in three, that no team can lead the league every year, neither Rome, nor Athens, nor London, nor Moscow, nor Washington. Those who wish to measure, summarize, predict, and change human behavior could do worse than model themselves after this so-called "game."

All behavior involves learned games. But only that rare Westerner we call "mystic" or who has had a visionary experience of some sorts sees clearly the game structure of behavior. Most of the rest of us spend our time struggling with roles and rules and goals and concepts of games which are implicit and confusedly not seen as games, trying to apply the roles and rules and rituals of one game to other games.

Worst of all is the not knowing that it is a game. Baseball is a clean and successful game because it is seen as a game. You can shift positions. You know the game is limited in space and in time. You know how you are doing. You sign your contract. You renew your contract. You can quit, start a new game.

Culturally, stability is maintained by keeping the members of any cultural group from seeing that the roles, rules, goals, rituals, language, and values are game structures. The family game is treated by most cultures as far more than a game, with its implicit contracts, limited in time and space. The nationality game. It is treason not to play. The racial game. The religious game. And that most treacherous and tragic game of all, the game of individuality, the ego game. The Timothy Leary game. Ridiculous how we confuse this game, overplay it. Our own mystics and the Eastern philosophers have been warning us about this danger for centuries.

Cultural institutions encourage the delusion that the games of life are inevitable givens involving natural laws of behavior. These fixed delusions tend to rigidify behavior patterns. This rigidity, as Professor Osgood pointed out in his significant opening address of the Copenhagen Congress, now threatens the very survival of the human species itself.

So now we come to behavior change. The currently popular method of behavior change is called psychotherapy. A medical game. A curing of the psyche. Psychotherapy interprets confusion and inefficiency in game playing as illness. We call it sickness and attempt to cure it employing the medical game. Consider the football player who doesn't know the rules. Perhaps he picks up the ball and runs off the field. He is punished for not playing the game correctly. He feels badly. Shall we pronounce him sick and call the doctor?

The failure to understand the game nature of behavior leads to confusion and eventually to helplessness. Helplessness. Let's look at this word for a moment. It's a big concept in understanding science, technology, rehabilitation and, for that matter, the working of the mind itself.

The basic aim of physical science is to reduce human helplessness in the face of the physical environment. Physical science has other goals, of course: to understand, explain, control, measure, predict. But certainly these are ends rather than means. Why explain? Why predict? To lessen fearful ignorance. The technologies which have grown up around the physical sciences, engineering, medicine, also take as their goal the reducing of human helplessness.

Do they not stem from the same survival motive? And the social technologies — psychiatry, social work, applied psychology — is not their goal the reduction of confusion and the increase in human freedom?

Judged by these criteria the game of Western science has not been a glorious success. Our helplessness in the face of physical disease has certainly diminished. Our control over natural forces has given us a sense of mastery. We live longer and healthier lives. Good.

We have created a game model — the subject-object model — which allows us on the one hand to dominate "object" but which has created a world full of human objects. Most of what we do in the name of science results in more and greater human helplessness.

The science game creates wonder drugs whose action is not understood by the user. And worse yet we turn over these drugs to those who play the doctor game, the medical game — whose roles, rules, rituals, language, goals and values place the patient into a passive object status.

The science game, the healing game, the knowledge game are magnificent human structures. They are our proudest game accomplishments. But they are great only as long as they are seen as game. When they go beyond this point the trouble begins — claims to a nongame reality status: the emergence of experts, professionals, priests, status-favored authorities; claims to power and control and priority. Look at the A.E.C. Look at the A.M.A. And watch out! At this point you will find that games which began with the goal of decreasing human helplessness end up increasing it.

Human beings inhabiting those areas of the globe which the geographic game calls East are, for the most part, well aware of the foregoing issues. It's hard for Westerners to back away, and see the artifactual game structures. We are so close to our games. We have been born into them. And we are born into a philosophic system which glorifies hierarchical expertise on the one hand and helplessness on the other: monotheism, the Judaic-Christian tradition. Monotheism, that game started by a few persecuted outcasts (game losers) in the Mid-Eastern desert: the subject-object game; the false quality game; the manipulating, predicting, controlling game. Montheism breeding helplessness.

Now, let's apply this general discussion of helplessness and the behavior game to the issue of behavior change. In spite of our apparent executive control over nature we have had small success in developing behavior change games. Indeed most of our attempts to change behavior increase human helplessness, lessen human freedom and thereby exaggerate the problem we set out to solve. Our behavior change games invariably set up structures which give more power to the few and less power to the many, invidious role models: doctor-patient; professor-student; inequitable rules involving secrecy and control; the one-upmanship language we call jargon.

When people come to us and ask us to change their behavior, why can't we do it? Why can't we teach them to see the game structure of human society? The problem seems simple enough. Why can't we find out what games they are caught up in? Find out what games they want to commit themselves to? Make them explicit? Help them discover the rules of the game, the role, the rituals, the goals, the concepts? Expose them to models of successful game playing; encourage them to practice; feed back objective appraisals of their performance; care for them and their game struggles? How do you care for them? You share time and space with them. Nothing else can substitute. We have little else to offer. If we don't, they'll learn the games of those who do share time and space. If they're prisoners, then who will teach them behavior games? Who shares the most time and space with prisoners? That's right, the other prisoners, older criminals and younger criminals. So who influences behavior in what direction? And who shares the most amount of time and space with prisoners? That's right, the prison guards who, in most American prisons, teach them how to play the role of robber in the game of "cops and robbers." And we professional middle-class experts? How much time and space do we share with the prisoners? An hour a week on the medical ward?

O.K. It sounds simple enough, doesn't it? Just show people that their social identity and their entire cultural commitment is a game. They aren't aware of it. Sure, just tell them.

Yes, you smile when I say this. It's not quite that easy, is it? Here's the rub. Few people, a very few people (and we Westerners call them mystics) are willing and able to admit that the game is a game. Most of our people become upset and even angry when the game is identified — the game of "I-and-all-I-stand-for."

At this point when you hear the word "mystic" you may be uneasily wondering if you are going to be subjected to a vague metaphysical discourse on general principles. Perhaps you will be surprised to hear me suggest the hypothesis that the most effective approach to the "practical" games of life is that of applied mysticism. Identify the game structure of the event. Make sure that you do not apply the rules and concepts of other games to this situation. Move directly to solve the problem avoiding abstractions and irrelevant rituals. A mystic Martian or a person from a different culture might be an excellent consultant for a behavioral problem. They might be able to cut through irrelevant games rules to what is most relevant to survival and peace of mind.

How can we make the point? How can we learn the lesson? How can we Westerners come to see that our own consciousness is infinitely greater than our little egos and the ego games into which we are so blindly caught up? That the universe within our skulls is infinitely more than the flimsy game world which our words and minds create?

Put in a sentence — the task is to see that the mind is a tiny fragment of the brain-body complex. It is the game-playing fragment — a useful and entertaining tool but quite irrelevant to survival, and indeed usually antagonistic to well-being.

The process of getting beyond the game structure, beyond the subject-object commitments, the dualities — this process is called the mystic experience. The visionary experience is the nongame, metagame experience. Change in behavior can occur with dramatic spontaneity once the game structure of behavior is seen. The visionary experience is the key to behavior change.

Consciousness and Its Change

How do we obtain the visionary state?

There are many methods for expanding consciousness beyond the game limits. Mr. Aldous Huxley this afternoon presented a scholarly history of the same classic and modern methods. Margaret Mead, the American anthropologist, has suggested several cross-cultural methods. Have a psychotic episode. (This is to say, just stop playing the social game for a while and they'll call you insane, but you may learn the great lesson.) Or expose yourself to some great trauma that shatters the gamesmanship out of you. Birth by ordeal is a well-documented phenomenon. The concentration camp experience has done this for some of our wisest men. Physical traumas can do it. Electric shock. Extreme fatigue. Live in another and very different culture for a year where your roles and rituals and language just don't mean a thing. Or separate yourself from the game pressure by institutional withdrawal. Live for a while in a monastic cell. Or marry a Russian. Sensory deprivation does it. Sensory deprivation cuts through the game.

Certain forms of sensory stimulation alter consciousness beyond games. The sexual orgasm is certainly the most frequent and natural, although so brief and so built into interpersonal courtship games that it has lost much of its mystical meaning in the West. We have recently learned from W. Grey Walters and William Burroughs about photostimulation as a means of consciousness alteration. Concentrated attention to a strobo-scope or flicker apparatus can produce visionary experiences.

The most efficient way to cut through the game structure of Western life is the use of drugs, consciousness-expanding drugs. From here on I shall use the abbreviation CE to refer to consciousness-expanding sub-stances, such as LSD, mescaline, psilocybin.

Now the reaction of the Western world to consciousness-expanding drugs is extremely interesting. We tend to apply our familiar game roles, rituals, goals, rules, concepts to the non-game experience produced by these substances. Those of you who have not had the shattering exposure to such old and worshipped plants as peyote and the sacred mushroom and cannabis or such startling newcomers as psilocybin[1] and lysergic acid will wonder at this point about the nature of these experiences. What do these substances do? The neuro-physiological answer — the answer from outside — to this question is not yet ready. The answer from the inside (from the awareness of the subject) can be cast in countless metaphors. Let's try a physiological analogy. Let's assume that the cortex, the seat of consciousness, is a millionfold network of neurones, a fantastic com-puting machine. Cultural learning has imposed a few, pitifully small programs on the cortex. These programs may activate perhaps one tenth or one one-hundredth of the potential neural connections. All the learned games of life can be seen as programs which select, censor, alert and thus drastically limit the available cortical response (Mr. Aldous Huxley's reducing valves).

The CE (i.e., consciousness-expanding) drugs unplug these narrow programs. They unplug the ego, the game machinery, and the mind (that cluster of game concepts). And with the ego and mind unplugged, what is left? Not the "id"; no dark, evil impulses. These alleged negative "forces" are, of course, part of the game, being simply antirules. What is left is something that Western culture knows little about: the open brain, the uncensored cortex — alert and open to a broad sweep. Huxley and Dr. Barron have told you in their own words what is left, and there is no need to add my lumbering prose.

There is need, however, to ask another question. Why is this ecstatic, brain-opening experience so strange and horrid to Western culture? Why have our ancestors and our colleagues tended to ignore and even to oppose the visionary experience? Mr. R. Gordon Wasson, banker, mycologist, anthropologist, gentleman-scholar turned mystic, has traced the persecu-tion of the divine and divinatory mushroom back through the millennia.

---

[1] Psilocybin is a synthetic of the active ingredients of the sacred mushroom of Mexico. The divinitory mushroom was introduced to the Western culture by Professor Roger Heim of Paris and R. Gordon Wasson of New York and synthesized by Dr. A. Hofmann of the Sandoz Laboratory in Basel, Switzerland, who is also known through his work on lysergic acid. We are grateful to Sandoz, Inc., for providing the research materials used in these studies.

Why the irrational fear so often aroused by research on CE drugs even to this day? Perhaps because our Western world is committed to over-playing the objective, external behavior game.

In particular we overvalue the mind — that flimsy collection of learned words and verbal connections; the mind, that system of paranoid delusions with the learned self as center. And we eschew the nonmind, non-game intuitive insight outlook which is the key to the religious experience, to the love experience.

We seem to oppose any process which puts the game of here and now onto the long evolutionary timetable. This is a natural opposition and a healthy one. It is the greatest game of "the game" versus the "nongame." Behavior versus consciousness. The universal brain-body versus the cultural mind. The ego versus the species. A dialogue old and holy, like the dialogue of sea against land.

But this old game should be made explicit if it is to be fun. Unfortunately, the West has no concepts for thinking and talking about this basic dialogue. There is no ritual for mystical experience, for the mindless vision. What should provoke intense and cheerful competition too often evokes suspicion, anger, and impatience. What can be holy and intensely educational in the action of CE drugs on the cortex finds no ritual for application. This is to me one of the greatest challenges of our times.

The nongame visionary experiences are, I submit, the key to behavior change — drug-induced *satori*. In three hours under the right circumstances the cortex can be cleared. The games that frustrate and torment can be seen in the cosmic dimension. But the West has no ritual, no game to handle the CE drug experience. In the absence of relevant rituals we can only impose our familiar games, the politics of the nervous system, the mind controlling the brain. Physicians seek to impose their game of control and prescription. The bohemians naturally strive to impose their games of back-alley secrecy. The police, the third member of the happy, symbiotic drug triangle, naturally move in to control and prosecute.

Clearly we need new rituals, new goals, new rules, new concepts to apply and use these precious substances for man's welfare, to give the brain back to the species.

A group of investigators in the United States and Europe are now at work building up new games for the visionary experience, trying to develop new roles, rules, rituals, concepts and values. While these will, of course, vary from group to group the goal remains constant: expansion of consciousness, freedom of brain from the mind, freedom of the cortex from those centers — reticular (?), diencephalic (?), prefrontal (?) — which control, alert, censor and select what the cortex attends to. The work has hardly begun. This much is clear. The theory of the new game will be simple and basic. Space and time will be among the few variables required. Human equality will be a central principle, for the mystic experience tells us that the game differences between men are infinitely small compared with the age-old species similarities.

In our research endeavors we have developed eleven egalitarian principles based on the game nature of the human contract: equality in determining role, rule, ritual, goal, language, commitment; equality in the explicit contractual definition of the real, the good, the true, the logical; equality of the right to speak and to have access to relevant information. Any contract between men should be explicit about any temporary suspension of these equalities.

This past year at the Center for Research in Personality, Harvard University, two research projects have attempted to put these egalitarian principles into operation. The first of these is a naturalistic study of drug-induced visions and the games which Americans impose on these new experiences. The second is a systematic study of the effects of consciousness-expanding drugs in a rehabilitation program. I hope that a description of these two projects will illustrate and clarify the preceding discussion.[2]

A Naturalistic Study of Psilocybin

The purpose of this study was to determine the effects of psilocybin when administered in a naturalistic, supportive setting, to observe the rituals and language imposed by Americans on an experience quite alien to their culture. One hundred and sixty-seven subjects were given the mushrooms, 43 female and 124 male. Of these, 26 were internationally distinguished intellectuals, scholars, artists; 10 were medical doctors, 73 were professional intellectuals, 21 nonprofessional normals; 27 were drug addicts (psychological or physical), and 10 were inmates in a state prison.

The eleven principles for the human contract led to the following operations:

1. Participants alternated roles of observer and subject, i.e., the researchers took the drug with the subjects. The humanizing effect of this procedure cannot be overestimated. Among other things the subject-object issue is clearly settled.

---

[3] The Director of the Center for Research in Personality, Prof. David C. McClelland, has provided these two projects with advice, support, and has labored to interpret our work to the nonvisionary world. All American psychologists are indebted to Professor Henry A. Murray for his pioneer explorations into the human condition. From his neighborly presence, friendly interest and deep understanding of man's potentialities we have benefited. Dr. Frank Barron and Dr. Richard Alpert have been coinvestigators in the mushroom research. Dr. W. Madison Presnell has lent psychiatric experience, administrative enthusiasm and clinical wisdom. George Litwin, James Ciarlo, Gunther Weil, Ralph Metzner, Ralph Schwitzgebel and Jonathan Shay have played important roles in charting the new realms of consciousness. Edward Travers, John Molinski, James Maloney, Frank Rafferty, Rodney Harrington, Henry Kinney, and Donald Levine have made significant contributions to the Concord project. Mr. George Litwin and his staff have taken responsibility for the computer analysis of the questionnaire data. Mrs. Pearl Chan, research administrator, has made things run.

2. Participants were given all available information about the drug. An atmosphere of mystery and secret experimentation was avoided.

3. Participants were given control of their own dosage. A maximum dosage was determined by the research team and this maximum number of tablets was given to the subject and he was free to dose himself at the rate and amount desired.

4. A comfortable, homelike environment was employed. The sterile impersonality of the laboratory was avoided.

5. Subjects were allowed to bring a relative or friend. No subject took the drug in a group where he was a stranger.

Three sets of data were obtained: questionnaires covering the reactions; written reports and tape recordings; observations by the research team.

While the results of this study are too extensive to summarize at this point, a few major conclusions can be stated: The psilocybin experience is pleasant and educational; seventy-three percent of our subjects reported the experience as "very pleasant" or ecstatic; ninety-five percent thought the experience had changed their lives for the better.

Three out of four subjects reported happy and insightful reactions. When we recall that the drug was given only once under informal circumstances, with no attempt to be therapeutic or problem-oriented, these data stimulate thoughts about the healing-educational possibilities of psilocybin. But how do these changes come about?

The most common reaction reported is the sudden perception of the effect of abstractions, rituals, learned-game routines — ecstastic pleasure at being temporarily freed from these limitations, a game-free honesty. Set and suggestive contexts account for ninety-nine percent of the specific response to the drug. Thus, you cannot sensibly talk about the effects of psilocybin. It's always the set and suggestive context triggered off by the drug. A fascinating tension between these two factors — set and context — inevitably develops. If both are positive and holy then a shatteringly sacred experience results. If both are negative then a hellish encounter ensues. There is, of course, the tendency for people to impose their familiar games on to the psilocybin experience. The more rigidly committed to the game, the stronger this tendency. If the drug-giving person is secure, flexible, supportive, then the experience is almost guaranteed to be pleasant and therapeutic. Intensely deep communication occurs. Deep insights of a personal, social, and philosophic nature take place.

The Use of Psilocybin in a Rehabilitation Program

For many people one or two psilocybin experiences can accomplish the goals of a long and successful psychotherapy, a deep understanding and game-free collaboration between participants plus insight. But what then? People vary tremendously in their readiness to move forward from this point. Many of the 167 subjects in our naturalistic study were able to exploit the close, honest relationship and the insight. They were already involved in rewarding games to which they could return with renewed vision and energy.

But many of our subjects came through the psilocybin experience with the knowledge that they were involved in nonrewarding games, caught in routines which they disliked. Some realized that they had no games they wanted to play. The "therapeutic" effect of the experience did not last for these subjects. Expanded consciousness narrowed back. They were left with pleasant memories of their visionary journey and nothing more.

After insight comes the deeper question as to the meaning of life: What games to play? Behavior change must follow change in consciousness.

Our research group is now committed to a series of investigations which seek to develop methods of perpetuating the positive effects of the psilocybin experience, methods for helping the subject select and learn new games which give meaning to life.

The first of these projects concerned itself with the rehabilitation of inmates in a state prison. In helping prisoners we have of course found that the prisoners have rehabilitated us — changed our notions about crime, punishment, taught us about their games, made us see the limitations of our middle-class conceptions, expanded our consciousness, and given deeper meaning to our lives.

Ten volunteer prisoners. A maximum security prison. The recidivism rate is eighty percent. Eight of the ten would be expected back in prison a year after release. In baseball terms, eighty percent is the error percentage our team attempted to lower.

After three orientation meetings with the prisoners, the drug was given. I was the first one to take the drug in that bare hospital room behind barred windows. Three inmates joined me. Two psychologists and the other inmates served as observers — taking the drug three hours later. The psilocybin session was followed by three discussions, then another drug session, then more discussions. At this point the inmates had taken the drug an average of four times. There had not been one moment of friction or tension in some forty hours of egoless interaction. Pre-post testing had demonstrated marked changes on both objective and projective instruments: dramatic decreases in hostility, cynicism, depression, schizoid ideation; definite increases in optimism, planfulness, flexibility, tolerance, sociability.

The group has become a workshop for planning future games. Some prisoners are being trained to take over the functions of research assistants. They are performing the tasks of a vocational guidance clinic — preparing occupational brochures for inmates about to be released, making plans to act as rehabilitation workers after their release, for organizing a halfway house for ex-convicts. Other prisoners are using their time to prepare for the games to which they will return — the family game, their old job.

The psilocybin experience made these men aware of the stereotyped games in which they had been involved, the game of "cops and robbers," the game of being a tough guy, the game of outwitting the law, the game of resentful cynicism. "My whole life came tumbling down and I was sitting happily in the rubble." But insight is the beginning, and the more demanding task is to help these men choose new games, help them learn the rules, the roles, the concepts, the rituals of the new game — practical, collaborative reality education. Of course, this phase of our work requires help from others. But the helpers get helped. The businessmen who helped our inmates get jobs are invited into a new and exciting game which gives more meaning to their lives.

Our work progresses slowly and against strong opposition. Our new game of allowing criminals to take over responsibility and authority and prestige as experts on "crime and rehabilitation" brings us into game competition with the professional middle class. Anger and anxiety is aroused. Society has always produced and needed a criminal class. When criminals drop their roles and begin to play a different game, incredulous panic can ensue. Can society play its game without some men acting the part of criminals? If criminals are no longer criminals, where do the rest of us stand? The game of rehabilitator and client (i.e., a professional and a criminal) is being threatened. People are upset when their games are changed.

But our new game has begun. The game statistic for measuring success is clearcut. Eighty percent of convicts return to prison. Next season will reveal how well we have played our game.

Summary

Let me summarize. We have been concerned with change in behavior and change in consciousness. It is considerably easier to change behavior if you understand the learned-game nature of behavior. This sort of insight can be brought about by the administration of consciousness-expanding drugs, of which psilocybin is the most effective. But insight must be followed by behavior change. In the "rehabilitation game" we have been developing, the role of the helper is threefold. He provides a serious, supportive context for the CE experience, sets up an atmosphere in which insight can quickly occur. He then joins with the subject in an all-out collaborative process of selecting and mastering new games. He keeps accurate records of his activities and those of his subjects so that the success of his game performance can be objectively appraised by his fellow men.

A final word of clarification: Those of us who talk and write about the games of life are invariably misunderstood. We are seen as frivolous, or cynical anarchists tearing down the social structure. This is an unfortunate misapprehension. Actually, only those who see culture as a game, only those who take this evolutionary point of view can appreciate and treasure the exquisitely complex magnificence of what human beings do and have done. To see it all as "serious, taken-for-granted reality" is to miss the point, is to derogate with bland passivity the greatness of the games we learn.

Those of us who play the game of "applied mysticism" respect and support good gamesmanship. You pick out your game. You learn the rules, rituals, concepts. You play fairly and cleanly. You don't confuse your games with other games. You do not impose your game rituals on others' games. You win today's game with humility. You lose tomorrow's game with dignity. Anger and anxiety are irrelevant because you see your small game in the context of the great evolutionary game which no one can win and no one can lose.

Tom Wolfe | # What Do You Think of My Buddha?

He had gone to Stanford University in 1958 on a creative-writing fellowship, and they had taken him in on Perry Lane because he was such a swell diamond in the rough. Perry Lane was Stanford's bohemian quarter. As bohemias go, Perry Lane was Arcadia, Arcadia just off the Stanford golf course. It was a cluster of two-room cottages with weathery wood shingles in an oak forest, only not just amid trees and greenery, but amid vines, honeysuckle tendrils, all buds and shoots and swooping tendrils and twitterings like the best of Arthur Rackham and *Honey Bear*. Not only that, it had true cultural cachet. Thorstein Veblen had lived there. So had two Nobel Prize winners everybody knew about though the names escaped them. The cottages rented for just $60 a month. Getting into Perry Lane was like getting into a club. Everybody who lived there had known somebody else who lived there, or they would never have gotten in, and naturally they got to know each other very closely too, and there was always something of an atmosphere of communal living. Nobody's door was ever shut on Perry Lane, except when they were pissed off.

It was sweet. Perry Lane was a typical 1950s bohemia. Everybody sat around shaking their heads over America's tailfin, housing-development civilization, and Christ, in Europe, so what if the plumbing didn't work, they had mastered the art of living. Occasionally somebody would suggest an orgy or a three-day wine binge, but the model was always that old Zorba the Greek romanticism of sandals and simplicity and back to first principles. Periodically they would take pilgrimages 40 miles north to North Beach to see how it was actually done.

The main figures on Perry Lane were two novelists, Robin White, who had just written the Harper Prize novel, *Elephant Hill*, and Gwen Davis, a kind of West Coast Dawn Powell. In any case, all the established Perry Laners could see Kesey coming a mile away.

He had Jack London Martin Eden Searching Hick, the hick with intellectual yearnings, written all over him. He was from Oregon — who the hell was ever from Oregon? — and he had an Oregon country drawl and too many muscles and callouses on his hands and his brow furrowed when he was thinking hard, and it was perfect.

White took Kesey under his wing and got him and his wife Faye a cottage on Perry Lane. The Perry Lane set liked the idea at once. He could always be counted on to do *perfect* things. Like the time they were all having dinner — there was a lot of communal dining — and some visitor was going on about the ineffable delicacy of James Baldwin's work, and Kesey keeps eating but also trying to edge a word in, saying, well, bub, I dunno, I cain't exactly go along with you there, and the fellow puts down his knife and fork very carefully and turns to the others and says,

"I'll be delighted to listen to what*ever* Mr. Kesey has to say — as soon as he learns to eat from a plate without holding down his meat with his thumb."

Perfect! He had been voted "most likely to succeed" at his high school in Springfield, Oregon, and had graduated from the University of Oregon, where he was all involved in sports and fraternities, the All-American Boy bit. He had been a star wrestler in the 174-pound class and a star actor in college plays. He had even gone to Los Angeles after he finished college, and knocked around Hollywood for a while with the idea of becoming a movie star. But the urge to write, to create, had burst up through all this thick lumpy All-American crap somehow, like an unaccountable purslane blossom, and he had started writing, even completing a novel about college athletics, *End of Autumn*. It had never been published, and probably never would be, but he had the longing to do this thing. And his background — it was great, too. Somehow the Perry Lane set got the idea that his family were Okies, coming out of the Dust Bowl during the Depression, and then up to Oregon, wild, sodden Oregon, where they had fought the land and shot bears and the rivers were swift and the salmon leaped silver in the spring big two-hearted rivers.

His wife Faye — she was from the same kind of background, only she came from Idaho, and they had been high-school sweethearts in Springfield, Oregon, and had run off and gotten married when they were both freshmen in college. They once made a bet as to which of them had been born in the most Low Rent, bottomdog shack, his old place in La Junta, or hers in Idaho. He was dead sure there was no beating La Junta for Rundown until they got to Idaho, and she sure as hell did win that one. Faye was even more soft-spoken than Kesey. She hardly spoke at all. She was pretty and extremely sweet, practically a madonna of the hill country. And their cottage on Perry Lane — well, everybody else's cottage was run-down in a careful bohemian way, *simplicity,* Japanese paper lamp globes and monk's cloth and blond straw rugs and Swedish stainless steel knives and forks and cornflowers sticking out of a handthrown pot. But theirs was just plain Low Rent. There was always something like a broken washing machine rusting on the back porch and pigweed, bladder-pods, scoke and scurf peas growing ragged out back. Somehow it was . . . *perfect* . . . to have him and Faye on hand to *learn* as the Perry Lane sophisticates talked about life and the arts.

Beautiful! . . . the current fantasy . . . But how to tell them? — about such arcane little matters as Captain Marvel and The Flash . . . and *The Life* — and the very *Superkids* —
". . . a considerable new message . . . the blissful counterstroke . . . "
— when they had such a nice clear picture of him as the horny-nailed son of the Western sod, fresh from Springfield, Oregon. It was true that his father, Fred Kesey, had started him and his younger brother, Joe, known as Chuck, shooting and fishing and swimming as early as they could in any way manage it, also boxing, running, wrestling, plunging down the rapids of the Willamette and the McKenzie Rivers, on inner-tube rafts, with a lot of rocks and water and sartin' death foamin' down below. But it was not so they could tame animals, forests, rivers, wild upturned convulsed Oregon. It was more to condition them to do more of what his father had already done a pretty good job of — claim what-ever he can rightly get by being man enough to take it, and not on the frontier, either . . . Kesey Sr. had been part of the 1940s migration from the Southwest — not of "Okies" but of Protestant entrepreneurs who looked to the West Coast as a land of business opportunity. He started out in the Willamette Valley with next to nothing and founded a market-ing cooperative for dairy farmers, the Eugene Farmers Cooperative, and built it into the biggest dairy operation in the area, retailing under the name of Darigold. He was one of the big postwar success stories in the Valley — and ended up not in an old homestead with wood sidings and lightning rods but in a modern home in the suburbs, lowslung and pastel, on a street called Debra Lane. The incredible postwar American electro-pastel surge into the suburbs! — it was sweeping the Valley, with super-highways, dreamboat cars, shopping centers, soaring thirty-foot Federal Sign & Signal Company electric supersculptures — Eight New Plexiglas Display Features! — a surge of freedom and mobility, of cars and the money to pay for them and the time to enjoy them and a home where you can laze in a rich pool of pale wall-to-wall or roar through the tech-

nological wonderworld in motor launches and, in the case of men like his father, private planes —

The things he would somehow suddenly remember about the old home town — over here, for example, is the old white clapboard house they used to live in, and behind it, back a ways, is the radio tower of station KORE with a red light blinking on top — and at night he used to get down on his knees to say his prayers and there would be the sky and the light blinking — and he always kind of thought he was praying to that red light. And the old highway used to take a bend right about here, and it seemed like there was always somebody driving through about three or four in the morning, half asleep, and they would see the lights over there in town where it was getting built up and they'd think the road headed straight for the lights and they'd run off the bend and Kesey and his dad would go out to see if they could help the guy draggle himself out of the muck — chasing street lights! — praying to the red beacon light of KORE! — and a little run-in at Gregg's Drive-In, as it used to be called, it is now Speck's, at Franklin Boulevard at the bridge over the river. That was the big high-school drive-in, with the huge streamlined sculpted pastel display sign with streaming streamlined superslick A-22 italic script, floodlights, clamp-on-trays, car-hop girls in floppy blue slacks, hamburgers in some kind of tissuey wax paper steaming with onions pressed down and fried on the grill and mustard and catsup to squirt all over it from out plastic squirt cylinders. Saturday nights when everybody is out cruising — some guy was in his car in the lot at Gregg's going the wrong way, so nobody could move. The more everybody blew the horns, the more determined the guy got. Like *this* was the test. He rolls up the windows and locks the doors so they can't get at him and keeps boring in. This guy vs. Kesey. So Kesey goes inside and gets a potato they make the french fries with and comes out and jams it over the guy's exhaust pipe, which causes the motor to conk out and you ain't going *any* which way now, bub. The guy brings charges against Kesey for ruining his engine and Kesey ends up in juvenile court before a judge and tries to tell him how it is at Gregg's Drive-In on a Saturday night: the Life — that *feeling* — The Life the late 1940s early 1950s American Teenage Drive-In Life was *precisely* what it was all about — but how could you tell anyone about it?

But of course! — the *feeling* — out here at night, free, with the motor running and the adrenaline flowing, cruising in the neon glories of the new American night — it was very Heaven to be the first wave of the most extraordinary kids in the history of the world — only 15, 16, 17 years old, dressed in the *haute couture* of pink Oxford shirts, sharp pants, snaky half-inch belts, fast shoes — with all this Straight-6 and V-8 power underneath and all this neon glamour overhead, which somehow tied in with the technological superheroics of the jet, TV, atomic subs, ultrasonics — Postwar American suburbs — glorious world! and the hell with the intellectual badmouthers of America's tailfin civilization . . . They couldn't know what it was like or else they had it cultivated out of them — the feeling — to be very Superkids! the world's first generation of the little devils — feeling immune, beyond calamity. One's parents remembered the sloughing common order, War & Depression — but Superkids knew only the emotional surge of the great payoff, when nothing was common any longer — The Life! A glorious place, a glorious age, I tell you! A very Neon Renaissance — And the myths that actually touched you at that time — not Hercules, Orpheus, Ulysses, and Aeneas — but Superman, Captain Marvel, Batman, The Human Torch, The Sub-Mariner, Captain America, Plastic Man, The Flash — but of course! On Perry Lane, what did they think it was — quaint? — when he talked about the comic-book Superheroes as the honest American myths? It was a fantasy world *already*, this electro-pastel world of Mom&Dad&Buddy&Sis in the suburbs. There they go, in the family car, a white Pontiac Bonneville sedan — *the family car!* — a huge crazy god-awful-powerful fantasy creature to begin with, 327-horsepower, shaped like twenty-seven nights of lubricious luxury brougham seduction — *you're already there, in Fantasyland*, so why not move off your snug-harbor quilty-bed dead center and cut loose — go ahead and say it — Shazam! — juice it up to what it's already aching to be: 327,000 horsepower, a whole superhighway long and *soaring*, *screaming* on toward . . . Edge City, and ultimate fantasies, current and future . . . Billy Batson said *Shazam!* and turned into Captain Marvel. Jay Garrick inhaled an experimental gas in the research lab . . .

    . . . and began traveling and thinking at the speed of light as . . . The Flash . . . the current fantasy. Yes. The Kesey diamond-in-the-rough fantasy did not last very long. The most interesting person on Perry Lane as far as he was concerned was not any of the novelists or other literary intellectuals, but a young graduate student in psychology named Vic Lovell. Lovell was like a young Viennese analyst, or at least a California graduate-school version of one. He was slender with wild dark hair and very cool intellectually and wound-up at the same time. He introduced Kesey to Freudian psychology. Kesey had never run into a system of thought like this before. Lovell could point out in the most persuasive way how mundane character traits and minor hassles around Perry Lane fit into the richest, most complex metaphor of life ever devised, namely, Freud's. . . . And a little experimental gas . . . Yes. Lovell told him about some experiments the Veterans Hospital in Menlo Park was running with "psychomimetic" drugs, drugs that brought on temporary states resembling psychoses. They were paying volunteers $75 a day. Kesey volunteered. It was all nicely calcimined and clinical. They would put him on a bed in a white room and give him a series of capsules without saying what they were. One would be nothing, a placebo. One would be Ditran, which always brought on a terrible experience. Kesey could always tell that one coming on, because the hairs on the blanket he was under would suddenly look like a field of hideously diseased thorns and he would put his finger down his throat and retch. But one of them — the first thing he knew about it was a squirrel dropped an acorn from a tree outside, only it was tremendously loud and sounded like it was not outside but right in the room with him and not actually a sound, either, but a great suffusing presence, visual, almost tactile, a great impacting of . . . *blue* . . . all around him and suddenly he was in a realm of consciousness he had never dreamed of before and it was not a dream or a delirium but part of his awareness. He looks at the ceiling. It begins moving. Panic — and yet there is no panic. The ceiling is moving — not in a crazed swirl but along its own planes its own planes of light and shadow and surface not nearly so nice and smooth as plasterer Super Plaster Man intended with infallible carpenter level bubble sliding in dim honey Karo syrup tube not so fool-proof as you thought, bub, little lumps and ridges up there, bub, and lines, lines like spines on crest of waves of white desert movie sand each one with MGM shadow longshot of the ominous A-rab coming up over the next crest for only the sinister Saracen can see the road and you didn't know how many subplots you left up there, Plaster Man, trying to smooth it *all* out, *all* of it, with your bubble in a honey tube carpenter's level, to make us all down here look up and see nothing but ceiling, because we all know ceiling, because it has a *name*, ceiling, therefore it is nothing but a ceiling — no room for A-rabs up there in Level Land, eh, Plaster Man. Suddenly he is like a ping-pong ball in a flood of sensory stimuli, heart beating, blood coursing, breath suspiring, teeth grating, hand moving over the percale sheet over those thousands of minute warfy woofings like a brush fire, sun glow and the highlight on a stainless-steel rod, quite a little movie you have going on in that highlight there, Hondo, Technicolors, pick each one out like fishing for neon gumballs with a steam shovel in the Funtime Arcade, a ping-pong ball in a flood of sensory stimuli, all quite ordinary, but . . . *revealing* themselves for the first time and happening . . . *Now* . . . as if for the first time he has entered a moment in his life and known exactly what is happening to his senses now, at this moment, and with each new discovery it is as if he has entered into all of it himself, is *one* with it, the movie white desert of the ceiling becomes something rich, personal, his, beautiful beyond description, like an orgasm behind the eyeballs, and his A-rabs — A-rabs behind the eyelids, eyelid movies, room for them and a lot more in the five billion thoughts per second stroboscope synapses — his A-rab heroes, fine Daily Double horsehair mustaches wrapped about the Orbicularis Oris of their mouths —

Face! The doctor comes back in and, marvelous, poor tight cone ass, doc, Kesey can now see *into him*. For the first time he notices that the doctor's lower left lip is trembling, but he more than *sees* the tremor, he understands it, he can — almost seen! — see each muscle fiber decussate, pulling the poor jelly of his lip to the left and the fibers one by one leading back into infrared caverns of the body, through transistor-radio innards of nerve tangles, each one on Red Alert, the poor ninny's inner hooks desperately trying to make the little writhing bastards *keep still in there*, I am Doctor, this is human specimen before me — the poor ninny has his own desert movie going on inside, only each horsehair A-rab is a threat — if only his lip, his face, would stay level, level like the honey bubble of the Official Plaster Man assured him it would —

Miraculous! He could truly *see into people* for the first time —

And yes, that little capsule sliding blissly blissly down the gullet was LSD.

Very soon it was already time to push on beyond another fantasy, the fantasy of the Menlo Park clinicians. The clinicians' fantasy was that the volunteers were laboratory animals that had to be dealt with objectively, quantitatively. It was well known that people who volunteered for drug experiments tended to be unstable anyway. So the doctors would come in in white smocks, with the clipboards, taking blood pressures and heart rates and urine specimens and having them try to solve simple problems in logic and mathematics, such as adding up columns of figures, and having them judge time and distances, although they did have them talk into tape recorders, too. But the doctors were so *out of it*. They never took LSD themselves and they had absolutely no comprehension, and it couldn't be put into words anyway.

Sometimes you wanted to paint it huge — Lovell is under LSD in the clinic and he starts drawing a huge Buddha on the wall. It somehow encompasses the whole — White Smock comes in and doesn't even look at it, he just starts asking the old questions on the clipboard, so Lovell suddenly butts in:

"What do you think of my Buddha?"

White Smock looks at it a moment and says, "It looks very feminine. Now let's see how rapidly you can add up this column of figures here ..."

Very feminine. Deliver us from the clichés that have locked up even these so-called experimenters' brains like the accordion fences in the fur-store window — and Kesey was having the same problem with his boys. One of them was a young guy with a lie-down crewcut and the straightest face, the straightest, blandest, most lineless awfulest Plaster Man honey bubble levelest face ever made, and he would come in and open his eyes wide once as if to make sure this muscular hulk on the bed were still *rational* and then get this smug tone in his voice which poured out into the room like absorbent cotton choked in chalk dust from beaten erasers Springfield High School.

"Now when I say 'Go,' you tell me when you think a minute is up by saying, 'Now.' Have you got that?"

Yeah, he had that. Kesey was soaring on LSD and his sense of time was *wasted*, and thousands of thoughts per second were rapping around between synapses, fractions of a second, so what the hell is a minute — but then one thought stuck in there, held . . . ma-*li*-cious, *de*-li-cious. He remembered that his pulse had been running 75 beats a minute every time they took it, so when Dr. Fog says 'Go,' Kesey slyly slides his slithering finger onto his pulse and counts up to 75 and says:

"Now!"

Dr. Smog looks at his stop watch. "Amazing!" he says, and walks out of the room.

You said it, bub, but like a lot of other people, you don't even know.

LSD; how can — now that those big fat letters are babbling out on coated stock from every newsstand . . . But this was late 1959, early 1960, a full two years before Mom&Dad&Buddy&Sis heard of the dread letters and clucked because Drs. Timothy Leary and Richard Alpert were french-frying the brains of Harvards boys with it. It was even before Dr. Humphry Osmond had invented the term "psych*o*delic," which was later amended to "psych*e*delic" to get rid of the nuthouse connotation of "psycho" . . . LSD! It was quite a little secret to have stumbled onto, a hulking supersecret, in fact — the triumph of the guinea pigs! In a short time he and Lovell had tried the whole range of the drugs, LSD, psilocybin, mescaline, peyote, IT-290 the superamphetamine, Ditran the bummer, morning-glory seeds. They were onto a discovery that the Menlo Park clinicians themselves never — mighty fine irony here: the White Smocks were supposedly using *them*. Instead the White Smocks had handed them the very key itself. *And you don't even know, bub . . . with these drugs your perception is altered enough that you find yourself looking out of completely strange eyeholes. All of us have a great deal of our minds locked shut. We're shut off from our own world. And these drugs seem to be the key to open these locked doors.* How many? — maybe two dozen people in the world were on to this incredible secret! One was Aldous Huxley, who had taken mescaline and written about it in *The Doors of Perception*. He compared the brain to a "reducing valve." In ordinary perception, the senses send an overwhelming flood of information to the brain, which the brain then filters down to a trickle it can manage for the purpose of survival in a highly competitive world. Man has become so rational, so utilitarian, that the trickle becomes most pale and thin. It is efficient, for mere survival, but it screens out the most wondrous part of man's potential experience without his even knowing it. *We're shut off from our own world.* Primitive man once experienced the rich and sparkling flood of the senses fully. Children experience it for a few months — until "normal" training, conditioning, close the doors on this other world, usually for good. Somehow, Huxley had said, the drugs opened these ancient doors. And through them modern man may at last go, and rediscover his divine birthright —

But these are *words*, man! *And you couldn't put it into words.* The

White Smocks liked to put it into words, like *hallucination* and *dissociative phenomena*. They could understand the visual skyrockets. Give them a good case of an ashtray turning into a Venus flytrap or eyelid movies of crystal cathedrals, and they could groove on that, *Kluver, op cit., p. 43n.* That was swell. *But don't you see?* — the visual stuff was just the décor with LSD. In fact, you might go through the whole experience without any true hallucination. The whole thing was . . . *the experience* . . . this certain indescribable *feeling* . . . Indescribable, because words can only jog the memory, and if there is no memory of . . . The *experience* of the barrier between the subjective and the objective, the personal and the impersonal, the *I* and the *not-I* disappearing . . . that *feeling!* . . . Or can you remember when you were a child watching someone put a pencil to a sheet of paper for the first time, to draw a picture . . . and the line begins to grow — into a nose! and it is not just a pattern of graphite line on a sheet of paper but the very miracle of creation itself and your own dreams flowed into that magical . . . growing . . . line, and it was not a picture but a *miracle* . . . an *experience* . . . and now that you're soaring on LSD that *feeling* is coming on again — only now the creation is of the entire universe —

Meanwhile, over on Perry Lane, this wasn't precisely the old Searching Hick they all knew and loved. Suddenly Kesey — well, he was soft-spoken, all right, but he came on with a lot of vital energy. Gradually the whole Perry Lane thing was gravitating around Kesey. Volunteer Kesey gave himself over to science over at the Menlo Park Vets hospital — and somehow drugs were getting up and walking out of there and over to Perry Lane, LSD, mescaline, IT-290, mostly. Being hip on Perry Lane now had an element nobody had ever dreamed about before, wild-flying, mind-blowing drugs. Some of the old Perry Lane luminaries' *cool* was tested and they were found wanting. Robin White and Gwen Davis were against the new drug thing. That was all right, because Kesey had had about enough of them, and the power was with Kesey. Perry Lane took on a kind of double personality, which is to say, Kesey's. Half the time it would be just like some kind of college fraternity row, with everybody out on a nice autumn Saturday afternoon on the grass in the dapple shadows of the trees and honeysuckle tendrils playing touch football or basketball. An hour later, however, Kesey and his circle would be hooking down something that in the entire world only they and a few avant-garde neuropharmacological researchers even knew about, drugs of the future, of the neuropharmacologists' centrifuge utopia, the coming age of . . .

Well shee-ut. An' I don't reckon we give much of a damn any more about the art of living in France, either, boys, every frog ought to have a little paunch, like Henry Miller said, and go to bed every night in pajamas with collars and piping on them — just take a letter for me and mail it down to old Morris at Morris Orchids, Laredo, Texas, boys, tell him about enough peyote cactus to mulch all the mouldering widows' graves in poor placid Palo Alto. Yes. They found out they could send off to a place called Morris Orchids in Laredo and get peyote, and one of the new games of Perry Lane — goodbye Robin, goodbye Gwen — got to be seeing who was going down to the Railway Express at the railroad station and pick up the shipment, since possession of peyote, although not of LSD, was already illegal in California. There would be these huge goddamned boxes of the stuff, 1,000 buds and roots $70; buds only — slightly higher. If they caught you, you were *caught*, because there was no excuse possible. There was no other earthly reason to have these goddamned fetid plants except to get high as a coon. And they would all set about cutting them into strips and putting them out to dry, it took days, and then grinding them up into powder and packing them in gelatin capsules or boiling it down to a gum and putting it in the capsules or just making a horrible goddamned broth that was so foul, so unbelievably vile, you had to chill it numb to try to kill the taste and fast for a day so you wouldn't have anything on your stomach, just to keep eight ounces of it down. But then — *soar*. Perry Lane, Perry Lane.

Miles
     Miles
          Miles
               Miles
                    Miles
                         Miles
                              Miles
                                   under all that good
vegetation from Morris Orchids and having visions of
Faces
     Faces
          Faces
               Faces
                    Faces
                         Faces
                              Faces
                                 so many faces
rolling up behind the eyelids, faces he has never seen before, complete with spectral cheekbones, pregnant eyes, stringy wattles, and all of a sudden: Chief Broom. For some reason peyote does this . . . Kesey starts getting eyelid movies of faces, whole galleries of weird faces, churning up behind the eyelids, faces from out of nowhere. He knows nothing about Indians and has never met an Indian, but suddenly here is a full-

blown Indian — Chief Broom — the solution, the whole mothering key, to the novel . . .

He hadn't even meant to write this book. He had been working on another one, called *Zoo*, about North Beach. Lovell had suggested why didn't he get a job as night attendant on the psychiatric ward at Menlo Park. He could make some money, and since there wasn't much doing on the ward at night, he could work on *Zoo*. But Kesey got absorbed in the life on the psychiatric ward. The whole system — if they set out to invent the perfect Anti-cure for what ailed the men on this ward, they couldn't have done it better. Keep them cowed and docile. Play on the weaknesses that drove them nuts in the first place. Stupefy the bastards with tranquilizers and if they still get out of line haul them up to the "shock shop" and punish them. Beautiful —

Sometimes he would go to work high on acid. He could *see into their faces.* Sometimes he wrote, and sometimes he drew pictures of the patients, and as the lines of the ball-point greasy creased into the paper the lines of their faces, he could — the *interiors* of these men came into the lines, the ball-point crevasses, it was the most incredible feeling, the anguish and the pain came right out front and flowed in the crevasses in their faces, and in the ball-point crevasses, the same — *one!* — crevasses now, black starling nostrils, black starling eyes, blind black starling geek cry on every face: "Me! Me! Me! Me! I am — Me!" — he could see clear into them. And — how could you tell anybody about this? they'll say you're a nut yourself — but afterwards, not high on anything, he could *still see into people.*

The novel, *One Flew Over the Cuckoo's Nest*, was about a roustabout named Randle McMurphy. He is a big healthy animal, but decides to fake insanity in order to get out of a short jail stretch he is serving on a work farm and into what he figures will be the soft life of a state mental hospital. He comes onto the ward with his tight reddish-blond curls tumbling out from under his cap, cracking jokes and trying to get some action going among these deadasses in the loony bin. They can't resist the guy. They suddenly want to *do* things. The tyrant who runs the place, Big Nurse, hates him for weakening . . . Control and the System. By and by, many of the men resent him for forcing them to struggle to act like men again. Finally, Big Nurse is driven to play her trump card and finish off McMurphy by having him lobotomized. But this crucifixion inspires an Indian patient, a schizoid called Chief Broom, to rise up and break out of the hospital and go sane; namely, run like hell for open country.

Chief Broom. The very one. From the point of view of craft, Chief Broom was his great inspiration. If he had told the story through McMurphy's eyes, he would have to end up with the big bruiser delivering a lot of homilies about his down-home theory of mental therapy. Instead, he told the story through the Indian. This way he could present a schizo-phrenic state the way the schizophrenic himself, Chief Broom feels it and at the same time report the McMurphy Method more subtly.

Morris Orchids! He wrote several passages of the book under peyote and LSD. He even had someone give him a shock treatment, clandestinely, so he could write a passage in which Chief Broom comes back from "the shock shop." Eating Laredo buds — he would write like mad under the drugs. After he came out of it, he could see that a lot of it was junk. But certain passages — like Chief Broom in his schizophrenic fogs — it was true *vision*, a little of what you could see if you opened the doors of perception, friends . . .

Right after he finished *One Flew Over the Cuckoo's Nest,* Kesey sublet his cottage on Perry Lane and he and Faye went back up to Oregon. This was in June, 1961. He spent the summer working in his brother Chuck's creamery in Springfield to accumulate some money. Then he and Faye moved into a little house in Florence, Oregon, about 50 miles west of Springfield, near the ocean, in logging country. Kesey started gathering material for his second novel, *Sometimes a Great Notion,* which was about a logging family. He took to riding early in the morning and at night in the "crummies." These were pickup trucks that served as buses taking the loggers to and from the camps. At night he would hang around the bars where the loggers went. He was Low Rent enough himself to talk to them. After about four months of that, they headed back to Perry Lane, where he was going to do the writing.

One Flew Over the Cuckoo's Nest was published in February, 1962, and it made his literary reputation immediately:

"A smashing achievement" — *Mark Schorer*
"A great new American novelist" — *Jack Kerouac*
"Powerful poetic realism" — *Life*
"An amazing first novel" — Boston *Traveler*
"This is a first novel of special worth" — New York *Herald Tribune*
"His storytelling is so effective, his style so impetuous, his grasp of characters so certain, that the reader is swept along . . . His is a large, robust talent, and he has written a large, robust book" — *Saturday Review*

And on the Lane — all this was a confirmation of everything they and Kesey had been doing. For one thing there was the old Drug Paranoia — the fear that this wild uncharted drug thing they were into would gradually . . . *rot your brain.* Well, here was the answer. Chief Broom!

And McMurphy . . . but of course. The current fantasy . . . he was a McMurphy figure who was trying to get them to move off their own snug-harbor dead center, out of the plump little game of being ersatz daring and ersatz alive, the middle-class intellectual's game, and move out to . . . Edge City . . . where it was scary, but people were whole people. And if drugs were what unlocked the doors and enabled you to do this thing and realize all this that was in you, then so let it be . . .

Not even on Perry Lane did people really seem to catch the thrust of the new book he was working on, *Sometimes a Great Notion*. It was about the head of a logging clan, Hank Stamper, who defies a labor union and thereby the whole community he lives in by continuing his logging operation through a strike. It was an unusual book. It was a novel in which the strikers are the villains and the strikebreaker is the hero. The style was experimental and sometimes difficult. And the main source of "mythic" reference was not Sophocles or even Sir James Frazer but . . . yes, Captain Marvel. The union leaders, the strikers, and the townspeople were the tarantulas, all joyfully taking their vow: "We shall wreak vengeance and abuse on all whose equals we are not . . . and 'will to equality' shall henceforth be the name for virtue; and against all that has power we want to raise our clamor!" Hank Stamper was, quite intentionally, Captain Marvel. Once known as . . . *Übermensch*. The current fantasy . . .

. . . on Perry Lane. Nighttime, the night he and Faye and the kids came back to Perry Lane from Oregon, and they pull up to the old cottage and there is a funny figure in the front yard, smiling and rolling his shoulders this way and that and jerking his hands out to this side and the other side as if there's a different drummer somewhere, different drummer, you understand, corked out of his gourd, in fact . . . and, well, Hi, Ken, yes, uh, well, you weren't *around*, exactly, you understand, doubledy-clutch, doubledy-clutch, and they told me you wouldn't mind, generosity knoweth no — ahem — yes, I had a '47 Pontiac myself once, held the road like a prehistoric bird, you understand . . . and, yes, Neal Cassady had turned up in the old cottage, like he had just run out of the pages of *On the Road*, and . . . what's next, Chief? Ah . . . many Day-Glo freaking curlicues —

All sorts of people began gathering around Perry Lane. Quite an . . . *underground* sensation it was, in Hip California. Kesey, Cassady, Larry McMurtry; two young writers, Ed McClanahan and Bob Stone; Chloe Scott the dancer, Roy Seburn the artist, Carl Lehmann-Haupt, Vic Lovell . . . and Richard Alpert himself . . . all sorts of people were in and out of there all the time, because they had heard about it, like the local beats — that term was still used — a bunch of kids from a pad called the Chateau, a wild-haired kid named Jerry Garcia and the Cadaverous Cowboy, Page Browning. Everybody was attracted by the strange high times they had heard about . . . the Lane's fabled Venison Chili, a Kesey dish made of venison stew laced with LSD, which you could consume and then go sprawl on the mattress in the fork of the great oak in the middle of the Lane at night and play pinball with the light show in the sky . . . Perry Lane.

And many puzzled souls looking in . . . At first they were captivated. The Lane was too good to be true. It was Walden Pond, only without any Thoreau misanthropes around. Instead, a community of intelligent, very open, out-front people — out front was a term everybody was using — out-front people who cared deeply for one another, and *shared* . . . in incredible ways, even, and were embarked on some kind of . . . *well*, adventure in living. Christ, you could see them trying to put their finger on it and . . . then . . . gradually figuring out there was something here they weren't *in on* . . . Like the girl that afternoon in somebody's cottage when Alpert came by. This was a year after he started working with Timothy Leary. She had met Alpert a couple of years before and he had been 100 percent the serious young clinical psychologist — legions of rats and cats in cages with their brainstorms, corpora callosa and optic chiasmas sliced, spliced, diced, iced in the name of the Scientific Method. Now Alpert was sitting on the floor in Perry Lane in the old boho Lotus hunker-down and exegeting very seriously about a baby crawling blindly about the room. Blindly? What do you mean, blindly? That baby is a very sentient creature . . . That baby sees the world with a completeness that you and I will never know again. His doors of perception have not yet been closed. He still experiences the moment he lives in. The inevitable bullshit hasn't constipated his cerebral cortex yet. He still sees the world as it really is, while we sit here, left with only a dim historical version of it manufactured for us by words and official bullshit, and so forth and so on, and Alpert soars in Ouspenskyian loop-the-loops for baby while, as far as this girl can make out, baby just bobbles, dribbles, lists and rocks across the floor . . . But she was learning . . . that the world is sheerly divided into those who have had *the experience* and those who have not — those who have been through that door and —

It was a strange feeling for all these good souls to suddenly realize that right here on woody thatchy little Perry Lane, amid the honeysuckle and dragonflies and boughs and leaves and a thousand little places where the sun peeped through, while straight plodding souls from out of the Stanford eucalyptus tunnel plodded by straight down the fairways on the golf course across the way — this amazing experiment in consciousness was going on, out on a frontier neither they nor anybody else ever heard of before.

Frank Zappa | # The New Rock

Rock music is a necessary element of contemporary society. It is functional. It is healthy and valid artistically. It is also educational (how to ask a girl for a date, what love is like). It has all the answers to what your mother and father won't tell you. It is also a big business. This is a brief history of rock and its relationship to our society.

LO: PFF PFF. A nifty questionnaire to get you interested so you'll read the rest of the article:

Part One: The 50s

1. Who remembers beer? White port and lemon juice? For 10 points, what was the name of the guy in your school who used to buy your juice for parties . . .

2. Who remembers making out and getting hot? For 10 points, how old were you when it happened . . .

3. Who remembers duck tails, peggers, leather jackets, bunny shoes, brogans, tight sweaters, teardrops, full skirts with a million starchy petticoats, Sir Guy shirts and khakis? For 10 points, how much did you pay for your St. Christopher medallion . . .

4. Who remembers gang fights, tire chains, boys with razor blades in the toes of their wedgies, girls with razor blades in their hair, blood and sickening crunch? For 10 points, tell why the cops were afraid of your gang . . .

Part Two: The 60s

5. Who remembers speed? Smoke? Acid? Transcendental meditation? For 10 points, name your connection or guru . . .

6. Who remembers getting stoned and having an orgy? For 10 points, how old were you when you learned you were incapable of relating to others in a tender, personal way and finally discovered you had become asexual . . .

7. Who remembers electric hair, bell bottoms, plastic jackets, sandals, high boots, bulky knit sweaters, Guccis, miniskirts, De Voss shirts and velvet pants? For 10 points, look around the house, find your beads and bells, and recite Hare Krishna without laughing . . .

8. Who remembers demonstrations, truncheons, Mace, police dogs, the Pentagon, Century City, blood and sickening crunch? For 10 points, tell

SOURCE: *Life*, June 28, 1968.

why you were afraid to cut your hair, infiltrate the establishment, and do it the easy way . . .

Our present state of sociosexual enlightenment is, to a certain extent, attributable to the evolution of rock and vice versa. Our story begins back in . . . the good old days, at the recreation centers, no Levis or capris please. "School functions" and "teen hops" were real swell and keen and acceptable to Mom and Dad. They were also dull unless you liked to dance a fox-trot as the high school swing band fumbled through an evening of Combo Orks and reprocessed Glenn Miller. The kids would be holding on to each other desperately and sweating. The chaperon would come along and say, "Seven inches apart please," and hold a sawed-off ruler between you and the girl.

Society was very repressed, sexually, and dancing was a desperate attempt to get a little physical contact with the opposite sex. Free love, groupies, the Plaster Casters of Chicago and such bizarre variants as the G.T.O.s of Laurel Canyon in L.A. didn't exist then. Preoccupation with sexual matters accounted for a disproportionate amount of the daily conscious thought process and diverted a lot of energy from school work.

This, and the low quality of teaching in many schools, caused kids to seek education in the streets. Youth gangs with marvelous names and frightening reputations cruised the streets at night, searching for ways to compensate for the lack of sexually approachable girls. Vandalism and assorted manglings became acceptable substitutes for "teen sex." Young men would compete, like cowboy gunfighters, to be "the baddest cat." This dubious honor would generally entitle its bearer to boss the gang and, in some instances, preferential treatment from those few daring girls who would go "all the way."

Parents, unfortunately, have a tendency to misunderstand, misinterpret, and, worst of all, ridicule patterns of behavior which seem foreign to them. When they noticed a growing interest among teen-agers in matters pertaining to the pleasure-giving functions of the body, they felt threatened. Mom and Dad were sexually uninformed and inhibited (a lot of things wrong with society today are directly attributable to the fact that the people who make the laws are sexually maladjusted) and they saw no reason why their kids should be raised differently. (Why should those dirty teen-agers have all the fun?) Sex is for making babies and it makes your body misshapen and ugly afterward and let's not talk about it shall we?

The Big Note: Digression I

In the Abnuceals Emuukha Electric Symphony Orchestra album *Lumpy Gravy* there is a section on side two where several unidentified characters discuss the origins of the universe. One of the characters explains the concept of the Big Note: everything in the universe is composed basically of vibrations — light is a vibration, sound is a vibration, atoms are composed of vibrations — and all these vibrations just might be harmonics of some incomprehensible fundamental cosmic tone.

How important is sound? I participated in a conversation recently with Herbie Cohen (our manager) about rumors of a government research project. The project, it seems, has been going on for several years. What does sound do to plants? According to Herbie, a field of corn increased its yield — the individual ears even got bigger — because the research team set up loudspeakers in the field and pumped in some music. According to Herbie, the next step is to find out what kind of music the vegetables like the best.

The ways in which sound affects the human organism are myriad and subtle. Why does the sound of Eric Clapton's guitar give one girl a sensation which she describes as "Bone Conduction"? Would she still experience Bone Conduction if Eric, using the same extremely loud thick tone, played nothing but Hawaiian music? Which is more important: the timbre (color-texture) of a sound, the succession of intervals which make up the melody, the harmonic support (chords) which tells your ear "what the melody means" (is it major or minor or neutral or what), the volume at which the sound is heard, the volume at which the sound is produced, the distance from source to ear, the density of the sound, the number of sounds per second or fraction thereof . . . and so on? Which of these would be the most important element in an audial experience which gave you a pleasurable sensation? An erotic sensation? Look at kids in school, tapping their feet, beating with their fingers. People try, unconsciously, to be in tune with their environment. In a variety of ways, even the most "unconcerned" people make attempts to "tune up" with their God. Hal Zeiger (one of the first big promoters of rock entertainment during the 50s) says, "I knew that there was a big thing here that was basic, that was big, that had to get bigger. I realized that this music got through to the youngsters because the big beat matched the great rhythms of the human body. I understood that. I knew it and I knew there was nothing that anyone could do to knock that out of them. And I further knew that they would carry this with them the rest of their lives."

Rock Around the Clock

In my days of flaming youth I was extremely suspect of any rock music played by white people. The sincerity and emotional intensity of their performances, when they sang about boyfriends and girl friends and breaking up, etc., was nowhere when I compared it to my high school Negro R&B heroes like Johnny Otis, Howlin' Wolf and Willie Mae Thornton.

But then I remember going to see *Blackboard Jungle*. When the titles flashed up there on the screen Bill Haley and his Comets started blurching "One Two Three O'Clock, Four O'Clock Rock. . . ." It was the loudest rock sound kids had ever heard at that time. I remember being inspired with awe. In cruddy little teen-age rooms across America, kids had been huddling around old radios and cheap record players listening to the "dirty music" of their life style. ("Go in your room if you wanna listen to that crap . . . and turn the volume all the way down.") But in the theater, watching *Blackboard Jungle*, they couldn't tell you to turn it down. I didn't care if Bill Haley was white or sincere . . . he was playing the Teen-Age National Anthem and it was so LOUD I was jumping up and down. *Blackboard Jungle*, not even considering the story line (which had the old people winning in the end) represented a strange sort of "endorsement" of the teen-age cause: "They have made a movie about us, therefore, we exist. . . ."

Responding like dogs, some of the kids began to go for the throat. Open rebellion. The early public dances and shows which featured rock were frowned upon by the respectable parents of the community. They did everything they could do to make it impossible for these events to take place. They did everything they could to shield their impressionable young ones from the ravages of this vulgar new craze. (Hal Zeiger: "They did everything they could to make sure their children were not moved erotically by Negroes.")

From the very beginning, the real reason Mr. & Mrs. Clean White America objected to this music was the fact that it was performed by black people. There was always the danger that one night — maybe in the middle of the summer, in a little pink party dress — Janey or Suzy might be overwhelmed by the lewd, pulsating jungle rhythms and do something to make their parents ashamed.

Parents, in trying to protect their offspring from whatever danger they imagined to be lurking within the secret compartments of this new musical vehicle, actually helped to shove them in front of it whereupon they were immediately run over. The attitude of parents helped to create a climate wherein the usage of rock music (as a pacifier or perhaps anesthetic experience) became very necessary. Parents offered nothing to their children that could match the appeal of rock. It was obvious to the kids that anyone who did not like (or at least attempt to understand) rock music, had a warped sense of values. To deny rock music its place in the society was to deny sexuality. Any parent who tried to keep his child from listening to or participating in this musical ritual was, in the eyes of the child, trying to castrate him.

There was much resistance on the part of the music industry itself. (Hal Zeiger: "I remember a conversation with M—D—, a very famous song-writer, who has written many of our all-time favorites, wherein he chided me for being involved with this kind of music and entertainment and I said to him, 'M—, you are just upset because it has been discovered and revealed that a song written by some young colored child in a slum area can capture the fancy of the American public more effectively than a song written by you, who lives in a Beverly Hills mansion.' ")

Every year you could hear people saying, "I know it's only a phase . . . it'll poop out pretty soon. The big bands will come back." Year after year, the death of rock was predicted . . . a few times, as I recall, it was even *officially* announced: "Rock 'n' roll is dead, calypso is all the rage. . . ."

Oh, Those Great Rhythms: Digression II

The function of the drums in a rock music ensemble is to keep the beat. ("It has a good beat . . . I give it 10 points, Dick.") On early R&B records, the drum part was usually executed with brushes. All the arrangements required, generally, was a dull thud on the second and fourth pulse of the bar. There were very few "breaks" or "fills." When the drum fill (a short percussion outburst, usually at a cadence or resting point of a musical phrase) became popular in rock arrangements, it most often took the form of groups of triplets (three-note rhythmic figures, squeezed into the space of two beats . . . sounding like: ya-da-da ya-da-da ya-da-da ya-da-da-whomp). For a while, during the mid-50s, it seemed like every record produced had one or more fills of this nature in it. Eventually, with the improvements in studios and recording techniques, the drummers began to use sticks on the sessions and the cadence fills became more elaborate but, before and after the fill, the drummer's job was still to keep the beat . . . that same old crappy beat . . . the beat that made the kids hop around and scream and yell and buy records. A long process of rhythmic evolution has taken place since the early 50s. It is laughable now to think of that dull thud on the second and fourth as lewd and pulsating.

Green Visors

Hal Zeiger: "The problem at the time was basically this: trying to make the music acceptable, or, to try to get the right to expose it, and that took some doing. I knew the kids were listening to the radio stations . . . it was just a matter of how to merchandise this to get their dollars, too. I told Bill Graham (founder of the Fillmore and former manager of the Jefferson Airplane), 'You've got to understand when these things are underground, that's one thing. But the minute it goes over ground, the minute, you see, it looks like money, everyone wants in.' "

So to make R&B acceptable, the big shots of the record industry hired a bunch of little men with cigars and green visors, to synthesize and imitate the work of the Negroes. The visor men cranked out phony white rock. Highly skilled couriers then delivered the goods to American Bandstand along with a lot of presents (tokens of their esteem) to Dick Clark for all his marvelous assistance in the crusade to jam these products down the kids' throats. Pat Boone was notable, too, for his humanistic activities (bleaching Little Richard and making him safe for teen-age consumption).

One of my favorite Negro R&B groups during the 50s was Hank Ballard and the Midnighters. Their work was some of the most important socio-sexual true-to-life commentary of that era, for instance: *Stingy Little Thing* (a song in protest about girls who wouldn't "put out"), *Work with Me Annie*, and *Annie Had a Baby*. Songs like these got played on the air every once in a while — the kids would hear *Annie Had a Baby* and say, "Hey, here's a song about a girl getting pregnant," and rush to tune it in — but an official of the station (with teen-age children of his own to protect) would "lay a pink memo on it," and the song would sort of "disappear."

The visor men, meanwhile, were magically purifying all this stuff. *Work with Me Annie* ("Please don't cheat/Give me all my meat") through the wisdom of their craft became *Dance with Me, Henry* ("If you want romancin'/You better learn some dancin'").

Vaseline

White rock, overproduced and shiny, nearly slickened itself to death. (Remember *Fats Domino with Strings?*) The music industry was slumping a bit. Was this to be the end of rock? Were we doomed to a new era of country & western tunes smothered in Vaseline? Then, just in the nick of time, Beatlemania. New hope. There they were: cute, safe, white. The kids took to them immediately. Their music had real energy; it was sympathetic to their life style. It was music made for young people by other young people. No green visors. It seemed to radiate a secret message: "You can be free. You can get away with it. Look, we're doing it!"

I'm sure the kids never really believed all the Beatles wanted to do was *hold your hand*. And the girls were provided with "kissable closeups" (enlarged views of their idols' lips, teeth and gums) which they could kiss, touch, rub and/or hang on the bedroom wall. Girls forgot Elvis Presley. He was too greasy, too *heavy business*: sullen pouting and all that stuff. The Beatles were huggable & cute & mop-tops & happy & positive. Beatlemania was fun to be involved in.

The record companies were at a loss to compete with the British threat. Zeiger relates another droll incident: "I remember Mike Maitland who was then vice president and sales manager of Capitol Records. He was decrying the fact that they couldn't get any hit singles, and I said to him, 'Well, Mike, the reason is because you have the wrong people working for you.' 'Well, what do you want me to do? Get some of these fellows with the tight pants to produce these records?' I said, 'Exactly. Two button records can't be produced by guys with three button suits. It's all a matter of buttons.' Look at Mike Maitland now. He's president of Warner Brothers Records and look at the kind of things they're putting out . . . fellows with tight pants . . . or no pants . . . are producing the records.' "

It might be interesting at this point to discuss the evolution of recording-studio techniques. In the very oldenest of days, the recording engineer's main function was to stand behind the singer holding him by the shoulders, and either push him forward or pull him away from a large funnel-shaped object attached to a bent pin or something that used to function as a primitive microphone to gather sounds to be transcribed on a wax cylinder.

During the early stages of R&B, most recording was done on very large acetate discs. Then came tape. Monaural recordings gave way to stereo . . . then to three-track . . . then four-track. Four-track recording was the "standard of the industry" for a while until some of those tight pants, no pants producers Zeiger mentioned put pressure on companies and manufacturers to obtain eight-track machines which would allow more creative freedom to the young musicians who were playing this wonderful new money-making form of music. Today, eight-track recording is common and the adventurous new breed of "pop experimenters" are hustling to get 12-track machines, 16-track machines, 24-track machines (the Beatles, I hear, are setting up a nifty studio with 72 tracks).

Audience Education

There seems to be a trend in today's music toward eclecticism. The people who make this music are examining a wide range of possible musical and nonmusical elements to incorporate into their bags. Through rock music, the audience is being exposed to an assortment of advanced musical and electronic techniques that five years ago might have sent them screaming into the street. Amazing breakthroughs have been made in the field of "audience education."

These improvements have been made almost against the will of the mass media. Suppression for racial and sexual reasons doesn't go on as much but radio stations still do not program progressive rock in proportion to the market which exists for it. Specific songs which seem most threatening to the established order don't get on radio and TV. Example: Society's Child by Janis Ian about interracial dating. (Mass media does more to keep Americans stupid than even the whole U.S. school system, that vast industry which cranks out trained consumers and technician-pawns for the benefit of other vast industries.) It is something of a paradox that companies which manufacture and distribute this art form (strictly for profit) might one day be changed or controlled by young people who were motivated to action by the products these companies sell.

The level of involvement with today's music is quite amazing. One example: Groupies. These girls, who devote their lives to pop music, feel they owe something personal to it, so they make the ultimate gesture of worship, human sacrifice. They offer their bodies to the music or its nearest personal representative, the pop musician. These girls are everywhere. It is one of the most amazingly beautiful products of the sexual revolution.

The Jimi Hendrix Phenomenon

Hendrix was one of the most revolutionary figures in today's pop culture, musically and sociologically. His success is a curious paradox in view of the historical prejudices outlined earlier.

Hendrix was 24 years old. He dropped out of a Seattle high school in the 11th grade. He was raised strictly by his parents: "They taught me to have manners." He was reasonably sincere and humble: "We are lucky to be listened to." He was apparently very happy with his commercial success. Partly because it allowed him to act out some of his childhood fantasies (in his clothing, for instance): "I always wanted to be a cowboy or a *hadji baba* or the Prisoner of Zenda. . . ."

His strongest appeal was to the white female audience ranging in age from about 13 to 30, with the highest concentration of victims between 19 and 22. "I just carry advantages with me in my back pocket when I go off at a gig." His charisma also extended to a white male audience, 15 to 25.

He was realistic about his market appeal: "The black people probably talk about us like dogs . . . until we play." "When I see some of them in the street, they say, 'I see you got those two white boys with you.' . . . I try to explain to them about all this new music. I play them some records. First I play Cream . . . and when they say, 'Hey that's great, who is that playing the guitar?', I tell them it's Eric Clapton and he's an Englishman. Then I might play them some of what we do. Sometimes they still think we're crazy."

Hendrix's music is very interesting. The sound of his music is extremely symbolic: orgasmic grunts, tortured squeals, lascivious moans, electric disasters and innumerable other audial curiosities are delivered to the sense mechanisms of the audience at an extremely high decibel level. In a live performance environment, it was impossible to merely listen to what the Hendrix group did . . . it ate you alive. (He was concerned about his live performance image: "I don't want everybody to solely think of us in a big flash of weaving and bobbing and groping and maiming and attacking and . . .")

In spite of his maiming and groping, etc., the female audience thought of Hendrix as being beautiful (maybe just a little scary), but mainly very sexy. The male audience thought of him as a phenomenal guitarist and singer. Boys brought girls backstage for autographs. While signing their scraps of paper, shoulder blades, handbags and pants, Hendrix was frequently asked: "Do you think of any particular girl while you're playing, or do you just think of sex itself?" Meanwhile, the boys asked, "What kind of equipment do you use? Do you get high before you go on stage?"

The boys seemed to enjoy the fact that their girl friends were turned on to Hendrix sexually; very few resented his appeal and showed envy. They seemed to give up and say: "He's got it, I ain't got it, I don't know if I'll ever get it . . . but if I do, I wanna be just like him, because he's really got it." They settle for vicarious participation and/or buy a Fender Stratocaster, an Arbiter Fuzz Face, a Vox Wah-Wah Pedal, and four Marshall amplifiers.

The Gas Co., The Electric Co. & The Music Co.: Digression IV

The loud sounds and bright lights of today are tremendous indoctrination tools. Is it possible to modify the human chemical structure with the right combination of frequencies? (Frequencies you can't hear are manifested as frequencies you can see in a light show.) Can prolonged exposure to mixed media produce mutations? If the right kind of beat makes you tap your foot, what kind of beat makes you curl your fist and strike? Do you cry if the violin is playing the melody *molto vibrato*?

Manifestations of response to music will vary according to the character of the music and the audience. Swooning to Kay Kyser is roughly equivalent to squealing for the Monkees or drooling over Jimi Hendrix. In each case the *swoonee, squealee,* or *droolee* is responding to the music in a manner which he feels is reasonably acceptable by current social standards in his peer group.

If you were drunk, and it was the middle of summer, Saturday night about 11:30, and you had your comfortable clothes on, and you were in a small beer joint dancing, and it's crowded (temperature about 82°), and the local Rock & Roll combo (Ruben and The Jets) is playing *Green Onions* (or something that sounds just like it . . . all full of parallel fifths moving monotonously through a root progression I, IIb, IV, IIIb . . . or something like that, over & over again), and the guitar player goes to take a solo and stomps his *fuzz-tone* into action and turns his amplifier all the way up so his guitar squeals and screams and sounds absolutely vicious, and he bends and mangles the strings & starts to really get it on, gyrating and going totally berserk and playing his ass off and everythin' . . . if you were drunk, and all this was going on, and you were out there dancing and sweating and really *feeling* the music (every muscle & fiber of your being, etc., etc.) and the music suddenly got louder and more vicious . . . louder and viciouser than you could ever imagine (and you danced harder and got sweaty & feverish) and got your unsuspecting self worked up into a total frenzy, bordering on electric Buddha nirvana total acid freak cosmic integration (one with the universe), and you were drunk & hot & not really in control of your body or your senses (you are possessed by the music), and all of a sudden the music gets EVEN LOUDER . . . and not only that: IT GETS FASTER & YOU CAN'T BREATHE (But you can't stop either; it's impossible to stop) and you know you can't black out because it feels too good . . . I ask you now, if you were drunk and all this stuff is happening all over the place and somebody (with all the best intentions in the world) MADE YOU *STOP* so he could ask you this question: *"Is a force this powerful to be overlooked by a society that needs all the friends it can get?"* Would you listen?

| Tom Nolan | # Groupies: A Story of Our Times |

The March of Time's issue about teen-age girls is worth seeing in the sense that one might examine with interest a slide of cancer tissue. These girls may be no worse than the teen-age girls of any other country, class, or generation, but I would be sorry really to believe that, and am sorrier still to imagine their children.

— JAMES AGEE, 1945

It was the warm Saturday afternoon blues concert at the Monterey Pop Festival, and Brian Jones of the Rolling Stones was sitting in the second row of wooden chairs in the press section sipping on a Budweiser, dressed in a tattered-looking nineteenth-century gown of lace-and-fur-and-Tudor-ragged cloth, an Iron Cross dangling from his neck. He looked, with his pallid face, like an attenuated, dissipated little man: lines about his eyes, bleached and wrinkled and wrapped in lace and fur — the washed-out face of a randy pan, Harpo touched with the acerbic leer of the sixties.

Sitting next to him was Nico, regal, untouchable, a slender reed in a velvet gown, sipping on a Lucky Lager.

The beer made everything hazily pleasant, even Monkee Peter Tork conspicuously walking up, conspicuously presenting his conspicuous hand. "It's a great honor, sir, it's a great *honour*," he beams, shaking, Monkee-bashful. Then, Monkee-cute, "You know . . . there's about a hundred photographers just *dying* to get that shot; would you mind, again?"

"Oh," says Brian, taken aback. "Oh, well . . . if you really *want* to."

They shake again, and Monkee Peter beams, golliwogs down the aisle, clowning for the cameras, a puppet on a string.

"Eeeaaaah," says Brian softly. "How . . . *embarrassing*."

Then someone asks Brian what he thinks about groupies; and he looks narrowly at the questioner. And thinks. And says carefully, noncommittally, "Well . . . sort of depends. Depends on your definition of *groupie*. All sorts of definitions, you know. Ah dunno, they're easily avoidable."

But later the question gets more specific. Brian is walking with Nico in the artist-and-press area, and someone comes up to him and asks what does he think of Sherry Sklar. Brian tosses his hair. "Uhmmmm, well . . . it's hard to say, actually. Oh, hallo!" and takes the opportunity to wave to someone he has just seen, and walkoffveryquickly because even though he doesn't like to talk about it, Brian Jones of the Rolling Stones knows Sherry Sklar.

Knows Sherry Sklar. *Knows* Sherry Sklar. Now Sherry Sklar isn't walking beside him; no, of course not — Nico is: Nico, silver-haired moon goddess in a velvet gown; Nico, the solitary queen in her midnight castle; Nico, the poets' lady. Dylan "discovered" her in Europe and he and Grossman, his manager, urged her to come to New York, where she soon became Andy Warhol's Chelsea Girl-of-the-Year; and French movie stars were known to call that summer, and then Eric Anderson and Timmy Hardin and Leonard Cohen and Jackson Browne and all the fine young men began writing songs *for* her, *about* her: Nico, the poets' lady — because Nico is, after all, the most awe-inspiring, lonely, ghostly-death's-head-of-a-god-awful-gorgeous-girl in the whole round world.

But Sherry Sklar is no Nico — not by a long long long long shot. Though she tries very hard; and she *has* attained a certain position.

At about this time Sherry is wandering around the same backstage area, looking as she does, pale, blond, reasonably attractive, in orange-tinted shades (which, if she removes them, reveal the faintly predatory look most often seen in Hollywood starlets-on-the-make, a look that always sadly surprises when found in one so young — Sherry is nineteen). But Sherry is not speaking to Brian, or to the ex-Raiders, or to any of the others she knows who are there; perhaps because of a certain propriety observed in such matters (after all, they are with other people, after *all*), or just because right now she is so very *involved* — as Sherry is always involved, *busy*, so many places to go, people to see. . . .

But right now she is busy because the most wonderful thing may be happening, all the incredible rumors are spreading like mad locusts: the Beatles are here, the Beatles are here, McCartney has checked into the Motor Inn and all their equipment stashed in the back (which is cordoned off); George is backstage with no beard or mustache; McCartney is traveling under the name of Mr. Webb; no the Beatles are all together and yes have registered under the name "Sgt. Pepper's Band"; yes they're going to close the show Sunday night; singing, no they're not going to sing but they will talk; yes it's decided; no nothing's decided until they see how the crowd is acting. . . .

And through all of this Sherry is going absolutely mad — she cannot pay attention to Monkee Micky Dolenz wandering around dressed as an American Indian, sitting down on the ground to lecture a group of twelve-year-olds on philosophy. She has enough problems trying to convince her friends to come back with her to the Motor Inn — they've *got* to get to him if he's there. And meanwhile the two girls she is with, the sister of the drummer-singer of America's No. 1 Clean-Cut-Wholesome-Group (whose group co-member is paying for Sherry's motel room — are you catching this? — even though she's driven up there with the drummer from yet *another* group, an Englishman) and *her* friend, and the other two girls don't like the coat she's wearing; it's a pink imitation-leather carcoat-jacket-thing and she *likes* it you see but the other girls want her to take it off (they are, all three of them, up on acid) and getting involved in their thing, she figures why should she take the coat off because the coat is *her* isn't it? and if they don't like her and want to accept her as she is, well that's just too bad isn't it and they know what they can do then, on the other hand, I mean, after all, if it's *bringing them down* — oh, what to *do!*

2

The excitement is everywhere. . . .

The two girls live together in a Hollywood apartment where the walls are covered with collages, more ambitious than accomplished, of rock-group members cut from teen magazines. They are finishing off a joint, and one girl is cocktailing the roach, placing it in the end of a Tareyton with the last inch of tobacco removed; the end is twisted and lit for a few drags; no tobacco, very stony.

"I heard Arthur Lee is leaving Love," she says.

"Oh no, *not* Arthur! They'll be *nothing* without him."

"Somebody on KFWB said it; BMR, or maybe it was Gene Weed, I forget which."

"Well, he'll be on the album at least, because he's in the picture on the billboard on Sunset."

She means the billboard on the Sunset Strip heralding their next record, captioned: "Watch for the Third Coming of Love." The Nitty Gritty Dirt Band has a billboard, too, as does Jim Kweskin's Jug Band and the Doors. The excitement is everywhere. The rock poets are today's Hemingways and Fitzgeralds; work-in-progress is eagerly awaited; its appearance causing critical discussion. Group members are watched closely: Zally's left the Spoonful to go it on his own, just like Harry James left Benny Goodman; three of the Stones got busted for drugs, just like Gene Krupa — pop fans being as interested today as in the days of swing. With an added interest.

The excitement is everywhere.

At the newsstands they cluster (the younger ones: thirteen, fourteen) on alternate Wednesdays, glomming through the new issues of *Tiget Beat, Teenset, Go!* — Look, Denny's back with the Springfield! And isn't McGuinn's beard *bitchen!* And all the Raiders are gone — what a bummer! And look, Brian Jones shaking hands with Peter!

They wait outside the RCA Hollywood Studios when word gets out that the Monkees or Stones are recording, and standing outside, hoping to catch a glimpse next to the Magic-marker autographs of Monkees Micky and Davy, they hesitantly leave scrawls of affection:

Peter	Mike	
o	is a	Mick Rules
R	Doll	
K		

"Micky rules all, especially me!" and others — nasties — which will eventually be obliterated by spray paint.

They go into the girls' room of the Hullabaloo (a club on Sunset for mostly pre-teenyboppers) and (along with general information like "Bullwinkle lives on in acid" and "A friend with weed is a friend indeed") leave anonymous judgments: "Larry of the Knack is bitchen," "Doors are outasite," "Lovin' Spoonful rule over all and everyone," and — hopefully — "Steve Boone and me."

They went to the Beatles' movies over and over and over and screamed and sighed and melted and Ringo is so sad — oh! — and laughed when he said, "I've 'ad a lotta *fun* with this finguh" — they knew what *that* meant! And they go to the Stones concerts — "O, God if he sings 'Lady Jane' I'll die! O, God if he sings 'Under My Thumb'! Or God if he sings 'Lady Jane' or 'Under My Thumb' I'll die!" — screaming and writhing and moaning, their apple asses a-tremble in flowered bell-bottoms while old Mick bumps and grinds and prances in the evening air, his tight white pants showing the lumpy shadow of his — *you* know — "Oh, *MICK*, oh, *MICK! UP HERE! Oh, that dancing* turns me on more than his *singing! OOAAWWHH!* Oh mister mister *please* mister *please please* mister let me use your binoculars please I'll do anything please I'll do anything if you let me use 'em, please mister please I'll do *anything!*"

But while all those legions of wistful bell-bottomed girls are dreaming about Paulie and screaming for Mick to come up here where I can get my *fingernails* into you! there are an ambitious few who are doing something about it. While all the nubile fans dream and wish and hope — well, maybe someday I could-might-would . . . *meet*, maybe, someday, maybe — and write pointless fan letters with flowers drawn on the envelopes (well, he *might* read it) — there are girls who are making the dream reality, the unattainable available . . .

In the girls' room of the Hullabaloo, a graffito proclaims: "I was screwed by Joe Naples and *wow!*"

Outside the RCA Studios the security guard says: "Yeah, I put twelve extra men out when the Stones are here, but a few girls still get in. They break locks; they bust doors. They get in."

Some don't even have to bust locks.

Baby baby baby you're
Out of time . . .

There are two session men on guitar recording a rock album, seasoned pros, and every time the tuba plays this part, the one on bass guitar, behind the rock leader's back, goes into his silly routine of an arm-flopping prancing elephantine fairy-child (all the while still seated in his metal folding chair), and this pretty much breaks up the other guitarist just about every time. The next coffee break the second guitarist starts building a riff off an old song (he used to be one of the most famous jazz guitarists in the country) — "Do you know what that is? 'Sweet Georgia Brown.' " No-gal-made-has-scadoobetyoopnscoobedybleeopmbliblip — "That's the trouble with these songs today; you just can't *jam* on 'em" — Guys-she-can't-get-scoodylyoopmatwidbbidybopmbleopblipblop-bli-blop — and then they get started talking about the kids today, and the fellow who's jamming away on Georgia is saying how the thing that really worries him, the thing that has *him* scared, is what happens when these kids today, who have no responsibility at *all* of *any* kind (just can't fathom the kind of things that can *happen* to them), is what happens to them when they have to face some kind of *stark reality*, like being confronted with the fact that *they're pregnant.* . . .

And then for some reason that reminds him of something he heard the other day, Jerry told him, you know Jerry? Well he was over at some studios, and he says *no*body could get in, but he was there on a session the other night, and those guys, the *Mmm*-mm-mmm, they were in there in Studio B, and they had two chicks from somewhere, and they were down there on the floor, two of the *Mmm*-mm-mmm, just . . . *doing* it . . . and everybody else was just standing around watching; I guess they were *producing* the session, right? Oh, *wow.* . . .

3

Have you seen your mother, baby,
Standing in the shadow?

Sherry's parents are sitting quietly in the living room of the closest-thing-residential-Bel-Air-can-come-to-a-minor-modern-palace. Her mother, a now mostly quiet woman exuding the somewhat sad air of one who has paid the dues of her husband's long ascent up the pyramid of corporate corridors, is sitting under the tasteful Tiffany lamp, braving her way through Chapter 18 of Elia Kazan's *The Arrangement*. Mr. Sklar, sitting in a somewhat garish orange armchair (the sole concession to *his* decorating taste), is watching the third night of ABC's Very Special Season in color (tomorrow he will watch the fourth night of NBC Week). The phone rings, it is for Sherry; even though Sherry has had her own phone disconnected, an incredible number of people manage to get the family number; and Mrs. Sklar smiles sweetly, gently, primly, and explains that Sherry is not at home this evening, she has gone to the library to return a book, no, she doesn't know when. . . .

At about this time Sherry, overdue library book in hand, is parked in her pink Mustang high in the Hollywood Hills, the city all a-twinkle below her, below her, and she watches the house she is about to enter, the house of the drummer of America's Number One Money-Making Group. She watches through the window of his den as he, unawares, flails away at his drums. His group is often accused of being blatant bogus-Beatles, and so it is somewhat ironic (and Sherry, cynical-sharp, is not unaware of this) that the record he is practicing to is the Beatles' "Lucy in the Sky with Diamonds"; and even though it is a fairly slow song, he can't . . . quite . . . keep the beat . . . and just before going in, she smiles slightly around the corners of her mouth and mind; she keeps her sense of perspective.

It all began for Sherry, all of it, when she formed the Boss Beatle Booster Fan Club in 1964, when she was fifteen and innocent. This was the year of the English Invasion: the Beatles, Stones, Gerry and the Pacemakers, Billy Jay Kramer and the Dakotas, the Dave Clark Five, the Searchers, Herman's Hermits, Peter and Gordon, Chad and Jeremy, Manfred Mann, Zombies, Kinks — and it was all so exciting and fun, and anyway it was something to *do*.

Because you must understand Sherry was really *innocent;* not that she had any particular scruples then, just a vague sort of sense of respectability, due mainly to her not yet being exposed to any intrusion (in the form of some randy back-seat young hard-breathing son of a golfing tycoon) that would break the vacuum of and expose the half-ridden hypocrisy behind her parents' country-club world of what proper young girls did and did not do — Sherry, then, was Innocent.

The idea of her Boss Beatle Booster Fan Club was that everyone who showed their Sincere Affection and joined could get a Boss Beatle Booster Fan Club Card, each of which is probably worth a small fortune now, expressions of Sincere Affection coming at a premium price these days; but still, Sherry was not content with what was, after all, really a minor sort of gesture. It was all somehow not quite right, there seemed to be something missing here; perhaps Sherry was slightly out-of-place.

At the giant Beatle Rally at the Coliseum, for instance, when all of L.A.'s pretty young things turned out merely to stand up and be counted; they came from Glendale and Pasadena and Pacoima for the Fab Four, Tarzana and Orange and Encino for the Lovely Liverpool Lads, Long Beach and Lakewood and Burbank for the Bashful Bragging Beautiful Boys — and — they wore almost-bursting bell-bottoms, the thin-tight cloth flower-painting their bods, they had just learned to love their mod-bods, tanned and lean and budding, and they shook their hair in the open air with just the touch of a frosted-pink slicker lipstick mist-kiss on their lips — and then — there was Sherry, a bit demure (as was only proper), blond of course but wearing the prim white dress-suit she and Mother had picked out because it was Her.

Well, she had to do something; something had to be done. Something large, and really *major*. She decided on a scroll, a really *major* scroll, with hundreds of names giving testimony to Great Affection and Sincere Loyalty (with each signer getting a Boss Beatle Booster Fan Club Card); she began collecting the signatures.

And yet — it somehow still didn't seem quite enough, and she noticed the beginnings of what she could only think of as . . . strange . . . *stirrings*, which began about the time she went to see the Rolling Stones on the Hollywood Palace TV Show, where Dean Martin kept cracking all his silly "jokes" about the Stones and all the old people in the audience, of course, they all *laughed;* and near the end of the show Sherry had run down from the balcony outside to the stage door to see the Stones, but really, it was something *else*, she couldn't say quite what, she'd never dreamed aloud, but it was . . . *strange;* and the handful of girls there seemed (she sensed) to be driven by the same strange Muse — and nothing happened, the Stones didn't show. But —

> Somethin' happened to me yesterday
> Somethin' I can't speak of right away

The oddness continued, through the next week and up to the Wednesday morning when she heard the one and only radio announcement that A—— and W—— were arriving at the airport, and naturally she hurried on down to welcome them and, as it turned out, was the only one there. Which was nice, because they talked to her. Alone. On and on they talked, and she welcomed them to California, and the one who had taken an especial interest in her, he smiled with his tired eyes, and leaned over; she was wearing a darling little A-line dress with rather large buttons over the, uh, breasts, and he just pressed the buttons; firmly. And this pretty little innocent little blond girl just didn't know what to *do*, she just didn't know *what* to do; so she went home. . . .

> Give it to me now,
> I've no objec-tion . . .

But it was a brush with fame, and Sherry had liked the hint of the something she had sniffed, and somehow couldn't just stop now. And so, to put it briefly, decided to take the Ultimate Step — not so hard as some might imagine, in fact ridiculously easy to arrange, and though details are boring, it was with a fairly popular English group that has since faded into obscurity, but they weren't a bad beginning, pretty auspicious in those days; and she would eventually make it with much much bigger groups. And once she got over her initial shyness, why, you'd think she had been doing it all her life! Rolling around in a giant bed, the four of them, she and her newfound friend Karen, and two members of a Philly White-Soul group, trading, switching, tumbling around — those guys, Sherry concedes, when she starts remembering the good old times in a misty-wistful kind of way, those guys, re*mem*ber? those guys were . . . *probably* . . . the best.

> No one knows,
> She comes, and goes . . .

She usually got in on the action by finding out when groups were in town and cruising the hotels on the Strip, looking up at balconies, and sooner or later — sure enough! there they'd be, shaggy-haired, lonely-looking, raunchy-looking . . . randy-looking. . . . She'd shout up and ask them their room numbers; and just in case the guys hadn't gotten the idea by then — and also for general use (she was going into this in a really big way), she had all these engraved cards printed up, plain little white cards printed up, plain little white cards that simply say I WANT YOU — though lately she has been having variations made up, like LET'S GET IT ON. And after a while she began collecting souvenirs, and now has a giant jingling chain full of keys from hotel rooms, the rooms of all the famous boys she has "been with."

> We love they
> We hope you love they too . . .

But of course the very best of boys were still the Beatles, and Sherry had by now, on the side, gathered hundreds of signatures for her major scroll which she planned to present to the Beatles, whose arrival was imminent. Finding them, though, was something else. She found out approximately where they'd be by going into a closet with a rock DJ and working on him for three hours — his stupid velour and his shades and Jay Sebring razorcut — boy was *he* terrible!

She had camped there then, up in Bel Air, at a strategic point; the Beatles could not leave without passing her, there being only one way down the hill; and even if the guard wouldn't let her in, why, she'd get a chance at them on their way to the airport. And sure enough, they finally came down, and saw her following them, and probably thought she'd stop once they got on the San Diego freeway to the airport, but they were wrong because Sherry kept up with them, pulled alongside, in fact (no small thing, as they were going about 85 mph). Sherry leaned out the window and there were the Beatles, dreamlike, in the next lane, rocketing down the freeway with the Beatles' driver trying to lose her or something. Sherry was just trying to throw her goddam scroll through their window but Brian Epstein (who was in the Beatle car too) thought she was trying to *hurl* herself from her car to theirs or something, and he started yelling "DON'T — JUMP! DON'T BE — A LITTLE — FOOL! YOU — WILL ONLY — INJURE — YOURSELF!" And by this time they were going about 95 mph, and finally she pulled back to the car behind, where one of the Beatles' staff was fondling some chick in his lap, and Sherry threw the goddam scroll through the window and he dumped the girl off his lap and started *reading* it! Wow! How funny! But then a cop pulled her over and she gets tagged for — tailgating! and that was that.

Not that she always goes to such extremes, because compared to some people she knows, that's a relatively primitive ploy. There was one girl, for instance, who along with her friends decided to find where the Beatles were staying one time by hiring a helicopter and flying all over Bel Air so she and her friends could wave to the Guys at poolside; she didn't get *in*, but they waved a lot. And the next day the Beatles held a press conference to which this girl managed to get herself invited through persuading some DJ — all these girls know *all* the DJ's — to let her in, providing she didn't cause a fuss.

So the girl hangs around for an hour or so, and then leaves just before it ends, hoping to beat the Beatles' cars to the Bowl; and just at that point some DJ is talking to Paul and saying there were these girls, you know, Paul, who rented a copter; you know, Paul, a *helicopter*, and flew over your house, did you know that Paul? And Paul says, oh yes, we'd like to meet them, are they here? Girls? Girls? and eager to please Paul, the murmur starts growing louder and louder, filling the room, girls? girls? GIRLS? That moment, when that girl remembers it, the moment she will never forget as long as she lives, that moment, drives her to moaning and turning green and writhing in agony and everything just short of pulling out all her lovely California-chic hair — she came — *so close!*

No, Sherry usually sticks to relatively less imaginative ways of finding groups, like the habit she developed of hiring limousines to cruise the streets in, up and down Sunset, that sort of thing. After a while the drivers got to know her, and what she was up to, and they'd point to likely-looking longhairs at bus stops: How 'bout him? Ya wanna pick him up? And now it's not too cool to take the limousines because all the drivers know about her and have started making big old hints like, *weeeeee!* now, wouldn't mind *havin'* some a' that there stuff yer givin' away there, nosirnosirnosirnosir. . . .

Of course Sherry has her memories, fond ones, many of them funny, like the time she and Karen decided to take their friend Linda to see her fave-rave English group leader at his hotel at some ungodly hour, and the girls drag her out of the shower, clinging wet, all this is sort of a joke anyway, because this girl is seventeen and *incredibly* pure, never been with *any*one, and they drag her into the poor guy's room, and he offers her his bathrobe, which she goes into the bathroom to put on. Meanwhile there is a knock on the door and in burst her parents, with the hotel manager, and Linda emerges from the bathroom in this star's dressing gown, with her father yelling about aliens! coming over here! and — oh! and everybody is shouting and explanations are demanded and papers are seized and — finally, this nice guy with his faggoty glasses and his beard is deported, and can never come back to America again, and — because record-plugging tours are often essential — will never have a hit here *ever again*. Wow, remembers Sherry, it's all too funny! And she wouldn't have even let him do anything with her! Oh *wow!*

Or the time she had lassoed two entire groups at the airport, and they were waiting for her by her car and she couldn't find the car keys! Here she is at the airport and they're standing around, about eight guys, shuffling their feet, and she's pouring out her handbag, shaking it out on the hood, just can't find them! Well! And she was laughing so hard she pissed in her pants! . . .

Of course a lot of things have happened since then; a lot of things have changed. And you must not get the idea that Sherry has no standards; some people, after all, are really just out-of-the-question; for instance, *Ne*-groes, well, that's really perverted, isn't it? and she doesn't go in for any of those *kinky* practices. And one group she wouldn't "be with" because when they switched from good-time music to intellectual-rock, well, they just went way out of their league, she wouldn't have a thing to do with them.

Following these somewhat strange standards, Sherry has attained a certain status. She is not your run-of-the-mill groupie: when she goes somewhere it is because she has been invited. At Monterey she travels with a member of one of the most famous groups: she is his guest, having all the privileges of same; she is part of pop society, even if only the fringes, but retrenching all the time; and even though she may not absolutely be *the numero uno* (there is a girl in New York rumored to have had *both* Jagger and McCartney, and another girl who has only had Keith Richard, which is, after all, not the same as having had Jagger, but this is made up for by her having had Lennon, who counts for two times with McCartney), nonetheless she is *known*, a person in her own right, and whenever major crises come up she is there to help. Like when a famous teenybopper idol raided one group to refill his own depleted ranks, causing a certain amount of bad feeling, why, Sherry was right in there, acting the intermediary, hopping in her car, let's find out what all this is all about! Let's settle this!

Meanwhile her old friend and sometime-companion Karen is beginning to wonder about it all, or at least certain parts of it, like the way she will ask strangers do they think she looks — well, *used* . . .

> Who wants yesterday's papers
> Who wants yesterday's girl . . .

and it is true that her fragile blonde prettiness is beginning to harden around the edges, and though she isn't quite as hard-looking as Sherry, maybe she has gotten to the point where the faces are all beginning to blur together in a hazy kind of fog. . . .

4

> Dying all the time;
> Lose your dreams and you will lose your mind —

I saw her first at my high school, where I would return melancholic to the scene of my past and most recent triumphs — she was awfully un-questionably pretty in a way that brought back the unbearable loneliness of a summer afternoon — in a pretty calendar-day-sort-of-way; some must have called her beautiful, but just as surely it was a sad beauty; for she was the girl who seemed somehow sadly older, this coming with the territory, and boys (and some girls too) would whisper jokes about her behind their hands. And she smiled often (though wistfully) and was touched deeply by any small act of kindness, that commodity being more precious to her, perhaps, and less given, than for the rest of us.

And she wanted to be a model, of course, like every other halfway decent-looking girl in town, and even some who weren't but made the trek anyhow from Racine, Wisconsin, with money for pictures and The School. But she didn't have to worry, she was beautiful; life for her was different, I thought — the candy apple of the month.

I had hardly spoken to her at all, only briefly, passing in a corridor — could she sense my clumsy, well-meaning feelings? But we saw her, my older cousin and I, he on a visit from Cleveland, Ohio, with his fine Marine sensibilities honed on a life of drive-in-theater passion with the rest of his buddies looking on from their own back seats — "Sure, they knew what we were doin' back there; after that I left her. She wanted me, but I left her, an' now you can see her at the dances up at Broadview Heights. Waitin' round. Tryin' to pick up somebody; anybody" — he shakes his head at her stupidity, the awful and comical depth of her fall.

And then we saw my friend on TV, some teen-age show; she was taking telephone votes for the dance contest and I said, "I *know* that girl; isn't she great looking?" and because (I knew) he didn't believe me (I had been making these claims through three days of watching television), I phoned her on the show, at which point my now-convinced cousin started whispering hoarsely, "Can-she-fix-me-up? Ask-her-can-she-fix-me-up!" and a double-date was arranged; and even though my cousin, an unbearable clod, had been just that — on our way to pick them up, for instance, I had asked why the blanket folded neatly on the back seat? "Oh, leave it, that's to show we're . . . *studs*" — and when we had gone (of all places) bowling, and he leaned over suavely with the ball poised suavely studying the length of the alley, his shirt pulled up to reveal his underwear — bad enough, but he had also comically managed to put his shorts on inside-out, so that in the small of his back is the little square cloth proclaiming "Fruit of the Loom" — and she looks at her friend — and s-i-l-e-n-t-l-y l-a-u-g-h-s . . . but in spite of my cousin, she is nice to me, and on the way back she allows me to kiss her and then, tentatively, fondle her breast, enough to impress my cousin, his eyes glued constantly to the rear-view mirror, she and I wrapped under his precious flannel studblanket.

I never saw her too often after that, either, but I kept in touch; she had fallen into a certain circle, calculated to enlarge her somewhat hazy plans of a singing-dancing-modeling career, and soon she was dancing on a go-go show, jerking swaying moaning bumping hips glistening with the best long-haired Strip-chicks of all, while the director who by-god knew his trade jockeyed the cameras for the up-the-skirt shot; and the groups who guested stared and licked their lips and smiled. (Oh the first one, yes, the first one: California Good-Time Music he made, he told her, in the back seat of his car.)

Connections of sorts developed — here and there; this and that. Plans to be made, something brewing all the time. This and that, here and there; a trip to Brazil for that TV show that never quite came off, but then again . . . maybe she would go on a tour, she and three other girls, they'd sing and dance, a little go-go revue; like, this guy was fixing it up, their manager, maybe next month. Things are coming, you know, okay, not bad, you know, pretty good, oh except for this and that — some dyke keeps phoning, says she's going to kill her — but then — acid is new and very large and there are always lots of famous people around, she is getting known in a small way, she's had some of the best of the less-known groups, this bass player, that lead singer, and one night Dylan even came over, a bunch of people brought him by, she could show the pictures to you. . . . And everything seemed to be fine, the world it seemed was turning ever-sweetly in a funny kind of way, if a bit slanted on its axis, but just . . . certain things . . .

Where she lived, the way she lived; the hint of something else (a plea perhaps) on the edge of a question. She stayed with a friend, another dancer, having moved out from her mother's some time ago. They had fixed the place up, she and her friend, with a lot of painfully artsy pop collages and the like, and there were always a lot of books lying around but she never quite got around to finishing any of them, and she and her friend would put on some campy little record, "Snow White and the Seven Dwarfs," and put on big floppy hats and jump all over and dance through the kitchen and into the living room and it was strangely sad; and upsetting.

Or the way you'd be talking and for no reason at all she'd say something like "Well, after all, who's to say what's Good and what's Bad?" and I didn't realize she might after all desperately want some kind of an answer.

After a while I fell out of touch and didn't see her for many months. When I did it was about one in the morning in front of a bittersweet coffeehouse in Hollywood, and any trace of that special spring-freshness she had once had seemed irretrievably lost; her face was drawn, dissipated, almost haggard; perhaps she ran through a Garbo beauty before her eyes turned harsh. Maybe it was the gonorrhea; she joked about being cured three different times, but most likely she had never lost it the first time. Surely it was one thing or another.

While her girl friend — the latest in a long succession of friends, boy and girl, none of whom stayed for much of the trip — was inside having her foot read by a kindly melancholy old German in spectacles, she told me about the spacemen. They had contacted her one night, now they wanted her to spy on the world for them, to spy on earth, and they would pay her very well, don't you know, very well indeed, and give her all the clothes she could ever imagine, and take her places, far away, but she didn't *know,* she just didn't know what to *do,* you see; she just didn't know what to do. . . .

5

> By the time you're thirty gonna look
> sixty-five
> You won't look purty and your
> friends will have kissed you good-bye . . .

Sherry is looking out the window of the Laurel Canyon house where she lives with Danny, a computer programmer in his twenties. (Karen cuts his hair.) Covering one window is a giant poster of James Dean. Sherry sits down on the floor, barefoot in white capris and sweater, starts playing with Pepper, their white kitten named after the Beatles' *Sgt. Pepper.* She grabs the rubber ball he is pawing, holding it just out of reach. "Hey, you're a sadist, you know, that's what you are. A sadist," Danny says. He grabs Kitten by the scruff of the neck, holds it up, drops it. Sherry goes to the window again to look out into the street. "Hey, here comes one of those freaky-looking guys," she says. "Wow! What a freaky-looking guy. Maybe he's in a group."

Sherry doesn't see too much of her old friends any more. There's really not that much to do, now that she's sort of settled down. Karen comes over about once a week, of course; but they don't . . . *go out.* And once in a while some of Danny's friends come over, and they'll all sing old Beatle songs, or the Mamas and Papas — she has a guitar and a big stack of songbooks — and Sherry sings in her strident slightly flat way and maybe Danny will make a joke, you know, just a little *remark* or something, and she'll flash her eyes at him, a trifle harsh, a trifle mean, and — "Well, mister, if it's so easy why don't *you* sing it!" — and it's just not the same; not like when she and Karen and who knows, maybe a guy or two, would go out *cruising,* looking for guys in rock groups, and maybe end up bribing the guard at the Hollywood Bowl with a cup of coffee and a doughnut (they'd cruised there so many times they knew to get him coffee. With cream. And now the guard — it was *too funny!* — he'd been starting to act a little randy, just a *l-e-e-t-l-e* bit, don't-you-know, looking at them, smiling, lips dry), and getting up on the stage at one in the morning, whatever and singing "If I Fell [for You]"; those were good times. Sherry doesn't see her friends any more.

Sherry stares out the window and the Stones are on the phonograph, and Sherry starts to chant along off-key:

> All of my friends from school grew
> up and settled down
> and they mortgaged off their lives.

Karen has enrolled in Ravi Shankar's Indian music school, hoping one day to get at George Harrison.

A Short Anthology of Rock Poetry

MY GENERATION

People try to put us down
Just because we get around
Things they do look awful cold
Hope I die before I get old.

This is my generation, baby.

Why don't you all f-f-f-fade away
Don't try and dig what we all say
I'm not trying to cause a big sensation
I'm just talking 'bout my generation.

This is my generation, baby,
My generation.

PETER TOWNSHEND (for the Who)

MORNING MORNING

Morning morning
Feel so lonesome in the morning
Morning morning
Morning brings me grief

Sunshine sunshine
Sunshine laughs upon my face
And the glory of the growing
Puts me in my rotting place

Evening evening
Feel so lonesome in the evening
Evening evening
Evening brings me grief

Moonshine moonshine
Moonshine drugs the hills with grace
And the secret of the shining
Seeks to break my simple face

Nighttime nighttime
Kills the blood upon my cheek
Nighttime nighttime
Does not bring me to relief

Starshine starshine
Feel so loving in the starshine
Starshine starshine
Darling kiss me as I weep

TULI KUPFERBERG (for the Fugs)

WONDERFUL

She belongs there
Left with her liberty,
Never known
As a non-believer,
She laughs and stays
In her wonderful . . .

She knew how
To gather the forest
When God reached softly
And moved her body,
One golden locket
Quite young and loving
Her mother and father.

Farther down
The path was a mystery,
Through the roses,
The chalk and numbers,
A boy bumped
Into her wonderful . . .

She'll return
In love with her liberty,
Never known
As a non-believer,
She'll smile and thank God
For wonderful . . .

BRIAN WILSON (for The Beach Boys)

SOURCE: © 1967, Tune Publishers, Inc. and Newkeys Music.

SAD-EYED LADY OF THE LOWLANDS[1]

With your mercury mouth in the missionary times
And your eyes like smoke and your prayers like rhymes
And your silver cross and your voice like chimes
Oh, who do they think could bury you?
With your pockets well-protected at last
And your streetcar visions which you place on the grass
And your flesh like silk and your face like glass
Who could they get to carry you?

Sad-eyed lady of the lowlands
Where the sad-eyed prophet said that no man comes
My warehouse has my Arabian drums
Should I put them by your gate
Oh sad-eyed lady, should I wait?

With your sheets like metal and your belt like lace
And your deck of cards missing the jack and the ace
And your basement clothes and your hollow face
Who among them did you think could outguess you?
With your silhouette when the sunlight dims
Into your eyes where the moonlight swims
And your matchbook songs and your gypsy hymns
Who among them could try to impress you?

Sad-eyed lady of the lowlands
Where the sad-eyed prophet said that no man comes
My warehouse has my Arabian drums
Should I put them by your gate
Oh sad-eyed lady, should I wait?

Oh, the farmers and the businessmen they all did decide
To show you where the dead angels are that they used to hide,
But why did they pick you to sympathize with their side
How could they ever stake you?
They wish you'd accepted the blame for the farm,
But with the sea at your feet and the phony false alarm
And with the child of a hoodlum wrapped up in your arms,
How could they ever have persuaded you?

SOURCE: Copyright © 1966 by Dwarf Music. Used by permission of Dwarf Music.

[1] Stanza three (3) of SAD-EYED LADY OF THE LOWLANDS has been deleted.

Sad-eyed lady of the lowlands
Where the sad-eyed prophet said that no man comes
My warehouse has my Arabian drums
Should I put them by your gate
Oh sad-eyed lady, should I wait?

With your sheet metal memory of Cannery Row
And your magazine husband who one day just had to go
And your gentleness now, which you just can't help but show
Who among them do you think would employ you?
Ah, you stand with your thief; you're on his parole
With your holy medallion and your fingertips that fold
And your saint-like face and your ghost-like soul
Who among them did ever think he could destroy you?

Sad-eyed lady of the lowlands
Where the sad-eyed prophet said that no man comes
My warehouse has my Arabian drums
Should I put them by your gate
Oh sad-eyed lady, should I wait?

Bob Dylan

SUZANNE

Suzanne takes you down
To her place near the river.
You can hear the boats go by,
You can stay the night beside her.
And you know that she's half-crazy
But that's why you want to be there,
And she feeds you tea and oranges
That come all the way from China,
And just when you mean to tell her
That you have no love to give her,
Then she gets you on her wave-length
And she lets the river answer
That you've always been her lover.

And you want to travel with her,
And you want to travel blind,
And you know that she can trust you
'Cause you've touched her perfect body
With your mind.

And Jesus was a sailor
When he walked upon the water
And he spent a long time watching
From a lonely wooden tower
And when he knew for certain
That only drowning men could see him,
He said, "All men shall be sailors, then,
Until the sea shall free them,"
But he, himself, was broken
Long before the sky would open.
Forsaken, almost human,
He sank beneath your wisdom
Like a stone.

And you want to travel with him,
And you want to travel blind,
And you think you'll maybe trust him
'Cause he touched your perfect body
With his mind.

Suzanne takes your hand
And she leads you to the river.
She is wearing rags and feathers
From Salvation Army counters,
And the sun pours down like honey
On our lady of the harbor;
And she shows you where to look
Among the garbage and the flowers.
There are heroes in the seaweed,
There are children in the morning.
They are leaning out for love,
And they will lean that way forever
While Suzanne, she holds the mirror.

And you want to travel with her,
You want to travel blind,
And you're sure that she can find you
'Cause she's touched her perfect body
With her mind.

LEONARD COHEN

MOTORCYCLE IRENE

There she sits a'-smokin'
Reefer in her mouth.
Her hair hanging northward
As she travels south.
Dirty, on her Harley,
(But her nails are clean.)
Super-powered, de-flowered,
Over-eighteen Irene.

I've seen her in the bare
Where her tatoos and her chains
Wrap around her body,
Where written are the names
Of prisons she's been in,
And lovers she has seen,
Curve-winding, bumping, grinding,
Motorcycle Irene

Ground round like hamburger
Laying in a splat
'Tis Irene, her sheen I seen
In pieces crumpled flat.
Her feet were in the bushes,
Her toes were in her hat,
Stark-ravin', un-shaven
Motorcycle Irene.

The Hunchback, the Cripple,
The Horseman, and the Fool,
Prayer books and candles, and
Carpets, cloaks, and jewels,
Knowing all the answers
Breaking all the rules,
With stark naked, unsacred,
Motorcycle Irene.

SKIP SPENCE (for Moby Grape)

SOURCE: Lyrics © 1968 South Star Music. (BMI)

THE LOVE YOU SAVE (MAY BE YOUR OWN)

People I've been misled
And I've been afraid
I've been hit in the head
And left for dead.
I've been abused,
And I've been accused
Been refused a piece of bread.

But I ain't never in my life before
Seen so many love affairs go wrong
As I do today.
I want you to stop!
Find out what's wrong.
Get it right, or just leave love alone
Because the love you save today
May very well be your own.

I've been pushed around.
I've been lost and found,
I've been given 'til sundown
To get out of town.
I've been taken outside,
And I've been brutalized
And I had to be always the one to smile
And apologize.

But I ain't never in my life before
Seen so many love affairs go wrong
As I do today.
I want you to stop!
Find out what's wrong.
Get it right, or just leave love alone
Because the love you save today
May very well be your own.

JOE TEX

SOURCE: Copyright © 1966 by TREE Publishing Co., Inc. All rights reserved.

WHITE RABBIT

One pill makes you larger
And one pill makes you small.
And the ones that mother gives you
Don't do anything at all.
Go ask Alice
When she's ten feet tall.

And if you go chasing rabbits
And you know you're going to fall.
Tell 'em a hookah smoking caterpillar
Has given you the call.
Call Alice
When she was just small.

When men on the chessboard
Get up and tell you where to go.
And you've just had some kind of mushroom
And your mind is moving low.
Go ask Alice
I think she'll know.

When logic and proportion
Have fallen sloppy dead,
And the White Knight is talking backwards
And the Red Queen's lost her head

Remember what the dormouse said:
"Feed your head.
Feed your head.
Feed your head."

GRACE SLICK (of The Jefferson Airplane)

A DAY IN THE LIFE

I read the news today, oh boy,
About a lucky man who made the grade
And though the news was rather sad
Well I just had to laugh
I saw the photograph.
He blew his mind out in a car
He didn't notice that the lights had changed
A crowd of people stood and stared
They'd seen his face before
Nobody was really sure
If he was from the House of Lords.

I saw a film today, oh boy,
The English army had just won the war
A crowd of people turned away
But I just had to look
Having read the book.
I'd love to turn you on.

Woke up, fell out of bed,
Dragged a comb across my head
Found my way downstairs and drank a cup,
And looking up I noticed I was late.
Found my coat and grabbed my hat
Made the bus in seconds flat
Found my way upstairs and had a smoke,
Somebody spoke and I went into a dream.

I read the news today, oh boy,
Four thousand holes in Blackburn,
Lancashire
And though the holes were rather small
They had to count them all
Now they know how many holes it takes to fill the Albert Hall.
I'd love to turn you on.

JOHN LENNON & PAUL MCCARTNEY (The Beatles)

THE ESTABLISHMENT

$\mathcal{2}$

■ Almost without thinking, everybody knows what it is: the "Establishment" of any society is the place where the real power is held. But after that the troubles begin at once, because in a modern society the diffusions and the concentrations of power are very hard to define. In earlier ages that complication hardly existed because Establishment power had an innocent way of manifesting itself in imposing symbols, and those symbols were likely to be the largest, finest, and most permanent buildings within view. There was no mistaking the meaning of Chartres cathedral, rising high above the humble roofs of the town, nor the significance of the grand expanse of Blenheim palace.

In these edifices the power of the church and the power of the aristocracy were magnificently visible. Even as a very young boy, Julien Sorel, the nineteenth century hero of Stendhal's *The Red and the Black*, could perceive that the Church and the Army were the headquarters of the Establishment in France. Ours is a time, on the other hand, when the locations of power are camouflaged and the exercise of power is far more hidden, indirect, and disguised. In a nation where almost every kind of activity is advertised and publicized, we tend to be most secretive about what is most potent.

Were the fictional Julien Sorel alive today, he would have difficulty in mapping out his road to the summit. If, like many students of the present time, he were prepared to dismantle the Establishment, he would be handicapped by the same lack of direction. In the fall of 1969 in the city of Chicago, there occurred an event that demonstrates this confusion very neatly.

The Weatherman faction of the SDS (Students for a Democratic Society) decided to demonstrate violently against the war in Vietnam, to "bring the war home" as a way of shocking the Establishment elite. The stage they chose for this experiment in living theatre was the old residential area where years ago many of the Chicago rich — the McCormicks, the Fieldses, and the Newberrys — had built their townhouses. But the Weathermen's plan was based on a legend some twenty-five years out of date. Over a quarter of a century prior to the demonstration, the real Establishment had moved on to broader fields and fresher air. There are still some rich families on Chicago's Gold Coast, but most residents are only marginally affluent or simply middle class — teachers, airline hostesses, salaried employees who live in three-room apartments there.

The Weathermen rallied in Lincoln Park and marched down Clark Street wrecking cars, breaking the windows of a small florist's shop, a stationery shop, a drugstore, and a neighborhood restaurant, and shattering some apartment-house plate glass. These were not exactly the haunts of the rich and powerful, who next day read about these distant events over their breakfasts in suburban Kenilworth or in their skyscraper offices in the Loop.

There have been several attempts to locate and describe this country's Establishment, but none has been entirely successful. One book that caused a stir was C. Wright Mills' *The Power Elite*, published in 1956. Mills put forward the thesis that the nation is directed no longer by an economically powerful "ruling class" but by an alliance of big-business executives, political leaders, and military chiefs, the "power elite" of the title. It is a managerial group whose importance arises from the political situation — mainly the cold war and huge defense expenditures — rather than an Establishment with any uniform or enduring dogma about how society should be ordered.

Richard Rovere took a different view in *The American Establishment and Other Reports, Opinions, and Speculations*, published in 1962. Rovere's title essay suffers from a kind of obscure hilarity, as if the Establishment were a kind of private joke or put-on. (There is considerable game-playing with what Rovere refers to as the "ins" and the "outs." We are told, for instance, that Billy Graham and Allen Ginsburg aren't Establishment members, while David Sarnoff and John McCloy are.) Rovere's serious argument is that the Establishment as he sees it is an informal association of the big-foundation, government, business, and cultural liberals who lent to the public affairs of the past two decades their own style of thought and action. Its members were intellectuals (such as Henry Kissinger and Arthur Burns), businessmen (such as David Sarnoff and Henry Luce) plus some bankers, labor leaders, government officials, and one theologian (Reinhold Niebuhr). This was the Establishment — with some changes in personalities — that reached its peak of influence under the Kennedy administration.

The main flaw in Rovere's half-serious essay is that he was assuming, or pretending to assume, that the Establishment is a kind of private club, a small, snobbish gathering, as it were, of *New Yorker* magazine characters who lay down rules for society. Politically at least, the influence of Establishment style diminished under Lyndon Johnson, declined further with its inability to nominate Nelson Rockefeller, and has had very uneven going under Richard Nixon.

According to Rovere's 1962 description, the Establishment runs a tight ship. He states that it "maintains effective control over the Executive and Judicial branches of government . . . it dominates most of American education and intellectual life . . . it has very nearly unchallenged power in deciding what is and what is not respectable opinion in this country. Its authority is enormous in organized religion . . . in science, and, indeed, in all the learned professions except medicine. It is absolutely unrivalled in the great new world created by the philanthropic foundations. . . ."

It was a neat diagram, and it seemed reasonable enough to believe in the relatively placid years of the 1950's and early 60's. Then came the shattering effect of the great argument over Vietnam. What had looked to Rovere like a confident, secure power structure suddenly began to sound like a debating society. Vietnam was not the only quarrel, but it was the biggest one, and it produced a good many offshoots.

Rovere's misapprehension is an example of the danger of looking at a situation as if it were an organism. In this vast, complex, and changeable society of ours, power is distributed among many groups and along different strata. An Establishment exists, but purely as a temporary alliance, the kind occurring when several tribes decide to pitch their tents on the same grounds. They form a dominant coalition on the order of the one that brought together the federal government, the military-industrial complex, the unions, the communications media, and the Civil Rights movement during the four Democratic administrations since World War II.

Times changed and the Establishment of the sixties suffered from turbulence, disarray, and defections. (Our concept of the Establishment has even had some additions. Rovere flatly denied that such an entity as the Mafia or the Cosa Nostra exists at all. We now know that it is not only alive but very powerful.) Besides the major sociopolitical split over Vietnam, many lesser divisions had appeared by 1970. Many senators with good Establishment credentials were opposing the Pentagon's wish to build an antiballistic missile system; government-workers' unions were striking against government; some prominent Establishment figures were attacking the big businesses that pollute and destroy our environment — to cite just a few examples.

Although the lineup changes from time to time, and we perceive new coalitions of forces forming the Establishment, the elements of power and influence endure, more or less the same in number and character. We live in a strange, sudden-grown, multiple society. Our original power structure was that of a fairly simple republic; superimposed on it we now have the enormously complex structure of empire. Certain paradoxes arise from this situation. We are sworn to conduct our public affairs in accordance with an eighteenth-century document of rather broad philosophical intent. That being impossible, the Supreme Court must create a modern gloss to fit the sophistication of our present social needs. In another area, a new President with a mandate to govern arrives in Washington intending to bring in his own team and make some drastic policy changes. He finds, however, that his options are much fewer than he imagined because a powerful civil service establishment will continue to do things much in its own way no matter who becomes President.

Even naming the various power-and-influence centers within the imperial superstructure is difficult to do in any clear and complete way. Sometimes they overlap, sometimes they almost merge, sometimes they compete. Still, for the sake of being specific, it's worthwhile to try a list. The reader is warned that this list is even more mixed than apples and oranges. Some of the headings are well-defined corporate organizations; other simply indicate a vested interest; some are almost broad enough to be called a viewpoint. They are in no special order and the parenthetical examples are just a few out of many:

Government: executive, legislative, and judicial branches
(the federal administration, Congress, the Supreme Court)

Organized religion
(The Roman Catholic Church; the National Council of Churches)

Education
(Ivy League universities; the large state universities)

Big business corporations, legitimate
(U.S. Steel; International Business Machines; American Telephone
and Telegraph; General Motors)

Big business organizations, illegitimate
(Cosa Nostra families)

Major investors of money
(The big insurance companies; banks; large mutual funds)

Class
(The individual rich, people in the 70 percent tax bracket)

The communications media
(The Times–Mirror Co., Time, Inc., RCA, CBS, *The New York
Times*)

Labor unions
(The AFL–CIO, The International Brotherhood of Teamsters)

Professional organizations
(the American Medical Association, the American Bar Association,
the American Association of University Professors)

Political parties
(The Republican Party, The Democratic Party)

The military
(the Joint Chiefs of Staff, high-ranking senior officer groups)

The characteristic that each of these has in common with all the others is simply the compound of money and power. The Establishment, of course, is an abstraction that arises from the nexus of many, or all, of these individual power systems. And though it is abstract, that does not mean that it is unreal. It acts. It has a dynamism of its own; and in our particular culture (though not in all cultures) it gets its way through persistent use of the M + P compound.

Radical critics of our society usually misunderstand the meaning of this phenomenon. They assume that the basic dynamism of the Establishment drives it simply to seek more money and power. They are wrong; in fact, what the Establishment desires fundamentally and most urgently is a stable world. In the sphere of policy, the Establishment will almost always spend vast amounts of money and power to buy stability.

After World War II, for instance, America followed two broad international policies, that of giving generous aid to countries in danger of political and economic disaster, and that of containing Communism. Both were meant to prevent a drastic imbalance of national wealth and national strength around the world. In Europe and Japan the policy worked. And as those areas recovered their prosperity and independence, American dominance — monetary and political — receded. The United States was willing to buy stability for a rather large price.

In Southeast Asia, in the 1960's, the policy did not work. Apparently, no matter how much money and force were applied, stability was not to be purchased, and the war dragged on through the decade and into the 70's. As we noted earlier, the Establishment split over the policy of continuing the war. Yet, even in great stress and by the thinnest of majorities, the Establishment clung to a national policy of settling the disruption by means of cash and force. It is not in the nature of Establishments to understand any other means. In Vietnam, however, conditions were such that the magic compound did not bring peace. (And the Establishment mind will probably never understand why; for years ahead, certain pundits will keep explaining that things would have turned out right if we had only used *more* force and *more* money.)

Any adequate portrait of the American Establishment would require a fairly large book. Here, we can do no more than offer a few clear snapshots of certain parts of its anatomy. One of the most striking things to note is the fact that the Establishment has gone through some changes of character in the twentieth century. In the early years, especially during the Coolidge Administration (1923–1929), business interests ruled Establishment thinking. Historian James Truslow Adams wrote in 1929, "the country is making the experiment of resting her civilization on the ideas of businessmen. The other classes dominated by the business one are rapidly conforming their philosophy of life to it." But, when the Depression descended on the country, the "business philosophy of life" went bankrupt.

The Establishment, not without bitter divisions, was able to adapt to history, and a new management took over under President Roosevelt. This was a liberal-professional establishment of lawyers, university political scientists, and economic planners.

The military, by American tradition, is supposed to be a specialized arm of the Establishment: it is to have no voice in policy-making, except in wartime. In the cold war years after World War II, however, new circumstances arose. In an area of huge military forces and enormous expenditures for the manufacture of armaments, corporations and Pentagon leadership formed a natural power alliance which has come to be known as the "Military-Industrial Complex." Undoubtedly it has had a definite effect on Establishment policy, despite President Eisenhower's strong warning against it. In a further comment, Eisenhower said, "The Military Establishment, not productive of itself, necessarily must feed on the energy, productivity, and brainpower of the country, and if it takes too much, our total strength declines." This section includes two views, from different angles, of the Military-Industrial Complex — Richard J. Barnet's analysis from *The Economy of Death*, and Gerald Green's chilling fictional speculation, *"The Dispatcher."*

Congress, always a major Establishment power in the past and a reflector of the varieties of Establishment opinion, resigned much of its leadership during the decades following World War II. Antiquated organization and procedure, key members who serve the Administration and the military better than the cause of congressional independence, and a tendency to be fascinated by peripheral matters all have contributed to the misfortune. A report on that situation comes from Joseph Alsop's book, *The Center.*

Organized crime, as a huge business enterprise, has seldom been recognized as an aspect of the Establishment. After the repeal of Prohibition and the law-and-order drive of the 1930's, corporate crime more or less dropped out of the public consciousness — until Senator Kefauver's investigations of 1951. Little came of these, but later, in the 1960's, there were more congressional investigations, a penetrating series in *Life*, and a number of books on organized crime (including even a 1969 best-seller, Mario Puzo's *The Godfather*). All information pointed to the fact that the crime syndicates, with their vast holdings in legitimate business and their high political connections, had become a kind of silent partner in the Establishment. A look at organized crime comes from *The Crime Confederation* by Ralph Salerno and John S. Tompkins.

The rich are always with us; they are one of the fundamental facts of any establishment. They no longer influence public matters as an organized aristocracy, but they make their weight felt through the various corporate bodies — businesses, political parties, and communications media — whence they derive power. *The Rich and the Super-Rich* by Ferdinand Lundberg is, as his subtitle puts it, a study of "the power of money today."

As America entered the 1970's, a new populist movement was trying to put the Establishment "up against the wall." Student demonstrations and *ad hoc* peace organizations attacked the draft and the war in Vietnam. Reformers such as Ralph Nader zeroed in on the large-scale manufacture of shoddy or dangerous consumer goods. Half a hundred vocal protest groups were denouncing the industries that pollute and destroy the environment. Articulate blacks were attacking Establishment lethargy about economic betterment of the black minority. There were even a few critics rash enough to question the munificent outpouring of money for the Establishment's most spectacular success of the late 1960's — the exploration of space.

The Establishment was not up against the wall yet. It was hardy; it had come through flood, fire, and famine before this, and had come through better, as the New Deal had proved. How well it would go about applying its traditional remedy, expenditure of vast resources of money and power to stabilize things again, should become clear in the decade of the 70's.

Gerald Green | # The Dispatcher

I could swear that my secretary, Miss Minihan, addressed my boss as *Colonel* Carter this morning. And did I hear him say to her, "Thank you, *Corporal?*" Having just assumed my new job as quality-control manager, I don't wish to seem too inquisitive.

Our firm is only indirectly involved in defense work, which makes me even more puzzled. Yesterday, for example, I overheard a conversation between two elderly mechanics in the shop. It went:

"Old man's on the warpath again."

"Eatin' ass like it was steak."

"You know how it is. With the I.G. on his back."

"They don't frighten me. Goddam brass. They'd strangle in their own snot if it wasn't for us."

At first I assumed the conversation was some kind of shop jargon. But now I am not so certain. What further disturbed me was that shortly after this conversation, Mr. Carter came to the assembly line to talk to these men. I could not hear the conversation, but a peculiar stiffness in the attitudes of the mechanics, a movement of their right arms, was evident.

Later I passed Carter in the corridor. He nodded at me and I suddenly felt my right arm moving toward my right temple, fingers extended and joined.

Carter smiled. "Go ahead, Dugan," he said. "It's all right, if you want to, even though we don't insist on it."

I pulled my arm back to my side, feeling embarrassed and confused, and I hurried to my office. Miss Minihan had a batch of invoices for me to check. I went about my work, trying to make some sense out of the strange work habits here. In the midst of the invoices, I saw a sheet of legal-size paper, headed:

TABLE OF ORGANIZATION

UNITED APERTURES, INC.

I called my secretary. "Miss Minihan, what is this?" I asked.

"Oh, that. The administrative chart."

SOURCE: Originally appeared in *Playboy* magazine. Copyright © 1967 by HMH Publishing Company, Inc. Reprinted by permission of the author and the author's agents, Scott Meredith Literary Agency, Inc., 580 Fifth Avenue, New York, N. Y. 10036.

"But it says *Table of Organization.* That is an Army expression. It is referred to as a T/O, and that's exactly what this paper is."

"Golly, I never thought of it that way." She giggled.

When she left, I searched for my name. I was listed under *Headquarters and Headquarters Company* with the rank of first lieutenant.

Dazed, I wandered about the plant for a few minutes and entered a half-hidden men's room on a fire-stair landing. As I approached the urinal, a sign over it greeted me:

PLEASE DO NOT THROW CIGAR BUTTS

IN HERE

IT MAKES THEM SOGGY AND

HARD TO LIGHT

I knew at once that I was involved in neither a joke nor a dream nor a corporate fancy. They had gotten me back in.

*   *   *

My present circumstances recall a series of curious incidents in which I was involved some years ago, beginning with the appearance of the *dispatcher* at my home.

After my discharge from military service, I was living with my parents in an old Spanish-style house in West Los Angeles. I had spent four years in the Army, including overseas duty, and was discharged with the rank of sergeant. Now I had returned to my studies in business administration at the University of California at Los Angeles. I note here that I was never a perpetual griper or a guardhouse lawyer. While I was not delighted with serving in the Army, I accepted it as a duty.

One spring morning, I was unable to locate the keys of the old Ford I drove to classes. We were a family of comfortable means and had three cars: my old Ford, a new Mercury driven by my father, an accountant for one of the film studios, and my mother's Nash. (We did not think ourselves in any way unusual, because there was virtually no public transportation to be had.) Having searched the house and the car for the keys, I went to the small room above our garage to look for them.

As I opened the screen door, I saw a man sleeping on the day bed. He was in an Army uniform. An overstuffed duffel bag was on the floor alongside him. On it was stenciled:

ESPOSITO SALVATORE ASN 32694853

My assumption was that he had been hitchhiking in the area (men were still being discharged and transferred) and he had wandered in to catch a night's sleep. I shook him firmly but gently.

"OK, Mac, let's hit it," I said. "Grab your socks."

The sleeper stirred. His eyes opened and he studied me irritably. "Jesus, I just got to sleep." He muttered something about "doing a frigging day's work without sleep," yawned enormously and sat up in bed. As he scratched himself, stretched and broke wind, I studied him.

Esposito was a squat, dark man in his early 20s. His features were blunt —the eyes hooded and suspicious, the mouth pouting. Black stubble covered his chin; he needed a haircut.

"Get a good night's sleep?" I asked.

"Lousy. Couldn' find da mess hall. You da CQ?"

"You're a little confused, soldier. This is a *private* house. I don't mind you catching some shut-eye, but don't you think you should have asked first?"

Esposito got up and stretched. His o.d. shirt came loose from his o.d. trousers. An o.d. undershirt peeked through the gap. "Ain't no terlet paper in da latrine. And dere better be a PX around, or I'll raise hell. I may be oney a lousy corporal, but I got rights."

Was he unbalanced? Some poor dope ready for a Section Eight discharge? I decided to be firm. "Esposito, you'd better get out of here. My father's got a bad temper and he won't like the idea. I'm a former enlisted man myself, so I don't mind. But you'd better clear out."

"I ain't goin' nowhere. I been *transferred* here."

"That's impossible. A soldier can't be transferred to a private home."

With that, he dragged the duffel bag to the bed, undid the cord and groped in its guts. Out came a wool-knit cap, half of a messtin, a cardboard stationery folder and some dirty socks. Then he located a single wrinkled sheet of mimeographed paper, which he thrust at me. "Dat's your copy, pal. File it or it'll be *your* ass."

I read it swiftly.

HOLABIRD ORDNANCE DEPOT
HOLABIRD, MARYLAND

Corporal ESPOSITO SALVATORE ASN 32694853 (NMI) Casual Detachment, 1145 Labor Supvn Co., Holabird Ordnance Depot, Holabird, Md., is transferred in rank and grade to 1125 Hampton Drive, West Los Angeles, California.

Cpl. ESPOSITO will on arrival at new post assume duties of DISPATCHER, Army Classification 562, and be responsible for dispatch of all vehicles, wheeled, tracked and half-tracked, at said installation.

No change of rank or pay involved. EM to draw six dollars per diem. Transfer at request and convenience of M.A.C.E., Washington, D.C.

Having at one time served as a battalion clerk, I realized that the orders were either the real thing or a perfect forgery. The language, the phrasing, the format were perfect.

As I puzzled over the sheet, Corporal Esposito seated himself at a table in the corner of the room. On it he placed a yellow pad and a few slips of carbon paper. These were *trip tickets*, standard Army forms for the use of a vehicle. Behind his ear he stuck a red pencil stub. He put his feet on the table and began to read a ragged copy of *Captain Marvel* comics.

"Just what do you think you're doing?" I protested.

"Look, Mac, I got a job to do, *you* got a job to do," he said thickly. His sullen eyes darted up from the comic book. "Anya you people wanna vehicle, you come see me foist for a trip ticket. No trip ticket, no vehicle."

At that moment I understood that Esposito was no lunatic, no practical joke, no error. He was real. He was the essential dispatcher. I knew his type — surly, slovenly, wary, a petty dictator, a wielder of power and influence. He wore exactly what you'd expect: a stained old-fashioned field jacket, the corporal's chevrons sloppily sewn to the sleeve; a sweat-marked overseas cap pushed back on his coarse black hair.

I wasn't ready to challenge him. I returned to the house and found my father eating his Bran Flakes and scowling at the *Los Angeles Times*. I told him about the intruder. My father, the late Francis James Dugan, was a short-tempered, choleric man. His reaction was what I expected.

"What are you worried about?" he asked. "I'll throw the bum out."

Esposito was smoking a foul cigar when we entered. He flicked ashes on the floor and called out: "Could use a coupla butt cans here!"

My father flew across the room and yanked the dispatcher from his chair by the lapels of his field jacket. "Beat it, you bum. Pack your bag and get out, or I'll throw you out."

Salvatore wriggled loose and backed against a wall. He did not seem frightened, merely annoyed at my father's obtuseness. Like all true dispatchers, Esposito had a snarling equanimity that never turned into genuine hate or permitted true fear.

"Hey, Mac," he appealed to me, "straighten yer old man out. Dis ain't my idea. Fa Chrissake, I'm here on orders, *orders*. Ya can't disobey orders. You seen 'em ya'self."

I took my father to the porch outside the study. "Pop, why start a fight? We'll call the police and let them handle it, OK?"

He agreed reluctantly and went back to the house. Suddenly I remembered my class at UCLA. I re-entered the spare room to look for my keys. Esposito studied me narrowly. "Lookin' for somethin', soljer?"

"Car keys."

He patted the pocket of his jacket. "Right here, Mac."

"Give them to me."

He took the keys out and jangled them tantalizingly. "Foist ya gotta ask for a trip ticket."

"Good God, this is lunacy. Give me those keys, Esposito."

"Oh, yeah?" he asked. His eyes were slits. "Who's aut'orizin' dis trip, anyway?"

"Captain Dugan of battalion public relations," I said glibly. "In the line of duty."

"Whyna hell dincha say so at foist?" He began to scrawl on the yellow pad. "Boy, you guys who go around keepin' secrets from da dispatcher. Jeez." He then ripped the carbon copy and thrust it at me with the keys. As I reached for them, he wickedly pulled his hand back. "Keep da ticket inna glove compartment and toin it in with the keys when ya get back."

I sat through my morning classes, hearing nothing, and got home before noon. My father had not gone to work. He was impatiently awaiting a call from Washington. He filled me in on what had happened. The local police had refused to throw Esposito out, after looking at his mimeographed orders. A call to the Ninth Service Command at Fort Douglas was even less helpful. They said the incident would have to be explained by the War Department in Washington.

"I asked them what the hell M.A.C.E. was, but they didn't know." He frowned. "I'll get to the bottom of this."

"Pop, I hate to tell you this, but I think that guy is *real*. He's a dispatcher and he's been assigned here."

The phone rang and I listened on the kitchen extension.

"Department of Defense?" asked my father.

A woman's nasal voice responded. "Who is calling?"

"This is Francis James Dugan of West Los Angeles, California. There's a goddamn soldier assigned to my house. I want him thrown out, but nobody'll take the responsibility. Let me talk to an outfit called M.A.C.E."

"I'm sorry, but no calls are permitted to that branch."

"The hell you say. I'm a taxpayer and a member of the American Legion. There's something in the Constitution about billeting soldiers in private homes."

"You will be reimbursed for the man's subsistence."

"I don't want to be. I want him out. And what does M.A.C.E. stand for?"

"I am sorry, I cannot help you, Mr. Dugan."

"Goddamn it, you'll hear from me again! Or my Congressman!"

But my father never carried out his threat. He worked long hours at the studio. My mother, a timid, retiring woman, had no stomach for conflict. As for myself, I was now convinced that Esposito was legally, actually and indisputably our dispatcher.

At first he was persistent in his efforts to make us accept his yellow trip tickets. He demanded the keys. When we refused, he removed the rotors from the engines (an old dispatcher's ruse). When we ourselves kept keys and rotors, he locked the steering wheels. He was frantic about his mission. Soon all three of us began to accommodate him, accepting his yellow chits and returning the keys.

So he lingered, taking his meals in the spare room (he dutifully gave my mother six dollars a day), reading comic books, presumably happy in his work. But he became lax. The keys were left in the cars; he did not demand trip tickets. I confronted him one day. He was sacked out on the day bed.

"Goofing off, Sal?"

"What's it to you?"

"As one enlisted man to another, Salvatore, I'd say you are gold-bricking. Isn't anyone checking up on you?"

He looked around warily. "S'posed to be an officer come around. But he ain't showed yet. You don't rat on me, I'll let yez drive a car all ya want."

"You got a deal, Sal." He could be managed.

The Sunday after his arrival, I drove out to the valley community of Sandoval to watch an old Army friend, Eddie Chavez, play sand-lot baseball. My parents had gone to La Jolla for the weekend. Esposito had been absent since noon Saturday. No doubt he had written himself a 36-hour pass.

I arrived at Sandoval just as the game was about to begin, found a seat in the rickety grandstand — there could not have been more than 200 people present — and waved to Eddie Chavez. He was at home plate discussing ground rules with the umpire and the captain of the visiting team, the Lock City Lions.

As Eddie was about to lead the Sandoval Giants into the field, three men in Army suntans appeared, walking from the third-base line to home plate. From my seat in back of third base, I could see their rank clearly: a captain bearing a manila envelope and two sweating sergeants, each porting huge barracks bags.

"Just a minute!" the captain called. "There'll be a change in procedure today!" The umpire, Eddie and the Lock City captain stared at him. The captain extracted a sheet of mimeo paper from his envelope and gave it to the umpire.

A crowd of ballplayers gathered around and I heard expressions such as "What the hell?" "Who's this guy?" "Where do they git off?"

The captain addressed the crowd with a bullhorn. "By order of the Defense Department, I am authorized to supervise this game. The first event will be a three-legged relay. Teams line up at home plate."

I jumped from my seat and raced to home plate. The argument was raging.

"Hey, Frank!" Eddie called. "This guy says he has the right to run the game today! You was a battalion clerk. Look at his papers."

I did. Again I saw the reference to M.A.C.E. and the formal language. The captain's name was Pulsifer. It seemed an appropriate name for a physical-training officer.

"All right, all right, we haven't got all day. Get those enlisted men lined up," Captain Pulsifer cried. "Sergeant, tie their legs together."

The ballplayers lined up in a column of twos. The sergeants bustled among them, joining them, left leg of one to right leg of another, for the three-legged race.

"I'm sure we'll all enjoy this!" Captain Pulsifer shouted.

He blew his whistle — a bronze whistle on a plaited red-and-yellow lanyard, a whistle only a P.T. officer would carry — and the three-legged race began. It was a dry, hot day, and the stumbling, cursing players kicked up great clouds of dust as they hopped off to the centerfield flag-pole.

"Faster, faster!" shouted Captain Pulsifer. "The winning team gets to bat last!"

"They do not!" I cried, trotting alongside the captain. "The home team bats last! You can't just change the rules like that!"

"Who says I can't?" he asked icily. "The Army can do anything it wants."

I could think of no response to this, but it hardly mattered, because the players refused to go on with the mad game. The crowd was booing, hissing. Pop bottles were thrown. But the captain was not through yet. Somehow — with threats, promises, frequent wavings of his orders, he got the teams to play short contests of underleg basketball relay, swat-the-baron and club-snatch. However, the games lasted only a few moments before the players stopped and began to yell again. How often I had played these same lunatic games during basic training!

"Play ball, goddamn it!" the umpire shouted. "Chavez, git yer team in the field. Lock City at bat! And you, you *jerk*, git lost!"

Captain Pulsifer walked off the field. But as the Lock City lead-off man stepped to the plate, the officer ordered one of his sergeants to bring a duffel bag forward. From it the captain took an olive-drab contraption — a gas mask.

"By order of the authority invested in me by the Defense Department, this game can proceed only under these conditions — *batter, pitcher, catcher and umpire are to wear gas masks at all times.*" He then attempted to affix the mask to the batter's head. The lead-off man recoiled, the captain came after him and then the ballplayer swung his bat at the officer. The sergeants leaped to help their superior — the blow had missed by a hair — and the fans swarmed onto the field.

Eddie Chavez, the umpire and I tried to calm people down. For a moment it looked as if the crowd was ready to pull the P.T.O. and his men to pieces. As it was, they merely gave them a bum's rush across the diamond and dumped them into a weapons carrier that had been parked near the left-field foul line.

"You personnel haven't heard the last of this!" I heard Captain Pulsifer mutter through bruised lips. And they drove off. The game resumed. Most of the people around me seemed to think that the whole thing was a dumb practical joke.

I went home feeling dizzy from too much sun and queasy with uncertainties. That night I had a terrifying dream (one that has been recurring since I took my new job) and I woke up shivering. In this dream, I am back in Service and I am a permanent latrine orderly. I protest that I have had two years of college and have been a model soldier, but I am nonetheless kept on latrine duty because I am a "troublemaker." The latrine occupies all five stories of a tall building, an endless vitreous enamel nightmare, never-ending urinals, toilet bowls, sinks, a latrine so huge that it spills out into the street, crosses a road and deposits its gleaming receptacles in private homes, stores, factories. It generates and reproduces itself. It is dotted with signs reading: BLOKES WITH SHORT HORNS STAND CLOSE, THE NEXT MAN MAY HAVE HOLES IN HIS SHOES; or, FLIES SPREAD DISEASE, KEEP YOURS BUTTONED; or, WE AIM TO PLEASE, YOU AIM, TOO, PLEASE; or, PLEASE DO NOT THROW CIGAR BUTTS IN THE URINAL, IT MAKES THEM SOGGY AND HARD TO LIGHT.

I did not feel well enough to attend classes on Monday. Lingering over my coffee, I tried to piece together Salvatore Esposito, the baseball game and the mysterious initials M.A.C.E.

My mother came in from the living room — I had heard the vacuum humming — and began to mop the kitchen floor.

"Where's Serena?" I asked. It was Monday, and Serena Hastings, a Negro lady from Watts, came every Monday to give the house a cleaning.

"She called to say she can't get here," my mother replied. "If it were anyone but Serena, I'd say they'd made the story up. Something about soldiers stopping her bus and making everyone get off."

"What?"

My mother continued mopping. Nothing ever rattled her. Her mind always seemed to be elsewhere, probably in Des Moines, where she was born and raised and where all of her family still lived.

"It sounded so silly, I really didn't pay attention, and at first I thought it was as if Serena had got drunk, or a little disturbed. But knowing Serena . . ."

"What, exactly, did she say, Mother?"

My mother paused and rested on her mop. "Well, she was on the Central Avenue bus, and it was filled, mostly with day workers like herself, and in downtown L.A. it was stopped by a soldier. He was armed and Serena knew he was an MP, because her brother was once an MP, and an officer got on and announced that the bus was being taken over for the day. He apologized and everything, but everyone had to get off."

"Then what happened?"

"Nothing. A bunch of officers got on and the bus drove off in a different direction. They put a sign or something on it — OFFFICERS' CLUB or something like that. Serena gave up and took a taxi home. You know how infrequently buses run. I can't blame the poor girl."

"But didn't anyone protest?"

"I didn't ask. Frank, could you please take these bottles into the garage?"

As I went on this errand, I began to feel faint. I decided to visit Dr. Cyril Mandelbaum, our family physician. I had not been to Dr. Mandelbaum's since my discharge. His pink-stucco house on a patched green plot off Pico Boulevard looked no better than before the War. An elderly nurse let me in and I settled into a sagging chair with a copy of the *Los Angeles Times*. There were five other people in the waiting room — a white-haired woman with a boy of about eight, a young Negro couple and a husky young man in denim work clothes.

"Dr. Mandelbaum has been delayed at the hospital," the nurse told us, "but I expect him any minute."

I paged through the *Times*, my vision blurred, my head throbbing. On the sports page, a small item drew my attention.

FUN AND GAMES AT SANDOVAL

A special program of unusual athletic contests highlighted yesterday's Inland League baseball game in which the Sandoval Giants defeated the Lock City Lions, 4–3.

Members of both squads volunteered for the amusing games, which included a three-legged race, underleg basketball relay and swat-the-baron. Sandoval was declared winner of the special pregame competition by Captain A. M. Pulsifer, United States Army, who supervised the program.

"This is the first of several such fitness programs," said Captain Pulsifer, "and we're delighted with the public acceptance. Fans and players both had a wonderful time."

I must have looked like an idiot to the other patients, shaking my head and muttering. "No, no," I mumbled, "it wasn't that way at all." How had this fiction gotten into print? Why hadn't they reported the near riot I had seen?

The newspaper slipped from my lap and I covered my eyes.

In a minute or so, the office doors opened and out stepped not Dr. Cyril Mandelbaum but two men in Army uniforms. One was a dapper first lieutenant with a yellow moustache and the caduceus on his starched collar. The other, a fat, ruddy man, was a master sergeant. Dr. Mandelbaum's perplexed nurse was trailing them.

"But can't you wait until Dr. Mandelbaum gets here?" she asked. "This must be a mistake."

"Prepare the infirmary for sick call," the officer snapped.

"But Dr. Mandelbaum should——"

"No time. I'm under orders to take this installation over until further notice. Don't stand there, nurse." He barked at the sergeant. 'Figler, tell the enlisted men to line up."

"Do they all have appointments with Dr. Mandelbaum?" she asked.

He waved a mimeographed sheet at her. "Government orders!"

I got up from my seat. "You're from M.A.C.E., aren't you?" I asked weakly.

"What business is that of yours?"

"I know a little bit about them. I was curious."

His yellow mustache quivered. "Figler, get that man's name, rank and serial number."

"Sir, I'm not sure he's in Service." Figler seemed a little confused. I guessed that these new assignments were so strange that even the personnel ordered to carry them out were puzzled, from time to time. "And the infirmary's ready anyway, sir. May we start sick call?"

"Very well. Tell them to line up outside. We'll do this as fast as possible."

The lieutenant then marched into Dr. Mandelbaum's office and sat at his desk. Figler followed him in, but emerged immediately, brushing by the astounded nurse. He carried a large glass beaker containing a half-dozen thermometers. Dumbly we lined up at the office door — the woman and the boy, the two Negroes, the man in work clothes and myself. With a speed and deftness that recalled to me every sick call I had ever attended, Figler flew down the line and jammed thermometers into our mouths. He had one left over, so he put *two* in my mouth. No sooner were they in than he raced back to the head of the line and yanked them out. Obviously, it had been impossible for a reading to register in so short a time, but that did not bother him. In any case, he barely glanced at the thermometers, putting them back into the beaker, which he gave to the nurse.

"Sir!" Figler called to the officer. Every one of these people is fit for duty. Not a sick one in the lot. We've had trouble with this outfit before."

The rugged man in denims looked appealingly to me. "What'n hell is this? Who are these jokers?"

"I'm not sure. But they're not joking."

The medical officer barely heard Figler. He was ripping pages from Dr. Mandelbaum's calendar, juggling paper clips, furiously dialing numbers and then hanging up. "Damn it, don't stand there all day! Come in! Wipe your feet before you do!"

Figler ushered the old woman and the boy to the desk. They stood there frightened. The lieutenant barked: "Well?"

"I ain't the patient," she said. "It's my grandson, Rollie. He gets dizzy and vomits."

The officer shook his head and gave her a small pillbox. "Take two of these every four hours and drink plenty of liquids! Next!"

"But I ain't sick," the woman pleaded. "It's Rollie."

"We are under no obligation to treat children of enlisted personnel. This is not an overseas installation."

"It isn't any kind of installation!" I shouted.

"Pipe down, soljer," Sergeant Figler said. "The lootenant's had about enough of you. We know your type. You wanna come on sick call, you keep yer mouth shut."

"This isn't sick call!" I protested.

"That's right," said the husky man. "Where's Doc Mandelbaum?"

"Yeah, wheah the *real* doctah?" the young Negro man asked.

"What's *your* outfit, soljer?" Figler asked the Negro. "Labor battalion? One of them troublemakers?"

"Labah battalion?" He grabbed his wife's arm. "Let's git outa heah. I din't come for no sick call." They left quickly. The white-haired woman and the little boy followed them out.

"This is terrible!" the nurse wailed. "You're driving away all of Dr. Mandelbaum's patients!"

"How do you think I feel?" the medical officer shouted. "I gave up a forty-thousand-dollar-a-year practice in Newark for this crap! Next!"

The big man in denim walked to the desk. He was rubbing his fists.

"What's your problem?" the officer asked.

"None of ya friggin' business," the man said. "I done doody already. Five years combat engineers. Where's Mandelbaum? What'd you jerks do wit' him?"

Figler moved toward him. "Watch yer language, soljer."

"You call me soljer oncet more, yer ass'll be suckin' wind."

"I'll handle this, Figler." The medical officer got up. His mustache bristled. "All right, you, what's your outfit?"

"I ain't tellin' you nothin'. Pill roller."

"You'll regret this," the officer said. He was trembling.

"Chancre mechanic."

"Figler——"

"Clap surgeon. Go run a pro station."

Seething, the officer began dialing. "I'll throw the book at you!" he yelled. "You'll be up for a general court-martial! Hello, hello — get me the military police!"

The rugged man yanked the phone from his hand and shoved the officer roughly. Sergeant Figler hurled himself at the man's back. Then the rear door of the office opened and Dr. Mandelbaum walked in. At that time, the doctor was in his 60s, but he was still as strong and as fit as when he was on the USC wrestling team.

"What the hell is this?" Dr. Mandelbaum shouted. His weeping nurse tried to explain.

The lieutenant retreated to a corner of the room. The big man, seeing Dr. Mandelbaum, stopped his lunge at the officer.

"Now, then, Mandelbaum," the medical officer snapped, "we've got a file on you. This mission will help all of us, including you, yourself. We are here in the national interest. That man threatened me and I'm having him brought up on charges of insubordination!" He was slightly hysterical. He was not carrying out his assignment as well as my dispatcher had.

"What are you talking about?" Dr. Mandelbaum yelled. "Who are you to bust into my office and abuse my patients? That's Al Zawatzkis. He's been my patient for years. I delivered him. He's never welshed on a bill in his life."

"Then you are prejudiced in his favor," the officer said. "I'll see to it that you don't testify at his court-martial!"

He began dialing again. "I want the military police, and if you can't get them, I'll talk to the Defense Department, office called M.A.C.E.——"

Dr. Mandelbaum grabbed him by his shoulder straps and shook him as if he were a rag doll. The lieutenant screamed for help. Figler tried to pry Doc Mandelbaum loose, but big Zawatzkis thundered at him. It was no contest. He plucked Sergeant Figler from Doc and threw him against a filing cabinet. While Figler lay there stunned, Zawatzkis tried to untangle the two physicians. I have to give credit to the Army officer; he was tenacious and brave. He clung to Mandelbaum, wheezing and hissing and protesting that we were all traitors, but he was no match for Zawatzkis. The medical officer sprawled on the X-ray table, then got a second wind and came at Zawatzkis, who smashed a jug of green soap over his head.

The lieutenant hit the floor. The jug broke clean. The medic wasn't cut, merely bruised and coated with the viscous fluid. "Get him out," Doc Mandelbaum said. I gave Zawatzkis a hand. We picked up the semiconscious officer and carted him out.

"He slipped!" I said loudly. "I saw it! He slipped on the floor!"

Dr. Mandelbaum helped Sergeant Figler to his feet and escorted him to the front door. "Be a nice boy, not a schlemiel," he was saying to him. "What is all this nonsense? Go get a job instead of being a bum in the Army all your life." The three of us — Doc, Zawatzkis and myself — stood on the sidewalk as Figler, crying softly, drove off in the jeep with his superior. Then we went into the office, where Doc took care of us in his usual considerate manner.

That evening at the dinner table, I kept my thoughts to myself. Esposito dropped down to pick up his dinner, greeted us sullenly and retreated to his sanctuary. We rarely saw him anymore. He had long stopped bothering us for car keys or trip tickets.

"I wish that tramp would go," my father said. It was exactly one week that Salvatore had been with us. "And I wish I knew why he's here."

"He doesn't bother anyone," my mother said. "And he is never behind with the six dollars a day."

"Who needs it?" my father grumbled.

"He keeps the room clean," my mother said defensively. "His personal appearance isn't much, but the bed is always made."

"*Bed,*" my father said. "Did you tell Frank what happened at the hotel in La Jolla yesterday?"

"You mean the tennis match?"

"No, no. That business with the beds. You know, what we saw when we were going down to the pool."

"What happened?" I asked.

My father stirred his coffee. "It was either a practical joke or else they were rehearsing for a movie or something. Maybe a publicity gimmick for a movie. That old hotel has been used a lot for locations."

"Francis, you asked the manager that and he said no."

"Yeah. But if it wasn't a movie stunt, what was it?"

My father shook his head.

"But what, exactly, happened?" I asked.

"Your mother and I were on our way down to the pool, when we passed this room with the door open. There was a lot of yelling going on and I peeked in. There were five people in the room — a young couple, a chambermaid and this Army officer and a sergeant. One with all those stripes up and down."

"First sergeant," I said. My hands were sweaty; a stone was growing in my stomach.

"This captain kept yelling that he was *gigging* — whatever that is — gigging the two guests because the beds weren't made with hospital corners."

"It *was* very strange," my mother said. "Like a silly motion picture, as Daddy says."

"This sergeant tried bouncing a dime off the bedspread a few times, but it wouldn't bounce, and this got the captain sore. He also had white gloves on and I saw him run his finger through the closet shelves."

"Didn't the guests object?" I asked.

"They were scared," said my father. "I think they were honeymooners and figured somebody was kidding them. The guy kept saying the chambermaid had made the bed and the officer kept shouting, 'We want results, not excuses, in this man's Army'. Probably be a funny story in the papers about it."

I wondered, would it be a funny story like the lying account of the baseball game at Sandoval? How would they handle inspection? As a cheerful course in modern hotelkeeping?

The last incident in this sequence of events — that is, the last up to my current listing on a *Table of Organization* as a first lieutenant — took place the next day.

Unhearing, I sat through morning classes and decided to spend the afternoon in the library. In the interests of economy, I had been driving home for lunch (we live a few minutes from the Westwood campus), but on this day I went to the school cafeteria. I arrived a moment after it had reopened for lunch and was greeted by an odd tableau.

The five colored ladies who manned the counter were clearly upset. They were huddled away from the steaming food vats. The manager, a

Mr. Sammartino, as I recall, was in front of the counter, gesticulating and appealing to—— Need I go on?

Looming behind the great aluminum bins of tuna-fish timbale, chicken and noodles, breaded veal cutlet and eggplant parmesan was one of the fattest men I have ever seen. He wore a filthy, sweat-stained fatigue suit with sergeant's stripes stenciled on the sleeves. On his head was a green fatigue cap, the brim upturned and stenciled with the name TEXAS. He brandished two enormous tools — a devil's fork and an ogre's ladle — and he sweat gallons into the food. A nauseating and disgusting figure, he was incontestably a mess sergeant. I needed no mimeographed orders to tell me so.

"Come and git it, fo' I throw it to the pigs!" he bellowed. "Yeah, hot today, hot today!"

He had an underling, a short, hairy man in dirty fatigues, who bustled through the kitchen doors, lugging a steaming pot of some appalling pink stew.

"Lady wit' a baby!" yelled the small man. "Hot stuff comin' through!"

"That's mah boy!" the mess sergeant beamed. "Li'l ole Hemsley. Hemsley a good ole boy. Look lak Hemsley brewed himself a mess of good ole S.O.S.! Shit on a shingle! Wahoo! Give us a ole rebel yell, Hemsley."

Hemsley obliged. The air shivered with the sound. The Negro ladies retreated even farther back. One, a bespectacled woman of great dignity, appealed to Mr. Sammartino.

"If this is a fraternity prank, Mr. S.," she said, "it gone far enough. The girls is fed up."

The manager paced feverishly. "But they said they had *orders*! They gave me *this*!" Mr. Sammartino waved a mimeographed sheet of paper. By now a queue of hungry students had formed in back of me. Most of them were amused by the insanity behind the steam table, assuming, as did the woman, that it was some form of undergraduate humor.

The mess sergeant stirred his pink S.O.S., stabbed at a gray sparerib, sniffed the okra soup. "Ole Hemsley. He a good ole boy. Hemsley, y'all got some grits back there, so's we can show the Yankees how rebels eat?"

"I wouldn't be for knowin', but I'll look."

Hemsley vanished into the kitchen, clanging empty pots. I took a clean tray and started down the line, as if drawn to some rendezvous with fate. The colored girls shrank away. The huge sergeant seemed to fill up all the space behind the counter.

He eyed me with contempt. "Y'all got an early chow pass?"

"Y-yes," I stammered. "Company and company headquarters. What's for chow, Sarge?"

A grin widened his pulpy face. He was in *control*. He had me. "Fly shit'n' brown pepper."

"That's OK," I said hoarsely. "So long as it ain't the same as what we had yesterday."

Chuckling, he began to load up my tray. A glop of mashed potatoes landed in the middle. Two slices of bread hit next and were promptly buried beneath the horrid S.O.S. A brownish mixture of vegetables was hurled, spattering the empty spaces of the tray. Several wilted leaves of lettuce were inserted in the brown ooze; a rubbery veal cutlet came to rest in the S.O.S. There remained but two square inches of inviolate mashed potatoes. The sergeant grinned at the tray. "Looks like we kinda missed a spot, right, buddy boy?" I said nothing. I knew what was coming. He ladled out a yellow cling peach, swimming in syrup like the inside of a roc's egg. Leaning over the counter, he deftly set the peach half in the midst of the potatoes, drowning everything else in the sweet juice.

"Now you all set," he beamed.

The blood roared to my skull. I breathed deeply, glanced at the wailing manager and lifted the tray high, as if sacrificing it to a god unknown. Then I hurled it at the fat sergeant. He took the blow — stunned, soaked, steaming — a great abstract work of food. I fled to cheers and laughter.

Upon returning home, I went to the spare room. Corporal Salvatore Esposito was sacked out, reading *Famous Funnies*.

"Get going, Salvatore," I said. "I am throwing you out."

"I don't go unless ya got orders for me."

"No, no, you must leave. And you tell your superiors you were thrown out, that we didn't want you and shouldn't have let you stay. The only reason you stayed so long was because of a delay in policy."

He sat up in bed. "I ain't goin' and you know it."

I walked to my father's golf bag and pulled out the driver. "Pack, soldier. I could handle you without this, but I want to make sure you leave in a hurry." I whipped the air a few times.

He struggled out of bed, a stumpy troll in droopy khaki drawers and socks. "Jeez. Din't think you was dat kind of guy." He dressed hastily, slung the bag over his shoulder and asked if he could make a telephone call. I permitted him to. He dialed swiftly, identified himself and asked that a jeep meet him at the corner, on Olympic Boulevard. I gave him his trip tickets, the carbon papers and the pencil, which he had carelessly left on the table. I wanted all traces of him obliterated. We walked to the street corner. Salvatore squatted on his sack.

"Who sent you here, Salvatore?" I asked.

"I dunno. I git assigned, I go."

"What is M.A.C.E.?"

"I dunno. All I know is someone's gonna get chewed out for throwin' me out." He glowered at me, but it was a meaningless glower, one for the record. "It'll be your ass, Dugan, not mine."

An open jeep, driven by a young second lieutenant, pulled up to us. "Spasita?" he asked.

"Dat's me." Salvatore didn't salute. He tossed his bag in the rear of the jeep and climbed in.

"Orders come through, Spasita. You transferred."

"They did not!" I shouted. "He was not transferred! I threw him out! Why was he sent to me anyway? I never wanted him!"

The shavetail studied me innocently. "Beats me, mistah. We git orders and folla them."

"All set, Spasita?" He gunned the engine.

"Just a minute," I said. "I demand an explanation. What does M.A.C.E. mean?"

"Never heard of it." And the jeep drove off.

"Remember what I said, Salvatore!" I shouted after them. "*I threw you out!* You tell them!"

Did I imagine it? Or did my dark dispatcher turn and answer my hysterical request with a nod of his head, a wink?

*　　　*　　　*

Today I sit in my air-conditioned office and think about my new job. Who decided I was first lieutenant? I have discharge papers at home showing that I was released from military service "for the convenience of the Government" some years ago. When was I commissioned? By whose authority?

I stopped Carter at the water cooler late this afternoon. My arm did not rise in salute, but he gauged the confusion on my face.

"I saw the T/O," I said. "Am I to call you Mr. or Colonel?"

"It doesn't matter, Dugan," he said pleasantly. "One way or the other. We don't stand on ceremony in this outfit."

"But what are we?"

He smiled. "Little bit of everything, you might say. You'll get used to it."

We walked down the corridor together. I glanced at his shoes — highly polished mahogany-brown officer's pumps with a strap instead of laces. They say to me: PX.

"Colonel, did you ever hear of an outfit called M.A.C.E.? Just after the War?"

"M.A.C.E.? Yes, I remember it. It was obsoleted a long time ago. We tried it out briefly. A pilot project, a really primitive one. We were just sort of fiddling around in those days."

"What did the letters stand for?"

"Military and Civilian Enterprises. Nothing mysterious about it."

"It was abandoned?"

"Naturally. We've got more sophisticated systems today. Data programming, circuitry. The whole operation is computerized. I must say, somebody in Washington is doing a marvelous job. M.A.C.E.! My goodness, I haven't thought about that old one-horse operation in years!"

He entered his office. I could hear people snapping to attention inside.

My nylon shirt is drenched; my knees are water. How did it happen? How in heaven's name did I get here? I curse Corporal Salvatore Esposito, my late dispatcher. He never told them that I threw him out. I am certain of that.

Stewart Alsop | The Sinking Hill

> Only ninety-nine other people in the world have
> as good a job, and no one has a better one.

There are three interesting questions about the Congress of the United States. They are:

a. How crooked is Congress?
b. Who really runs Congress?
c. How much power does Congress have in the American governmental system?

It is possible to give a short and roughly accurate answer to these three questions, as follows:

a. Not very.
b. The chairmen of the key standing committees of both houses.
c. Less and less.

Like all short answers to complex questions, these are only very roughly accurate. Moreover, all three are interrelated.

Thus the most important fact about Congress is (c) — the fact that its share of power in the American Government has been steadily dwindling. And (c) is directly related to both (a) and (b). The fact that many people suspect that Congress is crooked has eroded the prestige of Congress, and in Political Washington power and prestige go hand in hand. Moreover, the people who really run Congress — the committee chairmen and other members of the Congressional hierarchy — are well to the right of both Congress and the country. And this fact, too, is related to the dwindling power of Congress, for the Congressional system assigns to Congress an increasingly negative, or nay-saying, function.

SOURCE: Abridged and updated version of "The Sinking Hill" from *The Center: People and Power in Political Washington* by Stewart Alsop. Copyright © 1968 by Stewart Alsop. Reprinted by permission of Harper & Row, Publishers, Inc.

It is surprising how many citizens believe that Congress is very crooked indeed. As Senator Thruston Morton of Kentucky has observed, "All of us are under some sort of suspicion." To be a member of either house is automatically to be suspect at least of low crimes and misdemeanors. This is not a new phenomenon — Mark Twain described Congress as of a "distinctly American criminal class." But the prestige of Congress has not in modern times been lower than it is now, except perhaps during the brief McCarthy era. As Senator Morton says, "The public has lost confidence in Congress. . . . There has never been a time in my memory when Congress has been at such a low ebb in the judgment of the American people."

Three names suggest why so many people believe that a great many members of Congress are little better than crooks: Bobby Baker, Adam Clayton Powell, and Thomas Dodd. In fact, there is a sharp difference between the three.

Bobby Baker and Adam Clayton Powell are familiar figures in American politics, back to the time when Wicked Sam Ward served lobster tails stewed in champagne at his parties, and bought a Senator or two between courses. They are gay deceivers, honest rogues. They were entirely aware that they were cutting a few corners and entirely happy to do so as long as they could get away with it.

Senator Dodd, a sad old man with a sad old face, is quite different. Dodd, according to the findings of the Senate Ethics Committee, undisputed by him, collected close to half a million dollars from seven fund-raising dinners, and used a big chunk of the money for such purposes as paying his income tax, fixing up his house in Connecticut, club expenses, vacations, meals at luxury restaurants, and even buying a girdle for his wife. While this was going on, Dodd collected another $160,000 in legal and lecture fees, on top of his $33,000 a year as Senator.

This reporter went to see Dodd while the Senate was considering his case. He had done "nothing immoral or illegal," Dodd said. His "friends," who contributed to his testimonial dinners, were quite aware that they were making "gifts" to him for this personal use — not one of them had asked for his money back. And his "legal advisers" had told him that he did not have to pay income tax on these "gifts."

"It never occurred to me that there was anything wrong with what I did," he said sadly. "Never even occurred to me."

His tone carried conviction. It was quite clear that it really never *had* occurred to the Senator that there was anything wrong with what he did. This is the difference between the case of Tom Dodd and the cases of Bobby Baker and Adam Clayton Powell. Obviously, if there was "nothing immoral or illegal" about what Dodd did, the young man who aspires to a fortune should give up thoughts of oil or real estate and go into politics. For if it is both moral and legal for a Senator to collect large sums from interested citizens, pocket those sums, and pay no income tax on them, a seat in the Senate is potentially worth more than several oil wells. A really enterprising and influential Senator should be able to collect at least six million tax-free dollars in his six years in office, and even a Representative should be able to pile up a modest competence.

Thus the case of Tom Dodd is far more significant than the traditional shenanigans of a Bobby Baker or an Adam Clayton Powell. Almost all prominent politicians collect very large sums of money from interested constituents. They have to if they want to survive as politicians, unless they are very rich indeed in their own right. Moreover, the whole money-collecting process is a shadowy business, in which deception must be practiced in order to stay within the law. A lot of politicians have something like the "Nixon fund" — a fund provided by friends and admirers to support the politician's political career. As the Dodd case illustrated, the line between using this money for "political" and for "personal" purposes is not clear at all, and a politician with the limited perceptions of a Tom Dodd cannot be much blamed for crossing it.

There has, in fact, been a gradual but basic change in the way a man gets elected to high political office. The American mythos holds that any American boy can aspire to any office, up to and including the Presidency. That is still more or less true — especially if the boy is white, comes from a big state, and is not Jewish or a member of one of the other smaller racial or religious minorities. But there is now a further condition: he must be either very rich himself or willing to be beholden to very rich men.

The change is vividly illustrated by the sad case of Senator Truman Handy Newberry. Senator Newberry was a Michigan capitalist who had served as Teddy Roosevelt's Secretary of the Navy, and who was elected to the Senate in 1919. He spent what was regarded in those days as a vast sum of money on his nomination and election, and he was therefore tried and convicted in the Michigan courts on charges of corruption. The case was thrown out by the Supreme Court, and Newberry was exonerated by a sympathetic Senate committee. But the public outcry was such that he resigned from the Senate in 1922. Before resigning, he tearfully confessed on the Senate floor that he had been "astonished and amazed" when told by his employees that he had spent $195,000 on his election. The vastness of this sum brought gasps of disbelief.

Now the notion that a man could be elected Senator from a big industrial state like Michigan for so small a sum — or even double that sum, to allow for inflation — would still bring gasps of disbelief, but for the opposite reason. Expenditures on the order of $750,000 to $1 million are considered rather modest for a major political post. Television alone would eat up Truman Newberry's $195,000 before his campaign got off the ground. Television, in fact, which is responsible for so much else that is obnoxious in American life, is largely responsible for the immense cost of modern political campaigning.

More and more with every election, television has become the essential instrument of political persuasion. It is a very expensive instrument. Even in the smaller states television budgets in six figures have become standard for state-wide campaigns. Other instruments of persuasion have also greatly risen in cost.

The old notion that a man could run for office with the help of a few friends, getting his views known by making speeches here and there across the state, is long dead. Instead, the institution of the professional campaign manager, invented in California, has spread fast, and most campaigns these days are carefully prepackaged, with the aid of computer analysts, media specialists, and all the other paraphernalia of modern salesmanship.

Thus, while poor old Truman Newberry was chivied out of public life for his miserable $195,000 investment in his political future, nobody is a bit shocked when a Rockefeller or a Kennedy spends a million or so of his own or his family's money on a campaign; or when Ronald Reagan's rich friends raise a cool $5 million — more than $1.50 a voter — to make him Governor of California.

This kind of spending is illegal, of course, according to the plain English of the Corrupt Practices Act, passed by Congress in 1925 partly in reaction to the Newberry scandal. The act limits the spending of a candidate for the Senate to $25,000, and a candidate for the House to $5,000, such spending to include "each expenditure made by him or by any person for him with his knowledge and consent." If these words were taken at face value, a large majority of the members of Congress would have to be bundled off to jail; only a few members with safe seats would remain at liberty.

As this is written, efforts are being made to rewrite the rules to bring them into line with reality. Meanwhile, a way around the plain meaning of the act has of course been found: in any serious campaign, numerous committees are established, and these committees ostensibly collect and spend their hundreds of thousands, or even their millions, without the "knowledge and consent" of the candidate. This faintly ludicrous device has served to keep Congress out of jail, but it has also made liars out of most of the members of that body.

There are many techniques for extracting money from the citizenry for political purposes, but for a man not rich enough to finance his own campaigns the most painless and widely accepted method of money-grubbing is the "testimonial dinner," like the affairs that got Tom Dodd into trouble. These expensive repasts range upward from modest $25-a-plate affairs. For a major political dinner, $250-a-plate has become more or less standard.

The final flowering of this system is found in the $1,000-per-member "President's Club," to which many rich men, mostly important executives of corporations doing business with the government, belonged. In 1967 members of these not very exclusive clubs contributed more than $1 million to the coffers of the Democratic National Committee, ostensibly for the exquisite pleasure of mingling socially or breaking bread with the President. Such purposes are, of course, ostensible only. The dinner lists even of rather modest "plate dinners" in Washington are always studded with the names of lobbyists and others with a financial stake in the big business of big government. At some such affairs, the compliant lobbyists are even assigned a given number of plates to buy; a major lobbyist, for example, may be expected to buy a whole table, say, eight plates at $2,000.

"Who will buy a $250 plate?" Senator Albert Gore asked rhetorically on the Senate floor, of a routine Democratic fund-raising affair. "We know — and we are ashamed of it — the lobbyists and special interests, seeking favors of the Congress or this government, will buy those plates and tables."

In another speech, Senator Gore charged that "there is a degree of accepted and tolerated corruption inherent in our system of private subsidy of political campaigns. . . . The area of corruption is rapidly spreading." In fact, and rather surprisingly, the area of corruption has not really spread very far — at least not yet. It has not, for example, spread far enough for Senator Dodd's version of what is moral and legal to be widely accepted in the Senate.

In his passionate if somewhat irrational defense of Dodd, Senator Russell Long of Louisiana repeatedly said or implied that most of his colleagues regularly did what Dodd had done. He did not thereby endear himself to the Senate. And according to most close observers of the workings of Congress, what he said is, fortunately, simply not true.

Most of the Capitol Hill reporters agree that there are not more than two or three men really "on the take" in the Senate, and not many more in the House. There are corner-cutters, too, of course — men who profit from the political position via law partnerships or in other legal ways. And there are a few who, though less candidly, take the same position as the late Robert Kerr, the immensely rich Senator from Oklahoma who dominated the Senate between Lyndon Johnson's departure in 1960 and his own death in 1963. Kerr frequently and flatly stated that he was in the Senate to look after his own financial interests — mostly oil and banking — and the interests of his constituents similarly situated.

But such men are in the minority. Thruston Morton does not greatly exaggerate when he says that "99 percent of the members are thoroughly honest and reputable," by their own lights. Very few pocket the money given them as political contributions, or spend it to fix their houses or buy girdles for their wives. What most of those who are heavily dependent on such contributions do — what they almost have to do — is to listen with close and sympathetic attention to major contributors who are "seeking favors of the Congress or this government."

Indeed, most Capitol Hill reporters agree that it is rather surprising that the "lobbyists and special interests," who are in the market not only for "those plates and tables," do not own outright more Senators and Representatives. At the turn of the century, many influential Senators were known to be in the pay of the "trusts" — a Senator was known as "an oil man" or a "railroad man" or a "sugar man."

Nowadays a Texan, for example, is as unlikely to oppose the oil depletion allowance as an Iowan, say, is to be inimical to corn-fed hogs. But although members of Congress are — and in most cases ought to be — responsive to the major economic interests of their state, they are not directly in the pay of those interests. One reason is very simple. At present pay scales, although a member of Congress may badly need money for his election campaigns, he does not really have to have money to keep his wife in girdles — not unless he has especially extravagant tastes and a passionate desire to impress others with his importance.

In simple dollars-and-cents terms, the members of both houses are much better off than they have ever been before. They are thus *personally* — though not *politically* — more independent than they used to be. They are under no desperate compulsion to line their pockets with what Daniel Webster (one of the ablest and one of the most corrupt men ever to sit in Congress) used to call "the usual retainers." In money terms, being a member of Congress is not a bad job, and it has steadily gotten better in recent years.

A hundred years ago, Senators and Representatives received a measly allowance of $8 a day, and that only while Congress was in session. As recently as the early nineteen-fifties the pay was a mere $12,500, and as late as 1960 was $22,500. Now all members are paid $42,500 a year. Even allowing for inflation, they have never had it so good. And there are hidden perquisites, which mean that they have it even better than they seem to.

Until 1946, for example, there were no pensions for Congressmen; a defeated Congressman was expected to shift for himself. The first, very modest pensions were voted in that year, despite considerable public outcry. Since then Congressional pensions have been quietly but steadily rising — the cost of pensions for more than two hundred former members of the House or Senate now comes to nearly $2 million a year. Former members with long service draw $2,000 a month in pensions, and even those with relatively short service draw useful sums, especially if they have been in the armed services — every year in uniform is counted as the equivalent of a year in Congress. A man with, say, three terms in the House, plus a couple of years in uniform, has a pleasant additional income of $6,000 in pension rights until he dies.

A wife or son on the payroll also adds usefully to the family income, and nepotism is so common a practice that it is hardly noticed any more. Then there are also small perks and gimmicks which rarely come to public notice.

Perhaps the oddest gimmick is the cash rebate on the stationery allowance. In 1966, for example, $441,000 which was appropriated for stationery went unspent, and those who had underspent the $2,400 stationery allowance drew the balance in cash — often more than $1,000. Despite the surplus, the House in 1967 voted to increase the allowance to $3,000 — the equivalent of a useful increase in salary for most members.

A few Senators and Representatives have objected to this gimmickry — notably Senator John Williams of Delaware, who actually let the unused portion of his stationery allowance revert to the Treasury. But there was no general outcry; this kind of corner-cutting has come to seem the way the game is played.

One reason why such lagniappe as the extra stationery allowance is welcome is that a member of Congress — especially a Senator — is expected by his constituents and his fellow politicians to behave like a Big Shot. He is expected to pick up checks, dispense food and drink, ride in a large, new car, dress well, live in a good house, and display all the other status symbols of the modern American Big Shot. The cost of living like a Big Shot is not measured in the cost-of-living index, but there is no doubt that it has risen vertiginously.

In the earlier days of the Republic, when Washington was "scarce any better than a swamp," and when communications were slow and difficult, life was simpler for a member of Congress. Even in the early years of this century most members would leave their wives at home, and eat and sleep throughout the sessions (then mercifully much shorter) in boardinghouses, sometimes four to a room.

Some of the older members, especially from the South, still live simply in apartment hotels when in Washington. But Senators especially now find it politically rewarding — and rewarding also to their self-esteem — to maintain a Washington establishment in which important persons from back home and the denizens of Political Washington can be entertained. The really rich congregate in Georgetown. But Georgetown real estate prices — it is difficult to find a reasonably comfortable house there for less than $75,000 — has a filtering effect, and as a result only twenty-two members of Congress have Georgetown addresses, as of this writing. But even a Cleveland Park or Chevy Chase address runs into money.

The money it costs to live like a Big Shot contributed to the downfall of poor Tom Dodd, whose chief defense was, in effect, the plea that living like a Big Shot was part of a Senator's job. It is also one reason (the cost of campaigns is another and more important reason) why the number of poor men in Congress is constantly decreasing, by a process of natural selection, and the number of rich men constantly increasing. In the Senate, there are at least half a dozen multimillionaires and many more with capital in the high hundred thousands. . . .

For a man who is reasonably well off, being a member of Congress — and being a Senator especially — is an agreeable and rewarding life. "This is the most wonderful job in the world," Senator Claiborne Pell (who has no money worries) remarked exultantly soon after his first election. "Only ninety-nine other people in the world have as good a job, and no one has a better one."

Senators have always enjoyed being Senators. When he was urged to seek the Republican Presidential nomination, Warren Gamaliel Harding expostulated: "Why should I? . . . If I don't run for the Presidency I can stay in the Senate all my life. It is a very pleasant place." He would have died a happier man if he had stayed in that pleasant place.

There have, of course, been exceptions. Elihu Root, a contemporary of Harding's, Theodore Roosevelt's Secretary of State, and a brilliant, ambitious man, hated the Senate. It was galling to find himself, as a mere junior Senator, stripped of all real power. "I am tired of it," he said. "The Senate is doing such little things in such little ways."

John F. Kennedy in his Senate years also became visibly tired of doing little things in little ways. I once asked him an obvious question: why did he want to be President? He gestured with his right index finger in the direction of the White House. "Because that's where the real power is," he said. This clearly seemed to him an entirely adequate answer.

But most members of Congress like being members of Congress all the same. Unless he is very sick, or very old or very unelectable, a member hardly ever vacates his seat of his own accord. The fact that members of Congress, and Senators especially, very much like their jobs is a very important fact about Congress. It explains two otherwise mysterious things about Congress; why there are so many able men in the place, despite the "low ebb" referred to by Senator Morton; and why the peculiar system under which Congress works continues, after a fashion, to operate.

One reason most Congressmen like being Congressmen is the fact that Capitol Hill is, for a member of Congress, a curiously pleasant place to work. It has a special atmosphere of its own, cozy, clublike, and at the same time, thanks to its smell of the past, faintly and pleasantly awe-inspiring. The pictures, most of them awful and a few very good, the statuary, the Brumidi frescoes, the little cubbyholes and hideaways and subterranean passages, the almost palpable ghosts of those who have gone before — Calhoun and Clay and Randolph, Webster and Benton and Sumner, Vandenburg and Taft and Rayburn — all this gives a member a feeling of belonging, of being on the inside, which is to many men as pleasant a feeling as there is.

The general air of camaraderie among the members — most politicians are almost by definition jovial fellows — reinforces this sense of belonging. So does the endless parade of gawking tourists and awed constituents, the outsiders who don't know where the hideaways are, who aren't admitted to the members' restaurants or the lobbies with their overstuffed black-leather chairs, and who don't know Mike or Carl or Jerry.

Representatives, to be sure, tend to have more mixed feelings about their jobs than Senators, and almost any Representative who is not a committee chairman or high in the House hierarchy will willingly risk his seniority and his seat for a chance to go to "the other place." Freshmen Representatives tend to be lost in the crowd, and to feel, for a while at least, rather like new boys at school. As a freshman Representative, the reaction of George Bush of Texas is typical. He has described the experience as "fascinating but frustrating" — frustrating because it is so difficult for a freshman to get anything done, fascinating in large part because of the human relationships.

"Usually, a man makes his close friends in school or college, or in a war," says Bush, "and after that he just has acquaintances. But I think I may have made some real friends by the time I leave this place."

The experience of being a member of Congress in a certain session of a certain Congress is an experience both shared and unique, like the experience of going to a certain school in a certain year, or fighting a certain war in a certain unit. As in a school or a war, the members of Congress get caught up in the particular world in which they find themselves — the world of Capitol Hill. They want to shine in that world, for the same reason that they wanted to get that promotion or that medal in their war days, or to become a BMOC in their college days.

The desire to shine in the world of Capitol Hill is one of the intangible human factors which make the peculiar Congressional system work. The best way to shine in the world of Capitol Hill is to get on a good committee (or an important subcommittee), and stay on it until you head the committee itself. The committee system *is* the Congressional system.

For old habitués of the Senate galleries, it is always a bit amusing, and a bit sad too, to look at the faces of the tourists as they take their turn in the galleries. They invariably register, first surprise, then disappointment. Expecting to see something like the Webster-Hayne debate, they see instead a handful of elderly men, dozing or chatting, while another elderly man drones on inaudibly. The fact is, of course, that the real work of Congress is hardly ever done on the floor of either house. It is done in committee. In committee is where reputations are made and unmade.

To get on a good committee, to make a good reputation on it, and thus to shine in the world of Capitol Hill, it is important — indeed, it is essential — to get along well with the people who really run Congress. These people are collectively known as the Establishment (Senator Joseph Clark's designation) or the Inner Club (columnist William White's phrase). Their power over the rest of Congress is directly dependent on their desire to shine.

A man who defies or alienates the Establishment does not shine; or at least he shines, if at all, not within the world of Capitol Hill, but outside that world. This is why the members of the Inner Club have something of the same power over the other members of the Senate or House — although all are theoretically equal — as, say, the prefects in a boarding school, or the field-grade officers in a regiment, have over their juniors. The way that power is exercised and maintained makes an interesting study in the interrelationship between people and power.

Simple human likability has a lot to do with the maintenance of the Congressional power structure. Take, for example, Representative Wilbur Mills of Arkansas, chairman of the House Ways and Means Committee, and a leading member of the House Establishment — some would say *the* leading member.

The House has the constitutional responsibility for raising revenue, and the Ways and Means Committee is, of course, the tax committee, so Wilbur Mills would be a powerful man in any case. But what makes his power all but legendary is his ability to swing, first his committee, then the whole House, behind whatever position he may take on taxes. This ability derives in part from hard work, careful calculation, and a sensitive smell for the mood of the House. But Mills is also a notably courteous, fair-minded, and pleasant man, almost universally liked in the House, and especially on his own committee. Nobody wants to tangle with good old Wilbur, so Mills almost always has the last say on tax measures, which makes him one of the dozen or so most powerful men in Washington.

Most of the members of the Club are likable people; since most of them are Southerners, their charm often has the special Southern accent. They are also, without exception, Capitol Hill careerists — their lives and their ambitions are tied to the Senate or the House. This is why John F. Kennedy was never even a candidate member of the Club. John Kennedy was resented by some of the members of the Club, as was Robert Kennedy — the very essence of Clubmanship is that those who are not members must dearly wish they were, and John Kennedy quite obviously had no hankering at all to join the Club.

There is and always has been room for argument about who is in the Club and who isn't. But in general the Club consists of the official hierarchy of both parties in both houses; the chairmen of the important standing committees, plus most of the ranking minority members of the standing committees. There are also one or two, notably in the Senate — like Senator Edmund Muskie of Maine or Senator John Stennis of Mississippi or Senator John Pastore of Rhode Island — who have no exalted standing in the hierarchy or key committee chairmanships, but who are members of the Congressional ruling class for reasons of personality, intelligence, energy, or absorption in the affairs of Congress.

At the top of the hierarchy, of course, are the Majority Leader of the Senate and the Speaker of the House. When Lyndon Johnson and Sam Rayburn held those positions, the Congressional Establishment in both houses was wholly dominated by the two Texans. Nothing like the same degree of power was exercised by their successors, Mike Mansfield of Montana and John McCormack of Massachusetts.

The sharp decline in the power of both the Majority Leader and the

Speaker has contributed to the decline of the power and prestige of Congress itself. For a semivacuum of power at the top has created an impression of aimlessness, of talk without action. The impression accords with the reality. . . .

Since the days of the revolt against Speaker Joseph Cannon, the Speaker's power under the rules has been severely limited, and the Majority Leader's powers have been even less — before Lyndon Johnson, many Majority Leaders were nonentities. "The leadership," as Mike Mansfield has said, "has no special powers to lead." This is true enough. Rayburn and Johnson simply created their own "special powers to lead." . . .

There are, of course, actually two parties in both houses, and they are not, in terms of the political realities, the Democratic and Republican parties. They are the Congressional-Conservative and the Presidential-Liberal parties. The Congressional-Conservative Party is the normal majority party. . . . By and large, the Congressional-Conservative Party prevails, when it wants to prevail, over the Presidential-Liberal Party, partly because a big majority of the men who really run Congress belong to the Congressional-Conservative Party. The chief reason, of course, is the seniority system which operates with the force of law, and which guarantees that the men in the key positions will come from the safe seats. This in turn guarantees that at least two-thirds of the committee chairmen will be relatively conservative WASP's from the South or from the smaller Western and border states.

The result is that, especially when the Congressional-Conservative Party is in its normal majority position, Congress is catatonic. (Catatonia is defined in the dictionary as "a syndrome . . . with muscular rigidity and mental stupor, sometimes alternating with great excitement and confusion.") The periods of muscular rigidity and mental stupor prevail far more often than those of excitement and confusion. As a consequence, Congress, most of the time, is a bore. The boringness of Congress has hurt Congressional prestige far more than the Bakers and Powells and Dodds. Congress is a bore because Congress nowadays has the power to delay, or to emasculate, or to deny, but it almost wholly lacks the power to originate.

There was a time, not very long ago, when a Senator or even a lowly Representative could aspire to leave behind him a personal legislative monument — Representative Carter Glass's Banking Act, Senator Robert Wagner's labor law, Senator George Norris' TVA. Since World War II only one piece of major legislation was originated, debated, shaped, and passed by Congress wholly independent of the executive branch — Robert A. Taft's Taft-Hartley law. It may be the last such legislation Congress will ever originate.

Nowadays the role of Congress is to pass, or to refuse to pass, legislation originating in the executive branch — and sometimes, by not permitting an administration proposal to come to a vote, to do neither. This nay-saying power is still important, of course. But as the Congressional power becomes increasingly negative, Congress' slice of the whole pie of governmental power steadily becomes smaller.

The Constitution grants to Congress "the power to provide for the Common Defence and . . . to Declare War." The most obvious example of the withering of Congressional power is the fact that, since World War II ended, the country has fought two rather large wars without the formality of a declaration of war by Congress. The Congressional power to "provide for the Common Defence" has also been similarly eroded.

All the basic strategic decisions involving the "Common Defence" are now made in the executive branch. True, such Congressional grandees as Richard Russell and George Mahon are listened to with respect and attention. They can influence the major decisions. But they do not *make* the major decisions, and neither does Congress as a whole.

Consider two examples. With strong support from both Armed Services Committees, Congress in the early sixties began appropriating money to build a "follow-on manned bomber" — the B-70 — to replace the obsolescent B-52. Secretary of Defense McNamara thereafter curtly reported to Senator Russell that "the President chooses not to implement that section of the program." In short, the executive branch vetoed the clear intention of the Congress in "providing for the Common Defence," and the veto stuck.

Again, the Congressional grandees in the Armed Services Committees of both houses almost unanimously favored a "thick," or anti-Soviet, anti-ballistic-missile system, and in the mid-sixties money to start such an ABM system was twice voted. McNamara, with the backing of the President, simply refused to use the money — until, in September, 1967, he gave a reluctant yellow light to a "thin," or anti-Chinese, ABM system, which was not what the Armed Services Committee wanted.

In both cases — especially in the case of the B-70 — McNamara was almost certainly right. The plain fact is that "providing for the Common Defence" has become a matter so complex and technical that Congress cannot really do the job any more. In simpler days, Congress could intelligently debate whether the United States needed a standing army of ten or fifteen divisions; whether the United States fleet should match the British fleet; or whether there should be conscription. But a body of 535 men from all walks of life is not qualified to decide such arcane matters as the proportion of the national budget that should be devoted to the multiple-overhead ICBM as against the Nike-X; or even such relatively simple questions as the comparative merits of the nuclear-powered frigate as against the cheaper conventional-powered frigate. A few genuine experts in Congress, men like Russell and Mahon, may have intelligent opinions in such matters, but the final decision has to be taken after an infinitely complex process of technical analysis in the executive branch.

Even many areas of domestic policy have become so complex, as the power of the federal government has inexorably expanded, that Congress retains only a sort of vague watching brief over the activities of the executive branch. Consider, for example, a large volume published by Sargent Shriver's Office of Economic Opportunity, which is to be found in almost all Congressional offices. Its title is *Catalog of Federal Assistance Programs*, and it is about the size of a Sears Roebuck catalogue.

It lists all the ways in which Uncle Sam is ready to help his eager nephews and nieces, from such major programs as Medicare and the U.S. Employment Services to "Captioned Films for the Deaf" and "Farm Fish Pond Management." A total of 459 separate and distinct programs are listed, administered by 34 separate and distinct agencies. The "authorizing" legislation for each program is duly noted in the catalogue. But in virtually every case the program was actually originated in the executive branch, almost always in the agency charged with administering it. No Congressman (and nobody else) can hope to master the whole complex of "federal assistance programs." Most members of Congress use the catalogue to help them act as intermediaries, or tipsters for interested parties back home who want to get their share (or perhaps a bit more) of the federal gravy.

Moreover, both the executive and judicial branches have been invading, more than ever before, the lawmaking prerogative of Congress. Not only does almost all really important legislation now originate in the executive branch, a great body of "administrative law" has also been created by the administrative decisions of the regulatory agencies. These decisions have the force of law, and there are highly paid Washington lawyers who specialize in this kind of law and nothing else.

The Supreme Court has also created an increasingly large area of judicial law, or "judge-made law," as the Court's critics call it. The law on school integration, or the rights of criminal suspects, *or* legislative apportionment may be "judge-made." But it is the law of the land, all the same, to be obeyed by Congressmen like everybody else, and in certain areas this judge-made law affects the structure of American society more directly than legislation duly debated and passed by Congress. These are the areas, like school integration or voting rights, where Congress feared to tread; the Supreme Court, by boldly running into them, has seized a share of the power of Congress, as many anti-Court members of Congress are sulkily aware.

The loss of power by Congress should not be exaggerated. The power to delay, emasculate, and deny is a very great power, however negative. And the watching brief that Congress holds is also important. A major speech by a major Senator — Robert Kennedy's call in 1966 for incorporation of the National Liberation Front in a future Vietnamese government, for example; or Thruston Morton's hawk-to-dove speech on Vietnam in 1967 — remains an Event, to be covered on the front pages, and therefore capable of influencing national opinion.

The will of Congress, even when the legislative process is not involved, can still importantly affect national policy. It is most unlikely that Robert McNamara would have given even a yellow light to the "thin" ABM system, which he himself described as of "marginal" value, if he and the President had not been under heavy Congressional pressure. When Establishmentarians Richard Russell and John Stennis of Mississippi joined William Fulbright in denouncing the despatch of three cargo planes to the Congo's Mobutu during the creeping civil war there, all thoughts of further intervention in the Congo were hastily abandoned.

Incredible numbers of man-hours are wasted by the top appointed officials of the executive branch in testifying on the same subject before four or more Congressional committees. Sargent Shriver, for example, has estimated that he spent about 90 percent of his time defending his antipoverty program on Capitol Hill, and about 10 percent actually administering it. And yet the knowledge that they will have to answer a lot of questions — even stupid, repetitious, and irrelevant questions — is not necessarily an unhealthy knowledge for the presidential appointees and the powerful upper bureaucrats to labor under.

Moreover, most Capitol Hill reporters would agree not only that there are very few real crooks in Congress, but that there are a surprising number of surprisingly able men, especially in the Senate. Most reporters, asked to give a rough guess at the number of men of real ability in the Senate, come up with some such estimate as a quarter or a third. But when they go through the hundred-man list name by name, they find themselves checking off a much higher proportion. . . .

Here again, the fact that members of Congress like their jobs, and Senators especially love being Senators, is an important fact. A lot of intelligent and ambitious men scramble over each other to get into Congress, with the result that the Hill boasts so high a proportion of able men, along with a share, of course, of trimmers and pompous fools. This is one reason why the voters, who are by and large a remarkably ignorant and prejudiced lot, get better than they deserve.

And yet the fact is that the Congress of the United States has been rather steadily losing power and prestige. This is a process which has been going on elsewhere in the world — both the British and French Parliaments have also lost power and prestige, the latter more rapidly than the former. The conventional response to this loss of power and prestige is to express hand-wringing fears for the future of democracy.

If the process went too far — as it has in France, for example — it could indeed endanger the democratic system. But Congress is still capable of exercising the important nay-saying and watchdog functions. And it may be that those functions are, in fact, the only ones which a body of 535 men is capable of usefully exercising.

The periods of Congressional dominance, as after the Civil War, or in the nineteen-twenties, or in the early McCarthy period, have not been proud chapters in American political history. Especially in such times as these, the facts of life at home and abroad seem to dictate that the real policy-making power should rest increasingly with the executive branch, and that the power of Congress should become increasingly negative. In any case, that is what is happening.

Ferdinand Lundberg | **The Cream of the Quest**

The various attitudes and dispositions of the wealthy coterie — the up-and-coming, the active and established, the playful and the idly parasitic (artistic contrast on the social scene to the lethargic parasitic poor) — obviously have some sort of general end-in-view or goal. For a man ordinarily seeks to attain or retain great wealth for some more tangible reason than simple social security, which the American rich have achieved to an absurd and perhaps self-defeating degree. As seems evident, the common reason for attaining and retaining wealth, as displayed in specific careers, is to lead some personally determined insulated version of the Good Life. Considerable independence of others is an invariable hallmark of the good life as delineated by the rich. Power itself creates a barrier between those who possess it and those who do not.

As all of the rich have far more choices open to them than the nonrich in selecting personal roles and scheduling their time, the way they live should at least shadow forth their conception of how one should properly live. Manifestly, if they thought it a hardship to sleep in a gold canopied bed in a mansion they could, exercising free choice, instead sleep in a Bowery doorway, under a haystack or in a cabin small by a waterfall; some, in fact, prefer to sleep, occasionally at least, in remote hunting lodges or on damp, unsteady yachts. As far as that is concerned, they could, exercising choice, retire to a monastery on a cold Himalayan slope or join (or even buy) a circus. A few, to be sure, have satisfied profound inclinations by buying Broadway shows and square-rigged sailing ships.

Yet, despite the wide range of material choices open to them, recipes for living among the rich are so restricted and familiar as to have become historical clichés. Their general style of living has changed little since the days of the Pharaohs, both absolutely and relatively to the rest of society. The personal life of a rich man in truth is rather cut and dried and pretty

SOURCE: *The Rich and the Super-Rich* by Ferdinand Lundberg. Copyright © 1968 by Ferdinand Lundberg. Reprinted by permission of Lyle Stuart, Inc.

much follows a longstanding script; it is about as stylized and full of surprises as a minuet. Within a rather narrow range one can accurately predict his moves from collecting expensive objects to breeding horses and dogs. To be rich and not a collector is to be a fairly rare bird.

Certain broad patterns of living can be clearly discerned among the rich, although one may be a total abstainer and another a sturdy boozer; one may prefer blondes and another exotic non-Caucasians. It is no doubt because life for the rich is historically routinized, holding few surprises either enchanting or terrifying, that so many of them become addicted to gambling, from the stock market to the casino and horse race. Except for those who play out their gambling drive in politics or forms of business rulership, many of them are patently subject to boredom, as many photographs show.

While I would not go so far as to say that all of the rich are bored all of the time, boredom has historically been one of the occupational hazards of the upper classes; for people who have seen nearly everything and satisfied inclinations as much as they could each day acquire a considerable feeling of *déjà vu*. Unlike the common run of employee they have, for example, never had the unexpected thrill of being suddenly called to account. They have never suddenly been told: "You're fired," a dramatic experience known to thousands of poorer men, including university presidents.

Unlike the very poor they are not, even rarely, bemused by unexpected kindness or consideration; for they have learned to expect such attitudes from others, especially from officials and personnel, and might, perhaps, be diverted rather than otherwise moved by some rare outburst of rudeness that would annoy a humbler man. Some of the rich no doubt get some release from boredom by reading the overheated Marxist press and learning what aspiring back-alley commissars have in store for them. But such roaring historic adventure on the guillotine, they no doubt sadly realize, is not to be for them. They are fully aware of all the overlapping mechanisms of social control, from the Holy Ghost and the local schools to the police and the military, to say nothing of privately retained legislators and eager-beaver rank-and-file vigilantes ever ready to show their patriotic zeal by harassing bedraggled dissenters.

Whatever their orientation either as actives or passives on the social scene, the rich are all affected, almost without their knowledge, by the concentrated dynamic of money. Their assets, as it were, are constantly sending out invisible impulses to them to make some move, make some move, make some move. . . . To get away from the compulsively hypnotic influence of these assets is seemingly, for nearly all, virtually impossible. They are as Trilbys to the Svengali of their money. . . .

Most of the rich, whether they arrived by their own scheming or have inherited, are not taken by surprise. It was always understood by most of them that they were going to be rich as soon as some older relative passed to his reward. While no great alteration is required in the style of life of such they, too, have it gradually borne in upon them by bankers, lawyers, wives and friends that they are under some irresistible compulsion to make moves in which their money plays a major role, something like the queen in a game of chess. Few new heirs, if any, find that they can ignore or even tranquilly contemplate from afar their newly acquired assets. They are suddenly burdened with problems: an investment problem, a tax problem, a political problem, a donation problem, a general living problem. Where to spend the summer? The winter? Spring and fall? And what of the difficult periods between seasons, where there is an overlap? And what to wear? What clothing? Who to see and not see?

A generalization that applies with hardly an exception to all of the rich is that asceticism is rarely if ever an ingredient in their personal scheme of affairs. Not that it should be; it just is not. Rather is it the case that however the life of one rich person may differ from that of another both live at the opposite pole from asceticism. The elder J. P. Morgan was quite a bon vivant, a swinger, and Rockefeller was a teetotaler and homebody; yet Rockefeller, among other things, maintained four palatial estates, one for each season of the year, from Maine to Florida. Although a tight-lipped Baptist elder, he was far from monkish.

The personal life of the rich, almost without exception, comes down to sensory gratification on a grand scale, gratification attained in the light of standards generally considered luxurious. A simplistic material deter- minism seems to rule their lives as by an iron law. Here and there, it is true, have been persons frugal to the point of miserliness, such as Hetty Green, but in general the rich are found to live according to popular conceptions of extreme luxury even though one may be comparatively restrained and another an obvious sybarite. They do, broadly, precisely what the average man in the street would do, neither more nor less, were he on their lofty pecuniary perch. What one may say in the most extreme criticism of them is that they are so ordinary, so common, so vulgar, yet placed in positions of extraordinary advantage. Far more than they them-selves suppose, they are automatons, moved one way or the other almost always by considerations of money. To find a rich man, apart from an occasional eccentric inventor, living a life largely unmotivated by his money is, as I believe the record shows, a virtual impossibility. Successful inventors, yes; others, no.

The Gorgeous Setting

What unquestionably first strikes the most indolent observer about the personal lives of the rich compared with the nonrich is the opulence of their residential settings. These lush habitations, contrary to many hurried commentators, have more than a tintillating value for outsiders. They are, I submit, deeply symbolic of a self-conception and of actual objective social status. They are, contrary to the eagle-eyed Veblen, more than an exer-cise in ostentatious display and conspicuous consumption. They are, in fact, a dead giveaway of what it is all about.

Since the time of the Pharaohs, and no doubt even before, the head man in the kingdom always had the biggest house, a palace, and with the advent of progress in utilizing labor he came to have many palaces suitable to the different seasons of the year and different moods. The supporting nobility and priesthood had lesser but sufficiently palatial habitations, and it was only as some of these came to have more to say in ruling the realm that their homes began to rival in size that of the monarch.

At the risk of provoking the bargain-basement sages into charging that I am oversimplifying, let me lay it plainly on the line: The people with the most say-so have always had the largest and most elaborate domiciles. Big house historically means big man in the realm; conversely, small house means nobody in the realm.

As direct survivals of this tradition, embellished by Roman emperors, Louis XIV, the czars and a few others, we today see the pope, spiritual ruler over some 500 million precious immortal souls, living in a series of huge palaces, one of which is set in his own small city. We see the figure-head kings and queens of England still housed in extraordinarily large houses, some approaching the size of the Kennedys' Merchandise Mart in Chicago. And we see the successors to the czars living in the Kremlin, no shack.

From time to time a vast residence has been awarded at the expense of the realm to someone who has been of signal service to the rulers, as in the case of huge Blenheim Palace in Oxfordshire, England, awarded in Queen Anne's reign to John Churchill, first Duke of Marlborough, for his victory in 1704 over the French and Bavarians at the decisive battle of Blenheim in Bavaria. Winston Churchill spent much of his boyhood in this truly imperial edifice.

A very big house, then, or a series of big houses, means historically that the inhabitant is either a ruler or one very closely associated with rule. It is never, never, never the case that anyone functionally or otherwise dissociated from rule, anyone such as an artist, philosopher, civil service official or scientist, inhabits such a big house except as a guest. The big houses, then, are the outward signs writ plain of a class habituated to rule, reminding us of the principle of Roman law: *Cui bono?*

As the United States does not have anything like a ruling class, according to an extensive assortment of fully housebroken professors, we are confronted here by an apparent anomaly: People who in theory have no more to say about governance than the ordinary truck driver somehow inhabit some of the choicest and most expensive establishments of all history. In American political theory, to be sure, the rulers are fundamentally the whole people, who from time to time duly elect their representatives. These latter, if anyone, are held to be the real rulers. Yet these putative real rulers, unless they already belong to the very rich class, never inhabit dwellings of comparable opulence even if they reach the White House, which is itself a comparatively modest affair with a short-term lease. . . .

The big houses, in brief, are occupied by the basic decision makers, and this has been the rule down through history. A difference, however, is that in the United States the decisions are only indirectly and obliquely imposed.

It should not be supposed that the idea of this self-conception of rulership on the part of the rich is sustained only by the fact that they have a penchant for assorted ducal mansions and grounds. That this is the self-conception is shown, too, by the way many of them sign their names with Roman numerals appended, betokening an established family line in the style of European nobility. It is shown, furthermore, and more convincingly, in the affinity of the American rich, particularly with respect to their young women, for marriage with members of the European nobility.

It is obvious that the American industrial rich, not sharing the distaste of the Founding Fathers for titles, identified themselves with and saw themselves playing a role similar to European nobility and royalty.

True, a self-conception is not necessarily a reflection of reality; it could be pure fantasy. It is on other grounds, of actual rulership, that we see that the self-conception was not mistaken. The big-rich of the United States are in fact if not in form American dukes; the general populace pretty much enacts the role and has the outlook of peasantry, most of them quite gladly.

Patterns of Residence

While much has been written in detailed description of the opulent and vasty residences of the freedom-loving rich, and many photographs of them have been published, it has not been noticed as far as I am aware that they occur in distinct, different patterns.

These patterns are as follows:

1. The compound, or multiple estate, containing many large residences of different members of an extended family and sometimes including an entire village and much acreage.

2. The cluster or territorial grouping of separate estates of an extended family.

3. Scattered estates up to fifty or more of the different branches of an extended family.

4. The single country estate of a nuclear family, usually the mark of someone new to wealth.

In all cases it should be understood that the estate is merely the family center. There remain to be reckoned town houses, distant estates in non-urban terrain and foreign estates; many wealthy Americans own either European or Latin American estates and a few persons have them in northern Africa, particularly in Morocco.

One function of the large estate, of course, is to instil awe and thereby place social distance between the owner and the clamorous *hoi polloi*.

The question of preserving social distance is important for a variety of reasons, not the least of which is that it would be awkward in many ways if rich and poor were closely mingled. It would certainly be socially awkward when the rich man sat down to a feast and the poor man turned to his stew and grits. As a matter of common sociability the rich man would be expected to offer some of his steak and endive salad to the poor man and to accept some of the stew. If it were only one or a few poor men asked to partake of a sumptuous repast it would be one thing; but if the participation were quite general it would be another. A man worth $100 million would be broke over night, for example, if he treated all the families in the country to a single steak dinner at his expense.

Social distance, then, is seen to come down, among other things, to a matter of economy. One cannot invite everybody into the plantation and remain rich for long. The visitors will literally eat one out of house and home, like invading locusts. That the rich man is not ordinarily this open-handed does not signify that he is especially ungenerous; he is merely prudent and posts his various signs: "Private, Keep Out." Privacy becomes a cult. . . .

Cracks in the Compound Walls

What I have written thus far might tend to leave the impression that the rich are, relatively, in a cushy position. And so they are. But the enviableness of their position amid accumulating signs of storm on every hand can be easily exaggerated unless seen in perspective. In saying that the rich are faced by difficulties I simply state sober fact, not trying to gain for them any feeling that they are as heroes and heroines in an enveloping Greek tragedy. . . .

In speaking of the rich as of any collective group there is always the danger of tacitly assuming that all the units in the collection, because they share some characteristic, are as alike as peas. The rich, of course, differ among each other in age, constitution, temperament, intelligence and knowledge. They also differ as to source of wealth: inherited or self-accumulated, diversified or concentrated, held in the form of bonds, equities, real estate or a combination of all. Yet, despite individual differences, they are similar in that they are, most of them, held within the same social matrix, subject to the same external compulsions and pressures.

This fact is clearly brought into view when we consider that although the rich have much power, more than the common run of men surely, they also experience in general a deeper sense of frustration than most people owing to the fact that their greater power is exercised within the restraints of a certain system and under the scrutiny of other powerful people. This amounts to saying that, though great, their power has limits, often annoying limits.

We can see this at a glance by looking at the problem of air pollution. And New York City, financial center of the world, is fittingly held by experts to have the worst pollution problem in the country. True, the rich man can flee the city from time to time and has in his homes and offices the latest air filtration devices; he is not so badly off as the ordinary citizen who must breathe the lethal stuff without interruption. Yet he knows that his staff, to which he is as loyal as it is to him, is caught in the muck. And he knows various projects of interest to him — perhaps a big skyscraper promotion — are qualified in their attractiveness and even value.

Why, then, as he has power, does he not deal with the problem decisively?

He is unable to do so, no doubt to his chagrin, because of the very momentum and direction of the system. Although he may publicly deprecate stress on the health issue he understands it as well as anyone. He is, however, caught in the situation as depicted by Theodore B. Merrill, an editor of *Business Week*, who said in a comprehensive national survey as long ago as 1960 (and in the meantime the problem has become more urgent) that "Nobody is going to put in any kind of control devices that cost him money unless he has to. . . . It simply has to be unprofitable for an industry to pollute the air or else they are going to pollute it, because it is cheaper to use the air for a sewer than to pay for keeping it clean." The same holds true of polluting waterways.

Here, it would see, profit is being put before human life and health, a point made endlessly by nasty socialists. And it is not merely profit that is in question but the general standing of an institution, a particular company. Although a rich man may control this company and could instantly make it stop polluting the air, such unilateral action would not solve the pollution problem, to which other companies contribute. Unless all the companies acted in concert the action of one would have little effect.

And if all the companies in a particular region agreed to undergo the expense of reducing air pollution their costs would rise and profits fall in relation to companies in less populated regions not burdened with such costs. The inter-company position of the social-minded companies would decline. At this point multitudes of investors, some of them large but not controlling, would perhaps begin selling the stock of the social-minded companies because the relative return was diminishing in comparison with that of unsocial-minded companies. Dutch, Swiss, South American and ordinarily prudent domestic investors would sell out, realizing that these social-minded companies have expensive profit-eroding problems.

Investors, high or low, do not feel sympathetically identified with a company's problems, do not "forgive" it for making a poorer financial showing in a good cause. They simply analyze the figures and prospects of various companies. Some of these investors live in the bracing air of distant mountain resorts, by the seaside, off on distant healthy pampas. All they know is that as between company A and company B the latter, not burdened with many social-minded expenses, shows an ascending line of profitability and that this is better for *them*.

Why not then, it may be asked, make all companies uniformly comply to the maximum with all social-minded regulations, thus putting them on all fours and passing additional costs on in price? Doing this, however, would raise national costs vis-à-vis industries in other countries which could undersell the Americans. In the world market the lowest-cost producer, everything else being equal, has a profit advantage and most readily attracts new capital most cheaply. And the world market is an area of prime interest to capitalists.

It is, then, "The System," as socialists have long contended, that gives priority here to its own systemic needs over the larger question of human life and health in specific instances.

As many scattered stockholders begin selling out of a company with a declining relative level of profitability, the price of the stock, its value, declines, affecting multitudes, jeopardizing bank loans and inducing an endless train of economic troubles. And when it comes to new financing the capital is not readily available, must be obtained along the route of a fixed rate of high interest, itself damaging to profitability, rather than through the issuance of equities. Being unilaterally social-minded, then, is ruinous.

Although powerful, the rich man, even the grouping of all rich men, is not powerful enough to fly in the face of the requirements of the supporting system. Beyond a certain level they must all take the rough with the smooth as offered by that system, a point that no doubt makes disconsolate the more reflective of them. . .

The rich man wants for his children, whom he often loves passionately, the best in the way of education. He sends them to special schools that have the choice of teachers for small groups that are carefully supervised from dawn to nightfall. Most of these children, many of whom sign the family name with coveted large Roman numerals suffixed, go on to the best available in the way of colleges.

Yet the rich and powerful man cannot forever shield from his own children knowledge that they are going into a society bristling with avoidable destructive problems that *it is unable owing to its corporate systemic requirements to solve.* Many of these problems have their horns pointed directly at the children of the rich man.

Let us look at this neglected aspect.

All general disturbing and life-threatening social problems — air and water pollution; crime; overpopulation; vexed race relations; traffic tangles; accumulated causes of civil disturbance such as slums, unemployment and extreme poverty — intrude upon the young rich with about as much force as upon the young poor. The rich young person may have better oases to which to retreat; but he is nevertheless adversely affected by the same accumulating, neglected phenomena.

Even in their oases the young rich are by no means safe. They, like others, are subject to narcotic addiction, alcoholism and psychological disorders — and an inventory of all their tribulations along this line would be impressive. They, too, in various ways are assailed by hard types. And let us remember that their fathers are powerful men.

Of crime, against their own persons and in its aspect of crime against property a rising, low-grade, guerrilla variant of Marxist class war, they are steady direct and indirect targets. As the *Wall Street Journal* in many articles during the 1960's made clear, there is a broad and steady determined assault on the merchandise and cash of the big companies by shoplifters and employees — crime carried out by noncriminal classes. Losses here, contrived by people whose appetites are stimulated beyond the reach of their means through the agency of voracious advertising, are passed on to the general public as much as possible in higher prices; but some of these losses, running into billions annually, must be absorbed. There are not sufficient jails to hold most of the offenders, many of whom when caught are let off with suspended sentences, dire threats from the bench, paroles, disgracing publicity, etc.

That the rich are as subject as anyone to misadventures in a wide-open society (kept wide-open in general so as to facilitate double-dealing in profitable particulars) can be shown by the citation of a number of salient cases, abstracted from among many.

In 1966 the young daughter of Charles Percy, former chairman of Bell & Howell, camera manufacturers, and now junior senator from Illinois, was wantonly murdered in her bed in the family home in exclusive Kenilworth, Illinois, on the Gold Coast north of Chicago. Her unknown slayer was not apprehended. Wealth, power and exalted position did not protect her in a jungle society. In the same year a well-organized kidnapping plot against Leonard K. Firestone, rubber scion of Beverly Hills, California, was frustrated through the enterprise of an underworld tipster. . . .

Robberies in the homes of the rich are frequent and there is reason to believe they are not always reported. And this despite elaborate protective systems. While traveling, the rich are especially the targets of expert thieves, as in the case of Henry Ford II in New York City, also in 1966. His hotel suite was burglarized and jewels in the reported amount of $50,000 were taken. Servants in the homes of the affluent and rather wealthy, according to news reports, are pretty regularly trussed up by invading thieves and the premises ransacked. Burglaries are common in wealthy residential districts. . . .

What I want to say here for the methodologists is that the rich, almost as much as the poor in their slums, are the recurrent victims of violence in a cuckoo-clock political system. The profiteers and their poor-boys-who-made-good in the legislatures seem unable to give much protection to their own women and children, to say nothing of the women and children of the less well-heeled.

The rich, like the rest of us, are as readily victimized by deleterious products, dentifrices, cosmetics, pharmaceuticals, and various untested chemical applications to various parts of the body. After all, there is only a certain range of offerings of this kind; the rich have no more sophisticated choices open to them than the rest of the public in the way of deodorants, depilatories, mouth washes, unguents and the like. Their young gorge on rancid hot dogs and hamburgers at ball games like any other red-blooded, true-blue American.

That various of these products, including widely circulating food preparations, are dangerous to health is regularly made known by appropriate federal supervisory agencies, kept thoughtfully understaffed through the courtesy of a bought bucolic Congress. The rich here are often hoist by their own politico-economic petard. . . .

The situation is made clearer still in the case of the automobile. A rich man is obviously in a position to purchase the best there is in the way of automobiles and have his own private mechanics service them. But, as Ralph Nader has shown and as Detroit has more recently admitted through extensive recalls of delivered automobiles, many automobiles are not mechanically safe in a country crosshatched with roads literally clogged with cars. Even though a rich man may have a car that is in perfect working order, there is no guarantee that he will not be run into or run down by some automobile that is either mechanically defective or in the hands of a defective driver, of which numerous are disclosed from time to time. The rich man and his family, it is evident, are as exposed to the automobile menace as they are to poisonous smog. They are no better off in this respect, unless they remain permanently indoors, than the rest of society. And, sure enough, as newspaper reports from time to time show, top-drawer eminents and their children are from time to time cut down in the streets by cars or battered on the roads. A complete inventory of such cases would require many pages.

Although injured by avoidable accidents or made ill by detestable products, the rich man does have an edge in that he can procure, no matter where he is, the very best and most expensive medical services. But doctors cannot always save him, much as they would like to. . . .

One might suppose that a rich and powerful man, aware of the source of some patently deleterious influence, would take arms and gird himself against the common threat. Here we come to an aspect of inner *finpolitan* affairs to which most of the sociologists have turned a blind, uncomprehending eye. It is a *finpolitan* rule that one company does not take a public position against another — whatever it does — as long as it does not act directly as an adversary; and the members of one industry do not lead or join in the public denunciation of another industry. Each industry, each company is allowed to pursue its own way unless it tries to grab too big a share of the market.

Thus, when public criticisms gain momentum against one company or one industry, when that company or industry stands in the public dock, as it were, others preserve diplomatic silence. The mass media, too, stand aside if they do not offer outright defenses of the criticized practices. Thus we see the entire corporate world maintaining a studied silence as pharmaceuticals are criticized for pricing practices, automotives for safety factors, the oil industry for special tax shelters and any or all for monopoly, gouging prices, poor products or community pollution.

The reason for this impotent silence is simply that if one wealthy group opens fire on the cushy preserve of another wealthy group there will be retaliation in kind. For each industry has vulnerable points open to criticism. It is the need, then, to preserve some semblance of intramural harmony that causes the financial groups to maintain silence about the shortcomings of their various members. Higher capitalism is a little club holding within it diverse temperaments, true enough, but temperaments that must, under pain of direct reciprocal attack, preserve an appearance of outward solidarity to the world. . . .

Being bound to keep quiet when he sees obvious destruction being wrought by some reckless peer, at least the intelligently reflective capitalist cannot be entirely happy. And his unhappiness has an entirely different cause from that of most people. It is the unhappiness of a consciously powerful man who realizes he can do nothing effective against something he considers profoundly evil, cannot even fully protect his own children. Even though he may feel that his own enterprises are as far beyond criticism as ingenuity can make them, he knows that this is no defense against fabrications which can be circulated against him to his distress by powerful people his uncooperative crusading spirit has made angry.

It is for this reason, among others, that it is rare to find crusaders among capitalists, who all in one way or the other live in glass houses.

In the matter of divorce and broken families the rich are, if anything, worse off than most of the population; at least they are no better placed. For the divorce rate among the rich, with many of them such ardent believers in marriage that they remarry up to five and even ten times, is very much higher than the national rate. Divorce, even if one looks upon it as a desirable escape hatch from an untenable situation, is never taken as a sign of sound human relations; rather is it taken as an index of unresolvable interpersonal trouble. . . .

The rich, it is clear, are not immune to the general fallout from the existing socio-political system even though they may have compensations denied to others. Far from all the fallout upon the rich has been indicated and one could go on at considerable length about more. However, confining ourselves again to the young and innocent rich, it is clear that their minds are as subverted as those of poorer youth by the all-pervading influence of persuasive advertising.

If someone systematically splashed mud on the clothing of rich children their parents would soon take steps to see that the offender was laid by the heels. Yet the rich, for all their power, cannot protect their children from the subversive influence of advertisers who insistently confuse the intellect in various detectable ways. Most of the time they misuse language and pictures in the effort solely to sell.

True, the rich youth like the poor, if he makes his way into the higher and more recondite studies such as semantics, logic and epistemology, can overcome the enervating intellectual influences of advertising and home-spun propaganda, thus possessing himself at least of his own mind. But few find their way to such rarefied studies and the result is that the rich usually have as confused a view of the world as the poor, subject to exploded notions (particularly in economics) and with about the same general world view as that of a postman or bartender. That this is so is readily seen in the public utterances of the more vocal of them. Among the self-erected we have cracker-barrel philosophers like Henry Ford I and H. L. Hunt and among the more educated we have the sagging economic views of David Rockefeller and, on a much lower level of wealth, the socio-cultural divagations of William F. Buckley, Jr., who asserts the presence of "eternal verities." A B-minus undergraduate in epistemology at Swampwater College knows better than that even though Buckley's public vowel movements are intently studied by a select circle of admirers.

One would think that a rich man, with money at his fingertips, would get smart and hire an epistemologist who would at least straighten him out from time to time about the grounds for rational belief. For we may well suppose that a rich man, always wanting the best, does not wish to go about in a scatterbrained condition hawking absurdities. He must want the true view just as he wants a livewire girl, a prime steak and a sound wine. Yet we find him apparently no better off in this respect than the common man. Nor, considering the baneful social influences to which they are subject will most of his prized children be better off. Madison Avenue vomits on their minds as freely as on the battered mind of the ordinary clod. . . .

The fundamental difficulty of the rich has not yet been fully indicated. This difficulty consists of acquiring a sense of worthwhile function (and getting the world to agree with the self-estimate of this function) and, at the same time, of containing the many eruptions and breakdowns in a social system the obsolete structure of which is continually being strained by the introduction of new profit-making technology as well as by the rise of appropriately ferocious rivalry abroad. The situation in which the contemporary rich find themselves could be described by some pundit, brightly, as challenging.

As to function, it comes down largely to rule under various euphemistic rubrics. At times, as the pages of *Who's Who* attest, the claims to function are more flamboyant and see the subjects pathetically proclaiming themselves as financiers, investors, venture entrepreneurs, philanthropists and the like. After all, a financier is only a money lender, an investor is someone who owns something producing revenue for his own account, a venture entrepreneur a promoter for his own account and a philanthropist a lover of mankind. . . .

Function, among the rich, as we have seen, is most often stated in terms that boil down to rule: executive, public official, administrator, trustee and the like.

In the modern world, function is closely related to self-identity because the question is no longer who one is but what one does. To the question "Who are you?" the answer is generally that one is a truck driver, clerk, teacher, performer or what-not of a certain name. "I am a tuba player named John Jones" is, at least for a beginning, a satisfactory designation (if true) of one's identity.

The rich, however, have difficulty in stating any function for themselves that is dissociated from rule. While terms like financier, investor, venture entrepreneur and philanthropist suggest commendable, nonintrusive and possibly supportive roles, terms such as executive, director, official, trustee and administrator and the like are clearly epitomized in a revealing term: boss.

In the contexts in which they are publicly advanced, all these terms hazily suggest synonyms for "hero," and at times a halo is also indicated for the heroic figure as in "international financier" and "upper-echelon executive." As one hears and reads of such, one is literally stunned by the superhuman vistas suggested. And when one reads that messages are being exchanged — actually exchanged — between the president of the United States on the one hand and international financiers and upper-echelon executives on the other (subject: something or other) one can imaginatively feel the world grinding on its hinges.

Whether the rich recognize it or not, in most public roles they seem to feel qualified to play they appear as bosses, however disguised, and not necessarily unbenevolent. In any other function they may elect to attempt — of a physicist, a ballplayer, a soft-shoe dancer, an artist, a writer or a philosopher — they find that their money gives them no edge at all. In roles of nonrulership, where the competition is extremely lively, if they decided to go in for poetry they find that par for the course is set by hard-to-beat T. S. Eliot or Robert Lowell, if for ballplaying by Mickey Mantle and Joe DiMaggio, etc. Most of the rich seeking active roles therefore drift, by default as it were, to corporations, banks, brokerage houses, nonprofit funds and various political jurisdictions. These are all organizational havens for imprecision even though they all harbor aspects where precision may be required of underlings, and appreciated.

In attempting to establish his unique identity through some unfinanced achievement, the rich man is pretty much in the position of anyone else, even a pauper. If his claim to competence is that he is very good at chess, all he need do to establish it is to beat a few lower-rung chess experts and then move higher. If his forte is science all he need do is gain the accolade of other scientists, hard to do. Normally finding such feats difficult, his next recourse is to get for himself one of the vaguely heroic current designations, crown it with an adjectival halo and project it into print:

a public image. Most people will accept him, even applaud him, in his self-designation. The only ones who will ever question his bona fides will be dyspeptic churls, fit only for treasons, spoils and stratagems, perhaps to boot connoisseurs of pornography and arcane seances — in short, losers.

No matter what designation of puissance the rich man permits his media of publicity to allot him, however, there remains the harsh fact that he is operating within an increasingly obsolete social structure, politically designed for an agricultural and local commercial economy and culturally for the most part of even more antedated vintage. This social structure, under the impact of high-powered technology, is obviously increasingly inadequate to its supportive task, requires much change and is insulated against change by the resistance of many established economic groups, perhaps including his own.

What to do? One palliative after the other is embraced, resulting in an increasingly cross-stress, tension-producing patchwork. Where will it all lead? What will happen to the rich man's special stake, constantly threatened by science-derived innovations and requirements for more and more government intervention?

Obeying the maxim "If you can't lick 'em, join 'em," most of the rich appear increasingly to have joined forces with government in developing the welfare-warfare state, largely utilizing tax money from the labor force and thereby guaranteeing themselves one big profitable customer. Yet even this maneuver introduces endless new difficulties, and there remains to be contended with the rest of the terrestrial world exploding into smoggy industrialism.

The state of mind of a fully aware wealthy man, then, cannot be as tranquil as commonly supposed. And that it is not at all tranquil is shown by the endless fulminations of the various communications media against communism, socialism, statism, totalitarianism, radicalism, fascism, technocracy, liberalism, crime in the streets (where it clearly should not be), do-goodism, reformism, softism, sentimentalism, apathy, unpatriotism, unconstitutionalism, centralization, bureaucracy and the like, and by the stream of contributions to super-patriotic Pied Pipers. All persons who think seriously in terms of adjustment to modern conditions then find they must be extremely circumspect so as not to be suspected as subversive and un-American, in the ideological company of foreigners. . . .

While it appears a bit early to assert that the days of the rich are numbered, as socialists like to believe, it does appear they are in for some stormy times and, perhaps, for eventual extinction at the hands of rising forces. The rich, in any event, are in a time of many troubles as their wealth increases, and I conclude that the more thoughtful among them cannot be feeling as complacent as the bland-bland exterior of their power elite may suggest.

For it is veritably written: "So foul a sky clears not without a storm."

Richard J. Barnet | # The Military-Industrial Complex

The Economy of Death defies logic. A piece of technology like the ABM is virtually discredited again and again by every former science adviser to the President, a number of Nobel Prize physicists, and several former high officials of the Defense Department itself. Yet the juggernaut moves on. If one rationale for building a new weapons system is exposed as nonsense, others spring up to take its place. The Secretary of State talks about détente and coexistence, and the Secretary of Defense demands the build-up of a first-strike force. The Pentagon demands billions to counter a nonexistent Chinese missile force while ghetto and campus rebellions, police riots, and political assassinations tear away at American society. Why?

The institutions which support the Economy of Death are impervious to ordinary logic or experience because they operate by their own inner logic. Each institutional component of the military-industrial complex has plausible reasons for continuing to exist and expand. Each promotes and protects its own interests and in so doing reinforces the interests of every other. That is what a "complex" is — a set of integrated institutions that act to maximize their collective power. In this essay we shall look at the various structures of the military-industrial complex to try to understand how and why the decisions are made to allocate our national resources to the Economy of Death.

The defenders of the military establishment like to characterize the growing attacks on the military-industrial complex as conspiracy-mongering. Senator Henry Jackson, one of the staunchest defenders of big military budgets, calls the recent inquiries into military mismanagement and waste the "largest version of the devil theory of history." The injured brass, accustomed to twenty years of nineteen-gun salutes from the public, now charge their critics with the ancient military crime of showing disrespect to officers. When George Mahon, Chairman of the House Appropriations Committee and long-time advocate of big defense budgets, was boorish enough to suggest that perhaps the Navy had been a bit careless to let a $50 million nuclear submarine sink in thirty-five feet of water, L. Mendel Rivers, the Pentagon's most generous friend in Congress, attacked him on the floor of the House for "playing into the hands of the enemies of the military." The enemies he was talking about were not the Russians, but members of the U.S. Senate.

Nothing suggests the existence of a conspiracy more strongly than concerted efforts like these to protect the military establishment from public inquiry and debate. But conspiracy is not the answer. The sad truth is that it is not even necessary. To understand the hold of the Economy of Death on the country, one needs to look at the behavior of institutions, not individuals. To be sure, there are more than a few cases of profiteering, personal enrichment, conflict of interest, and graft. Eisenhower's first Secretary of the Air Force, Harold Talbott, who continued to receive over $400,000 a year from his former company while in office, wrote letters to defense contractors on Air Force stationery suggesting they might like to throw some business to his old firm. The Senate Permanent Subcommittee on Investigations reported in 1964 that numerous companies "pyramided" profits in connection with the missile procurement program. Western Electric, for example, on a contract for "checking over launcher loaders," earned $955,396 on costs totaling $14,293, a respectable profit of 6600 percent. Kennedy's Deputy Secretary of Defense, Roswell Gilpatric, played a major role in awarding the dubious TFX contract to his old client General Dynamics. The postwar successors to the merchants of death, such as Litton, Itek, Thiokol, and LTV, have earned quick fame and fortune. The present Deputy Secretary of Defense, David Packard, for example, parlayed an electronics shop in a garage into a $300 million personal fortune primarily through defense contracts.

A faint odor of corruption pervades the whole military procurement system. (Some early examples can be found in the House Armed Services. Committee Report *Supplemental Hearing Released from Executive Session Relating to Entertainment Furnished by the Martin Company of Baltimore, Md. of U.S. Government Officers, September 10, 1959*.) An officer who deals with a defense plant often has access to a variety of personal rewards, including a future with the company. He is likely to eat well, and he need never sleep alone.

But corruption and personal wrongdoing explain very little. In a sense, the managers of the Economy of Death conspire all the time. Men from the services and the defense contractors are constantly putting their heads together to invent ways of spending money for the military. Indeed, that is their job. As John R. Moore, President of North American Rockwell Aerospace and Systems Group, the nation's ninth-ranking defense contractor, puts it, "A new system usually starts with a couple of industry and military people getting together to discuss common problems." Military officers and weapons-pushers from corporations are "interacting continuously at the engineering level," according to Moore. A former Assistant Secretary of Defense who has followed the well-trodden path from the Pentagon to a vice-presidency of one of the nation's top military contractors says military procurement is a "seamless web": "Pressures to spend more . . . come from the industry selling new weapons ideas . . . and in part from the military." The problem, then, is not that those who make up the military-industrial complex act improperly, but that they do exactly what the system expects of them. Corruption is not nearly so serious a problem as sincerity. Each part of the complex acts in accordance with its own goals and in so doing reinforces all the others. The result is a government whose central activity is planning and carrying out wars. If we look at the military-industrial complex and how it operates, it will become clear why it has such a firm hold on American life and why it cannot be controlled without major institutional changes.

The Uniformed Military

Let us start our map of the military-industrial complex with the uniformed military. What are their interests? What do they believe?

The modern specialist in violence does not glorify war. He believes that diplomacy is a polite façade behind which nations calculate their killing power, and that political success ultimately depends upon the effective use of a war machine. Most military men now believe that total war in the nuclear age is not an effective way to use military power. The health of the modern state is not war but preparation for war. The military ethic firmly rejects the idea that the arms race itself could provoke an enemy into war. "They'll fortify the moon if you let them," Churchill once said of the military during the Second World War. Only a few years later a U.S. Air Force general was counseling a Congressional committee on the need to carry the arms race beyond the moon to Venus.

Generals and admirals invariably believe that what is good for the Air Force or the Navy is good for America. A few days after becoming Secretary of the Navy, Paul Nitze discovered a "power vacuum" in the Indian Ocean and a new "requirement" for the fleet. At a Congressional hearing on the B-36, a proposed new bomber for the Air Force, Admiral Arthur Radford denounced nuclear deterrence as "morally reprehensible." It was not until the Navy invented the Polaris submarine-launched nuclear missile that the Admiral decided that the peace of the world depended upon the hydrogen bomb. Each service embellishes "the threat" to serve its bureaucratic interests. The Office of Naval Intelligence is especially good at finding extra Soviet ships which Air Force intelligence always manages to miss. There are tens of thousands of mysterious objects in the Soviet Union which the Army is convinced are tanks but which any Air Force intelligence officer knows are really airplanes.

Each military service has also worked out a view of the world that justifies its own self-proclaimed mission. For the Army, the job is to preserve a "balance of power" and to keep order around the world through counter-insurgency campaigns and limited wars. It should be no surprise that the Air Force view of the world is much more alarmist. "The Soviet leadership is irrevocably committed to the achievement of the ultimate Communist objective, which is annihilation of the capitalist system and establishment of Communist dictatorship over all nations of the world," wrote former SAC Commander General Thomas Powers. According to General Nathan Twining, former Chief of Staff of the Air Force, "the leaders of an organized conspiracy have sworn to destroy America." It is essential to have an enemy worthy of your own weapons and your own war plans. A strategy based on the nuclear annihilation of the Soviet Union is far easier to accept if that country is the embodiment of evil. To rationalize a nuclear arsenal of 11,000 megaton bombs, it is vital to assume that the leaders in the Kremlin are too depraved to be deterred by less. The anti-Communist reflex is the Air Force's biggest political asset.

The preventive-war enthusiasts, vocal as they are in retirement, do not represent the dominant view of the military. True, there was the Air Force general who once exclaimed, "Let's start killing people. People need to respect the United States, and when we start killing people, then there will be more respect for the United States." But most professional military managers prefer to keep preparing for the big war that never comes. There is strong military support in the twentieth century for the view that fighting spoils armies. The Air Force used to define "victory" in nuclear war as having more missiles left than the Russians. It was hard to fire enthusiasm, however, for a war in which the weapons survive and the people die. Even to Air Force officers a full-scale "nuclear exchange" looks like the ultimate disaster in career-planning as well as national policy. This could change, however, if the U.S. continues to build up a "first-strike force" structure. As the Vietnam war illustrates, the military are susceptible to the illusion of victory. The availability of power or even the *appearance* of power tempts men to use it. The following exchange between the Chairman of the Joint Chiefs of Staff and the counsel of a Congressional committee shows how strong are the military man's psychological defenses to the implications of what he proposes:

MR. KENDALL: Suppose the numbers of casualties . . . were doubled [to 160 million for the U.S., 200 million for the Soviets]. . . . Obviously, you would have no country left, neither of us.

MR. WHEELER: Mr. Kendall, I reject the "better Red than dead" theory — lock, stock, and barrel.

But limited war has seemed much more promising. As former Marine Commandant General David Shoup puts it, "War justifies the existence of the establishment, provides experience for the military novice and challenges for the senior officer. Wars and emergencies put the military and their leaders on the front pages and give status and prestige to the professionals." During the early days of the Vietnam war, officers often greeted each other in Pentagon corridors with a standard quip, "It's not much of a war, but it's the only one we've got." In the pre-World War II period the only justification for mobilizing a huge army was to fight a moral crusade against the Kaiser or Hitler. But the permanent mobilization of the postwar period can be rationalized only by a "world responsibility" to be the "Guardian at the Gates."

Military bureaucrats have led exciting but not inordinately dangerous lives acting out the policeman's role. During the biggest pre-Vietnam military operation, the Korean war, the mortality rate of officers holding insurance policies with a leading company was below the average for industry as a whole. The incidence of death in battle fell from 104.4 per 1000 soldiers in the Civil War to 5.5 in the Korean conflict. Despite the heavy casualties among enlisted men and junior officers in Vietnam, the nation has never fought a war in greater comfort or relative safety. The higher officers need not normally confront their own death or anyone else's as part of their professional duties. In the antiseptic world of the Pentagon, captivated by the electronic magic of briefing charts that light up in six colors, instant global communications networks, and the power of Hell at the touch of a button, the top managers of the new constabulary can feel important, safe, and dedicated to a higher cause. "The naval profession is much like the ministry," a Naval captain wrote his son fifty years ago. "You dedicate your life to a purpose . . . You renounce your pursuit of wealth . . . In the final analysis your aims and objects are quite as moral as any minister's because you are not seeking your own good but the ultimate good of your country."

It is not altogether surprising that the military put such a high value on "security" for the nation through the "insurance" of new weapons systems. Military officers have exerted considerable efforts to achieve these goals in their personal lives and careers. The American military establishment is a well-protected, heavily subsidized enclave in American society which offers its constituents the best of the welfare state, including pensions unmatched in industry, complete medical care, travel, consumer bargains, and a steady supply of underlings who must show proper respect under penalty of law. Adventure with low personal risk is an ideal career for a man or a nation.

A very important element of personal security is the belief that your life and your work matter. The profoundly pessimistic view of a world full of enemies which military men invariably share is fundamentally self-serving. Man is evil. Nations are predatory. Therefore the nation must be armed to the teeth. This is not to say that the military man merely pretends to believe his own gloomy vision. He is usually quite serious. What is more, he can find plenty of evidence to support it. Men in charge of nations do use violence to solve political problems and have done so since the beginning of history. That is enough to justify the soldier's role to himself and to society. But the military man never examines his most fundamental assumptions. Challenging an enemy to an arms race is supposed to make him less dangerous and more accommodating, but the evidence is overwhelmingly discouraging, especially in an era when you cannot defeat him without destroying yourself. The effect of the military ideology on foreign policy is disastrous because it excludes all hope of moving international politics out of the Stone Age. In a world where there is no alternative to peace, as General Eisenhower put it, the standard military ideology denies the possibility of peace. "I would hate to see us enter any agreement with anybody," Major General William M. Creasy, the Army's man in charge of stockpiling and thinking up uses for nerve gases and bacterial agents, told a House Committee.

"Do you favor disarmament?" the General was asked.

"Yes, sir. I would like Utopia, too. I just don't believe it is practicable."

Although the armed services of the United States have developed increasingly sophisticated rationalizations for ever more military force, they have not improved on the succinct statement of the German High Command in 1938:

> Despite all attempts to outlaw it, war is still a law of nature which may be challenged but not eliminated. It serves the survival of the race and state or the assurance of its historical future. This high moral purpose gives war its total character and its ethical justification.

The Rise of the Military Establishment

How did the military establishment come to acquire such power in a nation which had a political tradition of condemning large standing armies and in 1938 ranked eighteenth among the nations of the world in land forces? What General Shoup calls the "new militarism" is an outgrowth of the Second World War. The federal government come to play a major managerial role in the economy and to help create and to dispose of a significant share of the national wealth. Within the federal bureaucracy the balance of power shifted decisively to those agencies which handled military power. In 1939 the federal government had about 800,000 civilian employees, about 10 percent of whom worked for national-security agencies. At the end of the war the figure approached 4 million, of whom more than 75 percent were in military-related activities.

Not only did the war radically shift the balance of power in the federal bureaucracy, catapulting the military establishment from a marginal institution without a constituency to a position of command over the resources of a whole society; it also redefined the traditional tasks of the military. The traditional semantic barriers between "political" and "military" functions were eroded; in the development and execution of strategy, the military were deep in politics. The major decisions of the war, those with the greatest obvious political impact, were made by the President, the Joint Chiefs of Staff, and Harry Hopkins. The Joint Chiefs prepared for diplomatic conferences, negotiated with the Allies. In the war theaters the military commanders, Eisenhower and MacArthur, were supreme. Each obtained the power to pass on all civilians sent to his theater and to censor their dispatches. "Through these controls of overseas communications," the military commentator Walter Millis observed, "JCS was in a position to be informed, forewarned, and therefore forearmed, to a degree no civilian agency could match."

At a time when Stalingrad was still under siege and it would have taken a lively imagination to conjure up a Soviet threat of world domination, United States military planners had already begun planning a huge postwar military machine. As the war ended, the Army demanded a ground force capable of expanding to 4.5 million men within a year. The Navy thought it wanted to keep 600,000 men, 371 major combat ships, 5000 auxiliaries, and a "little air force" of 8000 planes. The Air Force also had specific plans. It wanted to be a separate service and to have a seventy-group force with 400,000 men. With these plans the top military officers made it clear that they were through being fire-fighters called in when the diplomats had failed.

Under the pressure of war, new military instruments for manipulating the politics of other countries had been developed. Those who had put them together argued that the United States would need them in the post-war world, whatever the political environment. Thus the Joint Chiefs of Staff argued successfully for retaining most of the network of bases acquired in the war. The thinking of General William Donovan, the creator of OSS, America's first spy agency, shows the indestructibility of bureaucracies. His assistant Robert H. Alcorn has described his views:

> With the vision that had characterized his development of OSS, General Donovan had, before leaving the organization, made provision for the future of espionage in our country's way of life. Through both government and private means he had indicated the need for a long-range, built-in espionage network. He saw the postwar years as periods of confusion and readjustment affording the perfect opportunity to establish such networks. We were everywhere already, he argued, and it was only wisdom and good policy to dig in, quietly and efficiently, for the long pull. Overseas branches of large corporations, the expanding business picture, the rebuilding of war areas, Government programs for economic, social and health aid to foreign lands, all these were made to order for the infiltration of espionage agents.

A nation that for almost four years had performed stunning managerial feats in moving armies across seas, in producing clouds of airplanes, in training destructive power on an enemy with marvelous efficiency, and, finally, in extracting the abject surrender of two of the leading industrial nations of the world without having enemy soldiers or bombs on its soil or its wealth impaired, was ready to put its confidence in force as the primary instrument of politics. Americans, who had often felt swindled in the dreary game of diplomacy, looked in awe at the immense changes they had wrought in the world with their military power.

To maintain and extend their power in the postwar period, the military have been able to draw on a varied and effective arsenal. The most important weapon has been organization. As we have seen, the military bureaucracies came out of the war with their structures intact. Despite the rapid demobilization of millions of men and the sharp reduction of the defense budget from more than $80 billion to $11.7 billion in the first three postwar years, the institutional relationships of the Economy of Death created in the war were preserved and expanded. In this process the military establishment exploited two other weapons to the fullest: secrecy and fear.

In a bureaucracy knowledge is power. The military establishment has made particularly effective use of its jealously guarded monopoly of information on national-security matters. It has defined the threats, chosen the means to counteract them, and evaluated its own performance. Critics have been disarmed by the classification system and the standard official defense of policy, "If you only knew what I know." Academic consultants who have made their living advising the Department of Defense and writing about national-security affairs have protected their security clearances by discreetly accepting the Pentagon's assumptions. Except for a handful of Quakers, radicals, independent scientists, and incorrigible sceptics, no one during the 1940's and 1950's challenged the growing power of the military. The fact that the Pentagon was assuming a central position in American life was obvious. But the justification seemed equally obvious, and the danger was ignored.

Because of its exclusive hold on top-secret truth, the Pentagon was in a position to scare the public into supporting whatever programs the Administration put forward. The Department of Defense became a Ministry of Fear issuing regular warnings about a highly exaggerated threat of a Soviet attack in Europe and a nuclear strike against the United States long before the Soviets had the means to carry it out. Joseph R. McCarthy was a helpful ally in creating a climate of fear until he turned against the Army in a last suicidal gesture. But McCarthyism preceded McCarthy. Alger Hiss, the old China hands, the Poland losers, the Czechoslovakia losers, and other "vendors of compromise" in the State Department, as Senator John F. Kennedy would later call them, became tabloid celebrities long before Senator McCarthy advertised his "list" of 205 known Communists in the State Department. In this atmosphere anyone who dared to suggest that the country was spending too much money on defense was obviously either a traitor with a plan to leave the country "naked to attack" or a coward who preferred to be red rather than dead.

Military officers constantly held up to the public the specters of Hitler and Pearl Harbor. The only security in a dangerous and irrational world was to run it. On his office wall the first Secretary of Defense, James Forrestal, hung a framed card on which was printed the official lesson of World War II: "We will never have peace until the strongest army and the strongest navy are in the hands of the world's most powerful nation." It was now America's turn to be Number One in the world and to play out the historical role of earlier empires. It did not matter that the age of empire was over or that the age of nuclear weapons had come. In military bureaucracies it is standard procedure to pursue the most promising strategy for preventing the last war. . . .

The Militarized Civilians

"The country is looking for a scapegoat. First it was the draft, then recruiters, then Dow Chemical, and now it's the bloody generals," Major General Melvin Zais, Commander of the 101st Airborne Division in Vietnam, complained to an interviewer from *Time*. Many military officers view the belated but growing concern in Congress over uncontrolled military expenditure as an attack on the uniform. In a sense, it is. When General William Westmoreland appeared in full regalia before Congress to make claims about the Vietnam war which no one with a working television set could believe, the credibility gap assumed cavernous proportions. For the first time in a generation, the leaders of the military establishment have been challenged to produce facts and rational arguments to justify their claim to the biggest bite of the tax dollar. Credentials alone are no longer enough. Neither, one hopes, are the traditional national-security slogans about the Soviet Threat or the Chinese Threat, no matter how blood-curdling the rhetoric. Foolishness and waste in the Pentagon, the inevitable by-products of any institution with too much money to spend, are finally under attack. A patriotic American can only hope the attack will grow.

Nevertheless, the uniformed military are not the primary target of a serious political effort to shift from the Economy of Death to the Economy of Life. The principal militarists in America wear three-button suits. They are civilians in everything but outlook. Not the generals but the National Security Managers — the politicians, businessmen, and civil servants who rotate through the paneled offices of the Pentagon, the State Department, the Central Intelligence Agency, the Atomic Energy Commission, and the White House — have been in charge of national-security policy.

In the postwar years there have been, to be sure, some challenges to the traditional American principle of civilian control of the military. General MacArthur denounced as a "dangerous concept" the idea that members of the armed forces owe primary allegiance and loyalty "to those who temporarily exercise the authority of the executive branch of government." The President may be the Commander-in-Chief under the Constitution, but it is "the country," the General asserted, which the soldier must swear to serve. Yet President Truman was able to secure the unanimous assistance of the Joint Chiefs of Staff in removing MacArthur for insubordination in the conduct of the Korean war, and as the old soldier faded away, he became an advocate of nuclear disarmament. In the late Eisenhower years, according to Professor Samuel Huntington's studies, the Secretary of Defense rejected only four out of 2954 unanimous recommendations of the Joint Chiefs, yet many prominent generals resigned publicly in protest against Ike's budget-cutting. The top brass reluctantly went along with Robert McNamara's decisions to cut back on certain weapons systems favored by the Air Force, but they sniped at him in the press and, particularly in his final year at the Pentagon, grew bold in public criticism of the Secretary before the Armed Services Committees. Generals on active duty supplied information to right-wing groups like the American Security Council to assist them in their concerted campaign to discredit the Secretary. As Richard Goodwin, Special Assistant to Presidents Kennedy and Johnson, has pointed out, McNamara took office "with the avowed aim of establishing greater civilian control" over the military:

> Yet, the harsh fact of the matter is that when he left, the military had greater influence over American policy than at any time in our peacetime history. In the name of efficiency we unified many of the operations of the armed services, encouraged greater intimacy between the military and industry, and instituted the deceptive techniques of modern computer management, realistic or hard-headed, to solve problems and invest money and use power unguided by ultimate aims and values. . . . You can ask a computer whether you have the military capacity to accomplish an objective. It will answer either "yes" or "no." It will never say, "Yes, but it is not a good idea."

By the end of the Johnson Administration, the uniformed military had acquired considerable independent political power. They had powerful friends in Congress. Reserve commissions were held by 139 members, and several of these were generals. The Joint Chiefs had their terms of office extended from two to four years, which meant that a new President had to fire the nation's top military if he wanted to appoint his own men. A retired general ran for the Senate in New Hampshire, and General Curtis LeMay campaigned as George Wallace's running mate in the Presidential race of 1968. Both argued that the civilian leaders in the Pentagon were selling out the country. These were straws in the wind signifying the increasing frustration and anger of the military against civilian authorities who ordered them into war but would not let them win it. But the public was unimpressed. No man on horseback has yet emerged who appears able to challenge the civilian leadership in an election, and the supply of marketable war heroes is dwindling.

President Kennedy once confided to a close friend whom he had appointed Under Secretary of the Navy that a military coup along the lines of the one described in the popular novel *Seven Days in May* could happen in his Administration if, for example, the Bay of Pigs fiasco were ever repeated. Despite the frequency of military coups in the modern world, a seizure of government by the military in the United States still seems remote. But surrounding the White House with tanks is only one way to militarize the country. The Joint Chiefs of Staff possess sufficient power today so that the President of the United States cannot simply order them. He must negotiate with them. For example, as Elizabeth Drew of the

Atlantic has revealed, the Joint Chiefs of Staff exacted a price from President Johnson for their agreement to support the cessation of bombing over North Vietnam. They insisted upon taking the bombs they had counted on dropping on the North and dumping them on the South and Laos. There is a deep fear pervading the civilian leadership that the military, if sufficiently provoked, might pit their professional credentials against the "politicians" in a public confrontation.

Thus civilian control of the military has been maintained throughout the long years of the Cold War, but the price has been the militarization of the civilian leadership. Generals and admirals continue to take orders from the President as Commander-in-Chief, but the President spends about 90 percent of his time building and, to use the State Department term, "projecting" America's military power. Increasingly, the civilian managers have come to see the world through military eyes. They plan for "greater than expected threats." They avoid arms-control agreements that could "degrade" our military forces. They think a new "option" and a new airplane are the same thing. They seek "prestige" through intimidation of the weak.

It was a preacher's son from Wall Street, John Foster Dulles, who as Secretary of State spent most of his time building military alliances with more than forty nations. It was an economics professor from M.I.T., Walt Rostow, who made the earliest and most vigorous case for solving the problem of South Vietnam by bombing North Vietnam. It was an investment banker, James Forrestal, who designed the National Security Council without machinery to balance military requirements and domestic needs. It was a Washington lawyer, Dean Acheson, who thought that negotiating the Berlin crisis of 1961 instead of staging a military confrontation with a high risk of nuclear war was "weakness." It was a Massachusetts politican, John F. Kennedy, who was prepared to risk a minimum of 150 million lives to face down Khrushchev in the Cuban missile crisis of 1962. The instinctive approach to international conflict has been to reach for a gun.

Indeed, there is considerable evidence that the civilian managers, particularly at the beginning of the postwar period, have been far readier than the military to commit American forces to actual combat. Apprenticed to the military in World War II, the top civilian national-security elite absorbed the basic military outlook but not the soldier's professional caution. Perhaps because they lacked combat experience, they underestimated the difficulties and risks in using military power. In 1946 the Joint Chiefs of Staff cooled the State Department's enthusiasm for sending an ultimatum to Yugoslavia for shooting down an American plane. In the earliest days of the Cold War it was the State Department that kept urging a big military build-up to furnish "support for our political position," while the Defense Department set more modest goals for itself. Secretary of State Dean Acheson, not the Joint Chiefs of Staff, made the first recommendations to commit U.S. military forces to repel the Korean invasion. General

Matthew Ridgway, Chief of Staff of the Army, opposed John Foster Dulles' proposal to intervene militarily in Indo-China in 1954. The Joint Chiefs opposed Walt Rostow's plan to invade Laos in 1961. The military did not recommend commitment of forces either to aid the Hungarian revolution or to tear down the Berlin Wall. When David Lilienthal, the civilian chairman of the Atomic Energy Commission, asked the Joint Chiefs of Staff in 1949 what uses they would have for a hydrogen bomb, they couldn't think of one. The civilians directed the military to think harder.

The militarized civilians have surpassed the military themselves in embracing a "realism" which envisages no alternative to an escalating arms race but annihilation, perpetuates an aimless war by calling it a commitment, and measures the nation's greatness in megatons. Far more responsive to the bureaucratic interests of the services than to the wider political interests of the American people, they believe that America's principal role in the world is to acquire more power. Indeed, they see the accumulation of power as an end in itself. Thus it is they, rather than the uniformed military, who must assume responsibility for the distortion of national priorities. The armed services always want a more perfect fighting machine, but the civilian leadership does not have to give it to them. The military traditionally look upon the population as a mobilization base for the armed forces, forgetting that the army exists to serve the people and not the other way around. But the civilians at the top need not share that view.

Yet this is precisely what has happened. Civilian strategists and diplomats have developed a strategy that has made the American people instruments of political warfare. President Kennedy in 1962 was ready to risk the nuclear destruction of American society rather than negotiate with the Soviets about removing missiles no closer to our country than the U.S. missiles in Turkey were to theirs. To have bargained instead of threatened would have cost little. Indeed the decision to remove the Turkish missiles had been made months before the confrontation. "Your Daddy may have started World War III," Lyndon Johnson told his daughter on the day he accepted the advice of Dean Rusk, McGeorge Bundy, Walt Rostow, and Robert McNamara, and risked war with the Soviet Union and China by bombing their ally, North Vietnam. The side willing to take the greater risks with the lives of its own people wins this global version of the game of "chicken."

The temptation to try to solve political problems through violence is almost irresistible for the political leaders of a great power because the risk of retaliation seems low and the military man's "solutions" offer the illusion of toughness, practicality, and certitude. Factors which can be fed into computers such as "kill ratios" sound more persuasive than political analysis, which is hard to prepare and hard to comprehend. To understand the true interests of the American people in a remote area of the world, a diplomat must not only try to understand who the Vietnamese are and what they want, but must continually try to rediscover America's own interests. It is much easier to avoid both processes by treating the outside world as a collection of statistics, nuisances, and threats, ignoring domestic needs and treating international politics as gambling in a good cause. Arthur Schlesinger, Jr.'s account of the deliberations preceding the Bay of Pigs illustrates the point:

> The advocates of the adventure had a rhetorical advantage. They could strike virile poses and talk of tangible things — fire power, air strikes, landing craft, and so on. To oppose the plan, one had to invoke intangibles — the moral position of the United States, the reputation of the President, the response of the United Nations, "world public opinion" and other such odious concepts. These matters were as much the institutional concern of the State Department as military hardware was of Defense. . . . I could not help feeling that the desire to prove to the CIA and the Joint Chiefs that they were not soft-headed idealists but were really tough guys too influenced State's representatives at the Cabinet table.

Whatever the human dynamics that may explain it, the consequences of deferring to the military outlook have been disastrous. In recent years, under the tutelage of their civilian superiors, the military have managed to lose most of their earlier reticence. In 1962 the Joint Chiefs of Staff favored immediate bombing and invasion of Cuba. In Vietnam they have authorized the annihilation of population centers and urged the bombing of dikes and flooding as a strategy for winning the war. The abdication by the civilian leadership of their responsibility to find political rather than military solutions to the problems of twentieth-century man has encouraged the men in uniform to play an increasingly important and hawkish role in national policy.

The National Security Managers and the National Interest

Who are the key civilian foreign-policy decision-makers? How does one get to be a National Security Manager? Why do they think as they do? The questions are important, for the interests and beliefs which these men bring to their high office decide for the rest of us what the national interest is. "Foreign policies are not built on abstractions. They are the result of practical conceptions of national interest," Charles Evans Hughes noted when he was Secretary of State. The key word is *practical*. One man's Utopia is another man's Hell. Like the flag, the national interest can mean many different things to different people. In times past, those who managed the affairs of a great nation invariably defined the national interest in terms of power and glory. Whatever accrued to the majesty of the state was in its interest. It did not matter how much the people had to be taxed to pay for it or how many had to die. Anything that authorities decided was necessary to the health of the state was, by definition, in the national interest. President Johnson invoked the national interest to justify sending 600,000 troops to Vietnam and keeping them there despite the disastrous domestic consequences. In postwar America there has been a twenty-five-year consensus on the national interest. There is money for weapons, but not for people. Social decay must be accepted as the price of power. Security is to be achieved by preparing for the worst in meeting foreign threats and assuming that the crisis of our own society will take care of itself.

Who has decided that this is what the national interest is all about?

Since 1940 about 400 individuals have held the top civilian national-security positions. These men have defined the threats for the nation, made the commitments that were supposed to meet these threats, and determined the size of the armed forces. They have been above electoral politics. With few exceptions, the men who have designed the bipartisan foreign policy have never held elective office. Their skills have not been those of the politician, who must at least give the appearance of solving problems or reconciling competing interests if he hopes to get re-elected, but those of the crisis-manager. Dean Rusk characterized his personal goal in office as Secretary of State as handing the Berlin crisis over to his successor in no worse shape than he found it. This is the managerial or "keep the balls bouncing" view of statecraft characteristic of those who count on being somewhere else when the ball drops.

If we take a look at the men who have held the very top positions, the Secretaries and Under Secretaries of State and Defense, the Secretaries of the three services, the Chairman of the Atomic Energy Commission, and the Director of the CIA, we find that out of ninety-one individuals who held these offices during the period 1940–1967, seventy of them were from the ranks of big business or high finance, including eight out of ten Secretaries of Defense, seven out of eight Secretaries of the Air Force, every Secretary of the Navy, eight out of nine Secretaries of the Army, every Deputy Secretary of Defense, three out of five Directors of the CIA, and three out of five Chairmen of the Atomic Energy Commission.

The historian Gabriel Kolko investigated 234 top foreign-policy decision-makers and found that "men who came from big business, investment and law held 59.6 percent of the posts." The Brookings Institution volume *Men Who Govern*, a comprehensive study of the top federal bureaucracy from 1933 to 1965, reveals that before coming to work in the Pentagon, 86 percent of the Secretaries of the Army, Navy, and Air Force were either businessmen or lawyers (usually with a business practice). In the Kennedy Administration 20 percent of all civilian executives in defense-related agencies came from defense contractors. Defining the national interest and protecting national security are the proper province of business. Indeed, as President Coolidge used to say, the business of America is business.

In *Democracy in America*, Alexis de Tocqueville worried that the United States might not be successful in its foreign relations because "foreign politics demand scarcely any of those qualities which a democracy possesses; and they require on the contrary the perfect use of almost all those faculties in which it is deficient." He said that an aristocracy was better for running foreign policy because a government of the few could keep secrets, was invulnerable to the passions of the mob, and knew how to exercise great patience. Tocqueville would be greatly reassured by the way the conduct of foreign policy has evolved in America, for the National Security Managers exercise the power to make life-and-death decisions with very little interference from the rest of us.

They also constitute a social elite. At least a quarter of them are members of Washington's Metropolitan Club, a fair imitation of a London gentlemen's club. William Domhoff has noted that since 1944 five out of the seven Secretaries of State were listed in the *Social Register*. So also were many of the key figures in the War and Defense Departments, including Henry Stimson, Robert Patterson, John McCloy, Robert Lovett, James V. Forrestal, Thomas Gates, and Neil McElroy. The CIA, which is an outgrowth of the wartime OSS, has also put considerable emphasis on "background." (Unkind critics of OSS used to say the initials stood for "Oh So Social," so pervasive was the old-school-tie character of America's first spy agency.) The OSS roster included the most famous upper-class names in the country, including Paul Mellon, David Bruce, Albert DuPont, Junius S. Morgan, Lester Armour, and Lloyd Cabot Briggs. In more recent years Allen Dulles, William Bundy, Robert Amory, and John McCone have continued the tradition of bringing good breeding to the practice of espionage.

The collection of investment bankers and legal advisers to big business who designed the national-security bureaucracies and helped to run them for a generation came to Washington in 1940. Dr. New Deal was dead, President Roosevelt announced, and Dr. Win-the-War had come to take his place. Two men — Henry L. Stimson, Hoover's Secretary of State and a leading member of the Wall Street bar, and James V. Forrestal, president of Dillon Read Co., one of the biggest investment bankers — were responsible for recruiting many of their old friends and associates to run the war. In the formative postwar years of the Truman Administration, when the essential elements of U.S. foreign and military policy were laid down, these recruits continued to act as the nation's top National Security Managers. Dean Acheson, James V. Forrestal, Robert Lovett, John McCloy, Averell Harriman, all of whom had become acquainted with foreign policy through running a war, played the crucial roles in deciding how to use America's power in peace.

Once again it was quite natural to look to their own associates, each an American success story, to carry on with the management of the nation's military power. Thus, for example, Forrestal's firm, Dillon Read, contributed Paul Nitze, who headed the State Department Policy Planning Staff in the Truman Administration and ran the Defense Department as deputy to Clark Clifford in the closing year of the Johnson Administration. William Draper, an architect of U.S. postwar policy toward Germany and Japan, came from the same firm. In the Truman years twenty-two key posts in the State Department, ten in the Defense Department, and five key national-security positions in other agencies were held by bankers who were either Republicans or without party affiliation. As Professor Samuel Huntington has pointed out in his study *The Soldier and the State*, "they possessed all the inherent and real conservatism of the banking breed." Having built their business careers on their judicious management of risk, they now became expert in the management of crisis. Their interests lay in making the system function smoothly — conserving and expanding America's power. They were neither innovators nor problem-solvers. Convinced from their encounter with Hitler that force is the only thing that pays off in international relations, they all operated on the assumption that the endless stockpiling of weapons was the price of safety.

The Eisenhower Administration tended to recruit its National Security Managers from the top manufacturing corporations rather than from the investment banking houses. To be sure, bankers were not exactly unwelcome in the Eisenhower years. Robert Cutler, twice the President's Special Assistant for National Security Affairs, was chairman of the board of the Old Colony Trust Company in Boston; Joseph Dodge, the influential director of the Bureau of the Budget, was a Detroit banker; Douglas Dillon, of Dillon Read, was Under Secretary of State for Economic Affairs; Thomas Gates, the last Eisenhower Secretary of Defense, was a Philadelphia banker and subsequently head of the Morgan Guaranty Trust Company.

But most of the principal figures of the era were associated with the leading industrial corporations, either as chief executives or directors; many of these corporations ranked among the top 100 defense contractors. Eisenhower's first Secretary of Defense was Charles Wilson, president of General Motors; his second was Neil McElroy, a public-relations specialist who became president of Procter and Gamble. One Deputy Secretary of Defense was Robert B. Anderson, a Texas oilman. Another was Roger Kyes, another General Motors executive, and a third was Donald Quarles of Westinghouse.

In the Eisenhower Administration two fundamentally different views of defense spending and national security clashed. The advocates of each were National Security Managers with business backgrounds. Nelson Rockefeller, who had invested in such defense companies as Itek, McDonnell Aircraft, and Thiokol, was also a leading advocate of bigger military budgets. In the mid-1950's he and his brothers commissioned a report on *International Security — The Military Aspect*, drafted by Henry A. Kissinger, at present President Nixon's Special Assistant for National Security Affairs. The report called for a steady rise of $3 billion a year in the defense budget, and a follow-up report stated that the country should be prepared to spend $70 billion a year by 1970. (These recommendations, though slightly on the low side, turned out to be remarkably accurate projections.) At about the same time the Gaither Report, chaired jointly by H. Rowland Gaither, the man who was instrumental in setting up the Rand Corporation, the Air Force "think tank," and Robert C. Sprague, head of a Massachusetts military-electronics firm, called for "substantially increased expenditures" for national security including a $22 billion fallout-shelter program. Robert Lovett and John J. McCloy appeared before a meeting of the National Security Council on November 7, 1957, to assure the President that the financial community would support the steep increase in defense costs.

But Secretary of the Treasury George Humphrey, arguing that the Soviet strategy was to "make us spend ourselves into bankruptcy," refused to go along with the Gaither Committee recommendations. "You know how much money you're asking for?" the Secretary asked the staff director of the Gaither Committee. Pointing to the Washington Monument, which was clearly visible from his window, Humphrey estimated that if the amount of money requested were paid in $1000 bills, the pile would reach up to the top of the monument and fifty-six feet beyond. "As long as I'm here, you're not getting one of those bills." President Eisenhower went along with the fiscal conservatives and kept the budget below what Rockefeller and the defense contractors wanted, thus exposing his Administration to the "missile gap" charges of the 1960 campaign. In 1962 the former President publicly declared that "the defense budget should be substantially reduced."

The most influential of the National Security Managers were able to set the tone of national policy for a generation by combining perseverance and longevity. In 1938 Adolph Berle ran Latin American policy for F.D.R. In 1961 he designed the Alliance for Progress for J.F.K. In 1940 Dean Acheson was drafted into service to prepare the legal justification for giving Britain some old destroyers. In 1968 he was still a close (and hawkish) adviser to the White House. In 1941 Robert Lovett was Assistant Secretary of War in charge of the Air Corps. In the Truman Administration he served as Number Two in the State Department and the Defense Department. In 1961 President Kennedy offered him his choice of the three top Cabinet posts. He turned them all down, but left his enduring mark on American history by recommending his old assistant Dean Rusk. Rusk's service in the State Department spanned the Truman, Kennedy, and Johnson years. Paul Nitze, Averell Harriman, and Clark Clifford all occupied influential positions at the beginning of the Truman Administration and at the end of the Johnson Administration twenty-two years later.

When President Kennedy was elected on his campaign promise to "get the country moving again," the first thing he did was to reach back eight years for advice on national security. Many of the men he appointed as top National Security Managers of the New Frontier were the old faces of the Truman Administration. In addition to Dean Rusk, a strong MacArthur supporter in the Korean war who wrote the memorandum urging that U.N. forces cross the 38th Parallel in Korea, Kennedy's State Department appointments also included George McGhee, a successful oil prospector and principal architect of Truman's Middle East policy. Adolph Berle,

Averell Harriman, Paul Nitze, John McCone, John McCloy, William C. Foster, and other experienced hands from the national-security world also made it clear that the new Administration would follow familiar patterns.

However, the Kennedy Administration brought in some new faces, too. McGeorge Bundy, the Dean of the Faculty of Arts and Sciences at Harvard when Kennedy was an overseer, impressed the new President with his crisp, concise, and conventional analysis. The son of Henry Stimson's close wartime assistant, the Boston trust lawyer Harvey H. Bundy, McGeorge was a publicist who had put the Stimson papers in order and published a highly laudatory edition of Acheson's speeches while the Secretary (the father-in-law of Bundy's brother William) was under attack in the Congress. The teacher of a highly popular undergraduate course on power and international relations, Bundy appeared to have all the necessary qualifications to be the Special Assistant for National Security Affairs. Walt Rostow, the energetic M.I.T. professor who, in his own words, had not spent a year outside of the government since 1946, was promoted to a level appropriate to a man who had just published a book totally demolishing Marx. He was made Bundy's assistant.

Into the Defense Department also came a contingent of systems analysts and nuclear strategists from the Rand Corporation. These were not exactly new faces either. During the Eisenhower years they had been in and out of Washington, prodding the military services into more innovative thinking, which usually meant buying new hardware. Now they became the bosses of the men they had been advising. Charles Hitch, the Rand economist who had written a book on cost effectiveness in defense spending, was invited to put his program-packaging notions into effect as comptroller of the Defense Department. With Hitch came Alain Enthoven, Harry Rowan, and other Rand alumni, who became known as the "whiz kids."

However, the principal positions, with the exception of Bundy's, were filled according to the old patterns. Robert McNamara was president of Ford instead of General Motors; Roswell Gilpatric, appointed Deputy Secretary of Defense, was a partner of a leading Wall Street firm. In career experience he differed from his immediate Republican predecessor, James Douglas, in three principal respects. His law office was in New York rather than Chicago. He had been Under Secretary of the Air Force, while Douglas had been Secretary. He was a director of Eastern Airlines instead of American Airlines.

The Johnson Administration continued most of the Kennedy national-security appointments. Perhaps because of his generally bad relations with the academic community, Johnson appointed more professors to be National Security Managers than any of his predecessors. Lincoln Gordon and Covey Oliver, from the Harvard Business School and the University of Pennsylvania Law School, respectively, were made Assistant Secretaries of State in charge of Latin America. Although neither was a neophyte in government service and Gordon had a long history of business connections in Latin America, their appointments were departures from the Roosevelt and Truman practice of appointing the largest American investors in Latin America, notably Nelson Rockefeller and Spruille Braden, to oversee U.S. policy there.

The Nixon Administration brought in a veteran academic foreign-policy analyst, two business lawyers, one of the leading defenders of the military in the House, and one of California's most successful defense contractors to decide the national interest. Henry Kissinger, the academic, had made his reputation by advocating the judicious use of so-called "tactical" nuclear weapons on the battlefield. He then enhanced it by retracting his inherently mad proposal, thus demonstrating flexibility. The business lawyers, William Rogers and Elliot Richardson, had had no previous national-security or foreign-policy experience, which was no doubt an advantage. (Richardson's immediate prior experience had been in Massachusetts politics.) The Congressman, Melvin Laird, had an uncanny faculty for seeing all sorts of gaps in America's "security posture" and had written a book recommending that the U.S. launch a nuclear strike against the Soviet Union if "the communist empire further moves to threaten the peace."

The National Security Managers, like the uniformed military, have looked at the world through very special lenses, and the result has been a remarkable consensus. The policy toward NATO and German rearmament laid down by Dean Acheson in the late 1940's, the policy toward Vietnam laid down by John Foster Dulles in the early 1950's, and the policy of rearmament and nuclear strategy developed by the Truman Administration continue to this day without having been subjected to serious re-examination in five Presidencies. Most of the men who have set the framework of America's national-security policy, as I found when I studied the background of the top 400 decision-makers, have come from executive suites and law offices within shouting distance of one another in fifteen city blocks in New York, Washington, Detroit, Chicago, and Boston. It is not surprising that they emerge from homogeneous backgrounds and virtually identical careers with a standard way of looking at the world. They may argue with one another about means but not about ends. It has apparently never occurred to one of them to question seriously the basic assumptions of national-security policy.

The years of American supremacy have meant wealth, fame, comfort, excitement, and a sense of accomplishment for those who have operated at the top of the society. It is hardly surprising that those who have prospered equate the national interest and the status quo. When the term is stripped of geopolitical metaphor and ideological gloss, national security means nothing more complicated than making sure that the American Way of Life continues undisturbed by foreign challengers. But the American Way of Life means very different things to different people. To a Mississippi tenant farmer trying to keep out of his white neighbor's way and to eke out a subsistence living, the American Way of Life leaves something to be desired.

Scaring the Russians or the Chinese with an extra supply of missiles is not a first-priority concern. By the same token, it is difficult to see how the real security interests of a family battling rats in the ghetto or of a suburban housewife too fearful to venture out on the city streets connect with the measures that the National Security Managers are taking in their behalf.

Talleyrand once said that France had her conquests and Napoleon had his. In America the suggestion that the views of her leaders are colored by personal or class interests is generally dismissed as character-assassination or Marxism or both. Men who run for office seek "power," but the watch-words of the National Security Managers are "service" and "responsibility." It is easy to debunk the rhetoric of the National Security Managers, who have managed to concentrate greater power of life and death in their hands than Genghis Khan and to increase their fortunes at the same time. But to do so is to miss an important point. The patrician warriors are not cynics but complacent idealists who believe that America can ultimately enrich the world as she enriches them and their friends.

The National Security Manager is likely to be among the most shrewd, most energetic, and often most engaging men in America, but he has little feel for what is happening or should happen in this country. When Charles Wilson, the former president of General Motors who became Eisenhower's Secretary of Defense, blurted out his delightful aphorism, "What is good for the country is good for General Motors and vice-versa," he was merely restating the basic national-security premise. Using national power, including military force if necessary, to create a "good business climate" at home and abroad is more important than a good social climate in lower-class or middle-class America. An excited stock market rather than the depletion rate of the nation's human and natural resources is the index of America's progress. The National Security Manager sees his country from a rather special angle because, despite the thousands of miles he has logged, he is something of an émigré in his own society. The familiar itinerary takes him from one air-conditioned room to another across the continent — his office on Wall Street or LaSalle Street, his temporary office at the Pentagon or in the White House basement, a visit to a London or a Texas client, a dinner at the Council on Foreign Relations, and so forth. The closest he ever comes to seeing a hungry American is when his dinner companion is treated to bad service at one of Manhattan's declining French restaurants.

Under the stimulus of defense spending, the American economy has boomed, but its benefits have not been equitably shared. The disparity between rich and poor in America has widened. The National Security Managers have not regarded the redistribution of wealth as a priority concern, for they have had neither the experience nor the incentive to understand the problems of the poor. Their professional and personal interests are with the business and commercial interests which they serve and with which they identify. For a National Security Manager recruited from the world of business, there are no other important constituencies to which he feels a need to respond.

When planning a decision on defense policy, he does not solicit the views of civil-rights leaders, farmers, laborers, mayors, artists, or small businessmen. Nor do people from these areas of national life become National Security Managers. Indeed, when Martin Luther King expressed opposition to the Vietnam war, he was told that it was "inappropriate" for someone in the civil-rights movement to voice his views on foreign policy. The opinions which the National Security Manager values are those of his friends and colleagues. They have power, which is often an acceptable substitute for judgment, and since they view the world much as he does, they must be right. They are also the men with whom he will most likely have to deal when he lays down the burdens of office. "What will my friends on Wall Street say?" the Director of the Arms Control and Disarmament Agency once exclaimed when asked to endorse a disarmament proposal that would limit the future production of missiles.

The idea that spending one's life in the securities market is an essential qualification for dealing in national security is a confusion. There is no reason why the National Security Managers should not represent diverse interests, backgrounds, and ways of looking at the national interest. It is almost unbelievable that of the 400 top decision-makers who have assumed the responsibility for the survival of the species, only one has been a woman.

| *Ralph Salerno and* | Crime as a Business |
| *John S. Tompkins* | |

"We're bigger than U. S. Steel."

MEYER LANSKY

Mr. Lansky was being modest. In 1967, the United States Steel Corporation had assets of $5,600,000,000 and sales of $4,000,000,000 on which its profits after taxes were $172,500,000. Unless Lansky was talking only about his own activities, he understated the actuality. On the most conservative basis, the Confederation's gross from illegal activities alone is $40,000,000,000 a year, or ten times as much as U. S. Steel. And net profits, of course, are proportionally much much higher because the Syndicate

SOURCE: *The Crime Confederation* by Ralph Salerno and John S. Tompkins. Copyright © 1969 by Ralph Salerno and John S. Tompkins. Reprinted by permission of Doubleday & Company, Inc.

groups do not pay taxes on their illegal income, though payoffs and other overhead expenses do cut heavily into the gross.

The corporate giant of crime annually enjoys a profit greater than General Motors, Standard Oil, Ford, General Electric, and U. S. Steel combined. Its gross business is larger than that of all American automobile companies put together.

If the profits from one division alone (gambling) had been invested for the past seventeen years (since the Kefauver investigation) so as to earn only 5 percent on the principal, the sum today would be sufficient to purchase *every single share* of common stock in the ten largest corporate complexes in the United States (as listed in *Fortune* magazine) and the small change left over would buy up American Tel & Tel.

With a wide record of diversification, acquisitions and mergers this perfect conglomerate will never be investigated by the Federal Trade Commission. Freely employing restraints of trade and widely utilizing monopolistic practices, it need not fear the Anti-Trust Division of the Department of Justice.

Security regulations and the need to avoid jealousy and temptation make income figures within the Confederation a closely guarded internal secret. Only those with the need to know are privy to the income from any particular operation. Any numbers banker, loanshark, or narcotics pusher can give the dimensions of his own business, but he will not know anyone else's figures. He may not even know who else is in the same business. There is no over-all consolidated balance sheet or profit and loss statement for even one Cosa Nostra family, let alone the entire Confederation.

Aside from security, the main reason for the lack of over-all financial statements is that organized crime is not a single corporate entity with many subsidiaries and uniform accounting. It is more like a public market with many individuals occupying booths and stalls under the same roof. As long as they pay rent for their space, the owner of the market has no interest in the volume or profits of each entrepreneur. When a Cosa Nostra Boss gets tribute from his men, he does not know exactly how much their profits are; he depends on fear and respect to insure that his cut is proportionate.

Many criminals' *legal* business investments are unlikely to be known to their associates. Such separate activities, even as his home life, are kept distinct from illegal operations. Joseph Valachi told one of the authors (Salerno) that he had not known of most of the legal activities of the leaders of his own Cosa Nostra family until he heard them described to the hearings by the police.

Because of the lack of reliable statistics, estimates must be arrived at by deduction and extrapolation from known samples and benchmarks.

Gambling is the largest single income producer. The number of dollars bet illegally vastly exceeds the nearly $7,000,000,000 wagered in Las Vegas casinos, at the pari-mutuel tracks, and in the several state lotteries. The main reason for this is convenience. People who do not have the time or money to go out to the track, much less fly to Nevada, can bet over the phone, or hand a quarter to a man who comes around every day. Experts on gambling, such as John Scarne, have estimated that seven dollars are bet illegally for every dollar bet legally. And a five or four-to-one factor is considered conservative. (The various estimates are based on interviews with bookies, numbers bankers, and gamblers plus the actual sample data gleaned from gambling operations that the police have raided.)

In the late 1950s, William P. Rogers, President Eisenhower's Attorney General, estimated the total gross of organized crime at $20,000,000,000 a year, half of it from gambling. Around the same time, J. Edgar Hoover put the total at $22,000,000,000, with $11,000,000,000 coming from gambling. Then, Milton Wessel, who headed a special Justice Department group that looked into the Appalachian meeting, studied the problem and came up with a figure of $47,000,000,000 a year — *from gambling alone.* This reflects Scarne's seven-to-one ratio.

President Johnson's Commission on Law Enforcement and Administration of Justice also tackled the problem. Rufus King, a Washington lawyer, who had served as aide to Senator Kefauver during his crime hearings in the early 1950s, made his own study. Trying to be conservative, King decided to leave Nevada out of the legal total and use a three-to-one ratio of illegal to legal betting. His estimate is $20,000,000,000 a year gross, with a net income to organized crime of $6,000,000,000 to $7,000,000,000. King also estimates that $2,000,000,000 of the illegal gambling is spent on the corruption of public officials, including police.

Not generally appreciated is the fact that loansharking runs gambling a close second as a moneymaker for organized crime, and it is growing much faster. The annual take is now running about $10,000,000,000 on an investment of $5,000,000,000 in working capital, and most of the income is net income. One New York Boss invested $500,000 with his lieutenants in loansharking in 1959. By 1964 his money had been pyramided to $7,500,000. In 1965, a New York investigation identified Nicholas ("Jiggs") Forlano and his partner Charles ("Ruby") Stein as running the biggest loanshark operation in the city with up to $5,000,000 on the street (loaned out) at any one time. It was calculated that at an average 2 percent a week return, the two were taking in at least $100,000 a week.

Loansharking has proved an almost perfect medium for the investment of funds thrown off by gambling. In fact, having access to big-time loansharking as an investment is one of the advantages that Syndicate gamblers have over those who are still independent. Consider the case of "Newsboy" Moriarty, a Jersey City numbers racketeer who operated on a large scale, but managed to avoid being absorbed by any organized crime group. His independence may have been profitable and personally satisfying, but Moriarty found it impossible to do anything with the cash his business generated. He couldn't invest it fast enough without connections, he couldn't put it in banks, he couldn't even move it very far without help. So, Moriarity had to hide it and he did just that. In July 1962 $2,500,000 in cash was found crammed into his garage in Jersey City.

Not only is loansharking a high return investment, it is also a simple business to operate. A loanshark needs nothing but money and borrowers. He does not have to have an office: most loansharks meet their clients in restaurants and nightclubs. He needs no employees for he can call on his Syndicate backers for enforcers to help in collections. No special equipment is involved, and he does not require any particular skill or training in subtle intimidation or violence. Unlike gambling, the business has no odds or set rates or rules except for one: the borrower must pay.

The interest charged is, literally, whatever the traffic will bear. On a weekly basis rates have ranged between 1 percent and 150 percent, according to the relationship between the lender and the borrower, the intended use of the money, the size of the loan, and the ability of the customer to pay. Much of the time, the lender is more interested in perpetuating interest payments than in collecting the principal, so he will try to set the size and terms of the loan so that it is slightly more than the borrower can afford to carry. . . .

After gambling and loansharking, other income producing illegal activities pale into relative insignificance, though they add up to a gross of $7,500,000,000 to $10,000,000,000 a year. This area includes the importing and wholesaling of narcotics, and activities involving extortion, labor shakedowns and racketeering, counterfeiting, hijacking, cigarette smuggling, securities fraud, and bankruptcy fraud.

The Classic Pattern

In following the pattern of organized crime as a business [see p. 154] we have to separate two different kinds of violations of the law. The first are strategic and tactical crimes designed to create a state of mind; an acquiescence, a willingness of a victim or competitor to cooperate in whatever the Confederation wants him to do. These crimes are:

Arson, assault, blackmail, bribery, coercion, extortion, mayhem, murder, and sabotage.

Such crimes do not, and are not intended to, produce an immediate economic gain for the Syndicate using them. They are called on for short term or longer term gains. In this context, for example, arson might involve the burning out of a restaurant which would not install a Confederation jukebox or take its liquor supply or have its laundry done by a member firm. The arson is used as a form of warning or punishment. This kind of extortion is getting something of value (here, business for a service company) through the use or threat of force or fear — the value being one of future potential rather than immediate cash income.

Through the use of strategic and tactical crimes, organized crime has

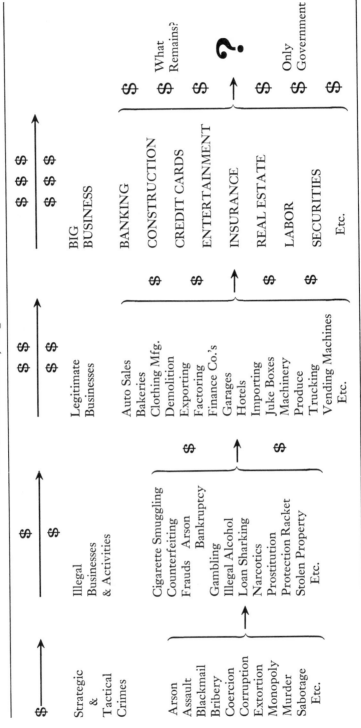

The Classic Pattern of Organized Crime.

been able to enter, dominate, and even control to varying degrees, all kinds of illegal businesses and activities. Arson is, of course, also used for fraud, as when a business is intentionally burned out after most of the inventory has been removed and the insurance money for the full value is collected from the insurer. Extortion is also used tactically for immediate economic gain, through "protection," where payments of cash are demanded for the right to continue in business without harm.

All of the violent crimes can contribute to a strategy: taking over the garbage collection business in a city, seizing control of independent bookmakers, dominating the restaurant-supply industry in an area.

As a result of operating illegal businesses, the Confederation began to gather in huge profits. Each of these activities has its own peculiar attraction or advantage to the men engaged in them. Gambling over the years has brought in the most money because of the volume of bettors; loansharking is extremely attractive because of the high yield on investment compared with the small legal penalties and the difficulty of conviction; and narcotics was attractive for the quick turnover and high return on investment, at least until the penalties became severe.

The Confederation takes these profits and couples them with further strategic and tactical crimes and uses both to penetrate legitimate businesses. While such businesses are themselves legal per se, they are run in such a way that the advantages of Syndicate membership can be used to move ahead of competition and make them even more profitable. Competitors can be intimidated by tactical crimes, and bribery and corruption can be used to cause them labor problems and higher operating costs. Having entered legitimate business, the Confederation seeks always to reduce free competition and establish monopoly whenever possible. The result is added profit, and a minimum of fuss.

It should be understood that throughout the progression from simple extortion and mayhem to the penetration and control of sophisticated larger businesses there is never an abandonment of illegal enterprises. In organized crime a man never goes completely "legit," though he may well move out of direct operation of illegal businesses. These will probably be run directly by lesser associates or even employees, with the higher ranking member giving only enough of his personal time and attention as is absolutely necessary. In addition to the increased profits to be gained from legitimate business, there is the added benefit of paying *some* taxes (from legal income) which helps to create a more convincing picture of legitimacy.

The main reason for entering legitimate business, though, is to make more money. It is a myth that proper taxes will be paid on all of the income of the legal business, or that respectability is the primary motive. The profits from legal and illegal businesses are melded so as to be indistinguishable. The Confederation man does not think in terms of "clean" money or "dirty" money. To him it is all money. He does use legal and financial advisers who tell him how much income he has to report on his tax forms to explain his standard of living.

The combined profits of legal and illegal businesses are now so substantial that the only place they can be invested is in big business and large industries. Once again, entry is made, operations safeguarded, and control effected by the use of strategic and tactical crimes. At this stage there will be less extortion, murder, arson, and assault, but much more blackmail, bribery, and coercion. The result is the same. The real danger of the Confederation invasion of big business is not that profits will go on to reach astronomical heights, but the fact that such enterprises have proved to be defenseless against penetration despite their large resources and educated managements.

What remains after the Confederation is solidly entrenched above ground? Like all other major industrialists, it will have lobbyists, favorite candidates for public office, and preferences in future legislation. In addition to the resources that legitimate industry normally uses with government, the Syndicate men will again have a competitive edge: strategic and tactical crimes. It is not ridiculous to conclude that the only area left to conquer will be the government itself.

Penetration Methods

A few case histories will show the mechanism by which organized crime moves in on a legitimate businessman, and does it so smoothly that it has taken control almost before the victim realizes what has happened to him.

Murray Packing Co., Inc. in New York City was a supplier of meat, poultry, and eggs to wholesale houses and markets. It was operated by Joseph Weinberg, his son Stanley, and David Newman. One of Murray Packing's many customers was Pride Wholesale Meat & Poultry Corp., headed by a man named Peter Castellana. He was a member of the Carlo Gambino family of Cosa Nostra and a second cousin of the Boss.

In December 1960 Murray Packing was short of working capital and a salesman for the firm, Joseph Pagano, told his employers that he could arrange a convenient loan for them. Pagano was a member of the Vito Genovese family. He arranged with Jo-Ran Trading Corp. — half-owned by Castellana — that Murray Packing be advanced $8500 at an interest charge of 1 percent a week. The other partner in Jo-Ran was Carmine Lombardozzi, a capo in the Gambino family.

In January 1961 the Weinbergs and Newman were required to help "protect the investment" by selling a one-third interest of Murray Packing to Pagano. He was made president of the company and became cosigner of every check it issued.

At this point, Pride Wholesale Meat, Castellana's company, which normally bought about $1000 a month in provisions from Murray Packing, began to buy huge quantities. In January it bought $241,000 worth, in

February, $298,000 worth, and in March, $922,000. These purchases were at prices below Murray Packing's own costs.

Castellana got Pagano to transfer Murray Packing's bank account to the bank where he did business. Pride Wholesale Meat checks payable to Murray Packing would be taken to the bank and presented by Pagano together with Murray Packing checks made out to him in the same amount. In this way, Murray Packing was milked of $745,000 in three months and forced into bankruptcy. Murray Packing's suppliers all over the country were left holding the bag and $112,000 more was siphoned out of the company during the bankruptcy proceedings.

Castellana, Pagano, the Weinbergs, and Newman were convicted in December 1964 of Federal bankruptcy fraud. Also convicted was Gondolfo Sciandria, an uncle of Castellana, who had acted as a messenger in transferring the money.

Mr. F[1] owned a fairly successful optical company with a factory in West Virginia. He needed some cash quickly for corporate development and was referred by a New Jersey businessman to First National Service and Discount Corp., located on Fifth Avenue in New York City.

First National was Julio Gazia, alias Julie Peters, related by marriage to Vito Genovese, a New York Cosa Nostra Boss. First National agreed to loan $22,000 to F at 5 percent interest a week. When asked how he came to agree to such an exorbitant rate (260 percent a year) F simply replied ". . . I needed the money." Three weeks after the first loan, F borrowed an additional $6500 without reducing the principal of the first loan. Now he found himself burdened by a $1425 weekly interest payment. In a short time, F's business was in a slump and he ran from friend to friend to borrow money for the loanshark payments.

Gazia became impatient, and the men at the top were also becoming concerned about their investment. The loanshark met with Thomas ("Tommy Ryan") Eboli, Underboss of the Genovese family, and Dominick Ferraro, in a Greenwich Village restaurant to decide their future course of action.

Ferraro was assigned to operate the company's plant in West Virginia, and F had to give him complete authority, including the right to sign company checks. Eboli ruled that F was to be held to complete repayment of the loan on their terms: the entire principal and as much interest as could be squeezed out of F and his company.

Other meetings were held concerning the future of the company, and another member suggested that he might be able to merge the optical business with another firm. A few months later F's company went bankrupt and was liquidated. The owner had paid $25,000 in interest on a $28,500 loan, and lost his business too. . . .

---

[1] The New York State Commission of Investigation gave the victim anonymity at his request.

These examples of corporate rape are known in the underworld as "scam" or the "bankruptcy caper." The action is usually reserved only for companies beyond easy salvage. Organized crime much prefers to have a business running at a profit, but profitable businesses are not such vulnerable targets for loansharks.

It is interesting to follow the progression of a typical figure through the classic pattern to see the new version of Horatio Alger.

Thomas Lucchese was born December 1, 1899, in Palermo, Sicily. He emigrated to the United States in 1911, though he did not become naturalized until 1943. In 1921 he was convicted of grand larceny (auto theft) and served a short prison sentence. In 1922 he set up a window-cleaning business in the East Harlem and Yorkville sections of Manhattan. The business employed a man with a mop and bucket and several kids with bricks. Storekeepers who did not pay to have their windows cleaned had them smashed instead.

Later in the 1920s, Lucchese graduated to the garment center, where some of his brick throwers were hired as labor goons. He also found time to involve himself in the Italian lottery in his own neighborhood. In 1923 he was arrested for receiving stolen goods but the case was dismissed. In 1927 he started the California Dried Fruit Importers, which is believed to have been a front for illegal alcohol manufacture. He was arrested again that year for stolen property, and the case was dismissed.

In 1930, Lucchese was affluent enough to move from an East Harlem tenement to a house in New Jersey. One day that year, Joseph Pinzola, a partner in the fruit business, was found shot to death on the office floor. Lucchese was charged with murder, but the Grand Jury refused to indict him.

In 1931 he was arrested in Cleveland while attending a championship prize fight with Lucky Luciano. During the 1930s, he got further involved in Seventh Avenue, and with the help of a brother-in-law who had a trucking business there, he became very influential. Lucchese also worked as a labor consultant, intimidating union representatives to keep garment shops from being organized. He plowed some of his own money into several dress and coat manufacturing firms.

During World War II, the Gaetano Gagliano family of Cosa Nostra, of which Lucchese was then Underboss, was heavily involved in the black marketing of sugar, gasoline ration stamps, and meat. Through his own clothing businesses, Lucchese was not only able to get government contracts to make uniforms, but was able to sell white shirts on the black market. He was also alleged to have developed gambling interests in Saratoga. Also, during this period he moved back from New Jersey to an exclusive colony of homes in suburban New York, one with its own private police force.

After the war, Lucchese moved up. He got deeper into the clothing business and a close associate started a construction company that built

2000 tract houses in upstate New York. Influence with one of the unions enabled them to offer the houses at reasonable prices and still make a large profit.

In 1949, Lucchese got the right to vote with a certificate of good conduct issued by the New York State Parole Department which wiped out the effect of his only conviction in 1921. His arrests for grand larceny, and two arrests for murder over the years had all resulted in dismissals. In 1953, Gagliano died of natural causes, and Lucchese succeeded him as Boss of the family. His wealth began to jump sharply. At this time he moved to Lido Beach, a conservative Long Island town, and bought a larger house and a power boat. Mr. Lucchese's son was given a Congressional appointment to the United States Military Academy and his beautiful daughter married a son of Carlo Gambino, another New York family Boss, when she graduated from a Catholic girls' school. At this time, Lucchese tried to buy a 10 percent interest in a popular singer who was having financial difficulties. The deal fell through, and the police have never revealed the singer's name.

By the 1960s Lucchese was believed to be a multimillionaire. The government had levied $162,000 against him for unpaid income taxes from 1947 through 1951. He had been investigated by the State Crime Commission, the Waterfront Commission, a Federal Grand Jury, and the McClellan Committee of the Senate. In 1963, he either owned or had interests in: Turbo Co., Gaucho LaForta Dresses, Amy DeFashion, Laurie Sportswear, Bewood Contracting, Debbie Petites, Budget Dress, Sherwood Fashions, Braunell, Ltd., Pleasant Coat Co., Bob-France Coat Co., and Fordham Hoisting Co. Many of his clothing companies were non-union.

Thomas Lucchese died after a long illness in July 1967.

Most businessmen who think that organized crime is moving in on them are unsure of where to turn for help and afraid to do anything. The safest thing for them to do is to make a collective approach, through a trade association or the like, to as many different law-enforcement agencies as possible. The local district attorney and police should be contacted as well as the United States Attorney and the Federal Bureau of Investigation. The collective approach may help save the individual businessman from the risk to himself of being a single complainant. Approaching many law-enforcement people will help insure that something is done, and will minimize the possibility that the man they approach is really organized crime itself in disguise.

SOCIAL AND
BIOLOGICAL IDENTITY

3

■ The nervous question, "What is an American?" was asked before the Revolution, repeated anxiously time and again in the early days of nationalism, and finally tackled head-on as the great and all-consuming American theme by the poet whose voice is still most strongly heard in modern American verse, Walt Whitman. With no established church to bind them in communion, no inherited class to bind them in fealty, and no single source of cultural origin to bind them in customs, Americans were a singularly heterogeneous lot anxiously in search of an identity. And the looming horror of their situation was not the chaos of diversity, but rather a compensatory characterlessness — a herding together in dull conformity to majority opinion as a dismal compensation for the lack of a confident sense of self.

Whitman faced the problem in one of his emblems:

ONE'S-SELF I sing, a simple separate person,
Yet utter the word Democratic, the word En-Masse.

How can Americans express their individuality without threatening the democratic principle of majority rule; how can they govern themselves free of feudal patterns and still respect the individual's right to be different?

The problem was exacerbated in Whitman's day by the larger questions of modern identity that were convulsing Europe as well as America. The spiritual alienation symbolized by Adam's fall and bridged by Christian theology had again opened awesomely in the wake of the Enlightenment's effect on science and philosophy. Blake and Wordsworth had been in full throat about it. And the social alienation brought about by industrialization and urbanization was accelerating as these processes accelerated. In their several ways, Thomas Carlyle, Charles Dickens, and Karl Marx made this alienation articulate.

But America had an openness in social relations derived from a belief in human equality, and this, Americans argued, would lead to a new and particularly modern and worthy identity. Whitman suggested boundless possibilities for the personality:

And I know that the hand of God is the elderhand of my own,
And I know that the spirit of God is the eldest brother of my own,
And that all the men ever born are also my brothers . . . . and the women my sisters and lovers,
And that a kelson of the creation is love.

Such a perception was rooted in American nature, even in that part of nature already defaced and neglected:

And limitless are leaves stiff or drooping in the fields,
And brown ants in the little wells, beneath them,
And mossy scabs of the wormfence, and heaped stones, and elder and mullen and pokeweed.

For a good part of the nineteenth century the leaves of America did seem limitless and a crisis in identity seemed infinitely deferable. Move west and you'll soon find out who you are. Ken Kesey's "Edge City," built by LSD and scary because of the creatures of the mind who prowl within and the officers of the law who prowl without, is nevertheless a place where you find your identity. It is a spiritual city clearly modelled on an image of the nineteenth-century frontier city.

So emphatically did the presence of the frontier mark American culture that, as Erik H. Erickson points out, mothers reared children in anticipation not just of their growing up but of their moving out to a new place that would give them their identity; the home itself need not face this task. What happens when the pattern of rearing remains but the new places disappear in a welter of cities? Where is the identity the home has never learned to give?

For a while such questions seemed unreal. Move to Edge City. Indeed, the cowboy who figures significantly in the national mythology is so prominent because he is the fantasy answer to questions of identity. His work is interchangeable with that of any other cowboy so that he is simultaneously free to be himself and yet remain a full member of a community of equals. Each day he undertakes tasks that assure him of his manhood since they require a high degree of direct action and few words. And as we follow him through his day we are impressed by how his identity is strengthened by the amount of space that organizes itself around his person. Everywhere about him are vast reaches of land, purple, grey, and sand-colored dimensions that etch him forth rather than diminish him. He has an identity: a consciousness of the self's sameness, purpose, and relationship with a society that by its very work is compelled to attune itself to the rhythms of nature. But now he lives on only as a symbol of mass nostalgia for something lost — an occasion for daydream in the dark of the movie theater, a suggestion that putting yourself behind this cigarette or that steering wheel will give you what you yearn for.

As Edge City grew suburbs and exurbs it nurtured the new man, the faceless man, whose identity was the financial and social status he had attained. He could not, with Whitman, sing of himself as a simple separate person because his work was a well-rewarded but anonymous part of a corporate enterprise. He could not, with Whitman, utter the word en-masse because his status, that sorry shred of a substitute for identity, was built on exclusion — what good a country club membership if anybody could join?

And then, quite unpredictably, in the sixties and seventies the children of the suburbs refused to serve. If they were not sure of what their identity should be, they were very certain of what it shouldn't be. In rhetoric that wraps its kernel of perceptive dismay in a husk of outrage, that generation attacks the anonymity of society by attacking the education offered it. Their schooling, its spokesmen assert, is not addressed to their need for self-discovery and desire for meaningful communal relationships but is, rather, a process by which society prepares them to serve impersonal social needs. It is a system based on the machine and unprepared to answer questions about identity because such have been left out of the program.

The term "relevance" sprang into use, misused and abused more often than not, but even at its most imprecise conveying the deep stirrings of a desire to penetrate through the walls of the university, the suburb, the structure of business, and the structure of government in order to make contact with that lost something that gives life dignity and purpose — in order to achieve identity.

As young Americans attempt to achieve this vital connection, the natural environment emerges again as a powerful potential source of self-discovery. Identity, they perceive, is biological as well as social, hence the redemption of the environment is crucial not just for the provision of an aesthetic amenity but for the very physical needs of the self. The ravagings of technology must be arrested and a new balance between man and the earth, although it may draw upon science for its means, must, finally, not be determined by science but by a new ethic that affirms the rights of nature.

Unlike the Romantic upheaval of the early 1800's, the present surge toward identity is based on the uses of technology even as it attacks technology's abuses. Indeed one of the most powerful influences on this surge is the sophisticated advance made in the production of contraceptive devices, because they enable men and women to plan a world in which sexuality and conception, for the first time in history, are separate. As a result many women are coming to see that the biological fact of being a woman does not carry with it absolute restrictions that are natural, but rather that the restrictions imposed on them in the name of nature are really instruments of the social process. With the spread of this awareness, especially in England and America, has come a consequent social philosophy that sees women in class rather than sexual terms, and in these terms finds them exploited. So profoundly has the history of mankind been shaped by other assumptions about the difference between the sexes that the potential of a redefinition of this difference, brought about by the Pill and its colleagues, is immense, capable ultimately of altering the foundation of daily life.

Technology also enters into the search for cultural identity. Although the endless line of consumable gadgets serves most obviously to insulate Americans against questions of ultimate meaning, those who had sought a road to a culture free of gadgetry, found themselves projecting a condition that was, at best, anachronistic. Their efforts in the battle against changing times broke down in exhaustion or led to a fragile, quaint, and subsidized artsy-craftiness. In the sixties there appeared a recognition that all the time Americans were mooning about the passing of the frontier and small town, they were imbibing another culture of which they were too mistakenly ashamed to dignify by the name. They shared in common the lore of Batman and Captain Marvel, the Marx Brothers and "B" gangster films, neon-lit drive-ins, and used cars. When one person even dared breathe that this too was culture, and culture that was not without its joys and comforts, that breath knocked over the dam and the flood descended in a riot of plays, poems, paintings, clothes, foods, and conversations that announced widespread recognition by individuals that their private fantasies and secret lore had all the while been generally, if covertly, held by others. Pop had arrived and although Pop will doubtless pass, it will not do so without leaving the reminder that what is widely known, enjoyed, and exchanged in a society is culture even though it is not classical tragedy or a sonata. This is not to say it is good culture or bad culture, only that it is the possession of the society, not the embarrassing memory of the individual.

Jerry Rubin, not everybody's candidate for patriot of the year, illustrates the coherence of an attachment to this kind of culture with a commitment to social revolution, when in a book that sings the praises of the unprogrammed revolution he also says:

> If I'm ever sent to Death Row for my revolutionary 'crimes', I'll order as my last meal: a hamburger, french fries and a Coke.
> I dig big cities.
> I love to read the sports pages and gossip column, listen to the radio and watch color TV.
> I dig department stores, huge supermarkets and airports. I feel secure (though not necessarily hungry) when I see Howard Johnson's on the expressway.
> I groove on Hollywood movies — even bad ones.[1]

---

[1] Jerry Rubin, *Do It!* (New York: Simon and Schuster, 1970), p. 12.

This "Yippie declaration" conforms easily to the more sober maxim guiding the Romantic search for identity of a century and a half ago: "A man must seek his salvation in the place of his birth." These sentiments are reminders that the search for identity must be a search, not an escape, and must, therefore, lead through the turnings of our own minds and bodies, the twistings of our own childhood streets and alleys. The sun behind the smog must be reclaimed rather than sought as it shines on greener pastures; the meaning of sexual difference must be an experience rather than a social habit; the condition of being an American must be interpreted in the illumination from neon tubing rather than in the glow of a gas lamp.

D. H. Lawrence | Benjamin Franklin

The Perfectibility of Man! Ah heaven, what a dreary theme! The perfectibility of the Ford car! The perfectibility of which man? I am many men. Which of them are you going to perfect? I am not a mechanical contrivance.

Education! Which of the various me's do you propose to educate, and which do you propose to suppress?

Anyhow I defy you. I defy you, oh society, to educate me or to suppress me, according to your dummy standards.

The ideal man! And which is he, if you please? Benjamin Franklin or Abraham Lincoln? The ideal man! Roosevelt or Porfirio Diaz?

There are other men in me, besides this patient ass who sits here in a tweed jacket. What am I doing, playing the patient ass in a tweed jacket? Who am I talking to? Who are you, at the other end of this patience?

Who are you? How many selves have you? And which of these selves do you want to be?

Is Yale College going to educate the self that is in the dark of you, or Harvard College?

The ideal self! Oh, but I have a strange and fugitive self shut out and howling like a wolf or a coyote under the ideal windows. See his red eyes in the dark? This is the self who is coming into his own.

The perfectibility of man, dear God! When every man as long as he remains alive is in himself a multitude of conflicting men. Which of these do you choose to perfect, at the expense of every other?

Old Daddy Franklin will tell you. He'll rig him up for you, the pattern American. Oh, Franklin was the first downright American. He knew what he was about, the sharp little man. He set up the first dummy American.

At the beginning of his career this cunning little Benjamin drew up for himself a creed that should "satisfy the professors of every religion, but shock none."

Now wasn't that a real American thing to do?

"That there is One God, who made all things."

(But Benjamin made Him.)

"That He governs the world by His Providence."

(Benjamin knowing all about Providence.)

"*That He ought to be worshipped with adoration, prayer, and thanksgiving.*"

(Which cost nothing.)

"*But — *" But me no buts, Benjamin, saith the Lord.

"*But that the most acceptable service of God is doing good to men.*"

(God having no choice in the matter.)

"*That the soul is immortal.*"

(You'll see why, in the next clause.)

"*And that God will certainly reward virtue and punish vice, either here or hereafter.*"

Now if Mr. Andrew Carnegie, or any other millionaire, had wished to invent a God to suit his ends, he could not have done better. Benjamin did it for him in the eighteenth century. God is the supreme servant of men who want to get on, to *produce*. Providence. The provider. The heavenly storekeeper. The everlasting Wanamaker.

And this is all the God the grandsons of the Pilgrim Fathers had left. Aloft on a pillar of dollars.

"*That the soul is immortal.*"

The trite way Benjamin says it!

But man has a soul, though you can't locate it either in his purse or his pocket-book or his heart or his stomach or his head. The *wholeness* of a man is his soul. Not merely that nice little comfortable bit which Benjamin marks out.

It's a queer thing, is a man's soul. It is the whole of him. Which means it is the unknown him, as well as the known. It seems to me just funny, professors and Benjamins fixing the functions of the soul. Why the soul of man is a vast forest, and all Benjamin intended was a neat back garden. And we've all got to fit in to his kitchen garden scheme of things. Hail Columbia!

The soul of a man is a dark forest. The Hercynian Wood that scared the Romans so, and out of which came the white-skinned hordes of the next civilization.

Who knows what will come out of the soul of man? The soul of man is a dark vast forest, with wild life in it. Think of Benjamin fencing it off!

Oh, but Benjamin fenced a little tract that he called the soul of man, and proceeded to get it into cultivation. Providence, forsooth! And they think that bit of barbed wire is going to keep us in pound forever? More fools them.

This is Benjamin's barbed wire fence. He made himself a list of virtues, which he trotted inside like a grey nag in a paddock.

TEMPERANCE Eat not to fulness; drink not to elevation.

SILENCE Speak not but what may benefit others or yourself; avoid trifling conversation.

ORDER Let all your things have their places; let each part of your business have its time.

RESOLUTION Resolve to perform what you ought; perform without fail what you resolve.

FRUGALITY Make no expense but to do good to others or yourself — i.e., waste nothing.

INDUSTRY Lose no time, be always employed in something useful; cut off all unnecessary action.

SINCERITY Use no hurtful deceit; think innocently and justly, and, if you speak, speak accordingly.

JUSTICE Wrong none by doing injuries, or omitting the benefits that are your duty.

MODERATION Avoid extremes, forbear resenting injuries as much as you think they deserve.

CLEANLINESS Tolerate no uncleanliness in body, clothes, or habitation.

TRANQUILLITY Be not disturbed at trifles, or at accidents common or unavoidable.

CHASTITY Rarely use venery but for health and offspring, never to dulness, weakness, or the injury of your own or another's peace or reputation.

HUMILITY Imitate Jesus and Socrates.

A Quaker friend told Franklin that he, Benjamin, was generally considered proud, so Benjamin put in the Humility touch as an afterthought. The amusing part is the sort of humility it displays. "Imitate Jesus and Socrates," and mind you don't outshine either of these two. One can just imagine Socrates and Alcibiades roaring in their cups over Philadelphian Benjamin, and Jesus looking at him a little puzzled, and murmuring: "Aren't you wise in your own conceit, Ben?"

"Henceforth be masterless," retorts Ben. "Be ye each one his own master unto himself, and don't let even the Lord put his spoke in." "Each man his own master" is but a puffing up of masterlessness.

Well, the first of Americans practised this enticing list with assiduity, setting a national example. He had the virtues in columns, and gave himself good and bad marks according as he thought his behaviour deserved. Pity these conduct charts are lost to us. He only remarks that Order was his stumbling block. He could not learn to be neat and tidy.

Isn't it nice to have nothing worse to confess?

He was a little model, was Benjamin. Doctor Franklin. Snuff-coloured little man! Immortal soul and all!

The immortal soul part was a sort of cheap insurance policy.

Benjamin had no concern, really, with the immortal soul. He was too busy with social man.

He swept and lighted the streets of young Philadelphia.

He invented electrical appliances.

He was the centre of a moralizing club in Philadelphia, and he wrote the moral humorisms of Poor Richard.

He was a member of all the important councils of Philadelphia, and then of the American colonies.

He won the cause of American Independence at the French Court, and was the economic father of the United States.

Now what more can you want of a man? And yet he is *infra dig*, even in Philadelphia.

I admire him. I admire his sturdy courage first of all, then his sagacity, then his glimpsing into the thunders of electricity, then his common-sense humour. All the qualities of a great man, and never more than a great citizen. Middle-sized, sturdy, snuff-coloured Doctor Franklin, one of the soundest citizens that ever trod or "used venery."

I do not like him.

And, by the way, I always thought books of Venery were about hunting deer.

There is a certain earnest naïveté about him. Like a child. And like a little old man. He has again become as a little child, always as wise as his grandfather, or wiser.

Perhaps, as I say, the most complete citizen that ever "used venery."

Printer, philosopher, scientist, author and patriot, impeccable husband and citizen, why isn't he an archetype?

Pioneer, Oh Pioneers! Benjamin was one of the greatest pioneers of the United States. Yet we just can't do with him.

What's wrong with him then? Or what's wrong with us?

I can remember, when I was a little boy, my father used to buy a scrubby yearly almanack with the sun and moon and stars on the cover. And it used to prophesy bloodshed and famine. But also crammed in corners it had little anecdotes and humorisms, with a moral tag. And I used to have my little priggish laugh at the woman who counted her chickens before they were hatched, and so forth, and I was convinced that honesty was the best policy, also a little priggishly. The author of these bits was Poor Richard, and Poor Richard was Benjamin Franklin, writing in Philadelphia well over a hundred years before.

And probably I haven't got over those Poor Richard tags yet. I rankle still with them. They are thorns in young flesh.

Because although I still believe that honesty is the best policy, I dislike policy altogether; though it is just as well not to count your chickens before they are hatched, it's still more hateful to count them with gloating when they *are* hatched. It has taken me many years, and countless smarts to get out of that barbed wire moral enclosure that Poor Richard rigged up. Here am I now in tatters and scratched to ribbons, sitting in the middle of Benjamin's America looking at the barbed wire, and the fat sheep crawling under the fence to get fat outside and the watchdogs yelling at the gate lest by chance anyone should get out by the proper exit. Oh America! Oh Benjamin! And I just utter a long loud curse against Benjamin and the American corral.

Moral America! Most moral Benjamin. Sound, satisfied Ben!

He had to go to the frontiers of his State to settle some disturbance among the Indians. On this occasion he writes:

"We found that they had made a great bonfire in the middle of the square; they were all drunk, men and women quarrelling and fighting. Their dark-coloured bodies, half naked, seen only by the gloomy light of the bonfire, running after and beating one another with fire-brands, accompanied by their horrid yellings, formed a scene the most resembling our ideas of hell that could well be imagined. There was no appeasing the tumult, and we retired to our lodging. At midnight a number of them came thundering at our door, demanding more rum, of which we took no notice.

"The next day, sensible they had misbehaved in giving us that disturbance, they sent three of their counsellors to make their apology. The orator acknowledged the fault, but laid it upon the rum, and then endeavoured to excuse the rum by saying: 'The Great Spirit, who made all things, made everything for some use; and whatever he designed anything for, that use it should always be put to. Now, when he had made rum, he said: "Let this be for the Indians to get drunk with." And it must be so.'

"And, indeed, if it be the design of Providence to extirpate these savages in order to make room for the cultivators of the earth, it seems not improbable that rum may be the appointed means. It has already annihilated all the tribes who formerly inhabited all the seacoast . . ."

This, from the good doctor, with such suave complacency is a little disenchanting. Almost too good to be true.

But there you are! The barbed wire fence. "Extirpate these savages in order to make room for the cultivators of the earth." Oh, Benjamin Franklin! He even "used venery" as a cultivator of seed.

Cultivate the earth, ye gods! The Indians did that, as much as they needed. And they left off there. Who built Chicago? Who cultivated the earth until it spawned Pittsburgh, Pa.?

The moral issue! Just look at it! Cultivation included. If it's a mere choice of Kultur or cultivation, I give it up.

Which brings us right back to our question, what's wrong with Benjamin, that we can't stand him? Or else, what's wrong with us, that we find fault with such a paragon?

Man is a moral animal. All right. I am a moral animal. And I'm going to remain such. I'm not going to be turned into a virtuous little automaton as Benjamin would have me. "This is good, that is bad. Turn the little handle and let the good tap flow," saith Benjamin and all America with him. "But first of all extirpate those savages who are always turning on the bad tap."

I am a moral animal. But I am not a moral machine. I don't work with a little set of handles or levers. The Temperance - silence - order - resolution - frugality - industry - sincerity - justice - moderation - cleanliness - tranquillity - chastity - humility keyboard is not going to get me going. I'm really not just an automatic piano with a moral Benjamin getting tunes out of me.

Here's my creed, against Benjamin's. This is what I believe:

"That I am I."
"That my soul is a dark forest."
"That my known self will never be more than a little clearing in the forest."
"That gods, strange gods, come forth from the forest into the clearing of my known self, and then go back."
"That I must have the courage to let them come and go."
"That I will never let mankind put anything over me, but that I will try always to recognize and submit to the gods in me and the gods in other men and women."

There is my creed. He who runs may read. He who prefers to crawl, or to go by gasoline, can call it rot.

Then for a "list." It is rather fun to play at Benjamin.

TEMPERANCE   Eat and carouse with Bacchus, or munch dry bread with Jesus, but don't sit down without one of the gods.

SILENCE   Be still when you have nothing to say; when genuine passion moves you, say what you've got to say, and say it hot.

ORDER   Know that you are responsible to the gods inside you and to the men in whom the gods are manifest. Recognize your superiors and your inferiors, according to the gods. This is the root of all order.

RESOLUTION   Resolve to abide by your own deepest promptings, and to sacrifice the smaller thing to the greater. Kill when you must, and be killed the same: the *must* coming from the gods inside you, or from the men in whom you recognize the Holy Ghost.

FRUGALITY   Demand nothing; accept what you see fit. Don't waste your pride or squander your emotion.

INDUSTRY   Lose no time with ideals; serve the Holy Ghost; never serve mankind.

SINCERITY   To be sincere is to remember that I am I, and that the other man is not me.

JUSTICE   The only justice is to follow the sincere intuition of the soul, angry or gentle. Anger is just, and pity is just, but judgment is never just.

MODERATION   Beware of absolutes. There are many gods.

CLEANLINESS   Don't be too clean. It impoverishes the blood.

TRANQUILLITY   The soul has many motions, many gods come and go. Try and find your deepest issue, in every confusion, and abide by that. Obey the man in whom you recognize the Holy Ghost; command when your honour comes to command.

CHASTITY   Never "use" venery at all. Follow your passional impulse, if it be answered in the other being; but never have any motive in mind, neither off-spring nor health nor even pleasure, nor even service. Only know that "venery" is of the great gods. An offering-up of yourself to the very great gods, the dark ones, and nothing else.

HUMILITY   See all men and women according to the Holy Ghost that is within them. Never yield before the barren.

There's my list. I have been trying dimly to realize it for a long time, and only America and old Benjamin have at last goaded me into trying to formulate it.

And now I, at least, know why I can't stand Benjamin. He tries to take away my wholeness and my dark forest, my freedom. For how can any man be free, without an illimitable background? And Benjamin tries to shove me into a barbed-wire paddock and make me grow potatoes or Chicagoes.

And how can I be free, without gods that come and go? But Benjamin won't let anything exist except my useful fellow-men, and I'm sick of them; as for his Godhead, his Providence, He is Head of nothing except a vast heavenly store that keeps every imaginable line of goods, from victrolas to cat-o-nine tails.

And how can any man be free without a soul of his own, that he believes in and won't sell at any price? But Benjamin doesn't let me have a soul of my own. He says I am nothing but a servant of mankind — galley-slave I call it — and if I don't get my wages here below — that is, if Mr. Pierpont Morgan or Mr. Nosey Hebrew or the grand United States Government, the great US, US or SOMEOFUS, manages to scoop in my bit along with their lump — why, never mind, I shall get my wages HEREAFTER.

Oh Benjamin! Oh Binjum! You do NOT suck me in any longer.

And why oh why should the snuff-coloured little trap have wanted to take us all in? Why did he do it?

Out of sheer human cussedness, in the first place. We do all like to get things inside a barbed-wire corral. Especially our fellow-men. We love to round them up inside the barbed-wire enclosure of FREEDOM, and make 'em work. *"Work, you free jewel,* WORK!" shouts the liberator, cracking his whip. Benjamin, I will not work. I do not choose to be a free democrat. I am absolutely a servant of my own Holy Ghost.

Sheer cussedness! But there was as well the salt of a subtler purpose. Benjamin was just in his eyeholes — to use an English vulgarism meaning he was just delighted — when he was at Paris judiciously milking money out of the French monarchy for the overthrow of all monarchy. If you want to ride your horse to somewhere you must put a bit in his mouth. And Benjamin wanted to ride his horse so that it would upset the whole apple-cart of the old masters. He wanted the whole European apple-cart upset. So he had to put a strong bit in the mouth of his ass.

"Henceforth be masterless."

That is, he had to break-in the human ass completely, so that much more might be broken, in the long run. For the moment it was the British Government that had to have a hole knocked in it. The first real hole it ever had: the breach of the American rebellion.

Benjamin, in his sagacity, knew that the breaking of the old world was a long process. In the depths of his own under-consciousness he hated England, he hated Europe, he hated the whole corpus of the European being. He wanted to be American. But you can't change your nature and mode of consciousness like changing your shoes. It is a gradual shedding. Years must go by, and centuries must elapse before you have finished. Like a son escaping from the domination of his parents. The escape is not just one rupture. It is a long and half-secret process.

So with the American. He was a European when he first went over the Atlantic. He is in the main a recreant European still. From Benjamin Franklin to Woodrow Wilson may be a long stride, but it is a stride along the same road. There is no new road. The same old road, become dreary and futile. Theoretic and materialistic.

Why then did Benjamin set up this dummy of a perfect citizen as a pattern to America? Of course he did it in perfect good faith, as far as he knew. He thought it simply was the true ideal. But what we *think* we do is not very important. We never really know what we are doing. Either we are materialistic instruments, like Benjamin, or we move in the gesture of creation, from our deepest self, usually unconscious. We are only the actors, we are never wholly the authors of our own needs or works. IT is the author, the unknown inside us or outside us. The best we can do is to try to hold ourselves in unison with the deeps which are inside us. And the worst we can do is to try to have things our own way, when we run counter to IT, and in the long run get our knuckles rapped for our presumption.

So Benjamin contriving money out of the Court of France. He was contriving the first steps of the overthrow of all Europe, France included. You can never have a new thing without breaking an old. Europe happens to be the old thing. America, unless the people in America assert themselves too much in opposition to the inner gods, should be the new thing. The new thing is the death of the old. But you can't cut the throat of an epoch. You've got to steal the life from it through several centuries.

And Benjamin worked for this both directly and indirectly. Directly, at the Court of France, making a small but very dangerous hole in the side of England, through which hole Europe has by now almost bled to death. And indirectly in Philadelphia, setting up this unlovely, snuff-coloured little ideal, or automaton, of a pattern American. The pattern American, this dry, moral, utilitarian little democrat, has done more to ruin the old Europe than any Russian nihilist. He has done it by slow attrition, like a son who has stayed at home and obeyed his parents, all the while silently hating their authority, and silently, in his soul, destroying not only their authority but their whole existence. For the American spiritually stayed at home in Europe. The spiritual home of America was and still is Europe. This is the galling bondage, in spite of several billions of heaped-up gold. Your heaps of gold are only so many muck-heaps, America, and will remain so till you become a reality to yourselves.

All this Americanizing and mechanizing has been for the purpose of overthrowing the past. And now look at America, tangled in her own barbed wire, and mastered by her own machines. Absolutely got down by her own barbed wire of shalt-nots, and shut up fast in her own "productive" machines like millions of squirrels running in millions of cages. It is just a farce.

Now is your chance, Europe. Now let Hell loose and get your own back, and paddle your own canoe on a new sea, while clever America lies on her muck-heaps of gold, strangled in her own barbed-wire of shalt-not ideals and shalt-not moralisms. While she goes out to work like millions of squirrels in millions of cages. Production!

Let Hell loose, and get your own back, Europe!

Erik H. Erikson | Mom

In recent years the observations and warnings of the psychiatric workers of this country have more and more converged on two concepts: the "schizoid personality" and "maternal rejection." Essentially this means

SOURCE: Reprinted from *Childhood and Society*, Revised, Second Edition, by Erik H. Erikson. By permission of W. W. Norton & Company, Inc. Copyright 1950, © 1963 by W. W. Norton & Company, Inc.

not only that many people fall by the wayside as a result of psychotic disengagements from reality, but also that all too many people, while not overtly sick, nevertheless seem to lack a certain ego tonus and a certain mutuality in social intercourse. One may laugh at this suggestion and point to the spirit of individualism and to the gestures of animation and of jovial friendliness characterizing much of the social life in this country; but the psychiatrists (especially after the shocking experience during the last war, of being forced to reject or to send home hundreds of thousands of "psycho-neurotics") see it differently. The streamlined smile within the perfectly tuned countenance and within the standardized ways of exhibiting self-control does not always harbor that true spontaneity which alone would keep the personality intact and flexible enough to make it a going concern.

For this the psychiatrists tend to blame "Mom." Case history after case history states that the patient had a cold mother, a dominant mother, a rejecting mother — or a hyperpossessive, overprotective one. They imply that the patient, as a baby, was not made to feel at home in this world except under the condition that he behave himself in certain definite ways, which were inconsistent with the timetable of an infant's needs and potentialities, and contradictory in themselves. They imply that the mother dominated the father, and that while the father offered more tenderness and understanding to the children than the mother did, he disappointed his children in the end because of what he "took" from the mother. Gradually what had begun as a spontaneous movement in thousands of clinical files has become a manifest literary sport in books decrying the mothers of this country as "Moms" and as a "generation of vipers."

Who is this "Mom"? How did she lose her good, her simple name? How could she become an excuse for all that is rotten in the state of the nation and a subject of literary temper tantrums? Is Mom really to blame?

In a clinical sense, of course, to blame may mean just to point to what the informed worker sincerely considers the primary cause of the calamity. But there is in much of our psychiatric work an undertone of revengeful triumph, as if a villain had been spotted and cornered. The blame attached to the mothers in this country (namely, that they are frigid sexually, rejective of their children, and unduly dominant in their homes) has in itself a specific moralistic punitiveness. No doubt both patients and psychiatric workers were blamed too much when they were children; now they blame all mothers, because all causality has become linked with blame.

It was, of course, a vindictive injustice to give the name of "Mom" to a certain dangerous type of mother, a type apparently characterized by a number of fatal contradictions in her motherhood. Such injustice can only be explained and justified by the journalistic habit of sensational contra-position — a part of the publicist folkways of our day. It is true that where the "psychoneurotic" American soldier felt inadequately prepared for life, he often implicitly and more often unconsciously blamed his mother; and that the expert felt compelled to agree with him. But it is also true that the road from Main Street to the foxhole was longer — geographically, culturally, and psychologically — than was the road to the front lines from the home towns of nations which were open to attack and had been attacked, or which had prepared themselves to attack other people's homelands and now feared for their own. It seems senseless to blame the American family for the failures, but to deny it credit for the gigantic human achievement of overcoming that distance.

"Mom," then, like similar prototypes in other countries — see the "German father" — is a composite image of traits, none of which could be present all at once in one single living woman. No woman consciously aspires to be such a "Mom," and yet she may find that her experience converges on this Gestalt, as if she were forced to assume a role. To the clinical worker, "Mom" is something comparable to a "classical" psychiatric syndrome which you come to use as a yardstick although you have never seen it in pure form. In cartoons she becomes a caricature, immediately convincing to all. Before analyzing "Mom," then, as a historical phenomenon, let us focus on her from the point of view of the pathogenic demands which she makes on her children and by which we recognize her presence in our clinical work:

1. "Mom" is the unquestioned authority in matters of mores and morals in her home, and (through clubs) in the community; yet she permits herself to remain, in her own way, vain in her appearance, egotistical in her demands, and infantile in her emotions.

2. In any situation in which this discrepancy clashes with the respect which she demands from her children, she blames her children; she never blames herself.

3. She thus artificially maintains what Ruth Benedict would call the discontinuity between the child's and the adult's status without endowing this differentiation with the higher meaning emanating from superior example.

4. She shows a determined hostility to any free expression of the most naïve forms of sensual and sexual pleasure on the part of her children, and she makes it clear enough that the father, when sexually demanding, is a bore. Yet as she grows older she seems unwilling to sacrifice such external signs of sexual competition as too youthful dresses, frills of exhibitionism, and "make-up." In addition, she is avidly addicted to sexual display in books, movies, and gossip.

5. She teaches self-restraint and self-control, but she is unable to restrict her intake of calories in order to remain within the bounds of the dresses she prefers.

6. She expects her children to be hard on themselves, but she is hypochondriacally concerned with her own well-being.

7. She stands for the superior values of tradition, yet she herself does not want to become "old." In fact, she is mortally afraid of that status

which in the past was the fruit of a rich life, namely the status of the grandmother.

This will be sufficient to indicate that "Mom" is a woman in whose life cycle remnants of infantility join advanced senility to crowd out the middle range of mature womanhood, which thus becomes self-absorbed and stagnant. In fact, she mistrusts her own feelings as a woman and mother. Even her overconcern does not provide trust, but lasting mistrust. But let it be said that this "Mom" — or better: any woman who reminds herself and others of the stereotype Mom — is not happy; she does not like herself; she is ridden by the anxiety that her life was a waste. She knows that her children do not genuinely love her, despite Mother's Day offerings. "Mom" is a victim, not a victor.

Assuming, then, that this is a "type," a composite image of sufficient relevance for the epidemiology of neurotic conflict in this country: to explain it would obviously call for the collaboration of historian, sociologist, and psychologist, and for a new kind of history, a kind which at the moment is admittedly in its impressionistic and sensational stages. "Mom," of course, is only a stereotyped caricature of existing contradictions which have emerged from intense, rapid, and as yet unintegrated changes in American history. To find its beginning, one would probably have to retrace this history back to the time when it was up to the American woman to evolve one common tradition, on the basis of many imported traditions, and to base on it the education of her children and the style of her home life; when it was up to her to establish new habits of sedentary life on a continent originally populated by men who in their countries of origin, for one reason or another, had not wanted to be "fenced in." Now, in fear of ever again acquiescing to an outer or inner autocracy, these men insisted on keeping their new cultural identity tentative to a point where women had to become autocratic in their demands for some order.

The American woman in frontier communities was the object of intense rivalries on the part of tough and often desperate men. At the same time, she had to become the cultural censor, the religious conscience, the aesthetic arbiter, and the teacher. In that early rough economy hewn out of hard nature it was she who contributed the finer graces of living and that spirituality without which the community falls apart. In her children she saw future men and women who would face contrasts of rigid sedentary and shifting migratory life. They must be prepared for any number of extreme opposites in milieu, and always ready to seek new goals and to fight for them in merciless competition. For, after all, worse than a sinner was a sucker. . . .

From the frontier, my historian-sociologist and I would have to turn to puritanism as a decisive force in the creation of American motherhood and its modern caricature, "Mom." This much-maligned puritanism, we should remember, was once a system of values designed to check men and women of eruptive vitality, of strong appetites, as well as of strong individuality. In connection with primitive cultures we have discussed the fact that a living culture has its own balances which make it durable and bearable to the majority of its members. But changing history endangers the balance. During the short course of American history rapid developments fused with puritanism in such a way that they contributed to the emotional tension of mother and child. Among these were the continued migration of the native population, unchecked immigration, industrialization, urbanization, class stratification, and female emancipation. These are some of the influences which put puritanism on the defensive — and a system is apt to become rigid when it becomes defensive. Puritanism, beyond defining sexual sin for full-blooded and strong-willed people, gradually extended itself to the total sphere of bodily living, compromising all sensuality — including marital relationships — and spreading its frigidity over the tasks of pregnancy, childbirth, nursing, and training. The result was that men were born who failed to learn from their mothers to love the goodness of sensuality before they learned to hate its sinful uses. Instead of hating sin, they learned to mistrust life. Many became puritans without faith or zest.

The frontier, of course, remained the decisive influence which served to establish in the American identity the extreme polarization which characterizes it. The original polarity was the cultivation of the sedentary and migratory poles. For the same families, the same mothers, were forced to prepare men and women who would take root in the community life and the gradual class stratification of the new villages and towns and at the same time to prepare these children for the possible physical hardships of homesteading on the frontiers. Towns, too, developed their sedentary existence and oriented their inward life to work bench and writing desk, fireplace and altar, while through them, on the roads and rails, strangers passed bragging of God knows what greener pastures. You had either to follow — or to stay behind and brag louder. The point is that the call of the frontier, the temptation to move on, forced those who stayed to become defensively sedentary, and defensively proud. In a world which developed the slogan, "If you can see your neighbor's chimney, it is time to move on," mothers had to raise sons and daughters who would be determined to ignore the call of the frontier — but who would go with equal determination once they were forced or chose to go. When they became too old, however, there was no choosing, and they remained to support the most sectarian, the most standardized adhesiveness. I think that it was the fear of becoming too old to choose which gave old age and death a bad name in this country. (Only recently have old couples found a solution, the national trailer system, which permits them to settle down to perpetual traveling and to die on wheels.)

We know how the problems of the immigrant and of the migrant, of the émigré and of the refugee, became superimposed on one another, as large areas became settled and began to have a past. To the new American, with a regional tradition of stratification, newcomers increasingly came to be characterized by the fact that they had escaped from something or other, rather than by the common values they sought; and then there were also the masses of ignorant and deceived chattels of the expanding industrial labor market. For and against all of these latter Americans, American mothers had to establish new moral standards and rigid tests of social ascendancy.

As America became the proverbial melting pot, it was the Anglo-Saxon woman's determination which assured that of all the ingredients mixed, puritanism — such as it then was — would be the most pervasive streak. The older, Anglo-Saxon type became ever more rigid, though at the same time decent and kind in its way. But the daughters of immigrants, too, frantically tried to emulate standards of conduct which they had not learned as small children. It is here, I think, that the self-made personality originated as the female counterpart of the self-made man; it is here that we find the origin of the popular American concept of a fashionable and vain "ego" which is its own originator and arbiter. In fact, the psychoanalysis of the children of immigrants clearly reveals to what extent they, as the first real Americans in their family, become their parents' cultural parents.

This idea of a self-made ego was in turn reinforced and yet modified by industrialization and by class stratification. Industrialization, for example, brought with it mechanical child training. It was as if this new man-made world of machines, which was to replace the "segments of nature" and the "beasts of prey," offered its mastery only to those who would become like it, as the Sioux "became" buffalo, the Yurok salmon. Thus, a movement in child training began which tended to adjust the human organism from the very start to clocklike punctuality in order to make it a standardized appendix of the industrial world. This movement is by no means at an end either in this country or in countries which for the sake of industrial production want to become like us. In the pursuit of the adjustment to and mastery over the machine, American mothers (especially of the middle class) found themselves standardizing and overadjusting children who later were expected to personify that very virile individuality which in the past had been one of the outstanding characteristics of the American. The resulting danger was that of creating, instead of individualism, a massproduced mask of individuality.

As if this were not enough, the increasing class differentiation in some not large but influential classes and regions combined with leftovers of European aristocratic models to create the ideal of the lady, the woman who not only does not need to work, but who, in fact, is much too childlike and too determinedly uninformed to even comprehend what work is all about. This image, in most parts of the country, except the South, was soon challenged by the ideal of the emancipated woman. This new ideal seemed to call for equality of opportunity; but it is well known how it came, instead, to represent often enough a pretense of sameness in equipment, a right to mannish behavior.

In her original attributes, then, the American woman was a fitting and heroic companion to the post-revolutionary man, who was possessed with the idea of freedom from any man's autocracy and haunted by the fear that the nostalgia for some homeland and the surrender to some king could ever make him give in to political slavery. Mother became "Mom" only when Father became "Pop" under the impact of the identical historical discontinuities. For, if you come down to it, Momism is only misplaced paternalism. American mothers stepped into the role of the grandfathers as the fathers abdicated their dominant place in the family, in the field of education, and in cultural life. The postrevolutionary descendants of the Founding Fathers forced their women to be mothers *and* fathers, while they continued to cultivate the role of freeborn sons.

I cannot try to appraise the quantity of emotional disturbance in this country. Mere statistics on severe mental disorders do not help. Our improved methods of detection and our missionary zeal expand together as we become aware of the problem, so that it would be hard to say whether today this country has bigger and better neuroses, or bigger and better ways of spotlighting them — or both. But I would, from my clinical experience, dare to formulate a specific *quality* in those who are disturbed. I would say that underneath his proud sense of autonomy and his exuberant sense of initiative the troubled American (who often looks the least troubled) blames his mother for having let him down. His father, so he claims, had not much to do with it — except in those rare cases where the father was an extraordinarily stern man on the surface, an old-fashioned individualist, a foreign paternalist, or a native "boss." In the psychoanalysis of an American man it usually takes considerable time to break through to the insight that there was a period early in life when the father did seem bigger and threatening. Even then, there is at first little sense of that specific rivalry for the mother as stereotyped in the oedipus complex. It is as if the mother had ceased to be an object of nostalgia and sensual attachment before the general development of initiative led to a rivalry with the "old man." Behind a fragmentary "oedipus complex," then, appears that deep-seated sense of having been abandoned and let down by the mother, which is the silent complaint behind schizoid withdrawal. The small child felt, it seems, that there was no use regressing, because there was nobody to regress to, no use investing feelings because the response was so uncertain. What remained was action and motion right up to the breaking point. Where action, too, failed, there was only withdrawal and the standardized smile, and later, psychosomatic disturbance. But wherever our methods permit us to look deeper, we find at the bottom of it all the conviction, the mortal self-accusation, that it was *the child who abandoned the mother,* because he had been in such a hurry to become independent.

Madison Avenue, Chicago

Ross Pelletier, 56

His office at the advertising agency, one of the largest in the world. It is after hours; the charwomen are appearing.

"I remember as a kid wanting to be a baggageman on a train. The D & I Railroad ran past our home, outside Duluth. Playing in the field, we'd see these trains going by and here's a baggageman leaning against the open door and looking at the passing countryside. I thought, oh my gosh, what a great job to have. That was one of the early things. Later, when you get to figuring out how you make any money doing that, to provide yourself with a new pair of shoes and so on, you, like everyone else, start to think, well, maybe I can do a little better than that."

To me, an executive is a man that makes things happen. He's executive something, some plan. He also helped devise that plan of action, whether this is military, let's say, or business or social, or church group or almost any kind of gathering of two or more people. You have to have someone that tries to make it go.

So in my work, it's been hiring and training of other men. So the job for me is to spot that talent, somewhat like a major league scout looking in baseball, trying to find a fella that can throw from the outfield straight and hit the ball hard and so on. So my job is to find and train these men in creating television and radio commercials.

Advertising is a very fascinating business to me. We think it's a very important business, sometimes not fully understood. It's hard to understand the other fellow's business, because no matter what he's doing, you kind of wonder well, what is the importance of this? But advertising has been so important in mass consumption. . . . There's no sense producing if people are not going to consume what you produce in masses. You need mass consumption to make use of the goods that are turned out by the dozens in the store, you know.

A product must stand up in the consumer's hands. I could, by advertising, maybe induce you to try a product. But you will not make a re-purchase if it is not satisfactory. I mean, if it's an off-brand, or if it's really too cheap a thing, you're not going to buy that coffee or soft drink or shirt or whatever it is. So you cannot put anything over — at least, not more than once. And who wants to stay in business putting something over once?

You have to tell a real story. One, is to sell him. But it's to let him know he has a choice. Our economy is an economy of choice. We, in this country, under this wonderful system we have, despite the fact that it has some faults, of course, have a tremendous choice. In worldly goods. And while life is more to it than just worldly goods, still, this man has appetites and needs. And here we have this great choice, be it a motorcar — you have a number of brands. They are all somewhat similar, but they all have their peculiar characteristics that make one of them maybe more desirable to you than another one would be.

Oh, another thing, business is quite competitive and people in executive life or even your good sharp clerks ... you must be on your toes. At least, that's what I and millions of other people feel about it. That's the way we're built, I guess.

I think most people want to do a darn good job and be known for that and have your name mean quality. I want that. So, in a sense, they're seeking status. I'd like to be known as an outstanding, sound human being. I would like to shoot for that. I think most of our fellow citizens have similar views. They want to be the best plumber there is, or the best whatever it is. Manager of a store, a salesman, or minister, or Pope. President Johnson, I'm sure, is driven to being the outstanding President we've ever had, if he can. So to me, status is wrapped up in striving to do the best you can with the material you have.

Often I think, status is used as a term of ... derision isn't quite the word. I think it stems from people who want to be known as this without putting in the sweat, let's say, to earn it. But people who have earned it, I don't think are thought of as status seekers.

So that means to me a certain amount of night work that I have to do. I think you would be a very smart person who could leave his problems at the office at night, and go home and not take his briefcase or his work home with him. I have not been able to do this. As a rule, I'd say, oh, eighty percent of the time that I take my briefcase home, and that is every single night, I will do some amount of work at home. Usually it involves the kind of reading and studying of business papers that I cannot handle in the office, because there's too many meetings, calls, conferences, and so on.

Again, this is violating a principle of my own ... which I violate constantly. Thinking about retirement slightly more as the years go by, I don't yet have a plan ... a particular hobby that would carry me through. I've seen and heard too much of people who go into retirement, finding themselves completely lost and just desolate. And finding themselves living without purpose. ...

My other interest at night involves Army. I'm still in the Army Reserves. And that takes another night or so a week for much of the year. And in the summer months I go on active duty, during one of the summer months. Now that's the kind of a hobby you would not carry into retirement. . . .

This has been fascinating to me. When I was drafted, I was routed into the Army like millions of others. I had to start out as an acting private. I went down to Camp Roberts, California, an infantry training center. Many of my friends, it seemed all of them, had big deals. They became commissioned right out of civilian life. I went to the infantry. I decided, all right, if this has to be my lot, I'll try and be as fine an infantry soldier as I can.

So what I had to start out with was an acting private. And then I finally fought my way up to a corporal.

That was almost the hardest promotion I ever got, to be an infantry corporal, to teach machine gun and BAR and M-1 and so on, and drilling people, of course. And getting my work done. All my life I'm sure it's getting my work done, whatever that work is. But anyway, I went to Fort Benning, Georgia, and was commissioned in the infantry after seventeen weeks there.

When I came out of the service as a first lieutenant, I thought I wouldn't stay in the Reserve, except that I didn't want to get drafted again if some other troubles came on the scene, and have to start back again as a private. I felt, by golly, I'm going to stay closer to this, because I saw already from my service overseas that the Russians were, oh, acting kinda tough. They really were. And I didn't know whether there'd be fighting or anything like that, but I thought I'd just better keep close to the scene. So I stayed there ever since, and that was 1946 when I got out of the service.

Here's what it's been since 1950: I've been in the Command General Staff College. I've been privileged, I claim, to be in it. It's a five-year course in the Reserve. You study all aspects of management and organization. The principle is the same, whether it be in business or, you know, military or political affairs. There are certain principles of organization . . .

In the military, you're studying how to serve on a staff, or be the commander of a unit. And you study personnel, all about it: from obtaining of personnel, training of personnel, the morale of personnel, and so on. It's all organizing men, training them to bring about the objective, winning battles. But that's what's so fascinating to me.

Let me reach over and get something and show it to you. Here's a book that's put out by the United States Army Commanding General Staff College. This is selected readings in management and in this book are articles by outstanding business and organizational minds, not necessarily military minds. Here as I flip through the contents, we find thirty-two articles in this book. And Ralph Cordiner, former president of General Electric, has an article in here. And there's one in here by a man from General Motors. And so on . . . Freedom, Authority, and Decentralization, there's another title for you. Managerial Skills for a New Age and so on. So, the Human Side of Enterprise. The Meaning of Control . . . where automatic data-processing fits into the Army future. . . .

You learn to be a commanding officer of a military unit. And to do it, it isn't just a matter of attention, right face, forward march. It isn't just marching men around. It's how do we organize the manpower of the country to preserve the country in case of an attack, let's say. That gets into mobilizing your manpower and your industry.

We've sent another division over to Vietnam, for example. All right, what kind of men, what kind of machines, what kind of weapons do they have? Where do they come from? How do you train these men? How do you exert leadership? How do you build loyalty and discipline? And how will a job get to be done? All those things are in this course. So having studied that for five years, I graduated in 1955 out of Fort Riley, and then was asked to serve on the faculty of our Chicago USAR School. And I've done that for the intervening ten years.

It's loyalty and discipline . . . serving the company then. But I don't think you set out blindly to serve or to just be a disciplined person. I think we all try to find expressions of ourself, an outlet. Also, I think most people want to do something for somebody, would like to do noble things, if possible. Now, most of all, of course we have to exist, I guess. That is, you have to earn a livelihood, let's say. So sometimes you do whatever has to be done.

So now the service years came next for me, the Army. Here I was with how many? . . . twelve million men in the total services. And so there I was, identifying with a tremendous group. So now out of the service and back to a firm like this. One of the largest agencies in the world. There are certain limitations, but it hasn't bothered me. I try to do the finest job of execution I can.

I mean, everybody can't have his own policy. There's never been a time, including our American Revolution, where every citizen thought that the policy was the best. But when the gavel falls and the policy is adopted, so to speak, we all want to — I think most of us certainly want to — to carry out this policy.

As a formal Catholic, I defer to what the bodies of the Catholic Church decide. I know in the matter of birth control, they are besieged by their own inner thoughts and by all the evidence that's mounting about the population explosion. And that we're going to control this, and control it in a way that will be an honorable way. But you have to support what your organization does.

In the same sense, you and I may not agree with what Congress and the President say, but we support it because they are our duly elected authorities. So I hope it isn't a war policy, believe me. . . . But as long as there is a draft going on, I think when a man is tapped, he should be given all the encouragement he can. And encourage a man rather than . . . Oh, wasn't it too bad a fella was caught, or something like that . . . you know.

Now, on the Bomb, I'm frightened by the implications of it, yes, and horrified by it, yes. But when I think you live with a threat or a horror for several years, or as many years as we have now, since 1945, and this is twenty years now, you begin to get adapted. They call it, like negative adaptation. Or you work in a foundry where they're pounding all the time, pretty soon you don't notice it. You don't hear it. The same with this A-Bomb threat. And I'm sure I speak for many, many people on this, don't from day to day worry and fret about it. We all hope that nothing will happen, but when you get so busy trying to work to support your family, or do some charitable works, or PTA or a youth movement, you don't have the time, thank heavens, to contemplate constantly the Bomb.

What I see coming is this wonderful conquest of outer space. Heaven only knows what we're going to find out there, there may be life out there and so on. But I think the opening up of outer space has helped ever so much in international relations, because if we find one speck of life out there, right away I think any aggressor nation or the United States, will somehow feel a little more closely bound to each other against what may be a common threat or a common unknown out there. Even in race relations, I think this helps a lot: the fact that we're going together out into outer space.

The conversation was resumed in a bar, frequented by advertising men. After a couple of martinis . . .

Yes, so much today is made of the matter of guilt, about bearing the guilt, and so on. I think we ought to throw off this burden. You and I were born into the world as we are, different religions and the color we were born with. And had nothing whatever to do with bringing slaves over here or with crucifying Christ or with defaming Buddha or whatever. So we have our own lives to live here, and are trying to do the best we can with our fellow man. And so to heck with the burdens of the past and guilt that spans down to us. I reject that.

I don't think any Negro, a bright, young, forward-looking Negro, expects you or me to bear any kind of guilt whatever. You and I also don't look at him to be any stereotype. We think he's a bright, young, up-and-coming fella and he's gonna earn his own way, and he's gonna be given the right, just as you and I have these rights, to vote and to make our way in life.

Here's what I mean: there's a lot of excess baggage that we attach unto ourselves in life, called this matter of guilt. We should quit calling up this old baggage of the past . . . and all the old photos and all the old wedding gowns and stuff that you find in the attic, old picture frames and what not. Quit taking them from place to place. Why should we, white or black, haul them into our new, nice, burgeoning homes in the suburbs or in the rebuilt areas of the city? Leave that in the past and let's forge our ways into the future, on our own merits. And I expect that of the young white man and the young colored man. And by golly, they expect that of themselves.

Where is it better to be a young Negro than in these states today? It's an exciting future for them. They don't have to be solemn and belligerent. They are coming in now and learning. To me, to be a Negro today is tremendous. How could you want a greater challenge? How could you find squarer, fairer rules than we have in our society?

I have a few Negro acquaintances. I wish I had more. We've had quite a few Negro women that have come out, whom I really know mostly by their first names. But I think we've treated them always as equal. Not equal in the sense as when you employ somebody you have to tell them what it is you're employing them for. To do. So you spell out the kind of work involved . . . gardening or maybe washing or cleaning the house. My wife and I have had many, many relationships this way, but not in a haughty, you know, sophisticated way at all. At least, I don't think so. I could say I love these people and I hope we've treated them very fairly.

The kingdom of God is within you. Someone said this, and I think it was Paul, who in turn was Saul, at one point and who was a prosecutor of the Jews, was he not? To subjugate the Christians or those who differed with him. I think that God is also within us, each and every one of us, and if we act badly with the gifts that he has given us, we become an anti-God or a devil or whatever you want to call it. But if we work for the good of our fellow man, we get rewards ourselves, and become a little bit of this omnipresent God . . .

Charlie Landesfahr, 34

He is copy chief at a middle-sized advertising agency. With his wife and two small children, he lives in an upper-class North Shore suburb.

"My father discovered the other day that the Landesfahrs came over in 1619, a year before the Pilgrims. I asked him whether they were indentured servants or something. He got kind of upset about it. I thought it was pretty funny."

He's a graduate of an Ivy League college; he was a Fulbright Fellow in Austria; and he toured Europe as a drummer in a jazz band. While working toward his Ph.D. in Germanic languages, he thought of going into teaching. He "discovered that faculty wives were possibly more shrewish than corporation wives." He came to the conclusion that the campus world was more restrictive than that of business: telling off a department head might hurt your chances for a job at some other college; the word is passed along. "In advertising, everything is so secret. If you insult the boss, he's not likely to tell the next guy about it, because he might be coming to you for a job three years hence. Three years is the average tenure at an agency." It enables men to blow up, without repercussions elsewhere.

On occasion, he writes articles, free-lance, for national magazines.

I find my job amusing. Soaps and cars, the differences are minute. If you're gonna write copy, *you* decide what the differences are gonna be. The dumb guys call it "image." The smart guys call it "a unit of communication." You become cynical, of course. One of our clients puts out a product in three different boxes. It's the same stuff, comes out of the same tube. It goes into different boxes with different labels. One advertising agency has one name to sell, another agency has another name to sell, and we have the third. Mrs. Housewife prefers one over all the others. If you approach it cynically, you find it amusing.

I know there's a guy, my counterpart somewhere, doing what I'm doing: trying to come up with a clever way of saying his is better than mine. A person is cynical if he is able to stand outside of the box he's in, right? So I stand outside and I say, "I'm doing what this guy's doing, and isn't he a funny man?" And I have to say, "Gee, I'm a funny man, too."

It takes a great deal of con to sound honest in this world. This is the crux of cynicism, I think. It's bigger than just the advertising world. The big lie is part of the outside world, too. Red versus white, yellow versus black, and what have you. This is the ball we're walking on. The big lie is promulgated by the advertising world, but it's a lot of little lies that add up to the big lie, okay?

It affects me both inside and outside. It affects me when I come home. There are some lucky ones who have a product that by its nature is unique. People are better off with it than without it. They're the easy ones. They don't make you feel cynical because you say, okay, I simply present this as *Consumer Reports* might do. My difficulty is that I get involved in something I don't believe in and I bring that cynicism home with me. You face ridiculous problems that nobody should bother to spend his time solving.

The great big white goods, the things that keep our economy going — refrigerators, stoves, all the things that used to be porcelain and white — they're now tinted. This is new. There's pop art that goes along with them. Very nice. Mandrake the Magician coming off the wall at you as you open your refrigerator to get your orange juice.

I'll use the word *creative* and bug you about that one, 'cause that's a gas, too. They're known as creative types in memos from heads of departments. "We just hired two more creative types." They don't say who they are or where they came from. The creative types have idols all right. Their idols are the modern communications heroes. They can list maybe five or six agencies in the whole country and these are the guys who do the Volkswagen ads, Polaroid ads, American Airlines, and maybe a few others. Gee, they aren't insulting my intelligence, see? So us guys that don't like to have our intelligence insulted admire these guys. . . .

The work pays too well. As a young man, moving from one agency to another, you can make a whole lot of money fast. Glibness, good appearance, and social acceptability, these are the three things really. With these three things, a guy will get ahead, no matter what company he's in.

The advertising business, like so many others, is becoming computerized in areas such as consumer research, motivational research, kinds of things machines can do in part. Of course, sociologists and psychologists are cutting in on the cake, too. There's a jumping on the bandwagon. It's terribly dependent on fads. The Ajax commercial, with the guy on the white horse and the long stiletto, who makes people white, has begun a whole new trend. This will last another three, four years. A white tornado coming out of your washing machine.

The consumer is a great big gaping jaw we're all trying to fill up with whatever we can cram down there, and the great hope is that the jaw will keep getting wider and wider. And the more products there are, the more, you know . . . The population explosion is a grand thing for business, of course. My God, think of all the machines we can sell to more people. A third of the population is going to be under the age of twenty in another year or two, I imagine. They got all the money to spend, that's great. We can sell them records and we can sell them cars and dresses and brassieres at that age, and the whole bit. We can make the whole world like us very fast and make a lot of money on it. We can make it an American middle-class universe. Sell this product against that product. And what you do is to try to find reasons why yours is better. If you can't find those, God help you. It takes time to realize they're identical. We're all conditioned to think this soap is different from that soap, until we go to the factory and see them coming off the same production line. There are times when I still believe they're different. It's a belief we have to hold on to.

Oh yeah, I'm established. And I'm digging tunnels like crazy to get out. Do I like my job? No. I deplore it. I hate it, I come home sick at night about it. I'm a pretty unhappy guy some nights. And a pretty mean father. I'm not able to divorce myself at five o'clock from what's happened to me all day long — or what I've been making happen to other people. As a consequence, evenings are not always pleasant.

I've discovered that I like writing. All right, a diaper pin's a useful thing, and ours is better than the next guy's because it's got a soft point and won't stick you. All right, we don't draw blood. What's wrong with it is you're not writing what you care about. You're writing what somebody else cares about. And you're a hack.

Call me a modern-day propagandist looking for a cause. When I was in college, there were no causes. We were known as the apathetic generation. All of a sudden there are a number of causes: civil rights, things like conservation, the population explosion, the H-Bomb.

The point is I've learned techniques, let's call them. Maybe I've even been brainwashed in a certain kind of way. Or I've learned how to use brainwash techniques, if you want to be cynical about it. Maybe it's just that I've learned a kind of persuasiveness and I'd like to put it to better use, okay?

It's a restlessness, something I've got to live with day in and day out. As you grow up, there are things more meaningful than others. Maybe it's because my dad took me to the North Woods when I was a kid, who knows? Trees, birds, wildlife — I don't want to call it a cause. But it's an important fact of man's existence, from which the urban community tends to cut him off. The more he gets cut off from certain roots . . . I'd like to do a series on conservation.

Maybe I'm ready to try to make it on my own. But at this point, it's irrelevant. I now have a family, two children, and I've got to weigh that balance against the other balances. I'm willing to take half the salary to do something I give a hoot in hell about. The trap, of course, is my past. I've been very successful writing for advertising agencies and I have a mortgage and a standard of living. . . .

Twice in my life I've reached for a knife, wanted to stick it into a guy's gut. We hold ourselves in check, fortunately. You learn to count to ten and you do all kinds of things, you bite something. The doctor's told me my safety valve's in my stomach. What I get, I get a very upset stomach. (Laughs.) That turns me off, that puts me flat on my back. You can't get in trouble there.

Kenneth Kenniston | # Moral Exhaustion and Student Revolution

---

Philippe Aries, in his remarkable book, "Centuries of Childhood," points out that, until the end of the Middle Ages, no separate stage of childhood was recognized in Western societies. Infancy ended at approximately 6 or 7, whereupon most children were integrated into adult life, treated as small men and women and expected to work as junior partners of the adult world. Only later was childhood recognized as a separate stage of

SOURCE: Appeared as "You Have to Grow Up in Scarsdale to Know. . ." by Kenneth Kenniston in *The New York Times Magazine* of April 27, 1969. Copyright © 1969 by The New York Times Company. Reprinted by permission.

life, and our own century is the first to "guarantee" it by requiring universal primary education.

The recognition of adolescence as a stage of life is of even more recent origin, the product of the 19th and 20th centuries. Only as industrial societies became prosperous enough to defer adult work until after puberty could they create institutions — like widespread secondary-school education — that would extend adolescence to virtually all young people. Recognition of adolescence also arose from the vocational and psychological requirements of these societies, which needed much higher levels of training and psychological development than could be guaranteed through primary education alone. There is, in general, an intimate relationship between the way a society defines the stages of life and its economic, political and social characteristics.

Today, in more developed nations, we are beginning to witness the recognition of still another stage of life. Like childhood and adolescence, it was initially granted only to a small minority, but is now being rapidly extended to an ever-larger group. I will call this the stage of "youth," and by that I mean both a further phase of disengagement from society and the period of psychological development that intervenes between adolescence and adulthood. This stage, which continues into the 20's and sometimes into the 30's, provides opportunities for intellectual, emotional and moral development that were never afforded to any other large group in history. In the student revolts we are seeing one result of this advance.

I call the extension of youth an advance advisedly. Attendance at a college or university is a major part of this extension, and there is growing evidence that this is, other things being equal, a good thing for the student. Put in an oversimplified phrase, it tends to free him — to free him from swallowing unexamined the assumptions of the past, to free him from the superstitions of his childhood, to free him to express his feelings more openly and to free him from irrational bondage to authority.

I do not mean to suggest, of course, that all college graduates are free and liberated spirits, unencumbered by irrationality, superstition, authoritarianism or blind adherence to tradition. But these findings do indicate that our colleges, far from cranking out only machinelike robots who will provide skilled manpower for the economy, are also producing an increasing number of highly critical citizens — young men and women who have the opportunity, the leisure, the affluence and the educational resources to continue their development beyond the point where most people in the past were required to stop it.

So, one part of what we are seeing on campuses throughout the world is not a reflection of how bad higher education is, but rather of its extraordinary accomplishments. Even the moral righteousness of the student rebels, a quality both endearing and infuriating to their elders, must be judged at least partially a consequence of the privilege of an extended youth; for a prolonged development, we know, encourages the individual to elaborate a more personal, less purely conventional sense of ethics.

What the advanced nations have done is to create their own critics on a mass basis — that is, to create an ever-larger group of young people who take the highest values of their societies as their own, who internalize these values and identify them with their own best selves, and who are willing to struggle to implement them. At the same time, the extension of youth has lessened the personal risks of dissent: These young people have been freed from the requirements of work, gainful employment and even marriage, which permits them to criticize their society from a protected position of disengagement.

But the mere prolongation of development need not automatically lead to unrest. To be sure, we have granted to millions the opportunity to examine their societies, to compare them with their values and to come to a reasoned judgment of the existing order. But why should their judgment today be so unenthusiastic?

What protesting students throughout the world share is a mood more than an ideology or a program, a mood that says the existing system — the power structure — is hypocritical, unworthy of respect, outmoded and in urgent need of reform. In addition, students everywhere speak of repression, manipulation, and authoritarianism. (This is paradoxical, considering the apparently great freedoms given them in many nations. In America, for example, those who complain most loudly about being suffocated by the subtle tyranny of the Establishment usually attend the institutions where student freedom is greatest.) Around this general mood, specific complaints arrange themselves as symptoms of what students often call the "exhaustion of the existing society."

To understand this phenomenon we must recognize that, since the Second World War, some societies have indeed begun to move past the industrial area into a new world that is post-industrial, technological, post-modern, post-historic or, in Brzezinski's term, "technectronic." In Western Europe, the United States, Canada and Japan, the first contours of this new society are already apparent. And, in many other less-developed countries, middle-class professionals (whose children become activists) often live in post-industrial enclaves within pre-industrial societies. Whatever we call the post-industrial world, it has demonstrated that, for the first time, man can produce more than enough to meet his material needs.

This accomplishment is admittedly blemished by enormous problems of economic distribution in the advanced nations, and it is in terrifying contrast to the overwhelming poverty of the Third World. Nevertheless, it is clear that what might be called "the problem of production" *can*, in principle, be solved. If all members of American society, for example, do not have enough material goods, it is because the system of distribution is flawed. The same is true, or will soon be true, in many other nations that are approaching advanced states of industrialization. Characteristically, these nations, along with the most technological, are those where student unrest has recently been most prominent.

The transition from industrial to post-industrial society brings with it a major shift in social emphases and values. Industrializing and industrial societies tend to be oriented toward solving the problem of production. An industrial ethic — sometimes Protestant, sometimes Socialist, sometimes Communist — tends to emphasize psychological qualities like self-discipline, delay of gratification, achievement-orientation and a strong emphasis on economic success and productivity. The social, political and economic institutions of these societies tend to be organized in a way that is consistent with the goal of increasing production. And industrial societies tend to apply relatively uniform standards, to reward achievement rather than status acquired by birth, to emphasize emotional neutrality ("coolness") and rationality in work and public life.

The emergence of post-industrial societies, however, means that growing numbers of the young are brought up in family environments where abundance, relative economic security, political freedom and affluence are simply facts of life, not goals to be striven for. To such people the psychological imperatives, social institutions and cultural values of the industrial ethic seem largely outdated and irrelevant to their own lives.

Once it has been demonstrated that a society *can* produce enough for all of its members, at least some of the young turn to other goals: for example, trying to make sure that society *does* produce enough and distributes it fairly, or searching for ways to live meaningfully with the goods and the leisure they *already* have. The problem is that our society has, in some realms, exceeded its earlier targets. Lacking new ones, it has become exhausted by its success.

When the values of industrial society become devitalized, the élite sectors of youth — the most affluent, intelligent, privileged and so on — come to feel that they live in institutions whose demands lack moral authority or, in the current jargon, "credibility." Today, the moral imperative and urgency behind production, acquisition, materialism and abundance has been lost.

Furthermore, with the lack of moral legitimacy felt in "the System," the least request for loyalty, restraint or conformity by its representatives — for example, by college presidents and deans — can easily be seen as a moral outrage, an authoritarian repression, a manipulative effort to "co-opt" students into joining the Establishment and an exercise in "illegitimate authority" that must be resisted. From this conception springs at least part of the students' vague sense of oppression. And, indeed, perhaps their peculiar feeling of suffocation arises ultimately from living in societies without vital ethical claims.

Given such a situation, it does not take a clear-cut issue to trigger a major protest. I doubt, for example, that college and university administrators are in fact *more* hypocritical and dishonest than they were in the past. American intervention in Vietnam, while many of us find it unjust and cruel, is not inherently *more* outrageous than other similar imperialistic interventions by America and other nations within the last century. And the position of blacks in this country, although disastrously and unjustifiably disadvantaged, is, in some economic and legal respects, better than ever before. Similarly, the conditions for students in America have never been as good, especially, as I have noted, at those élite colleges where student protests are most common.

But this is *precisely* the point: It is *because* so many of the *other* problems of American society seem to have been resolved, or to be resolvable in principle, that students now react with new indignation to old problems, turn to new goals and propose radical reforms.

So far I have emphasized the moral exhaustion of the old order and the fact that, for the children of post-industrial affluence, the once-revolutionary claims of the industrial society have lost much of their validity. I now want to argue that we are witnessing on the campuses of the world a fusion of *two revolutions* with distinct historical origins. One is a continuation of the old and familiar revolution of the industrial society, the liberal-democratic-egalitarian revolution that started in America and France at the turn of the 18th century and spread to virtually every nation in the world. (Not completed in any of them, its contemporary American form is, above all, to be found in the increased militancy of blacks.) The other is the new revolution, the post-industrial one, which seeks to define new goals relevant to the 20th and 21st centuries.

In its social and political aspects, the first revolution has been one of universalization, to use the sociologist's awkward term. It has involved the progressive extension to more and more people of economic, political and social rights, privileges and opportunities originally available only to the aristocracy, then to the middle class, and now in America to the relatively affluent white working class. It is, in many respects, a *quantitative* revolution. That is, it concerns itself less with the quality of life than with the amount of political freedom, the quantity and distribution of goods or the amount and level of injustice.

As the United States approaches the targets of the first revolution, on which this society was built, to be poor shifts from being an unfortunate fact of life to being an outrage. And, for the many who have never experienced poverty, discrimination, exploitation or oppression, even to *witness* the existence of these evils in the lives of others suddenly becomes intolerable. In our own time the impatience to complete the first revolution has grown apace, and we find less willingness to compromise, wait and forgive among the young, especially among those who now take the values of the old revolution for granted — seeing them not as goals, but as *rights*.

A subtle change has thus occurred. What used to be utopian ideals — like equality, abundance and freedom from discrimination — have now become demands, inalienable rights upon which one can insist without brooking any compromise. It is noteworthy that, in today's student confrontations, no one requests anything. Students present their "demands."

So, on the one hand, we see a growing impatience to complete the first revolution. But, on the other, there is a newer revolution concerned with newer issues, a revolution that is less social, economic or political than psychological, historical and cultural. It is less concerned with the quantities of things than with their qualities, and it judges the virtually complete liberal revolution and finds it is still wanting.

"You have to have grown up in Scarsdale to know how bad things really are," said one radical student. This comment would probably sound arrogant, heartless and insensitive to a poor black, much less to a citizen of the Third World. But he meant something important by it. He meant that *even* in the Scarsdales of America, with their affluence, their upper-middle-class security and abundance, their well-fed, well-heeled children and their excellent schools, something is wrong. Economic affluence does not guarantee a feeling of personal fulfillment; political freedom does not always yield an inner sense of liberation and cultural freedom; social justice and equality may leave one with a feeling that something else is missing in life. "No to the consumer society!" shouted the bourgeois students of the Sorbonne during May and June of 1968 — a cry that understandably alienated French workers, for whom affluence and the consumer society are still central goals.

What, then, are the targets of the new revolution? As is often noted, students themselves don't know. They speak vaguely of "a society that has never existed," of "new values," of a "more humane world," of "liberation" in some psychological, cultural and historical sense. Their rhetoric is largely negative; they are stronger in opposition than in proposals for reform; their diagnoses often seem accurate, but their prescriptions are vague; and they are far more articulate in urging the immediate completion of the first revolution than in defining the goals of the second. Thus, we can only indirectly discern trends that point to the still-undefined targets of the new revolution.

What are these trends and targets?

First, there is a revulsion against the notion of quantity, particularly economic quantity and materialism, and a turn toward concepts of quality. One of the most delightful slogans of the French student was, "Long live the passionate revolution of creative intelligence!" In a sense, the achievement of abundance may allow millions of contemporary men and women to examine, as only a few artists and madmen have examined in the past, the quality, joyfulness and zestfulness of experience. The "expansion of consciousness"; the stress on the expressive, the aesthetic and the creative; the emphasis on imagination, direct perception and fantasy — all are part of the effort to enhance the quality of this experience.

Another goal of the new revolution involves a revolt against uniformity, equalization, standardization and homogenization — not against technology itself, but against the "technologization of man." At times, this revolt approaches anarchic quaintness, but it has a positive core as well — the demand that individuals be appreciated, not because of their similarities or despite their differences, but because they *are* different, diverse, unique and noninterchangeable. This attitude is evident in many areas: for example, the insistence upon a cultivation of personal idiosyncrasy, mannerism and unique aptitude. Intellectually, it is expressed in the rejection of the melting-pot and consensus-politics view of American life in favor of a post-homogeneous America in which cultural diversity and conflict are underlined rather than denied.

The new revolution also involves a continuing struggle against psychological or institutional closure or rigidity in any form, even the rigidity of a definite adult role. Positively, it extols the virtues of openness, motion and continuing human development. What Robert J. Lifton has termed the protean style is clearly in evidence. There is emerging a concept of a lifetime of personal change, of an adulthood of continuing self-transformation, of an adaptability and an openness to the revolutionary modern world that will enable the individual to remain "with it" — psychologically youthful and on top of the present.

Another characteristic is the revolt against centralized power and the complementary demand for participation. What is demanded is not merely the consent of the governed, but the involvement of the governed. "Participatory democracy" summarizes this aspiration, but it extends far beyond the phrase and the rudimentary social forms that have sprung up around it. It extends to the demand for relevance in education — that is, for a chance for the student to participate in his own educational experience in a way that involves all of his faculties, emotional and moral as well as intellectual. The demand for "student power" (or, in Europe, "co-determination") is an aspect of the same theme: At Nanterre, Columbia, Frankfurt and Harvard, students increasingly seek to participate in making the policies of their universities.

This demand for participation is also embodied in the new ethic of "meaningful human relationships," in which individuals confront each other without masks, pretenses and games. They "relate" to each other as unique and irreplaceable human beings, and develop new forms of relationships from which all participants will grow.

In distinguishing between the old and the new revolutions, and in attempting to define the targets of the new, I am, of course, making distinctions that students themselves rarely make. In any one situation the two revolutions are joined and fused, if not confused. For example, the Harvard students' demand for "restructuring the university" is essentially the second revolution's demand for participation; but their demand for an end to university "exploitation" of the surrounding community is tied to the more traditional goals of the first revolution. In most radical groups there is a range of opinion that starts with the issues of the first (racism, imperialism, exploitation, war) and runs to the concerns of the second (experiential education, new life styles, meaningful participation, consciousness-expansion, relatedness, encounter and community). The first revolution is personified by Maoist-oriented Progressive Labor party factions within the student left, while the second is represented by hippies, the "acid left," and the Yippies. In any individual, and in all student movements, these revolutions coexist in uneasy and often abrasive tension.

Furthermore, one of the central problems for student movements today is the absence of any theory of society that does justice to the new world in which we of the most industrialized nations live. In their search for rational critiques of present societies, students turn to theories like Marxism that are intricately bound up with the old revolution.

Such theories make the ending of economic exploitation, the achievement of social justice, the abolition of racial discrimination and the development of political participation and freedom central, but they rarely deal adequately with the issues of the second revolution. Students inevitably try to adapt the rhetoric of the first to the problems of the second, using concepts that are often blatantly inadequate to today's world.

Even the concept of "revolution" itself is so heavily laden with images of political, economic and social upheaval that it hardly seems to characterize the equally radical but more social-psychological and cultural transformations involved in the new revolution. One student, recognizing this, called the changes occurring in his California student group, "too radical to be called a revolution." Students are thus often misled by their borrowed vocabulary, but most adults are even more confused, and many are quickly led to the mistaken conclusion that today's student revolt is nothing more than a repetition of Communism's in the past.

Failure to distinguish between the old and new revolutions also makes it impossible to consider the critical question of how compatible they are with each other. Does it make sense — or is it morally right — for today's affluent American students to seek imagination, self-actualization, individuality, openness and relevance when most of the world and many in America live in deprivation, oppression and misery?

The fact that the first revolution is "completed" in Scarsdale does not mean that it is (or soon will be) in Harlem or Appalachia — to say nothing of Bogotá or Calcutta. For many children of the second revolution, the meaning of life may be found in completing the first — that is, in extending to others the "rights" they have always taken for granted.

For others the second revolution will not wait; the question, "What lies beyond affluence?" demands an answer now. Thus, although we may deem it self-indulgent to pursue the goals of the new revolution in a world where so much misery exists, the fact is that in the advanced nations it is upon us, and we must at least learn to recognize it.

Finally, beneath my analysis lies an assumption I had best make explicit.

Many student critics argue that their societies have failed miserably. My argument, a more historical one perhaps, suggests that our problem is not only that industrial societies have failed to keep all their promises, but that they have succeeded in some ways beyond all expectations. Abundance was once a distant dream, to be postponed to a hereafter of milk and honey; today, most Americans are affluent. Universal mass education was once a Utopian goal; today in America almost the entire population completes high school, and almost half enters colleges and universities.

The notion that individuals might be free, en masse, to continue their psychological, intellectual, moral and cognitive development through their teens and into their 20's would have been laughed out of court in any century other than our own; today, that opportunity is open to millions of young Americans. Student unrest is a reflection not only of the failures, but of the extraordinary successes of the liberal-industrial revolution. It therefore occurs in the nations and in the colleges where, according to traditional standards, conditions are best.

But for many of today's students who have never experienced anything but affluence, political freedom and social equality, the old vision is dead or dying. It may inspire bitterness and outrage when it is not achieved, but it no longer animates or guides. In place of it, students (and many who are not students) are searching for a new vision, a new set of values, a new set of targets appropriate to the post-industrial era — a myth, an ideology or a set of goals that will concern itself with the quality of life and answer the question, "Beyond freedom and affluence, what?"

What characterizes student unrest in the developed nations is this peculiar mixture of the old and the new, the urgent need to fulfill the promises of the past and, at the same time, to define the possibilities of the future.

Juliet Mitchell | # Women:
The Longest Revolution

Production

The biological differentiation of the sexes and the division of labour have, throughout history, seemed an interlocked necessity. Anatomically smaller and weaker, woman's physiology and her psycho-biological metabolism appear to render her a less useful member of a work-force. It is always stressed how, particularly in the early stages of social development, man's physical superiority gave him the means of conquest over nature which was

SOURCE: *New Left Review*, November/December 1966. This excerpt is reprinted by permission.

denied to women. Once woman was accorded the menial tasks involved in maintenance whilst man undertook conquest and creation, she became an aspect of the things preserved: private property and children. All socialist writers on the subject mentioned earlier — Marx, Engels, Bebel, De Beauvoir — link the confirmation and continuation of woman's oppression after the establishment of her physical inferiority for hard manual work with the advent of private property. But woman's physical weakness has never prevented her from performing work as such (quite apart from bringing up children) — only specific types of work, in specific societies. In Primitive, Ancient, Oriental, Medieval and Capitalist societies, the *volume* of work performed by women has always been considerable (it has usually been much more than this). It is only its form that is in question. Domestic labour, even today, is enormous if quantified in terms of productive labour.[1] In any case women's physique has never permanently or even predominantly relegated them to menial domestic chores. In many peasant societies, women have worked in the fields as much as, or more than men.

The assumption behind most classical discussion is that the crucial factor starting the whole development of feminine subordination was women's lesser capacity for demanding physical work. But, in fact, this is a major oversimplification. Even within these terms, in history it has been woman's lesser capacity for violence as well as for work that has determined her subordination. In most societies woman has not only been less able than man to perform arduous kinds of work, she has also been less able to fight. Man not only has the strength to assert himself against nature, but also against his fellows. *Social coercion* has interplayed with the straightforward division of labour, based on biological capacity, to a much greater extent than generally admitted. Of course, it may not be actualized as direct aggression. In primitive societies women's physical unsuitability for the hunt is evident. In agricultural societies where women's inferiority is socially instituted they are given the arduous task of tilling and cultivation. For this coercion is necessary. In developed civilizations and more complex societies woman's physical deficiencies again become relevant. Women are no use either for war or in the construction of cities. But with early industrialization coercion once more becomes important. As Marx wrote: 'Insofar as machinery dispenses with muscular power, it becomes a means of

---

[1] Apologists who make out that housework, though time-consuming, is light and relatively enjoyable, are refusing to acknowledge the dull and degrading routine it entails. Lenin commented crisply: 'You all know that even when women have full rights, they still remain factually down-trodden because all housework is left to them. In most cases housework is the most unproductive, the most barbarous and the most arduous work a woman can do. It is exceptionally petty and does not include anything that would in any way promote the development of the woman'. (Collected Works xxx. 43). Today it has been calculated in Sweden, that 2,340 million hours a year are spent by women in housework compared with 1,290 million hours in industry. The Chase Manhattan Bank estimated a woman's overall working hours as averaging 99.6 per week.

employing labourers of slight muscular strength, and those whose bodily development is incomplete, but whose limbs are all the more supple. The labour of women and children was, therefore, the first thing sought for by capitalists who used machinery.'[2]

René Dumont points out that in many zones of tropical Africa today men are often idle, while women are forced to work all day.[3] This exploitation has no 'natural' source whatever. Women may perform their 'heavy' duties in contemporary African peasant societies not for fear of physical reprisal by their men, but because these duties are 'customary' and built into the role structures of the society. A further point is that coercion implies a different relationship from coercer to coerced than exploitation does. It is political rather than economic. In describing coercion, Marx said that the master treated the slave or serf as the 'inorganic and natural condition of its own reproduction.' That is to say, labour itself becomes like other natural things — cattle or soil: 'The original conditions of production appear as natural prerequisites, *natural conditions of the existence of the producer*, just as his living body, however reproduced and developed by him, is not originally established by himself, but appears as his *prerequisite*.'[4] This is preeminently woman's condition. For far from woman's physical weakness removing her from productive work, her social weakness has in these cases evidently made her the major slave of it.

This truth, elementary though it may seem, has nevertheless been constantly ignored by writers on the subject, with the result that an illegitimate optimism creeps into their predictions of the future. For if it is just the biological incapacity for the hardest physical work which has determined the subordination of women, then the prospect of an advanced machine technology, abolishing the need for strenuous physical exertion would seem to promise, therefore, the liberation of women. For a moment industrialization itself thus seems to herald women's liberation. Engels, for instance, wrote: 'The first premise for the emancipation of women is the reintroduction of the entire female sex into public industry . . . And this has become possible only as a result of modern large-scale industry, which not only permits of the participation of women in production in large numbers, but actually calls for it and, moreover strives to convert private domestic work also into a public industry.'[5] What Marx said of early industrialism is no less, but also *no more* true of an automated society: '. . . it is obvious that the fact of the collective working group being composed of individuals of both sexes and all ages, must necessarily, *under suitable conditions*, become

---

[2] Karl Marx, *Capital* I, 394.

[3] 'The African woman experiences a three-fold servitude: through forced marriage; through her dowry and polygamy, which increases the leisure time of men and simultaneously their social prestige; and finally through the very unequal division of labour.' René Dumont: *L'Afrique Noire est Mal Partie* (1962), p. 210.

[4] Karl Marx, *Precapitalist Economic Formations* op. cit., p. 87.

[5] Friedrich Engels, *op. cit.*, 11, 233 & 311.

a source of human development; although in its spontaneously developed, brutal, capitalistic form, where the labourer exists for the process of production, and not the process of production for the labourer, that fact is a pestiferous source of corruption and slavery.'[6] Industrial labour and automated technology both promise the preconditions for woman's liberation alongside man's — but no more than the preconditions. It is only too obvious that the advent of industrialization has not so far freed women in this sense, either in the West or in the East. In the West it is true that there was a great influx of women into jobs in the expanding industrial economy, but this soon levelled out, and there has been relatively little increase in recent decades. De Beauvoir hoped that automation would make a decisive, qualitative difference by abolishing altogether the physical differential between the sexes. But any reliance on this in itself accords an independent role to technique which history does not justify. Under capitalism, automation could possibly lead to an ever-growing structural unemployment which would expel women — the latest and least integrated recruits to the labour force and ideologically the most expendable for a bourgeois society — from production after only a brief interlude in it. Technology is mediated by the total social structure and it is this which will determine woman's future in work relations.

Physical deficiency is not now, any more than in the past, a sufficient explanation of woman's relegation to inferior status. Coercion has been ameliorated to an ideology shared by both sexes. Commenting on the results of her questionnaire of working women, Viola Klein notes: 'There is no trace of feminist egalitarianism — militant or otherwise — in any of the women's answers to our questionnaire; nor is it even implicitly assumed that women have a 'Right to Work.' "[7] Denied, or refusing, a role in *production*, woman does not even create the *pre*conditions of her liberation.

Reproduction

Women's absence from the critical sector of production historically, of course, has been caused not just by their physical weakness in a context of coercion — but also by their role in reproduction. Maternity necessitates periodic withdrawals from work, but this is not a decisive phenomenon. It is rather women's role in reproduction which has become, in capitalist society at least, the spiritual 'complement' of men's role in production.[8] Bearing children, bringing them up, and maintaining the home — these form the core of woman's natural vocation, in this ideology. This belief

---

[6] Karl Marx, *Capital* I, 394.

[7] Viola Klein, *Working Wives*, Institute of Personnel Management Occasional Papers, No. 15 (1960), p. 13.

[8] Maternity is *the* distinctive feature on which both sexes base their hopes: for oppression or liberation. The notion of woman's potential superiority on account of her procreative function reaches the absurd in Margherita Repetto: *Maternità e Famiglia, Condizioni per la Libertà della Donna, Rivesta Trimestrale* 11–12 (1964) but it is found even in Evelyne Sullerot: *Demain les Femmes* (1965).

has attained great force because of the seeming universality of the family as a human institution. There is little doubt that Marxist analyses have underplayed the fundamental problems posed here. The complete failure to give any operative content to the slogan of 'abolition' of the family is striking evidence of this (as well as of the vacuity of the notion). The void thus created has been quickly occupied by traditional beliefs such as Townsend's quoted above.

The biological function of maternity is a universal, atemporal fact, and as such has seemed to escape the categories of Marxist historical analysis. From it follows — apparently — the stability and omnipresence of the family, if in very different forms.[9] Once this is accepted, women's social subordination — however emphasized as an honourable, but different role (cf. the equal but 'separate' ideologies of Southern racists) — can be seen to follow inevitably as an *insurmountable* bio-historical fact. The casual chain then goes: Maternity, Family, Absence from Production and Public Life, Sexual Inequality.

The lynch-pin in this line of argument is the idea of the family. The notion that 'family' and 'society' are virtually co-extensive terms, or that an advanced society not founded on the nuclear family is now inconceivable, is widespread. It can only be seriously discussed by asking just what the family is — or rather what women's role in the family is. Once this is done, the problem appears in quite a new light. For it is obvious that woman's role in the family — primitive, feudal or bourgeois — partakes of three quite different structures: reproduction, sexuality, and the socialization of children. These are historically, not intrinsically, related to each other in the present modern family. Biological parentage is not necessarily identical with social parentage (adoption). It is thus essential to discuss: not the family as an unanalysed entity, but the separate *structures* which today compose it, but which may tomorrow be decomposed into a new pattern.

Reproduction, it has been stressed, is a seemingly constant atemporal phenomenon — part of biology rather than history. In fact this is an illusion. What is true is that the 'mode of reproduction' does not vary with the 'mode of production;' it can remain effectively the same through a number of different modes of production. For it has been defined till now, by its uncontrollable, natural character. To this extent, it has been an unmodified biological fact. As long as reproduction remained a natural phenomenon, of course, women were effectively doomed to social exploitation. In any sense, they were not masters of a large part of their lives. They had no choice as to whether or how often they gave birth to children (apart from repeated abortion), their existence was essentially subject to biological processes outside their control.

---

[9] Philippe Ariès in *Centuries of Childhood* (1962) shows that though the family may in some form always have existed it was often submerged under more forceful structures. In fact according to Ariès it has only acquired its present significance with the advent of industrialization.

Contraception

Contraception which was invented as a rational technique only in the 19th century was thus an innovation of world-historic importance. It is only now just beginning to show what immense consequences it could have, in the form of the pill. For what it means is that at last the mode of reproduction could potentially be transformed. Once child-bearing becomes totally voluntary (how much so is it in the West, even today?) its significance is fundamentally different. It need no longer be the sole or ultimate vocation of woman; it becomes one option among others.

Marx sees history as the development of man's transformation of nature, and thereby of himself — of human nature — in different modes of production. Today there are the technical possibilities for the humanization of the most natural part of human culture. This is what a change in the mode of reproduction could mean.

We are far from this state of affairs as yet. In France and Italy the sale of any form of contraception remains illegal. The oral contraceptive is the privilege of a moneyed minority in a few Western countries. Even here the progress has been realized in a typically conservative and exploitative form. It is made only for women, who are thus 'guineapigs' in a venture which involves both sexes.

The fact of overwhelming importance is that easily available contraception threatens to dissociate sexual from reproductive experience — which all contemporary bourgeois ideology tries to make inseparable, as the *raison d'être* of the family.

Reproduction and Production

At present, reproduction in our society is often a kind of sad mimicry of production. Work in a capitalist society is an alienation of labour in the making of a social product which is confiscated by capital. But it can still sometimes be a real act of creation, purposive and responsible, even in conditions of the worst exploitation. Maternity is often a caricature of this. The biological product — the child — is treated as if it were a solid product. Parenthood becomes a kind of substitute for work, an activity in which the child is seen as an object created by the mother, in the same way as a commodity is created by a worker. Naturally, the child does not literally escape, but the mother's alienation can be much worse than that of the worker whose product is appropriated by the boss. No human being can create another human being. A person's biological origin is an abstraction. The child as an autonomous person inevitably threatens the activity which claims to create it continually merely as a *possession* of the parent. Possessions are felt as extensions of the self. The child as a possession is supremely this. Anything the child does is therefore a threat to the mother herself who has renounced her autonomy through this misconception of her reproductive role. There are few more precarious ventures on which to base a life.

Furthermore even if the woman has emotional control over her child, legally and economically both she and it are subject to the father. The social cult of maternity is matched by the real socio-economic powerlessness of the mother. The psychological and practical benefits men receive from this are obvious. The converse of women's quest for creation in the child is men's retreat from his work into the family: 'When we come home, we lay aside our mask and drop our tools, and are no longer lawyers, sailors, soldiers, statesmen, clergymen, but only men. We fall again into our most human relations, which, after all, are the whole of what belongs to us as we are in ourselves.'[10]

Unlike her non-productive status, her capacity for maternity *is* a definition of woman. But it is only a physiological definition. So long as it is allowed to remain a substitute for action and creativity, and the home an area of relaxation for men, women will remain confined to the species, to her universal and natural condition.

Sexuality

Sexuality has traditionally been the most tabooed dimension of women's situation. The meaning of sexual freedom and its connexion with women's freedom is a particularly difficult subject which few socialist writers have cared to broach. Fourier alone identified the two totally, in lyrical strophes describing a sexual paradise of permutations — the famous phalansteries. 'Socialist morality' in the Soviet Union for a long time debarred serious discussion of the subject within the world communist movement. Marx himself — in this respect somewhat less liberal than Engels — early in his life expressed traditional views on the matter: '. . . the sanctification of the sexual instinct through exclusivity, the checking of instinct by laws, the moral beauty which makes nature's commandment ideal in the form of an emotional bond — (this is) the spiritual essence of marriage.'[11]

Yet it is obvious that throughout history women have been appropriated as sexual objects, as much as progenitors or producers. Indeed, the sexual relation can be assimilated to the statute of possession much more easily and completely than the productive or reproductive relationship. Contemporary sexual vocabulary bears eloquent witness to this — it is a comprehensive lexicon of reification. Later Marx was well aware of this, of course: 'Marriage . . . is incontestably a form of exclusive private property.'[12] But neither he nor his successors ever tried seriously to envisage the implications of this for socialism, or even for a structural analysis of women's condition. Communism, Marx stressed in the same passage, would not mean mere 'communalization' of women as common property. Beyond this, he never ventured.

---

[10] J. A. Froude: *Nemesis of Faith* (1849), p. 103.

[11] Karl Marx: *Chapitre de Marriage. Oeuvres Complètes* ed. Molitor *Oeuvres Philosophiques.* I, p. 25.

[12] Karl Marx, *Private Property and Communism, op. cit.* p. 153.

Some historical considerations are in order here. For if socialists have said nothing, the gap has been filled by liberal ideologues. A recent book, *Eros Denied* by Wayland Young, argues that Western civilization has been uniquely repressive sexually and in a plea for greater sexual freedom today compares it at some length with Oriental and Ancient societies. It is striking, however, that his book makes no reference whatever to women's status in these different societies, or to the different forms of marriage-contract prevalent in them. This makes the whole argument a purely formal exercise — an obverse of socialist discussions of women's position which ignores the problem of sexual freedom and its meanings. For while it is true that certain oriental or ancient (and indeed primitive) cultures were much less puritan than Western societies, it is absurd to regard this as a kind of 'transposable value' which can be abstracted from its social structure. In effect, in many of these societies sexual openness was accompanied by a form of polygamous exploitation which made it in practice an expression simply of masculine domination. Since art was the province of man, too, this freedom finds a natural and often powerful expression in art — which is often quoted as if it were evidence of the total quality of human relationships in the society. Nothing could be more misleading. What is necessary, rather than this naïve, hortatory core of historical example, is some account of the co-variation between the degrees of sexual liberty and openness and the position and dignity of women in different societies. Some points are immediately obvious. The actual history is much more dialectical than any liberal account presents it. Unlimited juridical polygamy — whatever the sexualization of the culture which accompanies it — is clearly a total derogation of woman's autonomy, and constitutes an extreme form of oppression. Ancient China is a perfect illustration of this. Wittfogel describes the extraordinary despotism of the Chinese *paterfamilias* — 'a liturgical semiofficial) policeman of his kin group.'[13] In the West, however, the advent of monogamy was in no sense an *absolute* improvement. It certainly did not create a one-to-one equality — far from it. Engels commented accurately: 'Monogamy does not by any means make its appearance in history as the reconciliation of man and woman, still less as the highest form of such a reconciliation. On the contrary, it appears as the subjugation of one sex by the other, as the proclamation of a conflict between the sexes entirely unknown hitherto in prehistoric times.'[14] But in the Christian era, monogamy took on a very specific form in the West. It was allied with an unprecedented régime of general sexual repression. In its Pauline version, this had a markedly anti-feminine bias, inherited from Judaism. With time this became diluted — feudal society, despite its subsequent reputation for ascetisim, practised formal monogamy with considerable actual acceptance of polygamous behaviour, at least within the ruling class. But here again

---

[13] Karl Wittfogel. *Oriental Despotism* (1957), p. 116.
[14] Friedrich Engels, *op. cit.*, 11, 224.

the extent of sexual freedom was only an index of masculine domination. In England, the truly major change occurred in the 16th century with the rise of militant puritanism and the increase of market relations in the economy. Lawrence Stone observes: 'In practice, if not in theory, the early 16th century nobility was a polygamous society, and some contrived to live with a succession of women despite the official prohibition on divorce . . . But impressed by Calvinist criticisms of the double standard, in the late 16th century public opinion began to object to the open maintenance of a mistress.'[15] Capitalism and the attendant demands of the newly emergent bourgeoisie accorded women a new status as wife and mother. Her legal rights improved; there was vigorous controversy over her social position; wife-beating was condemned. 'In a woman the bourgeois man is looking for a counterpart, not an equal.'[16] At the social periphery woman did occasionally achieve an equality which was more than her feminine function in a market society. In the extreme sects women often had completely equal rights: Fox argued that the Redemption restored Prelapsarian equality and Quaker women thereby gained a real autonomy. But once most of the sects were institutionalized, the need for family discipline was re-emphasized and woman's obedience with it. As Keith Thomas says, the Puritans 'had done something to raise women's status, but not really very much.'[17] The patriarchal system was retained and maintained by the economic mode of production. The transition to complete effective monogamy accompanied the transition to modern bourgeois society as we know it today. Like the market system itself, it represented a historic advance, at great historic cost. The formal, juridical equality of capitalist society and capitalist rationality now applied as much to the marital as to the labour contract. In both cases, nominal parity masks real exploitation and inequality. But in both cases the formal equality is itself a certain progress, which can help to make possible a further advance.

For the situation today is defined by a new contradiction. Once formal conjugal equality (monogamy) is established, sexual freedom as such — which under polygamous conditions was usually a form of exploitation — becomes, conversely, a possible force for liberation. It then means, simply, the freedom for both sexes to transcend the limits of present sexual institutions.

Historically, then, there has been a dialectical movement, in which sexual expression was 'sacrificed' in an epoch of more-or-less puritan repression, which nevertheless produced a greater parity of sexual roles, which in turn creates the precondition for a genuine sexual liberation, in the dual sense of equality *and* freedom — whose unity defines socialism.

---

[15] Lawrence Stone, *The Crisis of the Aristocracy* (1965), pp. 663–64.

[16] Simone de Beauvoir, *La Marche Longue* (1957), trans. *The Long March* (1958), p. 141.

[17] Keith Thomas, *Women and the Civil War Sects, Past and Present*, No. 13 (1958), p. 43.

This movement can be verified within the history of the 'sentiments.' The cult of *love* only emerges in the 12th century in opposition to legal marital forms and with a heightened valorization of women (courtly love). It thereafter gradually became diffused, and assimilated to marriage as such, which in its bourgeois form (romantic love) became a *free* choice for *life*. What is striking here is that monogamy as an institution in the West anticipated the idea of love by many centuries. The two have subsequently been officially harmonized, but the tension between them has never been abolished. There is a formal contradiction between the voluntary contractual character of 'marriage' and the spontaneous uncontrollable character of 'love' —the passion that is celebrated precisely for its involuntary force. The notion that it occurs only once in every life and can therefore be integrated into a voluntary contract becomes decreasingly plausible in the light of everyday experience — once sexual repression as a psycho-ideological system becomes at all relaxed.

Obviously, the main breach in the traditional value-pattern has so far been the increase in premarital sexual experience. This is now virtually legitimized in contemporary bourgeois society. But its implications are explosive for the ideological conception of marriage that dominates this society: that of an exclusive and permanent bond. A recent American anthology *The Family and the Sexual Revolution* reveals this very clearly: 'As far as extra-marital relations are concerned, the anti-sexualists are still fighting a strong, if losing, battle. The very heart of the Judeo-Christian sex ethic is that men and women shall remain virginal until marriage and that they shall be completely faithful after marriage. In regard to premarital chastity, this ethic seems clearly on the way out, and in many segments of the populace is more and more becoming a dead letter.'[18]

The current wave of sexual liberalization, in the present context, could become conducive to the greater general freedom of women. Equally it could presage new forms of oppression. The puritan-bourgeois creation of woman as 'counterpart' has produced the *precondition* for emancipation. But it gave statutory legal equality to the sexes at the cost of greatly intensified repression. Subsequently — like private property itself — it has become a brake on the further development of a free sexuality. Capitalist market relations have historically been a precondition of socialism; bourgeois marital relations (contrary to the denunciation of the *Communist Manifesto*) may equally be a precondition of women's liberation.

Socialization

Woman's biological destiny as mother becomes a cultural vocation in her role as socializer of children. In bringing up children, woman achieves her main social definition. Her suitability for socialization springs from her

---

[18] Albert Ellis, *The Folklore of Sex*, in *The Family and the Sexual Revolution*, ed. E. M. Schur (1964), p. 35.

physiological condition; her ability to lactate and occasionally relative inability to undertake strenuous work loads. It should be said at the outset that suitability is not inevitability. Lévi-Strauss writes: 'In every human group, women give birth to children and take care of them, and men rather have as their speciality hunting and warlike activities. Even there, though, we have ambiguous cases: of course, men never give birth to babies, but in many societies . . . they are made to act as if they did.'[19] Evans-Pritchard's description of the Nuer tribe depicts just such a situation. And another anthropologist, Margaret Mead, comments on the element of wish-fulfilment in the assumption of a *natural* correlation of feminity and nurturance: 'We have assumed that because it is convenient for a mother to wish to care for her child, this is a trait with which women have been more generously endowed by a careful teleological process of evolution. We have assumed that because men have hunted, an activity requiring enterprise, bravery, and initiative, they have been endowed with these useful aptitudes as part of their sex temperament.'[20] However, the cultural allocation of roles in bringing up children — and the limits of its variability — is not the essential problem for consideration. What is much more important is to analyse the nature of the socialization process itself and its requirements.

Parsons in his detailed analysis claims that it is essential for the child to have two 'parents,' one who plays an 'expressive' role, and one who plays an 'instrumental' role.[21] The nuclear family revolves around the two axes of generational hierarchy and of these two roles. In typically Parsonian idiom, he claims that 'At least one fundamental feature of the external situation of social systems — here a feature of the physiological organism — is a crucial reference point for differentiation in the family. This lies in the division of organisms into lactating and nonlactating classes.' In all groups, he and his colleagues assert, even in those primitive tribes discussed by Pritchard and Mead, the male plays the instrumental role *in relation* to the wife-mother. At one stage the mother plays an instrumental and expressive role *vis-à-vis* her infant: this is pre-oedipally when she is the source of approval and disapproval as well as of love and care. However, after this, the father, or male substitute (in matrilineal societies the mother's

---

[19] Claude Lévi-Strauss, *The Family*, in *Man, Culture and Society*, ed. H. L. Shapiro (1956), p. 274.

[20] Margaret Mead, *Sex and Temperament*, in *The Family and The Sexual Revolution*, *op. cit.*, pp. 207–8.

[21] Talcott Parsons and Robert F. Bales: *Family, Socialization and Interaction Process* (1956), p. 313. 'The instrumental-expressive distinction we interpret as essentially the differentiation of function, and hence of relative influence, in terms of 'external' vs. 'internal' functions of the system. The area of instrumental function concerns relations of the system to its situation outside the system, to meeting the adaptive conditions of its maintenance of equilibrium, and 'instrumentally' establishing the desired relations to *external* goal-objects. The expressive area concerns the 'internal' affairs of the system, the maintenance of integrative relations between the members, and regulation of the patterns and tension levels of its component units.' (Ibid., p. 47).

brother) takes over. In a modern industrial society two types of role are clearly important: the adult familial roles in the family of procreation, and the adult occupational role. The function of the family as such reflects the function of the women within it; it is primarily expressive. The person playing the integrated-adaptive-expressive role cannot be off all the time on instrumental-occupational errands — hence there is a built-in inhibition of the woman's work outside the home. Parson's analysis makes clear the exact role of the maternal socializer in contemporary American society.[22] It fails to go on to state that other aspects and modes of socialization are conceivable. What is valuable in Parsons' work is simply his insistence on the central importance of socialization as a process which is constitutive of any society (no Marxist has so far provided a comparable analysis). His general conclusion is that: 'It seems to be without serious qualification the opinion of competent personality psychologists that, though personalities differ greatly in their degrees of rigidity, certain broad fundamental patterns of 'character' are laid down in childhood (so far as they are not genetically inherited) and are not radically changed by adult experience. The exact degree to which this is the case or the exact age levels at which plasticity becomes greatly diminished, are not at issue here. The important thing is the fact of childhood character formation and its relative stability after that.'[23]

Infancy

This seems indisputable. One of the great revolutions of modern psychology has been the discovery of the decisive specific weight of infancy in the course of an individual life — a psychic time disproportionately greater than the chronological time. Freud began the revolution with his work on infantile sexuality; Klein radicalized it with her work on the first year of the infant's life. The result is that today we know far more than ever before how delicate and precarious a process the passage from birth to childhood is for everyone. The fate of the adult personality can be largely decided in the initial months of life. The preconditions for the latter stability and integration demand an extraordinary degree of care and intelligence on the part of the adult who is socializing the child, as well as a persistence through time of the same person.

These undoubted advances in the scientific understanding of childhood have been widely used as an argument to reassert women's quintessential maternal function, at a time when the traditional family has seemed increasingly eroded. Bowlby, studying evacuee children in the Second World War, declared: 'essential for mental health is that the infant and

---

[22] One of Parsons' main theoretical innovations is his contention that what the child strives to internalize will vary with the content of the reciprocal role relationships in which he is a participant. R. D. Laing, in *Family and Individual Structure* (1966) contends that a child may internalize an entire system — i.e. the family.

[23] Talcott Parsons, *The Social System* (1952), p. 227.

young child should experience a warm, intimate and continuous relationship with his mother,'[24] setting a trend which has become cumulative since. The emphasis of familial ideology has shifted away from a cult of the biological ordeal of maternity (the pain which makes the child precious, etc.) to a celebration of mother-care as a social act. This can reach ludicrous extremes: 'For the mother, breast-feeding becomes a complement to the act of creation. It gives her a heightened sense of fulfilment and allows her to participate in a relationship as close to perfection as any that a woman can hope to achieve . . . The simple fact of giving birth, however, does not of itself fulfil this need and longing. . . . Motherliness is a way of life. It enables a woman to express her total self with the tender feelings, the protective attitudes, the encompassing love of the motherly woman.'[25] The tautologies, the mystifications (an *act* of creation, a *process* surely?), the sheer absurdities . . . 'as close to perfection as any woman can hope to achieve' . . . point to the gap between reality and ideology.

Familial Patterns

This ideology corresponds in dislocated form to a real change in the pattern of the family. As the family has become smaller, each child has become more important; the actual *act* of reproduction occupies less and less time and the socializing and nurturance process increase commensurately in significance. Bourgeois society is obsessed by the physical, moral and sexual problems of childhood and adolescence.[26] Ultimate responsibility for these is placed on the mother. Thus the mother's 'maternal' role has retreated as her socializing role has increased. In the 1890's in England a mother spent 15 years in a state of pregnancy and lactation; in the 1960's she spends an average of four years. Compulsory schooling from the age of five, of course, reduces the maternal function very greatly after the initial vulnerable years.

The present situation is then one in which the qualitative importance of socialization during the early years of the child's life has acquired a much greater significance than in the past — while the quantitative amount of a mother's life spent either in gestation or child-rearing has greatly diminished. It follows that socialization cannot simply be elevated to the woman's new maternal vocation. Used as a mystique, it becomes an instrument

---

[24] John Bowlby, cit. Bruno Bettelheim, *Does Communal Education work? The Case of the Kibbutz*, in *The Family and the Sexual Revolution*, op cit., p. 295.

[25] Betty Ann Countrywoman, in *Redbook* (June, 1960), cit. Betty Friedan, *the Feminine Mystique* (1963), p. 58.

[26] David Riesman, while correctly observing this, makes a rather vain criticism of it: 'There has been a tendency in current social research influenced as it is by psychoanalysis, to over-emphasize and over-generalize the importance of very early childhood in character formation . . . It is increasingly recognized, however, that character may change greatly after this early period . . . Cultures differ widely not only in their timing of the various steps in character formation but also in the agents they rely on at each step.' *The Lonely Crowd* (1950), pp. 38–39.

of oppression. Moreover, there is no inherent reason why the biological and social mother should coincide. The process of socialization is, in the Kleinian sense, invariable — but the person of the socializer can vary.

Bruno Bettelheim observing Kibbutz methods notes that the child who is reared by a trained nurse (though normally maternally breast-fed) does not suffer the back-wash of typical parental anxieties and thus may positively gain by the system.[27] This possibility should not be fetishized in its turn. (Jean Baby, speaking of the post-four-year-old child, goes so far as to say that 'complete separation appears indispensable to guarantee the liberty of the child as well as of the mother.')[28] But what it does reveal is the viability of plural forms of socialization — neither necessarily tied to the nuclear family, nor to the biological parent.

Conclusion

The lesson of these reflections is that the liberation of women can only be achieved if *all four* structures in which they are integrated are transformed. A modification of any one of them can be offset by a reinforcement of another, so that mere permutation of the form of exploitation is achieved. The history of the last 60 years provides ample evidence of this. In the early 20th century, militant feminism in England or the USA surpassed the labour movement in the violence of its assault on bourgeois society, in pursuit of suffrage. This political right was eventually won. Nonetheless, though a simple completion of the formal legal equality of bourgeois society, it left the socio-economic situation of women virtually unchanged. The wider legacy of the suffrage was nil: the suffragettes proved quite unable to move beyond their own initial demands, and many of their leading figures later became extreme reactionaries. The Russian Revolution produced a quite different experience. In the Soviet Union in the 1920's, advanced social legislation aimed at liberating women above all in the field of sexuality: divorce was made free and automatic for either partner, thus effectively liquidating marriage; illegitimacy was abolished, abortion was free, etc. The social and demographic effects of these laws in a backward, semi-literate society bent on rapid industrialization (needing, therefore, a high birth-rate) were — predictably — catastrophic. Stalinism soon produced a restoration of iron traditional norms. Inheritance was reinstated, divorce inaccessible, abortion illegal, etc. 'The State cannot exist without the family. Marriage is a positive value for the Socialist Soviet State only if the partners see in it a lifelong union. So-called free love is a bourgeois invention and has nothing in common with the principles of conduct of a Soviet citizen. Moreover, marriage receives its full value for the State only if there is progeny, and the consorts experience

---

[27] Bruno Bettelheim, *Does Communal Education Work? The Case of the Kibbutz*, p. 303. From *The Family and Social Revolution, op. cit.*

[28] Jean Baby, *Un Monde Meilleur* (1964), p. 99.

the highest happiness of parenthood,' wrote the official journal of the Commissariat of Justice in 1939.[29] Women still retained the right and obligation to work, but because these gains had not been integrated into the earlier attempts to abolish the family and free sexuality no general liberation has occurred. In China, still another experience is being played out today. At a comparable stage of the revolution, all the emphasis is being placed on liberating women in *production*. This has produced an impressive social promotion of women. But it has been accompanied by a tremendous repression of sexuality and a rigorous puritanism (currently rampant in civic life). This corresponds not only to the need to mobilize women massively in economic life, but to a deep cultural reaction against the corruption and prostitution prevalent in Imperial and Kuo Ming Tang China (a phenomenon unlike anything in Czarist Russia). Because the exploitation of women was so great in the *ancien régime* women's participation at village level in the Chinese Revolution, was uniquely high. As for reproduction, the Russian cult of maternity in the 1930's and 1940's has not been repeated for demographic reasons: indeed, China may be one of the first countries in the world to provide free State authorized contraception on a universal scale to the population. Again, however, given the low level of industrialization and fear produced by imperialist encirclement, no all-round advance could be expected.

It is only in the highly developed societies of the West that an authentic liberation of women can be envisaged today. But for this to occur, there must be a transformation of all the structures into which they are integrated, and an '*unité de rupture*.'[30] A revolutionary movement must base its analysis on the uneven development of each, and attack the weakest link in the combination. This may then become the point of departure for a general transformation. What is the situation of the different structures today?

1. *Production*: The long-term development of the forces of production must command any socialist perspective. The hopes which the advent of machine technology raised as early as the 19th century have already been discussed. They proved illusory. Today, automation promises the *technical* possibility of abolishing completely the physical differential between man and woman in production, but under capitalist relations of production, the *social* possibility of this abolition is permanently threatened, and can easily be turned into its opposite, the actual diminution of woman's role in production as the labour force contracts.

This concerns the future, for the present the main fact to register is that woman's role in production is virtually stationary, and has been so for a

---

[29] *Sotsialisticheskaya Zakonnost* (1939. No. 2), cit. N. Timasheff, *The Attempt to Abolish the Family in Russia*, in *The Family*, ed. N. W. Bell and E. F. Vogel (1960), p. 59.

[30] See Louis Althusser, *op. cit.* See note 13.

long time now. In England in 1911 30 per cent of the work-force were women; in the 1960's 34 per cent. The composition of these jobs has not changed decisively either. The jobs are very rarely 'careers.' When they are not in the lowest positions on the factory-floor they are normally white-collar auxiliary positions (such as secretaries) — supportive to masculine roles. They are often jobs with a high 'expressive' content, such as 'service' tasks. Parsons says bluntly: 'Within the occupational organization they are analogous to the wife-mother role in the family.'[31] The educational system underpins this role-structure. 75 per cent of 18-year-old girls in England are receiving neither training nor education today. The pattern of 'instrumental' father and 'expressive' mother is not substantially changed when the woman is gainfully employed, as her job tends to be inferior to that of the man's, to which the family then adapts.

Thus, in all essentials, work as such — of the amount and type effectively available today — has not proved a salvation for women.

2. *Reproduction:* Scientific advance in contraception could, as we have seen, make involuntary reproduction — which accounts for the vast majority of births in the world today, and for a major proportion even in the West — a phenomenon of the past. But oral contraception — which has so far been developed in a form which exactly repeats the sexual inequality of Western society — is only at its beginnings. It is inadequately distributed across classes and countries and awaits further technical improvements. Its main initial impact is, in the advanced countries, likely to be psychological — it will certainly free women's sexual experience from many of the anxieties and inhibitions which have always afflicted it.[32] It will definitely divorce sexuality from procreation, as necessary complements.

The demographic pattern of reproduction in the West may or may not be widely affected by oral contraception. One of the most striking phenomena of very recent years in the United States has been the sudden increase in the birth-rate. In the last decade it has been higher than that of under-developed countries such as India, Pakistan and Burma. In fact, this reflects simply the lesser economic burden of a large family in conditions of economic boom in the richest country in the world. But it also reflects the magnification of familial ideology as a social force. This leads to the next structure.

3. *Socialization:* The changes in the composition of the work-force, the size of the family, the structure of education, etc. — however limited from an ideal standpoint — have undoubtedly diminished the societal function and importance of the family. As an organization it is not a significant unit in the political power system, it plays little part in economic production

---

[31] Parsons and Bales, *op. cit.*, p. 15n.

[32] Jean Baby records the results of an enquiry carried out into attitudes to marriage, contraception and abortion of 3,191 women in Czechoslovakia in 1959: 80 per cent of the women had limited sexual satisfaction because of fear of conception. *Op. cit.*, p. 82n.

and it is rarely the sole agency of integration into the larger society; thus at the macroscopic level it serves very little purpose.

The result has been a major displacement of emphasis on to the family's psycho-social function, for the infant and for the couple.[33] Parsons writes: 'The trend of the evidence points to the beginning of the relative stabilization of a *new* type of family structure in a new relation to a general social structure, one in which the family is more specialized than before, but not in any general sense less important, because the society is dependent *more* exclusively on it for the performance of *certain* of its vital functions.[34] The vital nucleus of truth in the emphasis on socialization of the child has been discussed. It is essential that socialists should acknowledge it and integrate it entirely into any program for the liberation of women. It is noticeable that recent 'vanguard' work by French Marxists — Baby, Sullerot, Texier — accords the problem its real importance. However, there is no doubt that the need for permanent, intelligent care of children in the initial three or four years of their lives can (and has been) exploited ideologically to perpetuate the family as a total unit, when its other functions have been visibly declining. Indeed, the attempts to focus women's existence exclusively on bringing up children, is manifestly harmful to children. Socialization as an exceptionally delicate process requires a serene and mature socializer — a type which the frustrations of a *purely* familial role are not liable to produce. Exclusive maternity is often in this sense 'counterproductive.' The mother discharges her own frustrations and anxieties in a fixation on the child. An increased awareness of the critical importance of socialization, far from leading to a restitution of classical maternal roles, should lead to a reconsideration of them — of what makes a good socializing agent, who can genuinely provide security and stability for the child.

The same arguments apply, *a fortiori*, to the psycho-social role of the family for the couple. The beliefs that the family provides an impregnable enclave of intimacy and security in an atomized and chaotic cosmos assumes the absurd — that the family can be isolated from the community, and that its internal relationships will not reproduce in their own terms the external relationships which dominate the society. The family as refuge in a bourgeois society inevitably becomes a reflection of it.

4. *Sexuality:* It is difficult not to conclude that the major structure which at present is in rapid evolution is sexuality. Production, reproduction, and socialization are all more or less stationary in the West today, in the sense that they have not changed for three or more decades. There is moreover, no widespread *demand* for changes in them on the part of women themselves — the governing ideology has effectively prevented critical consciousness. By contrast, the dominant sexual ideology is proving less and

---

[33] See Berger and Kellner, *Marriage and the Construction of Reality*, *Diogenes* (Summer 1964) for analyses of marriage and parenthood 'nomic-building' structure.

[34] Parsons and Bales, *op. cit.*, pp. 9–10.

less successful in regulating spontaneous behaviour. Marriage in its classical form is increasingly threatened by the liberalization of relationships before and after it which affects all classes today. In this sense, it is evidently the weak link in the chain — the particular structure that is the site of the most contradictions. The progressive potential of these contradictions has already been emphasized. In a context of juridical equality, the liberation of sexual experience from relations which are extraneous to it — whether procreation or property — could lead to true inter-sexual freedom. But it could also lead simply to new forms of neocapitalist ideology and practice. For one of the forces behind the current acceleration of sexual freedom has undoubtedly been the conversion of contemporary capitalism from a production-and-work ethos to a consumption-and-fun ethos. Riesman commented on this development early in the 1950's: '. . . there is not only a growth of leisure, but work itself becomes both less interesting and less demanding for many . . . more than before, as job-mindedness declines, sex permeates the daytime as well as the playtime consciousness. It is viewed as a consumption good not only by the old leisure classes, but by the modern leisure masses.'[35] The gist of Riesman's argument is that in a society bored by work, sex is the only activity, the only reminder of one's energies, the only competitive act; the last defence against *vis inertiae*. This same insight can be found, with greater theoretical depth, in Marcuse's notion of 'repressive de-sublimation' — the freeing of sexuality for its own frustration in the service of a totally co-ordinated and drugged social machine.[36] Bourgeois society at present can well afford a play area of premarital *non*-procreative sexuality. Even marriage can save itself by increasing divorce and remarriage rates, signifying the importance of the institution itself. These considerations make it clear that sexuality, while it presently may contain the greatest potential for liberation — can equally well be organized against any increase of its human possibilities. New forms of

---

[35] Riesman, *op. cit.*, p. 154.

[36] Marcuse offers the prospect of a leisure society produced by automation and the consequent shift from a Promethean to an Orphic ethos (eroticism over work-effort); and sees in this the true liberation of sexual energy for its own aesthetic end. Though he illustrates the difference (*Eros and Civilization* (1955), pp. 1978), this notion is too close to images of primitive societies dominated by the aura of maternal relaxation: '. . . satisfaction . . . would be *without toil* — that is, without the rule of alienated labour over the human existence. Under primitive conditions, alienation has *not yet* arisen because of the primitive character of the needs themselves, the rudimentary (personal or sexual) character of the division of labour, and the absence of an institutionalized hierarchical specialization of functions. Under the "ideal" conditions of mature industrial civilization, alienation would be completed by general automatization of labour, reduction of labour time to a minimum, and exchangeability of functions, . . . the reduction of the working day to a point where the mere quantum of labour time no longer arrests human development is the first prerequisite for freedom.' (Ibid., p. 138). Against the consumer use of sex illustrated by Riesman Marcuse poses the necessity for equal distribution of leisure, and hence the 'regression to a lower standard of life'; a new set of values ('gratification of the basic human needs, the freedom from guilt and fear . . . ') against an automated-TV culture. This is premature.

reification are emerging which may void sexual freedom of any meaning. This is a reminder that while one structure may be the *weak link* in a unity like that of woman's condition, there can never be a solution through it alone. The utopianism of Fourier or Reich was precisely to think that sexuality could inaugurate such a general solution. Lenin's remark to Clara Zetkin is a salutary if over-stated corrective: 'However wild and revolutionary (sexual freedom) may be, it is still really quite bourgeois. It is, mainly, a hobby of the intellectuals and of the sections nearest them. There is no place for it in the Party, in the class conscious, fighting, prole-tariat.'[37] For a general solution can only be found in a strategy which affects *all* the structures of women's exploitation. This means a rejection of two beliefs prevalent on the left:

Reformism: This now takes the form of limited ameliorative de-mands: equal pay for women, more nursery-schools, better retraining facilities, etc. In its contemporary version it is wholly divorced from any fundamental critique of women's condition or any vision of their real liberation (it was not always so). Insofar as it represents a tepid embellishment of the *status quo*, it has very little progressive content left.

Voluntarism: This takes the form of maximalist demands — the abo-lition of the family, abrogation of all sexual restrictions, forceful sepa-ration of parents from children — which have no chance of winning any wide support at present, and which merely serve as a substitute for the job of theoretical analysis or practical persuasion. By pitching the whole subject in totally intransigent terms, voluntarism objectively helps to maintain it outside the framework of normal political discussion.

What, then, is the responsible revolutionary attitude? It must include both immediate and fundamental demands, in a single critique of the *whole* of women's situation, that does not fetishize any dimension of it. Modern industrial development, as has been seen, tends towards the separating out of the originally unified function of the family — procreation, socializa-tion, sexuality, economic subsistence, etc — even if this 'structural differ-entiation' (to use a term of Parsons') has been checked and disguised by the maintenance of a powerful family ideology. This differentiation provides the real historical basis for the ideal demands which should be posed: structural differentiation is precisely what distinguishes an ad-vanced from a primitive society (in which all social functions are fused *en bloc*).[38]

---

[37] Clara Zetkin, *Reminiscences of Lenin* (1925, trans. 1929), pp. 52–53.

[38] (See Ben Brewster, *Introduction to Lukács on Bukharin, New Left Review*, No. 39, p. 25.) The capitalist mode of production separates the family from its earlier im-mediate association with the economy, and this marginality is unaffected directly by the transformation of the relations of production from private to public ownership in the transition to a socialist society. As the essence of woman's contemporary

In practical terms this means a coherent system of demands. The four elements of women's condition cannot merely be considered each in isolation; they form a structure of specific interrelations. The contemporary bourgeois family can be seen as a triptych of sexual, reproductive and socializatory functions (the woman's world) embraced by production (the man's world) — precisely a structure which in the final instance is determined by the economy. The exclusion of women from production — social human activity — and their confinement to a monolithic condensation of functions in a unity — the family — which is precisely unified in the *natural part* of each function, is the root cause of the contemporary *social* definition of women as *natural* beings. Hence the main thrust of any emancipation movement must still concentrate on the economic element — the entry of women fully into public industry. The error of the old socialists was to see the other elements as reducible to the economic; hence the call for the entry of women into production was accompanied by the purely abstract slogan of the abolition of the family. Economic demands are still primary, but must be accompanied by coherent policies for the other three elements, policies which at particular junctures may take over the primary role in immediate action.

Economically, the most elementary demand is not the right to work or receive equal pay for work — the two traditional reformist demands — but *the right to equal work itself*. At present, women perform unskilled, uncreative, service jobs that can be regarded as 'extensions' of their expressive familial role. They are overwhelmingly waitresses, office-cleaners, hair-dressers, clerks, typists. In the working-class occupational mobility is thus sometimes easier for girls than boys — they can enter the white-collar sector at a lower level. But only two in a hundred women are in administrative or managerial jobs, and less than five in a thousand are in the professions. Women are poorly unionized (25 per cent) and receive less money than men for the manual work they do perform: in 1961 the average industrial wage for women was less than half that for men, which, even setting off part-time work, represents a massive increment of exploitation for the employer.

Education

The whole pyramid of discrimination rests on a solid extra-economic foundation — education. The demand for equal work, in Britain, should above all take the form of a demand for an *equal educational system*, since this is at present the main single filter selecting women for inferior

---

problem derives from this marginality, for this problem, *but for this problem only*, the distinction between industrial and preindustrial societies is the significant one. Categories meaningful for one element of the social totality may well be irrelevant or even pernicious if extended to the whole of historical development. Similar arguments, but principally lack of space in a short article must excuse the total neglect of problems arising from class distinctions in the functions and status of women.

work-roles. At present, there is something like equal education for both sexes up to 15. Thereafter three times as many boys continue their education as girls. Only one in three 'A'-level entrants, one in four university students is a girl. There is no evidence whatever of progress. The proportion of girl university students is the same as it was in the 1920's. Until these injustices are ended, there is no chance of equal work for women. It goes without saying that the content of the educational system, which actually instils limitation of aspiration in girls needs to be changed as much as methods of selection. Education is probably the key area for immediate economic advance at present.

Only if it is founded on equality can production be truly differentiated from reproduction and the family. But this in turn requires a whole set of non-economic demands as a complement. Reproduction, sexuality, and socialization also need to be free from coercive forms of unification. Traditionally, the socialist movement has called for the 'abolition of the bourgeois family.' This slogan must be rejected as incorrect today. It is maximalist in the bad sense, posing a demand which is merely a negation without any coherent construction subsequent to it. Its weakness can be seen by comparing it to the call for the abolition of the private ownership of the means of production, whose solution — social ownership — is contained in the negation itself. Marx himself allied the two, and pointed out the equal futility of the two demands: '. . . this tendency to oppose general private property to private property is expressed in animal form; *marriage* . . . is contrasted with the community of women, in which women become communal and common property.'[39] The reasons for the historic weakness of the notion is that the family was never analysed structurally — in terms of its different functions. It was a hypostasized entity; the abstraction of its abolition corresponds to the abstraction of its conception. The strategic concern for socialists should be for the equality of the sexes, not the abolition of the family. The consequences of this demand are no less radical, but they are concrete and positive, and can be integrated into the real course of history. The family as it exists at present is, in fact, incompatible with the equality of the sexes. But this equality will not come from its administrative abolition, but from the historical differentiation of its functions. The revolutionary demand should be for the liberation of these functions from a monolithic fusion which oppresses each. Thus dissociation of reproduction from sexuality frees sexuality from alienation in unwanted reproduction (and fear of it), and reproduction from subjugation to chance and uncontrollable causality. It is thus an elementary demand to press for free State provision of oral contraception. The legalization of homosexuality — which is one of the forms of non-reproductive sexuality — should be supported for just the same reason, and regressive campaigns against it in Cuba or elsewhere should be unhesi-

---

[39] Karl Marx, *Private Property and Communism, op. cit.*, p. 153.

tatingly criticized. The straightforward abolition of illegitimacy as a legal notion as in Sweden and Russia has a similar implication; it would separate marriage civically from parenthood.

From Nature to Culture

The problem of socialization poses more difficult questions, as has been seen. But the need for intensive maternal care in the early years of a child's life does not mean that the present single sanctioned form of socialization — marriage and family — is inevitable. Far from it. The fundamental characteristic of the present system of marriage and family is in our society its *monolithism*: there is only one institutionalized form of inter-sexual or inter-generational relationship possible. It is that or nothing. This is why it is essentially a denial of life. For all human experience shows that intersexual and intergenerational relationships are infinitely various — indeed, much of our creative literature is a celebration of the fact — while the institutionalized expression of them in our capitalist society is utterly simple and rigid. It is the poverty and simplicity of the institutions in this area of life which are such an oppression. Any society will require some institutionalized and social recognition of personal relationships. But there is absolutely no reason why there should be only one legitimized form — and a multitude of unlegitimized experience. Socialism should properly mean not the abolition of the family, but the diversification of the socially acknowledged relationships which are today forcibly and rigidly compressed into it. This would mean a plural range of institutions — where the family is only one, and its abolition implies none. Couples living together or not living together, long-term unions with children, single parents bringing up children, children socialized by conventional rather than biological parents, extended kin groups, etc.— all these could be encompassed in a range of institutions which matched the free invention and variety of men and women.

Lynn White, Jr. | # The Historic Roots of Our Ecologic Crisis

A conversation with Aldous Huxley not infrequently put one at the receiving end of an unforgettable monologue. About a year before his lamented death he was discoursing on a favorite topic: Man's unnatural

SOURCE: *Machina Ex Deo* by Lynn White, Jr. Copyright © 1967 by the American Association for the Advancement of Science. Reprinted by permission of the M.I.T. Press.

treatment of nature and its sad results. To illustrate his point he told how, during the previous summer, he had returned to a little valley in England where he had spent many happy months as a child. Once it had been composed of delightful grassy glades; now it was becoming overgrown with unsightly brush because the rabbits that formerly kept such growth under control had largely succumbed to a disease, myxomatosis, that was deliberately introduced by the local farmers to reduce the rabbits' destruction of crops. Being something of a Philistine, I could be silent no longer, even in the interests of great rhetoric. I interrupted to point out that the rabbit itself had been brought as a domestic animal to England in 1176, presumably to improve the protein diet of the peasantry.

All forms of life modify their contexts. The most spectacular and benign instance is doubtless the coral polyp. By serving its own ends, it has created a vast undersea world favorable to thousands of other kinds of animals and plants. Ever since man became a numerous species he has affected his environment notably. The hypothesis that his fire-drive method of hunting created the world's great grasslands and helped to exterminate the monster mammals of the Pleistocene from much of the globe is plausible, if not proved. For 6 millennia at least, the banks of the lower Nile have been a human artifact rather than the swampy African jungle which nature, apart from man, would have made it. The Aswan Dam, flooding 5000 square miles, is only the latest stage in a long process. In many regions terracing or irrigation, overgrazing, the cutting of forests by Romans to build ships to fight Carthaginians or by Crusaders to solve the logistics problems of their expeditions, have profoundly changed some ecologies. Observation that the French landscape falls into two basic types, the open fields of the north and the *bocage* of the south and west, inspired Marc Bloch to undertake his classic study of medieval agricultural methods. Quite unintentionally, changes in human ways often affect non-human nature. It has been noted, for example, that the advent of the automobile eliminated huge flocks of sparrows that once fed on the horse manure littering every street.

The history of ecologic change is still so rudimentary that we know little about what really happened, or what the results were. The extinction of the European aurochs as late as 1627 would seem to have been a simple case of overenthusiastic hunting. On more intricate matters it often is impossible to find solid information. For a thousand years or more the Frisians and Hollanders have been pushing back the North Sea, and the process is culminating in our own time in the reclamation of the Zuider Zee. What, if any, species of animals, birds, fish, shore life, or plants have died out in the process? In their epic combat with Neptune have the Netherlanders overlooked ecological values in such a way that the quality of human life in the Netherlands has suffered? I cannot discover that the questions have ever been asked, much less answered.

People, then, have often been a dynamic element in their own environment, but in the present state of historical scholarship we usually do not know exactly when, where, or with what effects man-induced changes came. As we enter the last third of the 20th century, however, concern for the problems of ecologic backlash is mounting feverishly. Natural science, conceived as the effort to understand the nature of things, had flourished in several eras and among several peoples. Similarly there had been an age-old accumulation of technological skills, sometimes growing rapidly, sometimes slowly. But it was not until about four generations ago that Western Europe and North America arranged a marriage between science and technology, a union of the theoretical and the empirical approaches to our natural environment. The emergence in widespread practice of the Baconian creed that scientific knowledge means technological power over nature can scarcely be dated before about 1850, save in the chemical industries, where it is anticipated in the 18th century. Its acceptance as a normal pattern of action may mark the greatest event in human history since the invention of agriculture, and perhaps in nonhuman terrestrial history as well.

Almost at once the new situation forced the crystallization of the novel concept of ecology; indeed, the word *ecology* first appeared in the English language in 1873. Today, less than a century later, the impact of our race upon the environment has so increased in force that it has changed in essence. When the first cannons were fired, in the early 14th century, they affected ecology by sending workers scrambling to the forests and mountains for more potash, sulfur, iron ore, and charcoal, with some resulting erosion and deforestation. Hydrogen bombs are of a different order: a war fought with them might alter the genetics of all life on this planet. By 1285 London had a smog problem arising from the burning of soft coal, but our present combustion of fossil fuels threatens to change the chemistry of the globe's atmosphere as a whole, with consequences which we are only beginning to guess. With the population explosion, the carcinoma of planless urbanism, the now geological deposits of sewage and garbage, surely no creature other than man has ever managed to foul its nest in such short order.

There are many calls to action, but specific proposals, however worthy as individual items, seem too partial, palliative, negative: ban the bomb, tear down the billboards, give the Hindus contraceptives and tell them to eat their sacred cows. The simplest solution to any suspect change is, of course, to stop it, or, better yet, to revert to a romanticized past: make those ugly gasoline stations look like Anne Hathaway's cottage or (in the Far West) like ghost-town saloons. The "wilderness area" mentality invariably advocates deep-freezing an ecology, whether San Gimignano or the High Sierra, as it was before the first Kleenex was dropped. But neither atavism nor prettification will cope with the ecologic crisis of our time.

What shall we do? No one yet knows. Unless we think about fundamentals, our specific measures may produce new backlashes more serious than those they are designed to remedy.

As a beginning we should try to clarify our thinking by looking, in some historical depth, at the presuppositions that underlie modern technology and science. Science was traditionally aristocratic, speculative, intellectual in intent; technology was lower-class, empirical, action-oriented. The quite sudden fusion of these two, towards the middle of the 19th century, is surely related to the slightly prior and contemporary democratic revolutions which, by reducing social barriers, tended to assert a functional unity of brain and hand. Our ecologic crisis is the product of an emerging, entirely novel, democratic culture. The issue is whether a democratized world can survive its own implications. Presumably we cannot unless we rethink our axioms.

The Western Traditions of Technology and Science

One thing is so certain that it seems stupid to verbalize it: both modern technology and modern science are distinctively *Occidental*. Our technology has absorbed elements from all over the world, notably from China; yet everywhere today, whether in Japan or in Nigeria, successful technology is Western. Our science is the heir to all the sciences of the past, especially perhaps to the work of the great Islamic scientists of the Middle Ages, who so often outdid the ancient Greeks in skill and perspicacity: al-Razi in medicine, for example; or ibn-al-Haytham in optics; or Omar Khayyám in mathematics. Indeed, not a few works of such geniuses seem to have vanished in the original Arabic and to survive only in medieval Latin translations that helped to lay the foundations for later Western developments. Today, around the globe, all significant science is Western in style and method, whatever the pigmentation or language of the scientists.

A second pair of facts is less well recognized because they result from quite recent historical scholarship. The leadership of the West, both in technology and in science, is far older than the so-called Scientific Revolution of the 17th century or the so-called Industrial Revolution of the 18th century. These terms are in fact outmoded and obscure the true nature of what they try to describe — significant stages in two long and separate developments. By A.D. 1000 at the latest — and perhaps, feebly, as much as 200 years earlier — the West began to apply water power to industrial processes other than milling grain. This was followed in the late 12th century by the harnessing of wind power. From simple beginnings, but with remarkable consistency of style, the West rapidly expanded its skills in the development of power machinery, labor-saving devices, and automation. Those who doubt should contemplate that most monumental achievement in the history of automation: the weight-driven mechanical clock, which appeared in two forms in the early 14th century. Not in craftsmanship but in basic technological capacity, the Latin West of the

Middle Ages far outstripped its elaborate, sophisticated, and esthetically magnificent sister cultures, Byzantium and Islam. In 1444 a great Greek ecclesiastic, Bessarion, who had gone to Italy, wrote a letter to a prince in Greece. He is amazed by the superiority of Western ships, arms, textiles, glass. But above all he is astonished by the spectacle of water-wheels sawing timbers and pumping the bellows of blast furnaces. Clearly, he had seen nothing of the sort in the Near East.

By the end of the 15th century the technological superiority of Europe was such that its small, mutually hostile nations could spill out over all the rest of the world, conquering, looting, and colonizing. The symbol of this technological superiority is the fact that Portugal, one of the weakest states of the Occident, was able to become, and to remain for a century, mistress of the East Indies. And we must remember that the technology of Vasco da Gama and Albuquerque was built by pure empiricism, drawing remarkably little support or inspiration from science.

In the present-day vernacular understanding, modern science is supposed to have begun in 1543, when both Copernicus and Vesalius published their great works. It is no derogation of their accomplishments, however, to point out that such structures as the *Fabrica* and the *De revolutionibus* do not appear overnight. The distinctive Western tradition of science, in fact, began in the late 11th century with a massive movement of translation of Arabic and Greek scientific works into Latin. A few notable books — Theophrastus, for example — escaped the West's avid new appetite for science, but within less than 200 years effectively the entire corpus of Greek and Muslim science was available in Latin, and was being eagerly read and criticized in the new European universities. Out of criticism arose new observation, speculation, and increasing distrust of ancient authorities. By the late 13th century Europe had seized global scientific leadership from the faltering hands of Islam. It would be as absurd to deny the profound originality of Newton, Galileo, or Copernicus as to deny that of the 14th century scholastic scientists like Buridan or Oresme on whose work they built. Before the 11th century, science scarcely existed in the Latin West, even in Roman times. From the 11th century onward, the scientific sector of Occidental culture has increased in a steady crescendo.

Since both our technological and our scientific movements got their start, acquired their character, and achieved world dominance in the Middle Ages, it would seem that we cannot understand their nature or their present impact upon ecology without examining fundamental medieval assumptions and developments.

Medieval View of Man and Nature

Until recently, agriculture has been the chief occupation even in "advanced" societies; hence, any change in methods of tillage has much importance. Early plows, drawn by two oxen, did not normally turn the sod but merely scratched it. Thus, cross-plowing was needed and fields tended to be squarish. In the fairly light soils and semiarid climates of the Near East and Mediterranean, this worked well. But such a plow was inappropriate to the wet climate and often sticky soils of northern Europe. By the latter part of the 7th century after Christ, however, following obscure beginnings, certain northern peasants were using an entirely new kind of plow, equipped with a vertical knife to cut the line of the furrow, a horizontal share to slice under the sod, and a moldboard to turn it over. The friction of this plow with the soil was so great that it normally required not two but eight oxen. It attacked the land with such violence that cross-plowing was not needed, and fields tended to be shaped in long strips.

In the days of the scratch-plow, fields were distributed generally in units capable of supporting a single family. Subsistence farming was the presupposition. But no peasant owned eight oxen: to use the new and more efficient plow, peasants pooled their oxen to form large plow-teams, originally receiving (it would appear) plowed strips in proportion to their contribution. Thus, distribution of land was based no longer on the needs of a family but, rather, on the capacity of a power machine to till the earth. Man's relation to the soil was profoundly changed. Formerly man had been part of nature; now he was the exploiter of nature. Nowhere else in the world did farmers develop any analogous agricultural implement. Is it coincidence that modern technology, with its ruthlessness toward nature, has so largely been produced by descendants of these peasants of northern Europe?

This same exploitive attitude appears slightly before A.D. 830 in Western illustrated calendars. In older calendars the months were shown as passive personifications. The new Frankish calendars, which set the style for the Middle Ages, are very different: they show men coercing the world around them — plowing, harvesting, chopping trees, butchering pigs. Man and nature are two things, and man is master.

These novelties seem to be in harmony with larger intellectual patterns. What people do about their ecology depends on what they think about themselves in relation to things around them. Human ecology is deeply conditioned by beliefs about our nature and destiny — that is, by religion. To Western eyes this is very evident in, say, India or Ceylon. It is equally true of ourselves and of our medieval ancestors.

The victory of Christianity over paganism was the greatest psychic revolution in the history of our culture. It has become fashionable today to say that, for better or worse, we live in "the post-Christian age." Certainly the forms of our thinking and language have largely ceased to be Christian, but to my eye the substance often remains amazingly akin to that of the past. Our daily habits of action, for example, are dominated by an implicit faith in perpetual progress which was unknown either to Greco-Roman antiquity or to the Orient. It is rooted in, and is indefensible apart from, Judeo-Christian teleology. The fact that Communists share it merely helps to show what can be demonstrated on many other grounds: that Marxism, like Islam, is a Judeo-Christian heresy. We continue today to live, as we have lived for about 1700 years, very largely in a context of Christian axioms.

What did Christianity tell people about their relations with the environment?

While many of the world's mythologies provide stories of creation, Greco-Roman mythology was singularly incoherent in this respect. Like Aristotle, the intellectuals of the ancient West denied that the visible world had had a beginning. Indeed, the idea of a beginning was impossible in the framework of their cyclical notion of time. In sharp contrast, Christianity inherited from Judaism not only a concept of time as nonrepetitive and linear but also a striking story of creation. By gradual stages a loving and all-powerful God had created light and darkness, the heavenly bodies, the earth and all its plants, animals, birds, and fishes. Finally, God had created Adam and, as an afterthought, Eve to keep man from being lonely. Man named all the animals, thus establishing his dominance over them. God planned all of this explicitly for man's benefit and rule: no item in the physical creation had any purpose save to serve man's purposes. And, although man's body is made of clay, he is not simply part of nature: he is made in God's image.

Especially in its Western form, Christianity is the most anthropocentric religion the world has seen. As early as the 2nd century both Tertullian and Saint Irenaeus of Lyons were insisting that when God shaped Adam he was foreshadowing the image of the incarnate Christ, the Second Adam. Man shares, in great measure, God's transcendence of nature. Christianity, in absolute contrast to ancient paganism and Asia's religions (except, perhaps, Zoroastrianism), not only established a dualism of man and nature but also insisted that it is God's will that man exploit nature for his proper ends.

At the level of the common people this worked out in an interesting way. In Antiquity every tree, every spring, every stream, every hill had its own *genius loci*, its guardian spirit. These spirits were accessible to men, but were very unlike men; centaurs, fauns, and mermaids show their ambivalence. Before one cut a tree, mined a mountain, or dammed a brook, it was important to placate the spirit in charge of that particular situation, and to keep it placated. By destroying pagan animism, Christianity made it possible to exploit nature in a mood of indifference to the feelings of natural objects.

It is often said that for animism the Church substituted the cult of saints. True; but the cult of saints is functionally quite different from animism. The saint is not *in* natural objects; he may have special shrines, but his citizenship is in heaven. Moreover, a saint is entirely a man; he can be approached in human terms. In addition to saints, Christianity of course also had angels and demons inherited from Judaism and perhaps, at one remove, from Zoroastrianism. But these were all as mobile as the saints themselves. The spirits *in* natural objects, which formerly had protected nature from man, evaporated. Man's effective monopoly on spirit in this world was confirmed, and the old inhibitions to the exploitation of nature crumbled.

When one speaks in such sweeping terms, a note of caution is in order. Christianity is a complex faith, and its consequences differ in differing contexts. What I have said may well apply to the medieval West, where in fact technology made spectacular advances. But the Greek East, a highly civilized realm of equal Christian devotion, seems to have produced no marked technological innovation after the late 7th century, when Greek fire was invented. The key to the contrast may perhaps be found in a difference in the tonality of piety and thought which students of comparative theology find between the Greek and the Latin Churches. The Greeks believed that sin was intellectual blindness, and that salvation was found in illumination, orthodoxy — that is, clear thinking. The Latins, on the other hand, felt that sin was moral evil, and that salvation was to be found in right conduct. Eastern theology has been intellectualist. Western theology has been voluntarist. The Greek saint contemplates; the Western saint acts. The implications of Christianity for the conquest of nature would emerge more easily in the Western atmosphere.

The Christian dogma of creation, which is found in the first clause of all the Creeds, has another meaning for our comprehension of today's ecologic crisis. By revelation, God had given man the Bible, the Book of Scripture. But since God had made nature, nature also must reveal the divine mentality. The religious study of nature for the better understanding of God was known as natural theology. In the early Church, and always in the Greek East, nature was conceived primarily as a symbolic system through which God speaks to men: the ant is a sermon to sluggards; rising flames are the symbol of the soul's aspiration. This view of nature was essentially artistic rather than scientific. While Byzantium preserved and copied great numbers of ancient Greek scientific texts, science as we conceive it could scarcely flourish in such an ambience.

However, in the Latin West by the early 13th century natural theology was following a very different bent. It was ceasing to be the decoding of the physical symbols of God's communication with man and was becoming the effort to understand God's mind by discovering how his creation operates. The rainbow was no longer simply a symbol of hope first sent to Noah after the Deluge: Robert Grosseteste, Friar Roger Bacon, and Theodoric of Freiberg produced startlingly sophisticated work on the optics of the rainbow, but they did it as a venture in religious understanding. From the 13th century onward, up to and including Leibnitz and Newton, every major scientist, in effect, explained his motivations in religious terms. Indeed, if Galileo had not been so expert an amateur theologian he would have got into far less trouble: the professionals resented his intrusion. And Newton seems to have regarded himself more as a theologian than as a scientist. It was not until the late 18th century that the hypothesis of God became unnecessary to many scientists.

It is often hard for the historian to judge, when men explain why they are doing what they want to do, whether they are offering real reasons or merely culturally acceptable reasons. The consistency with which scientists during the long formative centuries of Western science said that the task and the reward of the scientist was "to think God's thoughts after him" leads one to believe that this was their real motivation. If so, then modern Western science was cast in a matrix of Christian theology. The dynamism of religious devotion, shaped by the Judeo-Christian dogma of creation, gave it impetus.

An Alternative Christian View

We would seem to be headed toward conclusions unpalatable to many Christians. Since both *science* and *technology* are blessed words in our contemporary vocabulary, some may be happy at the notions, first, that, viewed historically, modern science is an extrapolation of natural theology and, second, that modern technology is at least partly to be explained as an Occidental, voluntarist realization of the Christian dogma of man's transcendence of, and rightful mastery over, nature. But, as we now recognize, somewhat over a century ago science and technology — hitherto quite separate activities — joined to give mankind powers which, to judge by many of the ecologic effects, are out of control. If so, Christianity bears a huge burden of guilt.

I personally doubt that disastrous ecologic backlash can be avoided simply by applying to our problems more science and more technology. Our science and technology have grown out of Christian attitudes toward man's relation to nature which are almost universally held not only by Christians and neo-Christians but also by those who fondly regard themselves as post-Christians. Despite Copernicus, all the cosmos rotates around our little globe. Despite Darwin, we are *not*, in our hearts, part of the natural process. We are superior to nature, contemptuous of it, willing to use it for our slightest whim. The newly elected Governor of California, like myself a churchman but less troubled than I, spoke for the Christian tradition when he said (as is alleged), "when you've seen one redwood tree, you've seen them all." To a Christian a tree can be no more than a physical fact. The whole concept of the sacred grove is alien to Christianity and to the ethos of the West. For nearly 2 millennia Christian missionaries have been chopping down sacred groves, which are idolatrous because they assume spirit in nature.

What we do about ecology depends on our ideas of the man-nature relationship. More science and more technology are not going to get us out of the present ecologic crisis until we find a new religion, or rethink our old one. The beatniks, who are the basic revolutionaries of our time, show a sound instinct in their affinity for Zen Buddhism, which conceives of the man-nature relationship as very nearly the mirror image of the Christian view. Zen, however, is as deeply conditioned by Asian history as Christianity is by the experience of the West, and I am dubious of its viability among us.

Possibly we should ponder the greatest radical in Christian history since Christ: Saint Francis of Assisi. The prime miracle of Saint Francis is the fact that he did not end at the stake, as many of his left-wing followers did. He was so clearly heretical that a General of the Franciscan Order, Saint Bonaventura, a great and perceptive Christian, tried to suppress the early accounts of Franciscanism. The key to an understanding of Francis is his belief in the virtue of humility — not merely for the individual but for man as a species. Francis tried to depose man from his monarchy over creation and set up a democracy of all God's creatures. With him the ant is no longer simply a homily for the lazy, flames a sign of the thrust of the soul toward union with God; now they are Brother Ant and Sister Fire, praising the Creator in their own ways as Brother Man does in his.

Later commentators have said that Francis preached to the birds as a rebuke to men who would not listen. The records do not read so: he urged the little birds to praise God, and in spiritual ecstasy they flapped their wings and chirped rejoicing. Legends of saints, especially the Irish saints, had long told of their dealings with animals but always, I believe, to show their human dominance over creatures. With Francis it is different. The land around Gubbio in the Apennines was being ravaged by a fierce wolf. Saint Francis, says the legend, talked to the wolf and persuaded him of the error of his ways. The wolf repented, died in the odor of sanctity, and was buried in consecrated ground.

What Sir Steven Ruciman calls "the Franciscan doctrine of the animal soul" was quickly stamped out. Quite possibly it was in part inspired, consciously or unconsciously, by the belief in reincarnation held by the Cathar heretics who at that time teemed in Italy and southern France, and who presumably had got it originally from India. It is significant that at just the same moment, about 1200, traces of metempsychosis are found also in western Judaism, in the Provençal *Cabbala*. But Francis held neither to transmigration of souls nor to pantheism. His view of nature and of man rested on a unique sort of pan-psychism of all things animate and in-animate, designed for the glorification of their transcendent Creator, who, in the ultimate gesture of cosmic humility, assumed flesh, lay helpless in a manger, and hung dying on a scaffold.

I am not suggesting that many contemporary Americans who are con-cerned about our ecologic crisis will be either able or willing to counsel with wolves or exhort birds. However, the present increasing disruption of the global environment is the product of a dynamic technology and science which were originating in the Western medieval world against which Saint Francis was rebelling in so original a way. Their growth cannot be understood historically apart from distinctive attitudes toward nature which are deeply grounded in Christian dogma. The fact that most people do not think of these attitudes as Christian is irrelevant. No new set of basic values has been accepted in our society to displace those of Christianity. Hence we shall continue to have a worsening ecologic crisis until we reject the Christian axiom that nature has no reason for existence save to serve man.

The greatest spiritual revolutionary in Western history, Saint Francis, proposed what he thought was an alternative Christian view of nature and man's relation to it: he tried to substitute the idea of the equality of all creatures, including man, for the idea of man's limitless rule of creation. He failed. Both our present science and our present technology are so tinctured with orthodox Christian arrogance toward nature that no solution for our ecologic crisis can be expected from them alone. Since the roots of our trouble are so largely religious, the remedy must also be essentially religious, whether we call it that or not. We must rethink and refeel our nature and destiny. The profoundly religious, but heretical, sense of the primitive Franciscans for the spiritual autonomy of all parts of nature may point a direction. I propose Francis as a patron saint for ecologists.

Aldo Leopold | # The Land Ethic

When God-like Odysseus returned from the wars in Troy, he hanged all on one rope a dozen slave-girls of his household whom he suspected of misbehavior during his absence.

This hanging involved no question of propriety. The girls were property. The disposal of property was then, as now, a matter of expedience, not of right and wrong.

Concepts of right and wrong were not lacking from Odysseus' Greece: witness the fidelity of his wife through the long years before at last his black-prowed galleys clove the wine-dark seas for home. The ethical structure of that day covered wives, but had not yet been extended to human chattels. During the three thousand years which have since elapsed, ethical criteria have been extended to many fields of conduct, with corresponding shrinkages in those judged by expediency only.

SOURCE: *A Sand County Almanac with other essays on conservation from Round River* by Aldo Leopold. Copyright © 1949, 1953, 1966 by Oxford University Press, Inc. Reprinted by permission.

The Ethical Sequence

This extension of ethics, so far studied only by philosophers, is actually a process in ecological evolution. Its sequences may be described in ecological as well as in philosophical terms. An ethic, ecologically, is a limitation on freedom of action in the struggle for existence. An ethic, philosophically, is a differentiation of social from antisocial conduct. These are two definitions of one thing. The thing has its origin in the tendency of interdependent individuals or groups to evolve modes of co-operation. The ecologist calls these symbioses. Politics and economics are advanced symbioses in which the original free-for-all competition has been replaced, in part, by co-operative mechanisms with an ethical content.

The complexity of co-operative mechanisms has increased with population density, and with the efficiency of tools. It was simpler, for example, to define the anti-social uses of sticks and stones in the days of the mastodons than of bullets and billboards in the age of motors.

The first ethics dealt with the relation between individuals; the Mosaic Decalogue is an example. Later accretions dealt with the relation between the individual and society. The Golden Rule tries to integrate the individual to society; democracy to integrate social organizations to the individual.

There is as yet no ethic dealing with man's relation to land and to the animals and plants which grow upon it. Land, like Odysseus' slave-girls, is still property. The land-relation is still strictly economic, entailing privileges but no obligations.

The extension of ethics to this third element in human environment is, if I read the evidence correctly, an evolutionary possibility and an ecological necessity. It is the third step in a sequence. The first two have already been taken. Individual thinkers since the days of Ezekiel and Isaiah have asserted that the despoliation of land is not only inexpedient but wrong. Society, however, has not yet affirmed their belief. I regard the present conservation movement as the embryo of such an affirmation.

An ethic may be regarded as a mode of guidance for meeting ecological situations so new or intricate, or involving such deferred reactions, that the path of social expediency is not discernible to the average individual. Animal instincts are modes of guidance for the individual in meeting such situations. Ethics are possibly a kind of community instinct in-the-making.

The Community Concept

All ethics so far evolved rest upon a single premise: that the individual is a member of a community of interdependent parts. His instincts prompt him to compete for his place in that community, but his ethics prompt him also to co-operate (perhaps in order that there may be a place to compete for).

The land ethic simply enlarges the boundaries of the community to include soils, waters, plants, and animals, or collectively: the land.

This sounds simple: do we not already sing our love for and obligation to the land of the free and the home of the brave? Yes, but just what and whom do we love? Certainly not the soil, which we are sending helter-skelter downriver. Certainly not the waters, which we assume have no function except to turn turbines, float barges, and carry off sewage. Certainly not the plants, of which we exterminate whole communities without batting an eye. Certainly not the animals, of which we have already extirpated many of the largest and most beautiful species. A land ethic of course cannot prevent the alteration, management, and use of these "resources," but it does affirm their right to continued existence, and, at least in spots, their continued existence in a natural state.

In short, a land ethic changes the role of *Homo sapiens* from conqueror of the land-community to plain member and citizen of it. It implies respect for his fellow-members, and also respect for the community as such.

In human history, we have learned (I hope) that the conqueror role is eventually self-defeating. Why? Because it is implicit in such a role that the conqueror knows, *ex cathedra*, just what makes the community clock tick, and just what and who is valuable, and what and who is worthless, in community life. It always turns out that he knows neither, and this is why his conquests eventually defeat themselves.

In the biotic community, a parallel situation exists. Abraham knew exactly what the land was for: it was to drip milk and honey into Abraham's mouth. At the present moment, the assurance with which we regard this assumption is inverse to the degree of our education.

The ordinary citizen today assumes that science knows what makes the community clock tick; the scientist is equally sure that he does not. He knows that the biotic mechanism is so complex that its workings may never be fully understood.

That man is, in fact, only a member of a biotic team is shown by an ecological interpretation of history. Many historical events, hitherto explained solely in terms of human enterprise, were actually biotic interactions between people and land. The characteristics of the land determined the facts quite as potently as the characteristics of the men who lived on it. Consider, for example, the settlement of the Mississippi valley. In the years following the Revolution, three groups were contending for its control: the native Indian, the French and English traders, and the American settlers. Historians wonder what would have happened if the English at Detroit had thrown a little more weight into the Indian side of those tipsy scales which decided the outcome of the colonial migration into the cane-lands of Kentucky. It is time now to ponder the fact that the cane-lands, when subjected to the particular mixture of forces represented by the cow, plow, fire, and axe of the pioneer, became bluegrass. What if the plant succession inherent in this dark and bloody ground had, under the impact of these forces, given us some worthless sedge, shrub, or weed? Would Boone and Kenton have held out? Would there have been any overflow into Ohio,

Indiana, Illinois, and Missouri? Any Louisiana Purchase? Any transcontinental union of new states? Any Civil War?

Kentucky was one sentence in the drama of history. We are commonly told what the human actors in this drama tried to do, but we are seldom told that their success, or the lack of it, hung in large degree on the reaction of particular soils to the impact of the particular forces exerted by their occupancy. In the case of Kentucky, we do not even know where the bluegrass came from — whether it is a native species, or a stowaway from Europe.

Contrast the cane-lands with what hindsight tells us about the Southwest, where the pioneers were equally brave, resourceful, and persevering. The impact of occupancy here brought no bluegrass, or other plant fitted to withstand the bumps and buffetings of hard use. This region, when grazed by livestock, reverted through a series of more and more worthless grasses, shrubs, and weeds to a condition of unstable equilibrium. Each recession of plant types bred erosion; each increment to erosion bred a further recession of plants. The result today is a progressive and mutual deterioration, not only of plants and soils, but of the animal community subsisting thereon. The early settlers did not expect this: on the ciénegas of New Mexico some even cut ditches to hasten it. So subtle has been its progress that few residents of the region are aware of it. It is quite invisible to the tourist who finds this wrecked landscape colorful and charming (as indeed it is, but it bears scant resemblance to what it was in 1848).

This same landscape was "developed" once before, but with quite different results. The Pueblo Indians settled the Southwest in pre-Columbian times, but they happened *not* to be equipped with range livestock. Their civilization expired, but not because their land expired.

In India, regions devoid of any sod-forming grass have been settled, apparently without wrecking the land, by the simple expedient of carrying the grass to the cow, rather than vice versa. (Was this the result of some deep wisdom, or was it just good luck? I do not know.)

In short, the plant succession steered the course of history; the pioneer simply demonstrated, for good or ill, what successions inhered in the land. Is history taught in this spirit? It will be, once the concept of land as a community really penetrates our intellectual life.

The Ecological Conscience

Conservation is a state of harmony between men and land. Despite nearly a century of propaganda, conservation still proceeds at a snail's pace; progress still consists largely of letterhead pieties and convention oratory. On the back forty we still slip two steps backward for each forward stride.

The usual answer to this dilemma is "more conservation education." No one will debate this, but is it certain that only the *volume* of education needs stepping up? Is something lacking in the *content* as well?

It is difficult to give a fair summary of its content in brief form, but, as I understand it, the content is substantially this: obey the law, vote right, join some organizations, and practice what conservation is profitable on your own land; the government will do the rest.

Is not this formula too easy to accomplish anything worth-while? It defines no right or wrong, assigns no obligation, calls for no sacrifice, implies no change in the current philosophy of values. In respect of land-use, it urges only enlightened self-interest. Just how far will such education take us? An example will perhaps yield a partial answer.

By 1930 it had become clear to all except the ecologically blind that south-western Wisconsin's topsoil was slipping seaward. In 1933 the farmers were told that if they would adopt certain remedial practices for five years, the public would donate CCC labor to install them, plus the necessary machinery and materials. The offer was widely accepted, but the practices were widely forgotten when the five-year contract period was up. The farmers continued only those practices that yielded an immediate and visible economic gain for themselves.

This led to the idea that maybe farmers would learn more quickly if they themselves wrote the rules. Accordingly the Wisconsin Legislature in 1937 passed the Soil Conservation District Law. This said to farmers, in effect: *We, the public, will furnish you free technical service and loan you specialized machinery, if you will write your own rules for land-use. Each county may write its own rules, and these will have the force of law.* Nearly all the counties promptly organized to accept the proffered help, but after a decade of operation, *no county has yet written a single rule.* There has been visible progress in such practices as strip-cropping, pasture renovation, and soil liming, but none in fencing woodlots against grazing, and none in excluding plow and cow from steep slopes. The farmers, in short, have selected those remedial practices which were profitable anyhow, and ignored those which were profitable to the community, but not clearly profitable to themselves.

When one asks why no rules have been written, one is told that the community is not yet ready to support them; education must precede rules. But the education actually in progress makes no mention of obligations to land over and above those dictated by self-interest. The net result is that we have more education but less soil, fewer healthy woods, and as many floods as in 1937.

The puzzling aspect of such situations is that the existence of obligations over and above self-interest is taken for granted in such rural community enterprises as the betterment of roads, schools, churches, and baseball teams. Their existence is not taken for granted, nor as yet seriously discussed, in bettering the behavior of the water that falls on the land, or in the preserving of the beauty or diversity of the farm landscape. Land-use ethics are still governed wholly by economic self-interest, just as social ethics were a century ago.

To sum up: we asked the farmer to do what he conveniently could to save his soil, and he has done just that, and only that. The farmer who clears the woods off a 75 per cent slope, turns his cows into the clearing, and dumps its rainfall, rocks, and soil into the community creek, is still (if otherwise decent) a respected member of society. If he puts lime on his fields and plants his crops on contour, he is still entitled to all the privileges and emoluments of his Soil Conservation District. The District is a beautiful piece of social machinery, but it is coughing along on two cylinders because we have been too timid, and too anxious for quick success, to tell the farmer the true magnitude of his obligations. Obligations have no meaning without conscience, and the problem we face is the extension of the social conscience from people to land.

No important change in ethics was ever accomplished without an internal change in our intellectual emphasis, loyalties, affections, and convictions. The proof that conservation has not yet touched these foundations of conduct lies in the fact that philosophy and religion have not yet heard of it. In our attempt to make conservation easy, we have made it trivial.

Substitutes for a Land Ethic

When the logic of history hungers for bread and we hand out a stone, we are at pains to explain how much the stone resembles bread. I now describe some of the stones which serve in lieu of a land ethic.

One basic weakness in a conservation system based wholly on economic motives is that most members of the land community have no economic value. Wildflowers and songbirds are examples. Of the 22,000 higher plants and animals native to Wisconsin, it is doubtful whether more than 5 per cent can be sold, fed, eaten, or otherwise put to economic use. Yet these creatures are members of the biotic community, and if (as I believe) its stability depends on its integrity, they are entitled to continuance.

When one of these non-economic categories is threatened, and if we happen to love it, we invent subterfuges to give it economic importance. At the beginning of the century songbirds were supposed to be disappearing. Ornithologists jumped to the rescue with some distinctly shaky evidence to the effect that insects would eat us up if birds failed to control them. The evidence had to be economic in order to be valid.

It is painful to read these circumlocutions today. We have no land ethic yet, but we have at least drawn nearer the point of admitting that birds should continue as a matter of biotic right, regardless of the presence or absence of economic advantage to us.

A parallel situation exists in respect of predatory mammals, raptorial birds, and fish-eating birds. Time was when biologists somewhat over-worked the evidence that these creatures preserve the health of game by killing weaklings, or that they control rodents for the farmer, or that they prey only on "worthless" species. Here again, the evidence had to be economic in order to be valid. It is only in recent years that we hear the more honest argument that predators are members of the community, and that no special interest has the right to exterminate them for the sake of a benefit, real or fancied, to itself. Unfortunately this enlightened view is still in the talk stage. In the field the extermination of predators goes merrily on: witness the impending erasure of the timber wolf by fiat of Congress, the Conservation Bureaus, and many state legislatures.

Some species of trees have been "read out of the party" by economics-minded foresters because they grow too slowly, or have too low a sale value to pay as timber crops: white cedar, tamarack, cypress, beech, and hemlock are examples. In Europe, where forestry is ecologically more advanced, the non-commercial tree species are recognized as members of the native forest community, to be preserved as such, within reason. Moreover some (like beech) have been found to have a valuable function in building up soil fertility. The interdependence of the forest and its constituent tree species, ground flora, and fauna is taken for granted.

Lack of economic value is sometimes a character not only of species or groups, but of entire biotic communities: marshes, bogs, dunes, and "deserts" are examples. Our formula in such cases is to relegate their conservation to government as refuges, monuments, or parks. The difficulty is that these communities are usually interspersed with more valuable private lands; the government cannot possibly own or control such scattered parcels. The net effect is that we have relegated some of them to ultimate extinction over large areas. If the private owner were ecologically minded, he would be proud to be the custodian of a reasonable proportion of such areas, which add diversity and beauty to his farm and to his community.

In some instances, the assumed lack of profit in these "waste" areas has proved to be wrong, but only after most of them had been done away with. The present scramble to reflood muskrat marshes is a case in point.

There is a clear tendency in American conservation to relegate to government all necessary jobs that private landowners fail to perform. Government ownership, operation, subsidy, or regulation is now widely prevalent in forestry, range management, soil and watershed management, park and wilderness conservation, fisheries management, and migratory bird management, with more to come. Most of this growth in governmental conservation is proper and logical, some of it is inevitable. That I imply no disapproval of it is implicit in the fact that I have spent most of my life working for it. Nevertheless the question arises: What is the ultimate magnitude of the enterprise? Will the tax base carry its eventual ramifications? At what point will governmental conservation, like the mastodon, become hadicapped by its own dimensions? The answer, if there is any, seems to be in a land ethic, or some other force which assigns more obligation to the private landowner.

Industrial landowners and users, especially lumbermen and stockmen, are inclined to wail long and loudly about the extension of government ownership and regulation to land, but (with notable exceptions) they show little disposition to develop the only visible alternative: the voluntary practice of conservation on their own lands.

When the private landowner is asked to perform some unprofitable act for the good of the community, he today assents only with outstretched palm. If the act costs him cash this is fair and proper, but when it costs only forethought, open-mindedness, or time, the issue is at least debatable. The overwhelming growth of land-use subsidies in recent years must be ascribed, in large part, to the government's own agencies for conservation education: the land bureaus, the agricultural colleges, and the extension services. As far as I can detect, no ethical obligation toward land is taught in these institutions.

To sum up: a system of conservation based solely on economic self-interest is hopelessly lopsided. It tends to ignore, and thus eventually to eliminate, many elements in the land community that lack commercial value, but that are (as far as we know) essential to its healthy functioning. It assumes, falsely, I think, that the economic parts of the biotic clock will function without the uneconomic parts. It tends to relegate to government many functions eventually too large, too complex, or too widely dispersed to be performed by government.

An ethical obligation on the part of the private owner is the only visible remedy for these situations.

The Land Pyramid

An ethic to supplement and guide the economic relation to land presupposes the existence of some mental image of land as a biotic mechanism. We can be ethical only in relation to something we can see, feel, understand, love, or otherwise have faith in.

The image commonly employed in conservation education is "the balance of nature." For reasons too lengthy to detail here, this figure of speech fails to describe accurately what little we know about the land mechanism. A much truer image is the one employed in ecology: the biotic pyramid. I shall first sketch the pyramid as a symbol of land, and later develop some of its implications in terms of land-use.

Plants absorb energy from the sun. This energy flows through a circuit called the biota, which may be represented by a pyramid consisting of layers. The bottom layer is the soil. A plant layer rests on the soil, an insect layer on the plants, a bird and rodent layer on the insects, and so on up through various animal groups to the apex layer, which consists of the larger carnivores.

The species of a layer are alike not in where they came from, or in what they look like, but rather in what they eat. Each successive layer depends on those below it for food and often for other services, and each in turn furnishes food and services to those above. Proceeding upward, each successive layer decreases in numerical abundance. Thus, for every carnivore there are hundreds of his prey, thousands of their prey, millions of insects, uncountable plants. The pyramidal form of the system reflects this numerical progression from apex to base. Man shares an intermediate layer with the bears, raccoons, and squirrels which eat both meat and vegetables.

The lines of dependency for food and other services are called food chains. Thus soil-oak-deer-Indian is a chain that has now been largely converted to soil-corn-cow-farmer. Each species, including ourselves, is a link in many chains. The deer eats a hundred plants other than oak, and the cow a hundred plants other than corn. Both, then, are links in a hundred chains. The pyramid is a tangle of chains so complex as to seem disorderly, yet the stability of the system proves it to be a highly organized structure. Its functioning depends on the co-operation and competition of its diverse parts.

In the beginning, the pyramid of life was low and squat; the food chains short and simple. Evolution has added layer after layer, link after link. Man is one of thousands of accretions to the height and complexity of the pyramid. Science has given us many doubts, but it has given us at least one certainty: the trend of evolution is to elaborate and diversify the biota.

Land, then, is not merely soil; it is a fountain of energy flowing through a circuit of soils, plants, and animals. Food chains are the living channels which conduct energy upward; death and decay return it to the soil. The circuit is not closed; some energy is dissipated in decay, some is added by absorption from the air, some is stored in soils, peats, and long-lived forests; but it is a sustained circuit, like a slowly augmented revolving fund of life. There is always a net loss by downhill wash, but this is normally small and offset by the decay of rocks. It is deposited in the ocean and, in the course of geological time, raised to form new lands and new pyramids.

The velocity and character of the upward flow of energy depend on the complex structure of the plant and animal community, much as the upward flow of sap in a tree depends on its complex cellular organization. Without this complexity, normal circulation would presumably not occur. Structure means the characteristic numbers, as well as the characteristic kinds and functions, of the component species. This interdependence between the complex structure of the land and its smooth functioning as an energy unit is one of its basic attributes.

When a change occurs in one part of the circuit, many other parts must adjust themselves to it. Change does not necessarily obstruct or divert the flow of energy; evolution is a long series of self-induced changes, the net result of which has been to elaborate the flow mechanism and to lengthen the circuit. Evolutionary changes, however, are usually slow and local. Man's invention of tools has enabled him to make changes of unprecedented violence, rapidity, and scope.

One change is in the composition of floras and faunas. The larger predators are lopped off the apex of the pyramid; food chains, for the first time in history, become shorter rather than longer. Domesticated species from other lands are substituted for wild ones, and wild ones are moved to new habitats. In this world-wide pooling of faunas and floras, some species get out of bounds as pests and diseases, others are extinguished. Such effects are seldom intended or foreseen; they represent unpredicted and often untraceable readjustments in the structure. Agricultural science is largely a race between the emergence of new pests and the emergence of new techniques for their control.

Another change touches the flow of energy through plants and animals and its return to the soil. Fertility is the ability of soil to receive, store, and release energy. Agriculture, by overdrafts on the soil, or by too radical a substitution of domestic for native species in the superstructure, may derange the channels of flow or deplete storage. Soils depleted of their storage, or of the organic matter which anchors it, wash away faster than they form. This is erosion.

Waters, like soil, are part of the energy circuit. Industry, by polluting waters or obstructing them with dams, may exclude the plants and animals necessary to keep energy in circulation.

Transportation brings about another basic change: the plants or animals grown in one region are now consumed and returned to the soil in another. Transportation taps the energy stored in rocks, and in the air, and uses it elsewhere; thus we fertilize the garden with nitrogen gleaned by the guano birds from the fishes of seas on the other side of the Equator. Thus the formerly localized and self-contained circuits are pooled on a world-wide scale.

The process of altering the pyramid for human occupation releases stored energy, and this often gives rise, during the pioneering period, to a deceptive exuberance of plant and animal life, both wild and tame. These releases of biotic capital tend to becloud or postpone the penalties of violence.

This thumbnail sketch of land as an energy circuit conveys three basic ideas:

1. That land is not merely soil.
2. That the native plants and animals kept the energy circuit open; others may or may not.
3. That man-made changes are of a different order than evolutionary changes, and have effects more comprehensive than is intended or foreseen.

These ideas, collectively, raise two basic issues: Can the land adjust itself to the new order? Can the desired alterations be accomplished with less violence?

Biotas seem to differ in their capacity to sustain violent conversion. Western Europe, for example, carries a far different pyramid than Caesar found there. Some large animals are lost; swampy forests have become meadows or plowland; many new plants and animals are introduced, some of which escape as pests; the remaining natives are greatly changed in distribution and abundance. Yet the soil is still there and, with the help of imported nutrients, still fertile; the waters flow normally; the new structure seems to function and to persist. There is no visible stoppage or derangement of the circuit.

Western Europe, then, has a resistant biota. Its inner processes are tough, elastic, resistant to strain. No matter how violent the alterations, the pyramid, so far, has developed some new *modus vivendi* which preserves its habitability for man, and for most of the other natives.

Japan seems to present another instance of radical conversion without disorganization.

Most other civilized regions, and some as yet barely touched by civilization, display various stages of disorganization, varying from initial symptoms to advanced wastage. In Asia Minor and North Africa diagnosis is confused by climatic changes, which may have been either the cause or the effect of advanced wastage. In the United States the degree of disorganization varies locally; it is worst in the Southwest, the Ozarks, and parts of the South, and least in New England and the Northwest. Better land-uses may still arrest it in the less advanced regions. In parts of Mexico, South America, South Africa, and Australia a violent and accelerating wastage is in progress, but I cannot assess the prospects.

This almost world-wide display of disorganization in the land seems to be similar to disease in an animal, except that it never culminates in complete disorganization or death. The land recovers, but at some reduced level of complexity, and with a reduced carrying capacity for people, plants, and animals. Many biotas currently regarded as "lands of opportunity" are in fact already subsisting on exploitative agriculture, i.e. they have already exceeded their sustained carrying capacity. Most of South America is overpopulated in this sense.

In arid regions we attempt to offset the process of wastage by reclamation, but it is only too evident that the prospective longevity of reclamation projects is often short. In our own West, the best of them may not last a century.

The combined evidence of history and ecology seems to support one general deduction: the less violent the man-made changes, the greater the probability of successful readjustment in the pyramid. Violence, in turn, varies with human population density; a dense population requires a more violent conversion. In this respect, North America has a better chance for permanence than Europe, if she can contrive to limit her density.

This deduction runs counter to our current philosophy, which assumes that because a small increase in density enriched human life, that an indefinite increase will enrich it indefinitely. Ecology knows of no density relationship that holds for indefinitely wide limits. All gains from density are subject to a law of diminishing returns.

Whatever may be the equation for men and land, it is improbable that we as yet know all its terms. Recent discoveries in mineral and vitamin nutrition reveal unsuspected dependencies in the up-circuit: incredibly minute quantities of certain substances determine the value of soils to plants, of plants to animals. What of the down-circuit? What of the vanishing species, the preservation of which we now regard as an esthetic luxury? They helped build the soil; in what unsuspected ways may they be essential to its maintenance? Professor Weaver proposes that we use prairie flowers to reflocculate the wasting soils of the dust bowl; who knows for what purpose cranes and condors, otters and grizzlies may some day be used?

Land Health and the A-B Cleavage

A land ethic, then, reflects the existence of an ecological conscience, and this in turn reflects a conviction of individual responsibility for the health of the land. Health is the capacty of the land for self-renewal. Conservation is our effort to understand and preserve this capacity.

Conservationists are notorious for their dissensions. Superficially these seem to add up to mere confusion, but a more careful scrutiny reveals a single plane of cleavage common to many specialized fields. In each field one group (A) regards the land as soil, and its function as commodity-production; another group (B) regards the land as a biota, and its function as something broader. How much broader is admittedly in a state of doubt and confusion.

In my own field, forestry, group A is quite content to grow trees like cabbages, with cellulose as the basic forest commodity. It feels no inhibition against violence; its ideology is agronomic. Group B, on the other hand, sees forestry as fundamentally different from agronomy because it employs natural species, and manages a natural environment rather than creating an artificial one. Group B prefers natural reproduction on principle. It worries on biotic as well as economic grounds about the loss of species like chestnut, and the threatened loss of the white pines. It worries about a whole series of secondary forest functions: wildlife, recreation, watersheds, wilderness areas. To my mind, Group B feels the stirrings of an ecological conscience.

In the wildlife field, a parallel cleavage exists. For Group A the basic commodities are sport and meat; the yardsticks of production are ciphers of take in pheasants and trout. Artificial propagation is acceptable as a permanent as well as a temporary recourse — if its unit costs permit. Group B, on the other hand, worries about a whole series of biotic side-issues. What is the cost in predators of producing a game crop? Should we have further recourse to exotics? How can management restore the shrinking species, like prairie grouse, already hopeless as shootable game? How can management restore the threatened rarities, like trumpeter swan and whooping crane? Can management principles be extended to wild-flowers? Here again it is clear to me that we have the same A-B cleavage as in forestry.

In the larger field of agriculture I am less competent to speak, but there seem to be somewhat parallel cleavages. Scientific agriculture was actively developing before ecology was born, hence a slower penetration of ecological concepts might be expected. Moreover the farmer, by the very nature of his techniques, must modify the biota more radically than the forester or the wildlife manager. Nevertheless, there are many discontents in agriculture which seem to add up to a new vision of "biotic farming."

Perhaps the most important of these is the new evidence that poundage or tonnage is no measure of the food-value of farm crops; the products of fertile soil may be qualitatively as well as quantitatively superior. We can bolster poundage from depleted soils by pouring on imported fertility, but we are not necessarily bolstering food-value. The possible ultimate ramifications of this idea are so immense that I must leave their exposition to abler pens.

The discontent that labels itself "organic farming," while bearing some of the earmarks of a cult, is nevertheless biotic in its direction, particularly in its insistence on the importance of soil flora and fauna.

The ecological fundamentals of agriculture are just as poorly known to the public as in other fields of land-use. For example, few educated people realize that the marvelous advances in technique made during recent decades are improvements in the pump, rather than the well. Acre for acre, they have barely sufficed to offset the sinking level of fertility.

In all of these cleavages, we see repeated the same basic paradoxes: man the conqueror *versus* man the biotic citizen; science the sharpener of his sword *versus* science the searchlight on his universe; land the slave and servant *versus* land the collective organism. Robinson's injunction to Tristram may well be applied, at this juncture, to *Homo sapiens* as a species in geological time:

> Whether you will or not
> You are a King, Tristram, for you are one
> Of the time-tested few that leave the world,
> When they are gone, not the same place it was.
> Mark what you leave.

The Outlook

It is inconceivable to me that an ethical relation to land can exist without love, respect, and admiration for land, and a high regard for its value. By value, I of course mean something far broader than mere economic value; I mean value in the philosophical sense.

Perhaps the most serious obstacle impeding the evolution of a land ethic is the fact that our educational and economic system is headed away from, rather than toward, an intense consciousness of land. Your true modern is separated from the land by many middlemen, and by innumerable physical gadgets. He has no vital relation to it; to him it is the space between cities on which crops grow. Turn him loose for a day on the land, and if the spot does not happen to be a golf links or a "scenic" area, he is bored stiff. If crops could be raised by hydroponics instead of farming, it would suit him very well. Synthetic substitutes for wood, leather, wool, and other natural land products suit him better than the originals. In short, land is something he has "outgrown."

Almost equally serious as an obstacle to a land ethic is the attitude of the farmer for whom the land is still an adversary, or a taskmaster that keeps him in slavery. Theoretically, the mechanization of farming ought to cut the farmer's chains, but whether it really does is debatable.

One of the requisites for an ecological comprehension of land is an understanding of ecology, and this is by no means co-extensive with "education"; in fact, much higher education seems deliberately to avoid ecological concepts. An understanding of ecology does not necessarily originate in courses bearing ecological labels; it is quite as likely to be labeled geography, botany, agronomy, history, or economics. This is as it should be, but whatever the label, ecological training is scarce.

The case for a land ethic would appear hopeless but for the minority which is in obvious revolt against these "modern" trends.

The "key-log" whch must be moved to release the evolutionary process for an ethic is simply this: quit thinking about decent land-use as solely an economic problem. Examine each question in terms of what is ethically and esthetically right, as well as what is economically expedient. A thing is right when it tends to preserve the integrity, stability, and beauty of the biotic community. It is wrong when it tends otherwise.

It of course goes without saying that economic feasibility limits the tether of what can or cannot be done for land. It always has and it always will. The fallacy the economic determinists have tied around our collective neck, and which we now need to cast off, is the belief that economics determines *all* land-use. This is simply not true. An innumerable host of actions and attitudes, comprising perhaps the bulk of all land relations, is determined by the land-user's tastes and predilections, rather than by his purse. The bulk of all land relations hinges on investments of time, forethought, skill, and faith rather than on investments of cash. As a land-user thinketh, so is he.

I have purposely presented the land ethic as a product of social evolution because nothing so important as an ethic is ever "written." Only the most superficial student of history supposes that Moses "wrote" the Decalogue; it evolved in the minds of a thinking community, and Moses wrote a tentative summary of it for a "seminar." I say tentative because evolution never stops.

The evolution of a land ethic is an intellectual as well as emotional process. Conservation is paved with good intentions which prove to be futile, or even dangerous, because they are devoid of critical understanding either of the land, or of economic land-use. I think it is a truism that as the ethical frontier advances from the individual to the community, its intellectual content increases.

The mechanism of operation is the same for any ethic: social approbation for right actions: social disapproval for wrong actions.

By and large, our present problem is one of attitudes and implements. We are remodeling the Alhambra with a steam-shovel, and we are proud of our yardage. We shall hardly relinquish the shovel, which after all has many good points, but we are in need of gentler and more objective criteria for its successful use.

BLACK IDENTITY

4

■ In his preface to Frantz Fanon's *The Wretched of the Earth* Jean-Paul Sartre tells the white man that he should read the book, although it is not addressed to him, because it will show him the mechanism by which he has become estranged from himself. And, indeed, as the white reader in America proceeds through the writings of Malcolm X or Eldridge Cleaver or Stokely Carmichael the overwhelming impression he receives is one of the public "arrival" of a culture that was always there, a culture whose members, sure of their identity, are vitally attached to reality in a way that he, the white man trammeled by guilt and uncertain of direction, can only envy.

Crises aplenty swirl about the Black Protest movement in America, but one crisis that is notably missing is a crisis in identity. America's Negroes have been reminded of just who they are for centuries, compelled into a severe sense of self, and, so long as they kept their place, abandoned to develop their own language, their own manners, in short, their own culture. So long as society remained undisturbed in its habit of regarding the Negro as invisible, it could facilely assume that this other culture was either no culture at all or a very debased version of the dominant culture. But with the growth of black protest and the widespread awareness that "black is beautiful" has come not only social turmoil but a recognition even harder for white society to cope with — American Negroes have developed a strong and magnetic culture of their own. While the dominant society becomes increasingly uncertain of its direction, and its members, especially the young, become increasingly disturbed about its values, it discovers that in its midst there exists a structure of living free of the hesitancies produced by loss of purpose and overabundance of goods. Excluded from "cultural advantages" the black people of America developed their own pattern of reaction to the problems of leading the common life, a pattern that includes a distinct language and a distinct temperament. Society perceives that jazz that reached white ears (most often in an emasculated version) was not the isolated achievement of a deprived people but a strand in a cultural fabric the larger texture of which is now emerging.

The invisible men are not just beginning to have an identity because they are just beginning their fight for social justice. Rather, in this matter they are already fully armed, and in this sense are far more powerful than a mere count of numbers or examination of programs will suggest.

This is not to say that there do not exist within the black movement serious problems of political (as opposed to cultural) identity. The emergence since World War II of Third World nations has quite naturally suggested an analogy for American blacks. The metaphor of their having been colonized *within* America and their present striving to emerge into independence is attractive and useful, both as a model for internal action and as a source of international support for their aspirations. But one has only to glance at the diversity of styles among Marxist nations today to recognize the powerful counteracting force national habits exert on an international politico-economic theory. This, in turn, raises serious doubts about the effectiveness of the Third World metaphor for people who are, finally, Americans. The psychological strength gathered from Third World identity is great, but the patterns for action that are suggested by the model may hinder rather than advance social programs that are to be carried out in a technologically advanced nation by persons who are the inheritors of technological awareness however much they may have been excluded from its profits. Interwoven with his brilliance of mind and unshakably noble sense of purpose, Malcolm X, for example, had a belief in personal achievement that is more clearly related to Benjamin Franklin than to any Third World figure.

The principal governmental reaction to the powerful surge toward black identity has been a renewal of attempts to remove or lower barriers for those individuals who will qualify themselves, in conventional terms, for equality. This will assure the fact that if change comes it will come in an "American" fashion. As a result, although the struggle that most catches the eye is that which features die-hard reactionaries refusing to budge an inch, the crucial test does not lie here. It is taking place between the idea of integration of blacks as individuals as opposed to the idea of recognition of the black community as a valuable unit within the general society.

Speaking of the theory of individual advancement of the Negro, Stokeley Carmichael asserts:

> Its goal was to make the whole community accessible to 'qualified' Negroes and presumably each year a few more Negroes armed with their passport – a couple of university degrees – would escape into middle-class America and adopt the attitudes and life styles of that group; and one day the Harlems and the Wattses would stand empty, a tribute to the success of integration. This is simply neither realistic nor particularly desirable. You can integrate communities, but you assimilate individuals. Even if such a program were possible, its result would be not to develop the black

community as a functional and honorable segment of the total society, with its own cultural identity, life patterns, and institutions, but to abolish it — the final solution of the Negro problem.

Those who oppose such a solution point with some justice to the fact that ghetto schools teaching Negro children as if they had no language rather than a different but expressive idiom are interrupting rather than furthering their education. Institutions that attempt to do for Negroes what other communities prefer to do for themselves are oppressive even as they claim and believe themselves to be liberating.

One cannot confidently predict that the idea of integration of communities will prevail over that of assimilation of individuals. It is unAmerican in the sense that social advancement in America has always meant, according to the national mythology, being melted and recast into the common alloy. Communal attachments should not be permitted to stand in the way of this process. In the short run, however, it seems safe to assume that the white community's uncertainties about identity will encourage Negroes to retain their bitterly earned identity and therefore to choose advancement as a community. Certainly it is this aspect of Black Protest that most attracts the movement's thousands of young white supporters. Their acquaintance with the Negro struggle and with individual Negroes has promoted admiration for Negro culture. Some have quite bluntly attempted to enter that culture by adopting its lifestyle. This, on the face of it, would be ridiculous did not so many social institutions instantly cooperate in the transformation by oppressing them in a manner analogous to the traditional treatment of Negroes.

At the same time, Negro leaders are quarreling among themselves about whether their white admirers and allies constitute a threat to their movement through compromise. Eldridge Cleaver appears to welcome the alliance with young white radicals, envisioning a better society for all when the values and style of the black proletariat are shared by all. But Stokely Carmichael believes that a movement powered by the cultural identity of a community cannot include in its numbers those who have not paid the dues of membership — the price exacted by the white society for being Black. After all, a people are on the move, not a social theory.

The temptation is strong to go back over American history to identify that point at which the corrective measure should have been taken to avoid today's incendiary situation, to retain the notion that the past must have lessons for the present. Even as one does so, however, the conviction grows that the present is unique. Now there is no question of the stronger patronizing the weaker, and if the achieved visibility of the Negro community bring with it white fear and black hate — easily reversible terms — perhaps this is a better basis on which to proceed than the former hypocritical pretense of equality between two men, one of whom had dealt himself all the aces.

In this connection the Black Panthers are a very significant group. Numerically they may represent a small minority of the American Negro population. But their idealism and practices indicate the terms in which the situation must now be considered. Those ideals emphasize a severe code of self-discipline in recognition of the fact that men who will have no masters over them must master themselves. And those practices include the assumption by the Negro community of the institutional services, such as education, that have always come to it from the outside. Also among these services is policing, and even as this causes alarm in white society it symbolizes the determination of many in the black community to control their environment. The uproar over the Panthers' view of policing is often used by those in power as a screen to cover the real issue of whether a community will be permitted to advance as a community.

Nobody needs be reminded of how incendiary the situation is. But the Panthers have dramatized the real issues when most would prefer a complacent dialogue conducted in the vocabulary of the national mythology. It is difficult to escape the conclusion that unless all the roles in this drama are skillfully enacted and interpreted, the next act will be tragic.

Malcolm X | Saved

During the years that I stayed in the Norfolk Prison Colony, never did any official directly say anything to me about those letters, although, of course, they all passed through the prison censorship. I'm sure, however, they monitored what I wrote to add to the files which every state and federal prison keeps on the conversion of Negro inmates by the teachings of Mr. Elijah Muhammad.

But at that time, I felt that the real reason was that the white man knew that he was the devil.

Later on, I even wrote to the Mayor of Boston, to the Governor of Massachusetts, and to Harry S. Truman. They never answered; they probably never even saw my letters. I handscratched to them how the white man's society was responsible for the black man's condition in this wilderness of North America.

It was because of my letters that I happened to stumble upon starting to acquire some kind of a homemade education.

I became increasingly frustrated at not being able to express what I wanted to convey in letters that I wrote, especially those to Mr. Elijah Muhammad. In the street, I had been the most articulate hustler out there — I had commanded attention when I said something. But now, trying to write simple English, I not only wasn't articulate, I wasn't even functional. How would I sound writing in slang, the way I would *say* it, something such as, "Look, daddy, let me pull your coat about a cat, Elijah Muhammad —"

Many who today hear me somewhere in person, or on television, or those who read something I've said, will think I went to school far beyond the eighth grade. This impression is due entirely to my prison studies.

It had really begun back in the Charlestown Prison, when Bimbi first made me feel envy of his stock of knowledge. Bimbi had always taken charge of any conversation he was in, and I had tried to emulate him. But every book I picked up had few sentences which didn't contain anywhere from one to nearly all of the words that might as well have been in Chinese. When I just skipped those words, of course, I really ended up with little idea of what the book said. So I had come to the Norfolk Prison Colony still going through only book-reading motions. Pretty soon, I would have quit even these motions, unless I had received the motivation that I did.

SOURCE: *The Autobiography of Malcolm* X. Copyright © 1964 by Alex Haley and Malcolm X. Copyright © 1965 by Alex Haley and Betty Shabazz. Reprinted by permission of Grove Press, Inc.

I saw that the best thing I could do was get hold of a dictionary — to study, to learn some words. I was lucky enough to reason also that I should try to improve my penmanship. It was sad. I couldn't even write in a straight line. It was both ideas together that moved me to request a dictionary along with some tablets and pencils from the Norfolk Prison Colony school.

I spent two days just riffling uncertainly through the dictionary's pages. I'd never realized so many words existed! I didn't know *which* words I needed to learn. Finally, just to start some kind of action, I began copying.

In my slow, painstaking, ragged handwriting, I copied into my tablet everything printed on that first page, down to the punctuation marks.

I believe it took me a day. Then, aloud, I read back, to myself, everything I'd written on the tablet. Over and over, aloud, to myself, I read my own handwriting.

I woke up the next morning, thinking about those words — immensely proud to realize that not only had I written so much at one time, but I'd written words that I never knew were in the world. Moreover, with a little effort, I also could remember what many of these words meant. I reviewed the words whose meanings I didn't remember. Funny thing, from the dictionary first page right now, that "aardvark" springs to my mind. The dictionary had a picture of it, a long-tailed, long-eared, burrowing African mammal, which lives off termites caught by sticking out its tongue as an anteater does for ants.

I was so fascinated that I went on — I copied the dictionary's next page. And the same experience came when I studied that. With every succeeding page, I also learned of people and places and events from history. Actually the dictionary is like a miniature encyclopedia. Finally the dictionary's A section had filled a whole tablet — and I went on into the B's. That was the way I started copying what eventually became the entire dictionary. It went a lot faster after so much practice helped me to pick up handwriting speed. Between what I wrote in my tablet, and writing letters, during the rest of my time in prison I would guess I wrote a million words.

I suppose it was inevitable that as my word-base broadened, I could for the first time pick up a book and read and now begin to understand what the book was saying. Anyone who has read a great deal can imagine the new world that opened. Let me tell you something: from then until I left that prison, in every free moment I had, if I was not reading in the library, I was reading on my bunk. You couldn't have gotten me out of books with a wedge. Between Mr. Muhammad's teachings, my correspondence, my visitors — usually Ella and Reginald — and my reading of books, months passed without my even thinking about being imprisoned. In fact, up to then, I never had been so truly free in my life.

The Norfolk Prison Colony's library was in the school building. A variety of classes was taught there by instructors who came from such places as Harvard and Boston universities. The weekly debates between inmate teams were also held in the school building. You would be astonished to know how worked up convict debaters and audiences would get over subjects like "Should Babies Be Fed Milk?"

Available on the prison library's shelves were books on just about every general subject. Much of the big private collection that Parkhurst had willed to the prison was still in crates and boxes in the back of the library — thousands of old books. Some of them looked ancient: covers faded, old-time parchment-looking binding. Parkhurst, I've mentioned, seemed to have been principally interested in history and religion. He had the money and the special interest to have a lot of books that you wouldn't have in general circulation. Any college library would have been lucky to get that collection.

As you can imagine, especially in a prison where there was heavy emphasis on rehabilitation, an inmate was smiled upon if he demonstrated an unusually intense interest in books. There was a sizable number of well-read inmates, especially the popular debaters. Some were said by many to be practically walking encyclopedias. They were almost celebrities. No university would ask any student to devour literature as I did when this new world opened to me, of being able to read and *understand*.

I read more in my room than in the library itself. An inmate who was known to read a lot could check out more than the permitted maximum number of books. I preferred reading in the total isolation of my own room.

When I had progressed to really serious reading, every night at about ten P.M. I would be outraged with the "lights out." It always seemed to catch me right in the middle of something engrossing.

Fortunately, right outside my door was a corridor light that cast a glow into my room. The glow was enough to read by, once my eyes adjusted to it. So when "lights out" came, I would sit on the floor where I could continue reading in that glow.

At one-hour intervals the night guards paced past every room. Each time I heard the approaching footsteps, I jumped into bed and feigned sleep. And as soon as the guard passed, I got back out of bed onto the floor area of that light-glow, where I would read for another fifty-eight minutes — until the guard approached again. That went on until three or four every morning. Three or four hours of sleep a night was enough for me. Often in the years in the streets I had slept less than that.

The teachings of Mr. Muhammad stressed how history had been "whitened" — when white men had written history books, the black man simply had been left out. Mr. Muhammad couldn't have said anything that would have struck me much harder. I had never forgotten how when my class, me and all of those whites, had studied seventh-grade United States history back in Mason, the history of the Negro had been covered in one paragraph, and the teacher had gotten a big laugh with his joke, "Negroes' feet are so big that when they walk, they leave a hole in the ground."

This is one reason why Mr. Muhammad's teachings spread so swiftly all over the United States, among *all* Negroes, whether or not they became followers of Mr. Muhammad. The teachings ring true — to every Negro. You can hardly show me a black adult in America — or a white one, for that matter — who knows from the history books anything like the truth about the black man's role. In my own case, once I heard of the "glorious history of the black man," I took special pains to hunt in the library for books that would inform me on details about black history.

I can remember accurately the very first set of books that really impressed me. I have since bought that set of books and have it at home for my children to read as they grow up. It's called *Wonders of the World*. It's full of pictures of archeological finds, statues that depict, usually, non-European people.

I found books like Will Durant's *Story of Civilization*. I read H. G. Wells' *Outline of History*. *Souls Of Black Folk* by W. E. B. Du Bois gave me a glimpse into the black people's history before they came to this country. Carter G. Woodson's *Negro History* opened my eyes about black empires before the black slave was brought to the United States, and the early Negro struggles for freedom.

J. A. Rogers' three volumes of *Sex and Race* told about race-mixing before Christ's time; about Aesop being a black man who told fables; about Egypt's Pharaohs; about the great Coptic Christian Empires; about Ethiopia, the earth's oldest continuous black civilization, as China is the oldest continuous civilization.

Mr. Muhammad's teaching about how the white man had been created led me to *Findings In Genetics* by Gregor Mendel. (The dictionary's G section was where I had learned what "genetics" meant.) I really studied this book by the Austrian monk. Reading it over and over, especially certain sections, helped me to understand that if you started with a black man, a white man could be produced; but starting with a white man, you never could produce a black man — because the white chromosome is recessive. And since no one disputes that there was but one Original Man, the conclusion is clear.

During the last year or so, in the *New York Times*, Arnold Toynbee used the word "bleached" in describing the white man. (His words were: "White (i.e. bleached) human beings of North European origin. . . .") Toynbee also referred to the European geographic area as only a peninsula of Asia. He said there is no such thing as Europe. And if you look at the globe, you will see for yourself that America is only an extension of Asia. (But at the same time Toynbee is among those who have helped to bleach history. He has written that Africa was the only continent that produced no history. He won't write that again. Every day now, the truth is coming to light.)

I never will forget how shocked I was when I began reading about slavery's total horror. It made such an impact upon me that it later became one of my favorite subjects when I became a minister of Mr. Muhammad's. The world's most monstrous crime, the sin and the blood on the white man's hands, are almost impossible to believe. Books like the one by Frederick Olmstead opened my eyes to the horrors suffered when the slave was landed in the United States. The European woman, Fannie Kimball, who had married a Southern white slaveowner, described how human beings were degraded. Of course I read *Uncle Tom's Cabin*. In fact, I believe that's the only novel I have ever read since I started serious reading.

Parkhurst's collection also contained some bound pamphlets of the Abolitionist Anti-Slavery Society of New England. I read descriptions of atrocities, saw those illustrations of black slave women tied up and flogged with whips; of black mothers watching their babies being dragged off, never to be seen by their mothers again; of dogs after slaves, and of the fugitive slave catchers, evil white men with whips and clubs and chains and guns. I read about the slave preacher Nat Turner, who put the fear of God into the white slavemaster. Nat Turner wasn't going around preaching pie-in-the-sky and "non-violent" freedom for the black man. There in Virginia one night in 1831, Nat and seven other slaves started out at his master's home and through the night they went from one plantation "big house" to the next, killing, until by the next morning 57 white people were dead and Nat had about 70 slaves following him. White people, terrified for their lives, fled from their homes, locked themselves up in public buildings, hid in the woods, and some even left the state. A small army of soldiers took two months to catch and hang Nat Turner. Somewhere I have read where Nat Turner's example is said to have inspired John Brown to invade Virginia and attack Harper's Ferry nearly thirty years later, with thirteen white men and five Negroes.

I read Herodotus, "the father of History," or, rather, I read about him. And I read the histories of various nations, which opened my eyes gradually, then wider and wider, to how the whole world's white men had indeed acted like devils, pillaging and raping and bleeding and draining the whole world's non-white people. I remember, for instance, books such as Will Durant's story of Oriental civilization, and Mahatma Gandhi's accounts of the struggle to drive the British out of India.

Book after book showed me how the white man had brought upon the world's black, brown, red, and yellow peoples every variety of the suffering of exploitation. I saw how since the sixteenth century, the so-called "Christian trader" white man began to ply the seas in his lust for Asian and African empires, and plunder, and power. I read, I saw, how the white man never has gone among the non-white peoples bearing the Cross in the true manner and spirit of Christ's teachings — meek, humble, and Christ-like.

I perceived, as I read, how the collective white man had been actually nothing but a piratical opportunist who used Faustian machinations to make his own Christianity his initial wedge in criminal conquests. First, always "religiously," he branded "heathen" and "pagan" labels upon ancient non-white cultures and civilizations. The stage thus set, he then turned upon his non-white victims his weapons of war.

I read how, entering India — half a *billion* deeply religious brown people — the British white man, by 1759, through promises, trickery and manipulations, controlled much of India through Great Britain's East India Company. The parasitical British administration kept tentacling out to half of the sub-continent. In 1857, some of the desperate people of India finally mutinied — and, excepting the African slave trade, nowhere has history recorded any more unnecessary bestial and ruthless human carnage than the British suppression of the non-white Indian people.

Over 115 million African blacks — close to the 1930's population of the United States — were murdered or enslaved during the slave trade. And I read how when the slave market was glutted, the cannibalistic white powers of Europe next carved up, as their colonies, the richest areas of the black continent. And Europe's chancelleries for the next century played a chess game of naked exploitation and power from Cape Horn to Cairo.

Ten guards and the warden couldn't have torn me out of those books. Not even Elijah Muhammad could have been more eloquent than those books were in providing indisputable proof that the collective white man had acted like a devil in virtually every contact he had with the world's collective non-white man. I listen today to the radio, and watch television, and read the headlines about the collective white man's fear and tension concerning China. When the white man professes ignorance about why the Chinese hate him so, my mind can't help flashing back to what I read, there in prison, about how the blood forebears of this same white man raped China at a time when China was trusting and helpless. Those original white "Christian traders" sent into China millions of pounds of opium. By 1839, so many of the Chinese were addicts that China's desperate government destroyed twenty thousand chests of opium. The first Opium War was promptly declared by the white man. Imagine! Declaring *war* upon someone who objects to being narcotized! The Chinese were severely beaten, with Chinese-invented gunpowder.

The Treaty of Nanking made China pay the British white man for the destroyed opium; forced open China's major ports to British trade; forced China to abandon Hong Kong; fixed China's import tariffs so low that cheap British articles soon flooded in, maiming China's industrial development.

After a second Opium War, the Tientsin Treaties legalized the ravaging opium trade, legalized a British-French-American control of China's customs. China tried delaying that Treaty's ratification; Peking was looted and burned.

"Kill the foreign white devils!" was the 1901 Chinese war cry in the Boxer Rebellion. Losing again, this time the Chinese were driven from Peking's choicest areas. The vicious, arrogant white man put up the famous signs, "Chinese and dogs not allowed."

Red China after World War II closed its doors to the Western white world. Massive Chinese agricultural, scientific, and industrial efforts are described in a book that *Life* magazine recently published. Some observers inside Red China have reported that the world never has known such a hate-white campaign as is now going on in this non-white country where, present birth-rates continuing, in fifty more years Chinese will be half the earth's population. And it seems that some Chinese chickens will soon come home to roost, with China's recent successful nuclear tests.

Let us face reality. We can see in the United Nations a new world order being shaped, along color lines — an alliance among the non-white nations. America's U.N. Ambassador Adlai Stevenson complained not long ago that in the United Nations "a skin game" was being played. He was right. He was facing reality. A "skin game" *is* being played. But Ambassador Stevenson sounded like Jesse James accusing the marshal of carrying a gun. Because who in the world's history ever has played a worse "skin game" than the white man?

Mr. Muhammad, to whom I was writing daily, had no idea of what a new world had opened up to me through my efforts to document his teachings in books.

When I discovered philosophy, I tried to touch all the landmarks of philosophical development. Gradually, I read most of the old philosophers, Occidental and Oriental. The Oriental philosophers were the ones I came to prefer; finally, my impression was that most Occidental philosophy had largely been borrowed from the Oriental thinkers. Socrates, for instance, traveled in Egypt. Some sources even say that Socrates was initiated into some of the Egyptian mysteries. Obviously Socrates got some of his wisdom among the East's wise men.

I have often reflected upon the new vistas that reading opened to me. I knew right there in prison that reading had changed forever the course of my life. As I see it today, the ability to read awoke inside me some long dormant craving to be mentally alive. I certainly wasn't seeking any degree, the way a college confers a status symbol upon its students. My homemade education gave me, with every additional book that I read, a little bit more sensitivity to the deafness, dumbness, and blindness that was afflicting the black race in America. Not long ago, an English writer telephoned me from London, asking questions. One was, "What's your alma mater?" I told him, "Books." You will never catch me with a free fifteen minutes in which I'm not studying something I feel might be able to help the black man.

Yesterday I spoke in London, and both ways on the plane across the Atlantic I was studying a document about how the United Nations proposes to insure the human rights of the oppressed minorities of the world. The American black man is the world's most shameful case of minority oppression. What makes the black man think of himself as only an internal United States issue is just a catch-phrase, two words, "civil rights." How is the black man going to get "civil rights" before first he wins his *human* rights? If the American black man will start thinking about his *human* rights, and then start thinking of himself as part of one of the world's great peoples, he will see he has a case for the United Nations.

I can't think of a better case! Four hundred years of black blood and sweat invested here in America, and the white man still has the black man begging for what every immigrant fresh off the ship can take for granted the minute he walks down the gangplank.

But I'm digressing. I told the Englishman that my alma mater was books, a good library. Every time I catch a plane, I have with me a book that I want to read — and that's a lot of books these days. If I weren't out here every day battling the white man, I could spend the rest of my life reading, just satisfying my curiosity — because you can hardly mention anything I'm not curious about. I don't think anybody ever got more out of going to prison than I did. In fact, prison enabled me to study far more intensively than I would have if my life had gone differently and I had attended some college. I imagine that one of the biggest troubles with colleges is there are too many distractions, too much panty-raiding, fraternities, and boola-boola and all of that. Where else but in a prison could I have attacked my ignorance by being able to study intensely sometimes as much as fifteen hours a day?

Schopenhauer, Kant, Nietzsche, naturally, I read all of those. I don't respect them; I am just trying to remember some of those whose theories I soaked up in those years. These three, it's said, laid the groundwork on which the Fascist and Nazi philosophy was built. I don't respect them because it seems to me that most of their time was spent arguing about things that are not really important. They remind me of so many of the Negro "intellectuals," so-called, with whom I have come in contact — they are always arguing about something useless.

Spinoza impressed me for a while when I found out that he was black. A black Spanish Jew. The Jews excommunicated him because he advocated a pantheistic doctrine, something like the "allness of God," or "God in everything." The Jews read their burial services for Spinoza, meaning that he was dead as far as they were concerned; his family was run out of Spain, they ended up in Holland, I think.

I'll tell you something. The whole stream of Western philosophy has now wound up in a cul-de-sac. The white man has perpetrated upon himself, as well as upon the black man, so gigantic a fraud that he has put himself into a crack. He did it through his elaborate, neurotic necessity to hide the black man's true role in history.

And today the white man is faced head on with what is happening on the Black Continent, Africa. Look at the artifacts being discovered there, that are proving over and over again, how the black man had great, fine, sensitive civilizations before the white man was out of the caves. Below the Sahara, in the places where most of America's Negroes' foreparents were kidnapped, there is being unearthed some of the finest craftsmanship, sculpture and other objects, that has ever been seen by modern man. Some of these things now are on view in such places as New York City's Museum of Modern Art. Gold work of such fine tolerance and workmanship that it has no rival. Ancient objects produced by black hands . . . refined by those black hands with results that no human hand today can equal.

History has been so "whitened" by the white man that even the black professors have known little more than the most ignorant black man about the talents and rich civilizations and cultures of the black man of millenniums ago. I have lectured in Negro colleges and some of these brainwashed black Ph.D.'s, with their suspenders dragging the ground with degrees, have run to the white man's newspapers calling me a "black fanatic." Why, a lot of them are fifty years behind the times. If I were president of one of these black colleges, I'd hock the campus if I had to, to send a bunch of black students off digging in Africa for more, more and more proof of the black race's historical greatness. The white man now is in Africa digging and searching. An African elephant can't stumble without falling on some white man with a shovel. Practically every week, we read about some great new find from Africa's lost civilizations. All that's new is white science's attitude. The ancient civilizations of the black man have been buried on the Black Continent all the time.

Here is an example: a British anthropologist named Dr. Louis S. B. Leakey is displaying some fossil bones — a foot, part of a hand, some jaws, and skull fragments. On the basis of these, Dr. Leakey has said it's time to rewrite completely the history of man's origin.

This species of man lived 1,818,036 years before Christ. And these bones were found in Tanganyika. In the Black Continent.

It's a crime, the lie that has been told to generations of black men and white men both. Little innocent black children, born of parents who believed that their race had no history. Little black children seeing, before they could talk, that their parents considered themselves inferior. Innocent black children growing up, living out their lives, dying of old age — and all of their lives ashamed of being black. But the truth is pouring out of the bag now.

Eldridge Cleaver | # The White Race and Its Heroes

White people cannot, in the generality, be taken as models of how to live.
Rather, the white man is himself in sore need of new standards,
which will release him from his confusion and place him once again
in fruitful communion with the depths of his own being.

— JAMES BALDWIN — *The Fire Next Time*

Right from the go, let me make one thing absolutely clear: I am not now, nor have I ever been, a white man. Nor, I hasten to add, am I now a Black Muslim — although I used to be. But I *am* an Ofay Watcher, a member of that unchartered, amorphous league which has members on all continents and the islands of the seas. Ofay Watchers Anonymous, we might be called, because we exist concealed in the shadows wherever colored people have known oppression by whites, by white enslavers, colonizers, imperialists, and neo-colonialists.

Did it irritate you, compatriot, for me to string those epithets out like that? Tolerate me. My intention was not necessarily to sprinkle salt over anyone's wounds. I did it primarily to relieve a certain pressure on my brain. Do you cop that? If not, then we're in trouble, because we Ofay Watchers have a pronounced tendency to slip into that mood. If it is bothersome to you, it is quite a task for me because not too long ago it was my way of life to preach, as ardently as I could, that the white race is a race of devils, created by their maker to do evil, and make evil appear as good; that the white race is the natural, unchangeable enemy of the black man, who is the original man, owner, maker, cream of the planet Earth; that the white race was soon to be destroyed by Allah, and that the black man would then inherit the earth, which has always, in fact, been his.

I have, so to speak, washed my hands in the blood of the martyr, Malcolm X, whose retreat from the precipice of madness created new room for others to turn about in, and I am now caught up in that tiny space, attempting a maneuver of my own. Having renounced the teachings of Elijah Muhammad, I find that a rebirth does not follow automatically, of its own accord, that a void is left in one's vision, and this void seeks constantly to obliterate itself by pulling one back to one's former outlook. I have tried a tentative compromise by adopting a select vocabulary, so that now when I see the whites of *their* eyes, instead of saying "devil" or "beast" I say "imperialist" or "colonialist," and everyone seems to be happier.

In silence, we have spent our years watching the ofays, trying to understand them, on the principle that you have a better chance coping with the known than with the unknown. Some of us have been, and some still are, interested in learning whether it is *ultimately* possible to live in the same territory with people who seem so disagreeable to live with; still others want to get as far away from ofays as possible. What we share in common is the desire to break the ofays' power over us.

At times of fundamental social change, such as the era in which we live, it is easy to be deceived by the onrush of events, beguiled by the craving for social stability into mistaking transitory phenomena for enduring reality. The strength and permanence of "white backlash" in America is just such an illusion. However much this rear-guard action might seem to grow in strength, the initiative, and the future, rest with those whites and blacks who have liberated themselves from the master/slave syndrome. And these are to be found mainly among the youth.

Over the past twelve years there has surfaced a political conflict between the generations that is deeper, even, than the struggle between the races. Its first dramatic manifestation was within the ranks of the Negro people, when college students in the South, fed up with Uncle Tom's hat-in-hand approach to revolution, threw off the yoke of the NAACP. When these students initiated the first sit-ins, their spirit spread like a raging fire across the nation, and the technique of non-violent direct action, constantly refined and honed into a sharp cutting tool, swiftly matured. The older Negro "leaders," who are now all die-hard advocates of this tactic, scolded the students for sitting-in. The students rained down contempt upon their hoary heads. In the pre-sit-in days, these conservative leaders had always succeeded in putting down insurgent elements among the Negro people. (A measure of their power, prior to the students' rebellion, is shown by their success in isolating such great black men as the late W. E. B. DuBois and Paul Robeson, when these stalwarts, refusing to bite their tongues, lost favor with the U.S. government by their unstinting efforts to link up the Negro revolution with national liberation movements around the world.)

The "Negro leaders," and the whites who depended upon them to control their people, were outraged by the impudence of the students. Calling for a moratorium on student initiative, they were greeted instead by an encore of sit-ins, and retired to their ivory towers to contemplate the new phenomenon. Others, less prudent because held on a tighter leash by the whites, had their careers brought to an abrupt end because they thought they could lead a black/white backlash against the students, only to find themselves in a kind of Bay of Pigs. Negro college presidents, who expelled students from all-Negro colleges in an attempt to quash the demonstrations, ended up losing their jobs; the victorious students would no longer allow them to preside over the campuses. The spontaneous protests on southern campuses over the repressive measures of their college administrations were an earnest of the Free Speech upheaval which years later was to shake the UC campus at Berkeley. In countless ways, the rebellion of the black students served as catalyst for the brewing revolt of the whites.

What has suddenly happened is that the white race has lost its heroes. Worse, its heroes have been revealed as villains and its greatest heroes as the arch-villains. The new generations of whites, appalled by the sanguine and despicable record carved over the face of the globe by their race in the last five hundred years, are rejecting the panoply of white heroes, whose heroism consisted in erecting the inglorious edifice of colonialism and imperialism; heroes whose careers rested on a system of foreign and domestic exploitation, rooted in the myth of white supremacy and the manifest destiny of the white race. The emerging shape of a new world order, and the requisites for survival in such a world, are fostering in young whites a new outlook. They recoil in shame from the spectacle of cowboys and pioneers — their heroic forefathers whose exploits filled earlier generations with pride — galloping across a movie screen shooting down Indians like Coke bottles. Even Winston Churchill, who is looked upon by older whites as perhaps the greatest hero of the twentieth century — even he, because of the system of which he was a creature and which he served, is an arch-villain in the eyes of the young white rebels.

At the close of World War Two, national liberation movements in the colonized world picked up new momentum and audacity, seeking to cash in on the democratic promises made by the Allies during the war. The Atlantic Charter, signed by President Roosevelt and Prime Minister Churchill in 1941, affirming "the right of all people to choose the form of government under which they may live," established the principle, although it took years of postwar struggle to give this piece of rhetoric even the appearance of reality. And just as world revolution has prompted the oppressed to re-evaluate their self-image in terms of the changing conditions, to slough off the servile attitudes inculcated by long years of subordination, the same dynamics of change have prompted the white people of the world to re-evaluate their self-image as well, to disabuse themselves of the Master Race psychology developed over centuries of imperial hegemony.

It is among the white youth of the world that the greatest change is taking place. It is they who are experiencing the great psychic pain of waking into consciousness to find their inherited heroes turned by events into villains. Communication and understanding between the older and younger generations of whites has entered a crisis. The elders, who, in the tradition of privileged classes or races, genuinely do not understand the youth, trapped by old ways of thinking and blind to the future, have only just begun to be vexed — because the youth have only just begun to rebel. So thoroughgoing is the revolution in the psyches of white youth that the traditional tolerance which every older generation has found it necessary to display is quickly exhausted, leaving a gulf of fear, hostility, mutual misunderstanding, and contempt.

The rebellion of the oppressed peoples of the world, along with the Negro revolution in America, have opened the way to a new evaluation of history, a re-examination of the role played by the white race since the beginning of European expansion. The positive achievements are also there in the record, and future generations will applaud them. But there can be no applause now, not while the master still holds the whip in his hand! Not even the master's own children can find it possible to applaud him — he cannot even applaud himself! The negative rings too loudly. Slave-catchers, slaveowners, murderers, butchers, invaders, oppressors — the white heroes have acquired new names. The great white statesmen whom school children are taught to revere are revealed as the architects of systems of human exploitation and slavery. Religious leaders are exposed as condoners and justifiers of all these evil deeds. Schoolteachers and college professors are seen as a clique of brainwashers and whitewashers.

The white youth of today are coming to see, intuitively, that to escape the onus of the history their fathers made they must face and admit the moral truth concerning the works of their fathers. That such venerated figures as George Washington and Thomas Jefferson owned hundreds of black slaves, that all of the Presidents up to Lincoln presided over a slave state, and that every President since Lincoln connived politically and cynically with the issues affecting the human rights and general welfare of the broad masses of the American people — these facts weigh heavily upon the hearts of these young people.

The elders do not like to give these youngsters credit for being able to understand what is going on and what has gone on. When speaking of juvenile delinquency, or the rebellious attitude of today's youth, the elders employ a glib rhetoric. They speak of the "alienation of youth," the desire of the young to be independent, the problems of "the father image" and "the mother image" and their effect upon growing children who lack sound models upon which to pattern themselves. But they consider it bad form to connect the problems of the youth with the central event of our era — the national liberation movements abroad and the Negro revolution at home. The foundations of authority have been blasted to bits in America because the whole society has been indicted, tried, and convicted of injustice. To the youth, the elders are Ugly Americans; to the elders, the youth have gone mad.

The rebellion of the white youth has gone through four broadly discernible stages. First there was an initial recoiling away, a rejection of the conformity which America expected, and had always received, sooner or later, from its youth. The disaffected youth were refusing to participate in the system, having discovered that America, far from helping the under-dog, was up to its ears in the mud trying to hold the dog down. Because of the publicity and self-advertisements of the more vocal rebels, this period has come to be known as the beatnik era, although not all of the youth affected by these changes thought of themselves as beatniks. The howl of the beatniks and their scathing, outraged denunciation of the sys-tem — characterized by Ginsberg as Moloch, a bloodthirsty Semitic deity to which the ancient tribes sacrificed their firstborn children — was a seri-ous, irrevocable declaration of war. It is revealing that the elders looked upon the beatniks as mere obscene misfits who were too lazy to take baths and too stingy to buy a haircut. The elders had eyes but couldn't see, ears but couldn't hear — not even when the message came through as clearly as in this remarkable passage from Jack Kerouac's *On the Road:*

> At lilac evening I walked with every muscle aching among the lights of 27th and Welton in the Denver colored section, wishing I were a Negro, feeling that the best the white world had offered was not enough ecstasy for me, not enough life, joy, kicks, darkness, music, not enough night. I wished I were a Denver Mexican, or even a poor overworked Jap, any-thing but what I so drearily was, a "white man" disillusioned. All my life I'd had white ambitions. . . . I passed the dark porches of Mexican and Negro homes; soft voices were there, occasionally the dusky knee of some mysterious sensuous gal; the dark faces of the men behind rose arbors. Little children sat like sages in ancient rocking chairs.

The second stage arrived when these young people, having decided em-phatically that the world, and particularly the U.S.A., was unacceptable to them in its present form, began an active search for roles they could play in changing the society. If many of these young people were con-tent to lay up in their cool beat pads, smoking pot and listening to jazz in a perpetual orgy of esoteric bliss, there were others, less crushed by the system, who recognized the need for positive action. Moloch could not ask for anything more than to have its disaffected victims withdraw into safe, passive, apolitical little nonparticipatory islands, in an economy less and less able to provide jobs for the growing pool of unemployed. If all the unemployed had followed the lead of the beatniks, Moloch would gladly have legalized the use of euphoric drugs and marijuana, passed out free jazz albums and sleeping bags, to all those willing to sign affidavits promising to remain "beat." The non-beat disenchanted white youth were attracted magnetically to the Negro revolution, which had begun to take on a mass, insurrectionary tone. But they had difficulty understanding their relationship to the Negro, and what role "whites" could play in a "Negro revolution." For the time being they watched the Negro activists from afar.

The third stage, which is rapidly drawing to a close, emerged when white youth started joining Negro demonstrations in large numbers. The presence of whites among the demonstrators emboldened the Negro leaders and allowed them to use tactics they never would have been able to employ with all-black troops. The racist conscience of America is such that murder does not register as murder, really, unless the victim is white. And it was only when the newspapers and magazines started carrying pictures and stories of white demonstrators being beaten and maimed by mobs and police that the public began to protest. Negroes have become so used to this double standard that they, too, react differently to the death of a white. When white freedom riders were brutalized along with blacks, a sigh of relief went up from the black masses, because the blacks knew that white blood is the coin of freedom in a land where for four hundred years black blood has been shed unremarked and with impunity. America has never truly been outraged by the murder of a black man, woman, or child. White politicians may, if Negroes are aroused by a particular murder, say with their lips what they know with their minds they should feel with their hearts — but don't.

It is a measure of what the Negro feels that when the two white and one black civil rights workers were murdered in Mississippi in 1964, the event was welcomed by Negroes on a level of understanding beyond and deeper than the grief they felt for the victims and their families. This welcoming of violence and death to whites can almost be heard — indeed it can be heard — in the inevitable words, oft repeated by Negroes, that those whites, and blacks, do not die in vain. So it was with Mrs. Viola Liuzzo. And much of the anger which Negroes felt toward Martin Luther King during the Battle of Selma stemmed from the fact that he denied history a great moment, never to be recaptured, when he turned tail on the Edmund Pettus Bridge and refused to all those whites behind him what they had traveled thousands of miles to receive. If the police had turned them back by force, all those nuns, priests, rabbis, preachers, and distinguished ladies and gentlemen old and young — as they had done the Negroes a week earlier — the violence and brutality of the system would have been ruthlessly exposed. Or if, seeing King determined to lead them on to Montgomery, the troopers had stepped aside to avoid precisely the confrontation that Washington would not have tolerated, it would have signaled the capitulation of the militant white South. As it turned out, the March on Montgomery was a show of somewhat dim luster, stage-managed by the Establishment. But by this time the young whites were already active participants in the Negro revolution. In fact they had begun to transform it into something broader, with the potential of encompassing the whole of America in a radical reordering of society.

The fourth stage, now in its infancy, sees these white youth taking the initiative, using techniques learned in the Negro struggle to attack problems in the general society. The classic example of this new energy in action was the student battle on the UC campus at Berkeley, California — the Free Speech Movement. Leading the revolt were veterans of the civil rights movement, some of whom spent time on the firing line in the wilderness of Mississippi/Alabama. Flowing from the same momentum were student demonstrations against U.S. interference in the internal affairs of Vietnam, Cuba, the Dominican Republic, and the Congo and U.S. aid to apartheid in South Africa. The students even aroused the intellectual community to actions and positions unthinkable a few years ago: witness the teach-ins. But their revolt is deeper than single-issue protest. The characteristics of the white rebels which most alarm their elders — the long hair, the new dances, their love for Negro music, their use of marijuana, their mystical attitude toward sex — are all tools of their rebellion. They have turned these tools against the totalitarian fabric of American society — and they mean to change it.

From the beginning, America has been a schizophrenic nation. Its two conflicting images of itself were never reconciled, because never before has the survival of its most cherished myths made a reconciliation mandatory. Once before, during the bitter struggle between North and South climaxed by the Civil War, the two images of America came into conflict, although whites North and South scarcely understood it. The image of America held by its most alienated citizens was advanced neither by the North nor by the South; it was perhaps best expressed by Frederick Douglass, who was born into slavery in 1817, escaped to the North, and became the greatest leader-spokesman for the blacks of his era. In words that can still, years later, arouse an audience of black Americans, Frederick Douglass delivered, in 1852, a scorching indictment in his Fourth of July oration in Rochester:

What to the American slave is your Fourth of July? I answer: a day that reveals to him, more than all other days in the year, the gross injustice and cruelty to which he is the constant victim. To him your celebration is a sham; your boasted liberty, an unholy licence; your national greatness, swelling vanity; your sounds of rejoicing are empty and heartless; your denunciation of tyrants, brass-fronted impudence; your shouts of liberty and equality, hollow mockery; your prayers and hymns, your sermons and thanksgivings, with all your religious parade and solemnity, are, to him, more bombast, fraud, deception, impiety and hypocrisy — a thin veil to cover up crimes which would disgrace a nation of savages. . . .

You boast of your love of liberty, your superior civilization, and your pure Christianity, while the whole political power of the nation (as embodied in the two great political parties) is solemnly pledged to support and perpetuate the enslavement of three millions of your countrymen. You hurl your anathemas at the crown-headed tyrants of Russia and Austria and pride yourselves on your democratic institutions, while you yourselves consent to be the mere *tools* and *bodyguards* of the tyrants of Virginia and Carolina.

You invite to your shores fugitives of oppression from abroad, honor them with banquets, greet them with ovations, cheer them, toast them, salute them, protect them, and pour out your money to them like water; but the fugitive from your own land you advertise, hunt, arrest, shoot, and kill. You glory in your refinement and your universal education; yet you maintain a system as barbarous and dreadful as ever stained the character of a nation — a system begun in avarice, supported in pride, and perpetuated in cruelty.

You shed tears over fallen Hungary, and make the sad story of her wrongs the theme of your poets, statesmen and orators, till your gallant sons are ready to fly to arms to vindicate her cause against the oppressor; but, in regard to the ten thousand wrongs of the American slave, you would enforce the strictest silence, and would hail him as an enemy of the nation who dares to make these wrongs the subject of public discourse!

This most alienated view of America was preached by the Abolitionists, and by Harriet Beecher Stowe in her *Uncle Tom's Cabin*. But such a view of America was too distasteful to receive wide attention, and serious debate about America's image and her reality was engaged in only on the fringes of society. Even when confronted with overwhelming evidence to the contrary, most white Americans have found it possible, after steadying their rattled nerves, to settle comfortably back into their vaunted belief that America is dedicated to the proposition that all men are created equal and endowed by their Creator with certain inalienable rights — life, liberty and the pursuit of happiness. With the Constitution for a rudder and the Declaration of Independence as its guiding star, the ship of state is sailing always toward a brighter vision of freedom and justice for all.

Because there is no common ground between these two contradictory images of America, they had to be kept apart. But the moment the blacks were let into the white world — let out of the voiceless and faceless cages of their ghettos, singing, walking, talking, dancing, writing, and orating *their* image of America and of Americans — the white world was suddenly challenged to match its practice to its preachments. And this is why those whites who abandon the *white* image of America and adopt the *black* are greeted with such unmitigated hostility by their elders.

For all these years whites have been taught to believe in the myth they preached, while Negroes have had to face the bitter reality of what America practiced. But without the lies and distortions, white Americans would not have been able to do the things they have done. When whites are forced to look honestly upon the objective proof of their deeds, the cement of mendacity holding white society together swiftly disintegrates. On the other hand, the core of the black world's vision remains intact, and in fact begins to expand and spread into the psychological territory vacated by the non-viable white lies, i.e., into the minds of young whites. It is remarkable how the system worked for so many years, how the majority of whites remained effectively unaware of any contradiction between their view of the world and that world itself. The mechanism by which this was rendered possible requires examination at this point.

Let us recall that the white man, in order to justify slavery and, later on, to justify segregation, elaborated a complex, all-pervasive myth which at one time classified the black man as a subhuman beast of burden. The myth was progressively modified, gradually elevating the blacks on the scale of evolution, following their slowly changing status, until the plateau of separate-but-equal was reached at the close of the nineteenth century. During slavery, the black was seen as a mindless Supermasculine Menial. Forced to do the backbreaking work, he was conceived in terms of his ability to do such work — "field niggers," etc. The white man administered the plantation, doing all the thinking, exercising omnipotent power over the slaves. He had little difficulty dissociating himself from the black slaves, and he could not conceive of their positions being reversed or even reversible.

Blacks and whites being conceived as mutually exclusive types, those attributes imputed to the blacks could not also be imputed to the whites — at least not in equal degree — without blurring the line separating the races. These images were based upon the social function of the two races, the work they performed. The ideal white man was one who knew how to use his head, who knew how to manage and control things and get things done. Those whites who were not in a position to perform these functions nevertheless aspired to them. The ideal black man was one who did exactly as he was told, and did it efficiently and cheerfully. "Slaves," said Frederick Douglass, "are generally expected to sing as well as to work." As the black man's position and function became more varied, the images of white and black, having become stereotypes, lagged behind.

The separate-but-equal doctrine was promulgated by the Supreme Court in 1896. It had the same purpose domestically as the Open Door Policy toward China in the international arena: to stabilize a situation and subordinate a nonwhite population so that racist exploiters could manipulate those people according to their own selfish interests. These doctrines were foisted off as *the epitome of enlightened justice, the highest expression of morality*. Sanctified by religion, justified by philosophy and legalized by the Supreme Court, separate-but-equal was enforced by day by agencies of the law, and by the KKK & Co. under cover of night. Booker T. Washington, the Martin Luther King of his day, accepted separate-but-equal in the name of all Negroes. W. E. B. DuBois denounced it.

Separate-but-equal marked the last stage of the white man's flight into cultural neurosis, and the beginning of the black man's frantic striving to assert his humanity and equalize his position with the white. Blacks ventured into all fields of endeavor to which they could gain entrance. Their goal was to present in all fields a performance that would equal or surpass that of the whites. It was long axiomatic among blacks that a black had to be twice as competent as a white in any field in order to win grudging recognition from the whites. This produced a pathological motivation in the blacks to equal or surpass the whites, and a pathological motivation in the whites to maintain a distance from the blacks. This is the rack on which black and white Americans receive their delicious torture! At first there was the color bar, flatly denying the blacks entrance to certain spheres of activity. When this no longer worked, and blacks invaded sector after sector of American life and economy, the whites evolved other methods of keeping their distance. The illusion of the Negro's inferior nature had to be maintained.

One device evolved by the whites was to tab whatever the blacks did with the prefix "Negro." We had *Negro* literature, *Negro* athletes, *Negro* music, *Negro* doctors, *Negro* politicians, *Negro* workers. The malignant ingeniousness of this device is that although it accurately describes an objective biological fact — or, at least, a sociological fact in America — it concealed the paramount psychological fact: that to the white mind, prefixing anything with "Negro" automatically consigned it to an inferior category. A well-known example of the white necessity to deny due credit to blacks is in the realm of music. White musicians were famous for going to Harlem and other Negro cultural centers literally to steal the black man's music, carrying it back across the color line into the Great White World and passing off the watered-down loot as their own original creations. Blacks, meanwhile, were ridiculed as *Negro* musicians playing inferior coon music.

The Negro revolution at home and national liberation movements abroad have unceremoniously shattered the world of fantasy in which the whites have been living. It is painful that many do not yet see that their fantasy world has been rendered uninhabitable in the last half of the twentieth century. But it is away from this world that the white youth of today are turning. The "paper tiger" hero, James Bond, offering the whites a triumphant image of themselves, is saying what many whites want desperately to hear reaffirmed: *I am still the White Man, lord of the land, licensed to kill, and the world is still an empire at my feet.* James Bond feeds on that secret little anxiety, the psychological white backlash, felt in some degree by most whites alive. It is exasperating to see little brown men and little yellow men from the mysterious Orient, and the opaque black men of Africa (to say nothing of these impudent American Negroes!) who come to the UN and talk smart to us, who are scurrying all over *our* globe in their strange modes of dress — much as if they were new, unpleasant arrivals from another planet. Many whites believe in their ulcers that it is only a matter of time before the Marines get the signal to round up these truants and put them back securely in their cages. But it is away from this fantasy world that the white youth of today are turning.

In the world revolution now under way, the initiative rests with people of color. That growing numbers of white youth are repudiating their heritage of blood and taking people of color as their heroes and models is a tribute not only to their insight but to the resilience of the human spirit. For today the heroes of the initiative are people not usually thought of as white: Fidel Castro, Che Guevara, Kwame Nkrumah, Mao Tse-tung, Gamal Abdel Nasser, Robert F. Williams, Malcolm X, Ben Bella, John

Lewis, Martin Luther King, Jr., Robert Parris Moses, Ho Chi Minh, Stokeley Carmichael, W. E. B. DuBois, James Forman, Chou En-lai.

The white youth of today have begun to react to the fact that the "American Way of Life" is a fossil of history. What do they care if their old baldheaded and crew-cut elders don't dig their caveman mops? They couldn't care less about the old, stiffassed honkies who don't like their new dances: Frug, Monkey, Jerk, Swim, Watusi. All they know is that it feels good to swing to way-out body-rhythms instead of dragassing across the dance floor like zombies to the dead beat of mind-smothered Mickey Mouse music. Is it any wonder that the youth have lost all respect for their elders, for law and order, when for as long as they can remember all they've witnessed is a monumental bickering over the Negro's place in American society and the right of people around the world to be left alone by outside powers? They have witnessed the law, both domestic and international, being spat upon by those who do not like its terms. Is it any wonder, then, that they feel justified, by sitting-in and freedom riding, in breaking laws made by lawless men? Old funny-styled, zipper-mouthed political night riders know nothing but to haul out an investigating committee *to look into the disturbance* to find the cause of unrest among the youth. Look into a mirror! The cause is you, Mr. and Mrs. Yesterday, you with your forked tongues.

A young white today cannot help but recoil from the base deeds of his people. On every side, on every continent, he sees racial arrogance, savage brutality toward the conquered and subjugated people, genocide; he sees the human cargo of the slave trade; he sees the systematic extermination of American Indians; he sees the civilized nations of Europe fighting in imperial depravity over the lands of other people — and over possession of the very people themselves. There seems to be no end to the ghastly deeds of which his people are guilty. GUILTY. The slaughter of the Jews by the Germans, the dropping of atomic bombs on the Japanese people — these deeds weigh heavily upon the prostrate souls and tumultuous consciences of the white youth. The white heroes, their hands dripping with blood, are dead.

The young whites know that the colored people of the world, Afro-Americans included, do not seek revenge for their suffering. They seek the same things the white rebel wants: an end to war and exploitation. Black and white, the young rebels are free people, free in a way that Americans have never been before in the history of their country. And they are outraged.

There is in America today a generation of white youth that is truly worthy of a black man's respect, and this is a rare event in the foul annals of American history. From the beginning of the contact between blacks and whites, there has been very little reason for a black man to respect a white, with such exceptions as John Brown and others lesser known. But respect commands itself and it can neither be given nor withheld when it is due. If a man like Malcolm X could change and repudiate racism, if I myself and other former Muslims can change, if young whites can change, then there is hope for America. It was certainly strange to find myself, while steeped in the doctrine that all whites were devils by nature, commanded by the heart to applaud and acknowledge respect for these young whites — despite the fact that they are descendants of the masters and I the descendant of the slave. The sins of the fathers are visited upon the heads of the children — but only if the children continue in the evil deeds of the fathers.

Stokeley Carmichael | **Toward Black Liberation**

One of the most pointed illustrations of the need for Black Power, as a positive and redemptive force in a society degenerating into a form of totalitarianism, is to be made by examining the history of distortion that the concept has received in national media of publicity. In this "debate," as in everything else that affects our lives, Negroes are dependent on, and at the discretion of, forces and institutions within the white society which have little interest in representing us honestly. Our experience with the national press has been that where they have managed to escape a meretricious special interest in "Git Whitey" sensationalism and race-war-mongering, individual reporters and commentators have been conditioned by the enveloping racism of the society to the point where they are incapable even of objective observation and reporting of racial *incidents*, much less the analysis of *ideas*. But this limitation of vision and perceptions is an inevitable consequence of the dictatorship of definition, interpretation and consciousness, along with the censorship of history that the society has inflicted upon the Negro — and itself.

Our concern for black power addresses itself directly to this problem, the necessity to reclaim our history and our identity from the cultural terrorism and depredation of self-justifying white guilt.

To do this we shall have to struggle for the right to create our own terms through which to define ourselves and our relationship to the society, and to have these terms recognized. This is the first necessity of a free people, and the first right that any oppressor must suspend. The white

---

SOURCE: *Black Fire*, edited by Leroi Jones and Larry Neal.

fathers of American racism knew this — instinctively it seems — as is indicated by the continuous record of the distortion and omission in their dealings with the red and black men. In the same way that southern apologists for the "Jim Crow" society have so obscured, muddied and misrepresented the record of the Reconstruction period, until it is almost impossible to tell what really happened, their contemporary counterparts are busy doing the same thing with the recent history of the civil rights movement.

In 1964, for example, the National Democratic Party, led by L. B. Johnson and Hubert H. Humphrey, cynically undermined the efforts of Mississippi's black population to achieve some degree of political representation. Yet, whenever the events of that convention are recalled by the press, one sees only that version fabricated by the press agents of the Democratic Party. A year later, the House of Representatives, in an even more vulgar display of political racism, made a mockery of the political rights of Mississippi's Negroes when it failed to unseat the Mississippi Delegation to the House which had been elected through a process which methodically and systematically excluded over 450,000 voting-age Negroes, almost one-half of the total electorate of the state. Whenever this event is mentioned in print it is in terms that leave one with the rather curious impression that somehow the oppressed Negro people of Mississippi are at fault for confronting the Congress with a situation in which they had no alternative but to endorse Mississippi's racist political practices.

I mention these two examples because, having been directly involved in them, I can see very clearly the discrepancies between what happened, and the versions that are finding their way into general acceptance as a kind of popular mythology. Thus the victimization of the Negro takes place in two phases: first it occurs in fact and deed, then — and this is equally sinister — in the official recording of those facts.

The "Black Power" program and concept that is being articulated by SNCC, CORE, and a host of community organizations in the ghettoes of the North and South has not escaped that process. The white press has been busy articulating their own analyses, their own interpretations, and criticisms of their own creations. For example, while the press had given wide and sensational dissemination to attacks made by figures in the civil rights movement — foremost among which are Roy Wilkins of the NAACP and Whitney Young of the Urban League — and to the hysterical ranting about black racism made by the political chameleon that now serves as Vice-President, it has generally failed to give accounts of the reasonable and productive dialogue which is taking place in the Negro community, and in certain important areas in the white religious and intellectual community. A national committee of influential Negro churchmen affiliated with the National Council of Churches, despite their obvious respectability and responsibility, had to resort to a paid advertisement to articulate their position, while anyone shouting the hysterical yappings of "Black Racism" got ample space. Thus the American people have gotten at best a superficial and misleading account of the very terms and tenor of this debate. I wish to quote briefly from the statement by the national committee of churchmen which I suspect that the majority of Americans will not have seen. This statement appeared in *The New York Times* of July 31, 1966.

We an informal group of Negro Churchmen in America are deeply disturbed about the crisis brought upon our country by historic distortions of important human realities in the controversy about "black power." What we see shining through the variety of rhetoric is not anything new but the same old problem of power and race which has faced our beloved country since 1619.

. . . The conscience of black men is corrupted because, having no power to implement the demands of conscience, the concern for justice in the absence of justice becomes a chaotic self-surrender. Powerlessness breeds a race of beggars. We are now faced with a situation where powerless conscience meets conscience-less power, threatening the very foundations of our Nation.

. . . We deplore the overt violence of riots, but we feel it is more important to focus on the real sources of these eruptions. These sources may be abetted inside the Ghetto, but their basic cause lies in the silent and covert violence which white middleclass America inflicts upon the victims of the inner city.

. . . In short; the failure of American leaders to use American power to create equal opportunity in *life* as well as *law*, this is the real problem and not the anguished cry for black power.

. . . Without the capacity to *participate with power*, *i.e.*, to have some organized political and economic strength to really influence people with whom one interacts — integration is not meaningful.

. . . America has asked its Negro citizens to fight for opportunity as *individuals*, whereas at certain points in our history what we have needed most has been opportunity for the *whole group*, not just for selected and approved Negroes.

. . . We must not apologize for the existence of this form of group power, for we have been oppressed as a group and not as individuals. We will not find our way out of that oppression until both we and America accept the need for Negro Americans, as well as for Jews, Italians, Poles, and white Anglosaxon Protestants, among others to have and to wield group power.

Traditionally, for each new ethnic group, the route to social and political integration into America's pluralistic society, has been through the organization of their own institutions with which to represent their communal needs within the larger society. This is simply stating what the advocates of Black Power are saying. The strident outcry, *particularly* from the liberal community, that has been evoked by this proposal can only be understood by examining the historic relationship between Negro and white power in this country.

Negroes are defined by two forces, their blackness and their powerlessness. There have been traditionally two communities in America: the white community, which controlled and defined the forms that all institutions within the society would take; and the Negro community, which has been excluded from participation in the power decisions that shaped the society, and has traditionally been dependent upon, and subservient to, the white community.

This has not been accidental. The history of every institution of this society indicates that a major concern in the ordering and structuring of the society has been the maintaining of the Negro community in its condition of dependence and oppression. This has not been on the level of individual acts of discrimination between individual whites against individual Negroes, but as total acts by the white community against the Negro community. This fact cannot be too strongly emphasized — that racist assumptions of white superiority have been so deeply ingrained in the structure of the society that it infuses its entire functioning, and is so much a part of the national subconscious that it is taken for granted and is frequently not even recognized.

Let me give an example of the difference between individual racism and institutionalized racism, and the society's response to both. When unidentified white terrorists bomb a Negro church and kill five children, that is an act of individual racism, widely deplored by most segments of the society. But when in that same city, Birmingham, Alabama, not five but five hundred Negro babies die each year because of a lack of proper food, shelter and medical facilities, and thousands more are destroyed and maimed physically, emotionally and intellectually because of conditions of poverty and deprivation in the ghetto, that is a function of institutionalized racism. But the society either pretends it doesn't know of this situation, or is incapable of doing anything meaningful about it. And this resistance to doing anything meaningful about conditions in that ghetto comes from the fact that the ghetto is itself a product of a combination of forces and special interests in the white community, and the groups that have access to the resources and power to change that situation benefit, politically and economically, from the existence of that ghetto.

It is more than a figure of speech to say that the Negro community in America is the victim of white imperialism and colonial exploitation. This is, in practical economic and political terms, true. There are over twenty million black people comprising ten per cent of this nation. They, for the most part, live in well-defined areas of the country — in the shantytowns and rural black-belt areas of the South, and increasingly in the slums of Northern and Western industrial cities. If one goes into any Negro community, whether it be in Jackson, Mississippi, Cambridge, Maryland or Harlem, New York, one will find that the same combination of political, economic and social forces is at work. The people in the Negro community do not control the resources of that community, its political decisions, its law enforcement, its housing standards; and even the physical ownership of the land, houses and stores *lie outside that community*.

It is white power that makes the laws, and it is violent white power in the form of armed white cops that enforces those laws with guns and nightsticks. The vast majority of Negroes in this country live in these captive communities and must endure these conditions of oppression because, and only because, *they are black and powerless.* I do not suppose that at any point the men who control the power and resources of this country ever sat down and designed these black enclaves, and formally articulated the terms of their colonial and dependent status, as was done, for example, by the apartheid government of South Africa. Yet, one cannot distinguish between one ghetto and another. As one moves from city to city, it is as though some malignant racist planning-unit had done precisely this — designed each one from the same master blueprint. And indeed, if the ghetto had been formally and deliberately planned, instead of growing spontaneously and inevitably from the racist functioning of the various institutions that combine to make the society, it would be somehow less frightening. The situation would be less frightening because, if these ghettoes were the result of design and conspiracy, one could understand their similarity as being artificial and consciously imposed, rather than the result of identical patterns of white racism which repeat themselves in cities as far apart as Boston and Birmingham. Without bothering to list the historic factors which contribute to this pattern — economic exploitation, political impotence, discrimination in employment and education — one can see that to correct this pattern will require far-reaching changes in the basic power-relationships and the ingrained social patterns within the society. The question is, of course, what kinds of changes are necessary, and how is it possible to bring them about?

In recent years, the answer to these questions which has been given by most articulate groups of Negroes and their white allies — the "liberals" of all stripes — has been in terms of something called "integration." According to the advocates of integration, social justice will be accomplished by "integrating the Negro into the mainstream institutions of the society from which he has been traditionally excluded." It is very significant that each time I have heard this formulation it has been in terms of "the Negro," the individual Negro, rather than in terms of the community.

This concept of integration had to be based on the assumption that there was nothing of value in the Negro community and that little of value could be created among Negroes, so the thing to do was to siphon off the "acceptable" Negroes into the surrounding middle-class white community. Thus the goal of the movement for integration was simply to loosen up the restrictions barring the entry of Negroes into the white community. Goals around which the struggle took place, such as public accommodation, open housing, job opportunity on the executive level (which is easier to deal with than the problem of semi-skilled and blue-collar jobs which involve more far-reaching economic adjustments), are quite simply middle-class goals, articulated by a tiny group of Negroes who had middle-class aspirations. It is true that the student demonstrations in the South during the early Sixties, out of which SNCC came, had a similar orientation. But while it is hardly a concern of a black sharecropper, dishwasher, or welfare recipient whether a certain fifteen-dollar-a-day motel offers accommodations to Negroes, the overt symbols of white superiority and the imposed limitations on the Negro community had to be destroyed. Now, black people must look beyond these goals, to the issue of collective power.

Such a limited class orientation was reflected not only in the program and goals of the civil rights movement, but in its tactics and organization. It is very significant that the two oldest and most "respectable" civil rights organizations have constitutions which *specifically* prohibit partisan political activity. CORE once did, but changed that clause when it changed its orientation toward Black Power. But this is perfectly understandable in terms of the strategy and goals of the older organizations. The civil rights movement saw its role as a kind of liaison between the powerful white community and the dependent Negro one. The dependent status of the black community apparently was unimportant since — if the movement were successful — it was going to blend into the white community anyway. We made no pretense of organizing and developing institutions of community power in the Negro community, but appealed to the conscience of white institutions of power. The posture of the civil rights movement was that of the dependent, the suppliant. The theory was that, without attempting to create any organized base of political strength itself, the civil rights movement could, by forming coalitions with various "liberal" pressure organizations in the white community — liberal reform clubs, labor unions, church groups, progressive civic groups, and at times one or other of the major political parties — influence national legislation and national social patterns.

I think we all have seen the limitations of this approach. We have repeatedly seen that political alliances based on appeals to conscience and decency are chancy things, simply because institutions and political organizations have no consciences outside their own special interests. The political and social rights of Negroes have been and always will be negotiable and expendable the moment they conflict with the interests of our "allies." If we do not learn from history, we are doomed to repeat it, and that is precisely the lesson of the Reconstruction. Black people were allowed to register, vote and participate in politics because it was to the advantage of powerful white allies to promote this. But this was the result of white decision, and it was ended by other white men's decision before any political base powerful enough to challenge that decision could be established in the southern Negro community. (Thus at this point in the struggle Negroes have no assurance — save a kind of idiot optimism and faith in a society whose history is one of racism — that if it were to become necessary, even the painfully limited gains thrown to the civil rights movement by the Congress will not be revoked as soon as a shift in political sentiments should occur.)

The major limitation of this approach was that it tended to maintain the traditional dependence of Negroes, and of the movement. We depended upon the goodwill and support of various groups within the white community whose interests were not always compatible with ours. To the extent that we depended on the financial support of other groups, we were vulnerable to their influence and domination.

Also, the program that evolved out of this coalition was really limited and inadequate in the long term, and one that affected only a small select group of Negroes. Its goal was to make the white community accessible to "qualified" Negroes and presumably each year a few more Negroes armed with their passport — a couple of university degrees — would escape into middle-class America and adopt the attitudes and life styles of that group; and one day the Harlems and the Wattses would stand empty, a tribute to the success of integration. This is simply neither realistic nor particularly desirable. You can integrate communities, but you assimilate individuals. Even if such a program were possible, its result would be not to develop the black community as a functional and honorable segment of the total society, with its own cultural identity, life patterns and institutions, but to abolish it — the final solution to the Negro problem. Marx said that "the working class is the first class in history that ever wanted to abolish itself." If one listens to some of our "moderate" Negro leaders, it appears that the American Negro is the first race that ever wished to abolish itself. The fact is that what must be abolished is not the black community, but the dependent colonial status that has been inflicted upon it. The racial and cultural personality of the black community must be preserved and the community must win its freedom while preserving its cultural integrity. This is the essential difference between integration as it is currently practised and the concept of Black Power.

What has the movement for integration accomplished to date? The Negro graduating from M.I.T. with a doctorate will have better job opportunities available to him than to Lynda Bird Johnson. But the rate of unemployment in the Negro community is steadily increasing, while that in the white community decreases. More educated Negroes hold executive jobs in major corporations and federal agencies than ever before, but the gap between white income and Negro income has almost doubled in the last twenty years. More suburban housing is available to Negroes, but housing conditions in the ghetto are steadily declining. While the infant mortality rate of New York City is at its lowest rate ever in the city's history, the infant mortality rate of Harlem is steadily climbing. There has been an organized national resistance to the Supreme Court's order to integrate the schools, and the federal government has not acted to enforce that order. Less than fifteen per cent of black children in the South attend integrated schools; and Negro schools, which the vast majority of black children still attend, are increasingly decrepit, overcrowded, understaffed, inadequately equipped and funded.

This explains why the rate of school dropouts is increasing among Negro teenagers, who then express their bitterness, hopelessness and alienation by the only means they have — rebellion. As long as people in the ghettoes of our large cities feel that they are victims of the misuse of white power without any way to have their needs represented — and these are frequently simple needs: to get the welfare inspectors to stop kicking down your doors in the middle of the night, the cops from beating your children, the landlord to exterminate the vermin in your home, the city to collect your garbage — we will continue to have riots. These are not the products of Black Power, but the absence of any organization capable of giving the community the power, the black power, to deal with its problems.

SNCC proposes that it is now time for the black freedom movement to stop pandering to the fears and anxieties of the white middle class in the attempt to earn its "goodwill," and to return to the ghetto to organize these communities to control themselves. This organization must be attempted in Northern and Southern urban areas as well as in the rural black-belt counties of the South. The chief antagonist to this organization is, in the South, the overtly racist Democratic Party, and in the North, the equally corrupt big-city machines.

The standard argument presented against independent political organization is, "But you are only ten per cent." I cannot see the relevance of this observation, since no one is talking about taking over the country, but taking control over our own communities.

The fact is that the Negro population, ten per cent or not, is very strategically placed because — ironically — of segregation. What is also true is that Negroes have never been able to utilize the full voting potential of our numbers. Where we could vote, the case has always been that the white political machine stacks and gerrymanders the political subdivisions in Negro neighborhoods so the true voting strength is never reflected in political strength. Would anyone looking at the distribution of political power in Manhattan, ever think that Negroes represented sixty per cent of the population there?

Just as often, the effective political organization in Negro communities is absorbed by tokenism and patronage — the time-honored practice of "giving" certain offices to selected Negroes. The machine thus creates a "little machine," which is subordinate and responsive to it, in the Negro community. These Negro political "leaders" are really vote-deliverers, more responsible to the white machine and the white power structure than to the community they allegedly represent. Thus the white community is able to substitute patronage-control for audacious Black Power in the Negro community. This is precisely what Johnson tried to do even before the Votings Rights Act of 1966 was passed. The National Democrats made it very clear that the measure was intended to register Democrats, not Negroes. The President and top officials of the Democratic Party called in almost one hundred selected Negro "leaders" from the Deep South.

Nothing was said about changing the policies of the racist state parties, nothing was said about repudiating such leadership figures as Eastland and Ross Barnett in Mississippi or George Wallace in Alabama. What was said was simply, "Go home and organize your people into the local Democratic Party — *then* we'll see about poverty money and appointments." (Incidentally, for the most part, the War on Poverty in the South is controlled by local Democratic ward heelers — and outspoken racists who have used the program to change the form of the Negroes' dependence. People who were afraid to register for fear of being thrown off the farm are now afraid to register for fear of losing their Head Start jobs.)

We must organize black community power to end these abuses, and to give the Negro community a chance to have its needs expressed. A leadership which is truly "responsible" — not to the white press and power structure, but to the community — must be developed. Such leadership will recognize that its power lies in the unified and collective strength of that community. This will make it difficult for the white leadership group to conduct its dialogue with individuals in terms of patronage and prestige, and will force them to talk to the community's representatives in terms of real power.

The single aspect of the Black Power program that has encountered most criticism is this concept of independent organization. This is presented as third-partyism, which has never worked, or a withdrawal into black nationalism and isolationism. If such a program is developed, it will not have the effect of isolating the Negro community, but the reverse. When the Negro community is able to control its local office, and negotiate with other groups from a position of organized strength, the possibility of meaningful political alliances on specific issues will be increased. That is a rule of politics and there is no reason why it should not operate here. The only difference is that we will have the power to define the terms of these alliances.

The next question usually is, "So — can it work, can the ghettoes in fact be organized?" The answer is that this organization must be successful, because there are no viable alternatives — not the War on Poverty, which was at its inception limited to dealing with effects rather than causes, and has become simply another source of machine patronage. And "Integration" is meaningful only to a small chosen class within the community.

The revolution in agricultural technology in the South is displacing the rural Negro community into Northern urban areas. Both Washington, D.C. and Newark, New Jersey have Negro majorities. One-third of Philadelphia's population of two million people is black. "Inner city," in most major urban areas, is already predominantly Negro, and with the white rush to suburbia, Negroes will, in the next three decades, control the heart of our great cities. These areas can become either concentration camps with a bitter and volatile population whose only power is the power to destroy, or organized and powerful communities able to make constructive contributions to the total society. Without the power to control their lives and their communities, without effective political institutions through which to relate to the total society, these communities will exist in a constant state of insurrection. This is a choice that the country will have to make.

Rules of the Black Panther Party

CENTRAL HEADQUARTERS
OAKLAND, CALIFORNIA

Every member of the BLACK PANTHER PARTY throughout this country of racist America must abide by these rules as functional members of this party. CENTRAL COMMITTEE members, CENTRAL STAFFS, and LOCAL STAFFS, including all captains subordinate to either national, state, and local leadership of the BLACK PANTHER PARTY will enforce these rules. Length of suspension or other disciplinary action necessary for violation of these rules will depend on national decisions by national, state or state area, and local committees and staffs where said rule or rules of the BLACK PANTHER PARTY WERE VIOLATED.

Every member of the party must know these verbatum by heart. And apply them daily. Each member must report any violation of these rules to their leadership or they are counter-revolutionary and are also subjected to suspension by the BLACK PANTHER PARTY.

THE RULES ARE:

1. No party member can have narcotics or weed in his possession while doing party work.

2. Any party member found shooting narcotics will be expelled from this party.

3. No party member can be DRUNK while doing daily party work.

4. No party member will violate rules relating to office work, general meetings of the BLACK PANTHER PARTY, and meetings of the BLACK PANTHER PARTY ANYWHERE.

5. No party member will USE, POINT, or FIRE a weapon of any kind unnecessarily or accidentally at anyone.

6. No party member can join any other army force other than the BLACK LIBERATION ARMY.

7. No party member can have a weapon in his possession while DRUNK or loaded off narcotics or weed.

SOURCE: The Black Panther Party.

8. No party member will commit any crimes against other party members or BLACK people at all, and cannot steal or take from the people, not even a needle or a piece of thread.

9. When arrested BLACK PANTHER MEMBERS will give only name, address, and will sign nothing. Legal first aid must be understood by all Party members.

10. The Ten Point Program and platform of the BLACK PANTHER PARTY must be known and understood by each Party member.

11. Party Communications must be National and Local.

12. The 10-10-10-program should be known by all members and

13. All Finance officers will operate under the jurisdiction of the Ministry of Finance.

14. Each person will submit a report of daily work.

15. Each Sub-Section Leader, Section Leader, Lieutenant, and Captain must submit Daily reports of work.

16. All Panthers must learn to operate and service weapons correctly.

17. All Leadership personnel who expel a member must submit this information to the Editor of the Newspaper, so that it will be published in the paper and will be known by all chapters and branches.

18. Political Education Classes are mandatory for general membership.

19. Only office personnel assigned to respective offices each day should be there. All others are to sell papers and do Political work out in the community, including Captains, Section Leaders, etc.

20. COMMUNICATIONS — all chapters must submit weekly reports in writing to the National Headquarters.

21. All Branches must implement First Aid and/or Medical Cadres.

22. All Chapters, Branches, and components of the BLACK PANTHER PARTY must submit a monthly Financial Report to the Ministry of Finance, and also the Central Committee.

23. Everyone in a leadership position must read no less than two hours per day to keep abreast of the changing political situation.

24. No chapter or branch shall accept grants, poverty funds, money or any other aid from any government agency without contacting the National Headquarters.

25. All chapters must adhere to the policy and the ideology laid down by the CENTRAL COMMITTEE of the BLACK PANTHER PARTY.

26. All Branches must submit weekly reports in writing to their respective Chapters.

8 POINTS OF ATTENTION

1. Speak politely.
2. Pay fairly for what you buy.
3. Return everything you borrow.
4. Pay for anything you damage.
5. Do not hit or swear at people.

6. Do not damage property or crops of the poor, oppressed masses.
7. Do not take liberties with women.
8. If we ever have to take captives do not ill-treat them.

3 MAIN RULES OF DISCIPLINE

1. Obey orders in all your actions.
2. Do not take a single needle or a piece of thread from the poor and oppressed masses.
3. Turn in everything captured from the attacking enemy.

Black Panther Party | # What We Want, What We Believe

1. We want freedom. We want power to determine the destiny of our Black Community.

We believe that black people will not be free until we are able to determine our destiny.

2. We want full employment for our people.

We believe that the federal government is responsible and obligated to give every man employment or a guaranteed income. We believe that if the white American businessmen will not give full employment, then the means of production should be taken from the businessmen and placed in the community so that the people of the community can organize and employ all of its people and give a high standard of living.

3. We want an end to the robbery by the white man of our Black Community.

We believe that this racist government has robbed us and now we are demanding the overdue debt of forty acres and two mules. Forty acres and two mules was promised 100 years ago as restitution for slave labor and mass murder of black people. We will accept the payment in currency which will be distributed to our many communities. The Germans are now aiding the Jews in Israel for the genocide of the Jewish people. The Germans murdered six million Jews. The American racist has taken part in the slaughter of over fifty million black people; therefore, we feel that this is a modest demand that we make.

4. We want decent housing, fit for shelter of human beings.

We believe that if the white landlords will not give decent housing to our black community, then the housing and the land should be made into

---

SOURCE: *Black Panther* NEWSPAPER.

cooperatives so that our community, with government aid, can build and make decent housing for its people.

5. We want education for our people that exposes the true nature of this decadent American society. We want education that teaches us our true history and our role in the present day society.

We believe in an educational system that will give to our people a knowledge of self. If a man does not have knowledge of himself and his position in society and the world, then he has little chance to relate to anything else.

6. We want all black men to be exempt from military service.

We believe that Black people should not be forced to fight in the military service to defend a racist government that does not protect us. We will not fight and kill other people of color in the world who, like black people, are being victimized by the white racist government of America. We will protect ourselves from the force and violence of the racist police and the racist military, by whatever means necessary.

7. We want an immediate end to POLICE BRUTALITY and MURDER of black people.

We believe we can end police brutality in our black community by organizing black self-defense groups that are dedicated to defending our black community from racist police oppression and brutality. The Second Amendment to the Constitution of the United States gives a right to bear arms. We therefore believe that all black people should arm themselves for self-defense.

8. We want freedom for all black men held in federal, state, county and city prisons and jails.

We believe that all black people should be released from the many jails and prisons because they have not received a fair and impartial trial.

9. We want all black people when brought to trial to be tried in court by a jury of their peer group or people from their black communities, as defined by the Constitution of the United States.

We believe that the courts should follow the United States Constitution so that black people will receive fair trials. The 14th Amendment of the U.S. Constitution gives a man a right to be tried by his peer group. A peer is a person from a similar economic, social, religious, geographical, environmental, historical and racial background. To do this the court will be forced to select a jury from the black community from which the black defendant came. We have been, and are being tried by all-white juries that have no understanding of the "average reasoning man" of the black community.

10. We want land, bread, housing, education, clothing, justice and peace. And as our major political objective, a United Nations-supervised plebiscite to be held throughout the black colony in which only black colonial subjects will be allowed to participate, for the purpose of determining the will of black people as to their national destiny.

When, in the course of human events, it becomes necessary for one people to dissolve the political bands which have connected them with another, and to assume, among the powers of the earth, the separate and equal station to which the laws of nature and nature's God entitle them, a decent respect to the opinions of mankind requires that they should declare the causes which impel them to the separation.

We hold these truths to be self-evident, that all men are created equal; that they are endowed by their Creator with certain unalienable rights; that among these are life, liberty, and the pursuit of happiness. That, to secure these rights, governments are instituted among men, deriving their just powers from the consent of the governed; that, whenever any form of government becomes destructive of these ends, it is the right of the people to alter or to abolish it, and to institute a new government, laying its foundation on such principles, and organizing its powers in such form, as to them shall seem most likely to effect their safety and happiness. Prudence, indeed, will dictate that governments long established should not be changed for light and transient causes; and, accordingly, all experience hath shown, that mankind are more disposed to suffer, while evils are sufferable, than to right themselves by abolishing the forms to which they are accustomed. But, when a long train of abuses and usurpations, pursuing invariably the same object, evinces a design to reduce them under absolute despotism, it is their right, it is their duty, to throw off such government, and to provide new guards for their future security.

Ronald Steel | ## Letter from Oakland: The Panthers

For the time being it is clear that the ghettos are potentially the most explosive places in the country. This is where the Panthers are organized (although they are trying to establish closer contacts with the revolutionary union movements, as well as with student groups) and where they draw their main support. Much of their appeal for ghetto youths (shared by many whites) is their image of a powerful black man with a rifle. In his recent book of essays Eldridge Cleaver describes his own first encounter with the Panthers at a meeting in the Fillmore district ghetto of San Francisco: "I spun round in my seat and saw the most beautiful sight I had ever seen: four black men wearing black berets, powder blue shirts, black

SOURCE: Reprinted with permission from *The New York Review of Books.* Copyright © 1969 The New York Review.

leather jackets, black trousers, shiny black shoes — and each with a gun!"

Since then Cleaver has learned that there is more to being a Panther than carrying a gun. But the image of power and violence is still the basic one created by the Panthers. When ghetto youths learn that party membership is not like joining a street gang but more like taking religious vows, many of them become disillusioned and turn away from the Panthers. They are put off by the strict discipline, the political indoctrination, the discouragement of racism, and such community service projects as the Panther program to provide free breakfast to ghetto children. The Panthers have had to purge people who turned out to be basically criminals or racists unable to relate to the party's political and intellectual program.

Unlike many of the ghetto youth, who want action, retribution, and loot, young black idealists are drawn to the Panthers' philosophy of social justice and equality through power. Where there have been spontaneous black riots, such as those following the assassination of Martin Luther King, the Panthers have tried to cool it, to discourage violence that could lead only to further repression without any political gains. Unfortunately the political leadership in most cities is too dense to realize that the Panthers are actually a force for stability in the ghettos. An intelligent white ruling class would encourage the Panthers rather than try to destroy them; that it has failed to understand this does indeed argue for its own inherent instability.

Lately the Panthers have been emphasizing programs directly related to the needs of the ghetto community, such as free breakfasts and health clinics. This summer they have also been setting up black "liberation schools," where children between two and sixteen are taught some things about American history, economics, and politics that they never learn in the public schools. Clearly much of this is indoctrination, although the Panthers claim that they are correcting the distorted image that black children receive of themselves and their society.

White middle-class revolutionaries tend to patronize such activities as reformist. But the breakfasts, the schools, and the clinics have won the Panthers support within the ghetto that they never could have gained by guns alone or by Marxist-Leninist analyses of the internal contradictions of capitalism. In Oakland, where the party has existed for nearly three years, it is an important element of the black community, respected even though it is not often fully understood. Just as the police have been forced to respect the power of the Panthers, so the white power elite has had to deal with an organized, politically conscious force within the black community. Throughout much of the Bay area, where the Panthers are particularly well organized, they are an articulate, alert defender of black people's interests. The Panthers are there when the community needs them, and they are there when no one else seems to be listening.

An example that comes to mind, simply because it occurred while I was in San Francisco, concerned a sixteen-year-old boy who was shot in the back by a member of San Francisco's Tactical Squad while he was fleeing the scene of an alleged auto theft. The shooting occurred near his home and was heard by his mother, a practical nurse, who was thrown to the ground by the police when she ran to his side screaming, "Don't shoot my boy again." The wounded boy was thrown into a police truck and nearly an hour elapsed before he actually reached the hospital. It is the sort of thing that happens every day in Hunter's Point and a hundred other black ghettos around America. The only difference is that, miraculously, the bullet was deflected by a rib bone and the boy was not killed, and that the Panthers brought it to the attention of the public by calling a press conference which Bobby Seale, David Hilliard, and Masai, the party's three top leaders, attended.

At the conference were a few representatives of the local press (the television stations were invited but refrained from sending anyone), myself, a few Panthers, their lawyer, Charles Garry, the boy, Jimmie Conner, and his parents. The boy, soft-spoken and composed, spoke of the incident as though it were a normal part of life, and when asked why he ran away, replied, with the tedium of one explaining the obvious, "Why did I run? Because I'm scared of police." With him sat his parents, an attractive, quiet woman in her mid-thirties and a handsome, somewhat stocky, graying man who works in aircraft maintenance. Both very light-skinned, eminently respectable, and both bitter and confused about what had happened to them.

Had they been white, their son would have been reprimanded, or at most taken to court. But they are black and their son was almost killed, as other boys have been killed in Hunter's Point and elsewhere for even lesser crimes — if indeed Jimmie Conner was guilty of a crime. When asked about the incident, Mrs. Conner replied, "Just another Negro gone, that's the way we believe that they think about the kids up here. Too many of our kids are dying for nothing. They see police three blocks away and they start running because they're scared. I'm gonna fight them. If I have to go to jail OK. If I have to work for the rest of my life, I will. If they shoot me that's fine. I'm gonna fight, this has got to stop." The story so far has included the radicalization of Mrs. Ozella Conner, housewife, mother, nurse, and now friend of the Black Panthers.

How did the Panthers get involved in this incident, although none of the Conners is a member of the party? Because a doctor at the hospital where Jimmie was taken was so shocked at his treatment by the police that he called Charles Garry, who in turn called Bobby Seale. What followed was a press conference, followed by a lawsuit under the 1964 Civil Rights Act, followed by press coverage — which of course could never have occurred had the Panthers not been called in.

The cynical would say that the Panthers have something to gain from this publicity, which indeed they have. But that is to miss the point, which is that by such actions they are establishing themselves, in the eyes of the black community, as the defenders of the black man too humble to interest anyone else. They can sink their roots in the black community and win its allegiance partly because no one else is fulfilling that role. This is one of the things that the Panthers mean by "educating" the people, informing them of their rights and making them activist defenders rather than passive victims. This education is carried on through meetings, discussions, leaflets, and the party newspaper. While their tactics have shifted several times since the formation of the party in October 1966, their objectives remain the ones set out in their ten-point program of black liberation.

Looking at this program and talking to the Panthers, as well as reading their newspaper, *The Black Panther* (which everyone interested enough to read this essay ought to do in order to gain, if nothing else, an idea of the atrocities that are going on under the name of law and order), make one realize that the "revolution" they talk about is not necessarily the cataclysmic upheaval that sends the white middle class into spasms. Rather, it is the achievement of constitutional guarantees and economic justice for black people. These gun-carrying, Mao-quoting revolutionaries want what most middle-class Americans take for granted. As Huey Newton has said, if reformist politicians like the Kennedys and Lindsay could solve the problems of housing, employment, and justice for blacks and other Americans at the bottom of the social heap, there would be no need for a revolution. And, it goes without saying, little support for such groups as the Black Panther Party.

The Panthers have a voice in the black community (although not necessarily so large as many whites imagine) because they offer hope for change to ghetto people whom the civil rights movement and the poverty program bureaucrats have been unable to touch. They walk proudly through the streets of Oakland in their black leather jackets, and they hold mass rallies for the liberation of Huey Newton in the shadow of the Alameda County Court House where he was sentenced. They speak to the black man's image of himself. They tell him that he is no longer powerless against the forces that oppress him, and that his struggle for freedom is part of a world-wide liberation movement. In this sense they fulfill a real psychological need.

While they have not yet shed white blood, except in self-defense, does this mean that they never will, that their talk of guerrilla warfare is simply rhetoric? It would be rash to say so, for the Panthers have declared that they are ready to kill anyone who stands in the way of "black liberation." And they are convinced that racism in this society is so pervasive and deeply rooted that there can be no freedom for black people until it is extirpated by some form of revolution. Even Gene Marine, who, in his highly informative book, *The Black Panthers*, freely admits his admiration for the Panthers, confesses, "I am frightened by them." Like some of the white revolutionaries who emulate them, the Panthers seem to have overlearned *The Battle of Algiers*, and have tried to apply its lesson to a society where the situation is totally different. The United States today is not

Algeria of 1954, nor Cuba of 1958, nor even France of 1968. It is a deeply troubled, but nonetheless largely stable society which is capable of putting down an insurrection ruthlessly and quickly.

Don't the Panthers realize this? They seem to, at the present moment anyway. This is why they are serving free breakfasts to ghetto children; attempting to form alliances with white radicals, liberals, workers, and pacifists; and urging people to sign petitions for the decentralization of the police. They may be going through a temporary stage, but the direction in which they are heading is clearly marked reformism. Right now they seem interested in maximum publicity, which is why they hold meetings and press conferences, and complain about the way the mass media ignores or distorts their actions. Some of their sympathizers fear that the Panthers are pushing themselves too much in the public eye, and that this only aids the enemies who are trying to destroy them. But since the police and politicians are out to get the Panthers in any case, perhaps such an effort to convince the public that they are not really monsters is their only chance for survival.

It is curious, to say the least, that the federal government has decided to come down hard on the Panthers at the very time that they are emphasizing ballots and petitions, community self-help, and political alliances, rather than shoot-outs. The severe harassment and repression they are now suffering may, if anything, improve the Panthers' appeal among the black bourgeoisie and white liberals. It would be one of the ironies of our irrational political life if John Mitchell and J. Edgar Hoover, together with the so-called "liberal" mayors of cities like San Francisco and Chicago, succeeded in giving the Panthers a new vitality just at the time when the party seemed in difficulty.

Mention of the word "revolution" is enough to send most politicians and police officers into a rage. Like radicals in general, the Panthers naturally talk a good deal about revolution, and use such other catch-words as fascism, imperialism, and the dictatorship of the proletariat. They connect racism with the evils of capitalism, and quote freely from the sacred texts of Marx, Lenin, and Mao. Walk into any Panther office and you are likely to find not only Little Red Books lying about, but the officer of the day with his nose buried in the works of Mao, or one of Lenin's many pamphlets. Slogans, often vague and even meaningless in the context in which they are used, become part of the revolutionary vocabulary. This is true not only of the Panthers, who use such slogans to reach an audience with little formal education, but of young radicals generally. The deliberate inflation and distortion of language is a disease of the Left.

The Panthers, however, realize that racism is deeply embedded in the cultural history of Europe and America and is not, as certain Marxists still argue, simply a by-product of class society. As Huey Newton has said, "Until you get rid of racism . . . no matter what kind of economic system you have, black people will still be oppressed." What revolution seems to mean for the Panthers is the transformation of the ghetto and the "liberation" of black people, and of all oppressed people, from lives of poverty, degradation, and despair. The steps by which this will take place are not specified precisely, but they need not be violent ones unless every other road to radical change is closed. Having defined the problem, the Panthers now ask white America what kind of solution it proposes. So far as the Panthers are concerned, the answer has been harassment, repression, and even murder.

The Panthers are not racist, but they refuse to take any instructions from their white sympathizers. Indeed, this may be what makes it possible for them to be anti-racist. Commenting on the anti-white sentiment in SNCC before it became an all-black organization, Huey Newton recently said, "We have never been controlled by whites, and therefore we don't fear the white mother-country radicals." Their willingness to work with allied white radicals is not shared by most black militant groups. When Stokely Carmichael recently left the Panthers, his stormy letter of departure centered on just this issue.

As the Carmichael–Cleaver exchange indicated, the black militants are just as fragmented into feuding factions as are the whites. Their rivalry, however, is a good deal more violent, and the struggle between the Panthers and the "cultural nationalist" US group of Ron Karenga led to the murder of two Panthers in Los Angeles last year. The Panthers are serious about wanting to carry on programs of education, and in spite of the terrible repression they are now facing have an enduring faith in the democratic system of petitions and ballots — far more than do the young white radicals. But like most revolutionaries, they are highly authoritarian and want loyal and unquestioning followers (as Stokely Carmichael rightly pointed out in his letter) rather than critical colleagues.

Unlike the white revolutionaries, however, the Panthers do have some fairly clear ideas of what they want — even though they are uncertain about the best way to get it. Whatever their shortcomings, they did not seem to me self-indulgent, romantic, or part-time players at revolution. They are in this struggle for keeps. Anyone who is a Panther today, or who contemplates joining the party, knows that there is a good chance that he will be jailed or die a violent death. Panthers have already been murdered by the police, many have been beaten and wounded, and others are almost certain to be killed in the months and years ahead. It takes courage to join the party, to submit to its discipline, and to face the likely prospect of imprisonment or death. But for some there is no other way. As Eldridge Cleaver has written, "A slave who dies of natural causes will not balance two dead flies on the scale of eternity."

The Panthers have come a long way since Huey Newton and Bobby Seale first formed the party three years ago in Oakland. It has spread across the nation and has eclipsed such groups as SNCC and CORE to become the most powerful black militant organization in America. This rapid expansion has created problems — not only increasing police harassment and repression as the Panthers become more influential within the black community, but also the difficulty of maintaining the high standard of membership that its leaders would like. Not all Panthers have the organizing ability of Bobby Seale or the analytical minds of David Hilliard, Eldridge Cleaver, and Huey Newton. Which is to say that the Panthers are not super-human, as some white radicals would like to believe, any more than they are devils.

Beneath an inflammatory vocabulary of ghetto hyperbole and a good deal of facile Marxist sloganizing, the Panthers seemed to me serious, hard-working, disciplined, and essentially humanistic in their work within the black community and in their vision of a more just society. For the Panthers, weapons are an instrument of self-protection, and ultimately the means to achieve the revolution that, in the absence of a peaceful alternative, will make liberation possible. For some of the white militants I spoke to around Berkeley, however, it seemed that revolution is the means, and denouncing or shooting up the "fascists" (who seem to include just about everyone who disagrees on tactics or strategy) is conceived as the end. Since Chicago, and particularly since the brutal suppression by the police during the battle of People's Park, some West Coast militants seem to have become traumatized by violence, convinced there is no other way to carry on radical politics.

But Che's prescription is no more relevant in the tree-lined streets of Berkeley or Cambridge than it was in the mountains of Bolivia. The Panthers are prepared for guerrilla warfare, as a last-ditch stand, because they think they may have no other alternative. There are white revolutionaries, on the West Coast and elsewhere, who, in the impatience of their rage and their inability seriously to change a society whose policies they find oppressive, accept this prescription uncritically, and, in view of the forces marshalled against them on the Right, with a half-conscious quest for martyrdom. As its frustration increases, the New Left becomes more shrill in its rhetoric and dogmatic in its politics. Instead of focusing on the most blatant inequalities and injustices of American life, it is assaulting the periphery. Instead of trying to educate the people to inequities of the social-economic system and the cost of maintaining an empire, it has successfully alienated the working class without whose support no radical change, let alone "revolution," is possible.

In its resistance to the draft, the war, and racism, the radical Left has aroused parts of the nation. More people now realize there is something seriously wrong with American society but are not certain how to deal with it. Many are frightened and attribute all unrest to a conspiracy of "troublemakers." Others know that change must come, but would like it to be as unobtrusive as possible. It remains to be seen how many can be reached, whether it be on the plane of morality or self-interest, and convinced that change need not be personally threatening to them. To do this radicals must have plausible ideas on how a transformed society would produce a better existence for the mass of people. It does little good for the radical Left to dismiss everyone who disagrees as "fascist," for these are a majority, and if they are treated as fascists long enough, they may begin behaving in such a way as to make the current repression seem like libertarianism in comparison.

America is not now a "fascist" country, nor is it likely soon to become one, although this is not impossible. Probably it will continue to be an advanced capitalist society in which cruel inequalities and repression, un-livable cities, and inhuman conditions of work continue to exist along with considerable liberty to take political action, while our rulers control an empire of poor nations abroad. It is the duty of the Left to find ways to change this system: to educate people rather than simply abuse them; to understand what is happening in the factories and farms and lower-middle-class neighborhoods and be in touch with the people in them; to use the universities as places where the complex problems of replacing repressive capitalism and imperialism with a better system can be studied seriously; to stop playing Minutemen and begin acting like radicals. If there is ever going to be a revolution in this country, it will have to happen first in people's heads. What takes place in the streets of a society like this one has another name. It is called repression.

SAY IT LOUD — I'M BLACK AND I'M PROUD

Say it loud, I'm Black and I'm proud,
Say it loud, I'm Black and I'm proud.

Some people say we got a lot of malice,
Some say it's a lot of nerve,
But I say we won't quit moving
Until we get what we deserve.

We've been rebuked and we've been scorned,
We've been treated bad, talked about, as sure as you're born,
But just as sure as it takes two eyes to make a pair,
Brother we can't quit until we get our share.

Whooee out of sight, tomorrow night it's tough,
You're tough enough whooee it's hurting me,
Say it loud I'm Black and I'm proud,
Say it loud I'm Black and I'm proud.

SOURCE: Reprinted by permission of Golo Publishing.

I've worked on jobs with my feet and my hands,
But all that work I did was for the other man,
Now we demand a chance to do things for ourselves,
We're tired of beating our heads against the wall
And working for someone else.

We're people, we're like the birds and the bees,
But we'd rather die on our feet than keep living on our knees.
Say it loud, I'm Black and I'm proud,
Say it loud, I'm Black and I'm proud.

JAMES BROWN

WAR

■ Thomas Hobbes, writing in the middle of the seventeenth century, spoke of war as a condition in which "there is no place for industry; because the fruit thereof is uncertain: and consequently no culture of the earth; no navigation, nor use of the commodities that may be imported by sea; no commodious building; . . . no knowledge of the face of the earth; no account of time; no arts; no letters; no society; and, which is worst of all, continual fear, and danger of violent death; and the life of man, solitary, poor, nasty, brutish, and short."

All through recorded time philosophers, historians, and reasonable men of every kind have been saying much the same thing about war, and yet our century of civilization has been the most murderous and warlike of any. In World War I, at the beginning of the century, we killed vast numbers of people in a slow, painful, extremely laborious way. Now, toward its close, we have discovered the means of killing almost everybody in a very quick, expeditious way. It seems incredible that we should want so much to destroy our own species. And the truly astonishing thing about it all is that, until quite recently, we never studied ourselves to analyze why we seem impelled to put so much thought and energy into vast attempts to make our life on this earth nasty, brutish, and short.

Simple condemnations of war, eloquent though they might be, have had almost no real effect. Herodotus said, "In peace the sons bury their fathers; in war the fathers bury their sons." Cicero said, "an unjust peace is better than a just war," and Voltaire said "It is forbidden to kill; therefore all murderers are punished unless they kill in large numbers and to the sound of trumpets." And men in general might agree but nonetheless find some overriding reason to make an exception; every war begins in some kind of good, pious logic.

Thus it is that philosophers condemn selfish motives for war (such as expansionism, greed for plunder, xenophobia, or the ambition of princes), while apologists point out virtuous motives (such as defense of the homeland, suppression of dangerous rivals, the desire to impose order and peace on some unruly area, or an impulse to spread the True Faith among the heathen).

However true or half-true these casual explanations may be, they are all superficial. They may explain deception and self-deception, and they are part of the history of politics, but none of them gets at the basic motivation for war, which must have been grafted onto the psyche of primitive man thousands of years ago in our dim past. Only recently have anthropologists and other scientists begun a systematic attempt to understand the hidden motive deep in man's unconscious — the underlying motive of aggression.

The greatest and most systematic behavioral theory of the nineteenth century was, of course, that arising from Charles Darwin's theory of evolution. Darwin gave much weight to aggression as a factor in his principles of survival of the fittest and natural selection. Obviously, courage plus warlike ability were favorable qualities for survival. When he began to look at the matter in a more concrete social context, however, Darwin was not so sure. He ran up against one of the great paradoxes about human warfare: it tends to destroy the strongest and ablest. After the battle is over, there are many dead heroes and many live cowards.

Darwin's doubt appears when he says, "he who was ready to sacrifice his life, as many a savage has been, rather than betray his comrades, would leave no offspring to inherit his noble nature. The bravest men, who were always willing to come to the front in war, and who freely risked their lives for others, would on an average perish in larger numbers than other men. Therefore it seems hardly probable that the number of men gifted with such virtues, or that the standard of their excellence, could be increased through natural selection, that is, by the survival of the fittest. . . ."

Between 1914 and 1918, over 1,300,000 young Frenchmen were killed and almost 5,000,000 more were casualties. The best third of the nation's most vigorous generation was wiped out. England had over 3,000,000 casualties. That drastic pruning resulted in a notable poverty in leadership and national accomplishment in the postwar years, when the bled-out generation had to take command. World War I was the greatest modern example of the paradox Darwin encountered. War, apparently, worked against evolution by selecting the strongest and fittest to die.

Thus, the only explanation for war seems to be that some combination of death-wish and killer-instinct brings mankind to wage it. Freud thought that a "cruel aggressiveness" is "one of the instinctual passions" of man. Communist doctrine, on the other hand, asserts that man is instinctively good and humane; it is only the capitalist system with its artificial institution of private wealth that makes him warlike. A number of anthropologists take the view that early man lived and let live, on the whole, and became belligerent relatively recently (about 10,000 years ago) when rudimentary political states began to appear.

Within the past fifty years, however, a whole new view has begun to take shape. The work of certain naturalists in studying animal behavior and that of certain unorthodox anthropologists in exploring man's origin and evolution has produced some surprising implications. These scientists are concerned with the root of the matter — the living creature's impulse toward aggression — and not with actual warfare as it occurs in society. Beginning carefully at the very beginnings may tell us something about our deepest selves that we have never realized before.

In the 1950's and 60's, this new line of thought began to emerge in a number of books written less for the scientific specialist than the serious general reader. They are such books as *King Solomon's Ring* and *On Aggression* by Konrad Lorenz, *African Genesis* and *The Territorial Imperative* by Robert Ardrey, *The Naked Ape* by Desmond Morris, and *The Dawn Warriors* by Robert Bigelow.

The new analysis of aggressiveness is a most complex and extensive matter. Here we can do no more than outline the main ideas, putting aside the wealth of detailed observation and thought that the naturalists and anthropologists have used to construct them. In brief, this is the general line: most aggression among nonhuman creatures occurs within the species (or with closely-related species) and is connected with territoriality or status. Territory in this sense means the living-space that creatures define for themselves; aggression is displayed in border wars of attack and counter-attack. Aggression is also a means to determine status within the group. (That desperate battle between the two bull moose is largely over leadership in the herd; it has very little to do with the female standing by.)

Aggressiveness, which comes from a competitive-belligerent feeling, is quite different from the hunting instinct. As Konrad Lorenz points out, hunting is functional and not emotional. Aggression among creatures, however, seems to have natural limits and balances. There is no conquest for the mere sake of conquest, and battles to the death are rare. In fact, certain creatures armed with "ultimate" death-dealing weapons — such as the rattlesnake — can fight among themselves without ever using their deadly power.

Between 500,000 and 1,000,000 years ago, there emerged from the primates a unique creature, a carnivorous killer ape. Raymond Dart, the naturalist who discovered him near the Kalahari desert, named him *australopithecus africanus*, or southern ape. This creature, having no natural weapons with which he could compete against fiercer carnivores at ground level, armed himself with an antelope bone. He seems to have been the first creature to use a killing-tool, and this fact had a dramatic effect on his evolution. It gave him the first step on his long road to becoming, in the course of generations, man. As Ardrey puts it, "a rock, a stick, a heavy bone — to our ancestral killer ape it meant the margin of survival. But the use of the weapon meant new and multiplying demands on the nervous system for the co-ordination of muscle and touch and sight. And so at last came the enlarged brain; so at last came man."

Ardrey adds, "far from the truth lay the antique assumption that man had fathered the weapon. The weapon, instead, had fathered man." One line of *australopithecus* finally moved into the human realm with the sophistication of stone weapons and — as evidence in African caves and riverbeds reveals — he eliminated his relatives, who had never progressed beyond the antelope-bone club.

During the long Pleistocene age, man's brain size increased threefold. His aggressiveness was surely one of the main factors. The tribal hunting party or war party — remote forerunner of armies — demanded a high degree of organization and social cooperation. Acknowledging a leader, following through a plan of action to a set objective, observing some discipline — all these demanded a new dimension of intelligence. And the branches of the race that did this best won out. About 35,000 years ago in Europe, the primitive Neanderthal man began to die out when the more intelligent Cro-Magnon man appeared in his hunting grounds.

With the dawn of history, the competition became even more dramatic. Aggressive man, ruled by organizational intelligence, formed the most vigorous powers and the most potent cultures of the ancient world. The disciplined Macedonian phalanx overcame the badly-organized oriental armies. The Roman legions — with their generalship, their chain of command, and their uniform order of battle — made possible a vast, civilized empire. Aggressive man was forced to be inventive not only in his battle formations but in all things necessary to make good his conquests. Thus communications systems, supply systems, building, and political administration followed the eagles. Is it any wonder that man so dearly cherished the motive force that had brought him into dominance? By his aggression, he had overcome his primate rivals, enlarged his brain, created a social world, and taken command of his environment. He owed a great debt to his urge to subdue others by force. On the other hand, of course, that urge has been the cause of an immense amount of suffering, bloodshed, and destruction of man's peaceful accomplishments. Throughout history, aggression has maintained a perilous equilibrium between profit and loss for mankind.

Now at last in the twentieth century, the balance seems overwhelmingly upset. Aggression in the form of organized warfare, with the new, total weapons of this age, has vastly outgrown any evolutionary function. It threatens the extinction of man. It is clear that a nuclear war would be apocalyptic; it is becoming clear that even smaller twentieth-century wars — France's in Algeria, the United States' in Vietnam — can disrupt very strong societies.

Control of armaments and international efforts for the peaceful solution of painful issues are important. But they are just the superstructure. They must be grounded in widespread and deep understanding of man's aggressive instincts and a consequent renunciation of military aggression. At the moment, as some political scientists have suggested, the nuclear powers may be behaving in the manner of two rattlesnakes who struggle and wrestle but instinctively hold back from using the ultimate weapon. This may serve for the moment, but it is hardly dependable for the long run.

If mankind is to save itself from itself, there must be an enormous effort of intelligence, combining social and scientific thought, toward a solution. The fantastic threat to us demands something fantastic in the way of response — certainly an effort on the scale of the world's space program.

Are we doing it? In May, 1970, newspapers printed the story of Dr. William D. Davidson of Washington, the only psychiatrist ever hired by the Arms Control and Disarmament Agency of our State Department. Dr. Davidson had resigned in disgust. He pointed out that "arms control and war are problems of human psychology, yet these issues are being decided by physicists and lawyers." The ACDA spent 97 per cent of its modest budget (total: $9,000,000) on electronic surveillance equipment and computerized techniques and only 3 per cent on projects with any relation to cultural or psychological factors.

Dr. Davidson observed, "It seems inconceivable that major policy decisions involving issues intimately related to human conduct, rational and irrational, are still being made in the complete absence of men who are specialized by training and experience in conscious and unconscious human behavior."

Konrad Lorenz | # Ecce Homo!

Let us imagine that an absolutely unbiased investigator on another planet, perhaps on Mars, is examining human behavior on earth, with the aid of a telescope whose magnification is too small to enable him to discern individuals and follow their separate behavior, but large enough for him to observe occurrences such as migrations of peoples, wars, and similar great historical events. He would never gain the impression that human behavior was dictated by intelligence, still less by responsible morality. If we suppose our extraneous observer to be a being of pure reason, devoid of instincts himself and unaware of the way in which all instincts in general and aggression in particular can miscarry, he would be at a complete loss how to explain history at all. The ever-recurrent phenomena of history do not have reasonable causes. It is a mere commonplace to say that they are caused by what common parlance so aptly terms "human nature." Unreasoning and unreasonable human nature causes two nations to compete, though no economic necessity compels them to do so; it induces two political parties or religions with amazingly similar programs of salvation to fight each other bitterly, and it impels an Alexander or a Napoleon to sacrifice millions of lives in his attempt to unite the world under his scepter. We have been taught to regard some of the persons who have committed these and similar absurdities with respect, even as "great" men, we are wont to yield to the political wisdom of those in charge, and we are all so accustomed to these phenomena that most of us fail to realize how abjectly stupid and undesirable the historical mass behavior of humanity actually is.

Having realized this, however, we cannot escape the question why reasonable beings do behave so unreasonably. Undeniably, there must be superlatively strong factors which are able to overcome the commands of individual reason so completely and which are so obviously impervious to experience and learning. As Hegel said, "What experience and history teach us is this — that people and governments never have learned anything from history, or acted on principles deduced from it."

All these amazing paradoxes, however, find an unconstrained explanation, falling into place like the pieces of a jigsaw puzzle, if one assumes that human behavior, and particularly human social behavior, far from being determined by reason and cultural tradition alone, is still subject to all the laws prevailing in all phylogenetically adapted instinctive behavior. Of these laws we possess a fair amount of knowledge from studying the instincts of animals. Indeed, if our extramundane observer were a knowledgeable ethologist, he would unavoidably draw the conclusion that man's social organization is very similar to that of rats, which, like humans, are social and peaceful beings within their clans, but veritable devils toward all fellow members of their species not belonging to their own community. If, furthermore, our Martian naturalist knew of the explosive rise in human populations, the ever-increasing destructiveness of weapons, and the division of mankind into a few political camps, he would not expect the future of humanity to be more rosy than that of several hostile clans of rats on a ship almost devoid of food. And this prognosis would even be optimistic, for in the case of rats, reproduction stops automatically when a certain state of overcrowding is reached while man as yet has no workable system for preventing the so-called population explosion. Furthermore, in the case of the rats it is likely that after the wholesale slaughter enough individuals would be left over to propagate the species. In the case of man, this would not be so certain after the use of the hydrogen bomb.

It is a curious paradox that the greatest gifts of man, the unique faculties of conceptual thought and verbal speech which have raised him to a level high above all other creatures and given him mastery over the globe, are not altogether blessings, or at least are blessings that have to be paid for very dearly indeed. All the great dangers threatening humanity with extinction are direct consequences of conceptual thought and verbal speech. They drove man out of the paradise in which he could follow his instincts with impunity and do or not do whatever he pleased. There is much truth in the parable of the tree of knowledge and its fruit, though I want to make an addition to it to make it fit into my own picture of Adam: that apple was thoroughly unripe! Knowledge springing from conceptual thought robbed man of the security provided by his well-adapted instincts long, long before it was sufficient to provide him with an equally safe adaptation. Man is, as Arnold Gehlen has so truly said, by nature a jeopardized creature.

Conceptual thought and speech changed all man's evolution by achieving something which is equivalent to the inheritance of acquired characters. We have forgotten that the verb "inherit" had a juridic connotation long before it acquired a biological one. When a man invents, let us say, bow and arrow, not only his progeny but his entire community will inherit the knowledge and the use of these tools and possess them just as surely as organs grown on the body. Nor is their loss any more likely than the rudimentation of an organ of equal survival value. Thus, within one or two generations a process of ecological adaptation can be achieved which, in normal phylogeny and without the interference of conceptual thought, would have taken a time of an altogether different, much greater order of magnitude. Small wonder, indeed, if the evolution of social instincts and, what is even more important, social inhibitions could not keep pace with the rapid development forced on human society by the growth of traditional culture, particularly material culture.

Obviously, instinctive behavior mechanisms failed to cope with the new circumstances which culture unavoidably produced even at its very dawn. There is evidence that the first inventors of pebble tools, the African Australopithecines, promptly used their new weapon to kill not only game, but fellow members of their species as well. Peking Man, the Prometheus who learned to preserve fire, used it to roast his brothers: beside the first traces of the regular use of fire lie the mutilated and roasted bones of Sinanthropus pekinensis himself.

One is tempted to believe that every gift bestowed on man by his power of conceptual thought has to be paid for with a dangerous evil as the direct consequence of it. Fortunately for us, this is not so. Besides the faculty of conceptual thought, another constituent characteristic of man played an important role in gaining a deeper understanding of his environment, and this is curiosity. Insatiable curiosity is the root of exploration and experimentation, and these activities, even in their most primitive form, imply a function akin to asking questions. Explorative experimentation is a sort of dialogue with surrounding nature. Asking a question and recording the answer leads to anticipating the latter, and, given conceptual thought, to the linking of cause and effect. From hence it is but a step to consciously foreseeing the consequences of one's actions. Thus, the same human faculties which supplied man with tools and with power dangerous to himself, also gave him the means to prevent their misuse: rational responsibility. I shall now proceed to discuss, one by one, the dangers which humanity incurs by rising above the other animals by virtue of its great, specific gifts. Subsequently I shall try to show in what way the greatest gift of all, rational, responsible morality, functions in banning these dangers. Most important of all, I shall have to expound the functional limitation of morality.

In the chapter on behavior mechanisms functionally analogous to morality, I have spoken of the inhibitions controlling aggression in various social animals, preventing it from injuring or killing fellow members of the species. As I explained, these inhibitions are most important and consequently most highly differentiated in those animals which are capable of killing living creatures of about their own size. A raven can peck out the eye of another with one thrust of its beak, a wolf can rip the jugular vein of another with a single bite. There would be no more ravens and no more wolves if reliable inhibitions did not prevent such actions. Neither a dove nor a hare nor even a chimpanzee is able to kill its own kind with a single peck or bite; in addition, animals with relatively poor defense weapons have a correspondingly great ability to escape quickly, even from specially armed predators which are more efficient in chasing, catching, and killing than even the strongest of their own species. Since there rarely is, in nature, the possibility of such an animal's seriously injuring one of its own kind, there is no selection pressure at work here to breed in killing inhibitions. The absence of such inhibitions is apparent to the animal keeper, to his own and to his animals' disadvantage, if he does not take seriously the intra-specific fights of completely "harmless" animals. Under the unnatural conditions of captivity, where a defeated animal cannot escape from its victor, it may be killed slowly and cruelly. In my book *King Solomon's Ring*, I have described in the chapter "Morals and Weapons" how the symbol of peace, the dove, can torture one of its own kind to death, without the arousal of any inhibition.

Anthropologists concerned with the habits of Australopithecus have repeatedly stressed that these hunting progenitors of man have left humanity with the dangerous heritage of what they term "carnivorous mentality." This statement confuses the concepts of the carnivore and the cannibal, which are, to a large extent, mutually exclusive. One can only deplore the fact that man has definitely not got a carnivorous mentality! All his trouble arises from his being a basically harmless, omnivorous creature, lacking in natural weapons with which to kill big prey, and, therefore, also devoid of the built-in safety devices which prevent "professional" carnivores from abusing their killing power to destroy fellow members of their own species. A lion or a wolf may, on extremely rare occasions, kill another by one angry stroke, but, as I have already explained in the chapter on behavior mechanisms functionally analogous to morality, all heavily armed carnivores possess sufficiently reliable inhibitions which prevent the self-destruction of the species.

In human evolution, no inhibitory mechanisms preventing sudden manslaughter were necessary, because quick killing was impossible anyhow; the potential victim had plenty of opportunity to elicit the pity of the aggressor by submissive gestures and appeasing attitudes. No selection pressure arose in the prehistory of mankind to breed inhibitory mechanisms preventing the killing of conspecifics until, all of a sudden, the invention of artificial weapons upset the equilibrium of killing potential and social inhibitions. When it did, man's position was very nearly that of a dove which, by some unnatural trick of nature, has suddenly acquired the beak of a raven. One shudders at the thought of a creature as irascible as all pre-human primates are, swinging a well-sharpened hand-ax. Humanity would indeed have destroyed itself by its first inventions, were it not for the very wonderful fact that inventions and responsibility are both the achievements of the same specifically human faculty of asking questions.

Not that our prehuman ancestor, even at a stage as yet devoid of moral responsibility, was a fiend incarnate; he was by no means poorer in social instincts and inhibitions than a chimpanzee, which, after all, is — his irascibility not withstanding — a social and friendly creature. But whatever his innate norms of social behavior may have been, they were bound to be thrown out of gear by the invention of weapons. If humanity survived, as, after all, it did, it never achieved security from the danger of self-destruction. If moral responsibility and unwillingness to kill have indubitably increased, the ease and emotional impunity of killing have increased at the same rate. The distance at which all shooting weapons take effect screens the killer against the stimulus situation which would otherwise activate his killing inhibitions. The deep, emotional layers of our personality simply do not register the fact that the crooking of the forefinger to release a shot tears the entrails of another man. No sane man would even go rabbit hunting for pleasure if the necessity of killing his prey with his natural weapons brought home to him the full, emotional realization of what he is actually doing.

The same principle applies, to an even greater degree, to the use of modern remote-control weapons. The man who presses the releasing button is so completely screened against seeing, hearing, or otherwise emotionally realizing the consequences of his action, that he can commit it with impunity — even if he is burdened with the power of imagination. Only thus can it be explained that perfectly good-natured men, who would not even smack a naughty child, proved to be perfectly able to release rockets or to lay carpets of incendiary bombs on sleeping cities, thereby committing hundreds and thousands of children to a horrible death in the flames. The fact that it is good, normal men who did this, is as eerie as any fiendish atrocity of war!

As an indirect consequence, the invention of artificial weapons has brought about a most undesirable predominance of intra-specific selection within mankind. In the third chapter, in which I discussed the survival value of aggression, and also in the tenth, dealing with the structure of society in rats, I have already spoken of the manner in which competition between the fellow members of one species can produce unadaptive results when it exerts a selection pressure totally unrelated to extra-specific environment.

When man, by virtue of his weapons and other tools, of his clothing and of fire, had more or less mastered the inimical forces of his extra-specific environment, a state of affairs must have prevailed in which the counter-pressures of the hostile neighboring hordes had become the chief selecting factor determining the next steps of human evolution. Small wonder indeed if it produced a dangerous excess of what has been termed the "warrior virtues" of man.

In 1955 I wrote a paper, "On the Killing of Members of the Same Species": "I believe — and human psychologists, particularly psychoanalysts, should test this — that present-day civilized man suffers from insufficient discharge of his aggressive drive. It is more than probable that the evil effects of the human aggressive drives, explained by Sigmund Freud as the results of a special death wish, simply derive from the fact that in prehistoric times intra-specific selection bred into man a measure of aggression drive for which in the social order of today he finds no adequate outlet." If these words contain an element of reproach against psychoanalysis, I must here withdraw them. At the time of writing, there were already some psychoanalysts who did not believe in the death wish and rightly explained the self-destroying effects of aggression as misfunctions of an instinct that was essentially life-preserving. Later, I came to know one psychiatrist and psychoanalyst who, even at that time, was examining the problem of the hypertrophy of aggression owing to intraspecific selection.

Sydney Margolin, in Denver, Colorado, made very exact psychoanalytical and psycho-sociological studies on Prairie Indians, particularly the Utes, and showed that these people suffer greatly from an excess of aggression drive which, under the ordered conditions of present-day North American Indian reservations, they are unable to discharge. It is Margolin's opinion that during the comparatively few centuries when Prairie Indians led a wild life consisting almost entirely of war and raids, there must have been an extreme selection pressure at work, breeding extreme aggressiveness. That this produced changes in the hereditary pattern in such a short time is quite possible. Domestic animals can be changed just as quickly by purposeful selection. Margolin's assumption is supported by the fact that Ute Indians now growing up under completely different educational influences suffer in exactly the same way as the older members of their tribe who grew up under the educational system of their own culture; moreover, the pathological symptoms under discussion are seen only in those Prairie Indians whose tribes were subjected to the selection process described.

Ute Indians suffer more frequently from neurosis than any other human group, and again and again Margolin found that the cause of the trouble was undischarged aggression. Many of these Indians feel and describe themselves as ill, and when asked what is the matter with them they can only say, "I am a Ute!" Violence toward people not of their tribe, and even manslaughter, belong to the order of the day, but attacks on members of the tribe are extremely rare, for they are prevented by a taboo the severity of which it is easy to understand, considering the early history of the Utes: a tribe constantly at war with neighboring Indians and, later on, with the white man, must avoid at all costs fights between its own members. Anyone killing a member of the tribe is compelled by strict tradition to commit suicide. This commandment was obeyed even by a Ute policeman who had shot a member of his tribe in self-defense while trying to arrest him. The offender, while under the influence of drink, had stabbed his father in the femoral artery, causing him to bleed to death. When the policeman was ordered by his sergeant to arrest the man for manslaughter — it was obviously not murder — he protested, saying that the man would want to die since he was bound by tradition to commit suicide and would do so by resisting arrest and forcing the policeman to shoot him. He, the policeman, would then have to commit suicide himself. The more than short-sighted sergeant stuck to his order, and the tragedy took place exactly as predicted. This and other of Margolin's records read like Greek tragedies: an inexorable fate forces crime upon people and then compels them to expiate voluntarily their involuntarily acquired guilt.

It is objectively convincing, indeed it is proof of the correctness of Margolin's interpretation of the behavior of Ute Indians, that these people are particularly susceptible to accidents. It has been proved that accident-proneness may result from repressed aggression, and in these Utes the rate of motor accidents exceeds that of any other car-driving human group. Anybody who has ever driven a fast car when really angry knows — in so far as he is capable of self-observation in this condition — what strong inclination there is to self-destructive behavior in a situation like this. Here even the expression "death wish" seems apt.

It is self-evident that intra-specific selection is still working today in an undesirable direction. There is a high positive selection premium on the instinctive foundations conducive to such traits as the amassing of property, self-assertion, etc., and there is an almost equally high negative premium on simple goodness. Commercial competition today might threaten to fix hereditarily in us hypertrophies of these traits, as horrible as the intra-specific aggression evolved by competition between warfaring tribes of Stone Age man. It is fortunate that the accumulation of riches and power does not necessarily lead to large families — rather the opposite — or else the future of mankind would look even darker than it does.

Aggressive behavior and killing inhibitions represent only one special case among many in which phylogenetically adapted behavior mechanisms are thrown out of balance by the rapid change wrought in human ecology and sociology by cultural development. In order to explain the function of responsible morality in re-establishing a tolerable equilibrium between man's instincts and the requirements of a culturally evolved social order, a few words must first be said about social instincts in general. It is a widely held opinion, shared by some contemporary philosophers, that all human behavior patterns which serve the welfare of the community, as opposed to that of the individual, are dictated by specifically human rational thought. Not only is this opinion erroneous, but the very opposite is true. If it were not for a rich endowment of social instincts, man could never have risen above the animal world. All specifically human faculties, the power of speech, cultural tradition, moral responsibility, could have evolved only in a being which, before the very dawn of conceptual thinking, lived in well-organized communities. Our prehuman ancestor was indubitably as true a friend to his friend as a chimpanzee or even a dog, as tender and solicitous to the young of his community and as self-sacrificing in its defense, aeons before he developed conceptual thought and became aware of the consequences of his actions.

According to Immanuel Kant's teachings on morality, it is human reason (*Vernunft*) alone which supplies the categorical imperative "thou shalt" as an answer to responsible self-questioning concerning any possible consequences of a certain action. However, it is doubtful whether "reason" is the correct translation of Kant's use of the word "*Vernunft*," which also implies the connotation of common sense and of understanding and appreciation of another "reasonable" being. For Kant it is self-evident that one reasonable being cannot possibly want to hurt another. This unconscious acceptance of what he considered evident, in other words common sense, represents the chink in the great philosopher's shining armor of pure rationality, through which emotion, which always means an instinctive urge, creeps into his considerations and makes them more acceptable to the biologically minded than they would otherwise be. It is hard to believe that a man will refrain from a certain action which natural inclination urges him to perform only because he has realized that it involves a logical contradiction. To assume this, one would have to be an even more unworldly German professor and an even more ardent admirer of reason than Immanuel Kant was.

In reality, even the fullest rational insight into the consequences of an action and into the logical consistency of its premise would not result in an imperative or in a prohibition, were it not for some emotional, in other words instinctive, source of energy supplying motivation. Like power steering in a modern car, responsible morality derives the energy which it needs to control human behavior from the same primal powers which it was created to keep in rein. Man as a purely rational being, divested of his animal heritage of instincts, would certainly not be an angel — quite the opposite.

Supposing that a being entirely indifferent to values, unable to see anything worth preserving in humanity, in human culture, and in life itself, were examining the principle of its action in pressing the button releasing the hydrogen bomb and destroying all life on our planet, even a full realization of the consequences would, in such a monster, elicit no imperative forbidding the deed, but only a reaction tantamount to saying, "So what?" We need not even suppose this hypothetical creature to be actively evil and to share the view of Goethe's Mephistopheles that everything created is worthy of annihilation; mere absence of any emotional appreciation of values could make it react in the way described.

Always and everywhere it is the unreasoning, emotional appreciation of values that adds a plus or a minus sign to the answer of Kant's categorical self-questioning and makes it an imperative or a veto. By itself, reason can only devise means to achieve otherwise determined ends; it cannot set up goals or give us orders. Left to itself, reason is like a computer into which no relevant information conducive to an important answer has been fed; logically valid though all its operations may be, it is a wonderful system of wheels within wheels, without a motor to make them go round. The motive power that makes them do so stems from instinctive behavior mechanisms much older than reason and not directly accessible to rational self-observation. They are the source of love and friendship, of all warmth of feeling, of appreciation of beauty, of the urge to artistic creativeness, of insatiable curiosity striving for scientific enlightenment. These deepest strata of the human personality are, in their dynamics, not essentially different from the instincts of animals, but on their basis human culture has erected all the enormous superstructure of social norms and rites whose function is so closely analogous to that of phylogenetic ritualization. Both phylogenetically and culturally evolved norms of behavior represent motives and are felt to be values by any normal human being. Both are woven into an immensely complicated system of universal interaction to analyze which is all the more difficult as most of its processes take place in the subconscious and are by no means directly accessible to self-observation. Yet it is imperative for us to understand the dynamics of this system, because insight into the nature of values offers the only hope for our ever creating the new values and ideals which our present situation needs so badly.

Even the first compensatory function of moral responsibility, preventing the Australopithecines from destroying themselves with their first pebble tools, could not have been achieved without an instinctive appreciation of life and death. Some of the most intelligent and most social birds and mammals react in a highly dramatic way to the sudden death of a member of their species. Greylag geese will stand with outspread wings over a dying friend hissing defensively, as Heinroth saw after having shot a goose in the presence of its family. I observed the same behavior on the occasion of an Egyptian goose killing a greylag gosling by hitting it on the head with its wing; the gosling staggered toward its parents and collapsed, dying of cerebral hemorrhage. Though the parents could not have seen the deadly blow, they reacted in the described way. In the Munich zoo some years ago an essentially friendly bull elephant while playing with his keeper unintentionally injured him severely, severing an artery in the man's thigh. The elephant immediately seemed to realize that something dangerous had befallen his friend and with the best intentions did the worst thing he could do: he stood protectively over the fallen man, thus preventing medical aid from reaching him. Professor Bernhard Grzimek told me that an adult male chimpanzee, after having bitten him rather badly, seemed very concerned, after his rage had abated, about what he had done and tried to press together, with his fingers, the lips of Grzimek's worst wounds. It is highly characteristic of that dauntless scientist that he permitted the ape to do so.

It is safe to assume that the first Cain, after having stricken a fellow member of his horde with a pebble tool, was deeply concerned about the consequences of his action. He may have struck with very little malice, just as a two-year-old child may hit another with a heavy and hard object without foreseeing the effect. He may have been most painfully surprised when his friend failed to get up again; he may even have tried to help him get up, as the bull elephant is reported to have done. In any case we are safe in assuming that the first killer fully realized the enormity of his deed. There was no need for the information being slowly passed around that the horde loses dangerously in fighting potential if it slaughters too many of its members for the pot.

Whatever the consequences may have been that prevented the first killers from repeating their deed, realization of these consequences and, therewith, a primitive form of responsibility must have been at work. Apart from maintaining the equilibrium between the ability and the inhibition to kill, responsible morality does not seem to have been too severely taxed in the earliest communities of true men. It is no daring speculation to assume that the first human beings which really represented our own species, those of Cro-Magnon, had roughly the same instincts and natural inclinations as we have ourselves. Nor is it illegitimate to assume that the structure of their societies and their tribal warfare was roughly the same as can still be found in certain tribes of Papuans in central New Guinea. Every one of their tiny settlements is permanently at war with the neighboring villages; their relationship is described by Margaret Mead as one of mild reciprocal head-hunting, "mild" meaning that there are no organized raids for the purpose of removing the treasured heads of neighboring warriors, but only the occasional taking of the heads of women and children encountered in the woods.

Now let us suppose that our assumption is correct and that the men of such a paleolithic tribe did indeed have the same natural inclinations, the same endowment with social instincts as we have ourselves; let us imagine a life, lived dangerously in the exclusive company of a dozen or so close friends and their wives and children. There would be some friction, some jealousy about girls, or rank order, but on the whole I think that this kind of rivalry would come second to the continuous necessity for mutual defense against hostile neighboring tribes. The men would have fought side by side from earliest memory; they would have saved each other's lives many times; all would have ample opportunity to discharge intraspecific aggression against their enemies, none would feel the urge to injure a member of his own community. In short, the sociological situation must have been, in a great many respects, comparable to that of the soldiers of a small fighting unit on a particularly dangerous and independent assignment. We know to what heights of heroism and utter self-abnegation average, unromantic modern men have risen under these circumstances. Incidentally, it is quite typical of man that his most noble and admirable qualities are brought to the fore in situations involving the killing of other men, just as noble as they are. However cruel and savage such a community may be to another, within its bonds natural inclination alone is very nearly sufficient to make men obey the Ten Commandments — perhaps with the exception of the third. One does not steal another man's rations or weapons, and it seems rather despicable to covet the wife of a man who has saved one's life a number of times. One would certainly not kill him, and one would, from natural inclination, honor not only father and mother, but the aged and experienced in general, just as deer and baboons do, according to the observations of Fraser Darling, Washburn, and De Vore.

The imagination of man's heart is not really evil from his youth up, as we read in Genesis. Man can behave very decently indeed in tight spots, provided they are of a kind that occurred often enough in the paleolithic period to produce phylogenetically adapted social norms to deal with the situation. Loving your neighbor as yourself or risking your life in trying to save his is a matter of course if he is your best friend and has saved yours a number of times; you do it without even thinking. The situation is entirely different if the man for whose life you are expected to risk your own or for whom you are supposed to make other sacrifices, is an anonymous contemporary on whom you have never set eyes. In this case it is not love for the fellow human being that activates self-denying behavior — if indeed it is activated — but the love for some culturally evolved traditional norm of social behavior. Love of something or other is, in very many cases, the motivation behind the power of the categorical imperative — an assertion which, I think, Kant would deny.

Our Cro-Magnon warrior had plenty of hostile neighbors against whom to discharge his aggressive drive, and he had just the right number of reliable friends to love. His moral responsibility was not overtaxed by an exercise of function which prevented him from striking, in sudden anger, at his companions with his sharpened hand-ax. The increase in number of individuals belonging to the same community is in itself sufficient to upset the balance between the personal bonds and the aggressive drive. It is definitely detrimental to the bond of friendship if a person has too many friends. It is proverbial that one can have only a few really close friends. To have a large number of "acquaintances," many of whom may be faithful allies with a legitimate claim to be regarded as real friends, overtaxes a man's capacity for personal love and dilutes the intensity of his emotional attachment. The close crowding of many individuals in a small space brings about a fatigue of all social reactions. Every inhabitant of a modern city is familiar with the surfeit of social relationships and responsibilities and knows the disturbing feeling of not being as pleased as he ought to be at the visit of a friend, even if he is genuinely fond of him and has not seen him for a long time. A tendency to bad temper is experienced when the telephone rings after dinner. That crowding increases the propensity to aggressive behavior has long been known and demonstrated experimentally by sociological research.

On the other hand, there is, in the modern community, no legitimate outlet for aggressive behavior. To keep the peace is the first of civic duties, and the hostile neighboring tribe, once the target at which to discharge phylogenetically programmed aggression, has now withdrawn to an ideal distance, hidden behind a curtain, if possible of iron. Among the many phylogenetically adapted norms of human social behavior, there is hardly one that does not need to be controlled and kept on a leash by responsible morality. This indeed is the deep truth contained in all sermons preaching asceticism. Most of the vices and mortal sins condemned today correspond to inclinations that were purely adaptive or at least harmless in primitive man. Paleolithic people hardly ever had enough to eat and if, for once, they had trapped a mammoth, it was biologically correct and moral for every member of the horde to gorge to his utmost capacity; gluttony was not a vice. When, for once, they were fully fed, primitive human beings rested from their strenuous life and were as absolutely lazy as possible, but there was nothing reprehensible in their sloth. Their life was so hard that there was no danger of healthy sensuality degenerating into debauch. A man sorely needed to keep his few possessions, weapons and tools, and a few nuts for tomorrow's meal; there was no danger of his hoarding instinct turning into avarice. Alcohol was not invented, and there are no indications that man had discovered the reinforcing properties of alkaloids, the only real vices known of present-day primitive tribes. In short, man's endowment with phylogenetically adapted patterns of behavior met the requirements well enough to make the task of responsible morality very easy indeed. Its only commandment at the time was: Thou shalt not strike thy neighbor with a hand-ax even if he angers thee.

Clearly, the task of compensation devolving on responsible morality increases at the same rate as the ecological and sociological conditions created by culture deviate from those to which human instinctive behavior is phylogenetically adapted. Not only does this deviation continue to increase, but it does so with an acceleration that is truly frightening.

The fate of humanity hangs on the question whether or not responsible morality will be able to cope with its rapidly growing burden. We shall not lighten this burden by overestimating the strength of morality, still less by attributing omnipotence to it. We have better chances of supporting moral responsibility in its ever-increasing task if we humbly realize and acknowledge that it is "only" a compensatory mechanism of very limited strength and that, as I have already explained, it derives what power it has from the same kind of motivational sources as those which it has been created to control. I have already said that the dynamics of instinctive drives, of phyletically and culturally ritualized behavior patterns, together with the controlling force of responsible morality, form a very complicated systemic whole which is not easy to analyze. However, the recognition of the mutual functional interdependence of its parts, even at the present incomplete stage of our knowledge, helps us to understand a number of phenomena which otherwise would remain completely unintelligible.

We all suffer to some extent from the necessity to control our natural inclinations by the exercise of moral responsibility. Some of us, lavishly endowed with social inclinations, suffer hardly at all; other less lucky ones need all the strength of their sense of moral responsibility to keep from getting into trouble with the strict requirements of modern society. According to a useful old psychiatric definition, a psychopath is a man who either suffers himself from the demands of society or else makes society suffer. Thus in one sense we are all psycopaths, for each of us suffers from the necessity of self-imposed control for the good of the community. The above-mentioned definition, however, was meant to apply particularly to those people who do not just suffer in secret, but overtly break down under the stress imposed upon them, becoming either neurotic or delinquent. Even according to this much narrower interpretation of our definition, the "normal" human being differs from the psychopath, the good man from the criminal, much less sharply than the healthy differs from the pathological. This difference is analogous to that between a man with a compensated valvular deficiency of the heart and one with a decompensated heart disease. In the first case, an increase of the work performed by the heart muscles is sufficient to compensate for the mechanical defect of the valve, so that the over-all pumping performance of the heart is adapted to the requirements of the body, at least for the time being. When the muscle finally breaks down under the prolonged strain, the heart becomes "decompensated." This analogy also goes to show that the compensatory function uses up energy.

This explanation of the essential function of responsible morality resolves a contradiction in Kant's doctrine of morality which was noticed earlier by Friedrich Schiller. He whom Herder called "the most inspired of all Kantians" opposed Kant's devaluation of all natural inclinations and satirized it in the wonderful Xenie: "*Gerne dien' ich dem Freund, doch lieber tu' ich's aus Neigung, darum wurmt es mich oft, dass ich nicht tugendhaft bin*" — "I like serving my friend but alas, I do it from inclination, and thus it often vexes me that I am not virtuous."

However, not only do we serve our friend by inclination but we judge his acts of friendship according to whether it was warm, natural inclination that prompted him to perform them. If we were utterly logical Kantians, we would have to do the opposite and value most the man who instinctively dislikes us but who by responsible self-questioning is forced, much against his inclinations, to treat us kindly; however, in actual fact we can feel at most a tepid form of respect for such a benefactor, but we have a warm affection for the man who treats us as a friend because he "feels that way," without thinking that he is doing something worthy of gratitude.

When my unforgettable teacher, Ferdinand Hochstetter, at the age of seventy-one gave his valedictory address at Vienna University, the then Chancellor thanked him warmly for his long and inspired work. Hochstetter's answer put in a nutshell the whole paradox of value and nonvalue of natural inclination. This is what he said: "You are thanking me for something for which I deserve no gratitude. Thank my parents, my ancestors who transmitted to me these and no other inclinations. And if you ask me what I have done throughout my life in the fields of research and teaching then I must honestly say: I have always done the thing which, at the moment, I considered the greatest fun!"

What a strange contradiction! This great scientist who, as I know for a fact, had never read Kant, here shared the philosopher's standpoint in denying all value to natural inclination while, at the same time, the inestimable value of his work, accomplished "just for fun," reduces the Kantian theory of values and morality *ad absurdum* even more effectively than Friedrich Schiller's succinct stanza.

Yet it is easy to resolve this seeming contradiction, if we keep in mind that moral responsibility functions, as a compensatory mechanism, in a system of which natural inclination, by no means necessarily devoid of value, forms another indispensable part. If we are assessing the behavior of a certain person — of ourselves, for example — we will naturally rate any particular action the higher the less it is motivated by natural inclination. On the other hand, if we are assessing people as friends, we will naturally prefer the one whose friendship does not stem from rational considerations — however moral these may be — but from the warm feelings of natural inclination. It is no paradox but plain common sense that we use two different standards for judging the deeds of a man and the man himself.

The man who behaves socially from natural inclination normally makes few demands on the controlling mechanism of his own moral responsibility. Thus, in times of stress, he has huge reserves of moral strength to draw upon. But the man who, even in everyday life, has constantly to exert all his moral strength in order to curb his natural inclination into a semblance of normal social behavior, is very likely to break down completely in case of additional stress. Our parable of the compensated heart disorder applies quite exactly here, particularly regarding its energetical aspects.

The stress under which morally responsible behavior breaks down can be of varying kinds. It is not so much the sudden, one-time great temptation that makes human morality break down but the effect of any prolonged situation that exerts an increasing drain on the compensatory power of morality. Hunger, anxiety, the necessity to make difficult decisions, overwork, hopelessness and the like all have the effect of sapping moral energy and, in the long run, making it break down. Anyone who has had the opportunity to observe men under this kind of strain, for example in war or in prisoner-of-war camps, knows how unpredictably and suddenly moral decompensation sets in. Men in whose strength one trusted unconditionally suddenly break down, and others of whom one would never have expected it prove to be sources of inexhaustible energy, keeping up the moral of others by their example. Anyone who has experienced such things knows that the fervor of good intention and its power of endurance are two independent variables. Once you have realized this, you cease to feel superior to the man who breaks down a little sooner than you do yourself. Even the best and noblest reaches a point where his resistance is at an end: "*Eloi, Eloi, lama sabachthani?*"

As already mentioned, norms of social behavior developed by cultural ritualization play at least as important a part in the context of human society as instinctive motivation and the control exerted by responsible morality. Even at the earliest dawn of culture, when the invention of tools was just beginning to upset the equilibrium of phylogenetically evolved patterns of social behavior, man's newborn responsibility must have found a strong aid in cultural ritualization. Evidence of cultural rites reaches back almost as far as that of the use of tools and of fire. Of course we can expect prehistorical evidence of culturally ritualized behavior only when ritualization has reached comparatively high levels of differentiation, as in burial ceremonies or in the arts of painting and sculpture. These make their first appearance simultaneously with our own species, and the marvelous proficiency of the first known painters and sculptors suggests that even by their time, art had quite a long history behind it. Considering all this, it is quite possible that a cultural tradition of behavioral norms originated as early as the use of tools or even earlier. The beginnings of both have been found in the chimpanzee.

Customs and taboos may acquire the power to motivate behavior in a way comparable to that of autonomous instincts. Not only highly developed rites or ceremonies but also simpler and less conspicuous norms of social behavior may attain, after a number of generations, the character of sacred customs which are loved and considered as values whose infringement is severely frowned upon by public opinion. As has already been hinted earlier, sacred custom owes its motivating force to phylogenetically evolved behavior patterns of which two are of particular importance. One is response of militant enthusiasm by which any group defends its own social norms and rites against another group not possessing them; the other is the group's cruel taunting of any of its members who fail to conform with the accepted "good form" of behavior. Without the phylogenetically programmed love for traditional custom, human society would lack the supporting apparatus to which its owes its indispensable structure. Yet, like any phylogenetically programmed behavior mechanism, the one under discussion can miscarry. School classes or companies of soldiers, both of which can be regarded as models of primitive group structure, can be very cruel indeed in their ganging up against an outsider. The purely instinctive response to a physically abnormal individual, for instance the jeering at a fat boy, is, as far as overt behavior is concerned, absolutely identical with discrimination against a person who differs from the group in culturally developed social norms — for instance, a child who speaks a different dialect.

The ganging up on an individual diverging from the social norms characteristic of a group and the group's enthusiastic readiness to defend these social norms and rites are both good illustrations of the way in which culturally determined conditioned-stimulus situations release activities which are fundamentally instinctive. They are also excellent examples of typical compound behavior patterns whose primary survival value is as obvious as the danger of their misfiring under the conditions of the modern social order. I shall have to come back to the different ways in which the function of militant enthusiasm can miscarry and to possible means of preventing this eventuality.

Before enlarging on this subject, however, a few words must be said about the functions of social norms and rites in general. First of all I must recall to the reader's memory the somewhat surprising fact mentioned earlier: We have no immediate knowledge of the function and/or survival value of the majority of our own established customs, notwithstanding our emotional conviction that they do indeed constitute high values. This paradoxical state of affairs is explained by the simple fact that customs are not man-made in the same sense as human inventions are, from the pebble tool up to the jet plane.

There may be exceptional cases in which causal insight gained by a great lawgiver determines a social norm. Moses is said to have recognized the pig as a host of the Trichina, but if he did, he preferred to rely on the devout religious observance of his people rather than on their intellect when he asserted that Jehovah himself had declared the porker an unclean animal. In general, however, it is quite certain that it hardly ever was insight into a valuable function that gave rise to traditional norms and rites, but the age old process of natural selection. Historians will have to face the fact that natural selection determined the evolution of cultures in the same manner as it did that of species.

In both cases, the great constructor has produced results which may not be the best of all conceivable solutions but which at least prove their viability by their very existence. To the biologist who knows the ways in which selection works and who is also aware of its limitations it is in no way surprising to find, in its constructions, some details which are unnecessary or even detrimental to survival. The human mind, endowed with the power of deduction, can quite often find solutions to problems which natural selection fails to resolve. Selection may produce incomplete adaptation even when it uses the material furnished by mutation and when it has at its disposal huge time periods. It is much more likely to do so when it has to determine, in an incomparably shorter time, which of the randomly arising customs of a culture make it best fitted to survival. Small wonder indeed if, among the social norms and rites of any culture, we find a considerable number which are unnecessary or even clearly inexpedient and which selection nevertheless has failed to eliminate. Many superstitions, comparable to my little greylag's detour toward the window, can become institutionalized and be carried on for generations. Also, intraspecific selection often plays as dangerous a role in the development of cultural ritualization as in phylogenesis. The process of so-called status-seeking, for instance, produces the bizarre excrescences in social norms and rites which are so typical of intra-specific selection.

However, even if some social norms or rites are quite obviously maladaptive, this does not imply that they may be eliminated without further consideration. The social organization of any culture is a complicated system of universal interaction between a great many divergent traditional norms of behavior, and it can never be predicted without a very thorough analysis what repercussions the cutting out of even one single part may have for the functioning of the whole. For instance, it is easily intelligible to anybody that the custom of head-hunting, widely spread among tropical tribes, has a somewhat unpleasant side to it, and that the peoples still adhering to it would be better off, in many ways, without it. The studies of the ethnologist and psychoanalyst Derek Freeman, however, have shown that head-hunting is so intricately interwoven with the whole social system of some Bornean tribes that its abolition tends to disintegrate their whole culture, even seriously jeopardizing the survival of the people.

The balanced interaction between all the single norms of social behavior characteristic of a culture accounts for the fact that it usually proves highly dangerous to mix cultures. To kill a culture, it is often sufficient to bring it into contact with another, particularly if the latter is higher, or is at least regarded as higher, as the culture of a conquering nation usually is. The people of the subdued side then tend to look down upon everything they previously held sacred and to ape the customs which they regard as superior. As the system of social norms and rites characteristic of a culture is always adapted, in many particular ways, to the special conditions of its environment, this unquestioning acceptance of foreign customs almost invariably leads to maladaptation. Colonial history offers abundant examples of its causing the destruction not only of cultures but also of peoples and races. Even in the less tragic case of rather closely related and roughly equivalent cultures mixing, there usually are some undesirable results, because each finds it easier to imitate the most superficial, least valuable customs of the other. The first items of American culture imitated by German youth immediately after the last war were gum chewing, Coca-Cola drinking, the crew cut, and the reading of color comic strips. More valuable social norms characteristic of American culture were obviously less easy to imitate.

Quite apart from the danger to one culture arising from contact with another, all systems of social norms and rites are vulnerable in the same way as systems of phylogenetically evolved patterns of social behavior. Not being man-made, but produced by selection, their function is, without special scientific investigation, unknown to man himself, and therefore their balance is as easily upset by the effects of conceptual thought as that of any system of instinctive behavior. Like the latter, they can be made to miscarry by any environmental change not "foreseen" in their "programming," but while instincts persist for better or worse, traditional systems of social behavior can disappear altogether within one generation, because, like the continuous state that constitutes the life of any organism, that which constitutes a culture cannot bear any interruption of its continuity.

Several coinciding factors are, at present, threatening to interrupt the continuity of our Western culture. There is, in our culture, an alarming break of traditional continuity between the generation born at about 1900 and the next. This fact is incontestable; its causes are still doubtful. Diminishing cohesion of the family group and decreasing personal contact between teacher and pupil are probably important factors. Very few of the present younger generation have ever had the opportunity of seeing their fathers at work; few pupils learn from their teachers by collaborating with them. This used to be the rule with peasants, artisans, and even scientists, provided they taught at relatively small universities. The industrialization that prevails in all sectors of human life produces a distance between the generations which is not compensated for by the greatest familiarity, by the most democratic tolerance and permissiveness of which we are so proud. Young people seem to be unable to accept the values held in honor by the older generation, unless they are in close contact with at least one of its representatives who commands their unrestricted respect and love.

Another probably important factor contributing to the same effect is the real obsolescence of many social norms and rites still valued by some of the older generation. The extreme speed of ecological and sociological change wrought by the development of technology causes many customs to become maladaptive within one generation. The romantic veneration of national values, so movingly expressed in the works of Rudyard Kipling or C. S. Forester, is obviously an anachronism that can do nothing but damage today.

Such criticism is indubitably overstressed by the prevalence of scientific thought and the unrelenting demand for causal understanding, both of which are the most characteristic, if not the only, virtues of our century. However, scientific enlightenment tends to engender doubt in the value of traditional beliefs long before it furnishes the causal insight necessary to decide whether some accepted custom is an obsolete superstition or a still indispensable part of a system of social norms. Again it is the unripe fruit of the tree of knowledge that proves to be dangerous; indeed, I suspect that the whole legend of the tree of knowledge is meant to defend sacred traditions against the premature inroads of incomplete rationalization.

As it is, we do not know enough about the function of any system of culturally ritualized norms of behavior to give a rational answer to the perfectly rational question of what some particular custom is good for, in other words wherein lies its survival value. When an innovator rebels against established norms of social behavior and asks why he should conform with them, we are usually at a loss for an answer. It is only in rare cases, as in my example of Moses' law against eating pigs, that we can give the would-be reformer such a succinct answer as "You will get trichinosis if you don't obey." In most cases the defender of accepted tradition has to resort to seemingly lame replies, saying that certain things are "simply not done," are not cricket, are un-American or sinful, if he does not prefer to appeal to the authority of some venerable father-figure who also regarded the social norm under discussion as inviolable.

To anyone for whom the latter is still endowed with the emotional value of a sacred rite, such an answer appears as self-evident and satisfactory; to anybody who has lost this feeling of reverence it sounds hollow and sanctimonius. Understandably, if not quite forgivably, such a person tends to think that the social norm in question is just superstition, if he does not go so far as to consider its defender as insincere. This, incidentally, is very frequently the main point of dissension between people of different generations.

In order correctly to appreciate how indispensable cultural rites and social norms really are, one must keep in mind that, as Arnold Gehlen has put it, man is by nature a being of culture. In other words, man's whole system of innate activities and reactions is phylogenetically so constructed, so "calculated" by evolution, as to need to be complemented by cultural tradition. For instance, all the tremendous neuro-sensory apparatus of human speech is phylogenetically evolved, but so constructed that its function presupposes the existence of a culturally developed language which the infant has to learn. The greater part of all phylogenetically evolved patterns of human social behavior is interrelated with cultural tradition in an analogous way. The urge to become a member of a group, for instance, is certainly something that has been programmed in the prehuman phylogeny of man, but the distinctive properties of any group which make it coherent and exclusive are norms of behavior ritualized in cultural development. As has been explained, without traditional rites and customs representing a common property valued and defended by all members of the group, human beings would be quite unable to form social units exceeding in size that of the primal family group which can be held together by the instinctive bond of personal friendship.

The equipment of man with phylogenetically programmed norms of behavior is just as dependent on cultural tradition and rational responsibility as, conversely, the function of both the latter is dependent on instinctual motivation. Were it possible to rear a human being of normal genetic constitution under circumstances depriving it of all cultural tradition — which is impossible not only for ethical but also for biological reasons — the subject of the cruel experiment would be very far from representing a reconstruction of a prehuman ancestor, as yet devoid of culture. It would be a poor cripple, deficient in higher functions in a way comparable to that in which idiots who have suffered encephalitis during infantile or fetal life lack the higher functions of the cerebral cortex. No man, not even the greatest genius, could invent, all by himself, a system of social norms and rites forming a substitute for cultural tradition.

In our time, one has plenty of unwelcome opportunity to observe the consequences which even a partial deficiency of cultural tradition has on social behavior. The human beings thus affected range from young people advocating necessary if dangerous abrogations of customs that have become obsolete, through angry young men and rebellious gangs of juveniles, to the appearance of a certain well-defined type of juvenile delinquent which is the same all over the world. Blind to all values, these unfortunates are the victims of infinite boredom.

The means by which an expedient compromise between the rigidity of social norms and the necessity of adaptive change can be effected is prescribed by biological laws of the widest range of application. No organic system can attain to any higher degree of differentiation without firm and cohesive structures supporting it and holding it together. Such a structure and its support can, in principle, only be gained by the sacrifice of certain degrees of freedom that existed before. A worm can bend all over, an arthropod only where its cuticular skeleton is provided with joints for that purpose.

Changes in outer or inner environment may demand degrees of freedom not permitted by the existing structure and therefore may necessitate its partial and/or temporary disintegration, in the same way that growth necessitates the periodic shedding of the shell in crustacea and other arthropods. This act of demolishing carefully erected structures, though indispensable if better adapted ones are to arise, is always followed by a period of dangerous vulnerability, as is impressively illustrated by the defenseless situation of the newly molted soft-shelled crab.

All this applies unrestrictedly to the "solidified," that is to say institutionalized, system of social norms and rites which function very much like a supporting skeleton in human cultures. In the growth of human cultures, as in that of arthropods, there is a built-in mechanism providing for graduated change. During and shortly after puberty human beings have an indubitable tendency to loosen their allegiance to all traditional rites and social norms of their culture, allowing conceptual thought to cast doubt on their value and to look around for new and perhaps more worthy ideals. There probably is, at that time of life, a definite sensitive period for a new object-fixation, much as in the case of the object-fixation found in animals and called imprinting. If at that critical time of life old ideals prove fallacious under critical scrutiny and new ones fail to appear, the result is complete aimlessness, the utter boredom which characterizes the young delinquent. If, on the other hand, the clever demagogue, well versed in the dangerous art of producing supranormal stimulus situations, gets hold of young people at the susceptible age, he finds it easy to guide their object-fixation in a direction subservient to his political aims. At the postpuberal age some human beings seem to be driven by an overpowering urge to espouse a cause and failing to find a worthy one may become fixated on astonishingly inferior substitutes. The instinctive need to be the member of a closely knit group fighting for common ideals may grow so strong that it becomes inessential what these ideals are and whether they possess any intrinsic value. This, I believe, explains the formation of juvenile gangs whose social structure is very probably a rather close reconstruction of that prevailing in primitive human society.

Apparently this process of object-fixation can take its full effect only once in an individual's life. Once the valuation of certain social norms or the allegiance to a certain cause is fully established, it cannot be erased again, at least not to the extent of making room for a new, equally strong one. Also it would seem that once the sensitive period has elapsed, a man's ability to embrace ideals at all is considerably reduced. All this helps to explain the hackneyed truth that human beings have to live through a rather dangerous period at, and shortly after, puberty. The tragic paradox is that the danger is greatest for those who are by nature best fitted to serve the noble causes of humanity.

The process of object-fixation has consequences of an importance that can hardly be overestimated. It determines neither more nor less than that which a man will live for, struggle for, and, under certain circumstances, blindly go to war for. It determines the conditioned stimulus situation releasing a powerful phylogenetically evolved behavior which I propose to call that of militant enthusiasm.

Militant enthusiasm is particularly suited for the paradigmatic illustration of the manner in which a phylogenetically evolved pattern of behavior interacts with culturally ritualized social norms and rites, and in which, though absolutely indispensable to the function of the compound system, it is prone to miscarry most tragically if not strictly controlled by rational responsibility based on causal insight. The Greek word *enthousiasmos* implies that a person is possessed by a god; the German *Begeisterung* means that he is controlled by a spirit, a *Geist*, more or less holy.

In reality, militant enthusiasm is a specialized form of communal aggression, clearly distinct from and yet functionally related to the more primitive forms of petty individual aggression. Every man of normally strong emotions knows, from his own experience, the subjective phenomena that go hand in hand with the response of militant enthusiasm. A shiver runs down the back and, as more exact observation shows, along the outside of both arms. One soars elated, above all the ties of everyday life, one is ready to abandon all for the call of what, in the moment of this specific emotion, seems to be a sacred duty. All obstacles in its path become unimportant; the instinctive inhibitions against hurting or killing one's fellows lose, unfortunately, much of their power. Rational considerations, criticism, and all reasonable arguments against the behavior dictated by militant enthusiasm are silenced by an amazing reversal of all values, making them appear not only untenable but base and dishonorable. Men may enjoy the feeling of absolute righteousness even while they commit atrocities. Conceptual thought and moral responsibility are at their lowest ebb. As a Ukrainian proverb says: "When the banner is unfurled, all reason is in the trumpet."

The subjective experiences just described are correlated with the following, objectively demonstrable phenomena. The tone of the entire striated musculature is raised, the carriage is stiffened, the arms are raised from the sides and slightly rotated inward so that the elbows point outward. The head is proudly raised, the chin stuck out, and the facial muscles mime the "hero face," familiar from the films. On the back and along the outer surface of the arms the hair stands on end. This is the objectively observed aspect of the shiver!

Anybody who has ever seen the corresponding behavior of the male chimpanzee defending his band or family with self-sacrificing courage will doubt the purely spiritual character of human enthusiasm. The chimp, too, sticks out his chin, stiffens his body, and raises his elbows; his hair stands on end, producing a terrifying magnification of his body contours as seen from the front. The inward rotation of his arms obviously has the purpose of turning the longest-haired side outward to enhance the effect. The whole combination of body attitude and hair-raising constitutes a bluff. This is also seen when a cat humps its back, and is calculated to make the animal appear bigger and more dangerous than it really is. Our shiver, which in German poetry is called a *"heiliger Schauer,"* a "holy" shiver, turns out to be the vestige of a prehuman vegetative response of making a fur bristle which we no longer have.

To the humble seeker of biological truth there cannot be the slightest doubt that human militant enthusiasm evolved out of a communal defense response of our prehuman ancestors. The unthinking single-mindedness of the response must have been of high survival value even in a tribe of fully evolved human beings. It was necessary for the individual male to forget all his other allegiances in order to be able to dedicate himself, body and soul, to the cause of the communal battle. *"Was schert mich Weib, was schert mich Kind"* — "What do I care for wife or child," says the Napoleonic soldier in a famous poem by Heinrich Heine, and it is highly characteristic of the reaction that this poet, otherwise a caustic critic of emotional romanticism, was so unreservedly enraptured by his enthusiasm for the "great" conqueror as to find this supremely apt expression.

The object which militant enthusiasm tends to defend has changed with cultural development. Originally it was certainly the community of concrete, individually known members of a group, held together by the bond of personal love and friendship. With the growth of the social unit, the social norms and rites held in common by all its members became the main factor holding it together as an entity, and therewith they became automatically the symbol of the unit. By a process of true Pavlovian conditioning plus a certain amount of irreversible imprinting these rather abstract values have in every human culture been substituted for the primal, concrete object of the communal defense reaction.

This traditionally conditioned substitution of object has important consequences for the function of militant enthusiasm. On the one hand, the abstract nature of its object can give it a definitely inhuman aspect and make it positively dangerous — what do I care for wife or child; on the other hand it makes it possible to recruit militant enthusiasm in the service of really ethical values. Without the concentrated dedication of militant enthusiasm neither art, nor science, nor indeed any of the great endeavors of humanity would ever have come into being. Whether enthusiasm is made to serve these endeavors, or whether man's most powerfully motivating instinct makes him go to war in some abjectly silly cause, depends almost entirely on the conditioning and/or imprinting he has undergone during certain susceptible periods of his life. There is reasonable hope that our moral responsibility may gain control over the primeval drive, but our only hope of its ever doing so rests on the humble recognition of the fact that militant enthusiasm is an instinctive response with a phylogenetically determined releasing mechanism and that the only point at which intelligent and responsible supervision can get control is in the conditioning of the response to an object which proves to be a genuine value under the scrutiny of the categorical question.

Like the triumph ceremony of the greylag goose, militant enthusiasm in man is a true autonomous instinct: it has its own appetitive behavior, its own releasing mechanisms, and, like the sexual urge or any other strong instinct, it engenders a specific feeling of intense satisfaction. The strength of its seductive lure explains why intelligent men may behave as irrationally and immorally in their political as in their sexual lives. Like the triumph ceremony, it has an essential influence on the social structure of the species. Humanity is not enthusiastically combative because it is split into political parties, but it is divided into opposing camps because this is the adequate stimulus situation to arouse militant enthusiasm in a satisfying manner. "If ever a doctrine of universal salvation should gain ascendancy over the whole earth to the exclusion of all others," writes Erich von Holst, "it would at once divide into two strongly opposing factions (one's own true one and the other heretical one) and hostility and war would thrive as before, mankind being — unfortunately — what it is!"

The first prerequisite for rational control of an instinctive behavior pattern is the knowledge of the stimulus situation which releases it. Militant enthusiasm can be elicited with the predictability of a reflex when the following environmental situations arise. First of all, a social unit with which the subject identifies himself must appear to be threatened by some danger from outside. That which is threatened may be a concrete group of people, the family or a little community of close friends, or else it may be a larger social unit held together and symbolized by its own specific social norms and rites. As the latter assume the character of autonomous values, they can, quite by themselves, represent the object in whose defense militant enthusiasm can be elicited. From all this it follows that this response can be brought into play in the service of extremely different objects, ranging from the sports club to the nation, or from the most obsolete mannerisms or ceremonials to the ideal of scientific truth or of the incorruptibility of justice.

A second key stimulus which contributes enormously to the releasing of intense militant enthusiasm is the presence of a hated enemy from whom the threat to the above "values" emanates. This enemy, too, can be of a concrete or of an abstract nature. It can be "the" Jews, Huns, Boches, tyrants, etc., or abstract concepts like world capitalism, Bolshevism, fascism, and any other kind of ism; it can be heresy, dogmatism, scientific fallacy, or what not. Just as in the case of the object to be defended, the enemy against whom to defend it is extremely variable, and demagogues are well versed in the dangerous art of producing supranormal dummies to release a very dangerous form of militant enthusiasm.

A third factor contributing to the environmental situation eliciting the response is an inspiring leader figure. Even the most emphatically anti-fascistic ideologies apparently cannot do without it, as the giant pictures of leaders displayed by all kinds of political parties prove clearly enough. Again the unselectivity of the phylogenetically programmed response allows for a wide variation in the conditioning to a leader figure. Napoleon, about whom so critical a man as Heinrich Heine became so enthusiastic, does not inspire me in the least; Charles Darwin does.

A fourth, and perhaps the most important, prerequisite for the full eliciting of militant enthusiasm is the presence of many other individuals, all agitated by the same emotion. Their absolute number has a certain influence on the quality of the response. Smaller numbers at issue with a large majority tend to obstinate defense with the emotional value of "making a last stand," while very large numbers inspired by the same enthusiasm feel the urge to conquer the whole world in the name of their sacred cause. Here the laws of mass enthusiasm are strictly analogous to those of flock formation; here, too, the excitation grows in proportion, perhaps even in geometrical progression, with the increasing number of individuals. This is exactly what makes militant mass enthusiasm so dangerous.

I have tried to describe, with as little emotional bias as possible, the human response of enthusiasm, its phylogenetic origin, its instinctive as well as its traditionally handed down components and prerequisites. I hope I have made the reader realize, without actually saying so, what a jumble our philosophy of values is. What is a culture? A system of historically developed social norms and rites which are passed on from generation to generation because emotionally they are felt to be values. What is a value? Obviously, normal and healthy people are able to appreciate something as a high value for which to live and, if necessary, to die, for no other reason than that it was evolved in cultural ritualization and handed down to them by a revered elder. Is, then, a value only defined as the object on which our instinctive urge to preserve and defend traditional social norms has become fixated? Primarily and in the early stages of cultural development this indubitably was the case. The obvious advantages of loyal adherence to tradition must have exerted a considerable selection pressure. However, the greatest loyalty and obedience to culturally ritualized norms of behavior must not be mistaken for responsible morality. Even at their best, they are only functionally analogous to behavior controlled by rational responsibility. In this respect, they are no whit different from instinctive patterns of social behavior. Also they are just as prone to miscarry under circumstances for which they have not been "programmed" by the great constructor, natural selection.

In other words, the need to control, by wise rational responsibility, all our emotional allegiances to cultural values is as great as, if not greater than, the necessity to keep in check our other instincts. None of them can ever have such devastating effects as unbridled militant enthusiasm when it infects great masses and overrides all other considerations by its single-mindedness and its specious nobility. It is not enthusiasm in itself that is in any way noble, but humanity's great goals which it can be called upon to defend. That indeed is the Janus head of man: The only being capable of dedicating himself to the very highest moral and ethical values requires for this purpose a phylogenetically adapted mechanism of behavior whose animal properties bring with them the danger that he will kill his brother, convinced that he is doing so in the interests of these very same high values. *Ecce homo!*

Henry Slesar | # The Prisoner

Henry Slesar Bogash was dead, and Riley as good as, and Sergeant Harran was someplace in the cornfield with a bullet-shattered leg, so Private Tommy Dowd was alone with the decision to either attempt to rejoin his

---

SOURCE: Originally appeared in *Playboy* magazine. Reprinted by permission of the author and his agent, Theron Raines. Copyright © 1967 by HMH Publishing Company, Inc.

company or surrender. He was relieved when the tall sheaves began sprouting the gray-green uniforms of the enemy, and his only option was to discard the carbine and put his hands into the air. He was 20 years old, and the four-man patrol mission had been his first serious combat exercise. It had ended badly, but at least it had ended.

The enemy troopers didn't talk much when they marched Tommy back to their lines. Their faces under the helmet liners were ordinary faces, homogenized out of all racial differences by dust and fatigue. He had heard the tent-and-barrack rumors about prisoner treatment, ranging from outright torture to insidious indoctrination, but the indifferent faces of his captors calmed his apprehensions. They didn't care; why should he?

The march took three hours, but the sun was setting and the evening turning cool. He was in a truck by nightfall, with a handful of sullen prisoners. By morning, they were at the prison stockade, stripped, deloused, bathed and into their prison uniforms. Tommy's fit. It fit very well, better than his Army clothes. When he was summoned for interrogation, he patted the smooth gray twill on his hips and went half smiling into the presence of the camp's commanding officer. Maybe it was the smile that brought an answering curve to the lips of the silky-bearded colonel behind the desk.

"According to the rules of the Geneva convention," the officer said pleasantly, "you don't have to tell me anything but your name, rank and serial number. We already have those from your dog tags, so in truth, the only purpose of this meeting is to let you know who I am, and tell you that I expect you to obey our camp regulations. Understand?"

Tommy swallowed his answer — it was going to be "Yes, sir" — and merely nodded.

"How old are you, son?" the colonel said, and his smile became engaging. "You don't have to volunteer *that* information, either."

Tommy told him, and the officer looked saddened.

"You were a child when the war started," he said. "I'm sure your mother hoped it would be over by this time. Well, it won't be long now. Not very long."

Tommy, for whom the war had been a permanent fact of existence, wondered at the optimism. But he had something else to puzzle out a few minutes later when he was marched through the compound to his assigned quarters. The wood-framed structure was small, neatly built, but surely incapable of housing more than three or four prisoners. A single name had been stenciled on the door, and it read:

DOWD, THOMAS
PRIVATE

The double meaning of the word didn't strike him until a guard opened the door, and Tommy's first glimpse of the room's only bed told him that the quarters were, indeed, private. It was obviously some officer's billet, an officer whose high rank allowed him the indulgence of luxury. There was a thick, gold-colored carpet on the floor; a grouping of overstuffed furniture, the sofa half smothered in pillows; a credenza with open doors that revealed a back-lighted bar with bottles that glowed with amber lights; an elongated cabinet with hidden contents (later, he learned they were high-fidelity components). The bed was oversized, with a thick fur blanket; it was so inviting that Tommy fell face down into the soft nap the moment he was alone. He woke, startled, an hour later, and realized that he *was* the intended occupant of this plush apartment, that the name on the door had meant what it said, DOWD, THOMAS, PRIVATE. It made no sense, but it was true. Thinking that, he fell asleep again and dreamed of home; the magazine photos covering the wall cracks of his room; the smell of overcooked food and damp plaster in the flooded basement; the gargle of the plumbing and the grind and screech of the cutting machine he had operated. When he woke again, it was morning, and the alarm was ringing. No, not an alarm; he realized it was a telephone by the bedside. White. He picked it up and mumbled a bewildered "Hello."

"Good morning!" a man's voice said cheerily. "Ready for breakfast, Private? We'll be serving in the mess hall starting at seven."

He went outside. The sun was bright; he blinked as he caught up with the ragged parade of fellow prisoners heading for the source of the food smell. At the chow line, he caught the arm of one, a sleepy-eyed Southerner named Chester he had met briefly in basic, and whispered, "Hey, Chet, you been here long? What kind of joint is this?"

And the Southern boy grinned and shrugged. "Three weeks," he said. "And it's all right. Oh, my, yes."

"But what's it all about?" Tommy said desperately. "What are they fattening us up for? What's the *gimmick?*"

Chester winked. "Some of us figure it's, you know, brainwashing," and he laughed, with secret, dreamy pleasure. "Yeah, some of us figure that."

There were four kinds of eggs at breakfast. There were sausages — link or patties. French toast for those who wanted it, plenty of bacon, fried — but not overfried — potatoes; and the toast, miraculously, was buttered and hot. There wasn't much talking at the tables, but there were some easy, satisfied chuckles.

"Gimmick, gimmick, gimmick," Tommy muttered to himself, all the way back to his quarters. When he entered the room, he saw an enemy guard making up his bed. *Making up his bed.* He hadn't been as stunned since Bogash had bought his quick death in the cornfield.

"Hi," the guard said. It was probably the only English he knew. Even when he left, he said, "Hi."

Tommy spent the rest of the morning exploring the room. He took a luxurious shower, with plenty of hot water. He discovered the hi-fi set and a cache of records. They were disappointingly bland pop albums. Aloud, he said, "I'll have to complain about that," and laughed. Then he had the feeling that his complaint might even be taken seriously. He went out for a walk around the compound and discovered flower gardens, a ball field and a recreation hall appointed like a Las Vegas casino.

There was lobster salad at lunch. At dinner, the prisoners made joking comments about the bill of fare. "Shrimp cocktail *again*? Steak *again*? Corn on the cob? Chocolate layer cake? Hey, this place is going down-hill . . ."

He saw Chester grinning at him throughout the meal, and started getting annoyed. After dinner, on their way to a movie at the recreation building, he grabbed the Southerner's elbow, hard enough to show his irritation.

"What's so funny?" he said. "Something funny about me?"

"Heck, no, pal, don't get me wrong."

"Listen, you think we're getting this treatment for *nothing*? They've got something up their sleeves. A gimmick, a gimmick!"

"Sure," Chester said cordially. "Only I can't wait to find out. You better wait, too, pal."

"Wait for what?"

They went into the building together, but Tommy, feeling alienated by Chester's smugness, by *all* the smug faces of the prisoners, took a seat in the back. He left before the feature was concluded. He went back to his room, put the least offensive of the pop albums on the turntable and lay on his oversized bed, staring at the ceiling.

At ten o'clock, there was a soft rap on his door. He said, "Who is it?" but nobody answered. He opened the door and a woman came into his room, closed the door again, and leaned back with her shoulders pressed against it. Posed that way, smiling, a long cascade of silvery-blonde hair moving softly against her cheek, falling to the swelling contour of her bosom, her eyes both challenging and tender, she looked so unreal to Tommy, so much the magazine illustration rather than flesh-and-blood girl, that his mind rejected her presence.

Then she said, "Hello, Tommy, I'm Lisa," and laughed. It was more of a giggle, a sound of girlish amusement at his consternation, and it broke the spell.

"Who?" he said.

"Lisa. I'm going to be your friend here, if you want me."

She linked her arm with his and turned him toward the lighted liquor cabinet.

"Can a friend have a drink?" she said.

They had three drinks, and she poured them all. When Tommy asked bewildered questions, she ducked them adroitly and made him talk about himself, about his life back home, about his plans for the future. The wild thought that he was entertaining some latter-day Mata Hari crossed his mind and left it just as quickly; there was nothing of strategic importance he could reveal; she seemed interested only in Tommy Dowd. To prove it, she took him to bed.

She returned the next night, and the night after that, and the nights that followed. And shortly, he knew he was beginning to wear the same quietly satisfied expression worn by all the inmates of the camp.

Two months after his arrival, he was asked to appear before the commanding officer. For the first time in weeks, he forced himself to reconsider the meaning of his bizarre experience. Was it time for the switcheroo, the trap door, the gimmick? Was he going to be asked to make public statements about enemy ideology? Recruited for some traitorous errand? Somehow employed as a tool of enemy purpose? He steeled himself for the interview, hoping he would bear himself well, that these delicious, sybaritic days and nights hadn't drained him of courage and will.

He saluted the colonel stiffly, and the man with the silky beard and soft smile said, "Relax, son. I've got some good news for you."

"Yes, sir?" Tommy said.

"You're going home," the colonel told him. "This very afternoon. A truck convoy is taking you and five other prisoners back to a neutral zone. You'll be met by members of your command there."

"Home?" Tommy said.

"It's a prisoner exchange, arranged through the Red Cross. I'm sure you'll be happy to see your comrades again. Best of luck to you, son; I hope your Army sees fit to allow you a stretch of time back home."

"Thank you, sir," Tommy said, his heart sinking.

"You don't look very happy."

"I'm happy, sir."

"Good," said the colonel, and held out his hand. "It's not in the Geneva rules, either, but would you shake?"

Tommy shook the hand briefly, saluted again, less crisply, and went outside, thinking of Lisa. When he went to meet the truck, he found her waiting nearby, with tears in her eyes. He wanted to embrace her, but the truck was being loaded quickly, making loud, ugly noises within its engine. He could barely hear her murmured goodbye.

*   *   *

When the trucks had gone, a young lieutenant with a briefcase under his arm entered the commanding officer's quarters and beamed like a man bearing good tidings; which, in fact, he was.

"Just received the latest summations, Colonel," he said. "Since the inauguration of the plan, the total increase in enemy surrenders has been well over a thousand percent."

"Yes, and it should keep on increasing, the more 'exchange' prisoners we send back to spread the word. How many this month, Lieutenant?"

"Almost a hundred thousand surrenders," the younger officer said. "At this rate, the war might be over by Christmas."

"Ah," the colonel said contentedly. "Peace. Is there anything else like it?"

Joseph Heller | from Catch-22

Everyone was elated with this turn of events, most of all Colonel Cathcart, who was convinced he had won a feather in his cap. He greeted Milo jovially each time they met and, in an excess of contrite generosity, impulsively recommended Major Major for promotion. The recommendation was rejected at once at Twenty-seventh Air Force Headquarters by ex-P.F.C. Wintergreen, who scribbled a brusque, unsigned reminder that the Army had only one Major Major Major Major and did not intend to lose him by promotion just to please Colonel Cathcart. Colonel Cathcart was stung by the blunt rebuke and skulked guiltily about his room in smarting repudiation. He blamed Major Major for this black eye and decided to bust him down to lieutenant that very same day.

"They probably won't let you," Colonel Korn remarked with a condescending smile, savoring the situation. "For precisely the same reasons that they wouldn't let you promote him. Besides, you'd certainly look foolish trying to bust him down to lieutenant right after you tried to promote him to my rank."

Colonel Cathcart felt hemmed in on every side. He had been much more successful in obtaining a medal for Yossarian after the debacle of Ferrara, when the bridge spanning the Po was still standing undamaged seven days after Colonel Cathcart had volunteered to destroy it. Nine missions his men had flown there in six days, and the bridge was not demolished until the tenth mission on the seventh day, when Yossarian killed Kraft and his crew by taking his flight of six planes in over the target a second time. Yossarian came in carefully on his second bomb run because he was brave then. He buried his head in his bombsight until his bombs were away; when he looked up, everything inside the ship was suffused in a weird orange glow. At first he thought that his own plane was on fire. Then he spied the plane with the burning engine directly above him and screamed to McWatt through the intercom to turn left hard. A second later, the wing of Kraft's plane blew off. The flaming wreck dropped, first the fuselage, then the spinning wing, while a shower of tiny metal fragments began tap dancing on the roof of Yossarian's own plane and the incessant *cachung! cachung! cachung!* of the flak was still thumping all around him.

Back on the ground, every eye watched grimly as he walked in dull

SOURCE: *Catch-22* by Joseph Heller. Copyright © 1955 by Joseph Heller. Reprinted by permission of Simon & Schuster, Inc.

dejection up to Captain Black outside the green clapboard briefing room to make his intelligence report and learned that Colonel Cathcart and Colonel Korn were waiting to speak to him inside. Major Danby stood barring the door, waving everyone else away in ashen silence. Yossarian was leaden with fatigue and longed to remove his sticky clothing. He stepped into the briefing room with mixed emotions, uncertain how he was supposed to feel about Kraft and the others, for they had all died in the distance of a mute and secluded agony at a moment when he was up to his own ass in the same vile, excruciating dilemma of duty and damnation.

Colonel Cathcart, on the other hand, was all broken up by the event. "Twice?" he asked.

"I would have missed it the first time," Yossarian replied softly, his face lowered.

Their voices echoed slightly in the long, narrow bungalow.

"But *twice?*" Colonel Cathcart repeated, in vivid disbelief.

"I would have missed it the first time," Yossarian repeated.

"But Kraft would be alive."

"And the bridge would still be up."

"A trained bombardier is supposed to drop his bombs the first time," Colonel Cathcart reminded him. "The other five bombardiers dropped their bombs the first time."

"And missed the target," Yossarian said. "We'd have had to go back there again."

"And maybe you would have gotten it the first time then."

"And maybe I wouldn't have gotten it at all."

"But maybe there wouldn't have been any losses."

"And maybe there would have been more losses, with the bridge still left standing. I thought you wanted the bridge destroyed."

"Don't contradict me," Colonel Cathcart said. "We're all in enough trouble."

"I'm not contradicting you, sir."

"Yes you are. Even that's a contradiction."

"Yes, sir. I'm sorry."

Colonel Cathcart cracked his knuckles violently. Colonel Korn, a stocky, dark, flaccid man with a shapeless paunch, sat completely relaxed on one of the benches in the front row, his hands clasped comfortably over the top of his bald and swarthy head. His eyes were amused behind his glinting rimless spectacles.

"We're trying to be perfectly objective about this," he prompted Colonel Cathcart.

"We're trying to be perfectly objective about this," Colonel Cathcart said to Yossarian with the zeal of sudden inspiration. "It's not that I'm being sentimental or anything. I don't give a damn about the men or the airplane. It's just that it looks so lousy on the report. How am I going to cover up something like this in the report?"

"Why don't you give me a medal?" Yossarian suggested timidly.

"For going around twice?"

"You gave one to Hungry Joe when he cracked up that airplane by mistake."

Colonel Cathcart snickered ruefully. "You'll be lucky if we don't give you a court-martial."

"But I got the bridge the second time around," Yossarian protested. "I thought you wanted the bridge destroyed."

"Oh, I don't know what I wanted," Colonel Cathcart cried out in exasperation. "Look, of course I wanted the bridge destroyed. That bridge has been a source of trouble to me ever since I decided to send you men out to get it. But why couldn't you do it the first time?"

"I didn't have enough time. My navigator wasn't sure we had the right city."

"The right city?" Colonel Cathcart was baffled. "Are you trying to blame it all on Aarfy now?"

"No, sir. It was my mistake for letting him distract me. All I'm trying to say is that I'm not infallible."

"Nobody is infallible," Colonel Cathcart said sharply, and then continued vaguely, with an afterthought: "Nobody is indispensable, either."

There was no rebuttal. Colonel Korn stretched sluggishly. "We've got to reach a decision," he observed casually to Colonel Cathcart.

"We've got to reach a decision," Colonel Cathcart said to Yossarian. "And it's all your fault. Why did you have to go around twice? Why couldn't you drop your bombs the first time like all the others?"

"I would have missed the first time."

"It seems to me that *we're* going around twice," Colonel Korn interrupted with a chuckle.

"But what are we going to do?" Colonel Cathcart exclaimed with distress. "The others are all waiting outside."

"Why *don't* we give him a medal?" Colonel Korn proposed.

"For going around twice? What can we give him a medal for?"

"For going around twice," Colonel Korn answered with a reflective, self-satisfied smile. "After all, I suppose it did take a lot of courage to go over that target a second time with no other planes around to divert the antiaircraft fire. And he did hit the bridge. You know, that might be the answer — to act boastfully about something we ought to be ashamed of. That's a trick that never seems to fail."

"Do you think it will work?"

"I'm sure it will. And let's promote him to captain, too, just to make certain."

"Don't you think that's going a bit farther than we have to?"

"No, I don't think so. It's best to play safe. And a captain's not much difference."

"All right," Colonel Cathcart decided. "We'll give him a medal for being brave enough to go around over the target twice. And we'll make him a captain, too."

Colonel Korn reached for his hat.

"Exit smiling," he joked, and put his arm around Yossarian's shoulders as they stepped outside the door.

. . . . .

"Now he's butting into *my* business!" Colonel Scheisskopf cried.

"Don't let it worry you, Scheisskopf," said General Peckem, congratulating himself on how adeptly he had fit Colonel Scheisskopf into his standard method of operation. Already his two colonels were barely on speaking terms. "Colonel Cargill envies you because of the splendid job you're doing on parades. He's afraid I'm going to put you in charge of bomb patterns."

Colonel Scheisskopf was all ears. "What are bomb patterns?"

"Bomb patterns?" General Peckem repeated, twinkling with self-satisfied good humor. "A *bomb pattern* is a term I dreamed up just several weeks ago. It means nothing, but you'd be surprised at how rapidly it's caught on. Why, I've got all sorts of people convinced I think it's important for the bombs to explode close together and make a neat aerial photograph. There's one colonel in Pianosa who's hardly concerned any more with whether he hits the target or not. Let's fly over and have some fun with him today. It will make Colonel Cargill jealous, and I learned from Wintergreen this morning that General Dreedle will be off in Sardinia. It drives General Dreedle insane to find out I've been inspecting one of his installations while he's been off inspecting another. We may even get there in time for the briefing. They'll be bombing a tiny undefended village, reducing the whole community to rubble. I have it from Wintergreen — Wintergreen's an ex-sergeant now, by the way — that the mission is entirely unnecessary. Its only purpose is to delay German reinforcements at a time when we aren't even planning an offensive. But that's the way things go when you elevate mediocre people to positions of authority." He gestured languidly toward his gigantic map of Italy. "Why, this tiny mountain village is so insignificant that it isn't even there."

They arrived at Colonel Cathcart's group too late to attend the preliminary briefing and hear Major Danby insist, "But it *is* there, I tell you. It's there, it's there."

"It's where?" Dunbar demanded defiantly, pretending not to see.

"It's right there on the map where this road makes this slight turn. Can't you see this slight turn on your map?"

"No, I can't see it."

"I can see it," volunteered Havermeyer, and marked the spot on Dunbar's map. "And here's a good picture of the village right on these photographs. I understand the whole thing. The purpose of the mission is to knock the whole village sliding down the side of the mountain and create a roadblock that the Germans will have to clear. Is that right?"

"That's right," said Major Danby, mopping his perspiring forehead with his handkerchief. "I'm glad somebody here is beginning to understand. These two armored divisions will be coming down from Austria into Italy along this road. The village is built on such a steep incline that all the rubble from the houses and other buildings you destroy will certainly tumble right down and pile up on the road."

"What the hell difference will it make?" Dunbar wanted to know, as Yossarian watched him excitedly with a mixture of awe and adulation. "It will only take them a couple of days to clear it."

Major Danby was trying to avoid an argument. "Well, it apparently makes some difference to Headquarters," he answered in a conciliatory tone. "I suppose that's why they ordered the mission."

"Have the people in the village been warned?" asked McWatt.

Major Danby was dismayed that McWatt too was registering opposition. "No, I don't think so."

"Haven't we dropped any leaflets telling them that this time we'll be flying over to hit them?" asked Yossarian. "Can't we even tip them off so they'll get out of the way?"

"No, I don't think so." Major Danby was sweating some more and still shifting his eyes about uneasily. "The Germans might find out and choose another road. I'm not sure about any of this. I'm just making assumptions."

"They won't even take shelter," Dunbar argued bitterly. "They'll pour out into the streets to wave when they see our planes coming, all the children and dogs and old people. Jesus Christ! Why can't we leave them alone?"

"Why can't we create the roadblock somewhere else?" asked McWatt. "Why must it be there?"

"I don't know," Major Danby answered unhappily. "I don't know. Look, fellows, we've got to have some confidence in the people above us who issue our orders. They know what they're doing."

"The hell they do," said Dunbar.

"What's the trouble?" inquired Colonel Korn, moving leisurely across the briefing room with his hands in his pockets and his tan shirt baggy.

"Oh, no trouble, Colonel," said Major Danby, trying nervously to cover up. "We're just discussing the mission."

"They don't want to bomb the village," Havermeyer snickered, giving Major Danby away.

"You prick!" Yossarian said to Havermeyer.

"You leave Havermeyer alone," Colonel Korn ordered Yossarian curtly. He recognized Yossarian as the drunk who had accosted him roughly at the officers' club one night before the first mission to Bologna, and he swung his displeasure prudently to Dunbar. "Why don't you want to bomb the village?"

"It's cruel, that's why."

"Cruel?" asked Colonel Korn with cold good humor, frightened only momentarily by the uninhibited vehemence of Dunbar's hostility. "Would it be any less cruel to let those two German divisions down to fight with our troops? American lives are at stake, too, you know. Would you rather see American blood spilled?"

"American blood is being spilled. But those people are living up there in peace. Why can't we leave them the hell alone?"

"Yes, it's easy for you to talk," Colonel Korn jeered. "You're safe here in Pianosa. It won't make any difference to you when these German reinforcements arrive, will it?"

Dunbar turned crimson with embarrassment and replied in a voice that was suddenly defensive. "Why can't we create the roadblock somewhere else? Couldn't we bomb the slope of a mountain or the road itself?"

"Would you rather go back to Bologna?" The question, asked quietly, rang out like a shot and created a silence in the room that was awkward and menacing. Yossarian prayed intensely, with shame, that Dunbar would keep his mouth shut. Dunbar dropped his gaze, and Colonel Korn knew he had won. "No, I thought not," he continued with undisguised scorn. "You know, Colonel Cathcart and I have to go to a lot of trouble to get you a milk run like this. If you'd sooner fly missions to Bologna, Spezia and Ferrara, we can get those targets with no trouble at all." His eyes gleamed dangerously behind his rimless glasses, and his muddy jowls were square and hard. "Just let me know."

"I would," responded Havermeyer eagerly with another boastful snicker. "I like to fly into Bologna straight and level with my head in the bombsight and listen to all that flak pumping away all around me. I get a big kick out of the way the men come charging over to me after the mission and call me dirty names. Even the enlisted men get sore enough to curse me and want to take socks at me."

Colonel Korn chucked Havermeyer under the chin jovially, ignoring him, and then addressed himself to Dunbar and Yossarian in a dry monotone. "You've got my sacred word for it. Nobody is more distressed about those lousy wops in the hills than Colonel Cathcart and myself. *Mais c'est la guerre.* Try to remember that we didn't start the war and Italy did. That we weren't the aggressors and Italy was. And that we couldn't possibly inflict as much cruelty on the Italians, Germans, Russians and Chinese as they're already inflicting on themselves." Colonel Korn gave Major Danby's shoulder a friendly squeeze without changing his unfriendly expression. "Carry on with the briefing, Danby. And make sure they understand the importance of a tight bomb pattern."

"Oh, no, Colonel," Major Danby blurted out, blinking upward. "Not for this target. I've told them to space their bombs sixty feet apart so that we'll have a roadblock the full length of the village instead of in just one spot. It will be a much more effective roadblock with a loose bomb pattern."

"We don't care about the roadblock," Colonel Korn informed him. "Colonel Cathcart wants to come out of this mission with a good clean aerial photograph he won't be ashamed to send through channels. Don't forget that General Peckem will be here for the full briefing, and you know how he feels about bomb patterns. Incidentally, Major, you'd better hurry up with these details and clear out before he gets here. General Peckem can't stand you."

"Oh, no, Colonel," Major Danby corrected obligingly. "It's General Dreedle who can't stand me."

"General Peckem can't stand you either. In fact, no one can stand you. Finish what you're doing, Danby, and disappear. I'll conduct the briefing."

"Where's Major Danby?" Colonel Cathcart inquired, after he had driven up for the full briefing with General Peckem and Colonel Scheisskopf.

"He asked permission to leave as soon as he saw you driving up," answered Colonel Korn. "He's afraid General Peckem doesn't like him. I was going to conduct the briefing anyway. I do a much better job."

"Splendid!" said Colonel Cathcart. "No!" Colonel Cathcart countermanded himself an instant later when he remembered how good a job Colonel Korn had done before General Dreedle at the first Avignon briefing. "I'll do it myself."

Colonel Cathcart braced himself with the knowledge that he was one of General Peckem's favorites and took charge of the meeting, snapping his words out crisply to the attentive audience of subordinate officers with the bluff and dispassionate toughness he had picked up from General Dreedle. He knew he cut a fine figure there on the platform with his open shirt collar, his cigarette holder, and his close-cropped, gray-tipped curly black hair. He breezed along beautifully, even emulating certain characteristic pronunciations of General Dreedle's, and he was not the least bit intimidated by General Peckem's new colonel until he suddenly recalled that General Peckem detested General Dreedle. Then his voice cracked, and all confidence left him. He stumbled ahead through instinct in burning humiliation. He was suddenly in terror of Colonel Scheisskopf. Another colonel in the area meant another rival, another enemy, another person who hated him. And this one was tough! A horrifying thought occurred to Colonel Cathcart: Suppose Colonel Scheisskopf had already bribed all the men in the room to begin moaning, as they had done at the first Avignon mission. How could he silence them? What a terrible black eye that would be! Colonel Cathcart was seized with such fright that he almost beckoned to Colonel Korn. Somehow he held himself together and synchronized the watches. When he had done that, he knew he had won, for he could end now at any time. He had come through in a crisis. He wanted to laugh in Colonel Scheisskopf's face with triumph and spite. He had proved himself brilliantly under pressure, and he concluded the briefing with an inspiring peroration that every instinct told him was a masterful exhibition of eloquent tact and subtlety.

"Now, men," he exhorted. "We have with us today a very distinguished guest, General Peckem from Special Services, the man who gave us all our softball bats, comic books, and U.S.O. shows. I want to dedicate this mission to him. Go on out there and bomb — for me, for your country, for God, and for that great American, General P. P. Peckem. And let's see you put all those bombs on a dime!"

Robert Ardrey | Cain's Children

What are the things that we know about man? How much have the natural sciences brought to us, so far, in the course of a silent, unfinished revolution? What has been added to our comprehension of ourselves that can support us in our staggering, lighten our burdens in our carrying, add to our hopes, subtract from our anxieties, and direct us through hazard and fog and predicament? Or should the natural sciences have stayed in bed?

We know above all that man is a portion of the natural world and that much of the human reality lies hidden in times past. We are an iceberg floating like a gleaming jewel down the cold blue waters of the Denmark Strait; most of our presence is submerged in the sea. We are a moonlit temple in a Guatemala jungle; our foundations are the secret of darkness and old creepers. We are a thriving, scrambling, elbowing city; but no one can find his way through our labyrinthine streets without awareness of the cities that have stood here before. And so for the moment let us excavate man.

What stands above the surface? His mind, I suppose. The mind is the city whose streets we get lost in, the most recent construction on a very old site. After seventy million years of most gradual primate enlargement, the brain nearly trebled in size in a very few hundreds of thousands of years. Our city is spacious and not lacking in magnificence, but it has the problems of any boom town. Let us dig.

We are Cain's children. The union of the enlarging brain and the carnivorous way produced man as a genetic possibility. The tightly packed

SOURCE: *African Genesis* by Robert Ardrey. Copyright © 1961 by Literat S. A. Reprinted by permission of Atheneum Publishers.

weapons of the predator form the highest, final, and most immediate foundation on which we stand. How deep does it extend? A few million, five million, ten million years? We do not know. But it is the material of our immediate foundation as it is the basic material of our city. And we have so far been unable to build without it.

Man is a predator whose natural instinct is to kill with a weapon. The sudden addition of the enlarged brain to the equipment of an armed already-successful predatory animal created not only the human being but also the human predicament.. But the final foundation on which we stand has a strange cement. We are bad-weather animals. The deposit was laid down in a time of stress. It is no mere rubble of carnage and cunning. City and foundation alike are compacted by a mortar of mysterious strength, the capacity to survive no matter what the storm. The quality of the mortar may hold future significance far exceeding that of the material it binds.

Let us dig deeper. Layer upon layer of primate preparation lies buried beneath the predatory foundation. As the addition of a suddenly enlarged brain to the way of the hunting primate multiplied both the problems and the promises of the sum total, man, so the addition of carnivorous demands to the non-aggressive, vegetarian primate way multiplied the problems and promises of the sum total, our ancestral hunting primate. He came into his Pliocene time no more immaculately conceived than did we into ours.

The primate has instincts demanding the maintenance and defence of territories; an attitude of perpetual hostility for the territorial neighbour; the formation of social bands as the principal means of survival for a physically vulnerable creature; an attitude of amity and loyalty for the social partner; and varying but universal systems of dominance to insure the efficiency of his social instrument and to promote the natural selection of the more fit from the less. Upon this deeply-buried, complex, primate instinctual bundle were added the necessities and the opportunities of the hunting life.

The non-aggressive primate is rarely called upon to die in defence of his territory. But death from territorial conflict is second among the causes of lion mortality in the Kruger reserve. The nonaggressive primate seldom suffers much beyond humiliation in his quarrels for dominance. The lion dies of such conflicts more than of all other causes. The forest primate suppresses many an individual demand in the interests of his society. But nothing in the animal world can compare with the organization and the discipline of the lion's hunting pride or the wolf's hunting pack.

We can only presume that when the necessities of the hunting life encountered the basic primate instincts, then all were intensified. Conflicts became lethal, territorial arguments minor wars. The social band as a hunting and defensive unit became harsher in its codes whether of amity or enmity. The dominant became more dominant, the subordinate more disciplined. Overshadowing all other qualitative changes, however, was the coming of the aggressive imperative. The creature who had once killed only through circumstance killed now for a living.

As we glimpsed in the predatory foundation of man's nature the mysterious strength of the bad-weather animal, so we may see in the coming of the carnivorous way something new and immense and perhaps more significant than the killing necessity. The hunting primate was free. He was free of the forest prison; wherever game roamed the world was his. His hands were freed from the earth or the bough; erect carriage opened new and unguessed opportunities for manual answers to ancient quadruped problems. His daily life was freed from the eternal munching; the capacity to digest high-calorie food meant a life more diverse than one endless meal-time. And his wits were freed. Behind him lay the forest orthodoxies. Ahead of him lay freedom of choice and invention as a new imperative if a revolutionary creature were to meet the unpredictable challenges of a revolutionary way of life. Freedom — as the human being means freedom — was the first gift of the predatory way.

We may excavate man deeply and ever more deeply as we dig down through pre-primate, pre-mammal, and even pre-land-life levels of experience. We shall pass through the beginnings of sexual activity as a year-around affair, and the consequent beginnings of the primate family. But all the other instincts will be there still deeper down: the instinct to dominate one's fellows, to defend what one deems one's own, to form societies, to mate, to eat, and avoid being eaten. The record will grow dim and the outlines blurred. But even in the earliest deposits of our nature where death and the individual have their start, we shall still find traces of animal nostalgia, of fear and dominance and order.

Here is our heritage, so far as we know it today. Here is the excavated mound of our nature with *Homo sapiens'* boom town on top. But whatever tall towers reason may fling against the storms and the promises of the human future, their foundations must rest on the beds of our past for there is nowhere else to build.

Cain's children have their problems. It is difficult to describe the invention of the radiant weapon as anything but the consummation of a species. Our history reveals the development and contest of superior weapons as *Homo sapiens'* single, universal cultural preoccupation. Peoples may perish, nations dwindle, empires fall; one civilization may surrender its memories to another civilization's sands. But mankind as a whole, with an instinct as true as a meadow-lark's song, has never in a single instance allowed local failure to impede the progress of the weapon, its most significant cultural endowment.

Must the city of man therefore perish in a blinding moment of universal annihilation? Was the sudden union of the predatory way and the enlarged brain so ill-starred that a guarantee of sudden and magnificent disaster was written into our species' conception? Are we so far from being nature's most glorious triumph that we are in fact evolution's most tragic error, doomed to bring extinction not just to ourselves but to all life on our planet?

It may be so; or it may not. We shall brood about that in a moment. But to reach such a conclusion too easily is to oversimplify both our human future and our animal past. Cain's children have many an ancestor beyond *Australopithecus africanus*, and many a problem beyond war. And the first of our problems is to comprehend our own nature. For we shall fashion no miracles in our city's sky until we know the names of the streets where we live.

2

Man is a zoological group of sentient rather than sapient beings, characterized by a brain so large that he uses rather little of it, a chin distinctive enough to identify him among related animals, and an overpowering enthusiasm for things that go boom. Aside from these attributes — and the chin merely distinguishes *Homo sapiens* from earlier members of the human family — it is difficult to say where man began and the animal left off. We have a quality of self-awareness uncommon among animals, but whether this is a consequence of the enlarged brain or was shared with our extinct fathers, we do not know.

In any event, we do have the power to be aware of self, and to visualize ourselves in a present or future situation. And the power dictates as entirely natural our curiosity concerning the human outcome. Whether self-awareness will actually influence that outcome must strike any observer of human behavior, on the basis of past performance, as dubious. When human consciousness of potential disaster has in the past come into conflict with instincts of animal origin, our record has been one of impeccable poverty. No past situation, however, can compare with the contemporary predicament of potential nuclear catastrophe. And self-awareness, generating mortal fear, may at least partially forestall an evolutionary disaster.

How great will be the role of reason in such inhibition or diversion of the weapons instinct must be entirely of a collateral order. The human brain came too suddenly on to the evolutionary scene, and lacking animal foundation lacks the command of instinct to enforce its directives. The mind's decrees rank merely as learned responses, and we cannot expect too much of a learned power placed in opposition to an instinct. We cannot expect too much from the human capacity to reason, anyway, since its most elaborate energy is channelled as a rule into self-delusion and its most imposing construction erected so far has been that fairy-tale tower, the romantic fallacy.

The human mind, nevertheless, however sorry it may seem on a basis of past performance, cannot be ignored as a potential participant in some future human resolution. Granted a fresh comprehension of human nature and casting off pretence that reason carries power, the human mind can make alliance with animal instincts profound enough in our nature to engage forces for survival larger than the mind itself. We shall return to the thesis later in this chapter, but let us now look into the contemporary crisis of war and weapons, and see if our enhanced understanding of human behavior benefits us at all in the illumination of the possible outcome.

I find it convenient to consider the contemporary predicament in terms of three possible outcomes of varying probability, and the reader must forgive me if I do not seem to take the first two seriously. There is the first possibility — which I regard as remote — that *Homo sapiens* will obey his weapons instinct with minimum inhibition, put to full use his intellectual resources, and commit himself and his planet to a maximum explosion. The experiment of the enlarged brain, by its final action, will have been demonstrated a total failure. Allied to the vegetarian way, the big brain failed to survive as a significant evolutionary factor the dusty challenge of the Pliocene drought. Allied to the carnivorous way, reason in one fiery instant will have demonstrated its inadequacy as a guiding force for living beings.

To believe that man has the capacity, however, even through a maximum effort, to bring an end to all life on our planet is a melodramtic expression of the Illusion of Central Position. We have no such power. The ancient insect has mutational receptivity equal to our best efforts. While a giant effort on the part of man could conceivably bring extinction to all vertebrates, it is impossible to believe that a world of insects would not survive. We may regret the passing of the lion, of the elephant, of our partners the horse and the sparkling dog. But natural selection, regretting nothing, will turn its attention to the instinctual promise of the termite, the ant, and the subtle bee.

I find that I have small patience with this first outcome — purple in its hues, pat in its outline — which has so entranced our neo-romantics. And so I leave it to consider the far high probability of the second. This second field of probabilities grants like the first that man, sooner or later, will obey his weapons instinct. Though we be raised under canaries for four generations, as Marais raised his weaver birds, still no conditioning force can eradicate our genetic affinity for the weapon. Given access to traditional materials, Marais' weaver birds built their nests again complete to the horse-hair knot. Given access again to our traditional materials, we shall proceed with alacrity to blow up the place.

The second outcome presumes, however, that we fail to do quite such a job of it. The instinct to preserve the species runs deep in all animals, and it may compromise the effectiveness of our weapons compulsion. Or the enlarged brain may not succeed in perfecting a cataclysm of such devastating proportions. Whatever the ingredients of the partial disaster — whether instinctual, ineffectual, accidental, or even thoughtful — the second possible outcome presumes that a portion of mankind survives.

If I were a fox, or a reedbuck, or a rabbit, and I found myself among perhaps twenty per cent of my kind to survive a holocaust, I should face the future with equanimity. In a few generations select territories, abundant food supply, and compensatory breeding would restore my kind to its former fullness. But I am neither fox, nor reedbuck, nor rabbit. I am a human being dependent on society and technology. And were I to find myself among the twenty per cent of human beings to survive a contest of radiant weapons, I should much prefer to have been numbered among the victims.

One may of course take a hopeful view of such a colossal weeding of the human garden. Five hundred million people remain, but overpopulation will cease to be a problem in India, and traffic jams in New York. The Riviera will no longer be crowded in August, and there will be seats on commuter trains in the six o'clock rush. The diminished ranks of children will have school rooms in plenty, the diminished ranks of tenants, apartments galore. Were that all there was to it, we should all be as happy as unpursued foxes. But of course it is not.

Starkest in horror of the three probabilities is the partial catastrophe. The survivor will face plague unrivalled in the middle ages, and famine unknown in China's worst seasons. Social anarchy will grip him. The peasant will be murdered by marauding bands, the city man withered by his dependence on society. Disease, hunger, predation, and suicide will decimate the five hundred million, and mutuation will alter the remainder's descendants.

Yet a certain strange hope exists. We need not quarrel over the actuarial rates of post-apocalypse insurance companies. Premiums will be high. But there is something we know of a more exact order and of far greater evolutionary significance. Any radiant catastrophe killing a presumed four-fifths of the human population will induce mutations in the majority of the survivors. Ninety-nine out of every one hundred mutations will be unfavourable. One will be benevolent. And here, should the second outcome provide mankind with its fate, lies evolution's hope.

It is the paradox of the contemporary predicament that the force we have fashioned and that can destroy our species is the same force that can produce another.

Let us assume that among the five hundred million immediate survivors of a nuclear contest, one hundred million survive the post-apocalypse. Of the hundred million, perhaps half will have descendants suffering mutations. Forty-nine million five hundred thousand will be doomed. But a half million will have descendants with endowments superior to the ancestral line. And it is on the shoulders of this slim half million that primate hopes must rest.

What happens to the rest of us, the unmutated, is of small concern. Rats may eat us, or our fellow men. Mutant germs for which we have no resistance may sweep us away with diseases for which we have no names. Famine may waste us. Our predatory instinct, for which our intelligence was never a match, may now unchecked by social patterns drive us into ceaseless conflict until *Homo sapiens* becomes extinct.

A grand and tragic breed will have passed from the earth; and the engine of our creation will have proved the engine of our destruction. But we shall leave behind no barren tidings. Here and there, in unlikely valleys and on unlikely plains, a few mutant beings will roam the byways as others once haunted the Lake Victoria shore. And natural selection will find them, these superior creatures: a few here, in a moss-draped swamp of the Mississippi delta; a few there, in a windy Himalayan pass; a handful, wandering the green velvet of an Argentine grassland; a solitary figure on an old Greek island, pausing in wonder before a marble memory. Slowly, ever so slowly, the mutant beings of a fiery creation will assemble their genetic promises, and a new species will be born. Is it too much to hope that in such a species reason may not be an instinct?

The first outcome of the modern predicament must leave evolution to the neo-romantics. The second, more probable and more horrid in outline, at least allows man his evolutionary dignity. Our interest in either outcome, of course, must necessarily be of an academic nature. It is in part for this reason that I have treated neither too seriously, although in far larger part because I take neither too seriously. Likelihood, in vast array, rides with that group of probabilities centered on the third outcome, in which very little happens at all.

The third outcome assumes that we have already seen or shall shortly see the end of general warfare. Either a contest of ultimate weapons will never take place; or if it does take place, the contest will be of small biological significance in which no more than two or three hundred million people are killed. In either case, sufficient inhibition will have been created to hold in check the weapons instinct. And I regard this outcome as the most frightening if for no other reason than that it is the only one that we shall have to live with.

There are other and more immediate reasons for regarding the third outcome as a nightmare of unpredictables. For generations we have been enchanted by the romantic fallacy. Assuming that man is unique, innocent in his creation, noble by nature, and good in all his potentialities when not distorted by personal or social experience, modern thought has contented itself with the question, "How can we bring an end to war?" No one making such assumptions could be impelled to ask, "How can we get along without it?" Yet today the honest observer must conclude that man is noble in his nature only in the sense that he partakes of the nobility of all living things; that he is unique to no greater degree than that of any fellow species; that far from being created innocent, he originated as the most sophisticated predator the world has ever known; and that amity in his nature, while partly founded on animal values, must largely be erected as a learned response by the social conditioning of each baby born.

How can we get along without war? It is the only question pertaining to the future that bears the faintest reality in our times; for if we fail to get along without war, then the future will be as remarkably lacking in human problems as it will be remarkably lacking in men. Yet war has been the most natural mode of human expression since the beginnings of recorded history, and the improvement of the weapon has been man's principal preoccupation since Bed Two in the Olduvai Gorge. What will happen to a species denied in the future its principal means of expression, and its only means, in last appeal, of resolving differences? What will happen to a species that has dedicated its chief energy to the improvement and contest of the weapon, and that now arrives at the end of the road where further improvement and contest is impossible?

Let us not be too hasty in our dismissal of war as an unblemished evil. Are you a Christian? Then recall that Christendom survived its darkest hour in the fury of the Battle of Tours. Do you believe in law? The rule of law became a human institution in the shelter of the Roman legions. Do you subscribe to the value of individual worth? Only by the success of the phalanx at Marathon did the Greeks repel the Persian horde and make possible the Golden Age. Are you a materialist? Do you regard as a human good the satisfaction of economic want? The *Pax Britannica*, made possible by the unchallengeable supremacy of the British fleet, gave mankind the opportunity to lay the broad foundations of the Industrial Revolution.

I am free to uphold in the pages of this account certain views challenging the orthodoxies of my time because I belong to a nation that obtained freedom for its citizens through war, and that has successfully defended my freedom, by the same means, on all occasions since. You are free to read this book, and to consider, evaluate, reject or accept my views, because we are all members of a larger civilization that accept the free mind as a condition of such profound if painful value that on innumerable occasions it has been willing to fight for it. Do you care about freedom? Dreams may have inspired it, and wishes promoted it, but only war and weapons have made it yours.

No man can regard the way of war as good. It has simply been our way. No man can evaluate the eternal contest of weapons as anything but the sheerest waste and the sheerest folly. It has been simply our only means of final arbitration. Any man can suggest reasonable alternatives to the judgment of arms. But we are not creatures of reason except in our own eyes.

I maintain in these pages that the superior weapon, throughout the history of our species, has been the central human dream; that the energy focused on its continual development has been the central source of human dynamics; that the contest of superior weapons has been the most profoundly absorbing of human experiences; and that the issues of such contest have maintained and protected much that I myself regard as good. Finally, I maintain that deprived of the dream, deprived of the dynamics, deprived of the contest, and deprived of the issue, *Homo sapiens* stands on a darkened threshhold through which species rarely return.

The true predicament of contemporary man is not entirely unlike the Pliocene predicament of the gorilla. The bough was the focus of his experience as the weapon has been the focus of ours. It provided him with the fruit that was his nourishment, and with his means of locomotion. It dominated his existence even to the specialization of his anatomy: his hook-like thumbs, his powerful chest, his long arms, his weak and truncated legs. The bough was the focus of gorilla tradition, gorilla instinct, gorilla security, gorilla psyche, and of the only way of life the gorilla knew. Then a natural challenge deprived him of his bough. And the gorilla took to the ground. There we find him today, a depleted crew of evolutionary stragglers. Every night he builds a nest in tribute to ancestral memories. Every day he pursues the unequal struggle with extinction. His vitality sags. He defends no territory, copulates rarely. And the story of the gorilla will end, one day, not with a bang but a whimper.

Deprived of the contest of weapons that was the only bough he knew, man must descend to the cane-brakes of a new mode of existence. There he must find new dreams, new dynamics, new experiences to absorb him, new means of resolving his issues and of protecting whatever he regards as good. And he will find them; or he will find himself lost. Slowly his governments will lose their force and his societies their integration. Moral order, sheltered throughout all history by the judgement of arms, will fall away in rot and erosion. Insoluble quarrels will rend peoples once united by territorial purpose. Insoluble conflicts will split nations once allied by a common dream. Anarchy, ultimate enemy of social man, will spread its grey, cancerous tissues throughout the social corpus of our kind. Bandit nations will hold the human will a hostage, in perfect confidence that no superior force can protect the victim. Bandit gangs will have their way along the social thoroughfare, in perfect confidence that the declining order will find no means to protect itself. Every night we shall build our nostalgic family nest in tribute to ancestral memories. Every day we shall pursue through the fearful cane-brakes our unequal struggle with extinction. It is the hard way, ending with a whimper.

How can man get along without his wars and his weapons? It is the supreme question of the contemporary predicament. Have we within our human resource the capacity to discover new dreams, new dynamisms? Or are we so burdened by our illusions of central position, our romantic fallacies, and our pathetic rationalizations of the human condition that we can acknowledge no destiny beneath the human star but to go blindly blundering into a jingo jungle towards an indeterminate, inglorious, inexorable end?

The reader must sort out for himself, according to his own inclinations and judgement, the probabilities of the human outcome. But before we pass on to certain other consequences of our total animal legacy, I add a suggestion: If man is unique, and his soul some special creation, and his future is to be determined by his innate goodness, nobility, and wisdom, then he is finished. But if man is not unique, and his soul represents the product of hundreds of millions of patient years of animal evolution, and he approaches his crisis not as a lost lonely self-deluding being but as a proud creature bearing his in veins the tide of all life and in his genes the scars of the ages, then sentient man, sapient at last, has a future beyond the stormiest contradiction.

David Inglis | The Outlook for Nuclear Explosives

Nuclear weapons of the future will continue to be based on fission as the source of their energy. It is true that other ways of converting matter into energy are known to physicists, the most spectacular being the mutual annihilation of matter and "antimatter." Particles called antiprotons, antineutrons, and antielectrons (positrons) can be made in minute quantities and at great expense in high-energy experimental machines, and when one of these encounters its corresponding normal particle they both disappear, releasing a burst of energy. But the engineering problems of making and storing antimatter in militarily interesting quantities are so absurdly great that the possibility can be safely discounted for the foreseeable future.

It is likely, too, that existing explosives — uranium and plutonium for fission and lithium and heavy hydrogen for fusion — will continue to dominate in weapons. It is in principle possible that man-made elements heavier than plutonium might be used with the slight advantage of having smaller critical mass, but this is not a practical possibility, because it need not mean a much smaller weapon when the detonating device is included, because those heavier elements decay rapidly and thus cannot be stockpiled, and because their production and isolation in more than microscopic quantities is prohibitively expensive. For these reasons the postu-

SOURCE: *Unless Peace Comes: A Scientific Forecast of New Weapons,* edited by Nigel Calder. Copyright © 1968 by Nigel Calder. All rights reserved. Reprinted by permission of The Viking Press, Inc.

lated "californium bullet," for example, is no more than confusing fantasy.

Within the limitation of fission and fusion of the usual materials as the only energy sources, variations can be sought that may or may not have military significance. These include greater efficiency in using the nuclear explosives, and the development of very large or very "dirty" bombs, and very compact or relatively "clean" bombs.

The efficiency of existing bombs falls far short of one hundred per cent because the bomb blows itself apart so quickly that many nuclei do not have time to react. Much of the past effort to improve the bomb has been in this direction. The nature of recent testing programs suggests that the efficiency factor has been pushed about as far as is practicable; the situation is similar to that in automobiles — the current models are new in style but it is hard to discern any real improvement in terms of mileage per gallon.

For some purposes there will be a tendency toward more fusion and less fission, but for the biggest explosions the "dirty" bomb with much fission will probably be with us for a long time. There is no limit to how powerful an H-bomb may be made, nor to how dirty a "dirty" bomb may be made. It is possible that the arsenals of the future will include warheads much more powerful than present bombs. To put this possibility in perspective, one must, however, appreciate that a single large bomb is powerful enough practically to obliterate a large metropolitan area. There is thus no incentive to provide more powerful warheads than those in service, for the sake of destroying cities, or, more precisely, for being prepared to destroy them as part of the nuclear deterrent. But it is conceivable that incentives could be found for destroying still larger areas, such as whole forest regions, so as to ruin a land and deny sustenance to survivors of an all-city attack. During the last period of atmospheric testing the Soviet leaders talked of a one-hundred-megaton bomb, but actually did not go quite that far (fifty-seven megatons was the biggest they tested). The bigger bomb would have been feasible on either side, had this sort of incentive been felt. Such a bomb in appropriate weather would kindle forest fires over a radius of about 150 kilometers. It might also be useful in crushing blast shelters. If such a bomb is not made in the future, this will probably be either because restraining steps have been taken toward disarmament or because of the "law of diminishing returns"; six ten-megaton bombs would ignite as great an area as one dirty one-hundred-megaton bomb, with less world-wide radioactive fallout to react on the attacker.

It is technically possible to go very much further still, in deliberately making a very dirty bomb with the purpose of radioactive destruction of life on an entire hemisphere (northern or southern). In particular, the element cobalt when activated by a burst of neutrons from an H-bomb becomes a singularly powerful radioactive emitter of gamma radiation. The cobalt jacket would be wrapped around a big H-bomb, and there is no definite limit to the possible size of such a "cobalt bomb." Nevil Shute's novel *On the Beach*, set in Australia, carried a powerful message concerning the threat of nuclear war, but with a general euthanasia substituted for the horror of more likely forms of nuclear war and with some artistic license in the way the radioactivity destroyed all life on earth. The two main inaccuracies are that the attacking nation would have had no incentive to enter into a suicide pact with its enemies and that the nature of the atmospheric circulation would have confined the destruction to the northern hemisphere, at least for a longer time. Unless we can imagine an extremely hostile situation between the northern hemisphere as a whole and the southern hemisphere as a whole, we have little reason to worry that any nation will prepare a hemisphere bomb of this sort.

The strange name "doomsday machine" was introduced into nuclear strategy discussions to refer to a hypothetical instrument to obliterate life on earth at the push of a single button, a sort of *reductio ad absurdum* of the nuclear arms race. Such an infernal machine is not technically absurd. There is little doubt that it could be constructed — for example by means of a few widely dispersed cobalt bombs. It is of no use to anybody not bent on suicide, unless it be for blackmail by someone who can put on a convincing act of courting suicide, and it is not a serious candidate for future arsenals.

Improvements in the triggering process for H-bombs are difficult to predict with confidence, though it seems very likely that the possibilities have been practically exhausted. To be sure about sources of energy we only need to take inventory of the storehouse that nature has provided, but to anticipate triggering processes we have to predict limitations on future cleverness, and that is more difficult. The brute-force method of using chemical explosives alone — with a view to eliminating the fission stage of the present H-bomb — has not worked and is not expected to. I have already explained the need for violent collision to achieve fusion between nuclei. When the nuclei are as far apart as the size of an atom, the energy of the electric repulsion between them is only a little larger than typical chemical energies that also arise from electric forces at atomic distances — a few electron-volts. But nuclei are ten thousand times smaller than atoms, and the energies required to bang them together are more than ten thousand times the energy per atom given by a chemical explosion. For this reason a source of energy greatly surpassing chemical sources is needed to create the very high temperature to start the thermonuclear reaction between the light nuclei in an H-bomb. An A-bomb provides a concentration of energy about a million times as great as is available in an ordinary chemical explosive. There exist tricks for concentrating the energy of a large chemical explosive in a rather small volume, but it seems very unlikely that a factor of many thousand or a million can be gained in this way.

Beyond this one can imagine electromagnetic methods for concentrating energy, some of which have been tried in laboratory research on controlled, nonexplosive thermonuclear reactions. This field of technical development is being enthusiastically pursued on the basis of healthy, worldwide cooperation, in spite of the formidable difficulties of the instability that arises when one tries to concentrate sufficient energy in a small space to make a fusion process start on a modest scale in low-pressure gas. Although the situation is very different inside a solid body, it seems likely that difficulties of this general nature will also frustrate attempts to detonate an H-bomb without a fission trigger by electromagnetic means. On this point we cannot be sure, but even if such attempts should be successful in a large experimental device, it seems unlikely that the power plant to produce the electromagnetic heating could be miniaturized enough to be put in a practicable bomb or warhead. If both of these unlikely possibilities should materialize, we would have a somewhat cleaner and perhaps cheaper warhead — nothing to revolutionize warfare again. The fact that it would require no fissionable material would make the manufacture of H-bombs possible in countries that do not have the appropriate fissionable materials available. Less improbable, perhaps, is the eventual design of efficient H-bombs using a plutonium trigger if, indeed, present H-bomb triggers are essentially uranium-235, as is suggested by Sir John Cockcroft in the previous chapter. Then, with the rapid development of power reactors in many countries, which are potential sources of military-grade plutonium, it would become much easier for those countries to acquire H-bombs.

Thus an A-bomb has been necessary to trigger an H-bomb up till now, and will probably remain the only way to do it in the foreseeable future or, if not the only way, the only compact and convenient way. It is important to make this clear because the claim has been made that a fission-free fusion bomb might soon be developed. The claim was made most loudly by Senator Dodd of Connecticut while opposing the comprehensive test ban treaty in 1959. He implied that, if underground tests were allowed to go on another three years, such a bomb could be developed. They have and it hasn't, and for the reasons stated it is not expected.

In the category of "tactical" nuclear weapons, intended to be used as firepower for ground armies, some fantastic claims have been made about new possibilities, particularly concerning the "neutron bomb" that might slowly kill soldiers by neutron irradiation without doing as much property damage as is normal with nuclear weapons. Here the dream of a really cheap fission-free bomb has been hailed as making possible greatly increased firepower on the battlefield. Aside from the technical implausibility, this enthusiasm seems to be based on a lack of appreciation of the destructive power of even "small" nuclear weapons. They may be "only" about as powerful as the Hiroshima bomb and on down to a tenth or even a hundredth of that power. They have been made compact enough to be shot from large cannon (or presumably to be carried on the backs of saboteurs), but they will probably not be made much smaller. If ever used in more than extremely modest numbers they will make battling armies obsolete and defence of territory equivalent to its devastation. Field commanders are subject to the temptation to use nuclear blasts for special purposes such as creating transportation bottlenecks, but if once they were used in war conditions, escalation would be almost automatic up to the big nuclear weapons that hold the greater interest and terror. To avoid this, if there must be conventional wars at all, it is vitally important that they be restrained to stay below the well-defined line between conventional and nuclear weapons.

About the likely course of the future development of new kinds of nuclear bombs and warheads, as distinct from delivery vehicles, we can say in summary, then, that there seems to be no room for great new surprises, if we shun technical and strategic absurdities. Nuclear weapons of a given power may become slightly more compact, but not much more. The range of power per bomb can be extended, but it cannot be very much extended usefully because present bombs are already so terribly powerful. It is not impossible, though it is unlikely, that the requirement for a fission trigger of an H-bomb can be eliminated to make H-bombs cheaper, but they are already remarkably cheap relative to their destructive power, so that the increased cheapness, if it should materialize, would be important only in hastening proliferation of nuclear weapons among countries not yet possessing them.

Must the Bombs Multiply?

One might be tempted to conclude from this that there is nothing to worry about, that the worst of nuclear weapons have probably been developed, and that we've become accustomed to living with them. The conclusion is far from justified. The world situation that we have been so lucky to live through these last few years is an awfully unsafe one in which no sane race of beings would choose to live if it could help it. Our having been lucky does not mean that we are safe, even though most of us have permitted ourselves to become unaware of the nuclear threat under which we live.

There is already enough explosive power in the arsenals of the nuclear giants to provide the equivalent of over a hundred tons of TNT for each inhabitant of the world. An ounce of TNT exploded close to a person can be lethal. The total is already well over a million megatons and may soon, for reasons we shall see, be approaching a hundred million megatons. Less than ten years ago we were talking of stockpiles of ten thousand megatons as potentially almost unimaginably destructive, with one megaton being capable of destroying a large city.

Up to now, most of the missiles of each of the nuclear giants, the United States and the Soviet Union, have been aimed at the other giant, and the main danger, that of an outbreak of nuclear war between them, has been deterred by the respect each has for the power of the other. This is the apparently stable balance in which we have developed too much confidence. The prospect has been that a war would bring damage almost entirely to the giants and perhaps some of their immediate allies, with some serious local fallout spilling over the borders and with long-range fallout remaining not really very serious for most other countries. Here the most serious threat to the distant countries would be economic dislocation, unless it be some unanticipated world-wide plague. Bad as the prospect has been, it has been one that many of the countries of the world could reasonably view with greater complacency than could the nuclear giants who would bear the brunt of the attacks.

But in the absence of arms control, the moderately good side of even this bad situation cannot last. Even though the *kinds* of nuclear explosives may change very little, the increasing *number* of weapons can make the situation much worse in at least two ways, each of which makes the other more serious. The first is that the weight of explosives used in a prospective war between the nuclear giants will become so enormous that there will be "no place to hide" — that all countries will be disastrously damaged by the fallout. The second is that there will be so many nations equipped with nuclear weapons that the outbreak of nuclear war between some pair of them, possibly triggering one between the nuclear giants, will become very likely.

As matters have recently stood, there appeared to be signs that the total power of the nuclear weapons in the arsenals of the nuclear giants was leveling off, as though each side was becoming content with its possibility of inflicting terrible damage on the other and found it unnecessary to expend resources on a further build-up if the other side did not. The fact that the two opposing arsenals were not equal appeared to be considered relatively unimportant because the smaller was so enormous in its destructive power as to provide adequate deterrence.

Recently a new element has been introduced into the balance — the possibility of providing a partial defence against oncoming ballistic missiles. Although the idea of self-defence sounds innocuous, and an impenetrable defence could provide an entirely different basis for world stability, a merely partially effective defence can curiously be a very upsetting element in this otherwise fairly stable balance. There is no prospect of a completely impervious defence, but the possibility of a partly effective defensive system, based on the "antiballistic missile," or ABM, is at hand for both of the nuclear giants. Both the Soviet Union and, more recently, the United States, have started ABM deployment on a relatively small scale, probably for political more than military reasons. It is to be hoped that the scale will remain small, for a serious offence-defence race — as a new dimension of the arms race — would drastically increase international tension and the nuclear threat.

If, starting with stabilized numbers of intercontinental missiles, one side installs a substantial ABM system, the second side can respond by building more missiles to penetrate the defence and the first side is no safer than before. The interception by ABMS is estimated to be sufficiently inefficient for the cost to the second side of building the additional intercontinental missiles to be less than the cost of the ABM system to the first side. On a cost-effectiveness basis, there is thus no rational reason for the first side to start this step in the competition in the first place. However, military demands are seldom long delayed by cost-effectiveness arguments, and the usual experience is that what can be built will be built. The hope of arms control is to break this trend at some point, but lacking such artificial restraint, the likelihood is that the initiative in starting ABM deployment will be answered both by more intercontinental missiles and by some ABMS on the second side, to which the first side will respond with more ABMS to try to stop the missiles and more missiles to get past the ABMS, and so forth. Thus, in place of an arms race practically stopped, the ABM can, and probably will, carry a new arms race to entirely new dimensions.

The important point is that this process adds enormously to the numbers of nuclear weapons that would be used in a war between the nuclear giants and implies an amount of fallout that would spare no nation on earth, or at least none in the northern hemisphere.

The ABM possibility is thus a destabilizing factor, an effect arising partly from the uncertainty of performance of the ABMS. Suffice it to say here that future developments will probably involve several stages of counter-measures, the anti-anti-anti-ballistic missile, or methods to foil penetration aids and then ways to foil these methods, and that the ABMS themselves will have nuclear warheads.

For the types of ABMS that explode in the atmosphere and fairly near the targets they are trying to protect, the explosive power will be limited by the need to avoid damage by the ABM itself to the city being protected. Such close-in ABM bursts are being planned because of the necessity of distinguishing between an intercontinental-missile warhead and its accompanying swarm of light-metal "decoys" by the way they slow down in the atmosphere. Being limited in power, such an ABM must come fairly close to the warhead to destroy it, perhaps within a few hundred meters or so (the size of the fireball). But there will also be ABMS that explode outside the atmosphere far away from the defended area. They can be made very powerful, and the X-rays that they emit can be intense enough to damage an oncoming intercontinental missile at a distance of perhaps several miles. The desire to put up such an instantaneous X-ray shield to intercept as much of the swarm of unidentified decoys, including somewhere the warhead itself, as may be aimed at a large metropolitan area provides the incentive for using powerful warheads in the ABMS. Their power will be limited by the instantaneous radiation damage on the ground and people below, from the gamma rays (that make skin burns and leukemia as at Hiroshima), and from heat that starts fires. At heights of hundreds of kilometers, even these limitations permit bursts of tens of megatons, perhaps more powerful than the oncoming intercontinental missiles against which they are deployed. Even though they are exploded above the atmosphere, about half of their radioactive products descend into the atmosphere and contribute to fallout.

Such an ABM "shield" is only an instantaneous flash, so at least one ABM is needed for each oncoming intercontinental missile (since they won't attack in squad formation). An intercontinental attack may be concentrated on a region, so the defence might desire as many of these ABMS in *each* region to be defended as there are intercontinental missiles in the opponent's arsenal. Thus the potential military demands become enormous indeed in this defence-offence race. It seems likely that the cheapness and compactness of a "dirty" bomb will lead to its use in the above-the-atmosphere ABMS. It is conceivable that one day the size of the world's arsenal will be limited only by the available amount of fissionable material, although the limitation is more likely to remain, for the time being, in the cost of the delivery vehicles.

Without an ABM race, the hope remains that such enormous quantities will never be prepared for delivery, in keeping with the tendency for numbers of missiles to taper off toward a constant level. But if the world embarks on stage after stage of great competition, the demand for actual weapons will be unlimited and the prospect will be of a large part of the available explosive stuff being used in an all-out nuclear war.

Some proponents of ABMS favor them partly in the hope that their deployment would lead to their further improvement, so that they might eventually be able to intercept most of a massive attack. Enigmatically, this would probably only make the situation worse for the noncombatants and no better for the combatants. Without ABMS, an all-out war between the nuclear giants might be over in hours, one or both sides having been beaten into collapse or submission by use of considerably less than total stockpiles. With very efficient ABMS, let us say ninety-nine per cent efficient or more as an extreme hypothesis, the war might take years as initial arsenals were first exhausted and then improvised means of delivery were substituted to use more and more of the explosive material that had not been made into weapons in advance. The nuclear giants might be destroyed as before, but in this case would drag the rest of the world down with them by means of fallout.

In summary, increase in number is a more menacing aspect of the future of nuclear weapons than development in kind, though both types of change will make the future more difficult to handle and intensify the threat to civilization. Familiarity has bred contempt, while the world and its statesmen have become inured to "living with the bomb" and fatigued with patient negotiations that have done little more than hide a lack of decision. Yet we have actually lived through only a very few years, too few to be significant as a precedent, of the small end of a nuclear arms race that will become even more overwhelming if rational steps are not soon taken to terminate it and to deflect the efforts of mankind into more constructive channels.

Carl-Göran Hedén | # The Infectious Dust Cloud

The discovery of new weapons often becomes the subject of sensationalism and exaggeration, and one tends to forget that there is normally a considerable time lag between laboratory results and operational "hardware." However, this interval may be smaller in the case of biological weapons (BW) than for many other types of armament. There are now enough indications in military innovations in the biological field to predict a weapons system that will offer an enormous offensive potential at the same time as it will introduce staggering defence problems.

The offensive potential of biological weapons depends on five main factors:

1. the possibility of choosing a microorganism or a toxin tailored to the military need, whether it is to incapacitate the opponent temporarily (e.g., with certain viruses), to eliminate him permanently (e.g., with plague), or to attack his crops (e.g., with wheat rust);

2. a high effect on the human, animal, or plant targets, in relation to the weight and cost of the weapon;

3. a psychological effect based on the likelihood that very large groups of civilian and military personnel would be affected;

4. the imperceptible and insidious character of the attack, involving extremely difficult defence problems because of the large number of methods of delivery potentially available to the enemy;

5. the absence of physical damage to buildings and other structures would enable the attacker to take over the material resources of the territory.

Although infectious diseases have always been a serious problem for armies, biological warfare has, with few exceptions, been attempted only in a crude way and never as a major weapons system. In 1942 a military microbiologist could express the view that "it is highly questionable if biological agents are suitable for warfare" and as late as 1958 the American

SOURCE: *Unless Peace Comes: A Scientific Forecast of New Weapons,* edited by Nigel Calder. Copyright © 1968 by Nigel Calder. All rights reserved. Reprinted by permission of The Viking Press, Inc.

civil defence authorities still regarded the risk of biological and chemical attack as slight. Since then, however, there has been a re-evaluation of the situation, and several special investigations have emphasized the advances made in the handling of biological aerosols (dust clouds) and have put biological and chemical agents in the same class as nuclear weapons. One now comes acrosss authoritative statements like: "The offensive use of biological agents is feasible," and "Biological agents exist which can be used strategically to cause casualties in an area the width of a continent." A Russian colonel in 1959 went as far as to say that "from results of comparative studies of the losses of life from conventional weapons, war poisons, and atomic energy on one side and losses from biological weapons on the other, it is believed today that a biological war would have the greatest effect of all." Biological warfare has in fact given us the most forceful instance so far of the truth of Isador Rabi's observation that "the combining of military techniques and science makes it easy to apply scientific principles to kill people — who are not strong structures."

Very little has been published about the Soviet study of biological warfare, but a high level of civil defence preparedness indicates that it has attracted much attention; that would hardly have been the case were there no first-hand information on the offensive potential. In fact, it was claimed that, when the American program started to expand in 1959, the U.S.S.R. led the United States. The American level of expenditure for research and development in chemical and biological warfare then climbed from around $35 million per year to about $150 million by 1964, so it is conceivable that the supposed gap has now been closed, particularly if one adds the British and Canadian investments of funds and personnel.

Simple competition may partly explain the biological arms race, but technical factors have provided fuel for it. In the first place, strategy is becoming more and more dependent upon civil defence, and microbiological weapons are well suited for large-scale civilian targets. Some of their inherent characteristics, such as the incubation period and the possibilities for protection of one's own forces, add a certain amount of freedom to their strategic use and also offer advantages for counterinsurgency operations and in fighting limited wars.

Secondly, recent progress in medical and biological research is easily applicable to biological warfare. Our knowledge about the immunological and biochemical relations between the infectious agent and its victim has increased immensely. Methods for genetic manipulation of bacteria and viruses have been found, so that essentially new disease agents can be devised, against which defence preparations are almost impossible. Moreover, techniques for the mass production of most types of microorganism have been highly developed for the purposes of medical research and for making vaccines.

Again, earlier doubts about the striking power of isolated infectious agents have been rendered obsolete by extensive tests on animals and human volunteers. The doses needed for infection of humans have been established for several agents. For instance, about twenty-five inhaled cells of the bacterium *F. tularensis* are required to induce rabbit fever (a prostrating but not often fatal disease). In the case of Q-fever (a debilitating disease) even a single inhaled particle of *R. burneti* might be sufficient to cause infection, so that, in theory, three grams of embryonic chicken tissue inoculated with Q-fever might hold enough infectious doses for the entire human population of the world. Of course the logistics of distribution and the decay rate of infectivity are not considered in this estimate.

Finally, it has been shown that a large number of infectious agents and toxins can be disseminated in the form of aerosols. The discovery that diseases that are normally spread only by insects might be disseminated in this way is of particular interest because it means that in those cases there would be no person-to-person spread beyond the selected target area.

Present Inhibitions

Why, then, have biological weapons not yet been used on a large scale? This is a very difficult question to answer, but the following points may be considered:

1. that the military need has not yet arisen;
2. that critical problems in the production, storage, and delivery of some agents, judged necessary to make up a fully operational system, have not yet been solved;
3. that the potential attacker's own biological defences are not adequate or have not been fully tested. The existence of a sophisticated aerosol warning system in a country might for instance not be enough to induce that country to use infectious aerosols offensively, since this could invite biological sabotage acts that would circumvent that particular type of defence;
4. that the popular concept of biological weapons as terror agents makes their use most distasteful, at least in countries with a free press and a democratic system of government;
5. that the value of such weapons is relatively less to the nuclear-armed powers, which also have a great potential for biological warfare, than to the smaller, nonnuclear nations, which have a more limited capability;
6. that all the tactical and strategic implications — for example, the opportunities for small groups of men to bring about devastating reprisals — have not yet been given serious attention in discussions of military policy;
7. that the exact target area and the long-range ecological consequences are very difficult, and occasionally impossible, to predict. We actually lack much knowledge of the susceptibility of many of the mammals, birds, reptiles, amphibia, and insects that would be exposed during an aerosol

attack. Even the most perfect physical protection of man would be useless if he would later become the victim of newly established disease reservoirs in animals and insects;

8. that there exists a sort of *pactum turpae* based upon the unpredictability and complicated consequences of a biological attack. These must introduce very disturbing elements in the fashionable mathematical mode of military thinking. One simulated attack, for example, is said to have killed or incapacitated 600,000 friendly or neutral civilians at the same time as it eliminated seventy-five per cent of the opposing troops.

How long the period of grace may last, when it rests on as complex a foundation as this, is impossible to tell, but the psychological factors that underlie the Geneva Protocol of 1925 still seem to exert a strong inhibitory influence.

Delivering the Dose

The possibility of disseminating biological agents over very large areas has been demonstrated in field tests involving both inert particles and harmless bacterial spores. For instance, a cloud of inorganic particles (200 kilograms generated along a 250-kilometer stretch of coast) spread over about 88,000 square kilometers of land, where a minimum dose of fifteen and a maximum dose of 15,000 particles per minute were inhaled. In an experiment with bacterial spores, 600 liters of suspension were sprayed from the deck of a ship running on a three-kilometer course about three kilometers off shore, at right angles to an onshore wind. The meteorological situation was such that there was a slight tendency for the aerosol to rise and become diluted. Nevertheless, the cloud could be followed about thirty-seven kilometers, providing "infectious doses," even inside buildings, over some 250 square kilometers. Of course, the implications of a test of this sort can be downgraded in so far as it concerned a very hardy spore, but many years ago guinea pigs were successfully infected with bacteria in a more vulnerable (vegetative) form that had traveled nearly twenty-five kilometers in an aerosol. Indeed, aerosolized vegetative cells of a harmless bacterium have been made nearly as stable as the spores used in the field test mentioned earlier.

Besides a "biological decay," which is attributed to irradiation (notably by ultraviolet from the sun) or to unfavorable humidity, an infectious aerosol cloud is also subject to "physical decay." There is a progressive reduction in the effective particle concentration due to dilution, settling out under gravity, washing out by rainfall, and impact upon surfaces.

If an aerosol is generated along a line perpendicular to the wind direction, loss by lateral diffusion is significant only at the ends of the cloud: diffusion along the wind direction does not alter the total dose presented. Vertical mixing, on the other hand, may cause a rapid drop in the particle concentration. That is why an aerosol attack is most likely on a clear night when the ground loses heat by radiation and there is a "lid" of warm air to limit the upward movement of the aerosol. Very large areas could be involved by exploitation of the so-called polar outbreaks, wherein a layer of cold air a kilometer or more in thickness could carry an aerosol for hundreds of kilometers at speeds of thirty to forty kilometers per hour.

The effects of microbiological weapons, compared with their weight, are such that an attacker might easily increase the quantity released, to compensate for the decay, if he provides only "standard" protection for the active material and gives due consideration to its state at the time of release. If *F. tularensis* (rabbit fever) were aerosolized, it could perhaps be assumed that its capacity for infecting humans falls off at the same rate as it does on guinea pigs. Initially, the infectious dose for those animals is around ten to twenty cells, but it increases to about 150 to 200 when the aerosol is five and a half hours old. A relatively small amount of material would provide this dose over hundreds of square kilometers. Theoretical calculations clearly indicate the possibility of large-scale coverage, even allowing for a decay of, say, two per cent of the particles every minute. A midnight dispersion of five liters per kilometer of a suspension holding ten million million (10^{13}) particles per liter at an altitude of 100 meters along a fifty-kilometer line would — given a reasonable generator efficiency, certain meteorological conditions, and a wind speed of twenty kilometers per hour — set up a cylindrical cloud that would pass a downwind point in less than a minute. A person breathing at a rate of ten liters per minute would be exposed to about 150,000 particles. If this happened to him at 2 A.M., only 150 of those particles would still be active; in other words, the agent should have an infectious dose of not more than 150 viable particles in order to cause disease forty kilometers downwind. An individual exposed to the same cloud 120 kilometers downwind, at 6 A.M., would only contract the disease if the agent used had an infectious dose of 1.5 particles. By this time the coverage would be 6000 square kilometers.

The size of aerosol generators that would be used in limited attacks (on parliament buildings, military staff headquarters, and so on) would be so small that they could easily be concealed by a saboteur. He would certainly be vaccinated and could arrange to leave the scene in ample time before cases would start to appear; in the case of an attack with *F. tularensis*, for instance, some two to five days would elapse before the disease symptoms (fever, headache, malaise, sore throat, muscular ache, and chest pains) would begin to make themselves felt.

The conventional image of biological warfare, the covert "man with the suitcase" poisoning water supplies and ventilation systems, seems to have been discarded by many experts in the field, but this attitude may well prove to be premature, at least if one considers specific situations, for instance a sanitary breakdown due to a nuclear attack or mobilization, when the psychological repercussions of a covert biological attack might be very severe. A number of tendencies in a modern society pave the way for such attacks. Extensive and rapid communications increase the "coverage" by a lone man. Urbanization concentrates his targets in small areas. Increasing sizes in slaughterhouses, dairies, and food processing factories, and the extensive use of uniform cultivated crops, large herds of animals, and centralized fodder manufacture, make food supplies very vulnerable; similarly the development of large reservoirs increases the effectiveness of individual attacks on water supplies. Central ventilation systems in command centers, subways, cinemas, theaters, restaurants, and so on, provide a ready-made means of distributing biological agents, while society's dependence on key personnel — radar and missile operators, crews of ships, and workers in power communications, and transport services — makes them desirable targets. Such individuals are frequently confined to environments where conventional sabotage acts might be more difficult to carry out than the introduction of a biological agent with an incubation time giving a saboteur many days to escape.

Indeed, the most disturbing aspect of biological warfare is the possibility that it might give to small groups of individuals to upset the strategic balance. It is, for instance, hard to dismiss as unrealistic an example given by Dr. Brock Chisholm, formerly head of the World Health Organization. He has speculated about a hypothetical nation making an attack on the United States by 100 vaccinated agents using botulinus toxin as the weapon. Each would import a few pounds in a body belt and proceed to one of the major cities, power sites, or military centers. At a prearranged time each would take a small private plane from the local airport and then dust his target from the windward side with the aid of a small, easily made apparatus. Fatalities after such an attack might range from forty to nearly one hundred per cent, and the attack might well be blamed on the U.S.S.R. Nuclear weapons would then be fired, and retaliation from the U.S.S.R. would be automatic and immediate.

Why Defence is Difficult

The microbiological agents that might be used for offensive purposes represent a whole range of weapons systems rather than a single type of weapon. Antipersonnel, antianimal and anticrop agents all pose different defence problems; an open aerosol attack would represent one weapons system and a covert dissemination of infected insects another, quite different system. The situation is further complicated by the various means an enemy might employ in order to enhance his attack. Radiation from nuclear fallout would aggravate the results of an aerosol attack on man or animals by lowering natural resistance. Carriers like crystal needles might help viruses to penetrate plants. Elimination of chlorination would permit or simplify an attack on water supplies. And so on.

Specific prophylaxis, by vaccination for example, or cultivation of disease-resistant crop plants, has a very severe limitation because of the great range of weapons potentially available to the enemy, who might well use microorganisms made resistant to standard prophylactic and therapeutic measures. Consequently, nonspecific protection by physical and chemical means is essential. The possibilities include: particle filtration in gas masks; sterile ventilation in shelters and command centers at pressures above that of the atmosphere outside; sterilization and hermetic packaging in the food and beverage industries; conventional chlorination in waterworks, and so on. However, continuous physical protection would hardly be acceptable — particularly in "peacetime," when a surprise attack might well be launched — so an effective defence would presuppose a detection network including a sophisticated array of early-warning, sampling, and identification devices.

One of the technical difficulties in aerosol warning is the normal "background" of biological material in the air, and this changes with the time and place, making it necessary to base a setting of the alarm threshold on a thorough knowledge of the local situation. The concentration of viable aerobic bacteria is usually less than one per liter of outdoor air, and the protein content is around three billionths of a gram per liter. Automatic warning devices would have to measure such minute quantities of protein (or nucleic acid) continuously, and that involves a range of very difficult technical problems. Also the particle content in the narrow size range critical for infectivity would have to be monitored.

At the present time it seems necessary to combine several principles of detection and to rely on human integration of many factors, including weather conditions, in order to issue an alarm. Many sophisticated warning systems are conceivable, but considering the multitude of routes available for delivery and the great number of agents that the enemy might choose, it is highly improbable that any system will ever be able to prevent the occurrence of very significant numbers of clinical cases in the event of an attack.

Speed in the laboratory identification process is essential, since large groups of individuals would have to be detained and also because it may be too late to institute treatment by the time a clinical diagnosis is made. In the case of inhalation anthrax, treatment should start when the symptoms are vague and before the condition becomes alarming. Pneumonic plague has a mortality close to one hundred per cent if treatment is not instituted within twenty to twenty-four hours of exposure, and an early treatment is also important in the case of rabbit fever. Obviously the speed of identification required is a challenge to the microbiologist; only under exceptional conditions, where defective munitions, expended spray devices, or vector containers are recovered, would he have more than a minute amount of material available for study immediately after an attack. Microbiological laboratories themselves would be choice targets, and of course there is plenty of scope for using a multiplicity of agents to confuse the identifications.

However, biological warfare is a challenge to the microbiological profession, not only from a technical but also from an ethical point of view.

A Short Anthology of Poems About War

THE DEATH OF THE BALL TURRET GUNNER

From my mother's sleep I fell into the State,
And I hunched in its belly till my wet fur froze.
Six miles from earth, loosed from its dream of life,
I woke to black flak and the nightmare fighters.
When I died they washed me out of the turret with a hose.

RANDALL JARRELL

XXXVI

Here dead we lie because we did not choose
   To live and shame the land from which we sprung.
Life, to be sure, is nothing much to lose;
   But young men think it is, and we were young.

A. E. HOUSMAN

SOURCE: *The Complete Poems* by Randall Jarrell. Copyright © 1945, 1969 by Mrs. Randall Jarrell. Reprinted by permission of Farrar, Straus, and Giroux, Inc.

SOURCE: *The Collected Poems of A. E. Housman.* Copyright 1936 by Barclays Bank Limited. Copyright © 1964 by Robert E. Symons. Reprinted by permission of Holt, Rinehart and Winston, Inc., The Society of Authors as literary representatives of the estate of A. E. Housman, and Jonathan Cape, Ltd.

AN IRISH AIRMAN FORESEES HIS DEATH

I know that I shall meet my fate
Somewhere among the clouds above;
Those that I fight I do not hate,
Those that I guard I do not love;
My country is Kiltartan Cross,
My countrymen Kiltartan's poor,
No likely end could bring them loss
Or leave them happier than before.
No law, nor duty made me fight,
Nor public men, nor cheering crowds,
A lonely impulse of delight
Drove to this tumult in the clouds;
I balanced all, brought all to mind,
The years to come seemed waste of breath,
A waste of breath the years behind
In balance with this life, this death.

W. B. YEATS

THE GENERAL

'Good-morning; good-morning!' the General said
When we met him last week on our way to the line.
Now the soldiers he smiled at are most of 'em dead,
And we're cursing his staff for incompetent swine.
'He's a cheery old card,' grunted Harry to Jack
As they slogged up to Arras with rifle and pack.
. . . .
But he did for them both by his plan of attack.

SIEGFRIED SASSOON

SOURCE: *The Collected Poems of W. B. Yeats.* Copyright 1919 by the Macmillan Company, renewed 1947 by Bertha Georgie Yeats. Reprinted by permission of M. B. Yeats and Macmillan Company.

SOURCE: *The Collected Poems of Siegfried Sassoon.* Copyright 1918 by E. P. Dutton and Co., renewed 1946 by Siegfried Sassoon. Reprinted by permission of The Viking Press and George T. Sassoon.

MEDIA

6

In Paris in 1787, Thomas Jefferson followed reports from home of the framing of the Constitution. Shays' Rebellion had thrown many of the constitution drafters into a panic that was reflected in the strong power they proposed to give the federal government. The Bill of Rights was going to have to await Jefferson's return to his homeland, but, meanwhile, in letters Jefferson urged that the power of government be severely curtailed, telling James Madison, "I am not a friend to a very energetic government." He developed the line of argument that Thoreau so avidly seized upon a century and a half later when in "Civil Disobedience" he announced that that government was best that governed least.

But how meaningful could such assertions be in the face of the fact that if the government were not given repressive powers — especially the government of an infant nation — disorders would occur with such frequency the public welfare might be destroyed and the people could well become so distraught that they would accept tyranny so long as it restored order? Even as Jefferson asked himself this question he supplied the answer:

> And say, finally, whether peace is best preserved by giving energy to the government, or information to the people. This last is the most certain and the most legitimate engine of government. Educate and inform the whole mass of the people. Enable them to see that it is their interest to preserve peace and order and they will preserve them.

Law and order, or as Jefferson phrased it, peace and order, through the dissemination of information to the people rather than through energetic governmental action. The news media had their mandate.

The only press that could answer such a mandate was a free press and this created problems. The historian Charles Beard observed:

> In its origin freedom of the press had little or nothing to do with truth-telling. In fact most of the early newspapers established in the United

States after the adoption of the Constitution were partisan sheets devoted to savage attacks on party opponents. If we are to take George Washington's own statement at face value, it was scurrilous abuse by the press which drove him into retirement at the end of his second term. Freedom of the press means the right to be just or unjust, partisan or nonpartisan, true or false, in news column and editorial column.

The issue that developed in the course of American history, then, has been a question not so much of freedom versus repression as one of whether there could be such a thing as a press that combined freedom with responsibility. Under the ethic of *laissez-faire* capitalism prevalent for so much of that history the answer seemed to be no. One cynical New York newspaperman in the heyday of wide-open journalism put it this way: "The fundamental principle of metropolitan journalism is to buy white paper at three cents a pound and sell it at ten cents a pound. And in some quarters it does not matter how much the virgin whiteness of the paper is defiled so long as the defilement sells the paper."

Historians of journalism demonstrate that the situation improved greatly in the twentieth century and that especially since the 1930's American newspapers have, in the main, distinguished themselves by their responsible use of freedom. And surely the newspaper appears to be acting in the most responsible way when it takes as a fundamental right the people's "right to know" and acts as the agent of the people in persistently seeking access to information that some, especially politicians and government officials, just as persistently seek to withhold.

But the contemporary situation has a worrisome side to it. Big, wide-circulation metropolitan newspapers are diminishing in number, and, on the surface at least, the people have a narrower choice of where to go for their news. This is the direct result of the fact that enormous capital is required to run a newspaper. At the same time, the other news media, chiefly radio and television, also require such enormous capital investments that a porridge-like sameness seems to spread over all of them — indeed, in some areas organs of all three media have the same owners. The immense amount of money invested requires an immense number of customers, and whatever the positive rules are for acquiring such customers, the chief negative one appears to be "Don't offend!"

Thus, it can be argued that the large news media today even as they talk of freedom with responsibility more often emphasize freedom with respectability. The people's right to know may be a right while the people's desire to be left undisturbed by the discontented may be a weakness in need of correction, but it too is very often treated as a right. The talk and behavior of one or another odd group of people might be seen as a call for social justice, but since it is a minority view it can also be reported as something deviant and essentially unconnected with the reality of the mass of news consumers. Too often respectability dictates that the media make the latter response.

Television has had an important effect on this situation besides that which grows from its own financial need to be respectable. The instantaneous transmitted picture of the clubbing of a demonstrator surpasses in immediacy any written description that follows the event. Yet the ultimate effect seems far less powerful than that of the written word. The television picture arrives at the portals of the viewer's consciousness as an isolated and framed episode that possesses no vitality beyond its immediacy. Its appeal is to the observer in us rather than the participant.

An analogy may be drawn if we remember the difference in the feelings created by a baseball game and a play. Few baseball games build into a total experience. Rather, the most wretched fielding or decisive batting can occur out of any kind of order we would desire were we to write a plot of the game. The element of the unexpected, of course, is why we like baseball, but it is also why, after the day has faded, we are more likely to remember that we saw Joe Hero hit a home run or we saw Joe Goat drop a fly than we are to feel that we have participated in an experience that has in any way altered us.

The theater, on the other hand, does not ask us to be spectators but makes us participants. This is as true of the classical and Shakespearean theater as it is of the more raucous, self-proclaimed "total" theater. We do not go home remembering we were there the day Lear carried the body of his daughter, or the day Creon argued with Antigone; rather, we carry with us the effect of the whole — of the way in which the web of cause and effect was matched in our emotions by a series of expectations, dreads, fulfillments, and griefs that built into an integrated experience.

The television news item presents itself to consciousness like the home run. Stark and thrilling as it may be it yields almost immediately to a disconnected item, and once we become habituated, as we all do, to the uniformity of the series of episodes we watch on television, then in a subtle way the news becomes disconnected from us, inconsequential except as immediate spectacle. An increase in violence does not yield an increase in consequence. Indeed, the reverse may take place as we learn to peer in on war with the same equanimity we possess when the news ends with a look at the grand champion of a dog show.

The immediacy of television reporting and the uniformity of detail in its images create an emptiness of feeling. We develop a hunger for consequences, a whetted appetite that wants to *feel* when we learn what is happening to our fellow humans, not just to observe. The rise of underground radio, underground theater, and underground press may more accurately be attributed to the growth of this appetite than to any intellectual desire to get another point of view. Although it is true that the Underground, as its very name is designed to show, is offering opinions in opposition to established views, this opposition can easily be exaggerated. The underground, after all, offers the views to the converted rather than the heathen, and its audience has been converted by the information made available to it through more conventional channels. This is to say the underground media cannot be compared with the dissenting pamphlet of the eighteenth century (Tom Paine's *Common Sense* is a good example) that presented a point of view too often silenced by the Establishment and in presenting it moved the minds of many to a change in outlook.

But the Underground does work on our desire to escape the somnambulism of our spectatorship and to feel our common bond with the starved, the beaten, and the bombed of this world. The partiality of its views — more severe, more prejudiced, even, than the views of the Establishment — is not the essential fact its critics assume it to be. What is important is that through a variety of experimental devices, including prolonged exercises in bad taste, the Underground is responding to our urge to escape the numbness that television has produced with its pictures and to experience with commensurate feelings the joys and horrors of our fellow humans. The novocained lip yearns alike for the pleasure of the kiss and the pain of the bite.

However one may wish to do battle with Marshall McLuhan's specific contentions about media, his central contention that the medium is the message must be confronted. The effect of television is clearly far more potent than its content. Where McLuhan may be challenged is in his assumption that consciousness is, finally, smaller than the medium that acts upon it, and that therefore any reaction to the medium, such as that of the Underground, is inevitably committed to a program that imitates the medium.

If the establishment and most influential media in America may be accused of having confused respectability with responsibility, the rebellion against this situation — occurring chiefly in books, journals, and movies — may well be accused of confusing nonconformity with art. A greater legal freedom for the presentation of controversial matters, chiefly in the verbal and pictorial representation of sexual acts, has brought about a steeplechase to the frontiers of outrage. Those who believe themselves in the front of the race for freedom of artistic expression find themselves accompanied, stride for stride, by the pornographers. Voyeurism is a leisure activity and an industry has grown up to supply it just as industries have grown up in our wealthy society to support sports and do-it-yourself activities.

It is difficult if not impossible to keep artistic freedom and pornography apart. But more importantly, is it *necessary* at this juncture to keep them apart? That is, what benefit will society derive from continuing to maintain a legal distinction between the two? The real distinction that exists becomes clear on the open market when the two are permitted to compete side by side. Then pornography loses its novelty quickly and bores all save that relative few who, as Gillian Freeman argues, use it to fill a psychological need. But while the market is rigged by laws, the distinctions are blurred and neither the artistic nor the shoddy attain their potential, find their real value.

Indeed, with respect to the movies in particular, Pauline Kael's observations seem to indicate that greater permissiveness is damaging not because of any "harmful" new content that can now be exhibited, but because the freedom to present such has blinded too many film makers to the principles of their art. There is something "phonier" about a naturalistic, sexual epic shot with a hand-held camera and representing itself as a searching investigation into the modern condition, than there is about Fred Astaire and Ginger Rogers tap-dancing down a brilliantly lit crystal staircase in a world that never existed.

The world that never existed except as a place of escape in the dark is now discredited. Yet, as this brief view of the condition of the media has attempted to show, some advances in the media today, principally in reportage on television and sexual frankness in the movies, have transformed reality itself into a detached spectacle that has the distance of fantasy without fantasy's power to transform or at least refresh us. Perhaps this is why unabashed fantasies so different from one another as those of Tolkien and Henry Miller have both acquired a wide contemporary popularity.

At any rate, when it comes to the media we are all experts. Each of us has had as much experience with them as any of us. There is no reason in the world, therefore, why we should not all be vocal critics. This is one pot that is not, in the foreseeable future, going to be spoiled by too many cooks. Quite the reverse.

James Reston | # The News: What Can Be Done?

The Terrors of Competition

In the State Department, the Foreign Service officers have a fable. The grasshopper, worried about getting through the winter, sought advice from the cockroach, who seemed to thrive on cold weather. The cockroach was sympathetic. On the night of the first frost, he suggested, find a warm spot back of a radiator in a bakery, turn yourself into a cockroach, and stay happily there until spring. "But how," asked the grasshopper, "do I make myself into a cockroach?" "Look," the cockroach replied, "I'm merely giving you policy guidance."

Most critics of the press give much the same kind of policy guidance: change and be saved, they say. Transform yourselves into something quite different from what you are; stop giving the customers just anything they want — any amusement, any violence, anything that sells beer or cosmetics — and give them instead the information they need to know to be good citizens in a democracy.

I agree, of course, with fostering a better-informed citizenry, but it is not much use advising grasshoppers to be cockroaches, or newspapers to be monographs on foreign affairs. The problem is to see whether, human nature being what it is, the people who sell newspapers can change to meet all these new responsibilities without losing the patronage of the people who buy and advertise in newspapers. Obviously, newspaper publishers cannot serve the national interest by going broke.

The death of the *New York Herald Tribune* in 1966 is only the most spectacular reminder of the economic problems of even the most illustrious of American daily newspapers. At the end, this paper, whose heritage stemmed from two of the finest dailies of the nineteenth century, and whose criticism of the arts, sports, and politics was as good as any in America, had a circulation of only about 100,000 among the more than seven million people living in the five boroughs of New York City. Despite its history, its reputation for originality and innovation, and its staff of nationally famous critics, it simply could not get enough advertising to keep going and is reported to have lost more than $20 million during the last ten years of its existence. Lectures on the ideal newspaper, therefore, are not likely to have much effect on newspaper publishers, for in the postwar years even *The New York Times* has made more money by own-

SOURCE: *"What Can Be Done?"* from *The Artillery of The Press: Its Influence on American Foreign Policy* by James Reston. Copyright © 1966, 1967 by Council on Foreign Relations, Inc. Reprinted by permission of Harper & Row, Publishers, Inc.

ing a half-interest in a paper mill in Kapuskasing, Canada, and producing blank newsprint than it has earned by producing the best newspaper of record in the world.

This gives perhaps too gloomy a picture of the economics of American daily newspapers as a whole, however. The period of the great decline in the number of daily newspapers occurred between 1925, when there were 2,008 dailies, and 1945, when there were only 1,749. Actually, since 1945 and the rise of national television, the number of daily newspapers has remained fairly stable. Though they have not increased in proportion to the population, there are a few more now, mainly in the suburbs of the great cities, than there were in 1945.

Newspaper circulation and advertising have remained high despite the competition of television. More than sixty million papers are sold every day, and with the increase of higher education and the continued movement of the American people into large metropolitan areas where daily newspapers are most successful, there is every reason to believe that circulation demand will remain high. The main question is whether the newspapers will be able to keep their lead in advertising revenues over television, radio, magazines, and billboards in face of the steeply rising costs of newspaper labor, raw materials, production, and technical improvements.

Newspapers get about two-thirds of their operating revenues from advertising. Although they have continued to increase these revenues despite the competition of television, the rise is due largely to the fact that the economic prosperity of the postwar years has vastly increased the national investment in advertising of all kinds.

Nevertheless, the risks are high. All the modern instruments of communication in the United States are now caught up in a fierce competitive battle with one another and with the rising price of production. Everybody seems to be poaching on everybody else's preserve. The newspapers are now getting into the periodicals' field of "news significance"; the periodicals are invading the fields of both news and sociology, once dominated by the book publishers; the book publishers are producing "instant" paperback books on important news events; the television networks are bidding for the services of newspaper reporters, magazine writers, and historians; and all are engaged in a savage struggle for the advertising dollar. In this situation, it will not be very profitable to lecture publishers on their moral responsibilities unless it can be demonstrated that greater responsibility might produce greater prosperity. It is not a wholly new problem.

"To your request of my opinion of the manner in which a newspaper should be conducted, so as to be most useful," Thomas Jefferson wrote to John Norvell on June 14, 1807, "I should answer: by restraining it to true facts and sound principles only. Yet I fear such a paper would find few subscribers." Quite a few publishers have come to the same conclusion since then, and the competition for the citizen's time is increasing every year and tending to divert him from the most serious affairs.

The most insistent voices of America are now crying to the people night and day to think of other things: to buy and buy one more, to take in the Late Late Show, to join the Dodge Rebellion, or fly away from it all on Eastern Airlines — and on credit. We will only fool ourselves if we think we are going to compete on equal terms for the mass mind against the voice of the hawker, or bring about vast changes in the present ways of making, reporting, reading, and listening to the news. Some things, however, might be done in some important places.

The Advantages of Competition

Fortunately, some modern technical developments are forcing newspapers to be more responsible. I do not believe that journalists and officials in America are condemned by nature, like cats and dogs, to eternal hostility. There will always be times when the official will feel that it is his duty to conceal information and the reporter will believe it is his duty to publish it, but the area of conflict between them is narrowing and the area of cooperation is widening.

Newspapers are no longer the first messengers of the spot news. The radio deprived them of that function a generation ago. The noisy Horatio Alger urchin with a bundle of papers under his arm, shouting "Extra!" in the night, is a thing of the past. Though the radio and television reporters are competitive, they have never been as interested in "scoops" as the old newspaper reporters, and even now they are more concerned about sounding better and looking better than they are about going on the air first with some thumping disclosure.

Also, the television has deprived the newspaper of the great "picture" story. What poor scribbler can describe a political convention or the inauguration of a President as well as a television camera can capture such events? The modern newspaper is searching for a new role, or should be. That role, I believe, lies in the field of thoughtful explanation, which tends to make the reporter more of an ally of the government official than a competitor.

We are no longer merely in the transmitting business, but also in the education business. Actually, the mass communications of this country probably have more effect on the American mind than all the schools and universities combined, and the problem is that neither the officials who run the government nor the officials who run the newspapers, nor the radio and television news programs, have adjusted to that fact.

What Is "News"?

We are in trouble on the news side for a very simple reason: we have not kept our definition of news up to date. We are pretty good at reporting "happenings," particularly if they are dramatic. We are fascinated by events but not by the things that *cause* events. We will send five hundred correspondents to Viet Nam after the war breaks and fill the front pages with their reports, meanwhile ignoring the rest of the world, but we will not send one or two reporters there when the danger of war is developing. Even if we do, their reports of the danger will be minimized, by editors and officials alike, as "speculation" and hidden back among the brassiere ads if they are not hung on the spike.

We can see now that the conditions of life in Cuba under Batista were big news, but we paid very little attention to what was going on there at the time. The *effect* was Castro and the risk of war with the Soviet Union; but the *cause* was the social inequality under previous regimes, many of them in cahoots with American commercial interests, and all this was largely ignored.

Unfortunately, there is not much evidence that the news organizations of the country have learned the lesson. Occasionally a television network or a large newspaper will send a team of reporters into the Dominican Republic or some other infected spot and do a useful study of the problems there. Most of the time, however, we rush from crisis to crisis, like firemen, and then leave when the blaze goes out.

I believe that we in the news business are going to have to twist ourselves around and see the wider perspectives of the news: the causes as well as the effects, what is going to happen in addition to what governments do. The foreign correspondence of American newspapers was based very largely on British models in general and on *The Times* of London in particular, but *The Times* had a very special function, which was not necessarily applicable to the United States. It was a kind of house organ for the British government Establishment. It concentrated on the news of what governments all over the world did: who was up and who was down, who in and who out.

It is not governments that are transforming the world today, but the fertility of people, the creativity of scientists, the techniques of engineers and economists, and the discoveries of physicians. Almost all governments in the world today are merely rushing around trying to keep up with the consequences of what is happening outside their own offices. What the Roman Catholic Church does about birth control, for example, is probably going to be bigger news in the long run than what the American government does about foreign aid, which is overwhelmed each year by the staggering birth rate of the underdeveloped countries. The movement toward the unification of Europe did not start with governments but with private citizens like Jean Monnet. And it is being carried on by European businessmen — who like the larger markets and the fluidity of labor across national frontiers — rather than by governments.

Here again our profession, which prides itself on being up to date and is always shouting at governments to "keep up," is itself lagging behind the times. It has to go on covering "events," dealing with effects, and reporting the activities of governments; but, like the nation itself, its responsibilities have expanded. Ideas are news: see what John Maynard Keynes has done to our society with his ideas, what the conservatives backing Barry Goldwater did to the Republican Party and the balance of political power in America with their conservative revolt, what the Communists are doing to China with their savage ideology, what de Gaulle is doing to Europe with his patriotic yearning for national glory.

We are not covering the news of the mind as we should. Here is where rebellion, revolution, and war start, but we minimize the conflict of ideas and emphasize the conflict in the streets, without relating the second to the first. If the Secretary of Defense says, for the thousandth time, that the United States has enough hydrogen bombs on airplanes and submarines to wipe out both China and the Soviet Union, even after they destroy every major city in the United States, he is assured a big boxcar headline on the front page of every big-city newspaper in America and a prominent place on the Cronkite and Huntley-Brinkley shows. But if some thoughtful professor makes a speech demonstrating that the destruction of the human race can be avoided, he may easily be ignored even in his home town.

A Few Modest Proposals

What, then, can be done? Is there any way the flow of information can be increased, and the general understanding improved, without prohibitive costs?

I believe that the main hope lies in the expansion of the special correspondence in the large newspapers and news agencies, and of the special news events on the networks. All papers, agencies, and networks devote some time and money to serious studies of various social or political problems, but these "background" pieces tend to be irregular and are often cut down or squeezed out altogether by "hard news."

We are not likely to get much more serious correspondence in the big-city dailies until we stop making analytical articles compete for space with spot news. There is always more spot news, much of it trivial rubbish, than any paper can print. Nevertheless, an editor with two or three columns of serious correspondence on his desk is likely to fill up the paper with what happened "today" and leave out the special articles unless there is a specific policy on the paper to run several columns of this carefully prepared analysis every day. Most newspapers do print so-called "feature material." They do not make food recipes or fashions or comics compete every day with spot news for a place in the paper. They start with the proposition that they are going to publish these things each day for a special group of their readers. It would help if they did the same for their most thoughtful readers.

In the same way, the networks could help if they would set aside an hour each weekend in prime viewing time to review the important news of the week and put it into some historical perspective. Senator Fulbright stumbled into a fruitful pasture with his Viet Nam and China hearings. He brought together some of the best scholars of the nation and staged the first real debate on China policy since World War II. The purpose of the hearings was not to legislate but to educate. He merely noted: here is obviously a great question that needs to be discussed, and the television networks, after some scuffling in the corridors, took it from there.

The combination of Congressional hearings and network coverage has immense possibilities. Let the responsible committees of Congress explore the problems of population, of the Atlantic Alliance, of the balance of payments, of education and poverty — one great issue every month or so — and let the networks carry the principal parts of the testimony for an hour on the weekend. Again, we could easily lose by expecting too much. If this is to be done as a conscious effort to lift the level of attention on great issues, the networks will probably not carry the hearings live for hour after hour; but they might very well cooperate on an hour-a-week summary.

Ideally, the United States should have a radio and television service of special news and cultural events available on all sets and in all areas of the country. The National Educational Television network has made a beginning in this direction, but it does not have the scope or the funds to provide such a service for the entire nation. The Ford Foundation has suggested that the commercial networks, by using satellites for transmission of their programs, could save enough money to help finance an expanded educational television network, although it is probably a little idealistic to assume that the commercial networks will finance a competitor for the listening and viewing audience. No doubt, however, educational television can be expanded, by subscription or in some other way, so that there is a fuller flow of serious programming available to those families that wish to be informed as well as entertained.

Much more could also be done, through a nationwide educational television network and other ways, in the field of adult education on foreign affairs. This would require the preparation of the right kind of case studies on foreign-policy questions and their distribution to study groups in the churches, service clubs, and other nongovernmental organizations of the country. (We have seen how powerful the nongovernmental organizations of the United States can be in getting support for great acts of state like the Marshall Plan or the United Nations.) Though some of this goes on, more should be done.

The method of study is vital to its success. The problem is to present the great issues as a series of practical choices: let the people look at the alternatives as the President has to look at them and try at the end to decide among the hard and dangerous courses. We need simple case-study outlines containing, first, a statement of the facts of the policy question; second, a definition of one course of action, followed by arguments for and arguments against; and so on through definition of a second course, and a third and a fourth. The difficulty with the presentation of foreign-policy news to the people today is that it comes out a jumble of important and trivial things and personalities, so that the people cannot quite get clear the questions for decision, and end up either by giving up or by choosing up sides for or against the President. Even the Sunday newspapers might find room in their endless pages and sections for a syndicated case study of the issue of the month; and if not there, the foundations might take the project on.

If I may engage in a little heresy, it may be that news and analysis of news in a democracy are too serious to be left to newspapermen. The United States has been deeply involved in world affairs now for two generations. We have developed in the process a very large company of men and women in the universities, the foundations, international business, communications, and the government, who are well informed on international questions, some of them better informed on many subjects than any other people in the world. Unfortunately, not enough of these men and women are sharing with their fellow countrymen a great deal of what they know.

We are just beginning to develop a new class of public servants who move about in the triangle of daily or periodical journalism, the university or foundation, and government service. These roving writers and officials are a growing and hopeful breed — McGeorge Bundy, Arthur Schlesinger, Jr., John Kenneth Galbraith, Theodore Sorensen, Richard Goodwin, and Douglass Cater illustrate the point — but much more of such cross-fertilization could be done.

It is not sufficient that these men write occasionally for the Sunday *Magazine* of *The New York Times*. The great opportunity of the daily newspaper is that it reaches people when they are paying attention. Galbraith can write a learned, amusing, and provocative book about his diplomatic mission in India, which would probably come out when everybody's mind was on the Congo or the sad decline of the New York Yankees, and if he was lucky, 50,000 people would read it; but if he took a day in the middle of the Indian-Pakistani war to analyze the conflict for the newspapers, he could have an attentive audience of easily twenty million.

We need more open pages, preferably next to the editorial pages, where the best minds of the world could give their analyses of current developments; where the vivid passages out of the best speeches and periodical articles and editorials of the world could appear; where we could find the philosophers worrying not about the particular bill of the day but about the issue of the decade. These could, if edited by thoughtful minds, be among the liveliest pages, bringing continuity to the daily newspaper and some sense of balance and history to contemporary events. The "Letters to the Editor" columns of many papers have been dominated by publicists and crackpots for years. We should be able to do better than that and make the open pages into an exciting forum for the exchange of ideas and even for criticism of the papers themselves.

Unfortunately, the American newspapers seldom encourage this kind of morning-after analysis by outsiders. The British do. H. G. Wells, G. B. Shaw, G. K. Chesterton, J. B. Priestley, to mention only a few, all started in the free-lance tradition of the British daily newspaper. "I am a journalist," Wells once declared late in his career. "I refuse to play the artist. If sometimes I am an artist, it is a freak of the gods. I am a journalist all the time and what I write *goes now* — and will presently die." He recognized the main point about journalism: it can get ideas to a mass audience at the fleeting moment when they are listening, and he preferred to use his energies to do that rather than to write tedious volumes for the few. "Better the wild rush of the Boomster and the Quack," he told Henry James in 1912, "than the cold politeness of the established thing."

The Competition for Brains

The need to bring the most thoughtful minds of the nation into the columns of the best of our daily newspapers is only a symbol of a more fundamental question about the philosophy and techniques of both newspapers and radio and television networks, namely, whether the newspapers and the networks can continue to follow the old habits of emphasizing what is bright, dramatic, contentious, and superficial, and still attract and hold the most serious and intelligent young men and women of the day in competition with other institutions. The universities, the foundations, the law, and the government are also looking for the same talents that make a successful reporter.

Thus, newspapers find themselves in a wholly new competitive position. Many of our most intelligent young men find it difficult to pass up the fellowships and scholarships that enable them to stay on in the universities, avoiding the military draft in the meanwhile. They do not have to put up with the endless grind of daily deadlines in order to write on the problems of their time. No doubt many of these young men and women are fascinated by the conflicts of their generation and want to write about them, but attracting them into daily reporting is not easy.

It is even more important to the future of newspapers and the networks that these sensitive, intelligent young people find a useful and sympathetic life in the reporting of contemporary affairs than that the philosophic "outsiders" be encouraged to write for the daily papers or talk on radio and television. Both are important, but a newspaper and a network depend primarily, like a baseball team, on who is on the field every day.

The best of American newspapers understood this in the 1950s and 1960s. About that time they began to realize that they had to reappraise their economic assumptions of the past and pay their best reporters as well as they paid their best editors and even some of their best executives. The reappraisal was not easy for the owners of American newspapers because they had been accustomed to the idea that reporters were satisfied with the excitement of hobnobbing with political and commercial bigshots, and would be satisfied with the wages of schoolteachers, or even parsons.

Since then, the publishers of the best newspapers have learned that they are in a wholly new competitive situation for outstanding talent. At least some of them have seen that the best of their reporters were very much in demand by weekly news magazines that made more money than newspapers; by Big Business, whose public-relations activities were important enough to command fabulous salaries; by the universities and foundations, whose salary-level and work-year were more attractive than the routine of day-to-day news reporting; and even by the Federal government, which concluded during the Kennedy Administration that an effective newspaper reporter was competent enough to be a good Assistant Secretary of State or Defense or even an ambassador of the United States at a higher salary than even the most prestigious newspapers would normally pay.

Such recognition made a big difference, but the traditional editors of the newspapers, oriented to the spot news of the day, proved to be more of a problem for these reflective and analytical young men than the newspaper auditors. The reporters were looking for time and space to probe into the deeper meaning of the news. The editors were looking — not always, but a good deal of the time — for the main facts in a hurry. It would be wrong to say that the news editors were indifferent to detailed analysis of important stories, or that the new breed of intelligent reporters was uninterested in being first with the news or insensitive to the editors' problem of getting quick copy to the composing room in time to meet the pressing deadlines and railroad and airline schedules of the modern newspaper. But the preferences of the spot-news editor and the younger analytical reporter were different; and this was even more true of the editor and the reporter in the radio and television business, where a thoughtful reporter might gather a major story on some development in United States-Chinese relations and be told to present it in no more than forty-five seconds.

The whole point will be lost if we merely condemn the news editor. On a big city newspaper, he has to deal with a million words a day that pass through the office and select from them about 100,000 words for publication. Obviously, he cannot read the 100,000 words and, in most cases, not even the 10,000 that go into the major stories of the day. Thus he falls back most of the time on the old practice of printing the popular and cutting the rest to fit the limited space he has, which brings him into almost daily conflict with the reporter, who naturally thinks that nothing in the world is so important as the details of the beautiful story he has composed and finds mangled in the paper the following morning.

If I dwell on this point at the hazard of being tiresome, it is only because, first, the conflict of approach and philosophy must be resolved if the newspaper is to attain the level of intellectual excellence it needs in order to compete in the future; and second, the dominant role of the technicians in our newspapers is so typical of the crisis of leadership in so many American institutions today. John W. Gardner, formerly President of the Carnegie Corporation in New York and now Secretary of the Department of Health, Education, and Welfare in President Johnson's cabinet, has touched on these problems of the specialist, the technician, and the philosopher in the wider context of American life.

"One of them," Gardner wrote, "is that it is nobody's business to think about the big questions that cut across the specialties — the largest questions facing our society. Where are we headed? Where do we want to head? What are the major trends determining our future? Should we do anything about them? Our fragmented leadership fails to deal effectively with these transcendent questions.

"Very few of our most prominent people take a really large view of the leadership assignment. Most of them are simply tending the machinery of that part of society to which they belong. The machinery may be a great corporation or a great government agency or a great law practice or a great university. These people may tend it very well indeed, but they are not pursuing a vision of what the total society needs. . . . One does not blame them, of course. They do not see themselves as leaders of the society at large, and they have plenty to do handling their own specialized roles. Yet it is doubtful that we can any longer afford such widespread inattention to the largest questions facing us."

This is a perceptive and apt description of the leadership not only of American government but of American newspapers and networks today. In general, the men who select and display the news in newspapers, and plan and allocate the assignments and the time for news and special events on radio and television, are not thinking about "the society at large" but about the competition; they are "tending the machinery" rather than attending to "the largest questions facing us." It is not that they are indifferent to the larger questions. They talk about them after working hours a great deal, and occasionally they plan special reports and special projects that deal with the effects of science, population growth, the rich third and the hungry two-thirds of the human family, automation and the unskilled worker, the races and the cities, food surpluses in America and starvation in South Asia. But "tending the machinery" is the main thing for most editors, and this usually means what happened or what somebody said today rather than whether it is important to the relationship of today to tomorrow.

These modest suggestions for broadening and deepening the flow of serious news in America are not really beyond the capacity of the big papers and stations; nor are they, in my view, against their long-range commercial interests. No doubt it would cost a bit more to give reporters time to investigate the causes of developing problems and set aside a few columns of space to keep their reports appearing regularly. But the gains would not be worthless. In this field we are better able to compete with radio and television than in the field of hot news. It is hard to psycho-analyze a President with a television camera or take a film of what hasn't yet happened. Also, if we let our reporters use their minds as well as their legs on serious inquiries and then print their findings, we will un-doubtedly attract and keep more sensitive and perceptive men and women. At the same time, we would probably attract more and more of the intelli-gent young readers who are pouring out of our universities in an ever larger stream and are expecting from their newspapers a much more detailed and sophisticated account of world affairs.

To provide a fuller and more acute coverage is not a hopeless exercise by any means. The advertiser, at least in the large city, is no longer in a position to impose his views either of the President or of the Communists on the editor. I have never known a newspaper editor who was unalter-ably opposed to clear and vivid writing, though many of them tolerate some pretty shoddy stuff. There is a whole new generation of well-educated reporters who would welcome the opportunity to do more conscientious and careful work on major problems, and the more we get into this field of reporting, the less we are likely to be in conflict with officials.

The suggestion here is not that we try to make the daily American newspaper sound like a scholarly journal on affairs of state, that we put causes ahead of effects or ideas before facts, or the lonely professor's thoughts above the apocalyptic pronouncements of the Chairman of the Joint Chiefs of Staff, but merely that we give as much space to political ideas and social trends as we give, say, to new recipes on the women's page. It will not be easy to get a larger allocation of space or time for foreign and other serious news in the newspapers and radio and television stations, and it is silly to think that the reorganization of the political and social structure of Asia will ever get as much attention as sports or comics; but maybe a few papers and a few stations in the big cities might do better.

A little more self-analysis and a little less self-admiration would not hurt our business. We need to question not only our old definitions of news and our allocation of space and time but also many other popular assump-tions that have been accepted uncritically for much too long. For example, we have a very patriotic and even chauvinistic press on the whole, which is good in some ways but bad in others. The newspapers didn't help the country much, in my view, by taking a "my country right or wrong" attitude when Presidents Kennedy and Johnson began slipping into the war in Viet Nam. It is difficult to see how we can get a clear picture of the world as it is if we see it only from our own side, like a football game, and do not challenge the national assumptions that we can do almost anything anywhere in the world.

It was a jingoistic American press that whooped us into the Spanish-American War and then, having helped extend our commitments all the way to the Philippines, confirmed isolationism as the first article of faith. Officials, of course, tend to complain that we are not patriotic enough and that we are constantly criticizing their actions and providing propaganda for the enemy, which is true enough. But the opposite is worse. We will have to become more detached, more disinterested, more forehanded and farsighted if we are going to report accurately and criticize effectively in this kind of mixed-up world.

Greater detachment and impartial criticism probably mean that we are going to have to question the validity of the party-oriented newspaper, at least as far as party views of foreign affairs are concerned. Fortunately, the my-party-right-or-wrong habit is declining anyway, but why should it exist at all in the foreign field? In the first place, it is virtually impossible in America to know what a party's foreign policy is when the party is out of power. Yet many papers still look at the world from the viewpoint of the party, or some leader in the party, and this clearly adds one more subjective and perplexing consideration to the puzzle.

It is not clear to me why the modern newspaper should give its allegiance to any party's foreign policy. A newspaper may very well conclude today that this country badly needs a stronger opposition party and therefore argue for more Republicans in the Congress, but for an editor to support Johnson in Southeast Asia because he is the editor's party's man or back Goldwater because he is the titular head of the editor's party is putting party ahead of country and cheating the readers.

The press has one extremely important job to do. We must try to keep the issues for decision clearly before the people, a task which is not really being done in the present jumble of the average American newspaper or news program. There is, for example, a new kind of class war developing in the world today between the rich nations and the poor nations. It does not take much imagination to see the chaos ahead in international life if this gap between the white industrial nations and the nonwhite agricultural nations keeps widening. Yet the foreign aid bill in Washington runs into more and more opposition every year, and the debate on that bill tends to come over to the readers as a battle between the "bleeding hearts" and the "realists." Also, the debates in the U.N. Economic and Social Council are seldom reported, and the direct confrontations between the rich and poor nations at U.N. headquarters in Geneva are scarcely mentioned by press or radio.

What the Government Could Do

On the official side, too, some improvements are desirable and even possible. The attitude of the President toward the reporters is vital. If he regards them primarily as a problem and therefore tries to manipulate them, they eventually convey their suspicion and even hostility to the people. If, on the other hand, he regards them as an opportunity and tries to explain his problems to them, they can be a valuable educational force. It is the President, however, who has the initiative and the capacity to define the rules and set the tone of public discussion.

There has been a decline since President Roosevelt's day, for example, in the use of the informative Sunday evening fireside chat, which was often used to good effect by FDR to explain the background of his problems. Now the President is on the air more often, but with bits and pieces of information or with his argument when public opinion seems to be going against him. A revival of the calm philosophic talk or the quiet "conversation," which President Johnson does extremely well, could help keep the public mind on the larger questions and minimize the capacity of others to divert attention into narrow personal or petty political issues.

There has been a decline in recent years in the relations between the experts in the State Department and the reporters. The reason for this is that the experts know the President likes to dominate public announcements and are afraid that they might disclose something that would detonate his temper. Since this is not a thought that many officials contemplate with pleasure, they tend to hold back, and since the most useful information in this field usually comes not from the top leaders but from the men who brief the leaders, this chokes down a very valuable stream of information.

No government in history ever received such a torrent of information from abroad as the United States government does today. Not only the ambassadors in the capitals and the experts on agriculture, economics, and politics in the embassies, but also the consuls scattered throughout the world in major cities and towns inundate Washington every day with reports on every imaginable problem in their areas. A good deal of this reporting is interesting and unclassified and could help nourish the flow of information into the newspapers and periodicals of the nation, but it is not made available mainly because nobody thinks of making it available. The idea has grown up that all this official information "belongs to the government." Nobody is looking at it and asking, "Why should this *not* be put out?" They have lapsed into the habit of not even considering the possibility.

It should be possible for officials and reporters to do much better than they have done in discussing the problems and opportunities of their relationships. There is a great deal of chatter about it, of course, with the White House Press Secretary on the Presidential press plane flying between Washington and Texas. But all suggestions for more formal committees to analyze and correct obvious shortcomings, or, alternately, for the press to establish some way of correcting itself, have usually ended in useless vapor.

Proposals have been made for the formation of a press council, like the bar association, that could pass on the ethics of its members. But what do you do when Drew Pearson comes up with thousands of incriminating documents out of a Senator's private files: disbar him or give him the Pulitzer Prize?

"If there is ever to be an amelioration of the condition of mankind," John Adams wrote in 1815, "philosophers, theologians, legislators, politicians and moralists will find that the regulation of the press is the most difficult, dangerous and important problem they have to resolve. Mankind cannot now be governed without it, nor at present with it."

I am more hopeful. I believe that an increasingly educated electorate will provide a growing market for more serious papers and more serious radio and television. They will not drive out the bad, but they will supplement it for the thoughtful minority. As to the trickery of politicians, that, in the long run will prove, I think, to be a self-limiting disease simply because the people will catch on. Meanwhile, the willingness of serious men and women to discuss the question and moderate it in practical ways may prove to be more successful than we can now foresee.

Stuart B. Glauberman | # The News from Underground

If one is lucky, one can climb out of the underground unhurt, but it is impossible to escape unchanged. In the course of a year as a reporter for The Berkeley *Barb*, I learned the extent of what the underground press knows about the "straight" world above, and why and how they know it. More important, however, was what I learned about the vitality of papers like the *Barb*. They are not simply a variation on the old journalistic formula of sex plus crime plus political exposés. Their secret lies in the special relationship between the underground press and their readers throughout these Underground States of America.

The Berkeley *Barb*, or just *Barb* as staff members call it, is one of an estimated two hundred periodical newspapers which, for lack of a better name, call themselves the underground press. Few are more than two or three years old, but their combined circulation in this country may currently be well over two million readers. According to *The Wall Street Journal*, circulation is rising and profits are increasing. The underground has its own anti-Establishment press services, including the Underground

---

SOURCE: Reprinted with the author's permission.

Press Syndicate, the Intergalactic World Brain and the Liberation News Service. LNS, the largest and costliest of the services, has begun Telex communication between subscribers in New York, Washington, Detroit, and Berkeley.

Barb is neither the first, the largest, nor the best of the underground: however, it is one of the best known and, according to at least one "straight" critic, the most aggressive of them. The Los Angeles *Free Press* or *"FREEP"*, a two-sectioned goliath, with a circulation of 90,000 is more professional and analytical. The East Village *Other* (circ.: 60,000) is far more salacious and drug-oriented. The ephemeral San Francisco *Oracle* (circ.: unavailable) which blossomed briefly in 1967, was far more psychedelic and artistic. But *Barb* is an excellent example of the best and the worst of what the underground press has to offer. A complete set of the first 175 issues of the paper, described as "a social history of Berkeley and the Movement" is worth $500 according to one collector who is offering a set for sale in *Barb's* classified ad section.

In analyzing *Barb*, it is important to understand the man behind it. Max Scherr, at 52, is a grand daddy of the underground after three-and-a-half years as editor-publisher of *Barb*, seven years as the proprietor of an innovative bar in Berkeley, some years as a lawyer in Baltimore, a seller of gold watches in San Francisco, and a Bohemian in Mexico and other places. Among his own "Street People," Max is very much like a mayor whom anyone can approach publicly but few can reach personally. He likes to help, but does not like favors. Without writing a word of the copy or directly controlling what is written for him, Max makes *Barb* unique in the look-alike sound-alike field of the undergrounds. Part of its distinctive flavor according to the editor-publisher, is imparted by the headlines and illustrations he chooses to go along with the copy he edits. They are intricately related by "in" humor and satire to the material. The most notable quality of *Barb's* pages is the use of this slang, hip, and nonsense vocabulary which in itself helps make *Barb* whatever it is.

The use of Street vocabulary is an indispensable element of *Barb's* rapport with its readers. "Don't write down to the Street People. You write as if you were explaining what's happening in a postcard to your mother," Max once told me. "You know all those cracks and ruts in the pavement along Telegraph Avenue?" Max asked me when I was still new in Berkeley. "Well," he smiled, "I put them all there, myself. Been walking The Street here for twenty years. Those people on The Street today and every day — you write the paper for them. It's their paper."

In Berkeley, the name of The Street is Telegraph Avenue. In San Francisco, of course, it's the Haight. To judge by what appears in *Barb*, the residents of The Street include: fresh-smelling hippies and dewey-eyed runaways; pot smokers and pill poppers; university students and Regents; socialists, Communists, anarchists, and Yippies; draft resisters, black militants, grape strikers, and community organizers; Hell's Angels, police chiefs, Indian chiefs, city councilmen, the Pentagon, and the Bank of America; movie-goers and record-buyers; photographers and nudists; well-hung bi-guys, sadists, masochists, other assorted perverts and fetishists; a record number of venereal disease sufferers and a scattering of journalists and tourists.

The paper in which Max chronicles the life of The Street is an inky tabloid of from twelve to thirty-two pages, a little less than half of which is advertising. It comes out every Friday and its cover usually features a large black headline which reveals very little about what's inside. Most often there is a patchwork of photographs, or a photomontage of Movement heroes, barebreasted girls, and riot police beating students. Occasionally there is an original drawing of a somewhat less news-related origin.

The first issue of *Barb* that I wrote for contained the following major stories in the way of news: COPS RIOT IN HAIGHT, TALES OF TERROR, and FUZZ GO BERSERK IN THE HASH (personal accounts and reportage describing the San Francisco Tactical Squad moving in on hippies with clubs and gas), BLACK LEADERS DECLARE HUEY MUST GO FREE (three black militants speak on behalf of Black Panther martyr Huey P. Newton), CONS CALL IT WIN (a round-up of strike activity at Folsom and San Quentin prisons) and SAVIO FILES FOR PFP SENATE POST and MASS RALLY (the week's developments within the newly-formed Peace and Freedom Party). There were also a dozen shorter news notes on a wide variety of Movement-related activities. Besides local news, *Barb* offers much in the way of features. Notable among the features that week was the third installment of the testimony of Regis Debray at his trial in Camiri, Bolivia. Other kinds of in-depth features about such topics as drag queen championships and pornographic filmmakers which appear in *Barb* are borrowed from mother undergrounders like the East Village *Other* according to reciprocal sharing agreements.

Barb's host of features also includes half a dozen regular weekly columns. The most famous of *Barb's* columnists is Eugene Schoenfeld, M.D., a well-known Berkeley physician who is easily the most widely read person in the underground. As Doctor HIPpocrates, he answers questions on traditionally untalked about subjects concerning medicine, sex and drugs. A reader asks, "I have been getting a rather weird high by smoking a tobacco cigarette like a joint. A drag will start me up and two cigarettes will get me totally zonked. I usually don't smoke (except grass). Do you have any idea about the medical ramifications of this habit?" The good Dr. HIPpocrates answers: "Cigarettes are a known health hazard. Do you get them from The Friendly Stranger?"

The anonymous "Sgt. Pepper" is also featured weekly. The Sergeant's round up of each week's Vietnam and political news is compiled from "incredible" media sources as well as his own inside information and opinion. Another mysterious contributor is The Roving Rat Fink who writes a column of opinion for factotums. In the year I was with *Barb*, I saw the Rat Fink only once.

Other columns in *Barb* include "At The Flick With Lenny Lipton" and "Record Rap" by Jeff Jassen or Jef Jaisun (depending on what the author, a young musician, is calling himself that week). Both are intended as reviews, but Lipton, a Berkeley filmmaker, confuses his life with his film, and Jassen attempts to combine rock music with social criticism. Most readers would agree that the ADADADA classified ad section remains one of the *Barb's* best features, second only to HIPpocrates. Uniquely advertised in the People, the Pad-ads, and the Models columns are offers of uncommon roommates, sex partners, sex aids, bizarre photos and unusual jobs. ADADADA runs for at least two pages with six columns of ads on every page.

Anywhere from fifty to sixty thousand *Barbs* are printed weekly for sale primarily in the streets of Berkeley and to tourists in San Francisco, and by mail to subscribers and bookshops all over the world. Max told me that unlike its competitors for the underground readership, *Barb* is absolutely dependent on sale in the Street at home. Circulation is highest in the summer when there are more kids in the Street and "the papers sell themselves." In the autumn when sales begin to drop, Max has to find some people who are willing to do some real selling. (Vendors make 7½¢ per copy.)

Barb, begun on a barroom bet, is intended to cover only what the Street People are doing and what they, as Street People, are interested in, that being presumably news of the Movement in Berkeley and elsewhere. This is not my observation so much as it is Max's concept of the job he's doing. *Barb* is often associated with the politically explosive Berkeley campus of the University of California. (The barb of the newspaper's skeleton horseman symbol is actually the campus' Campanile clocktower turned over on its side.) However, Max apparently never saw the paper as being wholly important to the University or vice versa. Rather, it is more closely aligned to the general drift of The Movement. In underground terms, there are two camps: the great monolithic Establishment which the young, the Third World minorities and the hip of all ages are not responsible for nor responsive to; and the great monolithic Movement which they have built in protest and presumably live to defend.

Max hired me to write the kind of news that is of interest to those in the Movement. He looks forward each week to having several big stories, but he knows that stories don't necessarily sell the paper. Many regular "readers" start from the back. They read the Scenedrome Calendar, the ADADADA classifieds, the HIPpocrates column, and the entertainment and sex display ads. They never get to the stories. I remember telling a fellow student that I wrote for *Barb*. "What do you write," he asked, "the ads?" I told him no, that I covered the campus and the Black Panthers. "Oh," he said, "who writes the ads?"

While news is by no means the most important ingredient for many of *Barb's* readers, my job was to provide enough in the way of local news stories to fill at least a couple of pages.

Though I was not new to the underground when I became a *Barb* reporter, my experience had been limited to the grass roots of "The Sixth Estate." A college student with weak New Left sympathies, I had for some time been an interested reader and observer of the new underground since its birth during my last year in high school. In September, 1967, some friends and I at Northwestern University founded the *Real Press*, and I became its editor. At the time, we envisioned the underground press as a way to turn other students on to the events and "enlightened" attitudes ignored by the semi-official *Daily Northwestern* and the Chicago papers (which they weren't reading anyhow). For several months, our four-page weekly appeared on the day the campus daily didn't. As it turned out, the most difficult part of being in the underground at a traditionally conservative Midwestern university, was trying to give away our product to coeds who simply did not want to know where "it" was "at." Now, of course, the underground is more influential on many campuses than old American standbys like *Life* and *Look*. In New York City and in Los Angeles, high school students edit their own underground newspapers.

The underground business cannot be learned anywhere else but in the underground. Almost the last place one could hope to be trained for the loose discipline of underground journalism would be the school of journalism. The inverted pyramid style of newswriting in which all the facts are crammed into the first paragraph, and the use of proper grammar, spelling, and other journalistic necessities, are practically taboo. News stories are often written free of any journalistic interference. A staff member of the psychedelic San Francisco *Oracle* once explained to a straight newsman; "It's an oracle just like the Delphic Oracle, but there are no priests to interpret the babble." Many "untrained" *Barb* reporters will compose their stories in the style of a letter to a friend, complete with schoolgirl underscoring and unrestrained street language, and the piece will run as news. During my weeks as a copy editor, one particular young lady somehow found herself week after week amid a volley of bullets. Her story would begin, "DEAR BOSS, It happened again this week. . . ."

Most professors of journalism would think very poorly of this style. It is, however, communicative and apparently interesting enough to the audience at which *Barb* is aimed. And while the old inverted pyramid is the only acceptable way to recount the story of how a man bit a dog, the underground lends itself regularly to ways and means outside of the textbooks and stylebooks. They are far more concerned with, believe it or not, credibility than style. Dealing with the people who were forced to go underground was one of the real experiences of working there. When a young Berkeley couple came into the office and claimed to have been "maced" by police after a traffic offense, I believed them, as I learned to believe the others who came to *Barb* for help. The matters were not earth-shaking, nor were they of international importance. Many of them were just personal and human, the kind of stories editors love — if they come off the wire. "You say you were maced, but how do we know?" a city editor is likely to ask. "You were maced?" *Barb* asks. "Tell us all about it." Instant acceptance.

A good analogy for this is the dinner-table conversation after a member of the family has been arrested or suspended from school, for example. He tells the story, highlighting what he did and neglecting to mention, perhaps, a few items that his principal might emphasize. His family believes him, knowing that there may be a little more to the story but accepting the version presented. It is unlikely that someone at the table would ask, "What do the police say?" or "What did the principal think of the teacher's version of the story?"

Barb and other papers in the underground exist to provide a kind of family news that regular newspapers aren't interested in printing. Large city newspapers and even smaller ones have never been able to communicate effectively with subcultures. They are almost always directed at the middle class and owned by the upper class and as a result, they are totally unconcerned with the lower class until Christmas comes. Though they claim to be objective, they are usually infused with Protestant white middle-aged and middle-class attitudes and biases. There is only one possible side to a crime story, and that is the police side. There are only two established political parties — if there are that many. And when young people or minority people make news, it is generally held to be too insignificant for the majority of readers of the great gray journals of our great gray cities.

Those who have attempted to explain the success of the underground papers from their aboveground desks have generally turned first to the low costs of offset printing, and the new permissiveness of the U.S. Supreme Court regarding printed matter and obscenity. Then they suggest that the papers are capitalizing on the commercial appeal of the Love Summer of 1966 along with hippies and beads, which is not far from the truth chronologically. But these are far from the most important reasons for the appearance and success of underground newspapers. The real reason is that everyone likes to hear and read things their own way. "Telling it like it is" means telling it our way. The people at the City Desk tell it the way the majority of their readers supposedly would like to hear it. Young people and Third World people, no matter how many of them there are, will always be in the minority. For this reason, they want especially to read things their way. Like it is to them. For this reason, there is *Barb* and all of the others like it. For this reason also, there are magazines like the *National Review*, the *New Republic*, and the *New Statesman* whose readers want to learn the issues their way.

Besides telling things the way young people want to hear it, the underground press also reserves space, so to speak, for radical, political, economic, and other minority groups whose news and announcements would otherwise not appear in print. While a distributor's streetbox for automatic sale of *Barbs* may boast, "All The News They FEAR To Print," it is not really fear that keeps such news out of the overground press. The Bay area dailies, like those in other parts of the country, full of wire service copy and society news, make no claim to complete or even partial coverage of Street news, Movement news or sex revolution news. The Young Socialist Alliance, the Sexual Freedom League, the Women's Liberation Front, and a plethora of small community organizations, museums, art fairs and craft shows, are dependent on the underground for their notices. At *Barb* and at almost every other underground paper, black is beautiful and brown, red, and yellow make equally good copy. For like the young, the Third World have traditionally had no major media of their own.

When the Berkeley *Barb* hired me to write the local scene as I saw it, I had not a very good idea of who the Street People were and no idea of how they wanted their news. By chance one clear spring morning, I wound up with the Black Panther Party for a beat, and Bobby Seale, Chairman and co-founder of the Berkeley-based black militant organization, gave me my first lesson. After that, it was easy. What I learned from the underground press was largely what I learned from listening to the Panthers.

When I began covering the Black Panther stories which were popping out of Oakland and Berkeley with the secrecy of machine gun fire, few representatives of the straight press were on hand for the Panther part of the story. All that their papers would say about the Panthers was that several had been arrested at such and such a time and place, "the police said today." Inevitably, the story I wrote was just as one-sided, since I told only the Panthers' side. Consider, for example, the first big story I wrote for *Barb*. Headlined, D.A. BALKS AT PRE-DAWN CHARGES, it began like this:

> Sunday before dawn. Six cops with shotguns. The Berkeley police moving in on Bobby Seale.
> "They knocked on the door and said there had been a disturbance," Seale said. "Then they broke into my home — and pulled guns."
> "The pigs (cops) said they didn't need a warrant," he said.
> "They threw me against the wall. They got my wife out of her bed. And they ransacked the house with a shotgun jammed at me."

The Seale story broke the morning of February 25, 1968. According to the morning newspapers, Seale and five others were arrested the night before at his home on charges of conspiracy to commit murder. I hadn't anything specific in mind when I asked *Barb's* managing editor, Jim Schreiber, if I should follow the story up. Within forty-eight hours I was caught up in the world of the Black Panthers, of Seale, his lawyers, and the straight press. I spoke to Seale myself and listened to his charges. Seale denied everything that the papers had reported. He denied the conspiracy. He denied having possessed the illegal weapons that the police said they had seized. He accused the police of lying. He accused the newspapers of printing lies. He told me that the police had acted illegally, that they had tricked him into opening the door, that they had manhandled him and his wife. He said they told him that they didn't need warrants for search or arrest. I didn't know whether to believe the intense Seale or not, but I took it all down.

In the months that followed, I listened to hundreds of Seale's charges. I balked at believing almost each of them at the start, but later found that practically everything he told me was true. I began to believe in him and in the value of my own reporting.

Almost a year after the Seale raid, an Alameda County Superior Court judge ruled that the arrest and seizure in the predawn raid had been unlawful. Judge Lionel Wilson denounced the police action in raiding the Seale home and questioned the credibility of the testimonies offered by the Berkeley police, testimonies which the Bay area dailies presented and fought to preserve on their front pages.

The Panther stories I wrote were almost verbatim accounts of what Panther spokesmen had said, rearranged slightly for greater effect. My reports varied point for point with other newspaper accounts of the same incident. The metropolitan press uniformly printed police desk reports with little variation, and it was a long time before any daily paper paid attention to what was coming out of Panther headquarters or what was being printed in the Berkeley *Barb*.

Even after considering that the Panthers were telling me only what they wanted told, I still preferred what they said to anything I read in the other newspapers. From an objective standpoint, however, I realized that the newspapers that carried the police version and *Barb* were equally "honest" — and equally limited. The "credibility gap," even for myself, was neither bridged nor widened, but remained constant. The straight press is more culpable, however, since it is in a good position to cover both sides of a dispute, while *Barb* isn't. In the underground, there is little or no access to the "official" story; there are no press passes, no police permits, no briefings, no access to documents and files, and no advance notification. The Berkeley police will not talk to *Barb* reporters who identify themselves as such. The courts will not admit a *Barb*man when other media personnel are permitted. I have during my year's apprenticeship to the underground learned to sneak in or to listen from open windows and cracks in the door, and even, I admit, to overhear the conversation of other reporters.

(An interesting situation exists currently in Los Angeles where the *Free Press* is suing the city and the police department in order to obtain press privileges. *Freep, The New York Times* of the underground, feels that press passes would improve its reporting — partly by reducing the number of occasions on which the paper's reporters were arrested while trying to get the story. Should the *Free Press* win, however, the question arises as to whether or not it will still technically be in the underground. Police cooperation, and the press pass in particular, are the marks of what the underground has termed "the permitted press" in this country.)

The skilled underground reporter learns not so much how to write his story, but how to find it, or if necessary, how to create it. It becomes obvious that anything said about the Movement is usable and anything said against the Establishment is as good or better. I confess that after I developed the talent for recognizing underground material, I also learned how to create Movement mountains from established molehills. A large part of the news under the ground is of an announcement nature. By far the most numerous and most prosaic of the stories I did for *Barb* during the year, especially when I was doing office work, were spots for Movement groups. They call in, ask for Max, get the OK and describe the coming event and its significance to a reporter. Or, as is common in the real pressrooms of our country, they send press releases, often with complimentary tickets.

Aside from the announcements, the most common type of news story I found myself writing was the "rap." After the first big story, I discovered a very natural thing for an underground freelancer to do. Follow Seale, follow the other Panthers and the anti-Panther elements, find out who's saying what, copy it down, and sell it. At the same time I was investigating that first illegal police action against the Panthers, I learned from Kathleen Cleaver, Panther Communications Secretary, of her theory that police in the Bay area were embarked on a plan to harass and assault the Black Panther Party and each of its leaders. I reported that, too, in *Barb* a year ago, and then I spent the year following up each and every incident of harassment and assault by police on Panthers. There must have been at least fifty. Each resulted in at least one rap; often there were several. It got so that any time Seale (or later Eldridge Cleaver) said anything I would rap it out for *Barb*. The reporting was honest, the statements were more than interesting, and in the days before the Black Panther newspaper, *Barb* became an important source of information for the growing radical communities in the Bay area. *Barb*, incidentally, has the proud distinction of being the first publication to report on Panther founder Huey Newton while he was still developing his philosophy at Oakland's Merritt College. And while I was busy rapping out Panther statements those weeks following the Seale raid, I happened upon another important underground technique.

In April, the Seales came up for a preliminary hearing in Berkeley–Albany Municipal Court. After the session, an impromptu press conference was held by Seale and his attorney Charles Garry on the courthouse lawn. Present was Marlon Brando. I was a bit surprised to recognize him and thought that other people would be interested that he was there. Celebrities are celebrities, and Brando, having portrayed a number of underground types during his career, was in no way unwelcome underground. More importantly, Brando had come to stand with the Panthers, (he had conferred with Eldridge Cleaver) and "to find out why communication between black people and white people has broken down." Since I had been unable to talk my way into the courtroom that morning, Brando's appearance would help my story appreciably. A moment later, when I approached the actor, it became The Story — for the underground only. Brando was refusing to answer a question posed by an Oakland *Tribune* reporter. Straight papers are always on their scout's honor not to mention their competitors in anything but a pat-on-the-back fashion. When Brando very softly and matter-of-factly told the Trib man, "I have no wish to talk to you. I know that your paper is grossly unjust to the Negro people," I knew that I had an exclusive. It was, in effect, for *Barb* only. By the time we hit the streets, Brando had appeared on several local television interview shows to discuss his involvement with the Panthers, but for what it was worth, the story about the *Tribune* was a *Barb* exclusive. And to top it off, I picked up another inch or two of pay and an underground pat on the back, by obtaining an endorsement for *Barb* along with the anti-Establishment sentiment. "Do you ever read the *Barb?*" I asked Brando. "Yes, I've read the *Barb*. I like it," he replied, and I copied it down.

Thus the anti-Establishment media story became part of my repertoire. I decided that I didn't have to wait for someone like Brando to attack the straight press. I could interest readers just by pointing out paragraphs in the local papers that undergrounders might find hard to believe, given the "facts" presented in *Barb*.

It was in covering the killing of a young Panther named Bobby Hutton that my reporting differed most radically from the stuff appearing in other Bay area newspapers. The straight papers never mentioned "the Bobby Hutton murder" as I did; rather they played it as part of the Infamous Black Panther Ninety Minute Shootout With The Oakland Police. While I used the term "shootout" in several places, I remember that Max was very much against the term. It was too Wild West, a quality which the San Francisco papers delight in.

On April 7, the *Sunday Examiner & Chronicle* reported on its front page, ONE KILLED, FOUR SHOT IN OAKLAND; Two Police Hit In Ambush.

> An unidentified Negro was killed and two others, as well as two policemen, were wounded last night as violence exploded in West Oakland.
> One of the wounded men was Eldridge Cleaver, minister of education [sic] of the Black Panthers.

The remainder of the story, another fifteen paragraphs, described how the two police officers claimed to have been ambushed. In the page one follow-up story the next day, SILENCE ON KILLING OF "PANTHER", Hearst's Monarch of The Dailies reported:

> From reliable sources, The Examiner learned that Oakland police have reports that Black Panther leaders decided Friday night to bait "racist pig cops" into an incident that would escalate, with the help of white radicals, into a massive uprising.

It was one of several items which followed a statement that confirmation was not possible at *Examiner* press time.

Meanwhile in Oakland, the Sunday *Tribune* featured this account:

> One suspect was killed, two wounded, and Oakland police officers were shot and wounded Saturday night during a 90-minute gun battle and siege in West Oakland.
>
> The slain suspect, shot as he emerged from a barricaded house at 1218 28th Street, was tentatively identified as Bobby Hutton, about 18, a member of the Black Panthers.

(Note the use of the word "suspect.") Three paragraphs followed about the Panthers involved; the first of them about Cleaver and the second about Warren Wells, both of whom were wounded and arrested; the last was about Hutton's previous criminal record. There followed, in two days of reportage, a total of forty-two paragraphs directly based on the police version of the incident. One paragraph on the second day after the shooting related that "Black Panther Chairman Bobby Seale was bitterly critical of the police action. He told a news conference in Oakland yesterday that Hutton was shot while trying to surrender." The next paragraph described Seale's arrest record and current court cases. Three photographs were featured elsewhere in the same edition of the *Tribune*. There was one in which a police clerk was examining the seized Panther arsenal, one in which an Oakland policeman was firing upon the house on 28th Street from behind a car, and one showing Eldridge Cleaver in police custody.

In contrast, consider the human aspect of *Barb's* coverage of the story. *Barb's* front page on April 12 was one of its best ever, more serious than any I could remember. Kathleen Cleaver stood on the left side looking quite distraught, pictured above an exclusive interview with her, CHARGES COPS SPRUNG TRAP. The right half of the page was devoted to a photo of Bobby Hutton in Panther gear superimposed over a fragment of a bullet-blasted mirror. A dark headline hung over the top of the page: IN COLD BLOOD — How They Killed Him. The copy in large bold type began beneath the photograph:

> The first one out was Bobby Hutton.
>
> He emerged, his hands in the air, from a burning tear-gassed basement where eight of his Black Panther brothers were still holed up. He stepped into the bright searchlight. Oakland police shot him dead.

Bobby James Hutton, Black Panther treasurer, is now a martyr of the fight for black freedom. If he had survived the seven shots that shattered his life, Bobby Hutton would have been eighteen years old this month.

A lot happened in a very short time on that street in West Oakland on the night of April 6, 1968. Much of the story remained unclear for many weeks thereafter. The Bay area papers stuck to their story from their start, using the accounts given by two Oakland police officers. *Barb*, obtaining almost all of its information from interviews with Bobby Seale and Kathleen Cleaver, told Eldridge Cleaver's version of how the Oakland police ambushed the Panthers that night after following them for a week. Exactly what really happened has never been determined, but had it not been for *Barb*, no one would have been aware that there was another side to the ambush story.

One change in the reportage came twenty days later, when the *Cronicle* became interested in Eldridge Cleaver as a personality. Largely because of the Minister of Information's posture as a new hero and the author of a new book, the papers came to print portions of the Panther side of the story. By mid-May the *Chronicle* ran an "exclusive" series on the Black Panther Party by military editor Charles Howe. In *Barb*, Bobby Seale and Kathleen Cleaver called it a bomb in the most pejorative sense. In response to the *Chronicle's* conclusion that "a tense armed truce now exists between the Panthers and the Oakland police," Mrs. Cleaver told me: "That's absurd. You know, that's the first I've heard of that. Nobody told me," she said.

Papers like *Barb* are not obsessed with embarrassing or offending the straights as some have suggested, but they are still interested in the exposé story, which has traditionally been in the back of every journalist's mind. I admit that I was certainly no exception. There were, in fact, several kinds of exposés which I worked to find for the purposes of selling *Barb* and of course, for the thrill of exposing the "enemy" Establishment. The first of these was a variation of the anti-Establishment media story which I have already described.

Months after the Hutton murder, lawyers for the boy's family instituted a law suit against the City of Oakland for illegally murdering their son. One of my first "exposés" reported that the suit against the mayor, the police chief, and numerous John Does would amount to a total settlement of $175 million instead of a paltry $2.5 million as the straight media had reported. I've never heard anything about the suit since, but at the time, the correction alone was a big story for *Barb*. Many critics of the underground press have, in fact, described the purpose of the papers in terms of correcting the mistakes and distortions of the established media. While the quality of that kind of exposé is far from shocking, there were many others which were far more exciting and perhaps worthwhile.

The exposé stories often came from the outside — dare I say from an informer? — but the most important stories I found came once again from Movement sources who had been wronged by the power structure, the police or the press. In the last weeks of April, for example, Bay area newspapers responded to a grand jury indictment of the Panthers involved in the gun battle. Statements to the effect that the Panthers "had been out to do some shooting" were presented to the Alameda County Grand Jury's hearing on April 24, and the Grand Jury indicted all eight Panthers on charges of attempted murder against policemen.

The *Chronicle* and other papers ran front page accounts of the Grand Jury testimony, which contained excerpts from statements allegedly taken from the jailed Panthers. I spoke with Panther Chairman Bobby Seale once more, and interviewed Panther Captain David Hilliard, who had been one of those jailed. The exposé story which resulted began:

> "The pigs wrote the statements that appeared in the newspapers," Bobby Seale told BARB this week.
> "They forced the brothers to sign them. They put a gun to one brother's head, they brutalized and beat another. The pigs lied to them and threatened them. They told one brother he would be dragged from his cell and murdered if he didn't sign."

Seale said that the Panthers hadn't even seen the statements they were supposed to have signed, and Hilliard insisted that none of them had given any kind of statement. Eldridge Cleaver, who was imprisoned because of his alleged participation in the gun battle (in violation of his parole status), told me that the "official" version of the shootout was "a tissue of lies." For many months, Cleaver's imprisonment itself was the subject of a crusade of sorts in the underground press. *Barb* charged that the author and Panther leader was being held by the state "illegally." Five days after one of my exposés on the subject appeared, a superior court judge ruled the Cleaver confinement to be "illegal," and the Panther spokesman was freed.

Other *Barb* exposés at this time included a four-part series on the conditions which led to rioting behind the walls of San Quentin. Written by Jim Schreiber in February 1968, the articles were described as some of the best work ever done in the underground. Another *Barb* story, MACE MASKS A KILLER by Terry Reim, contained one of the first warnings about the dangerous effects of the chemical spray. Reaction to such stories came in heavy waves. The Mace story, for example, brought a flood of phone calls from the nation's newspapers, newsmagazines, and from law enforcement agencies. One call I handled was from the Nevada State Crime Commission. The caller said the Commission wanted more information, because it was considering using the dangerous preparation.

While doing desk work at *Barb*, I also wrote stories based on letters from outsiders. Thus I once reported that *Barb* had found its way into the commander's meeting of the First Battalion, Fourth Combat Support

Training Brigade at Fort Ord, where it discovered a search-and-destroy order against none other than the Berkeley *Barb*. Actually, the sleuthing was done by persons unknown, unpaid, and unheralded, who did their part for the underground by mailing the minutes of the Commander's Meeting to *Barb*. Letters from military personnel all over the world come to *Barb* almost daily to proudly report heavy drug use in barracks and on battlefields to their friends at home. Employees in police stations write in to warn *Barb* of what the guys are saying in the back room.

My greatest success in the underground came in May. At this point I was working a twenty-four hour week, almost all of it on Wednesday night. Much of my work was done from a desk. I got paid for original reportage, rewriting, editing, and off-the-wire copy (which in the underground means off the telephone wires). I was convinced I could write an underground story about anything including the day's stock market quotations, although I must admit I never attempted that one. My favorite of all the stories I did write and one which my mother could appreciate as well, was a playful account of the Mayor of San Francisco walking through the park.

I hadn't planned the piece. It wasn't assigned. It just happened. The papers had been full of the mayor's plans to stroll through Golden Gate Park on Saturdays to investigate charges that hippies, by their lewd behavior, were spoiling the park for straight citizens. A classic *Barb* cover appeared the first Friday after the mayor's announcement, featuring a photo of Mayor Joseph Alioto on such a Saturday walk with sandwich and Coke in hand, singing "As I Was Strolling Through The Park One Day." Surrounding him in every direction were represented dozens of naked hippies frolicking in a collage-satire of lewd and obscene park activities. The next day, while visiting the park with some friends, I happened to spot the mayor. I moved quickly to his side, watched him a few minutes, listened to what I could, and asked one question. I asked Mayor Alioto what he thought of *Barb's* cover. "I understand that it's all in fun," he said, "but I think it can only aggravate the situation." The mayor added that it might also defeat the cause, but I didn't get the opportunity to ask him what *Barb's* cause was. The story ran for sixteen inches, most of them describing how I had been unable to ask a second question of the mayor in order to find out what *Barb's* cause was. And yet, ALIOTO TAKES A TRIP AND NOBODY ROCKS THE BOAT is in my opinion a fine example of underground journalism. It is also, I imagine, the most favorable thing that's been written about San Francisco's mayor by any young person since he sent the Tac Squad into the Haight-Ashbury. The magic was that the article was entirely apolitical, and recaptured the spirit in which the underground papers are said to have been born. But they had already moved from flower power to political power and the Alioto story was merely a pleasant freak.

After the simple sylvan joys of strolling through Golden Gate Park with the Mayor of San Francisco, my education in the underground took two turns, both for the worst as far as Max and the Berkeley *Barb* were concerned. My experience is not, I think, uncommon in the underground.

In June I left for Europe and by the middle of July I had witnessed what I thought was a real revolution — the Bastille Day riots in the Latin Quarter of Paris. I was beaten as others have been before me, but saw for a brief moment beneath the club of a gendarme how stupid it all was. It occurred to me in Paris that the "high" ideals of student revolutionaries were not enough to oppose the weapons of the army and the riot police. Watching the French students, I realized that those who were first to antagonize the police, were also the first to run. The result was that those beaten most severely were bystanders, tourists, and café waiters. And my own misfortune led me to the thought that I, for one, am not that anxious for a New Left revolution, and never was. My reportage from a hospital bed was, under those conditions, as good as could be expected and was, I thought, a real windfall for *Barb*. Direct-from-Paris, etc. But rather than achieving those underground Halls of Fame, wherever they may be, I failed miserably. And for one reason. Max didn't approve of my tone. My true attitude toward what I was doing leaked out from behind the bandages. My false New Left face had been broken in the battering. Having assumed that I had a message (Don't get hurt), I was guilty of writing down. Max had warned me. The Revolution, Berkeley Style, had broken out in the meanwhile at home. Morale among the radicals and the Street People was high, and then along came my article, direct-from-Paris as it was, urging people not to get hurt for their foolishness. The article was apparently irretrievable. I didn't know until I returned. Max had paid me for it.

The end of the underground line for me was near when I returned to Berkeley, although I did go back to work for Max. At this point he suggested that Jim Schreiber and I should be writing pretty near the whole newspaper. It was the biggest mistake he ever made in dealing with me. Max, apparently having concluded that my Paris dispatch was the result of a temporary aberration, seemed unaware of my sagging attitude. I was at that time trying to think of a way out, but there arose a set of stories which needed writing and I knew I had to write them.

Panther coverage was being handled by Stew Albert, a friend of Cleaver and of Yippie mouthpiece Jerry Rubin, and a Movement spokesman in his own right. Albert's style was nothing like my own; nothing, in fact, like anyone's. Instead it was all his, with a little Cleaver and Rubin mixed in. and during the fifteen weeks that I was gone, it had begun to change *Barb's* personality. Somehow such reporting as his seemed perfect for *Barb's* pages: always inside the story, always imaginatively and outlandishly worded, very unjournalistic and yet very slick in an underground way. It was better for the audience Max had in mind. I couldn't write that way if I tried. It's not in me. If it ever was, it's been journalized out.

What I did, beginning in September, was to concentrate on the events taking place on the University of California campus. Late in October, as a result of the Regents' refusal to give academic credit for an experimental course in which Cleaver was the principal lecturer, there was a series of demonstrations and sit-ins. For the second time I found myself in a dual role, reporter for the underground and student at the University of California fearing further violence would result in unnecessary damage and injury. The picture changed when at 5:30 a.m. on the second day of sit-ins (October 24), almost one thousand riot-helmeted policemen and Highway Patrolmen marched onto the campus to "clean it up." I felt a slight wave of nausea come over me at the sight of the ugly police action and the memory of the burning streets of the student quarter of Paris. For the first time I allowed myself to use the word "Pigs" outside of a direct quotation. This emotional and semantic experience signalled the end of the underground for me. There were ten stories that I wrote for that issue of *Barb* totaling about 150 inches, and with NEW BATTLE CRY: PIGS OFF CAMPUS, HOW THEY HELD CLEAVER'S FORT BLOW BY BLOW, IT TOOK TILL NOW TO REACH WHAT'S UP, and FROM GLOWING FLAMES TO A BLOODY BUTT, I wrote myself out of a job.

The lesson of the underground is that you have to be where you are, doing what you're doing for those for whom you are doing it. I wanted only about a quarter's worth of the underground bag, and it wasn't enough. One crawls out of the underground with a feeling of accomplishment, of having come to understand a great deal about what is going on in this country. For one thing, I learned more about the American press than journalism professors generally know or would care to teach if they knew. And I have left with a profound respect for the integrity of the have-nots and an automatic desire to find out about the other side. I appreciate what *Barb* and other underground papers are attempting to do, and, to a large degree, accomplishing.

The future of the underground will be unrelated to the costs of offset printing and decisions of the Supreme Court. It will not disappear when the straight media proclaim "The Death of Hip" for the hundredth time. It will continue to criticize and prod and tease the established ways of doing things and the established ways of communicating. Perhaps it will refine itself out of the inky tabloid bag; many have already. But even if the child comes to the dinner table with dirty hands, he is loved and appreciated.

The most important asset of an underground paper is the character of its people. The underground press is a devoted press. There can, in theory, be no journalistic hacks below the ground. For one thing, the pay isn't good enough. Most work on a voluntary basis. At *Barb* freelancers can rarely make it on a 25-cent-per-published-inch basis. Even at the best of the papers, a full-time staffer makes only a subsistence wage of fifty or sixty dollars a week. For another thing, it takes dedication, and the desire to change the world. Men like Max, for whom the underground is a way of life, believe that those who have a great enough commitment will be happy just to do their part for the Movement. Unlike the straight media, for which anyone with a neat appearance and some standardized sign of achievement can qualify, the underground demands conviction, even before ability.

The people in the underground are a lot like the underground press. They are always changing, and because they are so fluid, there are never enough of them around. They learn quickly, grow quickly, and move quickly. They are, in their own way, very idealistic. They waver from pessimism to great optimism depending on whether they're up or down that week.

The problem facing the underground now is finding people who will stay on, and not just learn the lesson of the underground and then hop off at the next station as I did. As long as there are people who participate freely out of a desire to fight for the interest of their family, there will always be readers, no matter how seedy or silly the content of the underground press may appear to its adversaries, the rest of society.

I respect Max for having this kind of dedication, but there are very few who have both the ability and the devotion to share his dream. One of the few was Jim Schreiber, who joined Max in March, 1966, as managing editor and general miracle man. One day not very long ago, Jim walked into a double feature instead of going to the office on a deadline night. His shoulder-length hair disappeared a few days later. He dropped-in, so to speak, and became a stringer for *Time*, The Weekly Newsmagazine.

Gillian Freeman | # Pornography as a Necessity

Many of the magazines and books I have been able to obtain may — with obvious exceptions — be described as hard-core or soft-core pornography (I am not, of course, inferring that the serious and reputable novels and magazines mentioned because of a fantasy content are pornographic in any way whatever), and despite my aim to be scrupulously objective in the assessment of it, I have been inescapably led to the conviction that pornography is a real necessity in the lives of many people. So much so,

SOURCE: *The Undergrowth of Literature* by Gillian Freeman. Copyright © 1967 by Gillian Freeman. Reprinted by permission of Dell Publishing Company.

in fact, that I believe it should be on open sale — with the proviso that, as with alcohol and tobacco, it is not available to minors.

At present the English law — unlike the American law, which varies from state to state — forbids the publication of pornography under the Obscene Publications Act of 1959. The *Oxford English Dictionary* defines 'obscene, as 'repulsive, filthy, loathsome, indecent, lewd', etc. Supposing I see or read something obscene — and by the dictionary definition of the word I can see something obscene every time I open a newspaper — by what process can it be proved that I am morally harmed by it? The English law, in Section 1 (1) of the Act, states that an article shall be deemed to be obscene if its effect is, if taken as a whole, such as to tend to deprave and corrupt persons who are likely to read, see or hear the matter contained in it'. Yet on 6 July 1966 the British Attorney-General, Sir Elwyn Jones, stated in Parliament that the amount of pornography published in or imported into this country had reached 'saturation point'.[1] If this is so, where, then, is the wholesale 'corruption and depravity' the Obscene Libel Law was devised to prevent? From the Attorney-General's own lips the law is demonstrable nonsense so far as England is concerned.

It has been suggested that pornography can create anti-social behaviour — indecency, rape, and murder. This argument is, to say the least, unproven. No pictures or books can match the fantasies of the human mind, and to a diseased mind pornography is irrelevant; the sadistic murderer will commit his crime without the aid of pornography. If pornography has any effect at all, it is apt to be beneficial, acting as a mental aperient, a transference of need from the act to the image; at most it leads to onanism, which is innocuous enough. In some Scandinavian prisons it is on the library shelves for the inmates to read freely. I defy anyone to prove that people become depraved and corrupted by pornography. Excited perhaps, amused, sexually stimulated. So what? This results in no more than the excitement of an appetite, the selection of a stimulant as natural and as personal as the choice of food. One man's meat, in fact, is another man's pornography.

Most people find fantasy more satisfying than reality, and willingly enter into fantasy states. Sometimes these are self-induced and sometimes external elements incite them. A child will act out fantasies with no recourse to real life, temporarily allowing himself to believe he is a fictional character, just as, for a time, a male transvestite allows himself to believe he is a woman. Fantasy identity differs from the total identity in madness because the intrusion of reality kills the daydream. Often a child waits until he is in bed before embarking on an imaginary game, so that there are no interruptions. In the same way a young girl will lie in bed and invent romantic situations around real or unreal lovers. In love affairs

---

[1] During 1965 180,888 pornographic books and 1,076,139 magazines were seized by the police. At least the same number reached the intended market.

the truth is so involved with wish-fulfillment that it is difficult to assess. Anticipation and recollection are as satisfying and important as contact with the person.

Experiments have proved the absolute necessity of dreams in maintaining mental equilibrium; I am inclined to think that our conscious dreams are just as important in maintaining that stability, and that everyone, even those people who are considered to be unimaginative, indulge in them. Fantasy and hope are so closely allied that, without the mental freedom of daydreaming, life would not be worth living. People without hope, without dreams, often reject life altogether. Fantasy fills in the gaps which reality, sadly, fails to provide, particularly in sexual activity, when secret desires are often not voiced, or if they are, are then rejected so that actuality does not measure up to invention. Prostitutes are the recourse of many men who are afraid to tell their wives of deviations, but prostitutes merely act the desired part, and no one can pretend for long that it isn't pretence and therefore as unsatisfactory as solitary imaginings.

The trouble is that adult play, except at the nonparticipant level of fairly tales, or television shows like *The Avengers*, where it can be as kinky as you like without anxiety, acutely embarrasses us. This is the theme of John Osborne's play *Under Plain Cover*. Now and again, birds of a feather marry, the game becomes two-sided, the secret of a childhood secret (which is basically what it is) with loss of public anxiety. But in general we don't encourage such a secure comprehension. One has to be driven to be willing to be thought odd, especially by a life-partner.

Maybe the play is tension-reducing rather than life-changing, but so is most psychotherapy. This goes for sadism and masochism too, which express the factor — intersexual aggression — which now upsets us most. 'Except in border-line states, sado-masochistic fantasies are actually playful. The patients would be repelled by the opportunity to act them out: when the fantasy includes a partner, both are represented as knowing that the activity is playful.'[2] In other words, the frontier we ought to be fortifying isn't between love and aggression, but between play and spiteful reality. The worrying manifestations are those which escape from the bedroom: into politics, punishment, hooliganism, religion — the uncensorables.

I divide fantasy into levels, like the levels of an archaeological dig. At the lowest level, as close to the unconscious as anything outside our sleeping dreams, are those fantasies concerned with elaborate sexual fetish. At the top are the fantasies imposed on us and designed to stimulate. These the particularly common in advertising. Sometimes the intent is immediately evident as in a picture of a girl astride a giant lipstick — while in other instances it is more subtle. The dominant woman, so prevalent in

---

[2] S. S. Feldman in *Yearbook of Psychoanalysis, 8*, International University Press, New York, 1969.

pornography and male fantasy, appears more and more frequently in advertisements. In a series of petrol advertisements she is dressed as a cowboy and holds the filler hose like a whip or like a gun. In a soft drinks advertisement she carries an actual gun across her shoulder, slightly less obvious than the cigarettes which satisfy and are pictorially phallic, or the car ownership which is a gateway to sexual fulfillment, or the washing powder which makes a wife desirable.

Imposed fantasies are not always sexual. Romantic fantasies are recurrent in women's magazines and in novels intended for women. One American women's magazine, *Cosmopolitan*, has stories which are marginally erotic. 'She hummed a song to herself about a pretty girl is like a memory, and she smiled up at the moon and started taking off her clothes.' (To an audience.)

Now this kind of story is only suggestive, and differs from the pornographic story which is bought and read deliberately for sexual excitement. A person with deviate sexual desires will go out with the intention of buying a pornographic book with his particular interest as its theme. The pornographic book is sought out. No one reads pornography inadvertently; it is intended as an exercise in fantasy. A romantic or erotic story in a magazine arouses by chance and its effect is comparable to that brought about by an advertisement, which depends on the eventuality of its being seen. I doubt whether many people thumb through m   ines in the hope of finding a sexually motivated advertisement.

Another level at which fantasy plays an important role is the level of hopes and memories when fact is only a point of departure. There are the holidays to which we look forward, imagining ourselves — as we sit by the fire on a winter's day — standing on a terrace overlooking a beach we have never seen. Then we recall the holiday, blotting out the memories of mosquito bites and diarrhoea; making a fantasy of fact by being selective. Sometimes it is even necessary to retreat into fantasy as the only possible relief from memories which are too unpleasant or painful or desolating to be retained, and the conclusion in extreme cases is a complete rejection of reality.

In Fellini's film, *Juliet of the Spirits*, the middle-aged wife whose husband is unfaithful is haunted by fantasies derived from childhood. They become so overwhelming that, for a time, they are stronger than actuality and dominate her life. There is the real case of a boy who entered a German prison camp at the age of ten and, on release, lost his memory. Subsequently, brought up by Hungarians and given a new name, he dreamed continually of a woman and a white cottage. Seeking his identity, he underwent hypnosis, and spoke only Russian, a language he did not understand in his daily life. He was even able to give his name. Yet outside of hypnosis he is still unable to remember.

Ours is a comparatively rich and leisured society in which sex often becomes no more than a whimsical entertainment. The decline of religion and the obtaining of economic affluence have left, as they did in Ancient Rome, fetishes unattended by worship, which flourish on alone. The slaughtering of bulls is acceptable when the practice is a part of worship, but divorced from it it becomes a social pretension. Just as a ritual drinking ceremony has dwindled into a cocktail hour with a whole range of knicknacks produced for it alone, so sexual fetishism has become an end in itself. Stories of deviation are the products of leisured minds, the mechanical elaboration and detail planned with the care an interior decorator gives to a house; a showpiece, an entertainment and a ritual which has the woman or the penis as its object of worship.

Surveying the decadent contemporary scene, which was ultimately to produce the debaucheries and fetishism of Petronius' Rome ('Trimalchio's Feast'), Horace wrote:

> Boy, I detest the Persian style
> Of elaboration. Garlands bore me
> Laced up with lime bark. Don't run a mile
> To find the last rose of summer for me.
>
> None of your fussy attempts to refine
> On simple myrtle. Myrtle suits both
> Your pouring, my drinking, wine
> Under the trellised vine's thick growth.[3]

Perhaps automation will result in a vast new public avidity for pornography and perversion, as hard-working active men apparently don't require it.

'Sexual fantasy is as old as civilization (as opposed to as old as the race) [said Gore Vidal], and one of its outward and visible signs is pornographic literature, an entirely middle-class phenomenon since we are assured by many investigators (Kinsey, Pomeroy, et al.) that the lower orders seldom rely on sexual fantasy for extra-stimulus. As soon as possible the uneducated man goes for the real thing. This must be the last meaningful class distinction in the West.'[4]

Certainly it is only now, in England anyway, that pornographic books have been within the *reach* of the working class. In the past such reading was a prerogative of the rich, since it was obtainable not in London, but in Paris or Cairo on the Grand Tour; and at considerable cost. With the advent of higher incomes, greater literacy, and more free time, today's gigantic sales might well be explained. 'The fetishist has displaced his desire from an area in which it can be fulfilled to an area in which it cannot. It has been moved from a sensation to an idea.'[5]

The masturbation which almost always results from reading erotica

---

[3] *The Odes of Horace*, translated by James Michie, Rupert Hart-Davis, London, 1964.
[4] *New York Review*, March 1966.
[5] Anthony Storr, *Sexual Deviation*, Penguin Books, Harmondsworth, 1964.

must be unsatisfactory in the same way. An object or an idea is less rewarding than human contact.

Inge and Sten Hegeler make some sensible remarks about this in *An ABZ of Love*:[6]

'A very considerable part of masturbation is the fantasies which accompany the act. These flights of fancy are among the most private things we human beings have. But in the majority of instances these fanciful images accompany masturbation — i.e., parallel acts that supplement each other until the desired sexual satisfaction has been achieved. Nor is it unsual for these erotic fantasies, these sexual "accompanying" dreams, to be somewhat bolder than the reality which surrounds us. It is not unusual for our dreams to be somewhat wilder than our daily lives.

'It is not unthinkable, for instance, that a woman may select images of a homosexual nature — without this meaning that she would enter into homosexual relationships in real life. There are others who possibly toy with the thought of prostitution. . . . In the same way there are men whose images may be tinged with sadistic or masochistic ideas, but who in the course of their sex life keep strictly to the conventional, accepted pattern.'

I would add that not everyone is sexually attractive but that everyone has sexual desires. For millions of people masturbation must be the only form of sexual relief. If a man can't make love to a pretty girl because she would reject him, then the next best thing is to imagine he can. If he hasn't the courage to tell his wife he wants to bind her up and beat her or dress her in a frogman's suit, then at least he can sublimate his desires by doing it in fantasy.

Gore Vidal writes:

> . . . few lovers are willing to admit that in the sexual act to create and maintain excitement they may need some mental image as erotic supplement to the body in attendance; for those who find the classic positions of "mature" love-making unsatisfactory yet dare not distress the beloved with odd requests, sexual fantasy becomes inevitable and the shy lover soon finds himself imposing mentally all sorts of wild images upon his unsuspecting partner, who may also be relying on an inner theater of mind to keep things going.[7]

He also suggests that the economic necessity of a late marriage — sexual potency is very strong in the teens — and the social strictures that sex outside marriage is wrong, result in years of onanism and 'not unnaturally, in order to make that solitary act meaningful, the theater of the mind early becomes a Dionysian festival, and should he be a resourceful dramatist, he may find actual love-making disappointing when he finally gets to it.'[8]

---

[6] Translated by David Hohnen, Neville Spearman, London, 1963.

[7] Art. cit.

[8] Ibid.

The things that stimulate sexually are so varied, so complex, and so constricted by taboos that people are ashamed to admit that what they really want is to be chained or dressed in plastic or corsets, or to have their partner in boots, velvet, fur, or gagged. Clothes are generally more important than the bodies they conceal, and the long descriptions given to putting them on and taking them off, and the way they feel, outweigh those concerned with the sexual act.

Colin Spencer, in his novel, *Poppy Mandragora and the New Sex*,[9] creates a character, Dr. Berriman, who helps the sexually distressed.

' "There are in the home counties about twenty men and women who live with the Berriman life-sized doll. An invention of mine," he says modestly. "These in some cases of sexual frustration and impotence, of gross sexual inferiority are the perfect answer. The dolls are filled with hot water and they can be plugged in. They look and feel like human skin and they are hinged and painted in such a way that they can get into any position. Of course they make no sound and they comply with anything their lover demands. One poor boy ritually murders his doll every night." '

In the United States a life-sized inflatable doll has already been manufactured and marketed (it comes with a detachable wig, blonde, brunette, or redhead), and in a new film, originally entitled, *The Family is Sacred*, Marcio Ferrari has an epilogue set in a future in which men and women "marry" dolls, tailored to size.

'There sure are plenny er fetishes,' said the smiling bookseller in one of the many pornographic bookshops on Main Street, downtown Los Angeles. 'We try ter stock 'em all.' Of course he didn't. Small minorities are, on the whole, ignored. But some deviations are so common that there is a vast literature devoted to them; homosexuality, which comes in many guises of sun-worship and body-building and love of youth; undisguised transvestism, bondage, spanking, and torture. Yet it is a case of historical-pastoral, pastoral-comical, and comical-historical, for one can buy transvestite-bondage, bondage-spanking, spanking-transvestite, and torture for all.

As I have said, I think pornography is necessary to many people. Although personally I am bored by the bizarre deviations and sickened by the sado-masochism, I can accept that, however extreme and grotesque, it provides a catharsis for many whose sexual and emotional needs are otherwise unsatisfied. If at times I seem casual or flippant it is because my concern is with the literature and not with the conditions which promote it; with the written word and not with the personal despair, of which perhaps one of the saddest aspects is the guilt incurred. Even so, if one is amused at the gargantuan breasts and buttocks which many men find stimulating — and whose needs are easily catered for by the many legal publications which specialize in such fetishes — one has a deeper com-

---

[9] Anthony Blond, London, 1966.

miseration with the transsexualist who finds his body alien to his mind. If the research for this book has taught me anything, it is an increased sympathy for my fellow human beings whose erotic needs can only be served by fantasy literature which is often difficult to find, expensive, and illegal.

There, but for the grace of Aphrodite . . .

Pauline Kael | # from I Lost It at the Movies

When movies, the only art which everyone felt free to enjoy and have opinions about, lose their connection with song and dance, drama, and the novel, when they become cinema, which people fear to criticize just as they fear to say what they think of a new piece of music or a new poem or painting, they will become another object of academic study and "appreciation," and will soon be an object of excitement only to practitioners of the "art." Although *L'Avventura* is a great film, had I been present at Cannes in 1960, where Antonioni distributed his explanatory statement, beginning, "There exists in the world today a very serious break between science on the one hand . . . ," I might easily have joined in the hisses, which he didn't really deserve until the following year, when *La Notte* revealed that he'd begun to believe his own explanations — thus making liars of us all.

When we see Dwight Macdonald's cultural solution applied to film, when we see the prospect that movies will become a product for "Masscult" consumption, while the "few who care" will have their High Culture cinema, who wants to take the high road? There is more energy, more originality, more excitement, more *art* in American kitsch like *Gunga Din*, *Easy Living*, the Rogers and Astaire pictures like *Swingtime* and *Top Hat*, in *Strangers on a Train*, *His Girl Friday*, *The Crimson Pirate*, *Citizen Kane*, *The Lady Eve*, *To Have and Have Not*, *The African Queen*, *Singin' in the Rain*, *Sweet Smell of Success*, or more recently, *The Hustler*, *Lolita*, *The Manchurian Candidate*, *Hud*, *Charade*, than in the presumed "High Culture" of *Hiroshima Mon Amour*, *Marienbad*, *La Notte*, *The Eclipse*, and the Torre Nilsson pictures. As Nabokov remarked, "Nothing is more exhilarating than Philistine vulgarity."

Regrettably, one of the surest signs of the Philistine is his reverence for

SOURCE: *I Lost It at the Movies* by Pauline Kael. Copyright © 1961 and © 1964 by Pauline Kael. Reprinted by permission of Atlantic-Little, Brown & Co.

the superior tastes of those who put him down. Macdonald believes that "a work of High Culture, however inept, is an expression of feelings, ideas, tastes, visions that are idiosyncratic and the audience similarly responds to them as individuals." No. The "pure" cinema enthusiast who doesn't react to a film but feels he should, and so goes back to it over and over, is not responding as an individual but as a compulsive good pupil determined to appreciate what his cultural superiors say is "art." Movies are on their way into academia when they're turned into a matter of duty: a mistake in judgment isn't fatal, but too much anxiety about judgment is. In this country, respect for High Culture is becoming a ritual.

If debased art is kitsch, perhaps kitsch may be redeemed by honest vulgarity, may become art. Our best work transforms kitsch, makes art out of it; that is the peculiar greatness and strength of American movies, as Godard in *Breathless* and Truffaut in *Shoot the Piano Player* recognize. Huston's *The Maltese Falcon* is a classic example. Our first and greatest film artist D. W. Griffith was a master of kitsch: the sentiment and melodrama in his films are much more integral to their greatness than the critics who lament Griffith's lack of mind (!) perceive.

The movies are still where it happens, not for much longer perhaps, but the movies are still the art form that uses the material of our lives and the art form that we use. I am not suggesting that we want to see new and bigger remakes of the tired old standbys of the film repertory: who wants to see the new *Cimarron*, another *Quo Vadis?* And meanings don't have to be spread out for us like a free-lunch counter. There are movies that are great experiences like *Long Day's Journey into Night*, and just a few years back there were movies which told good stories — movies like *The Treasure of Sierra Madre, From Here to Eternity, The Nun's Story.*

People go to the movies for the various ways they express the experiences of our lives, and as a means of avoiding and postponing the pressures we feel. This latter function of art — generally referred to disparagingly as escapism — may also be considered as refreshment, and in terms of modern big city life and small town boredom, it may be a major factor in keeping us sane.

In the last few years there has appeared a new kind of filmgoer: he isn't interested in movies but in cinema. A great many of the film makers are in this group: they've never gone to movies much and they don't care about them. They're interested in what they can do in the medium, not in what *has* been done. This is, of course, their privilege, though I would suggest that it may explain why they have such limited approaches to film. I'm more puzzled by the large numbers of those who are looking for *importance* in cinema. For example, a doctor friend called me after he'd seen *The Pink Panther* to tell me I needn't "bother" with that one, it was just slapstick. When I told him I'd already seen it and had a good time at it, he was irritated; he informed me that a movie should be more than a waste of time, it should be an exercise of taste that will enrich your life.

Those looking for importance are too often contemptuous of the crude vitality of American films, though this crudity is not always offensive, and may represent the only way that energy and talent and inventiveness can find an outlet, can break through the planned standardization of mass entertainment. It has become a mark of culture to revere the old slapstick (the Mack Sennett two-reelers and early Chaplins that aren't really as great as all that) and put down the new. But in a movie as shopworn as *Who's Been Sleeping in My Bed?* there is, near the end, an almost inspired satirical striptease by Carol Burnett. *The Nutty Professor* is too long and repetitive, but Jerry Lewis has some scenes that hold their own with the silent classics. I enjoyed *The Prize*, which opens badly but then becomes a lively, blatant entertainment; but there's no point in recommending it to someone who wants his life enriched. I couldn't persuade friends to go see *Charade*, which although no more than a charming confectionery trifle was, I think, probably the best American film of last year — as artificial and enjoyable in its way as *The Big Sleep*. The word had got around that it isn't *important*, that it isn't serious, that it doesn't do anything for you.

Our academic bureaucracy needs something alive to nourish it and movies still have a little blood which the academics can drain away. In the West several of the academic people I know who have least understanding of movies were suddenly interested by Laurence Alloway's piece called "Critics in the Dark" in *Encounter*. By suggesting that movie criticism had never gotten into the right hands — i.e., theirs, and by indicating *projects*, and by publishing in the prestigious *Encounter*, Alloway indicated large vistas of respectability for future film critics. Perhaps also they were drawn to his condescending approach to movies as a pop art. Many academics have always been puzzled that Agee could *care* so much about movies. Alloway, by taking the position that Agee's caring was a maladjustment, re-established their safe, serene worlds in which if a man gets excited about an idea or an issue, they know there's something the matter with him. It's not much consolation, but I think the cinema the academics will be working over will be the cinema they deserve.

Recently, at a cocktail party of artists and professors, I noticed displayed on a table right next to the pickled Jerusalem artichokes, two French publications — Lo Duca's new volume on *Eroticism in the Cinema* and Kenneth Anger's *Hollywood Babylon*. Both books are like more elegantly laidout issues of *Confidential* and all those semi-nameless magazines which feature hideously outsized mammary glands, only these books are supposed to be chic — the latest intellectual camp. The Lo Duca book features stills from a Kenneth Anger movie in which nude ladies are wrapped in chains. Anger, you may recall, made his reputation with a film called *Fireworks*, in which a roman candle explodes inside a sailor's fly. His own book has a dust jacket photograph of Jayne Mansfield — an aerial view down her dress that makes her breasts look like long strips of cooked tripe. The book itself is a recounting of the legends (that is to say the dirty stories, scandals, and gossip) that Anger heard while growing up in southern California.

What struck me about these books, which function as entertainment to what might be called highbrows, was that their chic seemed to consist largely in a degradation of the female image. The stars and starlets are displayed at their most grotesque, just as they are in the cheapest American publications (in fact the photos are probably derived from those sources). This female image is a parody of woman — lascivious face, wet open mouth, gigantic drooping breasts. She has no character, no individuality: she's blonde or brunette or redhead, as one might consume a martini, an old-fashioned, or a gin and tonic.

Now I am told that even the junior-high-school boys of America use photographs like these as pinups, and that this is their idea of the desirable female. I don't believe it. I would guess that they pretend to this ideal because they're afraid they won't be considered manly and sexy if they admit they find this image disgusting. I don't believe that these photographs are erotic in any ordinary sense. I think that the grotesqueness of this female image is what people enjoy. Here are some possible reasons. First, these spongy, subhuman sex images reduce women to the lowest animal level. And in the modern world, where women are competent, independent, and free and equal, the men have a solid, competitive hostility — they want to see women degraded even lower than they were in the Victorian era. Here is woman reduced to nothing but a blob that will gratify any male impulse. And, of course, a woman who has no interest in life but love presents no challenge to the male ego. Second, there's the old split between sacred and profane love — and many men feel that the more degraded the female, the more potent they would become. Third, there's the vast homosexual audience which enjoys derision of the female. I would guess, and here's a big generalization, that more homosexuals than heterosexuals love to chortle over the nude photos of Anita Ekberg. She's so preposterous — a living satire of the female. It's my guess that the audience for nudie-cutie magazines uses them in much the same way the wealthy and educated use expensive French publications on the same theme: they want to laugh at the subjects and/or feel superior to them.

When the parodied female becomes known, becomes a "personality," derision gives way to admiration and sympathy and "understanding." In publications like the British *Sunday Times* you will find discussions with passages like "Marilyn Monroe grew up without affection and at times she was near suicide. When she talks about herself the awareness of her bitter past is never quite absent." *Time* and *Life* present her psychoanalytical comments on herself. And Dwight Macdonald in *Esquire* explains that "the expensive difficulties she makes for her employers are not so much prima donna assertiveness as symptoms of resentment and boredom." Sociologists read Zolotow's book on her character changes, and

Cecil Beaton rhapsodizes that "she was born the postwar day we had need of her. Certainly she has no knowledge of the past. Like Giraudoux's Ondine, she is only fifteen years old; and she will never die." He's right, at least, about her not having knowledge of the past: she seems to have swallowed all the psychoanalytical clichés about maltreated children, and when she talks about her past she simply spews them up. And the educated public loves the burbling bits of Freudian "insight" when they come out of the mouths of "babes." In *The Misfits*, our heroine, with the sure instincts of the faithful dog, and the uncorrupted clarity of the good clean peasant, looks at each character in the film and knows him for what he is. The innocent eye can see the inner man — she's the female of the species of the strong, silent hero, but she's also the traditional whore with the heart of gold. Her performance in *The Misfits* appears uncontrollably nervous, but it's almost as if her confused state were the final proof of her sincerity. The public loves her the more because life seems too much for her.

La Vérité is a tired and trite and mechanical piece of slick moviemaking. Conceptually, it's rather like *Of Human Bondage* — seen from Mildred's point of view. Although the title and the film's structure suggest that we are going to see the relativity of truth, the movie seems designed to show us the truth about Brigitte Bardot, just as *The Misfits* was written around Monroe. (These ladies are then congratulated for their histrionic achievements in playing themselves; certainly they are perfect in the roles — no one else could play them so well — but then, could they play anyone else?) This confusion of art and life which takes the form of sensationalism is becoming very popular in this Freudianized period. (Clouzot coyly plays with this confusion by having Bardot, the subject of a book by Simone de Beauvoir, accused in the courtroom of *La Vérité* of having read a book by de Beauvoir.)

It is supposed to be daring and modern to make these messed-up accounts of messed-up lives — though they may seem very much like the old Sunday supplements with their daring exposés. In this new form, however, the appeal is not only to the mass audience but also to the more literate, who are led to believe that they are getting some inside psychological dope.

Apparently these screen incarnations of male fantasies, Monroe (once a calendar girl come to comic strip life, an implausible but delicious affront to respectability) and Bardot (the distillation of all those irresponsible, petulant teen-agers who may never know that human experience has depth and expressiveness and potentialities beyond their immediate range of impulses) are objects of enthusiasm not so much for their (former or present) polymorphous-perverse physical charms and their (former or present) comedy talents, as for their messy, confused public-private lives — the nervous breakdowns, miscarriages, overweight problems, husband troubles, and all those mental and physical ills which now comprise the image of a great star. The new heroine of our film is becoming the wretched star herself. In the pre-Freudian age, the exploitation of personal ailments in films like *The Misfits* and *La Vérité* would have been regarded as disgusting. It *is* disgusting, and the condescending type of sympathetic "understanding" which is now widely purveyed is an insult to Freud and man. In the frivolous, absurd old days, stars were photographed in their bubble bath: now they bathe in tears of self-pity — while intellectual critics tap their understanding typewriters.

The "mass" audience looks up at the "stars"; the educated audience looks down sympathetically, as if reading a case history. They all stew in their own narcissism. The mass audience is beginning to catch up. On a recent television program Ed Sullivan clucked sympathetically at Brigitte Bardot and told her how much he sympathized with the hard life of glamour girls like her and Monroe and Taylor, and, final irony, told her how much he admired the way she had "handled herself."

The educated American is a social worker at heart: he feels especially sympathetic toward these slovenly ladies because their slovenliness marks them as misfits who couldn't function in his orderly world. The same man who is enchanted with Monroe in the seduction scene of *Some Like It Hot* — crawling all over Tony Curtis while hanging out of her dress both fore and aft — expects his girl friends or wife to be trim, slender and well-groomed. The decor in the homes and offices of the American professional classes is clean and functional — Scandinavian with a guilty dash of Japanese (as reparation for the bomb, we sit close to the earth). Upon occasion, the American will desert the art house for an American picture, particularly if it is advertised with the intellectually fashionable decor. For this decor is an article of faith: it is progressive and important; it calls businessmen and artists to conferences at Aspen, where it is linked with discussions of such topics as "Man the Problem Solver." And so American movies now often come, packaged as it were, with several minutes of ingenious, abstract, eye-catching titles. This send-off — the graphics look provided by Saul Bass and other designers — has virtually nothing to do with the style or mood of the picture, but it makes the movie look more *modern*. (How can the picture be dismissed as trash when it looks like your own expensive living room?) This type of design, using basic colors and almost no soft lines, was, of course, devised so that advertising would be clear and effective with a minimum of cost. In movies, a photographic medium, complexity and variety and shadings of beauty are no more expensive than simplification. But modern graphic design, which has built an aesthetic on advertising economics, has triumphed: new big productions (like *The Misfits*) open with such a proud array of flashy designs that the movie itself comes on rather apologetically.

The advertising campaign for new films often uses a motif that appears again at the opening of the film: presumably, if the ad was good enough to get you there, you'll appreciate having it amplified. Perhaps the next

Hollywood "genius" will be the man who can design the whole movie to look like the high-powered ad. At present, the movie that begins when the packaging is out of the way is in a different, and older, style of advertising art. This style was summed up by a member of the audience a few weeks ago when I was looking at a frightfully expensive, elaborately staged movie. The beautiful heroine, in pale blue, was descending an elegant beige staircase, when a voice from the dark piped up — "Modess, because . . ." When the beautiful heroine in pale blue finally got into her creamy white lace and the properly nondenominational clergyman intoned, "Wilt thou, Robert, take this woman . . . ," another voice in the theater groaned, "I wilt."

The social worker-at-heart finds true reassurance when the modern-designed movie also has modern design built into the theme: a movie like *Twelve Angry Men*. Ask an educated American what he thought of *Twelve Angry Men* and more likely than not he will reply, "That movie made some good points" or "It got some important ideas across." His assumption is that it carried these ideas, which also happen to be his ideas, to the masses. Actually it didn't: this tense, ingenious juryroom melodrama was a flop with the mass audience, a success only at revivals in art houses.

The social psychology of *Twelve Angry Men* is perfectly attuned to the educated audience. The hero, Henry Fonda — the one against the eleven — is lean, intelligent, gentle but strong; this liberal, fair-minded architect is *their* hero. And the boy on trial is their dream of a victim: he is of some unspecified minority, he is a slum product who never had a chance, and, to clinch the case, his father didn't love him. It isn't often that professional people can see themselves on the screen as the hero — in this case the Lincolnesque architect of the future — and how they loved it! They are so delighted to see a movie that demonstrates a proposition they have already accepted that they cite *Twelve Angry Men* and *The Defiant Ones* as evidence that American movies are really growing up.

It is a depressing fact that Americans tend to confuse morality and art (to the detriment of both), and that, among the educated, morality tends to mean social consciousness. Not implicit social awareness (Antonioni isn't "saying anything," they complain of *L'Avventura*) but explicit, machine-tooled, commercialized social consciousness. "The old payola won't work any more," announces the hero of *The Apartment*, and even people who should know better are happy to receive the message. How reassuring *The Apartment* is, with its cute, soft-hearted Jewish doctor and his cute, soft-hearted, fat, mama-comic Jewish wife — so unworldly and lovable that they take the poor frustrated sap for a satyr (almost as deadly in its "humor" as Rock Hudson being mistaken for a homosexual in *Pillow Talk*). In *The Apartment*, the little people are little dolls: the guys at the top are vicious and corrupt and unfaithful to their wives as well. The moral is, stick at the bottom and you don't have to do the dirty.

This is the pre-bomb universe; and its concept of the "dirty" is so old-fashioned and irrelevant, its notions of virtue and of vice so smugly limited, that it's positively cozy to see people for whom deciding to quit a plushy job is a big moral decision. The "social consciousness" of the educated is so unwieldy, so overstuffed, that the mass audience may well catch up before the intellectuals have found any grounds to move on to — though surely many should be happy to vacate the premises of Freud and Marx.

The art-house audience is at its dreamiest for Russian films like *Ballad of a Soldier* and *The Cranes Are Flying*. How eager they are to believe the best about the Soviet Union, to believe that love is back, propaganda is out, and it's all right to like Russian movies because the Russians are really nice people, very much like us, only better. These sentiments have been encouraged by the theaters and by the cultural exchange agreement, and at showings of *The Cranes Are Flying* there was a queasy little prefatory note: "At the same time you are watching this Soviet film, Soviet audiences are watching an American motion picture." I was happy for the voice in the theater which piped up, "But it's six A.M. in the Soviet Union."

The Cranes Are Flying and *Ballad of a Soldier* are both good examples of nineteenth-century patriotism and nineteenth-century family values; neither seems to belong to the Communist period at all — they're reminiscent of American war epics of the silent era. And sophisticated Americans love the simple, dutiful characters that they would laugh at in American movies. It's a long time since audiences at art houses accepted the poor, ravished unhappy heroine who has to marry the cad who rapes her. They go even farther toward primitivism at *Ballad of a Soldier:* they love the "touching" and "charming" hero and heroine who express such priggish repugnance at a soldier's unfaithful wife (how would these two react if they caught the wife sleeping with a German, like the heroine of *Hiroshima Mon Amour?*). *Ballad of a Soldier* takes us back to the days when love was sweet and innocent, authority was good, only people without principles thought about sex, and it was the highest honor to fight and die for your country. These homely values, set in handsome, well-photographed landscapes, apparently are novel and refreshing — perhaps they're even exotic — to art-house audiences. It's a world that never was, but hopeful people would love to associate it with life in the Soviet Union.

Are these recruiting posters so morally superior to American lingerie ads like *Butterfield 8?* Are they as effective in the U.S.S.R. as in the outside world? We can see the results of *Butterfield 8:* half the junior-high-school girls in America are made up to look like Elizabeth Taylor, and at the Academy Award Show it was hard to tell the stars apart — there were so many little tin Lizzies. It's more difficult to gauge the effects of Russia's antique middle-class morality. Perhaps educated Americans love the Russians more than the Russians do. All over America people are suddenly studying Russian; and they sometimes give the impression that the first word they want to learn is "Welcome."

A congressional subcommittee headed by Kathryn Granahan, a Democrat from Pennsylvania who is known as America's leading lady smut-hunter, is exploring the possibility that the influx of foreign films, most especially the French film *Les Liaisons Dangereuses,* may be a Communist plot to undermine American moral structure — that is to say that Americans are being offered a preoccupation with sex so that they will become degenerate, corrupt, too weak to combat the Communist threat. Mrs. Granahan has stated that the social, cultural and moral standards of France are among the greatest impediments to a strong NATO stand against international Communism.

In other words, she takes the position that a strong state, a state capable of defending itself, must be a Puritan state, and that individual freedom and the loosening of sexual standards threaten the state. This is, of course, the present Communist position; even American jazz is regarded as a threat. Nothing could be *cleaner* — in nineteenth-century terms — than Russian movies. Observers at the Moscow Film Festival reported that the Russians were quite upset after the showing of *The Trials of Oscar Wilde:* they had been under the impression that Wilde was imprisoned for his revolutionary politics — for socialism, not for sodomy. Russians have been protected from just such information, discussion and art as Mrs. Granahan would protect us from. Apart from what appears to be a wholly unfounded notion that the Russians are trying to poison us via French sexual standards, there is an interesting issue here. For absurd as the Granahan position seems to be, I have heard a variant of it from many people who would scoff at the way she puts it.

Everywhere in the United States enthusiasts for *La Dolce Vita* explain that it's a great lesson to us — that Rome fell because of sexual promiscuity and high living, and we will too — that the Communists are going to win because of our moral laxity, our decay. It's as if poor old Gibbon had labored in vain, and the churches' attitudes have triumphed. Even those who no longer believe in God seem to accept the idea that European and American habits and values are loose and sinful and will bring destruction down upon us.

May I suggest that this is just as nonsensical as the Granahan line? If all Europeans and all Americans suddenly became heterosexual and monogamous — if everyone took the pledge and there were no more drinking, if all nightclubs were closed, and if the rich turned their wealth over to the poor — I cannot see that our *power* position in this nuclear age would in any way be affected. And it's astonishing that sensible people can get so sentimental about Russian movies with their Puritan standards, the bourgeois morality that developed out of the rising salaried classes and the Stalinist drive to stamp out individual freedom. Queen Victoria squats on the Kremlin; and Americans who fought to rid themselves of all that repressive Victorianism now beat their breasts and cry, look how *good* they are, look how *terrible* we are — why, we don't *deserve* to win. Has Puritanism so infected our thinking that we believe a nuclear war would be won by the pure in heart?

Marshall McLuhan | # The TV Mosaic

The mode of the TV image has nothing in common with film or photo, except that it offers also a nonverbal *gestalt* or posture of forms. With TV, the viewer is the screen. He is bombarded with light impulses that James Joyce called the "Charge of the Light Brigade" that imbues his "soul-skin with sobconscious inklings." The TV-image is visually low in data. The TV image is not a *still* shot. It is not photo in any sense, but a ceaselessly forming contour of things limned by the scanning-finger. The resulting plastic contour appears by light *through*, not light *on*, and the image so formed has the quality of sculpture and icon, rather than of picture. The TV image offers some three million dots per second to the receiver. From these he accepts only a few dozen each instant, from which to make an image.

The film image offers many more millions of data per second, and the viewer does not have to make the same drastic reduction of items to form his impression. He tends instead to accept the full image as a package deal. In contrast, the viewer of the TV mosaic, with technical control of the image, unconsciously reconfigures the dots into an abstract work of art on the pattern of a Seurat or Rouault. If anybody were to ask whether all this would change if technology stepped up the character of the TV image to movie data level, one could only counter by inquiring "Could we alter a cartoon by adding details of perspective and light and shade?" The answer is "Yes," only it would then no longer be a cartoon. Nor would "improved" TV be television. The TV image is *now* a mosaic mesh of light and dark spots which a movie shot never is, even when the quality of the movie image is very poor.

As in any other mosaic, the third dimension is alien to TV, but it can be superimposed. In TV the illusion of the third dimension is provided slightly by the stage sets in the studio; but the TV image itself is a flat two-dimensional mosaic. Most of the three-dimensional illusion is a carry-

SOURCE: *Understanding Media: The Extensions of Man* by Marshall McLuhan. Copyright © 1964 by Marshall McLuhan. Reprinted by permission of McGraw-Hill Book Company.

over of habitual viewing of film and photo. For the TV camera does not have a built-in angle of vision like the movie camera. Eastman Kodak now has a two-dimensional camera that can match the flat effects of the TV camera. Yet it is hard for literate people, with their habit of fixed points of view and three-dimensional vision, to understand the properties of two-dimensional vision. If it had been easy for them, they would have had no difficulties with abstract art, General Motors would not have made a mess of motorcar design, and the picture magazine would not be having difficulties now with the relationship between features and ads. The TV image requires each instant that we "close" the spaces in the mesh by a convulsive sensuous participation that is profoundly kinetic and tactile, because tactility is the interplay of the senses, rather than the isolated contact of skin and object.

To contrast it with the film shot, many directors refer to the TV image as one of "low definition," in the sense that it offers little detail and a low degree of information, much like the cartoon. A TV close-up provides only as much information as a small section of a long-shot on the movie screen. For lack of observing so central an aspect of the TV image, the critics of program "content" have talked nonsense about "TV violence." The spokesmen of censorious views are typically semiliterate book-oriented individuals who have no competence in the grammars of newspaper, or radio, or of film, but who look askew and askance at all non-book media. The simplest question about any psychic aspect, even of the book medium, throws these people into a panic of uncertainty. Vehemence of projection of a single isolated attitude they mistake for moral vigilance. Once these censors became aware that in all cases "the medium is the message" or the basic source of effects they would turn to suppression of media as such, instead of seeking "content" control. Their current assumption that content or programming is the factor that influences outlook and action is derived from the book medium, with its sharp cleavage between form and content.

Is it not strange that TV should have been as revolutionary a medium in America in the 1950s as radio in Europe in the 1930s? Radio, the medium that resuscitated the tribal and kinship webs of the European mind in the 1920s and 1930s, had no such effect in England or America. There, the erosion of tribal bonds by means of literacy and its industrial extensions had gone so far that our radio did not achieve any notable tribal reactions. Yet ten years of TV have Europeanized even the United States, as witness its changed feelings for space and personal relations. There is new sensitivity to the dance, plastic arts, and architecture, as well as the demand for the small car, the paperback, sculptural hairdos and molded dress effects — to say nothing of a new concern for complex effects in cuisine and in the use of wines. Notwithstanding, it would be misleading to say that TV will retribalize England and America. The action of radio on the world of resonant speech and memory was hysterical. But TV has certainly made England and America vulnerable to radio where previously they had immunity to a great degree. For good or ill, the TV image has exerted a unifying synesthetic force on the sense-life of these intensely literate populations, such as they have lacked for centuries. It is wise to withhold all value judgments when studying these media matters, since their effects are not capable of being isolated.

Synesthesia, or unified sense and imaginative life, had long seemed an unattainable dream to Western poets, painters, and artists in general. They had looked with sorrow and dismay on the fragmented and impoverished imaginative life of Western literate man in the eighteenth century and later. Such was the message of Blake and Pater, Yeats and D. H. Lawrence, and a host of other great figures. They were not prepared to have their dreams realized in everyday life by the esthetic action of radio and television. Yet these massive extensions of our central nervous systems have enveloped Western man in a daily session of synesthesia. The Western way of life attained centuries since by the rigorous separation and specialization of the senses, with the visual sense atop the hierarchy, is not able to withstand the radio and TV waves that wash about the great visual structure of abstract Individual Man. Those who, from political motives, would now add their force to the anti-individual action of our electric technology are puny subliminal automatons aping the patterns of the prevailing electric pressures. A century ago they would, with equal somnambulism, have faced in the opposite direction. German Romantic poets and philosophers had been chanting in tribal chorus for a return to the dark unconscious for over a century before radio and Hitler made such a return difficult to avoid. What is to be thought of people who wish such a return to preliterate ways, when they have no inkling of how the civilized visual way was ever substituted for tribal auditory magic?

At this hour, when Americans are discovering new passions for skin-diving and the wraparound space of small cars, thanks to the indomitable tactile promptings of the TV image, the same image is inspiring many English people with race feelings of tribal exclusiveness. Whereas highly literate Westerners have always idealized the condition of integration of races, it has been their literate culture that made impossible real uniformity among races. Literate man naturally dreams of visual solutions to the problems of human differences. At the end of the nineteenth century, this kind of dream suggested similar dress and education for both men and women. The failure of the sex-integration programs has provided the theme of much of the literature and psychoanalysis of the twentieth century. Race integration, undertaken on the basis of visual uniformity, is an extension of the same cultural strategy of literate man, for whom differences always seem to need eradication, both in sex and in race, and in space and in time. Electronic man, by becoming ever more deeply involved in the actualities of the human condition, cannot accept the literate cultural strategy. The Negro will reject a plan of visual uniformity as definitely as women did earlier, and for the same reasons. Women found that they had been robbed of their distinctive roles and turned into fragmented citizens in "a man's world." The entire approach to these problems in terms of uniformity and social homogenization is a final pressure of the mechanical and industrial technology. Without moralizing, it can be said that the electric age, by involving all men deeply in one another, will come to reject such mechanical solutions. It is more difficult to provide uniqueness and diversity than it is to impose the uniform patterns of mass education; but it is such uniqueness and diversity that can be fostered under electric conditions as never before.

Temporarily, all preliterate groups in the world have begun to feel the explosive and aggressive energies that are released by the onset of the new literacy and mechanization. These explosions come just at a time when the new electric technology combines to make us share them on a global scale.

The effect of TV, as the most recent and spectacular electric extension of our central nervous system, is hard to grasp for various reasons. Since it has affected the totality of our lives, personal and social and political, it would be quite unrealistic to attempt a "systematic" or visual presentation of such influence. Instead, it is more feasible to "present" TV as a complex *Gestalt* of data gathered almost at random.

The TV image is of low intensity or definition, and, therefore, unlike film, it does not afford detailed information about objects. The difference is akin to that between the old manuscripts and the printed word. Print gave intensity and uniform precision, where before there had been a diffuse texture. Print brought in the taste for exact measurement and repeatability that we now associate with science and mathematics.

The TV producer will point out that speech on television must not have the careful precision necessary in the theater. The TV actor does not have to project either his voice or himself. Likewise, TV acting is so extremely intimate, because of the peculiar involvement of the viewer with the completion or "closing" of the TV image, that the actor must achieve a great degree of spontaneous casualness that would be irrelevant in movie and lost on stage.

For the audience participates in the inner life of the TV actor as fully as in the outer life of the movie star. Technically, TV tends to be a close-up medium. The close-up that in the movie is used for shock is, on TV, a quite casual thing. And whereas a glossy photo the size of the TV screen would show a dozen faces in adequate detail, a dozen faces on the TV screen are only a blur.

The peculiar character of the TV image in its relation to the actor causes such familiar reactions as our not being able to recognize in real life a person whom we see every week on TV. Not many of us are as alert as the kindergartner who said to Garry Moore, "How did you get off TV?" Newscasters and actors alike report the frequency with which they are approached by people who feel they've met them before. Joanne Woodward in an interview was asked what was the difference between being a movie star and a TV actress. She replied: "When I was in the movies I heard people say, 'There goes Joanne Woodward.' Now they say, 'There goes somebody I think I know.' "

The owner of a Hollywood hotel in an area where many movie and TV actors reside reported that tourists had switched their allegiance to TV stars. Moreover, most TV stars are men, that is, "cool characters," while most movie stars are women, since they can be presented as "hot" characters. Men and women movie stars alike, along with the entire star system, have tended to dwindle into a more moderate status since TV. The movie is a hot, high-definition medium. Perhaps the most interesting observation of the hotel proprietor was that the tourists wanted to see Perry Mason and Wyatt Earp. They did not want to see Raymond Burr and Hugh O'Brian. The old movie-fan tourists had wanted to see their favorites as they were in real life, not as they were in their film roles. The fans of the cool TV medium want to see their star in role, whereas the movie fans want the real thing.

A similar reversal of attitudes occurred with the printed book. There was little interest in the private lives of authors under manuscript or scribal culture. Today the comic strip is close to the preprint woodcut and manuscript form of expression. Walt Kelly's *Pogo* looks very much indeed like a gothic page. Yet in spite of great public interest in the comic-strip form, there is as little curiosity about the private lives of these artists as about the lives of popular-song writers. With print, the private life became of the utmost concern to readers. Print is a hot medium. It projects the author at the public as the movie did. The manuscript is a cool medium that does not project the author, so much as involve the reader. So with TV. The viewer is involved and participant. The role of the TV star, in this way, seems more fascinating than his private life. It is thus that the student of media, like the psychiatrist, gets more data from his informants than they themselves have perceived. Everybody experiences far more than he understands. Yet it is experience, rather than understanding, that influences behavior, especially in collective matters of media and technology, where the individual is almost inevitably unaware of their effect upon him.

Some may find it paradoxical that a cool medium like TV should be so much more compressed and condensed than a hot medium like film. But it is well known that a half minute of television is equal to three minutes of stage or vaudeville. The same is true of manuscript in contrast to print. The "cool" manuscript tended toward compressed forms of statement, aphoristic and allegorical. The "hot" print-medium expanded expression in the direction of simplification and the "spelling-out" of meanings. Print speeded up and "exploded" the compressed script into simpler fragments.

A cool medium, whether the spoken word or the manuscript or TV, leaves much more for the listener or user to do than a hot medium. If the medium is of high definition, participation is low. If the medium is of low intensity, the participation is high. Perhaps this is why lovers mumble so.

Because the low definition of TV insures a high degree of audience involvement, the most effective programs are those that present situations which consist of some process to be completed. Thus, to use TV to teach poetry would permit the teacher to concentrate on the poetic process of actual *making*, as it pertained to a particular poem. The book form is quite unsuited to this type of involved presentation. The same salience of process of do-it-yourselfness and depth involvement in the TV image extends to the art of the TV actor. Under TV conditions, he must be alert to improvise and to embellish every phrase and verbal resonance with details of gesture and posture, sustaining that intimacy with the viewer which is not possible on the massive movie screen or on the stage.

There is the alleged remark of the Nigerian who, after seeing a TV western, said delightedly, "I did not realize you valued human life so little in the West." Offsetting this remark is the behavior of our children in watching TV westerns. When equipped with the new experimental head-cameras that follow their eye movements while watching the image, children keep their eyes on the faces of the TV actors. Even during physical violence their eyes remain concentrated on the facial *reactions*, rather than on the eruptive *action*. Guns, knives, fists, all are ignored in preference for the facial expression. TV is not so much an action, as a re-action, medium.

The yen of the TV medium for themes of process and complex re-actions has enabled the documentary type of film to come to the fore. The movie *can* handle process superbly, but the movie viewer is more disposed to be a passive consumer of actions, rather than a participant in reactions. The movie western, like the movie documentary, has always been a lowly form. With TV, the western acquired new importance, since its theme is always: "Let's make a town." The audience participates in the shaping and processing of a community from meager and unpromising components. Moreover, the TV image takes kindly to the varied and rough textures of Western saddles, clothes, hides, and shoddy match-wood bars and hotel lobbies. The movie camera, by contrast, is at home in the slick chrome world of the night club and the luxury spots of a metropolis. Moreover, the contrasting camera preferences of the movies in the Twenties and Thirties, and of TV in the Fifties and Sixties spread to the entire population. In ten years the new tastes of America in clothes, in food, in housing, in entertainment, and in vehicles express the new pattern of interrelation of forms and do-it-yourself involvement fostered by the TV image.

It is no accident that such major movie stars as Rita Hayworth, Liz

Taylor, and Marilyn Monroe ran into troubled waters in the new TV age. They ran into an age that questioned all the "hot" media values of the pre-TV consumer days. The TV image challenges the values of fame as much as the values of consumer goods. "Fame to me," said Marilyn Monroe, "certainly is only a temporary and a partial happiness. Fame is not really for a daily diet, that's not what fulfills you. . . . I think that when you are famous every weakness is exaggerated. This industry should behave to its stars like a mother whose child has just run out in front of a car. But instead of clasping the child to them they start punishing the child."

The movie community is now getting clobbered by TV, and lashes out at anybody in its bewildered petulance. These words of the great movie puppet who wed Mr. Baseball and Mr. Broadway are surely a portent. If many of the rich and successful figures in America were to question publicly the absolute value of money and success as means to happiness and human welfare, they would offer no more shattering a precedent than Marilyn Monroe. For nearly fifty years, Hollywood had offered "the fallen woman" a way to the top and a way to the hearts of all. Suddenly the love-goddess emits a horrible cry, screams that eating people is wrong, and utters denunciations of the whole way of life. This is exactly the mood of the suburban beatniks. They reject a fragmented and specialist consumer life for anything that offers humble involvement and deep commitment. It is the same mood that recently turned girls from specialist careers to early marriage and big families. They switch from jobs to roles.

The same new preference for depth participation has also prompted in the young a strong drive toward religious experience with rich liturgical overtones. The liturgical revival of the radio and TV age affects even the most austere Protestant sects. Choral chant and rich vestments have appeared in every quarter. The ecumenical movement is synonymous with electric technology.

Just as TV, the mosaic mesh, does not foster perspective in art, it does not foster lineality in living. Since TV, the assembly line has disappeared from industry. Staff and line structures have dissolved in management. Gone are the stag line, the party line, the receiving line, and the pencil line from the backs of nylons.

With TV came the end of bloc voting in politics, a form of specialism and fragmentation that won't work since TV. Instead of the voting bloc, we have the icon, the inclusive image. Instead of a political viewpoint or platform, the inclusive political posture or stance. Instead of the product, the process. In periods of new and rapid growth there is a blurring of outlines. In the TV image we have the supremacy of the blurred outline, itself the maximal incentive to growth and new "closure" or completion, especially for a consumer culture long related to the sharp visual values that had become separated from the other senses. So great is the change in American lives, resulting from the loss of loyalty to the consumer package in entertainment and commerce, that every enterprise, from Madison Avenue and General Motors to Hollywood and General Foods, has been shaken thoroughly and forced to seek new strategies of action. What electric implosion or contraction has done inter-personally and inter-nationally, the TV image does intra-personally or intra-sensuously.

It is not hard to explain this sensuous revolution to painters and sculptors, for they have been striving, ever since Cézanne abandoned perspective illusion in favor of structure in painting, to bring about the very change that TV has now effected on a fantastic scale. TV is the Bauhaus program of design and living, or the Montessori educational strategy, given total technological extension and commercial sponsorship. The aggressive lunge of artistic strategy for the remaking of Western man has, *via* TV, become a vulgar sprawl and an overwhelming splurge in American life.

It would be impossible to exaggerate the degree to which this image has disposed America to European modes of sense and sensibility. America is now Europeanizing as furiously as Europe is Americanizing. Europe, during the Second War, developed much of the industrial technology needed for its first mass consumer phase. It was, on the other hand, the First War that had readied America for the same consumer "take-off." It took the electronic *implosion* to dissolve the nationalist diversity of a splintered Europe, and to do for it what the industrial *explosion* had done for America. The industrial explosion that accompanies the fragmenting expansion of literacy and industry was able to exert little unifying effect in the European world with its numerous tongues and cultures. The Napoleonic thrust had utilized the combined force of the new literacy and early industrialism. But Napoleon had had a less homogenized set of materials to work with than even the Russians have today. The homogenizing power of the literate process had gone further in America by 1800 than anywhere in Europe. From the first, America took to heart the print technology for its educational, industrial, and political life; and it was rewarded by an unprecedented pool of standardized workers and consumers, such as no culture had ever had before. That our cultural historians have been oblivious of the homogenizing power of typography, and of the irresistible strength of homogenized populations, is no credit to them. Political scientists have been quite unaware of the effects of media anywhere at any time, simply because nobody has been willing to study the personal and social effects of media apart from their "content."

America long ago achieved its Common Market by mechanical and literate homogenization of social organization. Europe is now getting a unity under the electric auspices of compression and interrelation. Just how much homogenization via literacy is needed to make an effective producer-consumer group in the postmechanical age, in the age of automation, nobody has ever asked. For it has never been fully recognized that the role of literacy in shaping an industrial economy is basic and archetypal. Literacy is indispensable for habits of uniformity at all times and places. Above all, it is needed for the workability of price systems and markets. This factor has been ignored exactly as TV is now being ignored, for TV fosters many preferences that are quite at variance with literate uniformity and repeatability. It has sent Americans questing for every sort of oddment and quaintness in objects from out of their storied past. Many Americans will now spare no pains or expense to get to taste some new wine or food. The uniform and repeatable now must yield to the uniquely askew, a fact that is increasingly the despair and confusion of our entire standardized economy.

The power of the TV mosaic to transform American innocence into depth sophistication, independently of "content," is not mysterious if looked at directly. This mosaic TV image had already been adumbrated in the popular press that grew up with the telegraph. The commercial use of the telegraph began in 1844 in America, and earlier in England. The electric principle and its implications received much attention in Shelley's poetry. Artistic rule-of-thumb usually anticipates the science and technology in these matters by a full generation or more. The meaning of the telegraph mosaic in its *journalistic* manifestations was not lost to the mind of Edgar Allan Poe. He used it to establish two startlingly new inventions, the symbolist poem and the detective story. Both of these forms require do-it-yourself participation on the part of the reader. By offering an incomplete image or process, Poe *involved* his readers in the creative process in a way that Baudelaire, Valéry, T. S. Eliot, and many others have admired and followed. Poe had grasped at once the electric dynamic as one of public participation in creativity. Nevertheless, even today the homogenized consumer complains when asked to participate in creating or completing an abstract poem or painting or structure of any kind. Yet Poe knew even then that participation in depth followed at once from the telegraph mosaic. The more lineal and literal-minded of the literary brahmins "just couldn't see it." They still can't see it. They prefer not to participate in the creative process. They have accommodated themselves to the completed packages, in prose and verse and in the plastic arts. It is these people who must confront, in every classroom in the land, students who have accommodated themselves to the tactile and nonpictorial modes of symbolist and mythic structures, thanks to the TV image.

Life magazine for August 10, 1962, had a feature on how "Too Many Subteens Grow Up Too Soon and Too Fast." There was no observation of the fact that similar speed of growth and precociousness have always been the norm in tribal cultures and in nonliterate societies. England and America fostered the institution of prolonged adolescence by the negation of the tactile participation that is sex. In this, there was no conscious strategy, but rather a general acceptance of the consequences of prime stress on the printed word and visual values as a means of organizing personal and social life. This stress led to triumphs of industrial production and political conformity that were their own sufficient warrant.

Respectabilty, or the ability to sustain visual inspection of one's life, became dominant. No European country allowed print such precedence. Visually, Europe has always been shoddy in American eyes. American women, on the other hand, who have never been equaled in any culture for visual turnout, have always seemed abstract, mechanical dolls to Europeans. Tactility is a supreme value in European life. For that reason, on the Continent there is no adolescence, but only the leap from childhood to adult ways. Such is now the American state since TV, and this state of evasion of adolescence will continue. The introspective life of long, long thoughts and distant goals, to be pursued in lines of Siberian railroad kind, cannot coexist with the mosaic form of the TV image that commands immediate participation in *depth* and admits of no delays. The mandates of that image are so various yet so consistent that even to mention them is to describe the revolution of the past decade.

The phenomenon of the paperback, the book in "cool" version, can head this list of TV mandates, because the TV transformation of book culture into something else is manifested at that point. Europeans have had paperbacks from the first. From the beginnings of the automobile, they have preferred the wraparound space of the small car. The pictorial value of "enclosed space" for book, car, or house has never appealed to them. The paperback, especially in its highbrow form, was tried in America in the 1920s and thirties and forties. It was not, however, until 1953 that it suddenly became acceptable. No publisher really knows why. Not only is the paperback a tactile, rather than a visual, package, it can be as readily concerned with profound matters as with froth. The American since TV has lost his inhibitions and his innocence about depth culture. The paperback reader has discovered that he can enjoy Aristotle or Confucius by simply slowing down. The old literate habit of racing ahead on uniform lines of print yielded suddenly to depth reading. Reading in depth is, of course, not proper to the printed word as such. Depth probing of words and language is a normal feature of oral and manuscript cultures, rather than of print. Europeans have always felt that the English and Americans lacked depth in their culture. Since radio, and especially since TV, English and American literary critics have exceeded the performance of any European in depth and subtlety. The beatnik reaching out for Zen is only carrying the mandate of the TV mosaic out into the world of words and perception. The paperback itself has become a vast mosaic world in depth, expressive of the changed sense-life of Americans, for whom depth experience in words, as in physics, has become entirely acceptable, and even sought after.

Just where to begin to examine the transformation of American attitudes since TV is a most arbitrary affair, as can be seen in a change so great as the abrupt decline of baseball. The removal of the Brooklyn Dodgers to Los Angeles was a portent in itself. Baseball moved West in an attempt to retain an audience after TV struck. The characteristic mode of the baseball game is that it features one-thing-at-a-time. It is a lineal, expansive game which, like golf, is perfectly adapted to the outlook of an individualist and inner-directed society. Timing and waiting are of the essence, with the entire field in suspense waiting upon the performance of a single player. By contrast, football, basketball, and ice hockey are games in which many events occur simultaneously, with the entire team involved at the same time. With the advent of TV, such isolation of the individual performance as occurs in baseball became unacceptable. Interest in baseball declined, and its stars, quite as much as movie stars, found that fame had some very cramping dimensions. Baseball had been, like the movies, a hot medium featuring individual virtuosity and stellar performers. The real ball fan is a store of statistical information about previous explosions of batters and pitchers in numerous games. Nothing could indicate more clearly the peculiar satisfaction provided by a game that belonged to the industrial metropolis of ceaselessly exploding populations, stocks and bonds, and production and sales records. Baseball belonged to the age of the first onset of the hot press and the movie medium. It will always remain a symbol of the era of the hot mommas, jazz babies, of sheiks and shebas, of vamps and gold-diggers and the fast buck. Baseball, in a word, is a hot game that got cooled off in the new TV climate, as did most of the hot politicians and hot issues of the earlier decades.

There is no cooler medium or hotter issue at present than the small car. It is like a badly wired woofer in a hi-fi circuit that produces a tremendous flutter in the bottom. The small European car, like the European paperback and the European belle, for that matter, was no visual package job. Visually, the entire batch of European cars are so poor an affair that it is obvious their makers never thought of them as something to look at. They are something to put on, like pants or a pullover. Theirs is the kind of space sought by the skin-diver, the water-skier, and the dinghy sailor. In an immediate tactile sense, this new space is akin to that to which the picture-window fad had catered. In terms of "view," the picture window never made any sense. In terms of an attempt to discover a new dimension in the out-of-doors by pretending to be a goldfish, the picture window does make sense. So do the frantic efforts to roughen up the indoor walls and textures as if they were the outside of the house. Exactly the same impulse sends the indoor spaces and furniture out into the patios in an attempt to experience the outside as inside. The TV viewer is in just that role at all times. He is submarine. He is bombarded by atoms that reveal the outside as inside in an endless adventure amidst blurred images and mysterious contours.

However, the American car had been fashioned in accordance with the *visual* mandates of the typographic and the movie images. The American car was an enclosed space, not a tactile space. And an enclosed space, as was shown in the chapter on Print, is one in which all spatial qualities have been reduced to visual terms. So in the American car, as the French observed decades ago, "one is not on the road, one is in the car." By contrast, the European car aims to drag you along the road and to provide a great deal of vibration for the bottom. Brigitte Bardot got into the news when it was discovered that she liked to drive barefoot in order to get the maximal vibration. Even English cars, weak on visual appearance as they are, have been guilty of advertising that "at sixty miles an hour all you can hear is the ticking of the clock." That would be a very poor ad, indeed, for a TV generation that has to be *with* everything and has to *dig* things in order to get at them. So avid is the TV viewer for rich tactile effects that he could be counted on to revert to skis. The wheel, so far as he is concerned, lacks the requisite abrasiveness.

Clothes in this first TV decade repeat the same story as vehicles. The revolution was heralded by bobby-soxers who dumped the whole cargo of visual effects for a set of tactile ones so extreme as to create a dead level of flat-footed dead-panism. Part of the cool dimension of TV is the cool, deadpan mug that came in with the teenager. Adolescence, in the age of hot media, of radio and movie, and of the ancient book, had been a time of fresh, eager, and expressive countenances. No elder states-man or senior executive of the 1940s would have ventured to wear so dead and sculptural a pan as the child of the TV age. The dances that came in with TV were to match—all the way to the Twist, which is merely a form of very unanimated dialogue, the gestures and grimaces of which indicate involvement in depth, but "nothing to say."

Clothing and styling in the past decade have gone so tactile and sculp-tural that they present a sort of exaggerated evidence of the new qualities of the TV mosaic. The TV extension of our nerves in hirsute pattern possesses the power to evoke a flood of related imagery in clothing, hairdo, walk, and gesture.

All this adds up to the compressional implosion—the return to non-specialized forms of clothes and spaces, the seeking of multi-uses for rooms and things and objects, in a single word—the iconic. In music and poetry and painting, the tactile implosion means the insistence on qualities that are close to casual speech. Thus Schönberg and Stravinsky and Carl Orff and Bartok, far from being advanced seekers of esoteric effects, seem now to have brought music very close to the condition of ordinary human speech. It is this colloquial rhythm that once seemed so unmelodi-ous about their work. Anyone who listens to the medieval works of Perotinus or Dufay will find them very close to Stravinsky and Bartok. The great explosion of the Renaissance that split musical instruments off from song and speech and gave them specialist functions is now being played backward in our age of electronic implosion.

THE FUTURE

7

■ You put an old woman in a cave, have her take a hallucinogen, then try to interpret her rambling speech. You open a copy of Vergil and stick a pin in a verse at random. You put a prisoner on a stone altar, cut his throat, and watch the pattern of the steam rising from the blood. You heat the dried bones of a tortoise and study the cracks. You observe the actions of wildlife, especially birds and snakes. You cut animals open and read something from their intestines. You decipher the meanings of dreams and you study the positions of the stars. All of these are ways in which men have tried, through magic, to discover the events of the future.

This endless fascination, reaching back through 6,000 years of history, oddly enough has almost never had much to do with the things that might affect the general condition of man. Oracles and soothsayers — some of whom are supposed to have produced remarkable forecasts — have almost always been concerned with personal fortunes or an occasional public disaster. And the notion has always been that the future was to be glimpsed through some kind of mystical revelation. Foresight, in the sense of projecting conditions to come in the light of a potential that already existed, came slowly and was hard to grasp.

The most ingenious early attempts to discover the shape of things to come by this kind of logic were mainly concerned with technology. We often forget what a slow learner and lazy inventor man has been in the past simply because we have done so much learning and inventing within the past two centuries. Humans, for instance, transported themselves across the earth at the end of the Roman Empire in A.D. 1453 exactly as they had at the founding of Rome 2,206 years earlier — with one revolutionary exception, the stirrup.

It was the technology of transportation and communication that first engaged Renaissance men in rational speculation about the future. In the fifteenth century Leonardo da Vinci was intrigued with the possibility of flight and had worked out the principle of the helicopter, and Sir Francis Bacon described functioning submarines and airplanes in *The New Atlantis,* published in 1626. Any broader or braver speculation about the future was slow to come — most people simply couldn't imagine the future as being qualitatively different from the past, except for random and incidental change. The concepts of progress, evolution, and chosen destiny took a long time for man to grasp. By 1771, however, Louis Sébastien Mercier, in his book *l'an 2440,* foresaw such things as movies and mechanical lamps. By 1881, Jules Verne was using "aeroplanes" and the great electric submarine "Nautilus," which was lighted by incandescent bulbs, in his fiction. It was not long before the novelists had "invented" television, telephones, atomic energy, and, in fact, most of the modern technical advances.

In the realm of social prophecy there were no real counterparts. The writers that came closest were portrayers of ideal states, or utopias. The first and most famous of the kind, Plato's Republic, was an aristocratic society ruled by philosopher-kings. St. Augustine's city of God was a dream of a theocracy. With the exception of a few points in Sir Thomas More's *Utopia* (1516), these philosophical states could not be called futuristic. (More did have some ideas that were very strange for his time: religious freedom and state education for both men and women.) They were simply conceptual, and they did not try to predict any dynamism of change from present-potential to future-possible.

The socialist utopias of the early nineteenth century — those sweet, agrarian visions of life — were likewise based on wishes. And the same was true of a spate of scientific utopias in the late nineteenth and early twentieth centuries, states in which man was freed for harmony and higher thought thanks to the slave labor of his many machines.

As Daniel Bell says in his introduction to *The Year 2000* by Kahn and Wiener, the social prophets lacked any notion of "how a society hangs together, how its parts are related to one another, which elements are more susceptible to change than others, and, equally important, any sense of method. They are not systematic, and they have no awareness of the nature of social systems."

If the social prophets were hardly prophetic, there was another kind of writer that was — in a nightmarish way. Mary Shelley's *Frankenstein* (1818) was a biological horror story that foreshadowed some of present-day theory about genetic manipulation. Ambrose Bierce's "Moxon's Master" (1909), about a chess-playing robot who finally strangles its inventor, is an early attempt to show the computer displacing man. H. G. Wells's *The War in the Air* (1908) imagined the world drawn into a catastrophic aerial conflict.

In fact it was Wells, a general believer in perfectibility through science, who combined social-science futurism and technological prophecy to produce some very depressing pictures (especially in *The Time Machine,*

1895). Wells was almost the first writer to be seriously troubled about the future effect of technology on the quality of human life and social organization, even though his pessimism was only occasional.

That pessimism is very much deepened in Aldous Huxley's *Brave New World* (1932), which is probably the first classic of modern science fiction (though it owes a great debt to Evgeny Zamiatin's *We* (1920) and E. M. Forster's "The Machine Stops" (1928)). A whole new generation of anti-utopian books came along with such novels as George Orwell's *1984*, Ray Bradbury's *Fahrenheit 451*, and Gore Vidal's *Messiah*. The recent writers are, if anything, the most pessimistic, anxiety-filled, and apocalyptic of all. Here are a few samples of their plots:

In the year 2103, the great cities of the earth are human jungles where black marketeers hunt people in the streets and parks — to kill them and sell their organs for transplant. (*Day Before Tomorrow* by Keith Laumer.)

After a nuclear war, radiation-affected women bear children that are entirely hairless; they acquire the name "Baldies." After a while, it becomes apparent that the Baldies are telepathic, and normal humans eventually outlaw them and begin to hunt them down like wild animals. (*Mutant* by Henry Kuttner.)

In the twenty-first century, a monstrous computer-despotism has taken over the earth and man no longer rules. The world has become a place where people fight desperately to get *into* prison, where real society has been replaced by exotic cults, where the insane are treated by having their fantasies turned into reality, and where everybody is on drugs and all sex is automatic. (*Journey Beyond Tomorrow* by Robert Sheckley.)

Then, of course, there have been a number of futurist novels, not frankly labelled science-fiction. John Barth's *Giles Goat-Boy* and Ira Levin's *This Perfect Day* repeat the theme of a world controlled by computer-gods.

Thus the literary futurists are filled with a sense of doom. In brief, their projection adds up to something like this: Our great technological advances conceal an inherent evil; scientific organization of society must end in a kind of totalitarianism; man himself is likely to be warped out of recognition by biological warfare or genetic experimentation. None of this is strikingly new, of course, but the science-fiction writers have it implanted firmly in their minds — a fact that causes a special chill when we remember how accurate their forerunners were about what would develop in our own time. We can only hope that the literary futurists have misread their runes or entrails. After all, history has recorded only the lucky guesses of the oracles — not their many wild errors.

H. Bruce Franklin, in a cogent article called "Fictions of the Future" (*The Futurist*, Vol. IV, No. 1, Feb., 1970), observes that "today Soviet and American future-scene fiction offer a perfect — and most revealing — contrast. . . . Whereas in the U.S.S.R. future-scene fiction almost always sees science as a great aid in human progress, in the U.S.A. many stories of the future see science as a destructive force, producing a society of robots or freaks or global catastrophe. Whereas the Soviet view of the future is almost universally optimistic, envisioning a world populated by heroes, ruled by love and ever-improving, the dominant American view is profoundly pessimistic, often envisioning futures filled with extrapolations of present problems or new horrors, calamities, decay, or extinction."

Franklin then goes on to make another point, which applies not only to futurist fiction but to the current factual projections as well. He says, "if there is a future, it seems safe to say that all life will become increasingly the product of visions of the future. . . . (They) will become a more vital part of the world's culture than the past."

In recent years there has been a tremendous boom in factual futurist studies. The field that was once left to the prophet and the imaginative writer has been invaded by the scientist and the social-scientist in strength. Projective studies in economics, political science, ecology, sociology, space, biology, communications, and technology in general appear on the publishers' lists in increasing numbers. There is a flourishing World Future Society in Washington, D.C., with an extensive study program and a magazine called *The Futurist*. The Ford Foundation, the Rand Corporation, the American Academy of Arts and Sciences, and the Hudson Institute have all set up ambitious study programs on the future. In France there are the *Futuribles* and the *Prospectives*. In Britain, the Social Science Research Council has set up the Committee on the Next Thirty Years.

Unlike the tragic view in fiction, most of the factual studies convey a sense of pragmatic optimism. At least they present the planners' belief that there is a choice between good and evil possibilities and a faith in the motto "forewarned is forearmed." The American experience has always been filled with a passion for bringing something new to pass and an anticipation for reaching goals. Our tragic flaw, of course, is a penchant for narrow, self-serving aims and our disregard of the massive side effects that technological change may bring with it. In the nineteenth century, for instance, we built huge cities with great enthusiasm and almost no planning. Now we are left with great urban deserts of obsolete brick-and-wood. This is just one of the kinds of sprawl that modern futurists hope we can avoid.

Daniel Bell, in the introduction cited previously, explains what is new about today's kind of future-study. He says that theories of social change used to be based on an analysis of impersonal processes — "theories of evolution, immanence, cycles, and the like." He says, "what is distinctive about the middle of the twentieth century is the deliberate intervention of human instruments, principally government, to control change for specified ends." We are aware, he says, that any given change will influence other social areas and all possible consequences have to be taken into account. "The rebuilding of American cities, for example, involves a thirty-five year cycle. The expansion of medical services, as another example, involves fifteen-year planning — the time it takes for a young man to enter college and complete his medical board exams. In fact, especially in a post-industrial society where human capital is the scarcest resource, planning necessarily involves long-run commitments and, with equal necessity, it requires long-run forecasting."

The Year 2000, subtitled "A Framework for Speculation on the Next Thirty-Three Years" by Herman Kahn and Anthony J. Wiener, offers a fascinating view of certain new methods of future-study. It uses various techniques worked out at The Hudson Institute for charting political, sociological, technological, and economic change. No more than a sketchy account of these elaborate methods can be given here.

Kahn and Wiener are interested in two things — important variables in future behavior and the circumstances that might arise from their interaction. To simplify that, we might say that they are trying to predict a drama or a series of dramas. Certain social and economic facts of today are the characters. We know what their present personalities are like. The futurist then tries to predict how they may behave — in action and reaction — when they are juxtaposed in projected situation. In other words, the authors are trying to predict a plot that will arise from a certain behavioral complex — and, of course, there are more plots than one possible.

One kind of plot assumes that most of the characters (present trends, present statistics) will run true to form, or continue on the same curve. The plot produced is something the authors call a "standard world" with "surprise-free projections." Then, certainly, more than one standard world ("canonical variations") can be imagined, depending on which issue or issues are emphasized — or, to call on the theatre again, depending on which character assumes a leading role.

What if some possible but unlikely things start to happen? (The young man who seemed to be cast as the hero dies unexpectedly in the first act, for instance.) To deal with this kind of development, the authors have worked out "alternative futures" from which come specific scenarios. The scenarios, Kahn and Wiener explain, are "hypothetical sequences of events constructed for the purpose of focusing attention on causal processes and decision points. They answer two kinds of questions: (1) precisely how might some hypothetical situation come about step by step? and (2) what alternatives exist for each actor, at each step, for preventing, diverting, or facilitating the process?"

One scenario, for example, explores the possibility of "inward-looking worlds" in which both the armaments competition and the international-aid competition between Russia and the United States slack off. Economic pressures at home and increasing disillusion with the notion of winning over the Third World cause an isolationist trend within the great powers.

The various nations of the Third World are then affected in contrasting ways by this abandonment, some being forced into greater self-sufficiency, some taking the road to dictatorship and aggression, some declining in hopelessness, and so forth.

This is no more than a glimpse of the activity now going on in future-studies. But, to predict something on our own account, future studies will undoubtedly increase in scope and sophistication as the twentieth century draws toward an end. We now seem to be more painfully aware of our mistakes — in ecology, politics, economics, and sociology — than ever before, and we are increasingly aware of the narrowing possibilities of life on this earth. Planning and shrewd judgment about the organization of society are needed as never before. Blunders are infinitely more costly than they were in a wide-open world. Santayana's observation that those who cannot remember the past are condemned to repeat it has to be supplemented by the idea that those who do not try to calculate the future are doomed to have none.

Arthur C. Clarke | # Hazards of Prophecy: The Failure of Nerve

Before one attempts to set up in business as a prophet, it is instructive to see what success others have made of this dangerous occupation — and it is even more instructive to see where they have failed.

With montonous regularity, apparently competent men have laid down the law about what is technically possible or impossible — and have been proved utterly wrong, sometimes while the ink was scarcely dry from their pens. On careful analysis, it appears that these debacles fall into two classes, which I will call "failures of nerve" and "failures of imagination."

The failure of nerve seems to be the more common; it occurs when *even given all the relevant facts* the would-be prophet cannot see that they point to an inescapable conclusion. Some of these failures are so ludicrous as to be almost unbelievable, and would form an interesting subject for psychological analysis. "They said it couldn't be done" is a phrase that occurs throughout the history of invention; I do not know if anyone has ever looked into the reasons *why* "they" said so, often with quite unnecessary vehemence.

It is now impossible for us to recall the mental climate which existed when the first locomotives were being built, and critics gravely asserted that suffocation lay in wait for anyone who reached the awful speed of thirty miles an hour. It is equally difficult to believe that, only eighty years ago, the idea of the domestic electric light was pooh-poohed by all the "experts" — with the exception of a thirty-one-year-old American inventor named Thomas Alva Edison. When gas securities nose-dived in 1878 because Edison (already a formidable figure, with the phonograph and the carbon microphone to his credit), announced that he was working on the incandescent lamp, the British Parliament set up a committee to look into the matter. (Westminster can beat Washington hands down at this game.)

The distinguished witnesses reported, to the relief of the gas companies, that Edison's ideas were "good enough for our transatlantic friends . . . but unworthy of the attention of practical or scientific men." And Sir William Preece, engineer-in-chief of the British Post Office, roundly declared that "Subdivision of the electric light is an absolute *ignis fatuus.*" One feels that the fatuousness was not in the *ignis.*

The scientific absurdity being pilloried, be it noted, is not some wild-

SOURCE: "Hazards of Prophecy: The Failure of Nerve" from *Profiles of the Future* by Arthur C. Clarke. Copyright © 1962 by HMH Publishing Company. Reprinted by permission of Harper & Row, Publishers, Inc.

and-woolly dream like perpetual motion, but the humble little electric light bulb, which three generations of men have taken for granted, except when it burns out and leaves them in the dark. Yet although in this matter Edison saw far beyond his contemporaries, he too in later life was guilty of the same shortsightedness that afflicted Preece, for he opposed the introduction of alternating current.

The most famous, and perhaps the most instructive, failures of nerve have occurred in the fields of aero- and astronautics. At the beginning of the twentieth century, scientists were almost unanimous in declaring that heavier-than-air flight was impossible, and that anyone who attempted to build airplanes was a fool. The great American astronomer, Simon Newcomb, wrote a celebrated essay which concluded:

> The demonstration that no possible combination of known substances, known forms of machinery and known forms of force, can be united in a practical machine by which man shall fly long distances through the air, seems to the writer as complete as it is possible for the demonstration of any physical fact to be.

Oddly enough, Newcomb was sufficiently broad minded to admit that some wholly new discovery — he mentioned the neutralization of gravity — might make flight practical. One cannot, therefore, accuse him of lacking imagination; his error was in attempting to marshal the facts of aerodynamics when he did not understand that science. His failure of nerve lay in not realizing that the means of flight were already at hand.

For Newcomb's article received wide publicity at just about the time that the Wright brothers, not having a suitable anti-gravity device in their bicycle shop, were mounting a gasoline engine on wings. When news of their success reached the astronomer, he was only momentarily taken aback. Flying machines *might* be a marginal possibility, he conceded — but they were certainly of no practical importance, for it was quite out of the question that they could carry the extra weight of a passenger as well as that of a pilot.

Such refusal to face facts which now seem obvious has continued throughout the history of aviation. Let me quote another astronomer, William H. Pickering, straightening out the uninformed public a few years *after* the first airplanes had started to fly.

> The popular mind often pictures gigantic flying machines speeding across the Atlantic and carrying innumerable passengers in a way analogous to our modern steamships. . . . It seems safe to say that such ideas must be wholly visionary, and even if a machine could get across with one or two passengers the expense would be prohibitive to any but the capitalist who could own his own yacht.
>
> Another popular fallacy is to expect enormous speed to be obtained. It must be remembered that the resistance of the air increases as the square of the speed and the work as the cube. . . . If with 30 h.p. we can now attain a speed of 40 m.p.h., then in order to reach a speed of 100 m.p.h. we

must use a motor capable of 470 h.p. . . . it is clear that with our present devices there is no hope of competing for racing speed with either our locomotives or our automobiles.

It so happens that most of his fellow astronomers considered Pickering far *too imaginative;* he was prone to see vegetation — and even evidence for insect life — on the Moon. I am glad to say that by the time he died in 1938 at the ripe age of eighty, Professor Pickering had seen airplanes traveling at 400 m.p.h., and carrying considerably more than "one or two" passengers.

Closer to the present, the opening of the space age has produced a mass vindication (and refutation) of prophecies on a scale and at a speed never before witnessed. Having taken some part in this myself, and being no more immune than the next man to the pleasures of saying, "I told you so," I would like to recall a few of the statements about space flight that have been made by prominent scientists in the past. It is necessary for *someone* to do this, and to jog the remarkably selective memories of the pessimists. The speed with which those who once declaimed, "It's impossible" can switch to, "I said it could be done all the time" is really astounding.

As far as the general public is concerned, the idea of space flight as a serious possibility first appeared on the horizon in the 1920's, largely as a result of newspaper reports of the work of the American Robert Goddard and the Rumanian Hermann Oberth. (The much earlier studies of Tsiolkovsky in Russia then being almost unknown outside his own country.) When the ideas of Goddard and Oberth, usually distorted by the press, filtered through to the scientific world, they were received with hoots of derision. For a sample of the kind of criticism the pioneers of astronautics had to face, I present this masterpiece from a paper published by one Professor A. W. Bickerton, in 1926. It should be read carefully, for as an example of the cocksure thinking of the time it would be very hard to beat.

> This foolish idea of shooting at the moon is an example of the absurd length to which vicious specialisation will carry scientists working in thought-tight compartments. Let us critically examine the proposal. For a projectile entirely to escape the gravitation of the earth, it needs a velocity of 7 miles a second. The thermal energy of a gramme at this speed is 15,180 calories. . . . The energy of our most violent explosive — nitroglycerine — is less than 1,500 calories per gramme. Consequently, even had the explosive nothing to carry, it has only one-tenth of the energy necessary to escape the earth. . . . Hence the proposition appears to be basically impossible. . . .

Indignant readers in the Colombo public library pointed angrily to the SILENCE notices when I discovered this little gem. It is worth examining it in some detail to see just where "vicious specialisation," if one may coin a phrase, led the professor so badly astray.

His first error lies in the sentence: "The energy of our most violent explosive — nitroglycerine . . ." One would have thought it obvious that *energy*, not violence, is what we want from a rocket fuel; and as a matter of fact nitroglycerin and similar explosives contain much less energy, weight for weight, than such mixtures as kerosene and liquid oxygen. This had been carefully pointed out by Tsiolkovsky and Goddard years before.

Bickerton's second error is much more culpable. What of it, if nitroglycerin has only a tenth of the energy necessary to escape from the Earth? That merely means that you have to use at least ten pounds of nitroglycerin to launch a single pound of payload.[1]

For the fuel itself has not got to escape from Earth; it can all be burned quite close to our planet, and as long as it imparts its energy to the payload, this is all that matters. When Lunik II lifted thirty-three years after Professor Bickerton said it was impossible, most of its several hundred tons of kerosene and liquid oxygen never got very far from Russia — but the half-ton payload reached the Mare Imbrium.

As a comment on the above, I might add that Professor Bickerton, who was an active popularizer of science, numbered among his published books one with the title *Perils of a Pioneer*. Of the perils that all pioneers must face, few are more disheartening than the Bickertons.

Right through the 1930's and 1940's, eminent scientists continued to deride the rocket pioneers — when they bothered to notice them at all. Anyone who has access to a good college library can find, preserved for posterity in the dignified pages of the January 1941 *Philosophical Magazine*, an example that makes a worthy mate to the one I have just quoted.

It is a paper by the distinguished Canadian astronomer Professor J. W. Campbell, of the University of Alberta, entitled "Rocket Flight to the Moon." Opening with a quotation from a 1938 Edmonton paper to the effect that "rocket flight to the Moon now seems less remote than television appeared a hundred years ago," the professor then looks into the subject mathematically. After several pages of analysis, he arrives at the conclusion that it would require *a million tons* of take-off weight to carry *one pound* of payload on the round trip.

The correct figure, for today's primitive fuels and technologies, is very roughly one ton per pound — a depressing ratio, but hardly as bad as that calculated by the professor. Yet his mathematics was impeccable; so what went wrong?

Merely his initial assumptions, which were hopelessly unrealistic. He chose a path for the rocket which was fantastically extravagant in energy, and he assumed the use of an acceleration so low that most of the fuel would be wasted at low altitudes, fighting the Earth's gravitational field. It was as if he had calculated the performance of an automobile — when

---

[1] The dead weight of the rocket (propellant tanks, motors, etc.) would actually make the ratio very much higher, but that does not affect the argument.

the brakes were on. No wonder that he concluded: "While it is always dangerous to make a negative prediction, it would appear that the statement that rocket flight to the moon does not seem so remote as television did less than one hundred years ago is overoptimistic." I am sure that when the *Philosophical Magazine* subscribers read those words, back in 1941, many of them thought, "Well, *that* should put those crazy rocket men in their place!"

Yet the correct results had been published by Tsiolkovsky, Oberth and Goddard years before; though the work of the first two would have been very hard to consult at the time, Goddard's paper "A Method of Reaching Extreme Altitudes" was already a classic and had been issued by that scarcely obscure body, the Smithsonian Institution. If Professor Campbell had only consulted it (or indeed *any* competent writer on the subject — there were some, even in 1941) he would not have misled his readers and himself.

The lesson to be learned from these examples is one that can never be repeated too often, and is one that is seldom understood by laymen — who have an almost superstitious awe of mathematics. But mathematics is only a tool, though an immensely powerful one. No equations, however impressive and complex, can arrive at the truth if the initial assumptions are incorrect. It is really quite amazing by what margins competent but conservative scientists and engineers can miss the mark, when they start with the preconceived idea that what they are investigating is impossible. When this happens, the most well-informed men become blinded by their prejudices and are unable to see what lies directly ahead of them. What is even more incredible, they refuse to learn from experience and will continue to make the same mistake over and over again.

Some of my best friends are astronomers, and I am sorry to keep throwing stones at them — but they do seem to have an appalling record as prophets. If you still doubt this, let me tell a story so ironic that you might well accuse me of making it up. But I am not that much of a cynic; the facts are on file for anyone to check.

Back in the dark ages of 1935, the founder of the British Interplanetary Society, P. E. Cleator, was rash enough to write the first book on astronautics published in England. His *Rockets through Space* gave an (incidentally highly entertaining) account of the experiments that had been carried out by the German and American rocket pioneers, and their plans for such commonplaces of today as giant multi-stage boosters and satellites. Rather surprisingly, the staid scientific journal *Nature* reviewed the book in its issue for March 14, 1936, and summed up as follows:

It must be said at once that the whole procedure sketched in the present volume presents difficulties of so fundamental a nature that we are forced to dismiss the notion as essentially impracticable, in spite of the author's insistent appeal to put aside prejudice and to recollect the supposed impossibility of heavier-than-air flight before it was actually accomplished.

An analogy such as this may be misleading, and we believe it to be so in this case. . . .

Well, the whole world now knows just how misleading this analogy was, though the reviewer, identified only by the unusual initials R.v.d.R.W., was of course fully entitled to his opinion.

Just twenty years later — *after* President Eisenhower had announced the United States satellite program — a new Astronomer Royal arrived in England to take up his appointment. The press asked him to give his views on space flight, and after two decades Dr. Richard van der Riet Woolley had seen no reason to change his mind. "Space travel," he snorted, "is utter bilge."

The newspapers did not allow him to forget this, when Sputnik I went up the very next year. And now — irony piled upon irony — Dr. Woolley is, by virtue of his position as Astronomer Royal, a leading member of the committee advising the British government on space research. The feelings of those who have been trying, for a generation, to get the United Kingdom interested in space can well be imagined.[2]

Even those who suggested that rockets might be used for more modest, though much more reprehensible, purposes were overruled by the scientific authorities — except in Germany and Russia.

When the existence of the 200-mile-range V-2 was disclosed to an astonished world, there was considerable speculation about intercontinental missiles. This was firmly squashed by Dr. Vannevar Bush, the civilian general of the United States scientific war effort, in evidence before a Senate committee on December 3, 1945. Listen:

> There has been a great deal said about a 3,000 miles high-angle rocket. In my opinion such a thing is impossible for many years. The people who have been writing these things that annoy me, have been talking about a 3,000 mile high-angle rocket shot from one continent to another, carrying an atomic bomb and so directed as to be a precise weapon which would land exactly on a certain target, such as a city.
>
> I say, technically, I don't think anyone in the world knows how to do such a thing, and I feel confident that it will not be done for a very long period of time to come. . . . I think we can leave that out of our thinking. I wish the American public would leave that out of their thinking.

A few months earlier (in May 1945) Prime Minister Churchill's scientific adviser Lord Cherwell had expressed similar views in a House of Lords debate. This was only to be expected, for Cherwell was an ex-

---

[2] In all fairness to Dr. Woolley, I would like to record that his 1936 review contained the suggestion — probably for the first time — that rockets could contribute to astronomical knowledge by making observations in ultraviolet light beyond the absorbing screen of the Earth's atmosphere. The importance of this is only now becoming apparent.

tremely conservative and opinionated scientist who had advised the government that the V-2 itself was only a propaganda rumor.[3]

In the May 1945 debate on defense, Lord Cherwell impressed his peers by a dazzling display of mental arithmetic from which he correctly concluded that a very long-range rocket must consist of more than 90 per cent fuel, and thus would have a negligible payload. The conclusion he let his listeners draw from this was that such a device would be wholly impracticable.

That was true enough in the spring of 1945, but it was no longer true in the summer. One astonishing feature of the House of Lords debate is the casual way in which much-too-well-informed peers used the words "atomic bomb," at a time when this was the best-kept secret of the war. (The Alamagordo test was still two months in the future!) Security must have been horrified, and Lord Cherwell — who of course knew all about the Manhattan Project — was quite justified in telling his inquisitive colleagues not to believe everything they heard, even though in this case it happened to be perfectly true.

When Dr. Bush spoke to the Senate committee in December of the same year, the only important secret about the atomic bomb was that it weighed five tons. Anyone could then work out in his head, as Lord Cherwell had done, that a rocket to deliver it across intercontinental ranges would have to weigh about 200 tons — as against the mere 14 tons of the then awe-inspiring V-2.

The outcome was the greatest failure of nerve in all history, which changed the future of the world — indeed, of many worlds. Faced with the same facts and the same calculations, American and Russian technology took two separate roads. The Pentagon — accountable to the taxpayer — virtually abandoned long-range rockets for almost half a decade, until the development of thermonuclear bombs made it possible to build warheads five times lighter yet several hundred times more powerful than the low-powered and now obsolete device that was dropped on Hiroshima.

The Russians had no such inhibitions. Faced with the need for a 200-ton rocket, they went right ahead and built it. By the time it was perfected, it was no longer required for military purposes, for Soviet physicists had bypassed the United States' billion-dollar tritium bomb cul-de-sac and gone straight to the far cheaper lithium bomb. Having backed the wrong horse in rocketry, the Russians then entered it for a much more important event — and won the race into space.

Of the many lessons to be drawn from this slice of recent history, the one that I wish to emphasize is this. Anything that is theoretically possible will be achieved in practice, no matter what the technical difficulties,

---

[3] Cherwell's influence — malign or otherwise — has been the subject of a vigorous debate since the publication of Lord Snow's *Science and Government*.

if it is desired greatly enough. It is no argument against any project to say: "The idea's fantastic!" Most of the things that have happened in the last fifty years have been fantastic, and it is only by assuming that they will continue to be so that we have any hope of anticipating the future.

To do this — to avoid that failure of nerve for which history exacts so merciless a penalty — we must have the courage to follow all technical extrapolations to their logical conclusion. Yet even this is not enough, as I shall now demonstrate. To predict the future we need logic; but we also need faith and imagination which can sometimes defy logic itself.

Arthur C. Clarke | Hazards of Prophecy:
The Failure of Imagination

Many of the negative statements about scientific possibilities, and the gross failures of past prophets to predict what lay immediately ahead of them, could be described as failures of nerve. All the basic facts of aeronautics were available — in the writings of Cayley, Stringfellow, Chanute, and others — when Simon Newcomb "proved" that flight was impossible. He simply lacked the courage to face those facts. All the fundamental equations and principles of space travel had been worked out by Tsiolkovsky, Goddard, and Oberth for years — often decades — when distinguished scientists were making fun of would-be astronauts. Here again, the failure to appreciate the facts was not so much intellectual as moral. The critics did not have the courage that their scientific convictions should have given them; they could not believe the truth even when it had been spelled out before their eyes, in their own language of mathematics. We all know this type of cowardice, because at some time or other we all exhibit it.

The second kind of prophetic failure is less blameworthy, and more interesting. It arises when all the available facts are appreciated *and* marshaled correctly — but when the really vital facts are still undiscovered, and the possibility of their existence is not admitted.

A famous example of this is provided by the philosopher Auguste Comte, who in his *Cours de Philosophie Positive* (1835) attempted to define the limits within which scientific knowledge must lie. In his chap-

SOURCE: "Hazards of Prophecy: The Failure of Imagination" from *Profiles of the Future* by Arthur C. Clarke. Copyright © 1962 by HMH Publishing Company. Reprinted by permission of Harper & Row, Publishers, Inc.

ter on astronomy (Book 2, Chapter 1) he wrote these words concerning the heavenly bodies:

> We see how we may determine their forms, their distances, their bulk, their motions, but we can never know anything of their chemical or mineralogical structure; and much less, that of organised beings living on their surface. . . . We must keep carefully apart the idea of the solar system and that of the universe, and be always assured that our only true interest is in the former. Within this boundary alone is astronomy the supreme and positive science that we have determined it to be . . . the stars serve us scientifically only as providing positions with which we may compare the interior movements of our system.

In other words, Comte decided that the stars could never be more than celestial reference points, of no intrinsic concern to the astronomer. Only in the case of the planets could we hope for any definite knowledge, and even that knowledge would be limited to geometry and dynamics. Comte would probably have decided that such a science as "astrophysics" was *a priori* impossible.

Yet within half a century of his death, almost the whole of astronomy *was* astrophysics, and very few professional astronomers had much interest in the planets. Comte's assertion had been utterly refuted by the invention of the spectroscope, which not only revealed the "chemical structure" of the heavenly bodies but has now told us far more about the distant stars than we know of our planetary neighbors.

Comte cannot be blamed for not imagining the spectroscope; *no one* could have imagined it, or the still more sophisticated instruments that have now joined it in the astronomer's armory. But he provides a warning that should always be borne in mind; even things that are undoubtedly impossible with existing or foreseeable techniques may prove to be easy as a result of new scientific breakthroughs. From their very nature, these breakthroughs can never be anticipated; but they have enabled us to bypass so many insuperable obstacles in the past that no picture of the future can hope to be valid if it ignores them.

Another celebrated failure of imagination was that persisted in by Lord Rutherford, who more than any other man laid bare the internal structure of the atom. Rutherford frequently made fun of those sensation mongers who predicted that we would one day be able to harness the energy locked up in matter. Yet only five years after his death in 1937, the first chain reaction was started in Chicago. What Rutherford, for all his wonderful insight, had failed to take into account was that a nuclear reaction might be discovered that would release more energy than that required to start it. To liberate the energy of matter, what was wanted was a nuclear "fire" analogous to chemical combustion, and the fission of uranium provided this. Once that was discovered, the harnessing of atomic energy was inevitable, though without the pressures of war it might well have taken the better part of a century.

The example of Lord Rutherford demonstrates that it is not the man who knows most about a subject, and is the acknowledged master of his field, who can give the most reliable pointers to its future. Too great a burden of knowledge can clog the wheels of imagination; I have tried to embody this fact of observation in Clarke's Law, which may be formulated as follows:

> When a distinguished but elderly scientist states that something is possible, he is almost certainly right. When he states that something is impossible, he is very probably wrong.

Perhaps the adjective "elderly" requires definition. In physics, mathematics, and astronautics it means over thirty; in the other disciplines, senile decay is sometimes postponed to the forties. There are, of course, glorious exceptions; but as every researcher just out of college knows, scientists of over fifty are good for nothing but board meetings, and should at all costs be kept out of the laboratory!

Too much imagination is much rarer than too little; when it occurs, it usually involves its unfortunate possessor in frustration and failure —unless he is sensible enough merely to write about his ideas, and not to attempt their realization. In the first category we find all the science-fiction authors, historians of the future, creators of utopias — and the two Bacons, Roger and Francis.

Friar Roger (c. 1214–1292) imagined optical instruments and mechanically propelled boats and flying machines — devices far beyond the existing or even foreseeable technology of his time. It is hard to believe that these words were written in the thirteenth century:

> Instruments may be made by which the largest ships, with only one man guiding them, will be carried with greater velocity than if they were full of sailors. Chariots may be constructed that will move with incredible rapidity without the help of animals. Instruments of flying may be formed in which a man, sitting at his ease and meditating in any subject, may beat the air with his artificial wings after the manner of birds . . . as also machines which will enable men to walk at the bottom of the seas. . . .

This passage is a triumph of imagination over hard fact. Everything in it has come true, yet at the time it was written it was more an act of faith than of logic. It is probable that all long-range prediction, if it is to be accurate, must be of this nature. The real future is not *logically* foreseeable.

A splendid example of a man whose imagination ran ahead of his age was the English mathematician Charles Babbage (1792–1871). As long ago as 1819, Babbage had worked out the principles underlying automatic computing machines. He realized that all mathematical calculations could be broken down into a series of step-by-step operations that could in theory, be carried out by a machine. With the aid of a government grant which eventually totaled £17,000 — a very substantial sum of money in the 1820's — he started to build his "analytical engine."

Though he devoted the rest of his life, and much of his private fortune, to the project, Babbage was unable to complete the machine. What defeated him was the fact that precision engineering of the standard he needed to build his cogs and gears simply did not exist at the time. By his efforts he helped create the machine-tool industry — so that in the long run the government got back very much more than its £17,000 — and today it would be a perfectly straightforward matter to complete Babbage's computer, which now stands as one of the most fascinating exhibits in the London Science Museum. In his own lifetime, however, Babbage was only able to demonstrate the operation of a relatively small portion of the complete machine. A dozen years after his death, his biographer wrote: "This extraordinary monument of theoretical genius accordingly remains, and doubtless will reman forever, a theoretical possibility."

There is not much left of that "doubtless" today. At this moment there are thousands of computers working on the principles that Babbage clearly outlined more than a century ago — but with a range and a speed of which he could never have dreamed. For what makes the case of Charles Babbage so interesting, and so pathetic, is that he was not one but *two* technological revolutions ahead of his time. Had the precision-tool industry existed in 1820, he could have built his "analytical engine" and it would have worked, much faster than a human computer, but very slowly by the standards of today. For it would have been geared — literally — to the speed with which cogs and shafts and cams and ratchets can operate.

Automatic calculating machines could not come into their own until electronics made possible speeds of operation thousands and millions of times swifter than could be achieved with purely mechanical devices. This level of technology was reached in the 1940's, and Babbage was then promptly vindicated. His failure was not one of imagination: it lay in being born a hundred years too soon.

One can only prepare for the unpredictable by trying to keep an open and unprejudiced mind — a feat which is extremely difficult to achieve, even with the best will in the world. Indeed, a completely open mind would be an empty one, and freedom from all prejudices and preconceptions is an unattainable ideal. Yet there is one form of mental exercise that can provide good basic training for would-be prophets: Anyone who wishes to cope with the future should travel back in imagination a single lifetime — say to 1900 — and ask himself just how much of today's technology would be, not merely incredible, but *incomprehensible* to the keenest scientific brains of that time.

1900 is a good round date to choose because it was just about then that all hell started to break loose in science. As James B. Conant has put it:

Somewhere about 1900 science took a *totally* unexpected turn. There had previously been several revolutionary theories and more than one epoch-making discovery in the history of science, but what occurred between 1900 and, say, 1930 was something different; it was a failure of a general prediction about what might be confidently expected from experimentation.

P. W. Bridgman has put it even more strongly:

> The physicist has passed through an intellectual crisis forced by the discovery of experimental facts of a sort which he had not previously envisaged, and which he would not even have thought possible.

The collapse of "classical" science actually began with Roentgen's discovery of X-rays in 1895; here was the first clear indication, in a form that everyone could appreciate, that the commonsense picture of the universe was not sensible after all. X-rays — the very name reflects the bafflement of scientists and laymen alike — could travel through solid matter, like light through a sheet of glass. No one had ever imagined or predicted such a thing; that one would be able to peer into the interior of the human body — and thereby revolutionize medicine and surgery — was something that the most daring prophet had never suggested.

The discovery of X-rays was the first great breakthrough into the realms where no human mind had ever ventured before. Yet it gave scarcely a hint of still more astonishing developments to come — radioactivity, the internal structure of the atom, relativity, the quantum theory, the uncertainty principle. . . .

As a result of this, the inventions and technical devices of our modern world can be divided into two sharply defined classes. On the one hand there are those machines whose working would have been fully understood by any of the great thinkers of the past; on the other, there are those that would be utterly baffling to the finest minds of antiquity. And not merely of antiquity; there are devices now coming into use that might well have driven Edison or Marconi insane had they tried to fathom their operation.

Let me give some examples to emphasize this point. If you showed a modern diesel engine, an automobile, a steam turbine, or a helicopter to Benjamin Franklin, Galileo, Leonardo da Vinci, and Archimedes — a list spanning two thousand years of time — not one of them would have any difficulty in understanding how these machines worked. Leonardo, in fact, would recognize several from his notebooks. All four men would be astonished at the materials and the workmanship, which would have seemed magical in its precision, but once they had got over that surprise they would feel quite at home — as long as they did not delve too deeply into the auxiliary control and electrical systems.

But now suppose that they were confronted by a television set, an electronic computer, a nuclear reactor, a radar installation. Quite apart from the complexity of these devices, the individual elements of which they are composed would be incomprehensible to any man born before this century. Whatever his degree of education or intelligence, he would not possess the mental framework that could accommodate electron beams, transistors, atomic fission, wave guides and cathode-ray tubes.

The difficulty, let me repeat, is not one of complexity; some of the simplest modern devices would be the most difficult to explain. A particularly good example is given by the atomic bomb (at least, the early models). What could be simpler than banging two lumps of metal together? Yet how could one explain to Archimedes that the result could be more devastation than that produced by all the wars between the Trojans and the Greeks?

Suppose you went to any scientist up to the late nineteenth century and told him: "Here are two pieces of a substance called uranium 235. If you hold them apart, nothing will happen. But if you bring them together suddenly, you will liberate as much energy as you could obtain from burning ten thousand tons of coal." No matter how farsighted and imaginative he might be, your pre-twentieth century scientist would have said: "What utter nonsense! That's magic, not science. Such things can't happen in the real world." Around 1890, when the foundations of physics and thermodynamics had (it seemed) been securely laid, he could have told you exactly why it was nonsense.

"Energy cannot be created out of nowhere," he might have said. "It has to come from chemical reactions, electrical batteries, coiled springs, compressed gas, spinning flywheels, or some other clearly defined source. All such sources are ruled out in this case — and even if they were not, the energy output you mention is absurd. Why, it is more than a *million* times that available from the most powerful chemical reaction!"

The fascinating thing about this particular example is that, even when the existence of atomic energy was fully appreciated — say right up to 1940 — almost all scientists would still have laughed at the idea of liberating it by bringing pieces of metal together. Those who believed that the energy of the nucleus ever could be released almost certainly pictured complicated electrical devices — "atom smashers" and so forth — doing the job. (In the long run, this will probably be the case; it seems that we will need such machines to fuse hydrogen nuclei on the industrial scale. But once again, who knows?)

The wholly unexpected discovery of uranium fission in 1939 made possible such absurdly simple (in principle, if not in practice) devices as the atomic bomb and the nuclear chain reactor. No scientist could ever have predicted them; if he had, all his colleagues would have laughed at him.

It is highly instructive, and stimulating to the imagination, to make a list of the inventions and discoveries that have been anticipated — and those that have not. Here is my attempt to do so.

All the items on the left have already been achieved or discovered, and all have an element of the unexpected or the downright astonishing about them. To the best of my knowledge, not one was foreseen very much in advance of the moment of revelation.

On the right, however, are concepts that have been around for hundreds or thousands of years. Some have been achieved; others will be achieved; others may be impossible. But which?

THE UNEXPECTED	THE EXPECTED
X-rays	automobiles
nuclear energy	flying machines
radio, TV	steam engines
electronics	submarines
photography	spaceships
sound recording	telephones
quantum mechanics	robots
relativity	death rays
transistors	transmutation
masers; lasers	artificial life
superconductors;	immortality
superfluids	invisibility
atomic clocks;	levitation
Mössbauer effect	teleportation
determining composition	communication with dead
of celestial bodies	observing the past,
dating the past	the future
(Carbon 14, etc.)	telepathy
detecting invisible	
planets	
the ionosphere;	
van Allen Belts	

The right-hand list is deliberately provocative; it includes sheer fantasy as well as serious scientific speculation. But the only way of discovering the limits of the possible is to venture a little way past them into the impossible. In the chapters that follow, this is exactly what I hope to do; yet I am very much afraid that from time to time I too will exhibit failure of imagination if not failure of nerve. For as I glance down the left-hand column I am aware of a few items which, only ten years ago, I would have thought were impossible. . . .

Herman Kahn
Anthony J. Weiner | # from The Year 2000

Success Breeds Failure: Affluence and the Collapse of Bourgeois[1] Values

John Maynard Keynes addressed himself to this dilemma in one of the earliest and still one of the best short discussions of some of the issues raised by the accumulation of wealth through investment.[2] As he put it,

> . . . the economic problem, the struggle for subsistence, always has been hitherto the primary, most pressing problem of the human race. If the economic problem is solved, mankind will be deprived of its traditional purpose.
>
> Will this be of a benefit? If one believes at all in the real values of life, the prospect at least opens up the possibility of benefit. Yet I think with dread of the readjustment of the habits and instincts of the ordinary man, bred into him for countless generations, which he may be asked to discard within a few decades. . . . thus for the first time since his creation man will be faced with his real, his permanent problem — how to use his freedom from pressing economic cares, how to occupy his leisure, which science and compound interest will have won for him, to live wisely and agreeably and well.

There are those who would argue that with increased freedom from necessity men will be freed for more generous, public-spirited, and humane enterprises. It is a commonplace of the American consensus that it is poverty and ignorance that breed such evils as Communism, revolutions, bigotry, and race hatred. Yet we know better than to expect that the absence of poverty and ignorance will result in a triumph of virtue or even of the benign. On the contrary, it is equally plausible that a decrease in the constraints formerly imposed by harsher aspects of reality will result in large numbers of "spoiled children." At the minimum many may become uninterested in the administration and politics of a society that hands out "goodies" with unfailing and seemingly effortless regularity.

One may choose almost at will from among available hypotheses that may seem to apply to the situation, and one reaches contrary conclusions

SOURCE: *The Year 2000* by Herman Kahn and Anthony J. Weiner. Copyright © 1967 by The Hudson Institute, Inc. Reprinted by permission of the Macmillan Company.

---

[1] We use this word in a somewhat special sense.

[2] "Economic Possibilities for our Grandchildren" (1930), reprinted in J. M. Keynes, *Essays in Persuasion* (New York: W. W. Norton, 1963), quoting from pp. 366–67.

depending upon the choice that is made; this indeterminacy is perhaps a measure of the inadequacy of contemporary social thought as a basis for generalization, relative to the complexity of human phenomena.

For example, one may take the Dollard et al.[3] frustration-aggression hypothesis and conclude that aggressiveness will be greatly tranquilized in a society that provides much less external and realistic frustration. This is opposed to the more complex and more psychoanalytically oriented point of view of Freud who points to the role that frustrations imposed by external reality may play in shoring up the defenses of the character structure — defenses that are crucial strengths and that were acquired through learning, with difficulty, as an infant to defer gratification and to mediate among conflicting energies of instinctual impulses, conscience, and the opportunities and dangers of the real world.[4] Research might show, if research could be done on such a subject, that many an infantile and narcissistic personality has matured only when faced with the necessity of earning a living — others only when faced with the necessity for facing up to some personal challenge, such as military service or participation in family responsibility. (The well-known finding that suicide rates drop sharply during wars and economic depressions is subject to diverse interpretation, but it may suggest that such external challenges can serve crucial integrative or compensatory functions for some personalities, and perhaps, less dramatically, for many others.) This not to say that equally effective or perhaps superior external challenges could not be found to substitute for the working role — or wartime experience — as a maturing or reality-focusing influence. If they are not found, however, while the economy and international and other threats make fewer demands, the decline of the values of work and national service may have some destructive effect.

Thus there may be a great increase in selfishness, a great decline of interest in government and society as a whole, and a rise in the more childish forms of individualism and in the more antisocial forms of concern for self and perhaps immediate family. Thus, paradoxically, the technological, highly productive society, by demanding less of the individual, may decrease his economic frustrations but increase his aggressions against the society. Certainly here would be fertile soil for what has come to be known as alienation.

The word alienation has been used in many different senses, some of them well defined and some in the context of systems of explanation and

---

[3] John Dollard et al., *Frustration and Aggression* (New Haven, Conn.: Yale University Press, 1939).

[4] As Freud pointed out, "Laying stress upon importance of work has a greater effect than any other technique of living in the direction of binding the individual more closely to reality; in his work he is at least securely attached to a part of reality, the human community . . . and yet . . . the great majority work only when forced by necessity, and this natural human aversion to work gives rise to the most difficult social problems." *Civilization and Its Discontents* (London: Hogarth Press, 1930), p. 34, note 1.

prescription for the ailment.[5] The young Karl Marx, for example, followed Ludwig Feuerbach (and to some extent anticipated Freud's *Civilization and its Discontents*) in the belief that alienation resulted from civilized man's "unnatural" repression of his instinctual, especially sexual, nature. Later, however, Marx concluded that alienation resulted from the worker's relationship to labor that had to be done for the profit of another; the cure was to have the worker "own" the means of production; thus alienation could be reduced by shortening the working day,[6] and "the worker therefore feels himself at home only during his leisure."[7]

The alienation that we speculate may result from affluence could have little or nothing to do with whether the society is capitalist or socialist. In either case the control of the decision-making apparatus would be perceived as beyond the reach of and in fact of little interest for the average person. Thus, whatever the economic system, the politics (and even the culture) of plenty could become one not of contentment but of cynicism, emotional distance, and hostility. More and more the good life would be defined in Epicurean or materialistic, rather than Stoic, or bourgeois terms. The enhancement of private values combined with the increased sense of futility about public values would also entail a kind of despair about the long-run future of the whole society. More and more people would act on the aphorism currently attributed to a leader of the new student left: "If you've booked passage on the Titanic, there's no reason to travel steerage."

Thus the classical American middle-class, work-oriented, advancement-oriented, achievement-oriented attitudes might be rejected for the following reasons:

1. Given an income per worker by the year 2000 of well over ten thousand dollars in today's dollars,[8] it may become comparatively easy for intelligent Americans to earn ten to twenty thousands dollars a year without investing very intense energies in their jobs — in effect they will be able to "coast" at that level.

2. It may become comparatively easy for an American to obtain several thousand dollars a year from friends and relatives or other sources, and to

---

[5] There is little doubt that this word has been used to refer to too many different phenomena, and too many different hypotheses concerning the causal relations among the phenomena. This is illustrated in the comprehensive but diffuse collection of materials edited by Gerald Sykes, *Alienation, The Cultural Climate of Our Time* (New York: George Braziller, 1964), 2 vols. For an interesting and critical historical survey, see Lewis Feuer, "What is Alienation? The Career of a Concept," in Stein and Vidich, eds., *Sociology on Trial*, (Englewood Cliffs, N.J.: Prentice-Hall, Inc., 1965). Feuer argues against the term on the ground that: "The career of this concept, from Calvin's depiction of man, the original sinner, alienated from God for all time, to the modern notion of man alienated somehow in every form of social organization, indicates indeed that its dominant overtone is social defeat."

[6] *Capital*, vol II.

[7] *Economic and Philosophical Manuscripts* (1844), p. 84.

[8] See projections of United States family income in Chap. III.

subsist without undergoing any real hardship, other than deprivation of luxuries. (Informal polls in the Cambridge, East Village, and Haight Ashbury areas indicate that many "hippies" get along on about ten dollars per week, as do many CORE and SNCC workers.)

3. Welfare services and public facilities will generally probably put a fairly high "floor" under living standards, even in terms of luxuries such as parks, beaches, museums, and so on.

4. With money plentiful, its subjective "marginal utility" would probably tend to diminish, and there would probably be a greatly increased emphasis on things that "money cannot buy."

5. Economic and social pressures to conform may diminish as the affluent society feels increasingly that it can "afford" many kinds of slackness and deviation from the virtues that were needed in earlier times to build an industrial society.

6. If the "Puritan ethic" becomes superfluous for the functioning of the economy, the conscience-dominated character type associated with it would also tend to disappear. Parents would no longer be strongly motivated to inculcate traits such as diligence, punctuality, willingess to postpone or forego satisfaction, and similar virtues no longer relevant to the socioeconomic realities in which children are growing up.

7. Yet the need to "justify" the new patterns may remain, and to the extent that there is any residual guilt about the abandonment of the nineteenth- and early twentieth-century values, there would be exaggerated feelings *against* vocational success and achievement. Many intellectuals and contributors to popular culture would help to make the case against "bourgeois," "managerial," "bureaucratic," "industrial," "Puritanical," and "preaffluent" values. There would then be considerable cultural support for feelings ranging from indifference to outright contempt for any sort of success or achievement that has economic relevance.

Other factors would augment these effects. For example, presumably by the year 2000 much more will be known about mood-affecting drugs, and these drugs will probably be used by many as a means of escape from daily life. At the same time, the young, those without responsibility in the social system, will be increasingly alienated by a society that conspicuously fails to meet what it judges to be minimal standards of social justice and purpose (standards which look impossibly Utopian to decision-makers). Ideological movements would form to rationalize and justify rebellion and renunciation of old "obsolete" values by youth from all classes and strata of society. Less articulate but equally rebellious young people would contribute to a great rise in crime and delinquency. Other symptoms of social pathology, such as mental illness, neurosis, divorce, suicide, and the like would also probably increase. Traditional religious doctrines might either continue to lose force or continue to be reinterpreted, revised, and secularized so as to pose few obstacles to the current general way of life.

On the other hand, the resources of society for dealing with these problems, perhaps in a (suffocatingly?) paternalistic way, would also have been greatly augmented. Before discussing the differences that might be made by social responses to these problems, let us see how they might affect various social groups.

Alienation and the Social Structure

Of course not everyone would suffer equally from the prevalence of affluence that we have just described. Among the voluntary poor, for example, there would be certain rock-bottom types who would insist on deprivation for reasons that have to do with personal psychopathology. Thus many skid-row derelicts, alcoholics, drug addicts, ambulatory schizophrenics, and other marginal or self-destructive personalities would insist on living at a level barely sufficient for survival. Some, indeed, would insist on slow forms of suicide through starvation, exposure, or malnutrition, as with some cases of alcoholism.

Most of the relatively poor members of society would, however, be amply subsidized. They would readily accept welfare as a means of support, and the feeling that the world owes them a living would go largely unquestioned. Incentives to take unskilled jobs would be minimal, nor would holding a job — particularly a marginal one — add much to self-esteem when relief and welfare have so much group approval. Extremist movements might flourish in the general climate of alienation from the "power structure." Many whites and middle-class Negroes might view race riots and acts of destruction with indifference, or even sympathy and approval. The following statement of a well-known poet of Negritude may well come to reflect the sympathies of a large segment of both populations:

> Mercy! mercy for our omniscient conquerors
> Hurray for those who never invented anything
> Hurrah for those who never explored anything
> Hurray for those who never conquered anything
> Hurray for joy
> Hurray for love
> Hurray for the pain of incarnate tears.[9]

At the same time, since what Oscar Lewis has described at the "culture of poverty"[10] — with its short-time perspectives and emphasis on immediate survival and pleasure, and the like — would have become, to some degree, also the culture of affluence, the assimilation of the impoverished

[9] Aimé Césaire, *Cahier D'un Retour Au Pays Natale*, as quoted in Colin Legum, *Pan-Africanism*, rev. ed. (London: Pall Mall Press Ltd.; New York: Frederick A. Praeger, 1965).

[10] Oscar Lewis, *La Vida, A Puerto Rican Family in the Culture of Poverty-San Juan and New York* (New York: Random House, 1966), esp. pp. xlii-lii.

ghetto-dweller into the larger society would pose less difficult psychological problems. The indolent spectator, the "hipster" and the "swinging cat" would have become in large degree the norm for very wide sectors of the population. Moreover, this group would be receptive to ideologies which welcome the downfall and dissolution of the American postindustrial way of life. These people would tend to be congregated in the major cities that they would probably not control politically but in which they would constitute major pressure groups and could exercise veto rights on many programs. They would probably live in rather uneasy and unstable alliance with the upper middle class, "responsible" people who would continue to control the economic structure and make use of the resources of the city. . . .

The lower middle classes (who in general will be making between ten and twenty 1965 dollars a year) would enjoy a greatly reduced work week with some emphasis on leisure. While their necessities and basic luxuries would be obtainable without great effort, they might still wish to increase income by moonlighting or by the wife's working. Some, of course, would have little motivation for expending extra effort and for them the problems of occupying leisure time would be a primary concern. Others would want to save money, pursue expensive hobbies, or emulate some aspect of the life patterns of the upper middle classes or even the wealthy. Both groups would provide a tremendous market for all kinds of sports and fads and particularly for various forms of mass entertainment. Year 2000 equivalents for the bowling alley, miniature slot-racing car tracks, and the outboard motor, would be everywhere. The drive-in church, the "museum-o-rama," and comparable manifestations of pressures toward a general degradation and vulgarization of culture would be a likely result of the purchasing decisions of this group. At the same time, these people might militate politically against civil rights and against the poor and relatively poor nonworking classes that they must support, and they would likely provide the primary support for both conservative national policies and political jingoism.

The upper middle class (most of whom will have annual income of perhaps twenty to sixty thousand 1965 dollars), by contrast, would, in many ways, be emulating the life-style of the landed gentry of the previous century, such as emphasizing education, travel, cultural values, expensive residences, lavish entertainments, and a mannered and cultivated style of life. For some there would be much effort to amass property and money for personal and family use. Getting away from the cities and from centers of population would be a difficult problem which only large amounts of money will solve. There would probably be some emphasis on "self-improvement" including cultural dilettantism. While among most members of this group we would expect a continuation of current well-to-do suburban patterns, in many cases patterns of life might be increasingly self-indulgent, marriages unstable, children alienated from their parents.

Interest in strange and exotic political ideologies, Eastern mysticism, and the like, might flourish, as could a cult of aestheticism and a shrinking from the "grubby" or "crass" aspects of society. Effete attitudes might be combined with contempt for the lower middle class and fear of the poor and of their propensity for violence. There may also be some romanticization of the "noble savage" (or "hippy") who lives outside the values of society, in voluntary poverty and/or minor or even major criminality.

The very wealthy would be able to buy considerable protection from these exigencies — that is, from all but the cultural confusion and normative conflicts. Because of their social power, many would have responsibility and there might be, in some groups, a sense of noblesse oblige, which would be shared by many in the upper middle class.

Youth could be especially self-indulgent or alienated, as the identity confusion typical of adolescence is exacerbated by the confusion, normlessness, and anomie of the society. Indifference to moral and ethical values and irresponsibility of personal behavior would be combined with feelings of outrage about the vast discrepancies between the wealth of the rich nations and the poor, and an especially painful situation would arise if these young people were drafted for military service in teeming, underdeveloped countries. Combined with pacifism and antipatriotic ideologies would be a strong feeling that American lives are too precious to be spent anywhere else in the world — or indeed to be wasted in America itself. Recruitment into any of the more difficult or demanding professions would be restricted to those (perhaps many) who have adopted Stoic patterns, and to the sons of fathers who are already in those professions and who identify with them. Conformers would — as always — work, aspire to comfortable sinecures, and look forward to early retirement — but now with great confidence. "Bumming around" and hip patterns of life could become increasingly common (though not the norm) in all but the lower middle-class groups. Many would live indefinitely on the resources of friends and relatives and on opportunistic sources of income without doing any sustained work, or in the upper middle-class pattern would cloak themselves in pretensions to artistic creativity. In spite of the prominence of symbols of rebellion and nonconformity, these youths, especially because of their anomie and alienation, would be subject to extreme fads of behavior and political, ethical, and religious ideas.

Of course, it is important to note that the lower middle class, making, say, five to twenty thousand dollars a year, are by 2000 not going to be very different from the lower middle and middle middle classes today. The upper (and middle) middle class in the year 2000 make, say, twenty to one hundred thousand dollars a year and will not necessarily feel independently wealthy. Both groups by and large will probably continue (with some erosion) with current work-oriented, advancement-oriented, achievement-oriented values. The extreme alienation we are talking about is restricted to minorities, which will be important in part because they are likely to be concentrated in the big cities, in part because they appeal to many of the more intellectual members of that ordinarily alienated group — adolescents — and mostly because their members will be literate and articulate and have a large impact on intellectuals and therefore on the culture generally.

It would be useful to make explicit the notions that determine these speculations and to discuss the alternative speculations that might be made. In particular, the evidence that might be found for or against the various alternative hypotheses and speculations should be given; only a small start can be made in this direction here.

Functions of Work

To arrive more precisely at an answer to the question, "What are the consequences of a reduction in the amount of work that needs to be done?" one must ask, "What are the various functions for the individual of the work he performs?" It is easy to make a long list of such benefits at various levels of analysis. For example, people derive from work such benefits as role; status; sense of striving; feeling of productivity, competency, and achievement; and relationships with others and advancement in a hierarchy, whether organizational or professional.

The following table shows some rough characterizations and generalizations about various roles work may play for different kinds of people in the year 2000. Those whose basic attitude toward work is that it is totally abhorrent or reprehensible are not listed, since on the whole they will find it possible to avoid employment entirely.

Basic Attitude Toward Work As:	Basic Additional Value Fulfilled by Work
1. Interruption	Short-run income
2. Job	Long-term income — some work-oriented values (one works to live)
3. Occupation	Exercise and mastery of gratifying skills — some satisfaction of achievement-oriented values
4. Career	Participating in an important activity or program. Much satisfaction of work-oriented, achievement-oriented, advancement-oriented values
5. Vocation (calling)	Self-identification and self-fulfillment
6. Mission	Near fanatic or single-minded focus on achievement or advancement (one lives to work)

As discussed later one could easily imagine that many Americans from "normal" (i.e., not deprived) backgrounds will increasingly adopt the first position, that work is an interruption, while many formerly in the lower and economically depressed classes will increasingly shift to the second or third positions which reflect more work-oriented and achievement-oriented values. On the other hand, the man whose missionary zeal for work takes priority over all other values will be looked on as an unfortunate, perhaps even a harmful and destructive neurotic. Even those who find in work a "vocation" are likely to be thought of as selfish, excessively narrow, or compulsive.

Many of the benefits of work could be derived from other forms of activity, provided they were available and, preferably, institutionalized. The model of the cultivated gentlemen, for example, is likely to be available and possibly generally usable in a democratic and upward mobile society like the United States. It may be argued that aristocrats are far more visible in Europe and that it is more respectable for the wealthy to live as landed gentry, rentiers, even as playboys in Europe than in the United States, and that for these reasons the transition to this pattern of life would be easier in Europe. Indeed, historically this has often been the aspiration and achievement (after a generation or two) of the upper middle class and even the lower class nouveaux riches. On the other hand, if it became the ideal it is probably more difficult for the typical European to think of making the social transition to such a status for himself than it would be for the typical American. Of course, the American has seen fewer examples of such lives, and has up to now respected them less. Therefore it seems less likely to be the American ideal.

In the economic structure we are describing, there may be a special problem of the service professions whose productivity per hour may not have gone up. Thus many believe there are probably important limits to the extent to which the efficiency of persons such as teachers, professors, doctors, lawyers, ministers, psychologists, social workers, and so forth can be increased. Others believe that not only can these professions be automated,[11] but that there are huge opportunities for increasing efficiency through better organization, specialization, and the very skilled use of computers. Nevertheless, there are likely to remain irreducible kinds of activities that defy rationalization or improvement, such as those that require face-to-face meeting and conversation. Thus programmed instruction, lectures, and sermons over television are not likely to displace face-to-face human communication, at least not without great loss to those involved. Therefore only part of the current activity in these fields is likely to increase in productivity.

---

[11] Thus much legal research can be done most easily through a computerized library. A physician may be able to phone a list of symptoms into a central computer and get back a print-out of suggested diagnostic possibilities. Many laboratory tests might be performable by methods which would present immediate results. Closed circuit television and various kinds of continuously reading tests presented on central display boards could even now make the utilization of hospital personnel also much more efficient. Other possibilities were mentioned in Chapter II.

To the extent that recruitment into the service professions is greatly expanded because of the reduced need for people in manufacturing, routine aspects of public administration, and automated administrative and managerial tasks, several problems will arise. One is that it will be perhaps more difficult to recruit people to do difficult and demanding work that either requires long and arduous training or requires working under difficult, dangerous, or frustrating conditions. If the hours of work of people in these professions go down severely, the incentives and psychological functions of membership in the profession may be somewhat diluted. For example, a hospital may have three head nurses if there are three shifts; what happens, however, when there are six or eight shifts? To what extent is authority, expertise, and satisfaction diluted when power, responsibility, and status are so fractionated?

Similar questions should be posed about other kinds of activities. In general, a threefold increase in GNP per capita is far from the equivalent of a threefold increase in productivity per capita in all relevant respects. As real productivity increases dramatically in certain industries, principally in manufacturing and heavily clerical industries, such as banking and insurance and many federal, state, and local governmental functions, which could be very much automated, the price structure would also change dramatically. This would result in enormous increase in the availability, variety, and quality of goods and many standardized services, since these items would become very much cheaper or very much better for the same price. A threefold increase in GNP per capita would probably imply a much greater increase in standard of living with respect to these items. Yet, at the same time, skilled, personal services requiring irreducible quantities of human time, training, and talent would become both absolutely and relatively expensive. Thus there would probably still be a very strong demand for, and probably also a much expanded supply of expensive and skilled professionals, managers, entrepreneurs, artisans, technicians and artists — for the most part, the well-educated upper middle class. This group may well be much too busy and well rewarded to be alienated.

Furthermore, even if one imagines the ordinary member of the labor force amply supplied with intricate technology affording innumerable needs and luxuries during his short work week, and even if he can travel anywhere in the less-developed world and easily buy vast quantities of domestic service and other personal attentions during his long vacations, many important consumer items are likely to remain too expensive for him to wish his work week to become *too* short. There will probably still be a class of "luxury items," consisting of such things as vacation houses in extremely exotic places, advanced or "sporty" personal vehicles such as perhaps ground-effect machines, or similar items for the most part well beyond today's technology and prohibitively expensive for ordinary workers by today's standards, that by the year 2000 will be still expensive, but perhaps within reach of the man who is interested in earning enough money — and many, no doubt, will be interested. . . .

Humanism and the Value of Time

It is possible to suppose that something else might happen. For example, John Adams, our second President, once suggested that: "my sons ought to study mathematics and philosophy, geography, natural history and naval architecture, in order to give their children a *right* to study painting, poetry, music, architecture, statuary, tapestry and porcelain. . . ." (emphasis added).

The passage is peculiarly American; almost no (correspondingly upperclass) European would use the word "right." The most he would have said would be that his sons *ought* to emphasize mathematics, philosophy, geography, and so on, in order that their sons *could* emphasize painting, poetry, music, and the like. He would feel that some interest in painting, poetry, and music was proper and unremarkable. On the other hand for most Americans a man who is deeply preoccupied with porcelain, or any of the fine arts, may still be, even in this less Philistine age, a bit suspect — whether as effeminate or as simply not sufficiently serious and practical. Adams's statement is characteristically American, in that it gives an overwhelming priority to the needs of national security and statemanship and asserts that no one has a *right* to devote his attention to "finer things" for their own sake, until these needs have been adequately met. A contemporary parallel is the American upper middle-class view of the proper relation between work and play. Typically an American businessman or professional man apologizes for taking a vacation by explaining it is only "in order to recharge his batteries"; he justifies rest or play mostly in terms of returning to do a better job. The European by contrast seems to enjoy his vacation as a pleasure in its own right, and does not hesitate to work for the express purpose of being able to afford to play in better style.

We have already suggested that in the postindustrial society that we are describing, in continental Europe the middle and upper classes could, in effect, return to or adopt the manner of the "gentleman." Many Europeans, of course, argue that things are now going the other way, that under the impact of a mass-consumption, materialistic culture the humanistic values that have been so characteristic in Europe are rapidly eroding or disappearing. One can fully concede that this is indeed the current phase and still note that there is likely to be a reaction in the not-too-distant future. Even today many Europeans seem to emphasize nonvocational aspects of their life much more intensely than even the family-oriented Americans do. For example, many Europeans seem to plan intensely, a year ahead, how they will spend their vacations. Once on vacation, they would resent any interruption for work — such as a business phone call — far more than any American would. It is the vacation that, at the time at least, deserves to be taken more seriously — not the work.

While the American has no sense of "staying in his place" and therefore could seek to emulate aristocratic ideals, the issue remains as to what extent the gentleman of leisure will be an ideal. It simply has not been one in the United States in the last one hundred and fifty years. On the other hand, the middle and upper middle class in Europe have often aspired to be gentlemen, and when tradesmen made fortunes they often made the transition, or at least their children did. In the United States, on the contrary, a member of the middle class who makes his fortune, or his descendants, such as those in the Yankee upper class, usually persists in the tradition of hard work and of service of one kind or another.

Thus if the average American had an opportunity to live on the beach for six months a year doing nothing, he might have severe guilt feelings in addition to a sunburn. If an American wishes to be broiled in the sun, he usually must go through a preliminary justification such as the following: "The system is corrupt, I reject it. Its values are not my values. To hell with these puritanical, obsolete concepts." Only at that point can he relax in the sun. If he is more guilty, or articulate, he may proclaim: "All of those robots who are working have sold out to the soulless, inhumane system with its obsolete and grubby, machine-based, materialistic values, and its empty goals of the Bitch-Goddess of monetary success. By refusing to be drawn in, I at least can preserve my humanity, individuality, integrity, dignity, and physical health, as well as my spontaneity, the freshness of my perceptions, the openness of my relating, and my capacity to love." Unless an American has taken an ideological and moralistic stance against the work-oriented value system, he cannot abandon work.

On the other hand, a good many Americans, and typically middle-class Americans, will have a sense of noblesse oblige. Some of the same pressures toward Stoic values that were important in the Roman Empire will be important here as well.

Let it be added that in this "super-affluent" society of year 2000, it is not likely that efficiency (defined by the criteria of maximizing profit or income) will still be primary, though it will doubtless remain important. To some degree this has already occurred and the situation in the United States is today very different from what it was before 1929. For example, it seems to be true that when a middle-class American looked for a job in 1929, he was interested in salary and prospects for advancement. Today, however, the first questions addressed to personnel interviewers are more likely to relate the satisfaction of the applicant's family with the new neighborhood and the quality of the schools. This is, of course, particularly true of professional and managerial workers, but it seems to be more widely spread as well. It is only after the requirements of home and children have been satisfied (and sometimes considerations of pension, vacation, and insurance as well), that salary and advancement are discussed.

We could think of this phenomenon as a shift to humanistic rather than vocational or advancement-oriented values, and conjecture that this tendency will increase over the next thirty-three years. Indeed, unless there is a surprising interruption in the exponential progress of prosperity, sensate-humanist and epicurean values almost surely will come to dominate older bourgeois virtues, and may even return, in some respects, to criteria that antedated the "bourgeois" element of the multifold trend, which has been a driving force for more than five centuries. . . .

The new values could not only be premature, they could also be wrong. The year 2000 conditions we have sketched could produce a situation in which illusion, wishful thinking, even obviously irrational behavior could exist to a degree unheard of today. Such irrational and self-indulgent behavior is quite likely in a situation in which an individual is overprotected and has no systematic or objective contact with reality. For example, there are probably many people for whom work is the primary touch with reality. If work is removed, or if important functions are taken from work, the contact these people have with reality will be to some degree impaired. The results — minor or widespread — may become apparent in forms such as political disruption, disturbed families, and personal tragedies — or in the pursuit of some "humanistic" values that many would think of as frivolous or even irrational.

Humanistic values are, of course, a question of definition. While some may judge certain ideologies that invoke humanistic language as better described as sentimental, self-indulgent, or rationalizations of quite irrational feelings of rebelliousness and selfishness, others will accept the ideology. (While this is, of course, more or less a value question, facts and analysis have some relevance to it.)

Consider this question of humanistic versus irrational or indulgent behavior. In 1926 the British economist Arthur Redford said, in describing the adjustment of British yeomen to industrialization: "In the course of a generation or two it becomes quite 'natural' . . . for a fixed number of hours each day, regulating their exertions constantly . . . there may be some temporary restlessness among the 'hands,' but the routine soon reestablishes itself as part of the ordinary discipline of life." While this may be a rather callous observation, "progress" and other conditions predominantly made the adjustment a necessary one.

In the post affluent, seemingly very secure world of the year 2000, we will not likely, and presumably should not, be willing to ask people to make sacrifices of this order. However, new issues will arise. Consider the following two statements put forth by Berkeley students on signs they were carrying while picketing and later on a BBC television broadcast:

I am a human being; please do not fold, spindle, or mutilate.

Life here is a living hell.

One can only agree with the first, assuming we understand precisely in what way the students believe they are not treated as well as IBM cards.

Thus it was widely believed, especially in the 1930's and 1940's, by people who thought they were "psychologically sophisticated," that any kind of discipline for children causes undesirable repression, inhibits creativity, and creates neuroses; that almost completely permissive upbringing is necessary for a parent not to "fold, spindle, or mutilate." Today psychoanalysts are emphasizing that a reasonable level of benevolent but firm discipline is very much needed by a child, and that excessive permissiveness is more likely to result in a child marred by guilty wilfulness, irresponsibility, and inadequacy.

Of course, the students would argue that they do not mean anything so extreme, but just that they ought to be treated better than items processed by machines. One can only sympathize with their lack of ability to communicate with a seemingly unfeeling, bureaucratic administration choosing to enforce computer decisions. But to argue that the idiosyncrasies of a computer that allows ten minutes between classes which require fifteen minutes to reach, or that assigns art classes to basements and engineering classes to top-floor rooms with windows, creates difficulties for students, is rather different from arguing that life is a "living hell." The most that students could reasonably say was that the administration made life unnecessarily complicated and frustrating, and had occasionally overstepped its proper bounds. Yet they chose to state (and no doubt felt) these issues in moralistic, politicized, ideological, and emotionally extreme terms. Similarly, increasing numbers of Americans are likely not only to reject currently held work-oriented, achievement-oriented, advancement-oriented attitudes, but are likely to adopt the kind of "spoiled child" attitudes that seem to have characterized at least some of the Berkeley protesters. . . .

Gordon Rattray Taylor | # New Minds for Old

'Everyone complains of his memory,' said the French wit la Rochefoucauld, 'but no one complains of his judgment.' However, most people would like to be able to improve both, and it looks as if they may be able to. Whether it will make mankind any happier is much less certain.

We stand on the threshold of a new era in understanding the mind, and more than one scientist has expressed the opinion that the biggest area of advance in biology during the next half-century may be that of neuro-

SOURCE: *The Biological Time Bomb* by Gordon Rattray Taylor. An NAL Book. Copyright © 1968 by Gordon Rattray Taylor. Reprinted by permission of The World Publishing Company.

physiology. Three major areas of excitement and progress can be detected among the numerous enquiries in the field. First, there is a growing power to intervene in the non-intellectual functions of the brain: a growing ability to alter moods and emotional states — a development which is based on the realization that the brain is not simply an electrical or computer-like mechanism, but a complex chemical system as well. Secondly, a spirit of extreme optimism has sprung up concerning the possibility of discovering the nature of memory. Finally, there is a guarded belief that one may be able to effect considerable improvements in the level of intelligence of future generations, even if the idea of an 'intelligence pill' which turns us all into geniuses in a week or two remains chimerical.

Ten years ago, Professor Jean Rostand foresaw the extraordinary significance of the early work on mood-control (as we may call it) and with Gallic wit declared: 'Special hormones or other chemical agents will be used to reinforce the vigour of a man's mind, to strengthen his character, to dispose him to virtuousness. Quite soon, perhaps, people will buy genius or sanctity at the chemist's just as now women buy the straightness of their nose or the depth of their gaze at the beauty parlour.'

It does not require much imagination to see that the power to regulate morality by drugs would raise unique ethical problems, and might change our whole system of life — politics, economics, war, the lot — even if we leave aside the probability that such powers would be misused. Equally, if we could shift levels of intelligence, the whole pattern of competitive interpersonal behaviour would be transformed, while if everyone were more intelligent, many of the precautions which we take against folly would become unnecessary. On the other hand, if only a minority acquire heightened intelligence, an élite system might develop which would put paid to democracy as most people now understand it. Yet again, if powers of memory can be greatly improved — still more, if ready-made memories can be bestowed — the whole educational system, based as it is largely on cramming in facts, will have to be reoriented.

And these three areas, mood, intelligence and memory, are merely the three currently most active fields: there are other areas of research still in a more exploratory stage which might, in due time, have just as dramatic an influence on our lives.

If the effects of the advance in biological understanding of the working of the body are disturbing, the effects of discovering in detail how the brain works are likely to be positively alarming. Society is adjusted to the basic facts of human mental attainment and weakness in many intricate ways. Any drastic change in parameters such as intelligence, memory-power, emotionality or ability to take decisions would create problems for which there is literally no precedent. And if such knowledge lent increased power to those who might misuse it to influence or control others, might not undreamed-of tyrannies arise?

It therefore seems worth looking rather closely at the state of play in this field in order to see whether the optimism (if that is the right word) of the research scientists is justified; and, if so, just where and how soon society had better begin preparing for the consequences.

To medieval man it was inconceivable that the brain, this few pounds of sloppy jelly, could perform the functions of thought and feeling, of decision and memory. It was easier to think of it as an anchorage point for some invisible soul or spirit, which would execute these functions, handing down the orders to the body to behave accordingly. Some, indeed, denied the brain responsibility for thought at all, and placed the seat of reason in the stomach. And that the feelings were located in the heart was a commonplace, as popular expressions in many languages show.

Perhaps the greatest breakthrough which has occurred in this century is the realization that the brain is a perfectly adequate device for thought; how it handles emotions and memory is less obvious, but the fact it does is now undoubted, and the structures within the brain which do so are now being investigated.

What has made its reasoning functions credible is the invention of the computer: a device consisting of thousands of identical switches, intricately wired together. The anatomists of the nineteenth century, like the Spaniard Ramon y Cajal, demonstrated that the brain consists not of thousands, but of hundreds of millions of inter-connected neurones, and these were later shown to be switches — rather fancy switches, but nevertheless switches. The way in which electric signals are transmitted through this system has become clear, though the details of the circuitry are only just beginning to be unravelled. The brain, whatever else it is besides, is certainly a very sophisticated computer. Or, as W. Nauta once said, it is four computers connected together. One monitors input, and filters out the trivial. One is an automatic pilot, executing all habitual functions. One is a calculating machine — and this is a double set of equipment, perhaps for the same reason that airline booking is often executed with double-banked equipment. It also appears to be the seat of memory. The last computer is concerned in some ill-understood way with feelings, and with primitive needs like hunger, thirst and sex.

The second new insight about the brain, and this one is only a decade or so old, is that the brain is also a complex chemical device. Its parts respond in subtle ways to the influence of substances in the fluids which bathe them, and contain specialized chemical agents — gangliosides, cerebrosides, sphingomyelin and so on — the functions of which are still obscure. Moreover, some brain cells secrete controlling substances, or neurohumours, which stimulate or calm other parts of the brain. To Sherrington, the great neurophysiologist who died in 1952, the brain was a vast electrical switchboard, and in the years between the wars his successors were busy trying to understand it in purely electrical terms, stimulating it electrically and measuring the electrical waves it produced.

Today, physiologists are busy dripping chemicals into it through fine tubes, analysing the substances in it and their distribution, and synthesizing a growing range of drugs which, when they reach it through the blood-stream, affect its functioning.

Each new approach reveals the brain as more complex than was thought previously, and it may well be fifty years or more before its mode of working is understood in any depth. But one does not have to understand a thing completely to be able to influence it, and the first-fruits of these new insights will ripen quite soon. Indeed, some of them have already been gathered. The somewhat superficial and fumbling research which is now going on has already yielded new techniques of practical importance and none more so than in the field of mood control.

Mood control

Of course, influencing affective states by chemical means is an old trick. Early in civilization man found he could use alcohol for this purpose, and chewed ivy and other plants for their effect on his mind. Berserk rage was probably induced in this way. Aphrodisiac smells and potions must have been discovered very early and the anaphrodisiac effect of some of these natural drugs has long been noted. Thus in the Yemen, a substance prepared from the buds or leaves of the plant *Catha edulis* is sold widely. It excites the central nervous system, producing gaiety and banishing hunger, but it also dulls desire and leads, if used frequently, to cardiac disorders. Or again in Gabon, iboga, derived from *Tabernanthe iboga,* is chewed to banish fatigue. It contains two alkaloids of unknown structure, christened ibogaine and iboganine, which have never been properly investigated.

The possibility of controlling our moods was thus always at hand, and it is perhaps surprising that it is only recently that it has been put on a scientific footing.

It was in 1947 that Professor Robert Robinson, a distinguished British chemist, asked the Swiss drug firm of CIBA if they could make ajmaline for him, and it was not until 1952 that they succeeded. Interest in ajmaline had been aroused by the use in India of the powdered root of *Rauwolfia,* known as sarpaganda, to combat heart disease; the active principle was found to be ajmaline. But besides reducing blood pressure it appeared to have a general calming effect on the patient. Soon, Dr Nathan Kline of the Rockland State Hospital, New York, tried using it to help psychotics, and got good results. At first his reports were greeted with scorn: insanity, psychiatrists said, was the product of childhood experience and not to be fought off with drugs. But in fact what Kline had pounced on what the first of the ataractics or, as they are now generally known, the tranquillizers.

The last twenty years have seen the emergence of three important groups of drugs acting on the mind: the analeptics or stimulants, such as pipradol, which counter depression and often act to produce a state of euphoria, or well-being, and do so without reducing appetite or interfering with sleep; the muscle-relaxants and tranquillizers, like chlorpromazine and meprobamate; and the hallucinogens, of which LSD-25 is known almost too well. In addition, we now have anticonvulsants for epilepsy: trimethadione for petit mal and diphenylhydantoin for grand mal.

Tranquillizers, it should be added, do more than soothe the nerves of harassed business men. In large doses, they calm frantic psychotics; in smaller ones they can make elderly patients more alert, active and co-operative. Variant forms, like methimazole, slow down the frenzied activity of the hyperthyroid patient, or like azacyclonal, block the psychotic episodes sometimes produced by LSD-25.

It would be absurd to suppose, however, that the discovery of new mind drugs will stop at this point. As the chemistry of the brain is gradually unravelled, an increasingly extensive and precise intervention in mood will surely become possible.

At present, the action of such drugs is often inconsistent and unreliable. They often produce startling effects in a minority of subjects, some effect in a majority and none at all in a few. Why this is so is a mystery. Moreover, their effect on psychotics and on normal people can be widely different. A dose of tranquillizer, such as chlorpromazine, which would calm a schizophrenic, improving his thinking and quelling his hallucinations, would leave a normal person numb, fatigued and miserable. We are not yet in a position to engineer drugs with precisely the effects we want; but that is clearly the end state towards which present research is tending.

We may actually be on the way to banish insanity. The success which has already been achieved with schizophrenia and the depressions is not always appreciated by the layman. Until twelve years ago, the figures of admission of mental cases were rising steadily. Then, following the introduction of the new drugs, they began to turn down for the first time in many years.

How far schizophrenia has a chemical cause is still a matter of warm controversy: there are those like Dr. H. Osmond of the Princeton Neuropsychiatric Service's Divisional Research Center, who says emphatically that it has. The older school are sceptical. Recently, a new drug, huphenazine enanthate, injected every two to four weeks, has been found to control the symptoms of schizophrenia for up to four weeks. The way things are going, it looks as if soon we shall be able not only to drive men mad with drugs, but also to drive them sane.

No longer will people be happy or sad, amiable or aggressive, active or lazy, calm or anxious, merely because it was their nature or because circumstances evoked the mood; they will be so because they took the appropriate pill. Humanists may feel that there is a personal loss involved in evading the various moods which life experiences bring us. Human beings protected from genuine emotion may be in some sense impoverished. Against this, it could be argued that even the most cloistered and unadventurous individuals will be able to experience pinnacles of emotion they would never otherwise have known — the rapture of gazing on a new ocean for the first time, the utter abandonment of the dark night of the soul. Such individuals might be richer, better able to appreciate the feelings of others, thanks to having had similar experiences themselves.

Socially, however, it may be disturbing not to know for sure if a person is genuinely himself. We feel some awkwardness in dealing with the intoxicated man, and still more in dealing with the insane, because society does not provide us with adequate conventions of behaviour. Insults which we would resent from a sober man, for instance, we may feel bound to ignore from a drunk. When a psychotic tries to persuade us to a course of action, we remain wary. When we try to reason with the psychotic and find our arguments produce action quite other than we intended, we feel baffled and impotent. It is probably this which is the main factor in the common objection to the use of behaviour-changing drugs.

Indeed, if the experience of the past few years is a guide, society will be prompt to prohibit the use of most of these drugs, except on a doctor's prescription. The tranquillizers, once sold freely, have been restricted in this way. The hallucinogens, although relatively harmless, have also been banned.

Among the arguments advanced to justify such bans have been that various disturbances of behaviour result — even that people may drive cars under their influence, and become involved in accidents. But of course this is also true of alcohol, which we do not ban: we restrict the freedom of young people to consume it, and we make special regulations to cover cases, such as car driving, where the safety of others may be affected. The readiness with which society has acted against non-addictive personality-changing drugs reflects, I suspect, rather deep unconscious anxieties concerning such matters. The fact that we are slow to prohibit many more dangerous and even lethal substances suggests that our motives are less pure than they look.

Recently, Dr. Heinz Lehmann of McGill University forecast the discovery of a drug which would dissipate aggression: an 'anti-aggression pill'. A drug of this kind would present a further set of ethical and social problems. He probably had in mind the work of Seegmiller, Rosenbloom and Kelley at the National Institute of Arthritis and Mental Disease. This team showed that over-production of uric acid can occur as the result of the absence of a certain enzyme (hypoxanthine-guanine-phosphoribosyl-transferase) though only in males. It is well established that too much uric acid causes compulsive aggressive behaviour and also results in mental retardation. It may well be that other disturbances in body chemistry are also associated with extreme irritability — the tetchiness of the gouty man is already proverbial.

It is not clear that such irritability is aggression in the strict sense; aggression is normally defined as an attempt to dominate others in order to achieve a sense of security, and sometimes as a form of revenge for remembered insults or deprivations. (The question is quite complex, but we need not analyse aggression in detail here.) To dissolve aggression of this type may call for therapies of a different type — perhaps even the dissolving of old, painful memories by the techniques discussed in the following section.

It is reasonable to assume, however, that at least in *some* cases it may be possible to banish aggression. The ethical question therefore arises whether society would be justified in compelling aggressive persons to take such treatment. Is this not a form of brain-washing? The answer must be yes, but at the same time the case is not very different from that of the manic-depressive psychotic who is given electroshock or who undergoes lobotomy. Society's problem is to decide when a man is dangerous enough to treat in this way. Up to now it has avoided treating anyone who was not directly physically violent. The person who expressed his aggression more deviously was and is exempt.

There is also a moral issue, raised by Anthony Burgess in his most unusual novel *The Clockwork Orange*. In it, a delinquent who obtains sexual excitement from violence, destructiveness and rape is conditioned to feel sick at the sight of violence. He becomes meek and fawning, offers to turn the other cheek. Is there any value, Burgess asks by implication, in virtuous behaviour which is not based on moral effort and moral choice? The boy has become a 'clockwork orange' — a simulacrum of the organic reality, with only crude mechanisms inside.

The scientist who sees organic life as based on mechanisms which differ from clockwork only by being immensely more complex will not be impressed by this image. But he should not dismiss the issue which Burgess raises because of this. Even without bringing in mystical, vitalistic assumptions about the nature of personality, it is still perfectly justifiable to say that the mechanisms which guide choice in a normal human being are so much more complex than the kind of simple conditioned response imposed on Burgess's anti-hero as to be greatly preferable in human terms. (To be sure there are scientists who do not recognize this fact. In particular, Professor H. J. Eysenck has hotly advocated the wider use of just such operant conditioning techniques for a long time, and in the U.S.A. they have recently become known through the work of Dr. J. Wolpé and others.)

Either way, as 'moral' behaviour becomes controllable, new problems will arise in penology and law. The British Lord Chancellor, Lord Gardiner, not long since attributed the large number of men in jail to 'lack of moral judgment.' On the other hand, Dr. W. M. Court Brown at Edinburgh showed not long ago that a significant proportion of anti-social persons possessed hereditary chromosomal defects — implying that their behaviour was, at least to some extent, the consequence of their imperfect physical development and to that extent not their 'fault' at all. The two assessments are not necessarily as far apart from each other as might seem to be the case. Most psychologists would agree that 'moral judgment' results from an appropriate sequence of learning experiences in early life and is also dependent on adequate emotional development. It can readily be shown in monkeys that deprivation in infancy restricts emotional development and leads to impoverished personal relationships.

It is becoming ever clearer that social behaviour derives from mechanisms which are understandable and therefore controllable. The familiar issue, that all crime is too readily excused on psychiatric grounds, is bound to become still more familiar, until society tires of trying to deal with crime by punishment, or even by rehabilitation after the event, and turns to mending the conditions which cause the distorted psychic development which manifests as 'lack of moral judgment'.

Lastly, a further set of moral problems would arise if a ruler or leader began to make use of mood-controlling drugs for political purposes. Thus he might feed aggression pills to his soldiers and airmen (for if it is possible to make anti-aggression pills it must be possible to make pro-aggression pills also) and anti-aggression pills and euphoriants to the public who might unseat him. The possibility that police forces might be equipped with anti-aggression sprays, in place of the hoses and tear gas which they now use, should be taken quite seriously.

But before discussing these wider issues, it will be as well to consider some other aspects of mind control, notably the growing understanding of the nature of memory and intelligence.

Memory lane

Current research into the nature of memory is in a highly controversial stage; nevertheless, it holds out the possibility of improvement of recall and the definite probability that erasure of memory may, in certain circumstances, be possible. It even hints at the weird prospect of being able to inject memories or of being able to transfer memories from one person to another after they have been formed.

What we loosely call memory comprises three distinct processes: read-in, storage and recall. The information must be entered in the filing system, must not fade or be destroyed while in it, and must be traceable when wanted. As anyone who has ever used a filing system knows, it is the third stage which gives most trouble. When we say that we have a poor memory, it is usually because we cannot bring something to mind when we want it. Nevertheless, we know that we know it, and afterwards, when it is too late, it often comes back to us.

If we receive a blow on the head, we may 'lose our memory' — suffer from amnesia — but later the memories return, and it is a curious fact that they return in the reverse order to that in which they were formed; the most recent are recovered first. It is almost as if they were buried layer upon layer. Clearly the filing system has remained intact: it is the much more vulnerable recovery system which has broken down.

Currently, scientists are preoccupied with the question of how memories are stored: once this is known it should be easier to investigate how they are read-in and recovered. The current air of optimism is due to the belief that the answer to the main question is in sight, and this optimism tends, I think, to obscure the fact that the other two questions remain almost wholly baffling.

A few years ago, when the brain was conceived of primarily as an electric machine, the popular line was that the storage was electrical. Since some early computers used resonating circuits as memory devices, it was thought that the brain might do the same. A succession of pulses, carrying information in much the same way that the Morse code does, would circle endlessly round a loop, to be tapped when required.

Then, when the development of molecular biology made it clear that information could be embodied in long-chain molecules, the idea was soon advanced that memory might be stored in molecules too, and was widely taken up.

It was Professor Holger Hydén of Gothenburg University in Sweden who, in 1961, first popularized this notion, saying that RNA was in fact the molecule in question. Analysing the brains of rats which had been trained in sundry tasks, he found not only increased quantities of RNA present, but a change in its composition.

The idea that the ultimate nature of memory is chemical, rather than electrical, is strongly supported by the fact that memories remain unimpaired after the brain's electrical activity has been temporarily stopped by cold, shock, drugs and many other kinds of stress. We have, however, a short-term memory — the one we employ in holding a telephone number while we dial it — which may well be electrical in nature.

Most such memories vanish rapidly, which is just as well, as we should be swamped by the mass of irrelevant detail, and should have difficulty finding the information we wanted among it. There are a number of experiments with animals which suggest that it takes some hours before a memory-trace is printed into long-term memory. They suggest, moreover, that the trace is held at first in an electrical form, but is finally embodied in a chemical form for permanent storage.

Only storage at the molecular level seems able to explain the vast capacity which man has for data. It has been estimated that, for a computer to have a memory rivalling a man's, it would require an area of magnetic tape equal to the entire surface of the earth. "Molecular neurology' is the still unfamiliar label which Francis O. Schmidt of MIT has coined for this new-born specialism.

The chemical approach to memory soon received strong support from the experiments of two young graduate students at the University of Texas. In the early 1950's, Robert Thompson and James V. McConnell began to carry out some experiments on memory that have since become widely known, not to say famous, and which have given a new impetus to research on memory. They chose as their research subject not human beings or higher mammals, as had most of their predecessors, but a lowly wormlike creature found in ditch-water and known as a planarian. In an evolutionary sense, it is the simplest creature to have anything which could reasonably be called a brain — a network of some 400 cells. But planarians are also the most complex of the creatures which can divide by fission. Cut one in half and not only will the head grow a new tail, but the tail will grow a new head.

Thompson and McConnell shone a bright light on each planarian; several seconds later it received a mild electric shock. The light merely caused it to stretch itself. The shock caused it to contract or to turn its head. After a hundred or so repetitions of this light/shock experience, the planarians usually started to contract when the light stimulus alone was given. Apparently, they had *learned* that light meant: 'shock coming'. The scientific world was sceptical: such a simple creature could not be expected to learn anything. Actually, an animal which receives a barrage of stimuli is irritated into a hypersensitive state, and this confuses the issue, as experimenters who had tried to 'condition' planaria forty years before found. Thompson and McConnell avoided this trap by requiring (a) that a planarian respond at least 23 times in every 25 tests, and (b) that, after it had been allowed to 'forget' the experience, it should relearn in fewer trials than previously.

The next step was to cut the trained planarians in half and let them regenerate. It was then found that not only did the head-half relearn in fewer trials than before, but the tail-half did also! How had the memory been preserved in the half which did not have a brain?

As I have mentioned, the idea had already been advanced by Holger Hydén that memory might be stored in the molecules of RNA, in much the same way that genetic information is stored in DNA. So William C. Corning of the University of Rochester, having cut his trained planarians in half, allowed them to regenerate in a solution of ribonuclease, an enzyme which specifically destroys RNA. He found that, whereas the head-half planarians still showed enhanced ability to relearn their lesson, the tail-halves had forgotten. This did not prove that RNA carried the memory. It could be that ribonuclease cannot get into head-halves, or that it destroyed the mechanism by which the tail-half put the memory back into the new head. But it did make RNA look very interesting in the context of memory.

Subsequently, the teams performed many other experiments which revealed the difficulty of interpreting planarian behaviour. At times it seemed as though the planarian was merely thrown into a state of anxiety, or hyper-irritability, rather than that it had learned in the strict sense of the word. The most sensational result of all was that in which planarians of a cannibalistic breed ate the chopped-up bodies of trained worms and then themselves showed enhanced learning power. Had they actually acquired the memories of the worms they ate? Professors of psychology, half seriously, envisaged the day when their class would learn their subject by eating their teachers.

That the molecules had survived the digestive processes seemed possible in planarians, improbable in higher organisms.

The destruction of memories and also their transfer to other organisms has thus been achieved, if McConnell's experiments were sound, at least in a lowly organism. A Californian team attempted to repeat this work, using more planarians, more kinds of stimuli and longer testing intervals. They reported negative results, but McConnell replied, in effect, that they lacked skill in handling planarians, and that other workers had repeated his experiments with success.

Experiments such as those described do not prove conclusively that RNA is the repository of memory. It seems slightly more likely, on the face of it, that memory should be embodied in specific proteins, and it is known that nerve cells manufacture proteins faster than other cells. The RNA may simply play an intermediary role in this process.

If you remove parts of the brain of an animal, you seem to impoverish its memory in a general way, rather than to eliminate specific memories, and it makes little difference which parts of the cortex you remove. It has several times been suggested that memories are diffused throughout the brain, and depend on the setting of innumerable 'switches'. If so, the function of the proteins made by the nerve cells may simply be to act as switches. If so, memory is *both* chemical *and* electrical, a solution which appeals to me as inherently probable.

It was in the early sixties that analogous experiments began to be conducted with mammals. Dr. Allan Jacobson (a former colleague of McConnell's) and co-workers at the University of California taught a number of animals, chiefly rats and hamsters, a task — to go to a feeding box when a light flashed or when a click was heard — then killed them and extracted the RNA from their brains. This was then injected into untrained rats which showed, not indeed an immediate grasp of the lesson, but a reduced learning time. Objectors said that RNA had merely acted as a stimulant. In a similar manner, Unger and Oceguera-Navaño at Baylor University habituated rats to noise and claimed to have transferred the tolerance to other rats. Jacobson also introduced a new note when he injected RNA from trained hamsters into rats and claimed that their learning performance was improved too.

Can memory cross the species barrier? Is memory based on identical coding throughout the whole range of living creatures? It seems that the coding for protein synthesis is basically the same, throughout the animal kingdom, so it was not inherently unlikely that memory would also be universal. Would-be humorists asked whether it was wise, any longer, to eat calves' brains.

Meanwhile, progress was also being made with the destruction of memories. Dr. Bernard W. Agranoff, at Michigan University's Mental

Health Research Institute, started from the fact that the antibiotic puromycin has the power of preventing the formation of protein. Using goldfish as his experimental animals, he taught them to ring a bell in order to obtain food, a trick which the Japanese sometimes teach their fish for fun. Then, at various stages in the process, he injected puromycin into their brains. When it was injected some hours after the conditioning process, it had no effect. Presumably the memory-proteins were already formed. But if it was injected just before the lesson, or even soon after, the lesson was not learned.

There are also substances which prevent the synthesis of RNA itself, such as 8-azaguanine, and they too cause impairment of learning if injected just before, but the dose has to be so high as to be almost lethal. Nevertheless, such experiments must be regarded as putting memory-erasure very much into the realm of possibility. Once the way has been shown, the rest is development.

It is not difficult to visualize a political use, or misuse, of the power of erasing memories as soon as they have been formed, or of preventing them forming. Indeed, when a reporter asked Dr. Agranoff whether the Central Intelligence Agency had been in touch with him about his work, he replied with a smile, 'I forget'. However, in these experiments the puromycin was injected directly into the brain, and in doses so massive as to be lethal if continued. This clearly rules out its use on human beings. But once the principle is established, the prospect opens up that one day someone may find a substance which can be introduced into the bloodstream by injection, or even swallowed, which will have the same effect. So the erasure of memory is a possibility which must be taken quite seriously.

Are we also to infer from experiments of this kind that memory can, or could, be transformed from one human being to another? No scientist, I suppose, would risk a definite forecast. In my opinion, provided it is quite definitely established that memory is encoded into molecules, there is a definite likelihood that, one day — probably quite a long time ahead — some degree of memory transfer may be effected. I do not foresee that students will ever be tempted to eat their teachers, like those tribesmen who eat their enemies in order to acquire their virtue; I should be surprised if the memory molecules would, first, survive the digestive processes. Nor am I convinced that they would reach the brain, even if injected into the bloodstream. There is an ill-understood protective mechanism, known as the blood-brain barrier, which guards the brain, to some extent, from circulating debris. It has not been shown that RNA, at all events, can cross this barrier. However, with the advance of knowledge, ways of temporarily abrogating the barrier may conceivably be developed. Even so, memory will hardly be sold in cans, like soup.

Success may come, more probably, by developing techniques currently used to drip fluids directly into the cavities within the brain, or on to its surface — but this involves drilling a hole through the skull. Finally, we do not know for sure that molecules, even when they reach the surface of a brain cell, will be admitted and there take their place alongside existing memory molecules without disturbance. The implication of the memory-transfer experiments is that they will. This work, therefore, calls for close attention.

The social implications of effective memory transfer would be almost too extraordinary to conceive. Firstly, education would be radically affected. The examination papers which ask the student to name the parts of a plant, or list the battles in a war, would become obsolete. Whether a student knew certain facts or not would depend entirely on whether his parents or teachers had chosen to have them injected. Tests would have to become, as many people already think they should anyway, tests of what a student can do with his knowledge.[1] Correspondingly, lectures and 'mugging up the answers' generally would become obsolete. And no doubt, by this time, the availability of computer memories will have made rote-learning even less useful.

The learning of foreign languages might become simple, and the world may finally escape from the confusion created at Babel. However, the pressure to standardize a small number of languages, thus reducing the cost of acquiring the ability to converse freely with no matter whom, may increase.

In place of the numerous class-rooms and lecture-rooms of today will the school need only a surgical suite? and pupils, instead of spending ten years of their life sitting in these rooms, pass only a few days in the school hospital?

If memories can be acquired then probably skills can be acquired also, for physical skills are memories of just how to co-ordinate certain sensations of weight, balance and muscle tension with certain muscular efforts and how to time them. Skills may also involve judgments of the position or movement of other objects, also based to a large extent on experience. Obviously, the whole of athletics as we know it would become futile, if any physically fit individual could be given the skill of the star performer overnight. The same would be true of musical performance, dancing and other artistic activities.

The interesting question, of course, is: who will be the donors? As with transplantation, we might expect social pressure on well-informed people to leave their brains to universities. Eventually, perhaps, it may be possible to synthesize memories, perhaps by copying the memory-molecules contained in a 'molecular library'. It will then be possible to make up any particular combination of memories which may be required, including even memories of things which never happened. The falsification of

---

[1] 'Open-book examinations', in which the student can consult any reference sources he wishes while preparing the answers required by the paper, have been tried by some western universities and schools, and are being generally used in China.

history for political ends will then take on a new aspect. The memory factories will become military targets of importance, and memory-spying will give espionage a new preoccupation.

There is still one other somewhat curious prospect to consider. Since, in some of Jacobson's experiments, memories acquired by hamsters were reported to have been conveyed to rats, it might therefore be possible for men to acquire the memories of animals. Perhaps the thrill-seekers who nowadays take a 'trip' with LSD-25 or psilocybin may seek to roam the jungle, in retrospect, like the kings of beasts, or know what it feels like to be a reptile or a tapeworm.

Meanwhile, what is being done to provide people like you and me with a less fallible memory than the one we have?

For older people at least there is a hope. In the early sixties, a Canadian doctor, Ewen Cameron, Director of the Allen Memorial Institute of Psychiatry at McGill, tried the experiment of giving RNA to elderly patients, suffering from senile memory defect, and detected some improvement, though deterioration resumed when the treatment stopped. The difficulty of obtaining sufficient RNA of suitable purity restricted his experiments, but he is confirming them in the U.S.A., in Albany. Then, around 1965, an American drug company, Abbott Laboratories of Chicago, announced the discovery of magnesium pemoline (trade name: Cylert), which improved recovery from the amnesia caused by electroshock. Dr. Alvin Glasky tested many products to find it. Dr. Cameron was quick to obtain the 'memory drug' for testing on human patients (not permitted at that time in the U.S.A.), and in 1966 reported his preliminary results. The drug was given by mouth to 24 patients with 'severe memory deficits due to senility or pre-senile psychosis' and precautions were taken against the possibility of suggestion. Placebos were employed on a double-blind basis: neither patients nor doctors knew, until after, which patient had had the drug and which the placebo.

For a week, there was no effect. Then the patients began to improve on memory tests. Relatives also reported improvement. 'My husband, who was an excellent bridge player and had to give it up, is now playing again,' said one wife. Another, who had forgotten how to switch on the television set, surely the ultimate disaster in our civilization, recovered this vital faculty. Experiments to see if Cylert will help those who have memory deficits due to carbon dioxide poisoning, overdose of anaesthetics or automobile accidents, are to follow.

Of course, we do not yet know what causes the impaired memory of old age, and in some cases it is total and may be due to a failure of read-in, as distinct from the failure of read-out which is what bothers us in middle life. Yet it would seem reasonable to hope at least for some improvement of the defects of senility — whether the same treatment will have any effect on normal people has yet to be shown. Dr. Cameron is optimistic.

'A century ago it was considered usual for men to be obese,' he says.

'And all mill girls had false teeth before they were forty years old. It was considered normal. . . . Now, with better dental care, it doesn't happen. So it *isn't* normal to have mental lapses.'

Memory, of course, is a factor in intelligence, as the word is generally used, for a person who knows nothing cannot behave intelligently. But to the psychologist, intelligence means something more specific — an ability to make use of data and to see the patterns it falls into. Most people admire intelligence, even if they distrust it; or perhaps it is intelligence divorced from feeling which they distrust. Certainly, most parents are concerned if their children rate low in IQ tests. The efforts which some researchers are making towards raising intelligence are therefore of more than academic importance.

Intelligence for all?

The great mathematician Karl Friedrich Gauss, probably one of the most acutely intelligent men who ever lived, was the son of a bricklayer. He showed signs of his superior intellectual powers from a very early age. Once, for instance, when at infant school, the teacher told the pupils to add up every number from one to a hundred. The other children started busily scratching away at their slates, but young Gauss put up his hand and announced the answer: 5050. He had immediately seen that 99 and 1 make a pair adding to 100; so do 98 and 2, 97 and 3 and so on. There are 49 such pairs, with a middle term of 50, making 4950. The addition of the final 100 brings the total to 5050. All done in the head, by a stroke of insight.

It would be a titanic thing for the human race if we were all a bit nearer Gauss in intelligence. What are the prospects? What was there about the grey matter within Gauss's head which differed from the grey matter in yours and mine? The answer to the latter question at least is becoming clear, and experiments are under way to exploit the knowledge.

Intelligence is only loosely connected with the size and weight of the brain-mass. While it is true that man has a bigger brain than an ape, and an ape than a cat, yet impressions taken from the skulls of eminent men show brain-masses well within the normal human range.[2] It seems almost certain that the prime factor in intelligence is the number and the nature of the interconnections between the hundred million cells in the brain.

The brain contains two types of cells: neurones which are believed to do the actual work, and glial cells which are believed to support them and supply them with energy. Glial cells may also conceivably be the repository of memory. They outnumber the neurones — indeed two-thirds of the brain's mass consists of neuroglia — and have been until recently

---

[2] Experiments on animals in which part of the cerebral cortex, the outer part of the brain, is removed, show little loss of capacity to perform learned routines, until the amount removed is considerable. The brain seems to have a good deal of spare capacity.

neglected, being regarded simply as a matrix for the neurones. There may be some surprises in store when they are more fully investigated.

The neurones, unlike most other cells, do not increase in number by division, so that the brain, once it is formed, cannot be developed in the way that muscles can, by actual growth. But each neurone puts out delicate processes which squirm about like living things and make contact with other neurones. If these contacts prove useful, they are consolidated, if not they are reabsorbed. Whether they are consolidated seems to depend upon whether, from time to time, an electric current passes along them — whether the circuit is proving to be needed. Thus every brain is 'wired' in a unique manner which reflects the life experience of its owner. The brain of a tennis player is wired differently from the brain of a philosopher but similarly, in some respects, to the brains of other tennis players. (This has not, of course, been demonstrated, owing partly to the difficulty of obtaining human brains of desired types, but mostly to the difficulty of tracing neuronal connections.)

Each neurone emits a tiny pulse of electricity when stimulated by the pulse arriving from a connecting neurone, provided the pulse is strong enough: its threshold of sensitivity to different neighbouring neurones varies, and is lowered with repeated use, raised if neglected. In this sense too, therefore, each brain is unique: the setting of the neuronal thresholds reflects the owner's life experience.

It follows, therefore, that there is no prospect of devising drugs or treatments which will instantly turn a mediocre adult brain into that of a Gauss, a Beethoven, a Shakespeare or even a brilliant athlete or tennis player. It is possible, however, that drugs may be developed which will bring about some lesser improvement of performance. Most of us do not make the best use of what we know, and there are times when we feel 'too tired to think'. Drugs like amphetamine dispel this tiredness, prolonging our thinking time and enabling us to marshal the facts we know, though they cannot tell us what we do not know.

It has been noticed, for instance, that the brains of rats which are cleverer at threading mazes contain more of the enzyme cholinesterase than the duller rats, and, as we come to see that brain function depends as much on chemistry as on electronics, some scientists have begun to visualize drugs which would improve brain function just as we intervene in nutrition with artificial vitamins. Thus Professor Jean Rostand writes:

> There is no prior reason why we should not succeed in stimulating the working of the brain, just as we do with other less exalted vital parts. . . .
> Even if the use of these future drugs resulted in no more than a few minutes of 'super thought' per day, and if these flashes were paid for by long periods of depression, mankind would still find it worth while to produce them. . . .

The probability is that most of us do not use the capacity that we already have to anything like the limit. The great Italian educator and physician

Mme Maria Montessori holds that children can do higher mathematics by the age of eight if they are encouraged to work to the limits of what they believe their own capacities to be.

We may therefore treat with some reserve a recent revolutionary suggestion for making use of the brain's spare capacity. The brain consists of two symmetrical halves. In right-handed people, it is the left half which does most of the work — it is said to be 'dominant'. The other half seems to be simply reserve capacity: there are numerous connections between the two halves and it has been shown, by separating the optic nerves so that each half-brain is connected to one eye only, that lessons learned by one half are soon written into the other also. This could explain why victims of 'stroke', with one half of their brain damaged, may gradually recover the use of their faculties: the unused half of the brain takes over.

Could we, then, exploit this reserve capacity? This is reported to be the aim of a group of neurologists, educators and other researchers who are busy organizing a group of Institutes for the Achievement of Human Potential. If they succeed, they might produce a new line of geniuses, equally at home in higher mathematics and in the kitchen garden. However, as Bertrand Russell has said, 'Men fear thought as they fear nothing else on earth — more than ruin, more even than death.' So they may not prove very popular.

While it seems unlikely that any drug or treatment will be found which will bestow on the adult human being a dramatically increased intelligence, the position is quite different for those who are still at the start of their programme of development. At this stage it is still possible to stimulate the development of the neuronal network. Thus Professor S. Zamenhof and his team at the University of California have tried injecting pregnant mice and rats with pituitary growth hormone, while the brain of the offspring was still maturing. They gave injections from the seventh to the twelfth day of pregnancy. Subsequently they killed the offspring and examined their brains closely. They found not only a significant increase in brain weight but also an increase in the ratio of neurones to the supporting glial cells. More important still, they discovered that the density of cells in the cortex, where reasoning is carried out, was increased and that the number and length of the dendrites — the branching interconnections — was greater. According to another group working on this idea, the chance of a neurone making contact with another brain cell is enhanced by an estimated fifty per cent in such animals. Similar brain enlargement was also found in parallel experiments on tadpoles, while other workers report that these hepped-up rats showed improved performance at standard maze-running tests.

While these results have been achieved with animals, a somewhat less drastic treatment has been applied to human babies in South Africa.

At the University of Witwatersrand, the Dean of the Medical Faculty,

Professor O. S. Heyns, developed a technique of keeping pregnant women with their abdomen and pelvis inside a plastic enclosure, the pressure in which is reduced by a pump to one-fifth atmospheric pressure, a procedure he calls decompression, or foetal oxygenation. The treatment is given for half an hour daily, during the last ten days of pregnancy and during the beginning of labour. The reduction in pressure on the uterus was planned to reduce the pains of childbirth, and it also helps the maternal blood to circulate more freely.

Professor Heyns was surprised when, a year or so after his first experiments, he began to get reports from their mothers that the children born in these conditions were exceptionally intelligent, and certainly forward in their physical development. At first these reports were ignored on the grounds that all mothers believe their new baby to be exceptional. But soon it was found that some of these super-oxygenated babies really were exceptional — like Katl Oertel, who was answering the telephone at 13 months, and was speaking in four languages by the age of three. (These babies commonly hear four languages spoken around them — English, German, Zulu and Afrikaans — but normal babies speak the tongue their mother speaks to them.) These super-children were bored at their nursery schools; they chat with adults in a fluent, unconcerned sort of way which suggests a maturity which usually comes far later. A vocabulary of 200 words by age 18 months is common with them: the average child speaks only half a dozen words at this age.

Critics say, however, that it is impossible to measure intelligence in two-year-old children in any reliable way, and several more years must pass before it can be proved that these children will make unusually intelligent adults. It is further objected that only the more intelligent mothers offered themselves to try Professor Heyns' new method and, since intellectual capacity may have hereditary components, the sample may be biased.

In the last weeks of pregnancy, the placenta does not grow any further, and the infant's heart becomes incapable of driving blood through it. Professor Heyns believes that, in consequence, the brains of most foetuses fail to develop to their full capacity since the foetus's oxygen demands outstrip the capacity of the mother to supply it. The oxygenation of the mother's blood helps to remedy this deficiency.

Whether these children continue to stay ahead is a matter to watch with close attention. This could prove one of the most significant experiments of our generation.

Apart from the rather macabre possibilities inherent in the work of Professors Zamenhof and Heyns, there is a very real possibility of achieving a small but definite improvement of intelligence, taking the population as a whole, by improving the environment in which the young child is brought up.

The fact that the children of intelligent parents tend to be above average in intelligence has long been noted; and it has been argued that this is not hereditary, but due to the fact that they find themselves in a more intellectually stimulating environment. (Against this, however, it has been shown that one-egg twins, separated at birth and brought up in widely different environments, tend to achieve similar IQ ratings. Thus, in a case where one twin was brought up in a university family at Oxford, and the other on a Welsh farm, their IQs were only a couple of points apart when measured. Brothers and sisters also show closer IQs, even when brought up separately, than do adopted children brought up in the same home. All of which argues a strong hereditary factor.) But that there is some truth in the view that environment matters is suggested by the work of Drs David Krech and Edward L. Bennett of Berkeley. They separated rats twenty-five days after birth and placed some in solitary confinement, the others in cages where there was plenty to do: ropes to climb, wheels to turn, and so on. Later, the first group scored lower on 'intelligence' tests than the latter. At fifteen weeks, they killed all the animals and dissected their brains. They found that, in the privileged group, the cortex was thicker and that the proportion of cortex to sub-cortex correlated with the speed at which they had learned to run mazes. The number of neurones was not increased, but their size and number of branchings seemed to be. There were certainly more glial cells, and more cholinesterase and acetyl-cholinesterase in them.

The British paper *Science Journal* commented:

> The most exciting implications of this research come from the strong probability that the results with rats can be extended to humans. This American work seems to be the first solid evidence from studies of the brain itself that intelligence can in fact be cultivated. This provides a wholly new line of support for the suggestions of some psychologists that the nature of the early environment has a critical bearing on the development of effective intelligence in later life. . . .

It also seems probable that undernourishment in early life permanently handicaps brain development.

It is safe to assume that a majority of the population in western countries does not benefit from an optimal environment in childhood, in the sense here considered. By improving this situation, IQs could almost certainly be raised by ten or fifteen points in many individuals. If this seems a small gain, compared with the dramatic possibilities discussed earlier, it should be borne in mind that a shift of only 1.5 per cent in the IQ of the entire population would more than double the number of people with IQs over 160 — sometimes described as the genius level, though perhaps highly talented would be a more realistic description.

In short, we can expect to see significant changes in global intelligence in those developing countries which are improving nutritional standards. Whether we shall see a decline in those western countries in which the quality of emotional relationships in the home is too often poor and elsewhere deteriorating raises issues so general that I shall leave them to another chapter.

Controlling pain

Before turning to wider issues, there is one further research area which demands our attention — the control of pain. Here, too, the rate of progress is accelerating.

It was in 1842 that Crawford W. Long of Jefferson, Georgia, performed the first operation under ether, the removal of a small tumour on the patient's neck. (Actually, this was not a 'first' in anaesthesia. The Greek doctor Dioscorides, who was surgeon-general of Nero's armies, knew of local and general anaesthesia, and even of rectal administration of narcotics, and was the first to use the word in its modern sense. The 'soporific sponge' is also mentioned from time to time in medieval writings.) But with Long's operation the modern era of chemical anaesthetics dawned, and in the century or so which has since elapsed, no radical changes have taken place. New and swifter anaesthetics have been found, with fewer side-effects, but until recently there has been nothing more than consolidation of the original advance.

Oddly enough, no one really understands why chemical anaesthetics produce their effect, or even where in the brain they act. Yet millions of people have reason to be grateful to those who fought down the prejudice which existed against the new chemical anaesthetics, and the idea that the best way to dull or banish pain is by chemical means has become taken for granted.

But nervous activity is electrical in nature, and at this very moment a new chapter in the control of pain is being opened — the use of electrical devices.

In 1965 two Harvard investigators exhibited a portable electronic device about the size of a transistor radio, capable of subduing even the intractable pain of cancer. The device is only for people with really severe pain, since it involves the insertion of electrodes into the brain through an opening drilled in the skull. The electrodes are placed in a structure known as the thalamus, and nine-volt thirty-cycles-per-second current can be administered by pressing a button. Pain is suppressed for many hours after about an hour's treatment, and there is no damage to brain tissue. The developers of this device are Dr. Frank Ervin, a neurosurgeon, and Dr. Vernon Mark, a neurologist. One patient with cancer of the larynx, Dr. Ervin reported, had required 100 mg. of a morphine analogue every two hours to relieve his pain. After using the 'pain box' he had gone for three months without having to take pain-relieving drugs. Dr. Mark reported similar results. Patients carry the box in the pocket of their dressing gown or pyjamas and turn it on whenever pain occurs. They report no side-effects.

But pain can also be controlled electronically, in some cases, by devices which do not call for anything so drastic as surgical insertion of electrodes in the skull.

Dr. Patrick Wall was struck by the fact that soldiers hit by a bullet often feel no pain for some hours, even though they may still feel the prick of the needle if blood is taken for analysis. Victims of motor and other accidents also display this self-induced anaesthesia. Dr. Wall argued from this that the body must includes 'gates' which can block or let through pain impulses. He believes these gates are located in a part of the spinal substance known as the substantia gelatinosa or gelatinous substance. Blocking occurs when specialized cells receive a large number of weak impulses — and this is why we scratch a wider area when we scratch an itch. The numerous weak impulses from the scratched area block the pain from the single nerve ending which constitutes the itching.

With Dr. William H. Sweet of the Department of Neurosurgery at Massachusetts General Hospital, Dr. Wall, who works in the Biology Department at MIT, attached electrodes to people suffering from pain in limbs or other superficial parts of the body, and fed them with brief pulses at 100 times a second. One of their patients was a man who had received a bullet wound through his shoulder. He reported an intense pain in his fingers, 'like a blowtorch being passed over them'. The electrical stimulation dispelled the pain, or as another patient, a pharmacist, put it: 'The buzzing masks the pain.' Success was also had in treating superficial cancers, though the use of surface electrodes did not act on pain in deeplying organs. After some months, it is true, the effectiveness of the treatment began to decline, and research is continuing.

The control of pain is also being approached in a different way. In the last few years it has been found that patients likely to suffer pain can be made drowsy and insensitive to pain, without becoming completely unconscious, by giving them analgesics such as phentanyl in conjunction with butyrophenones, such as haloperidol. For purposes such as an operation for Parkinsonism, or the insertion of bronchoscopes through the throat to inspect the lungs, it is better to have a patient who is awake and co-operative. This new technique, known as ataralgesia (meaning: no disturbance of mind or feeling of pain) is therefore superior to anaesthesia in such cases. The patient remains relaxed with a normally pink complexion and no feeling of nausea — very different from the pale, sweating, retching patient usually seen in bronchoscopy or intubation. Where an alert patient is not a requirement, however, light anaesthesia can be superimposed on the ataralgesia.

As dentists know, the unpleasantness of pain varies a great deal with one's attitude to it — the tense, worried person feels more pain than the relaxed one, from the same stimulus. This is the main reason that taking alcohol reduces the feeling of pain. The same is true of tranquillizers. As one scientist put it: chlorpromazine removes the harrowing element in pain.

Pain, in point of fact, is a more complex mechanism than is usually supposed. Why is it that, in some conditions, the lightest brushing of the affected part soon produces intense pain? The answer appears to lie in the fact that injured tissue can release substances, not yet fully understood, which in some way sensitize nerves to pain. These include histamine and 5-hydroxy-tryptamine, known as 5-HT for short. Wasps and hornets inject both these substances with their venom, as do octopuses and nettles. This is why their trifling stings, far less than a bramble scratch in a mechanical sense, are so painful. It may be, too, that some tumours also produce these substances.

Professor C. A. Keele, of the Department of Pharmacology and Therapeutics at Middlesex Hospital Medical School, is hopeful that in the next five or ten years a new drug with antagonistic effects on these substances will be isolated. There is already a drug named nalorphine which does so, but it has unwanted side-effects.

As these three reports show, both from the electrical and the chemical angle man's power to control pain is becoming steadily more absolute. It is logical to assume, therefore, that before very long now most, perhaps all, forms of pain will be in principle controllable, and control methods will become simpler and more reliable. Probably no one will be without his own portable pain-control unit, to be used in case of mischance. But, equally, this knowledge will give men increased power to inflict pain scientifically to any limit. Torturers will rely upon biochemists, and the latter may have to ask themselves whether to release their findings freely, and if so, how and to whom. When the technique of torture has thus become absolute, all expectation of captured personnel heroically remaining silent will become vain. International regulations will be desirable, but impossible to enforce. The prospect is not pleasant.

Mind control

"As we stand at the threshold of the chemopsychiatric era and look towards the future, some may feel disposed to cheer and some to shudder," Dr. Robert de Ropp has written. The shudder is caused, one assumes, by the fear that ability to modify the mind may lead to ability to control the mind. Is this a legitimate extrapolation? Does the ability to relieve the suicidal depression of a psychotic, or to calm the anxieties of a neurotic, really imply ability to impose moods and attitudes on people, at variance with their real nature?

The question is not an easy one, and raises, among other things, the question of what *is* one's real nature. If a man grows querulous and embittered with age, is this his 'real nature'? Do we have a basic personality on which life imposes distortions, or is our personality entirely the construct of our experience? In so far as the question originally raised reflects a fear that our personal uniqueness and individuality is at risk, these are relevant questions. If, on the other hand, we are simply concerned with how far political misuse could be made of our new powers, the matter becomes such simpler.

The drugs available at present are limited in scope. They consist, as we have seen, of ataractics (or tranquillizers), analeptics (or stimulants) and psychotomimetics. Drugs of this kind might be misused — for instance they might be given surreptitiously to prisoners of war, to reduce the likelihood of their attempting an escape. (True, anaesthetics can also be misused, for example by housebreakers or kidnappers, but at least it is clear to all when and if they have been used.)

It is hardly to be visualized, however, that they could be used surreptitiously to ensure support of a political programme, say, though conceivably a dictator could openly add them to the diet or distribute them like vitamin pills. Perhaps it is not out of the question that drugs might be found which greatly increased suggestibility, which could be convenient to a dictator controlling propaganda media.

Some years ago, there was a considerable stir when experiments were conducted in subliminal stimulation. Words were flashed on a cinema screen, in the course of running a film of general interest, so briefly that they were not consciously seen. Yet they could be shown to have registered on the brain by associative tests given afterwards. Advertisers at once thought this an interesting technique for stimulating the sale of their goods. If a word — such as a brand-name — could be presented subliminally, during television or cinema programmes, would not the viewers be more likely to ask for this product? In Britain, the U.S.A. and elsewhere, such techniques were soon banned or voluntarily renounced. It is not clear, however, whether they would have been effective. In one experimental run, before the ban, the word 'ice-cream' was subliminally presented to a cinema audience, in the expectation that the sale of ice-cream during the interval would increase. It did increase slightly, but other patrons complained to the management that the theatre was too cold, though it was in fact at the same temperature as usual. The outcome of such stimulation in action is therefore somewhat unpredictable, in the present state of the art.

There are also other directions in which behaviour might be influenced. For instance, Dr. R. P. Michael at the Institute of Psychiatry in London gave oestrogens to female rhesus monkeys and found that this evoked sexual excitement in near-by males. Apparently it stimulated the females to produce a sex-attractant, probably olfactory in nature. Such processes have been thoroughly studied in insects and were thought to be peculiar to them. Quite recently it has been realized they occur in mammals also. It is therefore highly probable that they also occur in man, and Dr H. Wiener of New York claims that they do, calling these chemical messengers ECM's. He believes that they can signal anger, hate and fear as well as desire.

Throughout the ages, of course, women have employed perfumes as sexual stimulants to the male, not wholly without effect. Such activity is related to the controlled chemistry of which I am speaking in much the same way that a witch's use of foxglove for dropsy is related to the medical use of digitalis today. We can reasonably expect that while perfumes sometimes unreliably perform what is expected of them, the synthesized attractants of the future will work wholly reliably and with precision.

(Incidentally, since oetrogens are the main component of contraceptive pills, it could be interesting to see whether their use by a woman affects her husband's desire.)

The British journal *New Scientist* saw in this development 'a possible clue to the little-understood factors regulating group and mass behaviour', and wondered whether dictators of the future might not 'maintain control by the use of appropriately formulated aerosols, piped from a central behaviour-plant to every factory, office and home'. The answer must surely be: only in the dictatorial world of Orwell's *1984*. In any other world the solution would be to put a sock in it.

More interesting perhaps is the reverse possibility: that one might be able to switch desire off, and embrace chastity without a further effort of will — such a course might be convenient, at least, for explorers, astronauts and others cut off from the society of the opposite sex. In prisons where abnormal sexual behaviour commonly occurs, as a result of such isolation, the use of such an anaphrodisiac might be justifiable, paralleling the alleged use of flowers of sulphur in the past for the same purpose.

Again, the hormone prolactin stimulates maternal behaviour in animals, and if injected into males, causes them to perform the appropriate maternal behaviour of their species. Humans are less under the sway of instinct, perhaps, and it would be interesting to see whether unsatisfactory mothers could be made more motherly by injections of such a drug; or indeed to discover whether their 'unnatural' behaviour was due to some constitutional lack of it — in which case its use would be fully justified as a form of 'replacement therapy'.

One form of mental control which has already become the subject of debate is the attempt to secure that a witness speaks the truth. The so-called 'lie detector' (which actually measures anxiety as reflected by changes in skin resistance, breathing or heart-rate) has been in use in some states of the U.S.A. for periods up to thirty years. The results are notoriously unreliable, since a man may have other reasons for anxiety than guilt, while some guilty men are preternaturally free from concern about their crime.

It is an interesting point that the subjects of such enquiries can also resort to scientific methods to resist the inquisition. Thus in December 1958, residents in Newbury, Vermont, were given lie-detector tests in connection with the violent death of a local farmer. He had been highly unpopular, and some people thought he had been put to death by neighbors in a 'white lynching'. The persons interrogated with the 'lie detector' all took the precaution of taking the tranquillizer meprobamate before undergoing the test: one effect of this drug is to raise the response-level of the skin. As a result the tests were of no value.

Where authority is in a position to expose an individual to prolonged stresses, as in the case of 'brain-washing', the withholding of information may become difficult, and there can be little doubt that these methods will be developed to the point where silence becomes impossible — if this is not already the case. This is not the place to go into the complex psychology of current techniques, but it may be well to justify the foregoing assertion by reference to a more physiological approach, currently being explored. There are centres in the brain which control eating, drinking, sleeping and perhaps other activities. If the appropriate centre is stimulated, an animal which is already sated with food will eat more, a waterlogged animal will drink. Some human patients with tumours or other disturbances of these regions are known: such people may eat to excess, for instance, or refuse food when starving. No one can resist these compulsions; equally when sexual needs are thus stimulated they become overwhelming. Other centres have an even more crucial role, and rats will ignore food and sex when they are stimulated, to the point of starvation. At present such stimulation can only be achieved by surgical intervention: electrodes must be inserted in the brain or chemicals dripped into it through a tube. But what if they could be stimulated by drugs or other methods which leave no visible scar? Would a soldier, the very mechanisms of whose brain had been tampered with, be able to resist the demand to supply information? It is most unlikely. Professor James G. Miller, the director of the Mental Health Research Institute of Ann Arbor, Michigan, has commented: 'Our present code of conduct for the military forces is not prepared for technical developments in brain-washing, any more than is the general concept of the average citizen.' To order a man to resist brain-washing, he adds, may be like ordering a man under anaesthesia to stand at attention.

Dr. Jonathan O. Cole, the Chief of the Psychopharmacology Service Center of the National Institutes of Health, takes an optimistic view: he maintains that we are not in a position to engineer drugs with the effect we want, since most of the known drugs have widely varying effects on different patients. He concludes:

> I consider it unlikely that current methods can be used to develop a new drug with any specific and reliable effect on either the freedom or the control of human mental processes, although I confidently expect that new types of drugs with different effects on brain functioning and behaviour will be uncovered by present drugs development methods. . . . The difficulties appear to be well-nigh insurmountable.

But Professor B. F. Skinner takes a different view. Arguing that behaviour can be, or is about to be, controlled effectively, he concludes that it is 'the duty of our society to attempt actively to control human behaviour in such a way as to achieve the effects we consider desirable before some other group becomes more proficient at controlling behaviour and directing it into paths we consider undesirable.'

All depends on what we do with this new knowledge. Professor Miller warns us that 'drug research could lead to a new tyranny beyond Jefferson's imagination . . . to control of man's acts by chemical strings. But it need not make him a puppet . . . it may increase the number of his alternatives of choice and so his individuality and freedom.'

There is also substance, I believe, in the fear that a hypertrophy of the memory and intelligence might lead to an 'inhuman' sort of society. By 'human' we tend to mean like ourselves and other human beings we know — and most of these will be of average intelligence, given to errors and misjudgments, often letting their emotions overrule their judgment, and so on. The kind of people which these developments may create will evidently be different from us, and we might find ourselves ill at ease with them. But then, the cruel and murderous knights of the thirteenth century would be extremely ill at ease in a modern drawing room or golf club. There is no reason to suppose that the intelligent denizens of future society will feel their world to be inhuman — since, for them, 'human' will mean like themselves.

But we can press the point a little further. The average man tends to distrust intelligence: he feels that high intelligence means low emotional involvement, and that where emotions are left out the reasoning power tends to arrive at decisions which, though logical, are not always acceptable. It is not an answer to say that a very intelligent person will allow for the emotional factors, since to allow for something and to feel it are by no means the same thing. It is possible, at this point, to proceed to split a good many philosophical hairs, but I think that the central point cannot be argued away; man needs to maintain a due balance between thinking and feeling, and often fails to do so. Unless, therefore, an appropriate amount of effort is put into the probably more difficult task of producing emotionally mature, responsive and balanced individuals, any recipe for the rapid improvement of intelligence might prove to have objectionable effects, even disastrous ones.

Besides this fundamental issue, there is in the shorter term the danger of creating an élite group, all the more dangerous socially because it will be genuinely an élite. Those who have been operated on at birth, or subjected to the oxygenating treatment, may well feel a genuine kinship with other super-brains, and as a group the super-brains may tend to work for their own preferential treatment, even if they do not actually seek to take over the reins of power. Even more in line with science-fiction thinking — and science-fiction writers tend to take a darkly pessimistic view of the future — is the possibility that such an élite, having assumed power, should deny the treatment which produces intelligence to any but a minority, perhaps their own offspring, thus perpetuating a two-caste society. By permitting varying degrees of treatment, a society with three, four or more intellectual castes could readily be produced.

Even if we do not push the prediction to these extremes, we can see that the possibility of a have and a have-not group, intellectually speaking, in society is a real one. Moreover, if the industrialized nations are the first to adopt such methods, there might be a widened gap between the developing and the developed countries, the latter tending to advance even more rapidly owing to their enhanced brain power.

The French statesman of science Pierre Auger has asked whether there are some operations beyond the capacity of the human brain as we know it. It may equally be asked whether an enlarged brain might not carry man above some threshold as yet uncrossed. When the brain became large enough and complex enough to compass speech, man diverged from the animals. Men with still better brains might have capacities which we cannot even envisage and as such would constitute a different species, even a different order of beings from ourselves.

Looking at brain research as a whole, I find it difficult to avoid the impression that it will create more serious social problems than any other area of biological enquiry. Professor Donald MacKay, of Keele University, who has written many papers and articles on the philosophical and religious aspects of what we know about the brain, declared recently in *Science Journal:* 'The possibilities of misapplication of the results of brain science are already frightening to many people. Could it be, they ask, that here at last we face the ultimate Pandora's Box, a secret whose uncovering would be the destruction of human society? Has brain research gone far enough, if not too far, already?'

To these questions he returns a negative answer on the shaky grounds that scientists have a duty to study everything and that one can never tell how anything will turn out. Personally, I think both these statements to be true, but that by no means convinces me that the future is not likely to be disastrous. Actually the premises and the conclusions are not logically connected and the remark may strike many people as typical of the woolly optimism to which so many scientists are given.

Willy Ley | # Atlantropa—
the Changed Mediterranean

Ever since the first long canal was dug, the first big bridge put up
successfully, and the first tunnel finished, modern man has found it difficult to look at a map without considering whether something else could
or should be done. To set the imagination working, a geographical feature on a map needs only to be narrow. There is that narrow piece of
land separating the Red Sea from the Mediterranean Sea; result, the Suez
Canal. There is the narrow strip of land tying North and South America
together; result, the Panama Canal. There is in Greece the narrow Isth-
mus of Korinthos (Corinth) separating the Gulf of Korinthos from the
Gulf of Aigina; the Corinth Canal was the inescapable consequence.

The separating element may also be a narrow strip of water, say the
East River between Manhattan and the tip of Long Island; the Brooklyn
Bridge was built to span it. And if we return to the Mediterranean Sea,
where narrow strips of land led to the Suez Canal and the Corinth Canal,
we also find narrow strips of water around it, in a highly interesting and
most challenging distribution.

At the eastern end of the Mediterranean Sea the small Sea of Marmara
lies between the Aegean Sea, a northern tongue of the Mediterranean
east of Greece, and the Black Sea. Both ends of the Sea of Mamara are
decided narrows. At the western end there are the Dardanelles, a natural
channel some 47 miles long, which has an average width of 3 to 4 miles
but is less than a mile wide at one point. At the eastern — or, better, the
northern — end of the Sea of Marmara is the strait which we call by the
Greek name of Bosporus but which the Turks, who own it, call Istanbul
Bogazi. It is 18 miles long, and almost 3 miles wide at the northern entrance. But it has a narrowest point with a width of only 2400 feet, with
a strong current running from the Black Sea into the Sea of Marmara and
on into the Mediterranean. At the southern end of the Istanbul Bogazi
there is Istanbul on one side and Scutari and Kadikoi on the other side.
The width at that point is a little less than a mile.

Decidedly this is a place which gives one the feeling that something
ought to be done. In about 1875 one J. L. Haddan, who was then director of public works at Aleppo in northern Syria, proposed a tunnel; a
bridge of the necessary length was impossible then. He even built a model
of the strait and of his tunnel, but the Turkish government of the time
would have nothing to do with it. The plan was rejected for political

SOURCE: *Engineers' Dreams* by Willy Ley. Copyright 1954, © 1964 by Willy Ley.
Reprinted by permission of The Viking Press, Inc.

reasons, but this was not stated; instead, Haddan's plan was branded as a "wild and impossible dream." It was not; such a tunnel could have been built. Much later (1949) an American engineer named Charles Andrew again suggested a tunnel under the Bosporus. The Turkish government remained noncommittal. It now looks as if they had already decided in favor of a bridge, because in July 1953, at the request of the Turkish government, the German firm of Stahlbau Rheinhausen submitted a plan and a bid for a bridge. The plan calls for a suspension bridge for automobiles and pedestrians (no railroad), with a length of 4550 feet.[1] But even if the bridge is started at once it will take 5 years to finish.

Moving westward in the Mediterranean area, we find another narrow strait near the middle of the sea. It is the Strait of Mesina, with Sicily on one side and the Italian province of Reggio di Calabria on the other. About 50 years ago some not very definite plans for a tunnel were under discussion, but these have been finally abandoned recently in favor of a plan for bridging the Strait of Messina. A design was prepared in 1953 by the New York engineer Dr. David B. Steinman, at the request of the Italian Steel Institute. The bridge would not have to be much longer than existing bridges, but one of the difficulties is that, in the Strait of Messina, it is not only the waters which are turbulent. The ground is earthquake territory — one of the most destructive earthquakes of this century is actually labeled the Messina earthquake. And violent windstorms are almost the rule in winter. Taking all these conditions into account, Dr. Steinman proposed a specially designed suspension bridge, similar in general shape to the George Washington Bridge. The span between the two towers would have to be 5000 feet, some 800 feet longer than the span of the Golden Gate Bridge. The two side spans, between the towers and the land, would each have to be 2400 feet long or about the length of the side spans of the largest bridges now in existence.

The western end of the Mediterranean is even more intriguing. Again we have the picture of two mighty land masses approaching each other until they almost touch. Almost, but not quite; they are separated along a 30-mile length by the Strait of Gibraltar. This opening, also characterized by a strong current flowing into the Mediterranean Sea, is considerably larger than the narrow straits at the eastern end. Its entrance, coming from the Atlantic Ocean, is more than 25 miles wide but narrows to about 7½ miles. What makes it so impressive is that it is flanked by two remarkable mountains, the Rock of Gibraltar on the north and Djebel Musa on the south. To the ancients these were the Pillars of Hercules. One version of the story has it that Hercules, having been sent to Spain to perform one of his superhuman labors, erected these two "pillars" to mark

---

[1] The George Washington Bridge in New York has a length of 3500 feet; the Golden Gate Bridge in San Francisco a length of 4200 feet.

his travels; another version, a bit more specific, states that Hercules made these two pillars by cleaving a single mountain into two.

That latter version may even be true, provided you substitute the force of Nature for the strength of the son of Alcmene. It is certain that the Strait of Gibraltar did not exist in the far past, but nobody can tell with any certainty when it came into existence, or whether the break between the two continents occurred suddenly or was a slow sinking or disintegration that took many thousands of years.

Naturally (I am tempted to say) the Strait of Gibraltar has its tunnel plan, just like the English Channel and the Bosporus. The Gibraltar tunnel was worked out by a French engineer named Berlier. Because the strait happens to be especially deep at its narrowest point, the location chosen for the tunnel is from Tangier on the African side to a point west of Tarifa on the European side. The actual shore-to-shore distance along that line is 20 miles, but the tunnel would have to be 25 miles long. It would have to go rather deep, requiring long approaches, with the center section 1500 feet below sea level. Berlier's tunnel does not create a political problem, since both ends would be on Spanish territory. Whether a group of banks could be convinced that it is an economic necessity and would therefore prove profitable is a different question.

However, all these tunnel and bridge plans are comparatively minor projects in relation to the Mediterranean Sea, which because of its peculiar structure, shape, and location has really caused people to think.

It was in March 1928 that scientists and engineers first read, with intense amazement about a plan outlining what could conceivably be done with the Mediterranean. The author was Herman Sörgel. Nothing much was known about him at the time, except that he was an architect employed by the government of Bavaria. At first Sörgel called his scheme the "Panropa Plan"; later, presumably to avoid confusion with a similarly named political association aiming at European confederation, he changed the name to "Atlantropa Plan." The magnitude of Sörgel's proposal was such that some readers wondered whether he was actually serious or was engaged in a huge if obscure joke. To show that he was serious he published in 1929 a more comprehensive statement which was printed in parallel columns in four languages: English, French, German, and Italian.

The title of this publication was *Mittelmeer Senkung*, which means "Reduction of the Mediterranean." Sörgel began with the statement that the Mediterranean Sea in its present shape is a recent body of water. According to some geologists — there is no complete agreement among them on the figures though they are agreed on the facts — about 50,000 years ago the level of the Mediterranean was about 3000 feet lower than it is now. Since 44 per cent of the area of the present sea is less than 3000 feet deep, the ancient sea was obviously much smaller. In fact, there was no Mediterranean Sea then, but only two large lakes, one of them east and one west of present-day Italy-Sicily. Europe was connected with Africa by three wide land bridges, one from present-day Spain to Morocco, one from Tunisia to Sicily and Italy, and one from Greece across the eastern end of the present sea. Later, when the glaciers of the Ice Age melted away, a great deal of fruitful and possibly even inhabited land was drowned. If we want to, said Sörgel, we can get much of this drowned land back. All we have to do is revoke the alleged feat of Hercules and plug the Strait of Gibraltar with an enormous dam.

It is an undisputed fact that the Mediterranean would shrink visibly if the Strait of Gibraltar were filled in, say, for argument's sake, by an earthquake. The Mediterranean is large, comprising a total of 970,000 square miles, just about ten times the area of the State of Wyoming. It is a warm sea, which means that much of its water is evaporating constantly. The evaporation losses are so high that the level of the sea would recede 5½ feet per year if the water were not replaced. The total mass of water which evaporates from the surface of the Mediterranean every year is a staggering figure — 4144 cubic kilometers, which is 146,343,-000,000,000 cubic feet![2]

Actually of course the level of the Mediterranean Sea does not recede because the evaporation losses are made up in various ways. Rain which falls into the sea replaces just about a quarter of the loss. Rivers also help, though not very much, since most of the rivers which empty into the Mediterranean are small and some of them are even seasonal. Only four of them can be called large, the Nile from Egypt, the Po from Italy, the Rhone from France, and the Ebro from Spain. The balance is maintained by water from the Black Sea and the Atlantic Ocean, hence the strong currents in the straits at both ends of the Mediterranean. The contribution of the Atlantic Ocean, which replaces two-thirds of the evaporation losses, results in a flow through the Strait of Gibraltar of 88,000 cubic meters (or 3,100,000 cubic feet) per second, which is twelve times the amount of the waters falling over Niagara Falls at high water!

In figures, the contributions of these four sources to the water budget of the Mediterranean are as follows:

| SOURCE | AMOUNT PER YEAR | | |
	(cubic kilometers)	(millions of cubic yards)	PERCENTAGE
Atlantic Ocean	2762	3,612,000	66.65
rain	1000	1,308,000	24.11
rivers	230	301,000	5.56
Black Sea	152	199,000	3.68
Total	4144	5,420,000	100.00

[2] A cubic kilometer is 1,000,000,000 cubic meters and each cubic meter equals 1.3079 cubic yards, or 35.314 cubic feet. A cubic yard equals 27 cubic feet.

This table is the basis of the Atlantropa Plan.

Obviously nothing can be done about the rain, and the rivers may as well be left alone. But it would be easy to build a dam across the Dardanelles. By itself this dam would not do any good because the Atlantic Ocean would simply provide an additional 200,000 million cubic yards per year. Still, Sörgel proposed to start at that end, largely because there would be no water-level difference on that dam during construction.

The big job would be the Gibraltar dam. Like Berlier's proposed tunnel, the dam is not planned to cross the strait at its narrowest because the depth there is more than 1600 feet. It would have the shape of a horseshoe, with its open end toward the east. Along the proposed curve of the dam there are many shallow places and the deepest point is about 1000 feet below sea level. The length of the dam would be 18 miles; its crown would be 165 feet wide but its foundation would have to have ten times that width to withstand the water pressure that would soon develop. The estimate of a drop of 5½ feet per year in the level of the Mediterranean is based on the assumption that the sea would receive no water from any source. Since the rain and the rivers would still provide some, the actual recession of the level would be about 40 inches per year. But this would cause a drop of 33 feet within 10 years after the completion of the dam, and this is enough of a difference in level to be utilized to produce electric current — and, considering the amount of water which could be sent through the turbines, to produce it in quantity.

In drawing up the plan, Sörgel did not think in terms of years, and only rarely in terms of decades, but often in terms of centuries. One century after the completion of the Gibraltar dam the level of the Mediterranean Sea would have gone down 330 feet, and by that time a total of 90,000 square miles of new land would have appeared above the surface, with the gains almost proportional for most of the countries bordering the sea. Spain's largest gains would be in the area of the mouth of the Ebro River, France's largest gains in the area of the mouth of the Rhone River. The two islands Mallorca and Minorca would have become one, as would Corsica and Sardinia. Italy would have gained on both coasts, and most of the northern end of the Adriatic Sea would have become the Adriatic Land. Sicily would have grown enormously, and Tunisia too; they would almost but not quite touch. A strait would still remain between Italy and Sicily but it would be a very narrow one.

From that point on, a further reduction of the sea's level would have little effect on the western part of the Mediterranean but much more on the eastern part. So Sörgel proposed as the second step, a hundred years after completion of the Gibraltar dam, two more dams: one across the remaining narrow strait between Sicily and Italy, say between Messina on the island to a point north of Reggio di Calabria on the toe of the Italian boot; the second to bridge the gap still remaining between Sicily and Tunisia.

After these dams were completed, the western half of the sea would be stabilized by permitting enough water to enter from the Atlantic to maintain that level. The eastern half would be permitted, in the course of another century, to sink for an additional 330 feet, which it would do all the more readily since virtually its only source of supply would be the Nile. Then the eastern half would also be stabilized, partly with water from the Sea of Marmara and hence from the Black Sea, partly with water from the western half. When completely adjusted in accordance with this plan, the Mediterranean Sea would hold 350,000 cubic kilometers less water than it does now. This amount of water would be distributed over all other oceans, since they are all interconnected, and would raise the sea level everywhere else by 3 feet.

In the Mediterranean area the final result would be 220,000 square miles of new land and hydroelectric power plants of virtually unlimited capacity in a number of places well distributed over the area: at least two in the Gibraltar dam, one each at the mouths of the Ebro, Rhone, Po, and Nile, at least one in the Dardanelles dam, and a minimum of two each in the two dams separating the western half of the sea from the eastern half. There would certainly be no lack of power for anything the inhabitants of the area might wish to do.

Sörgel considered that the final goal of the Atlantropa Plan was the fusion of the European and African continents; he titled a later book (published in 1938) *The Three Big A's* — America, Asia, and Atlantropa. But he also repeatedly pointed out that his plan could be stopped at any moment after the level of the sea had dropped, say, 50 feet, and still realize its chief purpose. Such a comparatively small reduction of the sea's level might not provide much new land, or any land of value, but it would create the means of producing enormous amounts of electric power.

If Sörgel's main idea — the dams across the Dardanelles and the Strait of Gibraltar — is ever carried out it is highly probable that the men entrusted with the Atlantropa project will stop when the sea level has fallen 50 or 75 feet. (This drop would be accelerated if the Gandrillon Plan for Palestine and the Qattara Depression plan, described in Chapter 4, were carried out simultaneously, since both take water from the Mediterranean.)

It is important to remember that none of this must interfere with shipping. Damming the Dardanelles might not be hard, but ships still would have to get from the Mediterranean to the Sea of Marmara and the other way round. For this, canals would have to be built, with a series of lock gates to take care of the difference in level. The Suez Canal would have to be lengthened and locks built at the Mediterranean end, and, most important, canals and locks would be required for the connection between the "inner sea" and the Atlantic Ocean.

The Gibraltar locks especially would have to be large enough to accommodate the largest ocean liners, battleships, and aircraft carriers. Every additional 50 feet of level difference to be overcome means one more lock

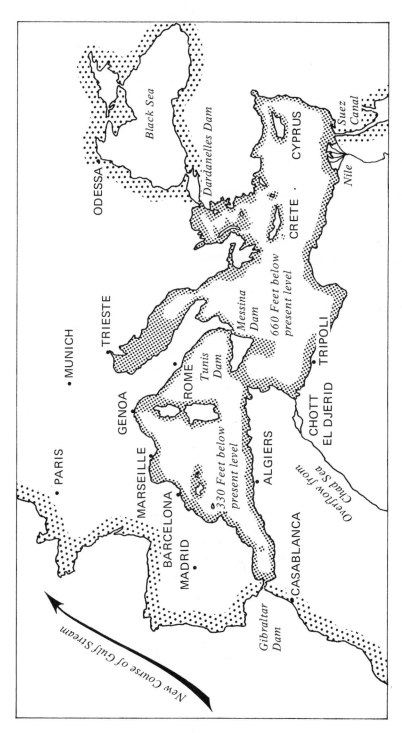

The Mediterranean Sea, showing the full extent of the Atlantropa Plan, after the eastern half has evaporated to a level 660 feet below the present level. The western half will be maintained at a level 330 feet below the present level. The black areas show the land that would be above the new sea levels.

in each canal and adds considerably to the length of the canal. The biggest gain would actually be made by the first 50 feet of level drop. This drop would provide power without doing too much harm to existing installations.

It would also accomplish something else which has not yet been mentioned. The figure of 3,100,000 cubic feet per second for the inflow through the Strait of Gibraltar represents the difference between two flows which take place there. At the surface the influx of water from the Atlantic is greater than that figure, but at the bottom there is, according to Sörgel, a flow in the opposite direction which brings cold bottom water from the Mediterranean into the open sea. This outflow is accused of forming a cold-water cushion outside western Europe which deflects the Gulf Stream into the northern Atlantic. Presumably, if this cold-water cushion were absent, the Gulf Stream would flow into the English Channel and thereby warm northern Europe more efficiently. A dam across the Strait, stopping any flow in either direction, would take care of that.

The reason many European experts who have studied the Atlantropa Plan, and many who are very much in favor of it, would like to stop after 12 or 15 years is that the continuation would prove costly. If the Mediterranean level were lowered 60 to 75 feet, about the only extra expenses required would be for equipping the Suez Canal with a lock somewhere near Port Said and deepening the Corinth Canal. But once the recession of the level goes beyond 100 feet, every single harbor along the shores of the Mediterranean stops being a harbor. Barcelona, Marseille, Genoa, Naples, Taranto, Trieste, Fiume, Haifa, Tel Aviv, Jaffa, Alexandria, Bengasi, Tunis, Bizerte, Algiers, Beirut, and Oran — to name only the larger ones that come to mind at once — would all be miles from the sea. Some of them might be "salvaged" by means of canals to the new shoreline, but many would become completely worthless, at least as harbors. Obviously, beyond a certain point the plan runs into the law of diminishing returns.

Another serious argument for stopping the Atlantropa Plan at an early stage is the volcanism of the Mediterranean area. Even now conditions are not as stable there as one would wish and it is feared that removal of the weight of water from these unstable areas may lead to earthquakes and volcanic eruptions. This, of course, is a field in which nobody can claim to have experience. It is possible that such fears are unfounded, but it is by no means possible for anybody to claim that they *are* unfounded. However, it seems logical to assume that the danger would increase roughly in proportion to the weight of water removed and that the results of a minor reduction in sea level would be minor too.

Of course under present conditions the Atlantropa Plan is politically impossible. It would need the cooperation of more than a dozen different nations. Some, such as Spain and Italy, would gain relatively much, while others would actually lose something; England, for example, would lose control of the Strait of Gibraltar. It is therefore unnecessary to discuss the engineering difficulties involved in the construction of a dam of such magnitude as the Gibraltar dam. The political situation of today makes the engineering problems future problems, and we can't tell how an engineer 50 years from now would go about solving them.

There can be no Atlantropa until a united Europe is a reality and until the control of the Strait of Gibraltar has developed into a purely commercial problem, with all military aspects absolutely missing.

Interestingly enough, the situation which prevails for the whole Mediterranean also holds true for a much smaller body of water in its immediate neighborhood — the Red Sea, part of the Great Rift Valley.

The Red Sea is, in round figures, 1200 miles long, and on the average less than 200 miles wide, except in its southern part where a maximum width of 250 miles occurs. Its surface has an area of about 180,000 square miles. The land bounding it along both shores is desert. Its northern end is closed except for the one artificial opening of the Suez Canal. Not a single river empties into the Red Sea. Its southern end is the sharply constricted Strait of Bab el Mandeb, which is further narrowed by the existence of the British-owned island of Perim, which divides the strait into two channels. The one to the east of the island is 2 miles wide, the one to the west 16 miles.

Since the Red Sea is a part of the Great Rift Valley it is much deeper than one would expect. The average depth is 1600 feet, but a number of extra-deep depressions have been measured, one of 4200 feet and one even of 7200 feet.

The "Red Sea Plan," worked out by the French engineer René Bigarre and published in 1940, shows many similarities to the Atlantropa Plan, with some features of Dead Sea development projects thrown in. It simply consists of a dam across the Strait of Bab el Mandeb with Perim as an off-center anchor. Naturally there would have to be a canal with lock gates connecting the Gulf of Aden with the Red Sea, and the Suez Canal would also need a lock gate at the Red Sea end, in the vicinity of Suez. After these had been built, evaporation could take its course. It is so enormous there that Matthew F. Maury, a United States naval officer whom many call the Father of Oceanography, estimated a century ago that the level of the Red Sea would sink 23 feet a year if no water could come in from the Gulf of Aden and the Indian Ocean.

René Bigarre thinks Maury's estimate too high and counts on only 0.4 inch per day or slightly more than 12 feet per year. Even this is enormous, amounting to a removal of 153,200 million cubic feet per 24-hour period. If Bigarre's figures are right, power generation could start about 5 years after completion of the dam; if Maury's should be correct, it could start in 2 years and a few months. If all the water then required to maintain the Red Sea at its new level were sent through turbines, the power output would be about 240 million kilowatt-hours daily. To produce that much by means of steam turbogenerators you would have to burn 200,000 tons of coal daily!

Some of the present Red Sea area would become dry land in the process, the area depending of course on the total level drop permitted. If the drop in level should be 100 feet, the dry areas would comprise 10 per cent of the present total area of the Red Sea, possibly 12 per cent. As land this land would be useless; as a source for salt it would be useful. The Red Sea is saltier than the open ocean right now and evaporation would make it saltier still. The yield would run into millions of tons.

From almost any angle the Red Sea Plan looks like a miniature version of the Atlantropa Plan. Carrying out Bigarre's plan would virtually provide a testing ground for Sörgel's ideas. It certainly should come first. The Bab el Mandeb dam is certainly an engineering possibility. The political difficulties are not so great that they might not be overcome. But nobody in the general area of the Strait of Bab el Mandeb needs such quantities of electric current.

J. G. Ballard | **Billenium**

All day long, and often into the early hours of the morning, the tramp of feet sounded up and down the stairs outside Ward's cubicle. Built into a narrow alcove in a bend of the staircase between the fourth and fifth floors, its plywood walls flexed and creaked with every footstep like the timbers of a rotting windmill. Over a hundred people lived in the top three floors of the old rooming house, and sometimes Ward would lie awake on his narrow bunk until 2 or 3 A.M., mechanically counting the last residents returning fróm the all-night movies in the stadium half a mile away. Through the window he could hear giant fragments of the amplified dialogue booming among the rooftops. The stadium was never empty. During the day the huge four-sided screen was raised on its davit and athletics meetings or football matches ran continuously. For the people in the houses abutting the stadium the noise must have been unbearable.

Ward, at least, had a certain degree of privacy. Two months earlier,

SOURCE: *Future Tense* by J. G. Ballard. Reprinted by permission of the author and his agents, Scott Meredith Literary Agency, Inc., 580 Fifth Ave., New York, N.Y. 10036.

before he came to live on the staircase, he had shared a room with seven others on the ground floor of a house in 755th Street, and the ceaseless press of people jostling past the window had reduced him to a state of chronic exhaustion. The street was always full, an endless clamour of voices and shuffling feet. By 6:30, when he woke, hurrying to take his place in the bathroom queue, the crowds already jammed it from sidewalk to sidewalk, the din punctuated every half minute by the roar of the elevated trains running over the shops on the opposite side of the road. As soon as he saw the advertisement describing the staircase cubicle he had left (like everyone else, he spent most of his spare time scanning the classifieds in the newspapers, moving his lodgings an average of once every two months) despite the higher rental. A cubicle on a staircase would almost certainly be on its own.

However, this had its drawbacks. Most evenings his friends from the library would call in, eager to rest their elbows after the bruising crush of the public reading room. The cubicle was slightly more than four and a half square metres in floor area, half a square over the statutory maximum for a single person, the carpenters having taken advantage, illegally, of a recess beside a nearby chimney breast. Consequently Ward had been able to fit a small straight-backed chair into the interval between the bed and the door, so that only one person at a time need to sit on the bed — in most single cubicles host and guest had to sit side by side on the bed, conversing over their shoulders and changing places periodically to avoid neckstrain.

"You were lucky to find this place," Rossiter, the most regular visitor, never tired of telling him. He reclined back on the bed, gesturing at the cubicle. "It's enormous, the perspectives really zoom. I'd be surprised if you hadn't got at least five metres here, perhaps even six."

Ward shook his head categorically. Rossiter was his closest friend, but the quest for living space had forged powerful reflexes. "Just over four and a half, I've measured it carefully. There's no doubt about it."

Rossiter lifted one eyebrow. "I'm amazed. It must be the ceiling then."

Manipulating the ceiling was a favorite trick of unscrupulous landlords — most assessments of area were made upon the ceiling, out of convenience, and by tilting back the plywood partitions the rated area of cubicle could be either increased, for the benefit of a prospective tenant (many married couples were thus bamboozled into taking a single cubicle), or decreased temporarily on the visits of the housing inspectors. Ceilings were criss-crossed with pencil marks staking out the rival claims of tenants on opposite sides of a party wall. Someone timid of his rights could be literally squeezed out of existence — in fact, the advertisement "quiet clientele" was usually a tacit invitation to this sort of piracy.

"The wall does tilt a little," Ward admitted. "Actually, it's about four degrees out — I used a plumb-line. But there's still plenty of room on the stairs for people to get by."

Rossiter grinned. "Of course, John. I'm just envious, that's all. My room's driving me crazy." Like everyone, he used the term "room" to describe his tiny cubicle, a hangover from the days fifty years earlier when people had indeed lived one to a room, sometimes, unbelievably, one to an apartment or house. The microfilms in the architecture catalogues at the library showed scenes of museums, concert halls and other public buildings in what appeared to be everyday settings, often virtually empty, two or three people wandering down an enormous gallery or staircase. Traffic moved freely along the centre of streets, and in the quieter districts sections of sidewalk would be deserted for fifty yards or more.

Now, of course, the older buildings had been torn down and replaced by housing batteries, or converted into apartment blocks. The great banqueting room in the former City Hall had been split horizontally into four decks, each of these cut up into hundreds of cubicles.

As for the streets, traffic had long since ceased to move about them. Apart from a few hours before dawn when only the sidewalks were crowded, every thoroughfare was always packed with a shuffling mob of pedestrians, perforce ignoring the countless "Keep Left" signs suspended over their heads, wrestling past each other on their way to home and office, their clothes dusty and shapeless. Often "locks" would occur when a huge crowd at a street junction became immovably jammed. Sometimes these locks would last for days. Two years earlier Ward had been caught in one outside the stadium, for over forty-eight hours was trapped in a gigantic pedestrian jam containing over 20,000 people, fed by the crowds leaving the stadium on one side and those approaching it on the other. An entire square mile of the local neighbourhood had been paralysed, and he vividly remembered the nightmare of swaying helplessly on his feet as the jam shifted and heaved, terrified of losing his balance and being trampled underfoot. When the police had finally sealed off the stadium and dispersed the jam he had gone back to his cubicle and slept for a week, his body blue with bruises.

"I hear they may reduce the allocation to three and a half metres," Rossiter remarked.

Ward paused to allow a party of tenants from the sixth floor to pass down the staircase, holding the door to prevent it jumping off its latch. "So they're always saying," he commented. "I can remember that rumour ten years ago."

"It's no rumour," Rossiter warned him. "It may well be necessary soon. Thirty million people packed into this city now, a million increase in just one year. There's been some pretty serious talk at the Housing Department."

Ward shook his head. "A drastic revaluation like that it almost impossible to carry out. Every single partition would have to be dismantled and nailed up again, the administrative job alone is so vast it's difficult to visualise. Millions of cubicles to be redesigned and certified, licenses to be issued, plus the complete resettlement of every tenant. Most of the buildings put up since the last revaluation are designed around a four-metre modulus — you can't simply take half a metre off the end of each cubicle and then say that makes so many new cubicles. They may be only six inches wide." He laughed. "Besides, how can you live in just three and a half metres?"

Rossiter smiled. "That's the ultimate argument, isn't it? They used it twenty-five years ago at the last revaluation, when the minimum was cut from five to four. It couldn't be done they all said, no one could stand living in only four square metres, it was enough room for a bed and suitcase, but you couldn't open the door to get in." Rossiter chuckled softly. "They were all wrong. It was merely decided that from then on all doors would open outwards. Four square metres was here to stay."

Ward looked at his watch. It was 7:30. "Time to eat. Let's see if we can get into the food bar across the road."

Grumbling at the prospect, Rossiter pulled himself off the bed. They left the cubicle and made their way down the staircase. This was crammed with luggage and packing cases so that only a narrow interval remained around the bannister. On the floors below the congestion was worse. Corridors were wide enough to be chopped up into single cubicles, and the air was stale and dead, carboard walls hung with damp laundry and makeshift larders. Each of the five rooms on the floors contained a dozen tenants, their voices reverberating through the partitions.

People were sitting on the steps above the second floor, using the staircase as an informal lounge, although this was against fire regulations, women chatting with the men queueing in their shirtsleeves outside the washroom, children diving around them. By the time they reached the entrance Ward and Rossiter were having to force their way through the tenants packed together on every landing, loitering around the notice boards or pushing in from the street below.

Taking a breath at the top of the steps, Ward pointed to the food bar on the other side of the road. It was only thirty yards away, but the throng moving down the street swept past like a river at full tide, crossing them from right to left. The first picture show at the stadium started at 9 o'clock, and people were setting off already to make sure of getting in.

"Can't we go somewhere else?" Rossiter asked, screwing his face up at the prospect of the food bar. Not only would it be packed and take them half an hour to be served, but the food was flat and unappetising. The journey from the library four blocks away had given him an appetite.

Ward shrugged. "There's a place on the corner, but I doubt if we can make it." This was two hundred yards upstream; they would be fighting the crowd all the way.

"Maybe you're right." Rossiter put his hand on Ward's shoulder. "You know, John, your trouble is that you never go anywhere, you're too disengaged, you just don't realise how bad everything is getting."

Ward nodded. Rossiter was right. In the morning, when he set off for the library, the pedestrian traffic was moving with him towards the down town offices; in the evening, when he came back, it was flowing in the opposite direction. By and large he never altered his routine. Brought up from the age of ten in a municipal hostel, he had gradually lost touch with his father and mother, who lived on the east side of the city and had been unable, or unwilling, to make the journey to see him. Having surrendered his initiative to the dynamics of the city he was reluctant to try to win it back merely for a better cup of coffee. Fortunately his job at the library brought him into contact with a wide range of young people of similar interests. Sooner or later he would marry, find a double cubicle near the library and settle down. If they had enough children (three was the required minimum) they might even one day own a small room of their own.

They stepped out into the pedestrian stream, carried along by it for ten or twenty yards, then quickened their pace and side-stepped through the crowd, slowly tacking across to the other side of the road. There they found the shelter of the shop-fronts, slowly worked their way back to the food bar, shoulders braced against the countless minor collisions.

"What are the latest population estimates?" Ward asked as they circled a cigarette kiosk, stepping forward whenever a gap presented itself.

Rossiter smiled. "Sorry, John, I'd like to tell you but you might start a stampede. Besides, you wouldn't believe me."

Rossiter worked in the Insurance Department at the City Hall, had informal access to the census statistics. For the last ten years these had been classified information, partly because they were felt to be inaccurate, but chiefly because it was feared they might set off a mass attack of claustrophobia. Minor outbreaks had taken place already, and the official line was that the world population had reached a plateau, levelling off at 20,000 million. No one believed this for a moment, and Ward assumed that the 3-per cent annual increase maintained since the 1960's was continuing.

How long it could continue was impossible to estimate. Despite the gloomiest prophecies of the Neo-Malthusians, world agriculture had managed to keep pace with the population growth, although intensive cultivation meant that 95 per cent of the population was permanently trapped in vast urban conurbations. The outward growth of cities had at last been checked; in fact, all over the world former suburban areas were being reclaimed for agriculture and population additions were confined within the existing urban ghettos. The countryside, as such, no longer existed. Every single square foot of ground sprouted a crop of one type or other. The one-time fields and meadows of the world were now, in effect, factory floors, as highly mechanized and closed to the public as any industrial area. Economic and ideological rivalries had long since faded before one overriding quest — the internal colonisation of the city.

Reaching the food bar, they pushed themselves into the entrance and joined the scrum of customers pressing six deep against the counter.

"What is really wrong with the population problem," Ward confided to Rossiter, "is that no one has ever tried to tackle it. Fifty years ago short-sighted nationalism and industrial expansion put a premium on a rising population curve, and even now the hidden incentive is to have a large family so that you can gain a little privacy. Single people are penalised simply because there are more of them and they don't fit conveniently into double or triple cubicles. But it's the large family with its compact, space-saving logistic that is the real villain."

Rossiter nodded, edging nearer the counter, ready to shout his order. "Too true. We all look forward to getting married just so that we can have our six metres."

Directly in front of them, two girls turned around and smiled, "Six square metres," one of them, a dark-haired girl with a pretty oval face, repeated. "You sound like the sort of young man I ought to get to know. Going into the real-estate business, Peter?"

Rossiter grinned and squeezed her arm. "Hello, Judith. I'm thinking about it actively. Like to join me in a private venture?"

The girl leaned against him as they reached the counter. "Well, I might. It would have to be legal, though."

The other girl, Helen Waring, an assistant at the library, pulled Ward's sleeve. "Have you heard the latest, John? Judith and I have been kicked out of our room. We're on the street right at this minute."

"What?" Rossiter cried. They collected their soups and coffee and edged back to the rear of the bar. "What on earth happened?"

Helen explained: "You know that little broom cupboard outside our cubicle? Judith and I have been using it as a sort of study hole, going in there to read. It's quiet and restful, if you can get used to not breathing. Well, the old girl found out and kicked up a big fuss, said we were breaking the law and so on. In short, out." Helen paused. "Now we've heard she's going to let it as a single."

Rossiter pounded the counter ledge. "A broom cupboard? Someone's going to live there? But she'll never get a licence."

Judith shook her head. "She's got it already. Her brother works in the Housing Department."

Ward laughed into his soup. "But how can she let it? No one will live in a broom cupboard."

Judith stared at him sombrely. "You really believe that, John?"

Ward dropped his spoon. "No, I guess you're right. People will live anywhere. God, I don't know who I feel more sorry for — you two, or the poor devil who'll be living in that cupboard. What are you going to do?"

"A couple in a place two blocks west are subletting half their cubicle to us. They've hung a sheet down the middle and Helen and I'll take turns sleeping on a camp bed. I'm not joking, our room's about two feet wide. I said to Helen that we ought to split up again and sublet one half at twice our rent."

They had a good laugh over all this and Ward said good-night to the others and went back to his rooming house.

There he found himself with similar problems.

The manager leaned against the flimsy door, a damp cigar butt revolving around his mouth, an expression of morose boredom on his unshaven face.

"You got four point seven two metres," he told Ward, who was standing out on the staircase, unable to get into his room. Other tenants milled, passed onto the landing, where two women in curlers and dressing gowns were arguing with each other, tugging angrily at the wall of trunks and cases. Occasionally the manager glanced at them irritably. "Four seven two. I worked it out twice." He said this as if it ended all possibility of argument.

"Ceiling or floor?" Ward asked.

"Ceiling, whaddya think? How can I measure the floor with all this junk?" He kicked at a crate of books protruding from under the bed.

Ward let this pass. "There's quite a tilt on the wall," he pointed out. "As much as three or four degrees."

The manager nodded vaguely. "You're definitely over the four. Way over." He turned to Ward, who had moved down several steps to allow a man and woman to get past. "I can rent this as a double."

"What, only four and a half?" Ward said incredulously. "How?"

The man who had just passed him leaned over the manager's shoulder and sniffed at the room, taking in every detail in a one-second glance. "You renting a double here, Louie?"

The manager waved him away and then beckoned Ward into the room, closing the door after him.

"It's a nominal five," he told Ward. "New regulation, just came out. Anything over four five is a double now." He eyed Ward shrewdly. "Well, whaddya want? It's a good room, there's a lot of space here, feels more like a triple. You got access to the staircase, window slit —" He broke off as Ward slumped down on the bed and started to laugh. "Whatsa matter? Look, if you want a big room like this you gotta pay for it. I want an extra half rental or you get out."

Ward wiped his eyes, then stood up wearily and reached for the shelves. "Relax, I'm on my way. I'm going to live in a broom cupboard. 'Access to the staircase —' that's really rich. Tell me, Louis, is there life on Uranus?"

Temporarily, he and Rossiter teamed up to rent a double cubicle in a semi-derelict house a hundred yards from the library. The neighbourhood was seedy and faded, the rooming houses crammed with tenants. Most of them were owned by absentee landlords or by the city corporation, and the managers employed were of the lowest type, mere rent-collectors who cared nothing about the way their tenants divided up the living space, and never ventured beyond the first floors. Bottles and empty cans littered the corridors, and the washrooms looked like sumps. Many of the tenants were old and infirm, sitting about listlessly in their narrow cubicles, wheedling at each other back to back through the thin partitions.

Their double cubicle was on the third floor, at the end of a corridor that ringed the building. Its architecture was impossible to follow, rooms letting off at all angles, and luckily the corridor was a cul-de-sac. The mounds of cases ended four feet from the end wall and a partition divided off the cubicle, just wide enough for two beds. A high window overlooked the area ways of the building opposite.

Possessions loaded on to the shelf above his head, Ward lay back on his bed and moodily surveyed the roof of the library through the afternoon haze.

"It's not bad here," Rossiter told him, unpacking his case. "I know there's no real privacy and we'll drive each other insane within a week, but at least we haven't got six other people breathing into our ears two feet away."

The nearest cubicle, a single, was built into the banks of cases half a dozen steps along the corridor, but the occupant, a man of seventy, was deaf and bedridden.

"It's not bad," Ward echoed reluctantly. "Now tell me what the latest growth figures are. They might console me."

Rossiter paused, lowering his voice. "Four per cent. *Eight hundred million extra people in one year* — just less than half the earth's total population in 1950."

Ward whistled slowly. "So they will revalue. What to? Three and a half?"

"Three. From the first of next year."

"Three square metres!" Ward sat up and looked around him. "It's unbelievable! The world's going insane, Rossiter. For God's sake, when are they going to do something about it? Do you realise there soon won't be room enough to sit down, let alone lie down?"

Exasperated, he punched the wall beside him, on the second blow knocked in one of the small wooden panels that had been lightly papered over.

"Hey!" Rossiter yelled. "You're breaking the place down." He dived across the bed to retrieve the panel, which hung downwards supported by a strip of paper. Ward slipped his hand into the dark interval, carefully drew the panel back on to the bed.

"Who's on the other side?" Rossiter whispered. "Did they hear?"

Ward peered through the interval, eyes searching the dim light. Suddenly he dropped the panel and seized Rossiter's shoulder, pulled him down on to the bed.

"Henry! Look!"

Rossiter freed himself and pressed his face to the opening, focused slowly and then gasped.

Directly in front of them, faintly illuminated by a grimy skylight, was a medium-sized room, some fifteen feet square, empty except for the dust silted up against the skirting boards. The floor was bare, a few strips of frayed linoleum running across it, the walls covered with a drab floral design. Here and there patches of the paper peeled off and segments of the picture rail had rotted away, but otherwise the room was in habitable condition.

Breathing slowly, Ward closed the open door of the cubicle with his foot, then turned to Rossiter.

"Henry, do you realise what we've found? Do you realise it, man?"

"Shut up. For Pete's sake keep your voice down." Rossiter examined the room carefully. "It's fantastic. I'm trying to see whether anyone's used it recently."

"Of course they haven't," Ward pointed out. "It's obvious. There's no door into the room. We're looking through it now. They must have panelled over this door years ago and forgotten about it. Look at that filth everywhere."

Rossiter was staring into the room, his mind staggered by its vastness.

"You're right," he murmured. "Now, when do we move in?"

Panel by panel, they pried away the lower half of the door, nailed it on to a wooden frame so that the dummy section could be replaced instantly.

Then, picking an afternoon when the house was half empty and the manager asleep in his basement office, they made their first foray into the room, Ward going in alone while Rossiter kept guard in the cubicle.

For an hour they exchanged places, wandering silently around the dusty room, stretching their arms out to feel its unconfined emptiness, grasping at the sensation of absolute spatial freedom. Although smaller than many of the subdivided rooms in which they had lived, this room seemed infinitely larger, its walls huge cliffs that soared upward to the skylight.

Finally, two or three days later, they moved in.

For the first week Rossiter slept alone in the room, Ward in the cubicle outside, both there together during the day. Gradually they smuggled in a few items of furniture: two armchairs, a table, a lamp fed from the socket in the cubicle. The furniture was heavy and Victorian; the cheapest available, its size emphasized the emptiness of the room. Pride of place was taken by an enormous mahogany wardrobe, fitted with carved angels and castellated mirrors, which they were forced to dismantle and carry into the house in their suitcases. Towering over them, it reminded Ward of the microfilms of gothic cathedrals, with their massive organ lofts crossing vast naves.

After three weeks they both slept in the room, finding the cubicle un-bearably cramped. An imitation Japanese screen divided the room ade-quately and did nothing to diminish its size. Sitting there in the evenings, surrounded by his books and albums, Ward steadily forgot the city out-side. Luckily he reached the library by a back alley and avoided the crowded streets. Rossiter and himself began to seem the only real inhabi-tants of the world, everyone else a meaningless byproduct of their own existence, a random replication of identity which had run out of control.

It was Rossiter who suggested that they ask the two girls to share the room with them.

"They've been kicked out again and may have to split up," he told Ward, obviously worried that Judith might fall into bad company. "There's always a rent freeze after a revaluation but all the landlords know about it so they're not re-letting. It's getting damned difficult to find anywhere."

Ward nodded, relaxing back around the circular red wood table. He played with a tassel of the arsenic green lampshade, for a moment felt like a Victorian man of letters, leading a spacious, leisurely life among over-stuffed furnishings.

"I'm all for it," he agreed, indicating the empty corners. "There's plenty of room here. But we'll have to make damn sure they don't gossip about it."

After due precautions, they let the two girls into the secret, enjoying their astonishment at finding this private universe.

"We'll put a partition across the middle," Rossiter explained, "then take it down each morning. You'll be able to move in within a couple of days. How do you feel?"

"Wonderful!" The goggled at the wardrobe, squinting at the endless reflections in the mirrors.

There was no difficulty getting them in and out of the house. The turn-over of tenants was continuous and bills were placed in the mail rack. No one cared who the girls were or noticed their regular calls at the cubicle.

However, half an hour after they arrived neither of them had unpacked her suitcase.

"What's up, Judith?" Ward asked, edging past the girls' beds in the narrow interval between the table and wardrobe.

Judith hesitated, looking from Ward to Rossiter, who sat on his bed, finishing off the plywood partition. "John, it's just that . . ."

Helen Waring, more matter-of-fact, took over, her fingers straighten-ing the bedspread. "What Judith's trying to say is that our position here is a little embarrassing. The partition is —"

Rossiter stood up. "For heaven's sake, don't worry, Helen," he assured her, speaking in the loud whisper they had all involuntarily cultivated. "No funny business, you can trust us. This partition is as solid as a rock."

The two girls nodded. "It's not that," Helen explained, "but it isn't up all the time. We thought that if an older person were here, say Judith's aunt — she wouldn't take up much room and be no trouble, she's really awfully sweet — we wouldn't need to bother about the partition — except at night," she added quickly.

Ward glanced at Rossiter, who shrugged and began to scan the floor.

"Well, it's an idea," Rossiter said. "John and I know how you feel. Why not?"

"Sure," Ward agreed. He pointed to the space between the girls' bed and the table. "One more won't make any difference."

The girls broke into whoops. Judith went over to Rossiter and kissed him on the cheek. "Sorry to be a nuisance, Henry." She smiled at him. "That's a wonderful partition you've made. You couldn't do another one for Auntie — just a little one? She's very sweet but she is getting on."

"Of course," Rossiter said. "I understand. I've got plenty of wood left over."

Ward looked at his watch. "It's seven-thirty, Judith. You'd better get in touch with your aunt. She may not be able to make it tonight."

Judith buttoned her coat. "Oh, she will," she assured Ward. "I'll be back in a jiffy."

The aunt arrived within five minutes, three heavy suitcases soundly packed.

"It's amazing," Ward remarked to Rossiter three months later. "The size of this room still staggers me. It almost gets larger every day."

Rossiter agreed readily, averting his eyes from one of the girls changing behind the central partition. This they now left in place as dismantling it daily had become tiresome. Besides, the aunt's subsidiary partition was attached to it and she resented the continuous upsets. Insuring she followed the entrance and exit drills through the camouflaged door and cubicle was difficult enough.

Despite this, detection seemed unlikely. The room had obviously been built as an afterthought into the central well of the house and any noise was masked by the luggage stacked in the surrounding corridor. Directly below was a small dormitory occupied by several elderly women, and Judith's aunt, who visited them socially, swore that no sounds came through the heavy ceiling. Above, the fanlight let out through a dormer window, its lights indistinguishable from the hundred other bulbs burning in the windows of the house.

Rossiter finished off the new partition he was building and held it upright, fitting it into the slots nailed to the wall between his bed and Ward's. They had agreed that this would provide a little extra privacy.

"No doubt I'll have to do one for Judith and Helen," he confided to Ward.

Ward adjusted his pillow. They had smuggled the two armchairs back to the furniture shop as they took up too much space. The bed, anyway, was more comfortable. He had never got completely used to the soft upholstery.

"Not a bad idea. What about some shelving around the wall? I've got nowhere to put anything."

The shelving tidied the room considerably, freeing large areas of the floor. Divided by their partitions, the five beds were in line along the rear wall, facing the mahogany wardrobe. In between was an open space of three or four feet, a further six feet on either side of the wardrobe.

The sight of so much space fascinated Ward. When Rossiter mentioned that Helen's mother was ill and badly needed personal care he immediately knew where her cubicle could be placed — at the foot of his bed, between the wardrobe and the side wall.

Helen was overjoyed. "It's awfully nice of you, John," she told him, "but would you mind if Mother slept beside me? There's enough space to fit an extra bed in."

So Rossiter dismantled the partitions and moved them closer together, six beds now in line along the wall. This gave each of them an interval two and a half feet wide, just enough room to squeeze down the side of their beds. Lying back on the extreme right, the shelves two feet above his head, Ward could barely see the wardrobe, but the space in front of him, a clear six feet to the wall ahead, was uninterrupted.

Then Helen's father arrived.

Knocking on the door of the cubicle, Ward smiled at Judith's aunt as she let him in. He helped her swing out the made-up bed which guarded the entrance, then rapped on the wooden panel. A moment later Helen's father, a small, grey-haired man in an undershirt, braces tied to his trousers with string, pulled back the panel.

Ward nodded to him and stepped over the luggage piled around the floor at the foot of the beds. Helen was in her mother's cubicle, helping the old woman to drink her evening broth. Rossiter, perspiring heavily, was on his knees by the mahogany wardrobe, wrenching apart the frame of the central mirror with a jimmy. Pieces of the wardrobe lay on his bed and across the floor.

"We'll have to start taking these out tomorrow," Rossiter told him. Ward waited for Helen's father to shuffle past and enter his cubicle. He had rigged up a small cardboard door, and locked it behind him with a crude hook of bent wire.

Rossiter watched him, frowning irritably. "Some people are happy. This wardrobe's a hell of a job. How did we ever decide to buy it?"

Ward sat down on his bed. The partition pressed against his knees and he could hardly move. He looked up when Rossiter was engaged and saw that the dividing line he had marked in pencil was hidden by the encroaching partition. Leaning against the wall, he tried to ease it back again, but Rossiter had apparently nailed the lower edge to the floor.

There was a sharp tap on the outside cubicle door — Judith returning from her office. Ward started to get up and then sat back. "Mr. Waring," he called softly. It was the old man's duty night.

Waring shuffled to the door of his cubicle and unlocked it fussily, clucking to himself.

"Up and down, up and down," he muttered. He stumbled over Rossiter's tool bag and swore loudly, then added meaningly over his shoulder: "If you ask me there's too many people in here. Down below they've only got six to our seven, and it's the same size room."

Ward nodded vaguely and stretched back on his narrow bed, trying not to bang his head on the shelving. Waring was not the first to hint that he move out. Judith's aunt had made a similar suggestion two days earlier. Since he left his job at the library (the small rental he charged the others paid for the little food he needed) he spent most of his time in the room, seeing rather more of the old man than he wanted to, but he had learned to tolerate him.

Settling himself, he noticed that the right-hand spire of the wardrobe, all he had been able to see for the past two months, was now dismantled.

It had been a beautiful piece of furniture, in a way symbolising this whole private world, and the salesman at the store told him there were few like it left. For a moment Ward felt a sudden pang of regret, as he had done as a child when his father, in a mood of exasperation, had taken something away from him and he knew he would never see it again.

Then he pulled himself together. It was a beautiful wardrobe, without doubt, but when it was gone it would make the room seem even larger.

Alvin Toffler | # from Future Shock

In the three short decades between now and the turn of the next millennium, millions of psychologically normal people will experience an abrupt collision with the future. Affluent, educated citizens of the world's richest and most technically advanced nations, they will fall victim to tomorrow's most menacingly malady: the disease of change. Unable to keep up with the supercharged pace of change, brought to the edge of breakdown by incessant demands to adapt to novelty, many will plunge into future shock. For them, the future will have arrived too soon.

SOURCE: *Future Shock* by Alvin Toffler. Copyright © 1970 by Alvin Toffler. Reprinted by permission of Random House, Inc.

Future shock is more than an arresting phrase. It may prove to be the most obstinate and debilitating social problem of the future. Its symptoms range from confusion, anxiety and hostility to helpful authority, to physical illness, seemingly senseless violence and self-destructive apathy. Future-shock victims manifest erratic swings in interest and life style, followed by a panicky sense that events are slipping out of their control and, later, a desperate effort to "crawl into their shells" through social, intellectual and emotional withdrawal. They feel continuously harassed and attempt to reduce the number of changes with which they must cope, the number of decisions they must make. The ultimate casualties of future shock terminate by cutting off the outside world entirely — dropping out, spiraling deeper and deeper into disengagement.

In the decades immediately ahead, we face a torrent of change — in our jobs, our families, our sexual standards, our art, our politics, our values. This means that millions of us, ill prepared by either past experience or education, will be forced to make repeated, often painful adaptations. Some of us will be simply unable to function in this social flux and, unless we learn to treat — or prevent — future shock, we shall witness an intensification of the mass neurosis, irrationalism and violence already tearing at today's change-wracked society.

The quickest way to grasp the idea of future shock is to begin with a parallel term — culture shock — that has begun to creep from anthropology texts into the popular language. Culture shock is the queasy physical and mental state produced in an unprepared person who is suddenly immersed in an alien culture. Peace Corps volunteers suffer from it in Ethiopia or Ecuador. Marco Polo probably suffered from it in Cathay. Culture shock is what happens when a traveler suddenly finds himself surrounded by newness, cut off from meaning — when, because of a shift of culture, a yes may mean no, when to slap a man's back in friendly camaraderie may be to offer a mortal insult, when laughter may signify not joy but fury. Culture shock is the bewilderment and distress — sometimes culminating in blind fury or bone-deep apathy — triggered by the removal of the familiar psychological cues on which all of us must depend for survival.

The culture-shock phenomenon accounts for much of the frustration and disorientation that plague Americans in their dealings with other societies. It causes a breakdown in communication, a misreading of reality, an inability to cope. Yet culture shock is relatively mild in comparison with future shock. This malady will not be found in *Index Medicus* or in any listing of psychological abnormalities. Yet, unless intelligent steps are taken to combat it, millions of human beings will find themselves increasingly incompetent to deal rationally with their environments. A product of the greatly accelerated rate of change in society, future shock arises from the superimposition of a new culture on an old one. It is culture shock in one's own society. But its impact is far worse. For most

Peace Corps men — in fact, most travelers — have the comforting knowledge that the culture they left behind will be there to return to. The victim of future shock does not.

Take an individual out of his own culture and set him down suddenly in an environment sharply different from his own, with a wholly novel set of cues to react to, different conceptions of time, space, work, love, religion, sex and everything else; then cut him off from any hope of retreat to a more familiar social landscape and the dislocation he suffers is doubly severe. Moreover, if this new culture is itself rife with change, and if, moreover, its values are incessantly changing, the sense of disorientation will be even further intensified. Given few clues as to what kind of behavior is rational under the radically new circumstances, the victim may well become a hazard to himself and others. Now, imagine not merely an individual but an entire society, an entire generation — including its weakest, least intelligent and most irrational members — suddenly transported into this new world. The result is mass disorientation, future shock on a grand scale.

This is the prospect man now faces. For a new society — superindustrial, fast-paced, fragmented, filled with bizarre styles, customs and choices — is erupting in our midst. An alien culture is swiftly displacing the one in which most of us have our roots. Change is avalanching upon our heads, and most people are unprepared to cope with it. Man is not infinitely adaptable, no matter what the romantics or mystics may say. We are biological organisms with only so much resilience, only a limited ability to absorb the physiological and mental punishment inherent in change. In the past, when the pace of change was leisurely, the substitution of one culture for another tended to stretch over centuries. Today, we experience a millennium of change in a few brief decades. Time is compressed. This means that the emergent superindustrial society will, itself, be swept away in a tidal wave of change — even before we have learned to cope adequately with it. In certain quarters, the rate of change is already blinding. Yet there are powerful reasons to believe that we are only at the beginning of the accelerative curve. History itself is speeding up.

This startling statement can be illustrated in a number of ways. It has been observed, for example, that if the past 50,000 years of man's existence were divided into lifetimes of approximately 62 years each, there have been about 800 such lifetimes. Of these 800, fully 650 were spent in caves. Only during the past 70 lifetimes has it been possible to communicate effectively from one lifetime to another — as writing made it possible to do. Only during the past six lifetimes have masses of men ever seen a printed word. Only during the past four has it been possible to measure time with any precision. Only in the past two has anyone anywhere used an electric motor. And the overwhelming majority of all the material goods we use in daily life today have been developed within the present, the 800th, lifetime.

Painting with the broadest of brush strokes, biologist Sir Julian Huxley informs us that "The tempo of human evolution during recorded history is at least 100,000 times as rapid as that of prehuman evolution." Inventions or improvements of a magnitude that took perhaps 50,000 years to accomplish during the early Paleolithic era were, he says, "run through in a mere millennium toward its close; and with the advent of settled civilization, the unit of change soon became reduced to the century." The rate of change, accelerating throughout the past 5000 years, has become, in his words, "particularly noticeable during the past 300 years." Indeed, says social psychologist Warren Bennis, the throttle has been pushed so far forward in recent years that "No exaggeration, no hyperbole, no outrage can realistically describe the extent and pace of change. . . . In fact, only the exaggerations appear to be true."

What changes justify such supercharged language? Let us look at a few — changes in the process by which man forms cities, for example. We are now undergoing the most extensive and rapid urbanization the world has ever seen. In 1850, only four cities on the face of the earth had a population of 1,000,000 or more. By 1900, the number had increased to 19. But by 1960, there were 141; and today, world urban population is rocketing upward at a rate of 6.5 per cent per year, according to Egbert de Vries and J. T. Thijsse of the Institute of Social Studies in The Hague. This single stark statistic means a doubling of the earth's urban population within 11 years.

One way to grasp the meaning of change on so phenomenal a scale is to imagine what would happen if all existing cities, instead of expanding, retained their present size. If this were so, in order to accommodate the new urban millions, we would have to build a duplicate city for each of the hundreds that already dot the globe. A new Tokyo, a new Hamburg, a new Rome and Rangoon — and all within 11 years. This explains why Buckminster Fuller has proposed building whole cities in shipyards and towing them to coastal moorings adjacent to big cities. It explains why builders talk more and more about "instant" architecture — an "instant factory" to spring up here, an "instant campus" to be constructed there. It is why French urban planners are sketching subterranean cities — stores, museums, warehouses and factories to be built under the earth — and why a Japanese architect has blueprinted a city to be built on stilts out over the ocean.

The same accelerative tendency is instantly apparent in man's consumption of energy. Dr. Homi Bhabha, the late Indian atomic scientist, once analyzed this trend. "To illustrate," he said, "let us use the letter Q to stand for the energy derived from burning some 33 billion tons of coal. In the 18½ centuries after Christ, the total energy consumed averaged less than ½ Q per century. But by 1850, the rate had risen to one Q per century. Today, the rate is about 10 Q per century." This means, roughly speaking, that half of all the energy consumed by man in the past 2000 years has been consumed in the past 100.

Also dramatically evident is the acceleration of economic growth in the nations now racing toward superindustrialism. Despite the fact that they start from a large industrial base, the annual percentage increases in production in these countries are formidable. And the rate of increase is itself increasing. In France, for example, in the 29 years between 1910 and the outbreak of World War Two, industrial production rose only five percent. Yet between 1948 and 1965, in only 17 years, it increased by more than 220 percent. Today, growth rates of from 5 to 10 percent per year are not uncommon among the most industrialized nations. Thus, for the 21 countries belonging to the Organization for Economic Cooperation and Development — by and large, the "have" nations — the average annual rate of increase in gross national product in the years 1960–1968 ran between 4.5 and 5 percent. The U.S., despite a series of ups and downs, grew at a rate of 4.5 percent, and Japan led the rest with annual increases averaging 9.8 percent.

What such numbers imply is nothing less revolutionary than a doubling of the total output of goods and services in the advanced societies about every 15 years — and the doubling times are shrinking. This means that the child reaching his teens in any of these societies is literally surrounded by twice as much of everything newly man-made as his parents were at the time he was an infant. It means that by the time today's teenager reaches the age of 30, perhaps earlier, a second doubling will have occurred. Within a 70-year lifetime, perhaps five such doublings will take place — meaning, since the increases are compounded, that by the time the individual reaches old age, the society around him will be producing 32 times as much as when he was born. Such changes in the ratio between old and new have, as we shall show, an electric impact on the habits, beliefs and self-images of millions. Never in history has this ratio been transformed so radically in so brief a flick of time.

Behind such prodigious economic facts lies that great, growling engine of change — technology. This is not to say that technology is the only source of change in society. Social upheavals can be touched off by a change in the chemical composition of the atmosphere, by alterations in climate, by changes in fertility and many other factors. Yet technology is indisputably a major force behind the accelerative thrust. To most people, the term technology conjures up images of smoky steel mills and clanking machines. Perhaps the classic symbol of technology is still the assembly line created by Henry Ford half a century ago and transformed into a potent social icon by Charlie Chaplin in *Modern Times*. This symbol, however, has always been inadequate — indeed misleading — for technology has always been more than factories and machines. The invention of the horse collar in the Middle Ages led to major changes in agricultural methods and was as much a technological advance as the invention of the Bessemer furnace centuries later. Moreover, technology includes techniques as well as the machines that may or may not be necessary to apply them. It includes ways to make chemical reactions occur, ways to breed fish, plant forests, light theaters, count votes or teach history.

The old symbols of technology are even more misleading today, when the most advanced technological processes are carried out far from assembly lines or open hearths. Indeed, in electronics, in space technology, in most of the new industries, relative silence and clean surroundings are characteristic — sometimes even essential. And the assembly line — the organization of armies of men to carry out simple repetitive functions — is an anachronism. It is time for our symbols of technology to change — to catch up with the fantastic changes in technology itself.

This acceleration is graphically dramatized by a thumbnail account of the progress in transportation. It has been pointed out, for example, that in 6000 B.C., the fastest transportation over long distances available to man was the camel caravan, averaging eight miles per hour. It was not until about 3000 B.C., when the chariot was invented, that the maximum speed was raised to roughly 20 mph. So impressive was this invention, so difficult was it to exceed this speed limit that nearly 5000 years later, when the first mail coach began operating in England, in 1784, it averaged a mere ten mph. The first steam locomotive, introduced in 1825, could muster a top speed of only 13 mph, and the great sailing ships of the time labored along at less than half that speed. It was probably not until the 1880s, that man, with the help of the more advanced steam locomotive, managed to reach a speed of 100 mph. It took the human race millions of years to attain that record. It took only 50 years, however, to quadruple the limit; so that by 1931, airborne man was cracking the 400-mph line. It took a mere 20 years to double the limit again. And by the 1960s, rocket planes approached speeds of 4000 mph and men in space capsules were circling the earth at 18,000 mph. Plotted on a graph, the line representing progress in the past generation would leap vertically off the page.

Whether we examine distances traveled, altitudes reached, minerals mined or explosive power harnessed, the same accelerative trend is obvious. The pattern, here and in a thousand other statistical series, is absolutely clear and unmistakable. Millenniums or centuries go by, and then, in our times, a sudden bursting of the limits, a fantastic spurt forward. The reason for this is that technology feeds on itself. Technology makes more technology possible, as we can see if we look for a moment at the process of innovation. Technological innovation consists of three stages, linked together into a self-reinforcing cycle. First, there is the creative, feasible idea. Second, its practical application. Third, its diffusion through society. The process is completed, the loop closed, when the diffusion of technology embodying the new idea, in turn, helps generate new creative ideas. There is evidence now that the time between each of the steps in this cycle has been shortened.

It is not merely true, as frequently noted, that 90 percent of all the scientists who ever lived are now alive and that new scientific discoveries are being made every day. These new ideas are put to work much more quickly than ever before. The time between original concept and practical use has been radically reduced. This is a striking difference between ourselves and our ancestors. Apollonius of Perga discovered conic sections, but it was 2000 years before they were applied to engineering problems. It was literally centuries between the time Paracelsus discovered that ether could be used as an anesthetic and the time it began to be used for that purpose. Even in more recent times, the same pattern of delay prevailed. In 1836, a machine was invented that mowed, threshed, tied straw into sheaves and poured grain into sacks. This machine was itself based on technology at least 20 years old at the time. Yet it was not until a century later, in the 1930s, that such a combine was actually marketed. The first English patent for a typewriter was issued in 1714. But a century and a half elapsed before typewriters became commercially available. A full century passed between the time Nicolas Appert discovered how to can food and the time when canning became important in the food industry.

Such delays between idea and application are almost unthinkable today. It isn't that we are more eager or less lazy than our ancestors, but that, with the passage of time, we have invented all sorts of social devices to hasten the process. We find that the time between the first and second stages of the innovative cycle — between idea and application — has been radically shortened. Frank Lynn, for example, in studying 20 major innovations, such as frozen food, antibiotics, integrated circuits and synthetic leather, found that since the beginning of this century, more than 60 percent has been slashed from the average time needed for a major scientific discovery to be translated into a useful technological form. William O. Baker, vice-president of Bell Laboratories, itself the hatchery of such innovations as sound movies, computers, transistors and Telstar, underscores the narrowing gap between invention and application by noting that while it took 65 years for the electric motor to be applied, 33 years for the vacuum tube and 18 years for the X-ray tube, it took only 10 for the nuclear reactor, 5 for radar and only 3 for the transistor and the solar battery. A vast and growing research-and-development industry is working now to reduce the lag still further.

If it takes less time to bring a new idea to the market place, it also takes less time for it to sweep through society. The interval between the second and third stages of the cycle — between application and diffusion — has likewise been cut, and the pace of diffusion is rising with astonishing speed. This is borne out by the history of several familiar household appliances. Robert A. Young, at the Stanford Research Institute, has studied the span of time between the first commercial appearance of a new electrical appliance and the time the industry manufacturing it reaches peak production of the item. He found that for a group of appliances introduced in the United States before 1920 — including the vacuum cleaner, the electric range and the refrigerator — the average span between introduction and peak production was 34 years. But for a group that appeared in the 1939–1959 period — including the electric frying pan, television and the washer-dryer combination — the span was only eight years. The lag had shrunk by more than 76 percent.

The stepped-up pace of invention, exploitation and diffusion, in turn, accelerates the whole cycle even further. For new machines or techniques are not merely a product, but a source, of fresh creative ideas. Each new machine or technique, in a sense, changes all existing machines and techniques, by permitting us to put them together into new combinations. The number of possible combinations rises arithmetically. Indeed, each new combination may, itself, be regarded as a new super-machine. The computer, for example, made possible a sophisticated space effort. Linked with sensing devices, communications equipment and power sources, the computer became part of a configuration that, in aggregate, forms a single new supermachine — a machine for reaching into and probing outer space. But for machines or techniques to be combined in new ways, they have to be altered, adapted, refined or otherwise changed. So that the very effort to integrate machines into supermachines compels us to make still further technological innovations.

It is vital to understand, moreover, that technological innovation does not merely combine and recombine machines and techniques. Important new machines do more than suggest or compel changes in other machines — they suggest novel solutions to social, philosophical, even personal problems. They alter man's total intellectual environment, the way he thinks and looks at the world. We all learn from our environment, scanning it constantly — though perhaps unconsciously — for models to emulate. These models are not only other people. They are, increasingly, machines. By their presence, we are subtly conditioned to think along certain lines. It has been observed, for example, that the clock came along before the Newtonian image of the world as a great clocklike mechanism, a philosophical notion that has had the utmost impact on man's intellectual development. Implied in this image of the cosmos as a great clock were ideas about cause and effect and about the importance of external, as against internal, stimuli that shape the everyday behavior of all of us today. The clock also affected our conception of time, so that the idea that a day is divided into 24 equal segments of 60 minutes each has become almost literally a part of us.

Recently, the computer has touched off a storm of fresh ideas about man as an interacting part of larger systems, about his physiology, the way he learns, the way he remembers, the way he makes decisions.

Virtually every intellectual discipline, from political science to family psychology, has been hit by a wave of imaginative hypotheses triggered by the invention and diffusion of the computer — and its full impact has not yet struck. And so the innovative cycle, feeding on itself, speeds up.

If technology, however, is to be regarded as a great engine, a mighty accelerator, then knowledge must be regarded as its fuel. And we thus come to the crux of the accelerative process in society. For the engine is being fed a richer and richer fuel every day.

The rate at which man has been storing up useful knowledge about himself and the universe has been spiraling upward for 10,000 years. That rate took a sharp leap with the invention of writing; but even so, it remained painfully slow over centuries of time. The next great leap in knowledge acquisition did not occur until the invention of movable type in the 15th Century by Gutenberg and others. Prior to 1500, by the most optimistic estimates, Europe was producing books at a rate of 1000 titles per year. This means that it would take a full century to produce a library of 100,000 titles. By 1950, four and a half centuries later, the rate had accelerated so sharply that Europe was producing 120,000 titles a year. What once took a century now took only ten months. By 1960, a single decade later, that awesome rate of publication had made another significant jump so that a century's work could be completed in seven and a half months. And by the mid-Sixties, the output of books on a world scale approached the prodigious figure of 1000 titles per *day*.

One can hardly argue that every book is a net gain for the advancement of knowledge, but we find that the accelerative curve in book publication does, in fact, roughly parallel the rate at which man has discovered new knowledge. Prior to Gutenberg, for example, only 11 chemical elements were known. Antimony, the 12th, was discovered about the time he was working on the printing press. It had been fully 200 years since the 11th, arsenic, had been discovered. Had the same rate of discovery continued, we would by now have added only two or three additional elements to the periodic table since Gutenberg. Instead, in the 500 years after his time, 73 additional elements were discovered. And since 1900, we have been isolating the remaining elements at a rate not of one every two centuries but of one every three years.

Furthermore, there is reason to believe that the rate is still rising sharply. The number of scientific journals and articles and the number of known chemical compounds are both doubling about every 15 years, like industrial production in the advanced countries. The doubling time for the number of asteroids known, the literature on non-Euclidean geometry, on experimental psychology and on the theory of determinants is only ten years. According to biochemist Philip Siekevitz, "What has been learned in the last three decades about the nature of living beings dwarfs in extent of knowledge any comparable period of scientific discovery in the history of mankind." The U. S. Government alone generates

over 300,000 reports each year, plus 450,000 articles, books and papers. On a world-wide basis, scientific and technical literature mounts at a rate of some 60,000,000 pages a year.

The computer burst upon the scene around 1950. With its unprecedented power for analysis and dissemination of extremely varied kinds of data in unbelievable quantities and at mind-staggering speeds, it has become a major force behind the latest acceleration in knowledge acquisition. Combined with other increasingly powerful analytical tools for observing the invisible universe around us, it has raised the rate of knowledge acquisition to dumfounding speeds.

Francis Bacon told us that knowledge is power. This can now be translated into contemporary terms. In our social setting, knowledge is change — and accelerating knowledge acquisition, fueling the great engine of technology, means accelerating change.

Discovery. Application. Impact. Discovery. We see here a chain reaction of change, a long, sharply rising curve of acceleration in human social development. This accelerative thrust has now reached a level at which it can no longer, by any stretch of the imagination, be regarded as "normal." The established institutions of industrial society can no longer contain it, and its impact is shaking up all our social institutions. Acceleration is one of the most important and least understood of all social forces.

This, however, is only half the story. For the speed-up of change is more than a social force. It is a *psychological* force as well. Although it has been almost totally ignored by psychologists and psychiatrists, the rising rate of change in the world around us disturbs our inner equilibrium, alters the very way in which we experience life. The pace of life is speeding up.

Most of us, without stopping to think too deeply about it, sense this quickening of the pace of events. For it is not just a matter of explosive headlines, world crises and distant technological triumphs. The new pace of change penetrates our personal lives as well. No matter where we are, even the *sounds* of change are there. Cranes and concrete mixers keep up an angry clatter on the Champs Elysées and on Connecticut Avenue. I happen to live in mid-Manhattan, where the noise level created by traffic and the incessant jackhammering is virtually intolerable. Recently, to escape the frenetic pace of New York and do some writing, I flew to a remote beach in Venezuela. At the crack of dawn on the first morning after arrival, I was awakened by the familiar sound of a jackhammer: The hotel was building an addition.

Other symptoms of change abound. In a 17th Century convent in a suburb of Paris, I walked through a long sun-dappled cloister, up several flights of rickety wooden stairs, in a mood of silent reverie — until I turned a corner and found the man I had come to see: a Berkeley-trained operations researcher with a desktop computer, busy studying long-range change in the French education system and economy. In Amsterdam and Rotterdam, streets built only five years ago are already ridiculously narrow; no one anticipated the rapidity with which automobiles would proliferate. As I can attest from unpleasant personal experience, change is also present in the form of bumper-to-boot traffic hang-ups on Stockholm's once-peaceful Strandvägen. And in Japan, the pace is so swift that an American economist says wryly: "Stepping off a plane in San Francisco after arriving from Tokyo gives one the feeling of having returned to the 'unchanging West.'"

In Aldous Huxley's *Point Counter-Point*, Lucy Tantamount declared that "Living modernly is living quickly." She should have been here now. Eating, once a leisurely semisocial affair, has become for millions a gulp-and-go proposition, and an enormous "fast-food" industry has arisen to purvey doughnuts, hamburgers, French fries, milk shakes, *tacos* and hot dogs, not to mention machine-vended hot soup, sandwiches, packaged pies and a variety of other quasi-edibles intended to be downed in a hurry. The critic Russell Lynes once attended a convention of fast-food executives. "I am not quite sure," he wrote, "whether the fast-food industry gets its name from the speed with which the food is prepared, served and eaten, or, on the other hand, from the fact that it is consumed by feeders of all ages on the run and, quite literally, on the wing." It was significant, he observed, that the convention was jointly held with a group of motelkeepers, whose prime passion in life is to keep the rest of us moving around.

As the pace accelerates, we seem to be always en route, never at our destination. The search for a place to stop, at least temporarily, is unwittingly symbolized by our increasingly hectic pursuit of that vanishing commodity — a parking place. As the number of autos grows and the number of places diminishes, so, too, does the allowable parking time. In New York and other major cities, what used to be one-hour meters have been converted to half-hour or 15-minute meters. The world awaits that crowning innovation: the 30-second parking slot. On the other hand, we may be bypassing that stage altogether by simply multiplying those disquieting signs that say NO STANDING.

Unconsciously, through exposure to a thousand such situations, we are conditioned to move faster, to interact more rapidly with other people, to expect things to happen sooner. When they don't, we are upset. Thus, economist W. Allan Beckett of Toronto recently testified before the Canadian Transport Commission that the country needed faster telephone service. Sophisticated young people, he declared, would not be willing to wait six seconds for a dial tone if it were technically possible to provide it in three.

* * *

Much of this might sound like subjective grousing based on impressionistic evidence — except that such facts fall into a rigorously definable, scientifically verifiable and historically significant pattern. They add up to a powerful trend toward transience in the culture; and unless this is understood, we cannot make sense of the contemporary world. Indeed, trying to comprehend the politics, economics, art or psychology of the present — let alone of the future — without the concept of transience is as futile as trying to write the history of the Middle Ages without mentioning religion.

If acceleration has become a primal social force in our time, transience, its cultural concomitant, has become a primal psychological force. The speed-up of change introduces a shaky sense of impermanence into our lives, a quality of transience that will grow more and more intense in the years ahead. Change is now occurring so rapidly that things, places, people, organizations, ideas all pass through our lives at a faster clip than ever before. Each individual's relationships with the world outside himself become foreshortened, compressed. They become transient. The throwaway product, the nonreturnable bottle, the paper dress, the modular building, the temporary structure, the portable playground, the inflatable command post are all examples of *things* designed for short-term, transient purposes, and they require a whole new set of psychological responses from man. In slower-moving societies, man's relationships were more durable. The farmer bought a mule or a horse, worked it for years, then put it out to pasture. The relationship between man and beast spanned a great many years. Industrial-era man bought a car, instead, and kept it for several years. Superindustrial man, living at the new accelerated pace, generally keeps his car a shorter period before turning it in for a new one, and some never buy a car at all, preferring the even shorter-term relationships made possible by leases and rentals.

Our links with *place* are also growing more transient. It is not simply that more of us travel more than ever before, by car, by jet and by boat, but more of us actually change our place of residence as well. In the United States each year, some 36,000,000 people change homes. This migration dwarfs all historical precedent, including the surge of the Mongol hordes across the Asian steppes. It also detonates a host of "microchanges" in the society, contributing to the sense of transience and uncertainty. Example: Of the 885,000 listings in the Washington, D.C., telephone book in 1969, over half were different from the year before. Under the impact of this highly accelerated nomadism, all sorts of once-durable ties are cut short. Nothing stays put — especially us.

Most of us today meet more people in the course of a few months than a feudal serf did in his lifetime. This implies a faster *turnover* of people in our lives and, correspondingly, shorter-term relationships. We make and break ties with people at a pace that would have astonished our ancestors. This raises all kinds of profound questions about personal commitment and involvement, the quality of friendship, the ability of humans to communicate with one another, the function of education, even of sex, in the future. Yet this extremely significant shift from longer to shorter interpersonal ties is only part of the larger, more encompassing movement toward high-transience society.

This movement can also be illustrated by changes in our great corporations and bureaucracies. Just as we have begun to make temporary products, we are also creating temporary *organizations*. This explains the incredible proliferation of *ad hoc* committees, task forces and project teams. Every large bureaucracy today is increasingly honeycombed with such transient organizational cells that require, among other things, that people migrate from department to department, and from task to task, at ever faster rates. We see, in most large organizations, a frenetic, restless shuffling of people. The rise of temporary organizations may spell the death of traditional bureaucracy. It points toward a new type of organization in the future — one I call Ad-Hocracy. At the same time, it intensifies, or hastens, the foreshortening of human ties.

Finally, the powerful push toward a society based on transience can be seen in the impermanence of knowledge — the accelerating pace at which scientific notions, political ideologies, values and life-organizing concepts are turning over. This is, in part, based on the heavier loads of information transmitted to us by the communications media. In the U.S. today, the median time spent by adults reading newspapers is 52 minutes per day. The same person who commits nearly an hour to the newspaper also spends some time reading other things as well — magazines, books, signs, billboards, recipes, instructions, etc. Surrounded by print, he "ingests" between 10,000 and 20,000 edited words per day of the several times that many to which he is exposed. The same person also probably spends an hour and a quarter per day listening to the radio — more if he owns an FM set. If he listens to news, commercials, commentary or other such programs, he will, during this period, hear about 11,000 preprocessed words. He also spends several hours watching television — add another 10,000 words or so, plus a sequence of carefully arranged, highly purposive visuals.

Nothing, indeed, is quite so purposive as advertising, and the average American adult today is assaulted by a minimum of 560 advertising messages each day. The verbal and visual bombardment of advertising is so great that of the 560 to which he is exposed, he notices only 76. In effect, he blocks out 484 advertising messages a day to preserve his attention for other matters. All this represents the press of engineered messages against his nervous system, and the pressure is rising, for there is evidence that we are today tampering with our communications machinery in an effort to transmit even richer image-producing messages at an even faster rate. Communications people, artists and others are consciously working to make each instance of exposure to the mass media carry a heavier informational and emotional freight.

In this maelstrom of information, the certainties of last night become the ludicrous nonsense of this morning and the individual is forced to learn and relearn, to organize and reorganize the images that help him comprehend reality and function in it. The trend toward telescoped ties with things, places, people and organizations is matched by an accelerated turnover of information.

What emerges, therefore, are two interlinked trends, two driving forces of history: first, the acceleration of change itself; and, second, its cultural and psychological concomitant, transience. Together, they create a new ephemeralized environment for man — a high-transience society. Fascinating, febrile but, above all, fast, this society is racing toward future shock.

One of the astonishing, as-yet-unpublicized findings of medical research, for example, bears directly on the link-up between change and illness. Research conducted at the University of Washington Medical School, at the U. S. Navy Neuropsychiatric Unit at San Diego, as well as in Japan, Europe and elsewhere, documents the disturbing fact that individuals who experience a great deal of change in their lives are more prone to illness — and the more radical and swift the changes, the more serious the illness. These studies suggest strongly that we cannot increase the rate at which we make and break our relationships with the environment without producing marked physiological changes in the human animal.

This is, of course, no argument against change. "There are worse things than illness," Dr. Thomas Holmes, a leader in life-change research, reminds us dryly. Yet the notion that change can be endlessly accelerated without harm to the individual is sharply challenged by the work of Holmes and many others. There are distinct limits to the speed with which man can respond to environmental change.

These limits, moreover, are psychological as well as physiological. The neural and hormonal responses touched off in the human body when it is forced to adapt to change may well be accompanied by a deterioration of mental functioning as well. Research findings in experimental psychology, in communications theory, in management science, in human-factors engineering and in space biology all point to the conclusion that man's ability to make sound decisions — to adapt — collapses when the rate at which he must make them is too fast. Whether driving a car, steering a space capsule or solving intellectual problems, we operate most efficiently within a certain range of response speeds. When we are insufficiently stimulated by change, we grow bored and our performance deteriorates. But, by the same token, when the rate of responses demanded of us becomes too high, we also break down.

Thus we see people who, living in the midst of the most turbulent change, blindly deny its existence. We meet the world-weary executive who smiles patronizingly at his son and mouths nonsense to the effect that nothing ever really changes. Such people derive comfort from the misleading notions that history repeats itself or that young people were always rebellious. Focusing attention exclusively on the continuities in experience, they desperately attempt to block out evidence of discontinuities, in the unconscious hope that they will therefore not have to deal with them. Yet change, roaring through the social order, inevitably overtakes even those who blind themselves to it. Censoring reality, blocking out important warning signals from the environment, the deniers set themselves up for massive maladaptation, virtually guaranteeing that when change catches up with them, it will come not in small and manageable steps but in the form of a single overwhelming crisis.

Others respond to future shock by burrowing into a specialty — a job, a hobby, a social role — and ignoring everything else. We find the electronics engineer who tries manfully to keep in touch with the latest work in his field. But the more world strife there is, the more outbreaks there are in the ghetto, the more campuses erupt into violence, the more compulsively he focuses on servomechanisms and integrated circuits. Suffering from tunnel vision, monitoring an extremely narrow slice of reality, he becomes masterful at coping with a tightly limited range of life situations — but hopeless at everything else. Any sudden shift of the external environment poses for him the threat of total disorientation.

Yet another response to future shock is reversion to previously successful behavioral programs that are now irrelevant. The reversionist clicks back into an old routine and clings to it with dogmatic desperation. The more change whirls around him, the more blindly he attempts to apply the old action patterns and ideologies. The Barry Goldwaters and George Wallaces of the world appeal to his quivering gut through the politics of nostalgia. Police maintained order in the past; hence, to maintain order, we need only supply more police. Authoritarian treatment of children worked in the past; hence, the troubles of the present spring from permissiveness. The middle-aged, right-wing reversionist yearns for the simple, ordered society of the small town — the slow-paced social environment in which his old routines were appropriate. Instead of adapting to the new, he continues automatically to apply the old solutions, growing more and more divorced from reality as he does so.

If the older reversionist dreams of reinstating a small-town past, the youthful, left-wing reversionist dreams of reviving an even older social system. This accounts for some of the fascination with rural communes, the bucolic romanticism that fills the posters and poetry of the hippie and post-hippie subcultures, the deification of Ché Guevara (identified with mountains and jungles, not with urban or post-urban environments), the exaggerated veneration of pretechnological societies and the exaggerated contempt for science and technology. The left reversionist hands out anachronistic Marxist and Freudian clichés as knee-jerk answers for the problems of tomorrow.

Finally, there is the future-shock victim who attempts to cope with the explosion of information, the pulsing waves of data, the novelty and change in the environment, by reducing everything to a single neat equation. Complexity terrifies him. The world slips from control when it is too complex. This helps explain the intellectual faddism that seizes on a McLuhan or a Marcuse or a Maharishi to explain all the problems of past, present and future. Upset by the untidiness of reality, the super-simplifier attempts to force it into an overneat set of dogmas. He then invests these with tremendous emotional force and clings to them with total conviction — until the next new world-explaining concept is merchandised by the media.

In the field of action and activism, the passionate pursuit of the super-simple leads to supersimple solutions — such as violence. For the older generation and the political establishment, police truncheons and military bayonets loom as attractive remedies, a way to end dissent once and for all. The vigilantes of the right and the brick-throwing cults of the left, overwhelmed by the onrushing complexities of change, employ violence to narrow their options and clarify their lives. Terrorism substitutes for thought.

These all-too-familiar forms of behavior can be seen as modes of response to future shock. They are the ways used by the future-shock victim to get through the thickening tangle of personal and social problems that seem to hit him with ever-increasing force and velocity. To the information scientist, these four responses — blocking out, overspecialization, reversion and supersimplification — are instantly recognizable, for they are classical ways of coping with overload. But classical or not, these tactics, pushed beyond a reasonable point, flower into full-blown pathology, endangering not merely the individual who employs them but the people around him as well.

Asked to adapt too rapidly, increasing numbers of us grow confused, bewildered, irritable and irrational. Sometimes we throw a tantrum, lashing out against friends or family or committing acts of senseless violence. Pressured too hard, we fall into profound lethargy — the same lethargy exhibited by battle-shocked soldiers or by change-hassled young people who, even without the dubious aid of drugs, all too often seem stoned and apathetic. This is the hidden meaning of the dropout syndrome, the stop-the-world-I-want-to-get-off attitude, the search for tranquillity or nirvana in a host of moldy mystical ideas. Such philosophies are dredged up to provide intellectual justification for an apathy that is essentially unhealthy and anti-adaptive, and that is often a symptom not of intellectual profundity, but of future shock.

For future shock is what happens to men when they are pushed beyond their adaptive tolerances. It is the inevitable and crushing consequence of a society that is running too fast for its own good — without even having a clear picture of where it wants to go.

Change is good. Change is life itself. The justifications for radical changes in world society are more than ample. The ghetto, the campus, the deepening misery in the Third World all cry out for rapid change. But every time we accelerate a change, we need to take into account the effect it has on human copability. Just as we need to accelerate some changes, we need to decelerate others. We need to design "future-shock absorbers" into the very fabric of the emergent society. If we don't, if we simply assume that man's capacity for change is infinite, we are likely to suffer a rude awakening in the form of massive adaptive breakdown. We shall become the world's first future-shocked society.

A B C D E F G H I J   9 8 7 6 5 4 3 2 1